2 VOL. SET; $279.95

VOL. I

Policing
Volume I

The International Library of Criminology, Criminal Justice and Penology
Series Editors: Gerald Mars and David Nelken

Titles in the Series:

Policing
Volume I
Cops, Crime and Control: Analysing the Police Function

Edited by

Robert Reiner

The London School of Economics and Political Science

Dartmouth
Aldershot • Brookfield USA • Singapore • Sydney

Published by
Dartmouth Publishing Company Limited
Gower House
Croft Road
Aldershot
Hants GU11 3HR
England

Dartmouth Publishing Company
Old Post Road
Brookfield
Vermont 05036
USA

British Library Cataloguing in Publication Data
Policing. – (The international library of criminology,
    criminal justice and penology)
    1. Police 2. Police administration 3. Criminology
    I. Reiner, Robert II. Cops, crime and control III. Controlling
    the controllers
    363.2

Library of Congress Cataloging-in-Publication Data
Policing / edited by Robert Reiner.
                p. cm.— (The international library of criminology, criminal
    justice, and penology)
        Includes bibliographical references and index.
        Contents: vol. 1. Cops, crime, and control: analysing the police
    function – vol. 2. Controlling the controllers: police discretion
    and accountability.
        ISBN 1–85521–390–7
        1. Police. 2. Law enforcement. I. Reiner, Robert, 1946–
    II. Series: International library of criminology, criminal justice and
    penology.
    HV7921.P579 1996
    363.2—dc20

                                                                    96–618
                                                                    CIP

ISBN 1 85521 390 7

Printed and bound by Athenaeum Press Ltd.,
Gateshead, Tyne & Wear

Contents

Acknowledgements

The editor and publishers wish to thank the following for permission to use copyright material.

American Sociological Association for the essays: Donald J. Black (1970), 'Production of Crime Rates', *American Sociological Review*, **35**, pp. 733–48; Egon Bittner (1967), 'The Police on Skid-Row: A Study of Peace Keeping', *American Sociological Review*, **32**, pp. 699–715.

Anderson Publishing Company for the essay: Cyril D. Robinson (1979), 'Ideology as History: A Look at the Way Some English Police Historians Look at the Police', *Police Studies*, **2**, pp. 35–49.

Blackwell Publishers for the essays: Robert Reiner (1992), 'Policing a Postmodern Society', *Modern Law Review*, **55**, pp. 761–81; Les Johnston (1993), 'Privatisation and Protection: Spatial and Sectoral Ideologies in British Policing and Crime Prevention', *Modern Law Review*, **56**, pp. 771–92. Copyright © The Modern Law Review Limited 1993.

Carnegie-Mellon University Press for the essay: Robert D. Storch (1976), 'The Policeman as Domestic Missionary: Urban Discipline and Popular Culture in Northern England, 1850–1880', *Journal of Social History*, **9**, pp. 481–509; Eric H. Monkkonen (1982), 'From Cop History to Social History: The Significance of the Police in American History', *Journal of Social History*, **15**, pp. 575–91.

The Gordon & Breach Publishing Group (Harwood Academic Publishers) for the essay: Anthony E. Bottoms (1990), 'Crime Prevention Facing the 1990s', *Policing and Society*, **1**, pp. 3–22. Copyright © 1990 Harwood Academic Publishers GmbH. Bob Hoogenboom (1991), 'Grey Policing: A Theoretical Framework', *Policing and Society*, **2**, pp. 17–30. Copyright © 1991 Harwood Academic Publishers S.A.

Kluwer Academic Publishers for the essay: Otwin Marenin (1982), 'Parking Tickets and Class Repression: The Concept of Policing in Critical Theories of Criminal Justice', *Contemporary Crises*, **6**, pp. 241–66. Copyright © 1982 Elsevier Scientific Publishing Co.

Law and Society Association for the essay: Cyril D. Robinson and Richard Scaglion (1987), 'The Origin and Evolution of the Police Function in Society: Notes Toward a Theory', *Law and Society Review*, **21**, pp. 109–53.

MCB University Press for the essay: William Watts Miller (1987), 'Party Politics, Class Interest and Reform of the Police 1829–56', *Police Studies*, **10**, pp. 42–60.

Oxford University Press for the essays: Joanna Shapland and Jon Vagg (1987), 'Using the Police', *British Journal of Criminology*, **27**, pp. 54–63; Nigel G. Fielding (1987), 'Being

Series Preface

The International Library of Criminology, Criminal Justice and Penology, represents an important publishing initiative designed to bring together the most significant journal essays in contemporary criminology, criminal justice and penology. The series makes available to researchers, teachers and students an extensive range of essays which are indispensable for obtaining an overview of the latest theories and findings in this fast changing subject.

This series consists of volumes dealing with criminological schools and theories as well as with approaches to particular areas of crime, criminal justice and penology. Each volume is edited by a recognised authority who has selected twenty or so of the best journal articles in the field of their special competence and provided an informative introduction giving a summary of the field and the relevance of the articles chosen. The original pagination is retained for ease of reference.

The difficulties of keeping on top of the steadily growing literature in criminology are complicated by the many disciplines from which its theories and findings are drawn (sociology, law, sociology of law, psychology, psychiatry, philosophy and economics are the most obvious). The development of new specialisms with their own journals (policing, victimology, mediation) as well as the debates between rival schools of thought (feminist criminology, left realism, critical criminology, abolitionism etc.) make necessary overviews that offer syntheses of the state of the art. These problems are addressed by the INTERNATIONAL LIBRARY in making available for research and teaching the key essays from specialist journals.

GERALD MARS
Professor in Applied Anthropology, University of Bradford
School of Management

DAVID NELKEN
Distinguished Research Professor, Cardiff Law School,
University of Wales, Cardiff

Introduction
Cops, Crime and Control: Analysing the Police Function

The Development of Police Research

Until the early 1960s research on the police was almost entirely non-existent in criminology, as indeed it was in every other academic discipline. Today, however, it constitutes one of the largest areas of research interest, as well as being a major focus of theoretical analysis and policy debate. At British and American criminology conferences for several years now, there have been more papers delivered on policing than on any other single topic.

Empirical research on the police has its origins in the same historical period – the early 1960s – in both Britain and North America. Spreading out from these centres of origin, there has been a proliferating research literature in many other countries as well, though particularly in other common-law, English-speaking jurisdictions.

Police research had somewhat similar conditions of origin on both sides of the Atlantic and, once in being, developments were accelerated by a considerable degree of international cross-fertilization. (I have analysed the origins and trajectory of police research in greater detail in Reiner 1994). The key intellectual precondition for research on policing was the epistemological shift in the problematic of academic criminology in the 1960s which is commonly referred to as 'labelling theory' (most famously identified with the seminal work of Becker 1964 and Lemert 1967).

This essential shift was from a 'correctional' to an 'appreciative' stance on deviance (in the terminology of Matza 1964, 1969), and then to a critical and radical one (Taylor, Walton and Young 1973 and 1975 are the flagships of the latter change). Instead of taking the values and epistemology of the criminal law and the criminal justice system as given (as the hitherto dominant positivists had done), criminologists began to question 'whose side' they were on (Becker 1967). This was partly the reflection in criminology of the more critical and conflictual counter-cultures of the 1960s. The shift was not solely one of values, however. Once the conceptual categories and correctionalist and control agendas of criminal law and punishment were no longer taken for granted, the structure and functioning of the criminal justice apparatus became legitimate targets for intellectual curiosity and empirical research.

The other source of police research was the centrality of policing issues to political debate in the early 1960s in both Britain and North America (Reiner 1992 traces this and subsequent developments in more detail). In Britain the police had stood as a symbol of national pride for a long period in the middle of the 20th century. However in the late 1950s a number of *causes célèbres* (which, with the hindsight of almost 40 years of deepening scandal and controversy, were very minor indeed) caused sufficient alarm in the political establishment to prompt the convening of a major Royal Commission on the Police which reported in 1962 after three years of deliberation. Its recommendations were translated into the Police Act of 1964, initiating the most significant transformation in the structure of British policing since its foundation in 1829 by Sir Robert Peel (until the profound changes launched since 1993 by the two most recent Home Secretaries, Kenneth Clarke and Michael Howard). However, these landmark policy developments of the early 1960s did not quell the growing debate about policing which has become increasingly fundamental and agonized ever since. Indeed, this debate is the most significant source of the flood of police research in the last 40 years.

In the US as well, the early 1960s saw major political concern and debate about law and order and civil rights, with the police in the cockpit of controversy. These were the years of the landmark Supreme Court (notably *Miranda* and *Escobedo*) decisions on the exclusionary rule governing evidence gathered by the police in violation of civil rights (Kaplan and Skolnick 1982, Ch. 5). They were also years of growing civil unrest, political demonstrations and urban rioting. By the late 1960s 'law and order' had become the dominant domestic political issue and the key focus of Richard Nixon's triumphant 1968 Presidential election campaign (Harris 1970). These concerns prompted a crescendo of research on policing – governmental, in-house and academic (Platt and Cooper 1974).

Although seldom made explicit until the development of a research literature on the police under the circumstances outlined above, the police seem doomed to be the centre of political controversy and to be regarded from conflicting perspectives. Policing is necessarily Janus-faced as it represents the exercise of authority over those who are – actually or potentially, explicitly or implicitly – recalcitrant to the dominant social order (whatever its particular character, democratic or authoritarian). Policing will inevitably be viewed differently by those who are policed against rather than policed for.

This dual aspect of policing was already evident in the earliest academic writings on the police. Jerome Skolnick, for example, focused his seminal analysis *Justice Without Trial* (1966) on the 'police dilemma' in a democratic society: how to balance the demands of law enforcement with the constraints of legality and due process. Mirroring political debates (and police practice), researchers implicitly divide into those primarily concerned with facilitating the achievement of 'crime control' and those prioritizing 'due process' (Packer 1968) – as well as those seeking the holy grail of balance between these values.

Although this divide may be exaggerated, and despite the many who consciously pursue synthesis, there does seem to be a broad distinction between two streams in police research: studies concerned primarily with the outputs of policing, and those aimed mainly at ensuring the accountability of the police. In a nutshell, some are more concerned with policing society; others with policing the police. This is the organizing principle of these two volumes which attempt to present a sample of the most significant aspects of the now massive research literature on policing. The first assembles work mainly examining the police function, the second police accountability. The two aspects are of course interdependent: concern about accountability arises from how the police perform their functions, whilst any issues of police functioning have implications for accountability. The two volumes similarly constitute two interdependent aspects of police research and not two hermetically-sealed compartments of specialist interest. The rest of this Introduction will discuss the organization and contents of Volume I in more detail. Volume II will be introduced separately.

Historical Development of the Police Function

There are numerous studies of the historical emergence of the police function primarily, but by no means only, in Great Britain and the US in modern times. The first essay in the volume, by Robinson and Scaglion, traces the origins and evolution of the police function in earlier societies by means of a fascinating analysis of the anthropological and historical literature. It adds not only to our historical knowledge but also to the theoretical understanding of policing, tracing the connections between social and political domination, inequality and the police function.

In the many studies which exist of the origins of modern policing, it is possible to trace three broad strands (these are discussed in more detail in Reiner 1992, Ch. 1). The earliest – often referred to as the 'orthodox' perspective – was the work mainly of amateur police buffs rather than professional historians. It is primarily a celebration of the emergence of an institution which is admired uncritically as a neutral and benign guarantor of civilized order. Chapter 4 by Robinson, 'Ideology as History', is a critical analysis of these studies.

The development of academic research on the police in the 1960s and 1970s coincided with the new and more critical approaches in both history and criminology. It is hardly surprising therefore that many histories of policing in this period were written from a 'revisionist' perspective, in many ways incorporating the obverse of the 'orthodox' school's assumptions. Where the latter saw neutral protection of the vulnerable and victimized as the police function, revisionists emphasized class control and political domination. The work of Robert Storch is the best known in this vein, especially his seminal paper 'The Plague of Blue Locusts' published in 1975 and frequently anthologized. I have instead chosen to represent Storch's work by his slightly less well-known paper on the police as 'domestic missionaries' (Chapter 2). This documents how modern police have performed the important symbolic and legitimating function of representing and diffusing the values of central and dominant authority by patrolling throughout society, initially in the face of considerable resistance.

More recently a post-revisionist approach has developed which incorporates the insights of the critical perspective into a more complex and ambivalent account of police development than either orthodoxy or its revisionist obverse. This has mainly been argued in a number of important books, notably Miller 1977, Monkkonen 1981 and Emsley 1991. I have represented this approach by Ignatieff's short piece on the origins and early development of Peel's Metropolitan Police – a model of compression and lucidity – and by Monkkonen's summary of American police history – (Chapters 3 and 6). Both emphasize the essentially mundane, bureaucratic reasons for police creation and expansion, and the synthesis of elements of social control and public service in their functioning.

The chapter by Watts Miller is a rigorous and highly illuminating analysis of the Parliamentary debates surrounding the creation of the New Police in 19th-century Britain. It shows the sources of the different strands of debate in terms of their party identification, social position, and political ideology.

The Role of the Police in Practice

Part II reviews one of the chestnuts of police research and debate, the question of balance between law enforcement and service elements in the police role. The first major empirical study of police in Britain, Michael Banton's 1964 *The Policeman in the Community* (which included some empirical research on the American police as well) emphasized the predominance in practice of peacekeeping and service tasks rather than law enforcement. This contrasted with the popular image of the police as primarily crime fighters. Banton stressed that the police tended to use their discretion to under-enforce the law, interpreting their job as the broader one of maintaining public peace.

This conception of the police as basically a social service rather than a crime control agency rapidly became a cliché of empirical studies on police work. It is represented here by two highly influential essays: Cumming, Cumming and Edell, an analysis of calls to the police in the US, and Punch and Naylor, a similar British study (Chapters 7 and 8). Both claim a preponderance of service calls in public demand for police intervention.

More recently, theoretical and empirical work has called this early research orthodoxy into question. Bittner's paper, 'Florence Nightingale in Pursuit of Willie Sutton', is probably the single most influential theoretical analysis of the police role. It develops an essentially Weberian account of the police as a body specialized in the use or potential use of legitimate force to deal with a miscellany of emergencies. On this view the police are distinguished, not by their function, but by their specific institutional capacity. Even apparently non-crime service calls involve emergencies where (as Bittner puts it) someone is doing something the caller wants stopped NOW! i.e. the police are called because of their perceived capacity for forceful and authoritative intervention.

Goldstein's essay on 'problem-oriented' policing is the seminal source of what is currently the most influential view of how to improve policing, popular amongst reform-minded police chiefs around the world today (together with the related but somewhat more nebulous notion of community policing). Goldstein urges that the sharp divisions between broad conceptions of the police role (force, service and such like) be abandoned. Instead he argues that the police should analyse the concrete problems worrying local people and develop specific targeted strategies to deal with these, possibly involving other agencies too.

Chapter 11 by Marenin, 'Parking Tickets and Class Repression', is rather less well-known, but is a penetrating and sophisticated theoretical critique – from a broadly Marxist perspective – of debates about the police role. The problem with such debates, he argues convincingly, is the polarization of views involved: the police are accepted on the one hand as a benign non-coercive social service or rejected on the other as agents of social oppression and political domination. The complexity of the police function lies in their performance of duties which are plausibly necessary in any contemporary, advanced, complex society ('parking tickets'), but which often also serve to perpetuate inequality because the social order which the police help reinforce is based on 'class repression'.

The debate between Shapland and Vagg in Chapter 12 and Fielding in Chapter 13 advances the issue mainly by new empirical findings, as well as by reconceptualizing some of the categories of older research. What Shapland and Vagg emphasize is the *potential* crime element in many of the demands for policing, such as in domestic disputes, which earlier researchers called service work. When this is recognized (and in view of the sheer rise in unequivocal crime calls), it becomes harder to say that, in most urban areas today, policing is mainly about uncontentious service work. Crime and potential crime are an increasing aspect of policing. Shapland and Vagg's research also highlights the considerable number of policing jobs done by the public. It thus underlines the distinction between a broader functional conception of policing, which may be achieved by the public and other bodies, and what the police undertake as a specific organization.

Fielding's critique of Shapland and Vagg raises several potential difficulties with the broadly promising idea of greater public involvement in policing. Above all it might encourage precisely the narrower, tougher approach to crime control which Shapland and Vagg seek to move away from.

Police and Crime Control

Part III considers in more detail the crime control element in police work. Donald Black's paper is one of the products of the massive observational study of police work he conducted with Professor Al Reiss for the Presidential Commission on Law Enforcement in 1967. It examines how and why police discretion operates to produce statistics on crime which, in political debate, are often taken as defining the crime problem. This happens even though they are partial and biased sub-sets of all offending, constructed by processes of social interaction and negotiation between complainants, witnesses, suspects and police officers, processes which are analysed in the study.

Chapter 16 by Wilson and Kelling has been enormously influential in policy debate in the US and in the British Home Office over the last decade. It argues that the sorts of order-maintenance and service work undertaken by patrol officers (e.g. dealing with the 'broken windows' of the title), though often seen as the antithesis of crime control, actually play a crucial part in preventing offending as well as reducing fear of crime (and thus the vicious cycle by which such fears become a self-fulfilling prophecy as people shun public places). Patrol work to combat incivilities and maintain accessibility to public spaces and amenities can prevent areas from slipping out of control altogether and becoming prey to serious crime. It is a spirited vindication of the potential of patrol work (even if based on a debatable and romanticized 'Golden Age' view of history).

In defending the value of patrol work in a broader sense, the 'broken windows' thesis qualifies the negative implications contained in a variety of studies of the impact of police patrol on crime, of which Kelling's own Kansas City Preventive Patrol Experiment in the early 1970s was the most rigorous and comprehensive. These studies of the impact of conventional police techniques on crime are reviewed by Kelling in Chapter 15 and brought up to date and extended to Britain by Hough in Chapter 17. Chatterton's response to Hough anticipates some recent attempts to qualify the 'nothing works' assumptions of most studies of police methods of crime control. The relatively recent paper by Sherman is a cogently presented critique of the pessimistic conventional wisdom of earlier studies that the impact of police tactics on crime was negligible. His thorough review of recent studies of innovative police strategies offers the tentative promise of some success in controlling crime.

Police and Order-Maintenance

Part IV comprises some influential work on police and the maintenance of public order.

Bittner's research is a classic study of everyday peacekeeping by patrol officers on skid row. Though on a small scale, it illustrates the centrality of maintaining public order in routine police work.

The exchange between Waddington and Jefferson (Chapters 21 and 22) is the latest round of a fairly long-running debate between them on the value and dangers of paramilitary methods in crowd and riot control. This issue became extremely controversial in Britain during the 1980s and 1990s as the country experienced levels of public disorder unprecedented in recent times and as police tactics stiffened to contain them. A fierce debate flourished about whether, in the light of increasing disorder, paramilitary policing had become inevitable and functioned to hold it in check (which Waddington argued), or whether it simply exacerbated a spiral of increasing tension and violence (which Jefferson contends).

Futures of Policing

The final section contains a variety of recent attempts to chart possible futures for policing. Holdaway's paper was one of the first to document a profound shift towards more action-oriented, tougher styles of everyday policing. This accentuates the permanent tension between the street cop's sense of professionalism based on experience and grounded knowledge, and the more bureaucratic and higher education-based 'professionalism' of the managerial ranks.

The other essays in this section all analyse the current predicament in which the police appear in danger of losing their position as monopolistic suppliers of security in society. The main direction of this is the growth of forms of policing other than by professional police officers. The mushrooming of private security organizations is the focus of work by Shearing and Stenning, Hoogenboom, Johnston and Reiner (Chapters 24, 26, 28 and 30 respectively). The proliferation of varieties of crime prevention functions outside or tangential to police organizations is examined by Bottoms. Newburn and Morgan argue that privatization and the development of alternative police forms are not merely a function of the aversion to state expenditure of the governments which held office in the 1980s. They are also rooted in wider structural trends which are inexorably driving up the demand for policing services beyond what any society can sensibly afford. Alternative ways of meeting this demand must be considered, including their own suggestion of different tiers of police for different tasks. Chapter 27 by Reiner on policing post-modern society looks at the sources of the spiralling pressures on the police by considering the relationship between wider and deeper economic, social and cultural trends – often referred to as post-modernity – and policing (as the profoundly challenging collection of papers in Nelken 1994 does for criminology as a whole).

Clearly there is no consensus in terms of crystal-ball gazing, and any areas of agreement will probably be rapidly falsified by events. However, the various speculations about the future suggest that the modern police organization, whose rise was charted by the essays in Part I, may be in a process of terminal diffusion and atrophy. As the review of anthropological material in Chapter 1 by Robinson and Scaglion suggested, whilst policing in some form may be universal, the modern type of police organization has definite historical conditions of existence. Future fragmentation and pluralism in society, in the state and in culture may render redundant the modern conception of police as a state bureaucracy with a monopoly to supply 'domestic missionaries' who symbolize and propagate to all one dominant view of morality and order.

References

Banton, M. (1964), *The Policeman in the Community*, London: Tavistock.

Becker, H. (1964), *Outsiders*, New York: Free Press.

Becker, H. (1967), 'Whose Side Are We On?', *Social Problems*, **14** (3), 239–45.

Emsley, C. (1991), *The English Police: A Political and Social History*, Hemel Hempstead: Wheatsheaf.

Harris, R. (1970), *Justice: The Crisis of Law, Order and Freedom in America*, London: Bodley Head.

Kaplan, J. and Skolnick, J. (1982), *Criminal Justice: Introductory Cases and Materials*, 3rd ed., New York: Foundation Press.

Lemert, E. (1967), *Human Deviance, Social Problems and Social Control*, Englewood Cliffs NJ: Prentice-Hall.

Matza, D. (1964), *Delinquency and Drift*, New York: Wiley.

Matza, D. (1969), *Becoming Deviant*, Englewood Cliffs NJ: Prentice-Hall.

Miller, W. (1977), *Cops and Bobbies*, Chicago: University of Chicago Press.

Monkkonen, E. (1981), *Police in Urban America*, Cambridge: Cambridge University Press.

Nelken, D. (ed.) (1994), *The Futures of Criminology*, London: Sage.

Packer, H. (1968), *The Limits of the Criminal Sanction*, Stanford: Stanford University Press.

Platt, A. and Cooper, L. (eds) (1974), *Policing America*, Englewood Cliffs NJ: Prentice-Hall.

Reiner, R. (1992), *The Politics of the Police*, 2nd ed., Hemel Hempstead: Wheatsheaf.

Reiner, R. (1994), 'Policing and the Police' in M. Maguire, R. Morgan and R. Reiner (eds), *The Oxford Handbook of Criminology*, Oxford: Oxford University Press.

Skolnick, J. (1966), *Justice Without Trial*, New York: Wiley.

Storch, R. (1975), 'The Plague of Blue Locusts: Police Reform and Popular Resistance in Northern England 1840–1857', *International Review of Social History*, **20** (1), 61–90.

Taylor, I., Walton, P. and Young, J. (1973), *The New Criminology*, London: Routledge.

Taylor, I., Walton, P. and Young, J. (eds) (1975), *Critical Criminology*, London: Routledge.

Part I
Historical Development
of the Police Function

[1]

THE ORIGIN AND EVOLUTION OF THE POLICE FUNCTION IN SOCIETY: NOTES TOWARD A THEORY

CYRIL D. ROBINSON

RICHARD SCAGLION

Our theory states that the police function, in its modern form, is linked to economic specialization and differential access to resources that occur in the transition from a kinship- to a class-dominated society. This theory shows the incremental steps by which this transition may come about, both historically and cross-culturally. In addition, we examine the implications of these steps for modern police-community relations.

Our theory is constructed from both anthropological and historical materials. It consists of four interdependent propositions: (1) The origin of a specialized police function depends upon the division of society into dominant and subordinate classes with antagonistic interests; (2) specialized police agencies are generally characteristic only of societies politically organized as states; (3) in a period of transition, the crucial factor in delineating the modern specialized police function is an ongoing attempt at conversion of the social control (policing) mechanism from an integral part of the community structure to an agent of an emerging dominant class; and (4) the police institution is created by the emerging dominant class as an instrument for the preservation of its control over restricted access to basic resources, over the political apparatus governing this access, and over the labor force necessary to provide the surplus upon which the dominant class lives.

We argue that the police institution has a double and contradictory origin and function, for at the same time and in the same society it may be both the agent of the people it polices and of the dominant class controlling these same people. An analysis linking the origin of the modern police function to social change in classless societies has important implications for an understanding of contemporary problems in police-community relations. It allows the dynamics of the social control function of police in small, homogeneous social units to be integrated with a consideration of its role in a complex society. Such an analysis also illuminates how an understanding of this specialized role may be obscured by the more general social control function of police displayed in simple social units, resulting in differential and conflicting expectations about the role and functions of police in the modern world.

I. INTRODUCTION

A society dominated by a ruling class needs a coercive instrument to maintain this class's control over basic resources and over a labor force necessary to produce the surplus product to support and sustain its class (Haas, 1982: 173–174). Our the-

LAW & SOCIETY REVIEW, Volume 21, Number 1 (1987)

110   ORIGIN AND EVOLUTION OF THE POLICE FUNCTION

ory, as proposed in this paper, is that because the police serve this function in contemporary, complex societies, modern policing contains the contradictory demands of the police function in kinship-based societies and the police function in state society (Claessen and Skalnik: 1978b). The development of the police function parallels the development of the state. The police function existing within a kinship-based society, as a product of the whole society, is transformed into a police function that predominantly represents the interests of the dominant class in a class-dominated society while at the same time purporting and appearing to represent the entire society. We attempt to reconstruct the means by which this transformation occurs. Because we consider the kinds of changes in community organization that make a police deemed necessary, our analysis has important implications for an understanding of contemporary problems in police-community relations. Our use of anthropological evidence to support a theory of police function also illustrates how that discipline can be used to elucidate contemporary problems in criminal justice.[1]

Modern writers on social control have been especially deficient in developing a conceptual and theoretical approach to the development of the police.[2] Given the functional perspective of much of the anthropological literature, it is surprising that so little attention has been given to the cross-cultural functions of police. Although almost every introductory anthropology text discusses social control in tribal societies, fundamental questions about the development of the police function remain unanswered: From what sort of "prepolice" structure did the police function develop into a specialized institution? Out of what perceived need did such a specialized form of social control evolve? To what kind or kinds of social structure is the police function linked? What is the relation of the incipient police to the community? What are the modifications in the economic

---

[1] Structures and changes may be less evident in complex societies than in structurally simpler societies. Moreover, certain characteristics that are subordinate in complex societies but dominant in simpler societies (reciprocity in social relations, for example) can be better understood in contemporary society by a study of them in structurally simpler societies (Sahlins, 1972: 135 n. 18).

[2] See, for instance, Galliher (1971: 308) and Center for Research on Criminal Justice (1977: 5). Manning (1979: 42) notes that "there is no comprehensive Marxist analysis of the rise of the police. . . ." Newman finds that

we still know very little about why particular kinds of societies exhibit the structures of conflict resolution they do. There has been a dearth of modern *comparative* work attempting to formulate typologies of legal institutions and determine what, if any, systematic causal links may be found between these institutions and the *types* of societies in which they occur (1983: 2 [emphasis in original]).

and social relations within a community that may encourage the development of the police function? What are the relations between coercive means of social control (police, for instance) and the noncoercive mechanisms?

Despite the enormous amount of writing on various aspects of police behavior, function, and history, no historian has attempted to answer such questions or to construct a cross-cultural, evolutionary theory of the police function. Historians, however, normally specialize in a limited time period or in some limited area of police history itself. For English and American historians, the accepted focal beginning of police history has been the formation of the organized police force in England in 1829.[3] Although the pre-1829 period seems to have been adequately documented by competent authors, especially Reith (1952), dealing with the years 600 to 1950, Critchley (1967), studying the period from 900 to 1966, and Radzinowicz (1956), examining the one hundred years between 1750 and 1850, their purpose has been restricted to recounting the events leading up to the formation of the organized police (Robinson, 1979). No historian has been interested in the prestate police institution for its own sake. The method used by most historians has not been designed to concentrate on questions involving the transition from one form of society to another (Terray, 1972: 32; Lewis, 1968: x).

Anthropology, on the other hand, has frequently been concerned with just such questions. However, although anthropologists have examined social control mechanisms of complex societies and in fact have been concerned with processual problems (Nader and Todd, 1978), most recent anthropological writings have focused on what has been called specific evolution (the study of the social system of one society) rather than with general evolution (the construction of theories of evolutionary stages based on the study of many societies) (Service, 1975). While there has been a recent surge of interest in general evolutionary theory,[4] neither of these two schools has studied the police as an institution.

---

[3] Richardson concludes that "academic or professional historians largely ignored the police until the 1960s when Roger Lane [1967] and James Richardson [1970] produced their accounts of the formative years of the Boston and New York departments respectively" (1979). In recent years, the literature on the police has grown enormously. A summary of much of this literature is found in Walker (1977) and Robinson (1983); a critical view is found in Center for Research on Criminal Justice (1977). A few exceptions to the lack of attention to nonindustrial police are collected in Greenberg (1976: 9 n. 1).

[4] Some recent literature that considers the evolution of the state is Fried (1967), Krader (1968; 1976; 1978), Carneiro (1970), Leacock (1972), Service (1975), Saxe (1977), Wright (1977), Sacks (1979), Haas (1982), and Newman

112   ORIGIN AND EVOLUTION OF THE POLICE FUNCTION

Related to the accent on specifics over general evolutionary
theory has been the movement toward specialization in all social sciences, with its emphasis on quantification and middle-
range theory over conceptualization, integration, and total systems theory (Leacock, 1972: 59–61; Rocher, 1972: 21). In anthropology, this approach began with the historical particularism of
Franz Boas, which in turn was a reaction to general theories of
social evolution proposed without sound ethnographic data. It
was also, in a sense, a reaction to the class-based theories of
Marx and Engels, which seemed to accept as their analytic focus the workings of the entire social system, employing what
appeared to be the evolutionary perspective as an integral part
of that analysis. This would suggest that an analysis of Marxist
anthropological literature might deal with questions of the origins of the police function. Marx and Engels, however, showed
only limited interest in precapitalist modes of production, concentrating principally on capitalist class relations (Hindess and
Hirst, 1975: 33). On the police they wrote little (Pearce, 1976:
61–66). It is understandable, therefore, that even Marxist scholars who are concerned with police history have largely ignored
early police forms, preferring to center their attention on the
function of the police during the more recent industrial era.[5]

Despite a lack of focus on the police function, however, the
literature reviewed above provides a detailed framework for
such an analysis. Anthropologists, who have written extensively on differences between state and stateless societies, have
provided a starting point. First, they provide us with a usable
analytic vocabulary. The state, for example, is generally defined as the societal institution having a monopoly of legitimate
force (the police function) over a specified territory.[6] In contrast, stateless societies are commonly agreed to have social
control mechanisms characterized by kinship-based, communal
security arrangements. Resources are generally collectively

(1983), although "there have been few research projects aimed at systematically collecting data directly relevant to questions of state evolution . . . . Only
within the past decade has archaeology turned its attention to such problems"
(Haas, 1982: 1, 131). There has been a particular void in theory development.

[5] One important Marxist work argues that the attempt to develop such
"concepts further would be a formalist and antiquarian exercise . . ." (Hindess
and Hirst, 1975: 20). For Marxist literature dealing with criminal justice, see
Center for Research on Criminal Justice (1977), the periodical *Crime and Social Justice*, and Pearce (1976: 61–67).

[6] A critical review of attempts to define the state from a Marxist perspective will be found in Balandier (1970: 123–157) and Newman (1983). See
also Krader (1968: 9, 21) and Vinogradoff (1920: 93). For more traditional definitions, see Sahlins (1972: 140, 179), Service (1962: 171; 1975: 10), Adams (1966:
14), Cohen (1978a: 52), Wright (1977: 52), Weber (1976: 10), Harris (1975: 370),
and Wright and Fox (1978: 73).

owned within significant social units, and there is evidence that
the police function, to the extent that such specialized functions
exist in the absence of state structure, remains part of and
serves the entire social unit or community (see, for example,
Service, 1962). In societies organized as states, however, the
community social control mechanism is replaced by a bureaucratic apparatus. This bureaucracy, of which the police function is a part, has "separated from" and is "above" the rest of
society, and tends to predominantly serve only one segment of
the community—the dominant class (Engels, 1972: 230).

On this point, a principal difference arises between Marxist
and non-Marxist anthropologists. While non-Marxists employ
the state-stateless dichotomy as a qualitative change point (Cohen and Service, 1978; Leacock, 1972: 48) or see merely "a continuum of directional change" (Service, 1975: 305–306), Marxists
see the crossover from kinship-dominated (primitive) to a class-
dominated (civil) society as a social discontinuity (Krader, 1976:
11–12, 1978: 94; White, 1959: 282, 329; Leacock, 1972: 61–62;
Claessen and Skalnik, 1978b: 33; Sacks, 1979: 194–195; Haas,
1982: 34–35). In general, the non-Marxist approach rests heavily on an assumption of an incremental increase in political
complexity until state organization is reached, while Marxist
analysis relies more on a belief that a change from a kinship- to
a class-dominated society results in a revolution in the entire
social fabric that requires a police mechanism to maintain the
social order of inequality (Engels, n.d.). From this standpoint,
the transition from a kinship- to a class-dominated society "is
not a continuity, but on the contrary, a rupture" (Althusser and
Balibar, 1968: 229). However, whatever disagreements there
are among theories of state formation, all Marxist proponents
seem to agree on one common feature of the state, namely its
rule as "a ruling body controlling production or procurement of
basic resources and exercising economic power over its population" (Haas, 1982: 15).

Our theory, which draws from both schools, consists of
four interdependent propositions:

1. The origin of the specialized police function depends upon the division of communal (kinship) society into dominant and subordinate classes with
antagonistic interests (Engels, 1972; White, 1959:
307).
2. Specialized police agencies are generally characteristic only of societies politically organized as states.
3. In a period of transition the crucial factor in delineating the modern specialized police function is
an ongoing attempt at the conversion of the social

114   ORIGIN AND EVOLUTION OF THE POLICE FUNCTION

control (policing) mechanism from an integral part
of the community structure to an agent of an
emerging dominant class.

4. The police institution is created by the emerging
    dominant class as an instrument for the preserva-
    tion of its control over restricted access to basic re-
    sources, over the political apparatus governing this
    access, and over the labor force necessary to pro-
    vide the surplus upon which the dominant class
    lives (Newman, 1983: 25).

Thus our theory suggests that developmentally the police have
a double, contradictory, and dynamic origin and function that
leads to its contemporary schizophrenic image (Reiner, 1978:
183–184). This is the case because the police are, at the same
time, the agent of both the people they police and the dominant
class controlling these same people in the interest of this class
(Robinson, 1978; Monkkonen, 1981).

The idea that the police really issue from the community
and are a part of that community has been a pervasive and essential prop to concepts of modern policing (Robinson, 1979). It
supplies the continuity between the ancient structural change
from police in and of the community to police as an agent of
the state. Therefore, before proceeding to develop our theory,
it is essential to examine the assumptions that give ideological
sustenance to the modern police function.

*A. The Traditional View of the History and Function of
Police in Western Society*

Traditional writing regarding the police function does not
view the police as an instrument of the state conceived to protect the interests of the few at the expense of the many.[7] On
the contrary, police in both England and the United States are
generally seen as protectors of the law and order that allow
democratic institutions to operate.

Early police history, from an American perspective, is English history, and most writers who have written on this period
are English (ibid.).[8] To them, England is a democracy, and the
police, like other English institutions, is either identical with or

---

[7] These assumptions are more explicitly set forth by English than by
American historians, although these themes become more evident in American writing on police-community relations (Robinson, 1979).

[8] We summarize only some of the major writers on early police history,
that is, those writing about the period before the organization of London police
in 1829. There is much relevant writing about law courts, prisons, local government, and the church that is not included. Our purpose here is not to set
forth all information available on English prestate police but merely to summarize the picture of that system provided by police historians.

representative of its people. American writers have generally accepted these propositions without question. What follows is a discussion of the logic behind these assumptions.

Crucial to the notion of the police as a democratic institution are the ideas that (1) the police institution in England has deep historical roots and is said to have experienced a slow but consistent growth (and progress) from ancient to modern times; (2) the police institution is unique to the English people, originates from the people, is dependent on them for its support, and that without that support, its effectiveness and even its existence would be in doubt; (3) the community is divided into a majority of good, law-abiding people and a minority of lawbreakers, and that one police function is to protect this virtuous majority from the criminal minority (ibid.).

One well known English police historian expresses the first of these themes as follows:

> Our English police system on the other hand, rests on foundations designed with the full approval of the people, we know not how many hundreds of years before the Norman conquest, and has been slowly moulded by the careful hand of experience, developing as a rule along the line of least resistance, now in advance of the general intelligence of the country, now lagging far behind, but always in the long run adjusting itself to the popular temper, always consistent with local self-government, and even at its worst, always English (Lee, 1971: xxvii).

This past is said to continue into the present. No structural or ideological breach between the police and the community is recognized. On the contrary, the unity of the two is affirmed: "The police . . . represent the collective interests of the community . . . . The device which is most characteristically English has been to arm the police with prestige rather than power, thus obliging them to rely on popular support" (Critchley, 1967: xiii–xiv).

One of the most important assertions of this viewpoint is that far from being policed from above, the English people police themselves. That the police and the people are one is embodied in the Seventh Principle adopted by the English police:

> To maintain at all times a relationship with the public that gives reality to the historic tradition that the police are the public and that the public are the police; the police being only members of the public who are paid to give full-time attention to duties which are incumbent on every citizen, in the interests of community welfare and existence (quoted in Reith, 1975: 163).

This same idea influenced the growth of American literature

116   ORIGIN AND EVOLUTION OF THE POLICE FUNCTION

on police-community relations (Radelet, 1973: vii–viii; National Advisory Commission on Criminal Justice Standards and Goals, 1973: 9; Bopp, 1972: 47; Momboisse, 1967: 4).

The Law Enforcement Assistance Administration, reviewing police-community relations efforts, combined these ideas into a philosophy of modern police-community relations:

> Sir Robert Peel, in the early 1800's set forth law enforcement principles which are particularly interesting today because of a notable prevailing emphasis on the important role to be played by the ordinary citizen in police service. . . .
> Within the context of the Peel philosophy and its assimilation into our society, at least three strongly prevailing themes have managed to stand the test of time. These points are:
> 1) The police are the public and the public are the police, the police accurately mirror the general culture of the society they represent;
> 2) The police function depends on a considerable amount of self-policing by every citizen. . . . Ideally, it is a matter of organic union, with police as part of, and not apart from the community they serve; and
> 3) The police are a living expression, and embodiment, an implementing arm of democratic law (1978: 3–4).

These assumptions obscure both the structural changes resulting from state formation—the switch in police loyalty from the community to the state—and the consequent conflicts between police and community groups. It is our intention to examine the processes through which societies become complex and to focus on the part played therein by the police function. We turn therefore to the development of our theory.

II. THE DEVELOPMENT OF THE POLICE FUNCTION IN SOCIETY: THE THEORY

A. *A Review of Prior Attempts to Construct Theories Relating to Police Origins*

Anthropologists have been divided as to the merits of approaching the development of civilization from an evolutionary basis. Early anthropologists advocated a stage theory in which they argued that all civilizations passed through or were destined to pass through specified stages (hunting-gathering, herding, pastoral, agricultural, and industrial) that were based on economic and social characteristics. Other evolutionists rejected the idea that there is any prescribed passage through specified stages and argued instead that the evolutionary pattern may vary, progressing or regressing depending on the ecological and cultural conditions to which any particular civilization is subject (Claessen and Skalnik, 1978b; Sacks, 1979: 194). Recently, neoevolutionists have focused upon energy capture and utilization as diagnostic variables indicating social evolution. As to the police function, most anthropologists have been satisfied with concluding that at a certain stage one group in a society has acquired a monopoly of force.

Much of the contemporary writing on the anthropology of law supports such a perspective, although it is rarely phrased in an evolutionary manner. A relationship between societal complexity and either bargaining or authority as the basis for conflict management is recognized. Kinship-based societies usually settle disputes through negotiation, mediation, or arbitration in loosely structured moot courts characterized by the absence of formal proceedings and authority, an emphasis on keeping peace rather than on assessing blame, and an attempt at decision making through consensus. Complex state societies base their dispute management on adjudication in formal courts characterized by authoritative decisions backed by legitimized coercion (Hoebel, 1954). There the emphasis is on rules or norms and fact situations related to the violation of these rules, and decisions are unilateral (Nader and Todd, 1978). While an evolutionary perspective is implicit in such a theoretical framework when we consider that societies have become more complex through time, we again must turn to Marxist anthropology for more detailed models.

There have been a number of attempts to express complete theories of evolution, the most well known being those of Morgan (1877), which in turn inspired those of Engels (1972) and Fried (1967). All three see the crucial point in societal development as the transition from stateless to state society, although for Engels class division precedes state formation. The latter represents a qualitative change from a noncoercive to a coercive, class-dominated society. Each theorist explains the appearance of the police function by the inability of the kinship means of social control to support or maintain a system of inequality and class domination.

Class divisions, in the process of their formation, decimated the kinship organization of society. As one of the conditions of the continued existence of a class-divided society and as a replacement for the kinship organization, a state apparatus came into existence. The former "self-acting armed organization" was no longer possible in a society consisting of antagonistic classes because society was no longer a "self-acting" organism

118   ORIGIN AND EVOLUTION OF THE POLICE FUNCTION

(Engels, 1972: 230). It was now directed from above, and from above emerged an agent of this state power—the police—that, "which, apparently standing about the warring classes, suppressed their open conflict and allowed the class struggle to be fought out at most in the economic field, in so-called legal form" (Engels, 1972: 228). Engels's thesis is useful as a starting point for comparative analysis but it does not "develop a very adequate theory about the causal mechanisms involved" (Pryor, 1977: 223; see also Balandier, 1970: 157). As Sacks (1979: 102–103) points out, Engels's "work is really not a history at all. It is evolution, a logical arrangement of static descriptions of a variety of social systems (or modes of production) frozen in time and truncated in space." Sacks further suggests that most other anthropological research has the same defect (ibid., p. 106).

Political anthropologist Fried (1967) argues that there are three stages of social organization that precede formation of the state, which he labels the egalitarian, ranking, and stratification stages. In the first two stages, individuals have equal access to the basic resources that are necessary to maintain human life. In the third stage, stratification, it is the control of these basic resources by some persons that makes it possible and necessary to develop means of coercive social control to maintain such limited access. Social control mechanisms to preserve such inequality are found within a state organization.

Thus, in general studies of societal evolution, the police have been mentioned as incidentally arising out of the transition from a stateless to a state society in that a society based on state organization, it is argued, is sustainable only through force. There is some disagreement among writers over whether a state bureaucracy produces a class structure or whether a class structure produces a state. In order to examine this problem, it is necessary to explore the nature of coercive kinship structures.

B.   The Evolution of a Coercive Kinship Structure

Kinship-based cultures, in which the people "produce most of what they consume and consume most of what they produce" (Fallers, 1964: 117), are often incorrectly pictured as totally egalitarian, idyllic societies with no divisions between producers and nonproducers and therefore no basis for a class structure. A related error is the attempt to distinguish stateless from complex societies merely by determining the stage at which they are capable of producing a surplus of food products that will support a class of nonproducers. In fact, many so-called simple societies are quite capable of producing a surplus with present technologies. Lee's data (1968: 1979) on the !Kung bushmen, for example, show that a surplus of mongongo nuts, the staple food, lies rotting on the ground for the lack of some-one with a reason to gather them. Likewise, Saffirio and Scag-lion (1982) show how a group of Yanomamo Indians, faced with ecological pressure, merely increased the use of a more efficient hunting technique.

The question then is not whether any particular society has a surplus but how labor, capable of producing a surplus, is ap-propriated and how the surplus products of that labor are dis-tributed.[9] A simple mode of production does not exclude the existence of arrangements that allow for collective and cooper-ative appropriation. Neither does it preclude coercion. It does, however, preclude a state apparatus to maintain such coercion. In most cases, production of a large surplus is of little benefit to individuals in simpler societies.

Communal appropriation of surplus value may be accom-plished by means of either simple or complex redistribution. *Simple redistribution* consists of the appropriation of natural products ready for use (such as nuts, roots, and animals) and their redistribution through a network of relations established on a temporary or semipermanent basis, as is seen in hunting-gathering societies in which people live in small bands. This type of distribution network is determined by the fragility and temporary nature of the social organization. Bands are small in size, variable in composition, and do not endure as units for long periods of time. There is therefore no basis for social rela-tions permanent enough to sustain the cooperation necessary to complete complex labor tasks. The dominant social division of labor in such societies is by age and sex (Sahlins, 1972: 79).

Complex redistribution, on the other hand, allows the dis-tribution of products throughout a permanent network of rela-tionships established in advance of any particular labor process. There is therefore the possibility of cooperation among work teams. Such redistribution is generally associated with (1) the increased productivity of labor; and (2) a greater number of la-borers and thus an increase in the amount of surplus labor ap-propriated for redistribution within the community. Such a community can support specialists who do not engage in food production but can receive their share of food just as if they

---

[9] The following analysis substantially relies on Hindess and Hirst (1975; 1977).

had produced it themselves. A larger nonproductive population can be sustained under this system. The presence of these non-producers has several results: (1) The maintenance of a high level of production depends on a continuing division of and complex cooperation among labor over long periods of time, which in turn encourages mechanisms to supervise and coordinate the labor process; (2) the appreciation of these mechanisms as a necessary part of the production of this surplus becomes an addition to the ideological component; (3) higher population density and therefore more producers become possible; (4) a group of persons forms who can devote time to ceremonial activities such as appeasing or opportuning the gods to increase or maintain production; and (5) relationships with other groups develop that tend to promote exchanges of items produced. In societies with such a system of distribution the elders receive the surplus and direct its redistribution. Distribution is based not on the relative amount of work done by the team or on the temporary relationships that might have been established between individuals, but on the position each person occupies in the kinship network, as determined by age, status, or sex.

The emergence of complex kinship relations is a necessary step in the transition from simple to complex redistribution. Kinship relations exist in societies in which there is simple redistribution, but their existence is unnecessary for the reproduction of the societies' economy. The kinship relations necessary for complex redistribution are those featuring hierarchical relations such as those within the household or lineage, between elders and youths, and between lineages and villages within a tribe (Lowie, 1927: 82). Although elders and adults of various statuses may supervise and coordinate the labor process, it is the kinship network of relationships that allows the direction, coordination, and supervision of labor by elders and other adults so as to extract surplus labor from those lower in the hierarchy. Division of labor, however, is limited by the social organization of kinship, which predetermines that the surplus will be redistributed to the community itself according to customary relations.

Meillassoux's work (1964) with the Guro of the Ivory Coast illustrates how coercive structures based on age may operate. Although most tools necessary to set the means of production in motion (wooden tools, mortars, pestles, canoes, and the like) are collectively available in this society, iron tools (such as machetes) remain in the exclusive possession of the elders. The hierarchical relationship between the elders and other adults allows the elders to assign land or work and to regulate marriage exchanges. Hindess and Hirst (1975: 66) suggest that "the coordination of labour and the regulation of marriages involves the existence of forms of coercion" such as the deprivation of food or slavery (forced labor). The coercive force is thus embodied in the capacity of the elders to withhold essential goods and services until their demands are met (Haas, 1982: 82). Similar situations may be seen in the redistribution of surplus by the chiefs in the Trobriand Islands and in the mobilization of labor for sea-going voyages (*Kula*), which were studied by Malinowski (1921).

We see, therefore, that a kinship-based society with a complex distribution system has, in addition to the usual accouterments of this type of society (such as reciprocal relations, relatively equal access to basic resources, and authority based on kinship rather than on political structure), a hierarchical order of kinship relations that permits the coercive use of traditions, rites, and customs by the elders for and on behalf of the tribal unit.

In addition to a hierarchical, coercive organization based on age, division may also be based on gender. Sacks (1979) shows how sex may form the basis for a coercive hierarchy in a variety of preindustrial societies. Godelier (1982) studied the Baruya people, a simple society living in seventeen villages and hamlets in a mountainous region of New Guinea. He describes how Baruya women are denied the ownership and control of the land they work as well as the ownership and production of the tools they use, thereby limiting their power, influence, and prestige in their lineage, which cooperatively owns its land. The women are likewise denied access to arms and forbidden to engage in war outside their tribal boundaries. Thus they are barred from gaining the prestige and glory acquired through the protection of the community. Neither can they engage in foreign trade, exchanges that bring to the tribe necessary products. Nor are they entitled to own sacred objects, which are the sole way the tribe can communicate with the supernatural forces that determine its well-being.

Having indicated that both age and sex divisions may underlie a coercive system in which a police mechanism does not necessarily exist, our next task will be to examine police mechanisms in societies in which the central authority and the police, acting for that authority, function on behalf of the whole community. Thereafter, we will suggest the transactional steps whereby a coercive, stateless society is converted to a society with a police institution acting on behalf of a dominant class.

122 ORIGIN AND EVOLUTION OF THE POLICE FUNCTION

C. *Police in Societies with Central Authorities Serving the Whole Community*

In non-Western societies, sodalities or associations occupy a transitional position between the absence of formal police functions and the existence of a formal police structure of state organization. The Plains societies of the American West were perhaps the simplest societies (from a point of view of social organization) to have such sodalities. In discussing these societies, Lowie describes how exigencies of the hunt precipitated the development of a police function in an essentially egalitarian society in which the thought of a chief having power over the life and property of others was foreign. However, to prevent a premature attack on the buffalo herd this situation changes:

> The personnel of the constabulary varies with the tribe; the duties may be linked with a particular society (Mandan, Hidatsa), or be assumed by various military societies in turn (Crow), or fall to the lot of distinguished men without reference to associational affiliations (Kansas). But everywhere the basic idea is that during the hunt a group is vested with the power forcibly to prevent premature attacks on the herd and to punish offenders by corporal punishment, by confiscation of the game illegally secured, by destruction of their property generally, and in extreme cases by killing them. . . . If, for example, a man had been murdered by another, the official peacemakers of the tribe—often identical with the buffalo police—were primarily concerned with pacifying the victim's kin rather than with meting out just punishment. There was thus a groping sentiment on behalf of territorial cohesion and against internecine strife. But there was no feeling that any impartial authority seated above the parties to the feud had been outraged and demanded penance or penalty. In juridical terminology, even homicide was a tort, not a crime. But with transgressions of the hunting regulations it was otherwise: they were treated as an attempt against the public, in short as a criminal act, and they were punished with all the rigor appropriate to political offenses (1927: 103–104).

Provinse sees the functions of these Plains Indians police as extending beyond their function in the hunt. Based on a number of references, he concludes that "police duties in connection with settling disputes, punishing offenders, and maintaining order in camp generally would seem to surpass in importance the police duties at the communal hunt" (1937: 348).

Llewellyn and Hoebel have produced the most detailed examination of police in an essentially egalitarian society. The

Cheyenne, numbering at most four thousand, separated into bands, except in summer when they came together for the communal hunts. Differences in wealth consisted mainly of horses, clothes, and adornments. The Cheyenne were a hunting society in which all shared the proceeds of the hunt. Government was by a council of chiefs who had ten-year terms. Each chief chose his own successor. A chief was appointed "because he approached the ideal qualities of leadership: wisdom, courage, kindness, generosity, and even temper" (1941: 73).

The Cheyenne had six military societies, in which membership was voluntary. Only one such society, the Dog Soldiers, remained together during the entire year, and that was because it constituted a band. The rest of the societies exercised their functions as units only during the summer hunting season. A major function of these societies was keeping the peace. They intervened in what would otherwise be private quarrels, but since every private disorder could result in a killing that could bloody the "Sacred Arrows, endangering thereby the well-being of the people . . . it was treated as a crime against the nation" (ibid., p. 132). The societies policed behavior of warriors in time of war and during communal bison hunts, supervised the division of meat, settled any resulting disputes, brought laggards to tribal religious ceremonies, and helped the poor and destitute.

Black cites a number of similar examples from the literature. There are, for example, the Yahgan nomadic bands, among which individuals appointed policed the initiation ceremonies. The Apinaye Indians of northern Brazil utilized policemen during the growing season, and anyone who harvested before that time was subject to punishment. Another Indian tribe "punished anyone who prematurely harvested wild rice," and "the early Ontong Javanese had officials . . . who guarded against theft of coconuts and other foodstuffs from the common lands" (1976: 90).

Regardless of the dramatic acts of these temporary police, it is important to emphasize that the individuals in the Cheyenne military societies, like those in other groups, remained an integral part of the community social fabric. Almost all mature males were members of such societies, and there were several such groups within the tribal structure. As a result, almost every man was at one time a member of a force policing the rest of the community and at other times a simple tribal member. In addition, such police service was temporary, lasting only while the Cheyenne camped together during the hunting season. Moreover, even when acting as police, Cheyenne remained bound by their kinship and tribal relations. Police who

124   ORIGIN AND EVOLUTION OF THE POLICE FUNCTION

overstepped their power would have to pay for such an action on returning to tribal life. Moreover, the separate associations acted as checks and balances on each other (Lowie, 1927: 103–104; Llewellyn and Hoebel, 1941: 130; Krader, 1976: 33–35).

After citing numerous incidents such as the above, Mac-Leod concludes that the

> policing of these hunts was of vital economic impor-tance [to the Plains Indians] and absolutely essential to prevent failure as a result of the behavior of any indi-viduals who might be selfish enough to scare the herd off by individual action. . . . The Plains police were, therefore, a rather democratic organization devoted to the maintenance of law and order in the interest of the people as a whole (1937: 186, 200).

D.   *Transitional Mechanisms of Moving from a Coercive but Classless Society to a Class-Dominated Society*

In attempting to construct an evolutionary approach to the police function, it does not seem profitable to try to provide a series of stages through which the police function necessarily "progressed" to its modern guise; neither does it seem fruitful to search for the point at which the police function suddenly appeared (Godelier, 1972: 124; Price, 1978: 168; Claessen and Skalnik, 1978b: 15). Rather, we should be searching for key ar-eas of development likely to be related to the police function. We believe that the most pertinent developmental changes are modifications in productive and distributional relations, polit-ical and community structure, social relations, and ideology.

We agree with the way in which Fried posed and then an-swered a pertinent question in this analysis:

> Why have people permitted themselves to be seduced, bilked, murphied, or otherwise conned into relinquish-ing a condition of egalitarianism for one of inequality? . . . I believe that stratified society and the state emerged in the same quiet way and were institution-ally fully present before anyone fumbled for a word by which to designate them (1967: 182–183).

The key to this development would seem to be in the conscious accumulation of surplus. Once one is a chief within a complex redistribution system, he has captive the kinds of virtues and material possessions that can attract to him the means to sub-stantially increase his ability to appropriate and thus systemati-cally accumulate surplus. This accumulation of wealth in turn increases his capability to add to his work force and so on (Sah-lins, 1972). He remains as chief because he appears to embody the virtues of liberality, reciprocity, and mutual aid, which is so important to tribal survival,[10] and thus it is upon him that tribal survival seems to depend (Saxe, 1977: 122). Redistribution of foodstuffs appears to be the material realization of tribal custom and virtues. In fact as well as in appearance, redistribution tends to enhance reciprocity by allowing more cooperative enterprise (Polanyi, 1968: 225; White, 1959: 234).

Thus, as Sahlins so neatly expresses, "what begins with the would-be head-man putting his production to others' benefit, ends, to some degree, with others putting their production to the chief's benefit" (1972: 140). But this transformation in the material social relationship between the chief and his kinsmen is compensated for by increased production and the evolution of an ideology that was unnecessary in earlier stages of development (Service, 1962: 170–177).

The redistributive function may then lead to the development of a hereditary office in which lineage or position rather than the individual ability of the kinsman is the determinant (White, 1959: 234; Lenski, 1966: 109; Ruyle, 1973). Core or privileged lineages may arise around which the lesser clans then group (Sanders and Price, 1968: 131, 132); slaves may be taken, again distributed unevenly, thereby differentially increasing productive capacity (Terray, 1974: 328–329); ownership or symbolic representation of the common lands may justify the chief in levying taxes and rents (Ruyle, 1973: 614); conquered or community land may become *state* land and thereby be converted into the private property of the sovereign (Skalnik, 1978: 604); or the sovereign, acting as "the ultimate source of order and justice," may determine that offenses against his dignity are in contravention of the common good (Mair, 1964: 204; Lenski, 1966: 181). Dominant-subordinate relations become the focus of political-social relations and finally of *"emergent* social classes" (Claessen and Skalnik, 1978c: 642 [emphasis in original]). Deference, loyalty, and obedience to hierarchical superiors replace individual striving as a means of achievement (Cohen, 1978b: 67–69). The former kinsman becomes thereby the ruler-father and the people his subject-children (Rounds, 1979: 78; Ruyle, 1973: 616).

How can we explain the means by which an egalitarian society (that is, a society without the sort of inner conflicts inher-

---

[10] In fact, there may be myths about how bad things were when there was no ruler: "The belief is common among [the Ganda, a Bantu people of East Africa] that a time when there is no ruler is a time of lawlessness and anarchy, though this may only be a metaphorical way of expressing their conception of the king as the ultimate source of order and justice" (Mair, 1964: 208). For a modern example, see Robinson (1979).

ent in a class-dominated society, a society that has the capacity
to be fulfilling for all—the strong as well as the weak) experiences a structural change radically modifying its class base?
(Harris, 1975: 308, 366; Leacock, 1972: 25). One rather obvious
mechanism involves a takeover of one group by another culture. Such a situation activates the ethnocentric attitudes
found in all cultures that relegate "others" to an inferior status.
The victors constitute a dominant class controlling both the
mode of production and the labor of the defeated, subordinate
class. One such example is the kingdom of Gyaman, which was
founded at the end of the seventeenth century in the northeast
part of present day Ivory Coast and northwest Ghana (Terray,
1974: 320). Originally, judicial, political, and administrative
power was in the hands of a warrior aristocracy. The principal
means of acquiring wealth was through long-distance trading in
gold. Terray shows that the control of the gold trade depended
on the labor of slaves, which was available only to an aristocracy, that to reproduce and defend this social order it was necessary for the aristocracy to maintain an armed presence both
outside and inside the society, and that this institutionalization
of force to supply the surplus product to support this elite class
resulted in the creation of a state society in which the continuity of kinship relations was a subordinate rather than a
dominant mode of production.

While in Gyaman society the dynamic force in the formation of a class-dominated society was the conversion by the ruling aristocracy of the dominant mode of production from kinship to slavery, in Aztec society a centralized elite gradually
seduced and coopted local lineage leadership away from their
kinship-based communities so as to produce a stratified, class-
dominated state organization.[11] In the mid-thirteenth century,
Aztec people migrated to the Valley of Mexico. They were organized in *calpulli* (groups of households) that were politically
arranged into clans with fictive kin relationships. Land was
corporately owned but individually cultivated. Separate plots
were communally farmed on behalf of *calpulli* leaders, not because the *calpulli* leaders could command it but because such
work was due by ancestral custom in payment "for the care he
[the leader] took of them, and for his expenditure on the annual meeting held in his house in support of the general welfare" (Adams, 1966: 92; see also Kurtz, 1978: 171).

Wealth was unequally distributed; some lineage lines were

---

[11] The material presented here on the Aztec state substantially follows
the work of Adams (1966) and Rounds (1979). See also Wolf (1959).

ranked higher than others, with some families receiving more land; those less favored might be forced into slavery or to migrate. There appeared to be a complex redistribution system operating through the *calpulli*. The authority of the *calpulli* and the *tlatoani* (literally, speaker; the term designated the central overall leader) was limited, in part because of the competition among the *calpulli* leaders. These leaders, apparently concerned with military threats from more centralized states around them, decided to adopt the style of their enemies. This plan was implemented by bringing in a foreign noble as *tlatoani*.

Thereafter the death of the leader of a rival people that had until then dominated the valley was followed by an internal power struggle, which allowed the Aztecs to attain hegemony over the valley and all its riches. With this tribute the *tlatoani* moved to consolidate his power by using the newly found wealth to bring *calpulli* leaders closer to central authority while at the same time separating them from their own local community power base.

The *tlatoani* set about to develop the *calpulli* into a self-consciously elite class by distributing titles of nobility, some lands, and other spoils; by requiring nobles to lodge separately and to wear distinctive clothing and jewelry; and by forbidding others to do likewise. He provided elaborate feasts and ceremonies in which only the designated nobles could participate and linked the *calpulli* leaders and the throne by marriage. The *tlatoani* thus defined nobles as those directly receiving tribute from him. All this was conceived to channel the local leaders' immediate self-interest to the political ends of the *tlatoani*.

The *tlatoani* also required that all administrative business be attended to at the central palace, asserted the right to name *calpulli* successors (over time the *calpulli* had changed from leaders elected by the community to hereditary leaders), and increased the significance of this power by making the hereditary succession of lands dependent on acquisition of the *calpulli* office. In addition, his control of trade and tribute allowed the *tlatoani* to determine the distribution of luxury goods to the nobles (cf. Lenski, 1966: 220). In sum, he was able to invert the source of the *calpulli* leaders' power. Instead of issuing from the *calpulli*, power now came from—or seemed to come from— the *tlatoani*. All this took a number of generations to accomplish. Nevertheless, the *tlatoani* left the political and economic organization of the *calpulli* community relatively untouched. Tribute or surplus, which the *calpulli* leaders were obligated to send to the Aztec state, was collected by the *calpulli* leaders on

128   ORIGIN AND EVOLUTION OF THE POLICE FUNCTION

the same basis as before, that is, through communal labor service accorded by ancient custom. Thus the unit of responsibility to the Aztec state was not the individual citizen but the corporate *calpulli* unit, as it had been earlier.

This use of a lineage-based kinship mode of production by a
centralized stratified structure to collect surplus to sustain an
elite class is characteristic of "weak states," which employ the
lineage elite as "hinge figures or brokers linking the lineage
territory to state authority" (Fox, 1976: 100). But equally important with the appearance of the dominant state organization
is the continuation of the kinship mode of production, even
though it may be in an attenuated form (White, 1959: 141, 310;
Krader, 1976: 11–12; Fox, 1971: 157).

Police control of large populations over long periods of
time is abnormal. In fact, states that endeavor to control their
populations by such methods receive the designation "police
states." A social control mechanism much more effective than
the police is the economiç system itself, especially the market
exchange system. Of supreme importance as a control of peasant populations is the self-regulating market, that is, an economic system regulated and directed by market forces and in
which order in the production and distribution of goods is assured by price alone (Polanyi, 1957: 68). In simple states, religious institutions also supply significant overt ideological support to the dominant elite (White, 1959: 218–220; Ruyle, 1973,
1976: 24; Cohen, 1978b: 63–65; Skalnik, 1978: 606).

For example, Adams suggests that the movement of Aztec
society from a stateless to state organization was accompanied
by the transformation of humanlike gods representing growth
and fertility into gods "more remote and awesome in their powers . . . , the emergence of representational art . . . [and] an elite
. . . that promoted those aspects of individuality for which por-
traiture became necessary as an enduring symbol and monu-
ment" (1966: 124; see also Kurtz, 1978: 178–179).

In societies of this type, the temple, like the chief, represented a redistributional center where offerings could be made,
craftsmen could gather, writing could develop, and records
could be kept. It thus functioned as an economic as well as a
religious institution (Sedov, 1978: 122). It came to have a life
separated from the community, with a monopoly of knowledge,
encouraging "a sense of detachment from and superiority to the
day-to-day concerns of secular life" (Adams, 1966: 126; see also
Saxe, 1977: 133; Lenski, 1966: 208–210).

"[R]eligion fulfilled the role of disseminating state propa-
ganda and inculcating in the common people a sense of loyalty

toward the state and its sovereign . . ." (Skalnik, 1978: 607).
Conversely, it was religion that maintained the myth of a continuous, harmonious, integrated, nonexploitative, and ideal
community. In emphasizing moral and individual concerns and
responsibilities, it replaced kin and territorial loyalties with a
universalistic perspective (ibid.; Eisenstadt, 1963: 63–65). The
king became the center of a priestly created universe with the
priest as the interpreter of the laws of a divine order in which
each individual had his preordained place (Campbell, 1959:
146–149).

E. The Evolution of the Police Function in a Class-Dominated Society

Earlier we demonstrated how a police could exist in a
stateless society and could act on behalf of the whole community. Our present task is to show how a police function might
arise within a class-dominated society. We have argued that
such a society results from a series of incremental steps. A major thesis of ours is that the police institution is a reflection of
the class organization of the state. We would expect the evolution of the police function to follow and parallel the evolution
of class society.

The appearance of a specialized police institution is related
to the appropriation of surplus labor. Like other specialists,
such as craftsmen, police are nonproducers of subsistence foodstuffs. If men are to be substantially engaged in police activity,
they must be maintained from the surplus labor appropriated
by some central authority (Harris, 1975: 374). A society that
cannot support other specialists because it has no apparatus to
appropriate a surplus for an elite class of nonproducers is unlikely to have a police (Lenski, 1966: 62). In addition, of course,
as Engels (1964) and Fried (1967) have pointed out, a society
based on kinship relations has adequate mutual aid mechanisms
to resolve internal divisions without having to resort to "law-
and-order specialists" (White, 1959: 85; see also Harris, 1975:
357).

In the case of the simple states we have discussed, the kinship mode of production has been maintained for the greatest
part of the population; for the emerging noble class other in-
ducements were available. Such a society may well be in transition from a hunting-and-gathering society to an agricultural
one in which extra people, instead of being a burden, become a
source of prestige and power to the chief through his use of the
additional labor to increase his surplus. Thus "person acquisi-

130   ORIGIN AND EVOLUTION OF THE POLICE FUNCTION

tion" through "increased birth rates . . . adoption, polygyny, bridewealth, clientage, fostering, and even . . . forcible capture and enslavement of strangers" becomes advantageous (Claessen and Skalnik, 1978b: 43). These societies carry within them the seeds of a stratified society, often encouraging mechanisms that eventually develop into a police function.

Haas (1982: chap. 4) attempts to determine whether the integrative or conflict theory of the evolution of the state is supported by the greater weight of empirical evidence. In concluding that the balance is on the side of the conflict position, he cites a number of examples from the literature showing that both forceful and nonforceful means have been used to maintain unequal access to scarce basic resources. In Hawaii, paramount chiefs used a mix of redistribution and force to maintain their power, exercising

> their control over land and water to dispossess from the means of subsistence those persons who failed to produce sufficient resources, or who secretly accumulated resources [citations omitted]. More direct physically coercive sanctions were applied against commoners who committed criminal acts or misdeeds. Particularly severe sanctions were applied when the misdeeds affected the paramount chiefs (ibid., p. 116).

Haas also cites the Zulu rulers' use of violence against their subordinate chiefs as a "critical component of the governing process" to keep the people in a position of subordination (ibid., p. 118). He likewise offers numerous cases of archaeological finds that indicate the existence of stratified societies among the first civilizations (ibid., p. 121). He concludes that although more evidence supports the conflict theory that holds that force was used to sustain stratification, it may be further argued that the material benefits gained through centralization were used by the rulers of the early civilizations as positive mechanisms to govern their respective populations (ibid., pp. 128–129).

One such mechanism of control is clientage—the combination of forceful and nonforceful relations involving the personal dependence of a subordinate on a superior. We suggest that the birth of the police institution is to be found in the building up of such a system outside of kinship and the gradual replacement of kinship with a system of personal dependency (Skalnik, 1978: 599–600). Although there is no description of such evolution of a police institution, there are many references to various types of clientage relationships in which police duties form one part of the overall duties owed by the client to his patron.

One of the clearest descriptions of such a relationship is

that provided by Mair in her discussion of several East African societies. Mair gives considerable attention to clientage, believing the "relationship to be the germ from which state power springs" (1964: 166). For example, "for a Hutu in Ruanda the value of clientship was that it got him the use of cattle even if he did not actually own them, and protection against marauders who might seize them" (ibid., p. 172).

Clientage is a reciprocal relationship and is therefore a fictive reproduction of the kinship relationship on a vertical (superior-inferior) rather than on a horizontal (equal) basis. Mair describes the case of the Getutu, a Kenya people who took in refugees from other related tribes that had been driven from their homelands. In exchange for various services such as serving as soldiers, working land, or tending cattle, the clients were given cattle, land, and protection. It becomes evident how these clients began to be used for police duties in ways that contributed to the deterioration of kinship ties:

> If a man wished to demand payment of a debt from someone at a distance, he would first persuade the elder in his own part of the country that he had a good claim. Then the elder would send one of his sons, carrying his staff, to the debtor's home to order him to pay. . . . But if the elder was afraid that the debtor would defy the order, he would send a number of his "bought persons" to enforce it. If they had to seize a cow from the debtor, and this led to fighting and perhaps killing, it would not be a fight between real "sons of Nyakundi," who ought to remain at peace (ibid., p. 112).

Mallon describes a patron-client relationship in an early Peruvian economy in which Spanish colonialists employed traditional structures to maintain their power, working through a class of Indian elites to control the labor force:

> Though rich peasants in the villages had at best a tenuous connection to the old communal traditions of authority, their position of influence did depend on fulfilling certain expectations of generosity and service to the community as a whole. If they financed the community's fiestas, gave aid to individuals in times of need, acted as godparents to neighbors' children (*campadrazgo*), served the village as political authorities, represented the community in court cases or petitions to the government, and organized and financed public works, they could expect preferential access to labor and resources. The poorer villagers, if they accepted the "generosity" of the rich, were bound to pay it back in individual or communal work; special "grants" of usufruct over community lands, pasture or water; or

132   ORIGIN AND EVOLUTION OF THE POLICE FUNCTION

with a more generalized and vague sense of loyalty and
deference which prompted them always to be ready to
do a favor, to serve their patrons in whatever way they
could (1983: 84–85).

Middle-level merchants thus served as mediators with village
elites. "In exchange, they received—and made available to
their patrons—a link to local client networks, through which it
was possible to obtain a labor force for the mule trade, hacien-
das, and mines" (ibid., p. 86 [emphasis in original]). An elite's
first choice in this society was to manipulate this traditional relationship to serve his new master, but when this means failed
"they did not hesitate to try intimidation and physical violence. . . ." Given the naked exploitation inherent in many of
these relationships, their continued effectiveness depended on
the ultimate capacity to use force . . ." (ibid., pp. 89, 90).

A central government must enforce its decrees and supervise any administrative apparatus in place. These tasks may be
accomplished by "extensive *travels* through the state on the
sovereign's part. . . . The use of messengers, envoys, plenipo-
tentiaries . . . ; the employment of *spies* . . . ; the *forced entertainment* of relatives of regional and/or local functionaries
in the capital" (Claessen, 1978: 584 [emphasis in original]).

Loyal clients were important to a chief's power and prestige, especially in Africa, because the ability to attract men to
cultivate his fields was "the most problematic factor" in the
chief's accumulating a surplus to distribute to increase his faithful supporters (Fallers, 1964: 126). Generosity, particularly in
the distribution of foodstuffs, is one source of followers, or may
be shown selectively to those who protect the chief (Pospisil,
1971: 68–69; Ruyle, 1973: 610). Fox suggests that in early Scottish society, large groups of "broken men," unattached to any
kin group, were "driven from their natal clan region or having
voluntarily foresworn their brethren . . . were a large mobile
population allied with any dominant clan or chief who would
guarantee them safety and land" (1976: 111). In India, "the
elite commonly settled foreign families, kin groups and
Brahmans on their kin lands in order to establish a loyal class
of retainers apart from the kin order" (ibid., p. 101). Other
sources of retainers were poorer relations and people in debt
who placed themselves in pawn (Ruyle, 1973: 620; Terray, 1974:
335; Winks, 1972: 53). In some societies, the institution of slavery performed the same function.

Somewhat more formal and permanent police functions are
performed by the African age-grade societies. Together with
sex, division of labor based on age is common to tribal societies.

From an early age boys in tribal societies learn to obey elders (Lowie, 1927: 82). When such customs are worked into the kind of evolving stratified structure we have described, an incipient police institution is present.

There appear to be two basic types of age-grade societies in operation: one in which the secret societies acted as a check on the power of the chief and another in which the secret societies were controlled by and acted on behalf of the chief. When a secret society, such as the Poro Society of the Kpelle of Liberia, acted to balance the power of the chief, the disruptive consequences were not conducive to state formation. In contrast to this situation is the well known and historically documented development of the Zulu state. Shaka, who brought the Zulu state into supreme dominance, and his predecessor Dingiswayo, who solidified and organized the Mthethwa paramount chiefdom, both increasingly employed age societies as police to protect their own interests. Originally, these societies had been age grades not dissimilar to the Poro Society of the Kpelle. When a group of young men reached puberty, they underwent a circumcision rite of passage and were formally constituted as a group. Gradually, these chiefs increased their use of these age grades for their own ends until the various grades became rather firmly attached to a specific chief. Walter describes the situation immediately before Dingiswayo's coalescence of the Mthethwa:

> Before Dingiswayo, the military force of each chiefdom was a small "standing army" made up of young bachelors in the warrior age grade. Adolescent boys lived a barracks life in military kraals, serving as aids and herd boys until their age set was organized ceremonially as *iButho*, a new guild or regiment, and they were elevated to the status of warriors. Carrying out military and police functions and for certain purposes acting as a labor gang, the warriors constituted the staff, not permanent but assembled according to circumstance, which enforced the chief's will. They fought the battles of the chiefdom, executed judgments by killing people accused of crimes, confiscating their property in the chief's name, and when the supply of the chief's cattle was low, replenished the bovine treasury by making raids on other communities. They cultivated the fields of the chief, built and maintained his kraals, and manufactured his war shields (1969: 121).

At some point, which is not historically clear, circumcision rites were abolished, perhaps under Dingiswayo's paramount chieftainship, and chiefs continued to assemble and name sets of young men of warrior age. This stage was a crucial depar-

134   ORIGIN AND EVOLUTION OF THE POLICE FUNCTION

ture, however, since these regiments were not constituted solely by and on behalf of the chiefs. They took on permanent and formalized police functions, clearly in keeping with our central hypothesis. The formation of the Zulu state soon followed.

Sacks (1979: chap. 8) provides an example of how a lineage structure was further undermined and illustrates one transformation of a kinship into a class structure mode of production. In the seventeenth century, Buganda, on the northern shore of Victoria Nyanza in Uganda, was a "small client" of a more powerful neighboring country. A king of Buganda won some lands from this neighbor, and divided the captured lands among his war leaders and other loyal followers. As more land was taken, this group of leaders grew in number compared to the clan leaders. By the end of the eighteenth century, in order to consolidate his rule, the king began killing or imprisoning his brothers and their sons.

> In this process relations of production were transformed from direct patrician control over productive means to control by a network of chiefly families of a few of these clans who held hereditary rights to goods and plunder by virtue of their ties to each other through the king . . . . Clans and their component lineages were decorporatized rather than destroyed. Kinship became a basis for establishing vertical, dyadic clientage relations, the central relation of men to productive means. Clans were deprived of their independent base of power by expropriation of clan land and installation of appointed officials, together with co-optation, or harnessing clanship to class organization (ibid., pp. 200–201).

By granting special rights such as hereditary positions to certain clans in return for their becoming the king's clients, potential clan unity in opposition was breached and instead was "transformed into class-centered patronage networks" (ibid., p. 201). In the nineteenth century, military expeditions became a way of life, with Buganda having the capability to "field a huge army" (ibid., p. 202). The spoils of war—women, children, and cattle—were distributed according to the class system. "The Buganda rulers relied on their control of armed forces to maintain their rule. The king and district chiefs had their own armed bodyguards even before Mutesa [a nineteenth-century king] was said to have created a standing army. The king also had his own secret police and executioners" (ibid., p. 204). Bugandan men were obligated to pay the king a tax of bark cloth, supply the labor to build his palaces and roads, carry his

firewood, and do his hunting (ibid., p. 207). Sacks summarizes
the resulting "gender and class relations of production" with
the following description:

> Ruler and peasants had diametrically opposed re-
> lations of production. The former owned the land and
> the bulk of the livestock, especially cattle. They deter-
> mined peasants' land allotments, could evict peasants
> at will, and could seize their livestock. Peasants ob-
> tained access to land by entering into clientage rela-
> tions in which they provided labor and tax to their pa-
> tron (ibid., p. 208).

Under this system, therefore, people entered the productive
process through clientage arrangements and not by kinship relations (ibid., p. 210).

F. Police Functions

In addition to the occasional enforcement of a chief's orders, for what other matters are police employed? The various
functions that the police have historically fulfilled can be gathered only from scattered references in the literature. Observers, whether anthropologists or not, have rarely recorded detailed descriptions of police forces. As one writer commented
after an extensive survey of traditional societies, "the data on
the existence of a police force are very scanty. In only four
cases was such a force mentioned. In five cases royal servants
or guards maintained public order . . ." (Claessen, 1978: 560).
There is an occasional allusion to a police or militia being used
to compel labor (Finley, 1973: 65–66), but as we have indicated,
commoners are more apt to be compelled to work by market
forces. Police are used to control the market, not the workers
(Pryor, 1977: 120; Smith, 1976: 336; Harris, 1975: 287). But police
are used to maintain the mode of production by controlling the
freedom of choice of the labor force. One of the distinctions between a stateless and state society is that "the state is a system
specifically designed to restrain" tendencies toward segmenta-
tion (Cohen and Service, 1978: 4). Thus police can be used to
prevent discontented groups from leaving a chief's jurisdiction
(Llewellyn and Hoebel, 1941: 94–96; Skalnik, 1978: 609), or, on a
larger scale, "to try and overcome any ethnic differences in the
total society" (ibid., p. 607). Over the long term this has meant
the crushing of ethnic in favor of state loyalties (Claessen and
Skalnik, 1978c: 632).

Inequalities and opposition incident to a class-dominated
society lead to struggle among common people for access to the
limited scarce resources that remain after the elite appropriate

136   ORIGIN AND EVOLUTION OF THE POLICE FUNCTION

the surplus; force must often be used to assert the elite's rights to control these resources; such conflict leads to the ideological justification of the use of arbiters to settle resulting disputes; and these arbiters in turn need to use detectives to search for evidence and police to execute judicial decisions (Pospisil, 1971: 16, 123; Harris, 1975: 357–358). Thus for the people's own apparent good, the ruler and his top officials need protection "against attempts at supplantation by pretenders to the supreme power" (Skalnik, 1978: 610). In early states, these hypothetical and real threats generally led to the creation of a bodyguard for the sovereign (Claessen, 1978: 563).

Thus we can hypothesize that in its early stage, the police mechanism was used for regulation of class conflict, acting as a neutral force, loyal only to the state, without ties to either side in the dispute (Mair, 1964). Its function was to permit a "class struggle . . . at most in the economic field, in so-called legal form" (Engels, 1972: 228).

III.   CROSS-CULTURAL EVIDENCE SUPPORTING THE THEORY

Until this point in our analysis we have drawn mainly upon evidence from societies whose development from a kinship-based system to a state system could be historically traced, at least at the critical stage. We have suggested a relationship between levels of economic and political organization and the presence of certain types of police functions in society. If our theory is correct, given any society at any level of economic and political development, we should be able to predict the corresponding police function. Thus if we examine a sample of societies at a single point in time, we should have a synchronic test of our theory.

For our cross-cultural analysis, we used the typology of the degree of specialization and institutionalization of police functions established by Tuden and Marshall (1972). Variables related to political organization were coded for some 186 societies in a world sample selected for representativeness and independence (Murdock and White, 1969). Data concerning the function of police were available for 181 of these societies. Results are tabulated in Table 1.

We may conclude that roughly 70 percent of these societies do not have a specialized police function and that about 25 percent have a specific specialized and institutionalized function. Since few intermediary cases existed, we decided to dichotomize societies according to the specialization of their police

Table 1. Degree of Specialization and Institutionalization of Police Functions

Degree of Specialization and Institutionalization	Number of Societies	Percentage	
Police functions are not specialized or institutionalized at any level of political integration, with the maintenance of law and order left exclusively to informal mechanisms of social control, private retaliation, or sorcery	125	69.1	
Police functions display only incipient specialization, as when groups with other functions are assigned police functions in emergencies	4	2.2	(Palauns, Gros Ventre, Omaha, Pawnee)
Police functions are assumed by the retainers of chiefs	4	2.2	(Suku, Tikopia, Natchez, Warrau)
Police functions are assumed by the military organizations	6	3.3	(Azande, Fur, Konso, Babylonians, Zuni, Haitians)
Police functions are specialized and institutionalized on at least some level or levels of political integration	42	23.2	
Total	181	100.0	

Source: Tuden and Marshall, 1972: 441, 444–451.

138   ORIGIN AND EVOLUTION OF THE POLICE FUNCTION

function. Accordingly, we established two groups: (1) those societies having neither police nor an incipient police function,
and (2) those societies having specialized police functions, including the retainers of chiefs and military organizations. We
then attempted to determine the level of political integration
associated with the presence of specialized police functions. If
our theories about police function are correct, we would expect
to find specialized police functions associated with state societies having ruling elites (proposition two). Following the definitions of Tuden and Marshall (ibid., p. 438), we have consequently distinguished between petty chiefdoms, small states,
and large states as representing increasing levels of complexity.
Petty chiefdoms are defined as "a petty paramount chief ruling
a district composed of a number of local communities." They
are societies in which effective sovereignty transcends the local
community at a single level. Small states are defined as "a
small state comprising a number of administrative districts
under subordinate functionaries" and thus have two levels of
sovereignty transcending the local community. Large states are
defined as "administrative provinces which are further subdivided into lesser administrative districts" and have at least
three levels of sovereignty transcending the local community.

   Using the total sample available in Tuden and Marshall
(1972), we have prepared a contingency table (Table 2) consisting of the presence or absence of specialized police functions as
one variable and the level of political organization as the other
variable to provide a cross-cultural test for proposition two. It
is apparent that, in broad outline, proposition two is supported
by these data. The presence of a specialized police function is
associated with state organization of society. State societies
generally have specialized police functions whereas stateless societies generally do not. But what of the relationship between
police function and a ruling elite? Proposition one suggests
that specialized police functions would be related to societal
stratification, or the existence of social classes.

   Murdock (1967) has been concerned with the identification
of particular societies according to their level of social stratification. Murdock's typology of class differentiation is not rank
ordered; we have consequently restructured the typology by
combining certain categories. We identified societies as having
complex stratification, noncomplex stratification (Murdock's
dual stratification, elite stratification, and wealth distinctions),
or an absence of significant class distinctions among freemen.
When Murdock's sample of societies identified according to
levels of stratification is combined with the sample for which

Table 2. Political Organization and Specialization of Police Functions*

Sovereignty Level (Societal Type)	No Specialization or Only Incipient Specialization	Specialization at Some Level of Political Integration (Including Retainers of Chiefs and Military Organizations)	Number of Societies
Stateless	99	5	104
Petty chiefdom	26	9	35
Small state	8	7	15
Large state	7	33	40
Total	140	54	194

* $\gamma = 0.88$; $\chi^2 = 89.7$; $p < .0001$.
Source: Tuden and Marshall, 1972: 444–451.

police functions are known, a sample of 169 societies results, distributed as shown in Table 3. It is clear that specialized police functions are strongly associated with more complex social stratification (proposition one) and with the presence of the state (proposition two).

In sum, we find that of the societies studied (Table 1), most (70%) have a specialized police function, that the presence of a specialized police function is associated with state organization (Table 2), and that specialized police functions are strongly associated with social stratification (Table 3), that is, a class structure (Black, 1976: 13).

Several works provide cross-cultural tests of aspects of our theory, most notably Schwartz and Miller (1964) and more recently Newman (1983). Schwartz and Miller sought to determine factors in the evolution of legal organizations. They concluded that "elements of legal organization emerge in a sequence, such that each constitutes a necessary condition for the next" (1964: 160). Defining police as a "specialized armed force used partially or wholly for norm enforcement" (ibid., p. 161) they found that of the fifty-one societies studied, twenty had police. For the most part, these societies were characterized by sufficient economic advancement to use money, while the presence of full-time priests, teachers, and government officials indicated a considerable degree of specialization. The authors concluded that police are found "only in association with a substantial degree of division of labor" (ibid., p. 166) and that mediation and the development of damages as compensation for injury almost always precede the police institution.

Newman's cross-cultural study of legal institutions is very similar to our research. Specifically, her work is a test of "a materialist theory of comparative legal institutions," that is, one "concerned with the nature of material production in societies and the internal distribution of the fruits of labor" (1983: 4). She sets forth six specific hypotheses for testing:

Hypothesis 1. The greater the degree of development of the forces of production, the greater the degree of social stratification. . . .

Hypothesis 2. The greater the opportunities for some individuals to control the surplus labor of others, the greater the degree of social stratification in a society. . . .

Hypothesis 3. The more stratified a society, the more complex its legal institutions. . . .

Hypothesis 4. Holding stratification constant (i.e., within each given level of stratification), the more developed the forces of production in a society, the more complex its legal institutions. . . .

ROBINSON AND SCAGLION 141

Table 3. Specialization of Police Functions and Social Stratification*

| Police Functions | Stratification Level | | | Number of Societies |
	Complex	Noncomplex	None	
No specialization or only incipient specialization	4	58	61	123
Specialization at some level of political integration (including retainers of chiefs and military organizations)	17	20	9	46
Total	$\overline{21}$	$\overline{78}$	$\overline{70}$	$\overline{169}$

* $\gamma = 0.67$; $\chi^2 = 38.0$; $p < .0001$.
Source: Murdock, 1967; Tuden and Marshall, 1972: 444-451.

142   ORIGIN AND EVOLUTION OF THE POLICE FUNCTION

Hypothesis 5. Holding the forces of production constant (i.e., within each subsistence type), the more stratified a society, the more complex its legal institutions. . . .

Hypothesis 6. The greater the development of the forces of production, social relations of production, and social stratification, the more complex a society's legal institutions (ibid., pp. 116–117).

Having carried out her analysis using the Standard Cross-Cultural Sample (Murdock and White, 1969), Newman concludes

that the degrees of development of the forces of production, "exploitive" social relations of production, and social stratification are strong independent predictors of legal complexity . . . .

In sum, one cannot simply take any dimension of social life and argue that the more complex that dimension, the more complex the law. All aspects of social reality are *not* equally effective in predicting levels of legal development. Even within the model developed here, it is the *interaction* between three distinct dimensions—the forces and social relations of production, and social stratification—that seems to best explain the variance in legal complexity (1983: 204, 205 [emphasis in original]).

Newman sees the dynamics of social inequality to be dependent on unequal access to limited means of production; in turn such unequal access triggers social inequalities, for some families use this unequal access to make others work for them, thereby setting the stage for class stratification (ibid., p. 205).

IV. ENGLISH POLICE HISTORY SEEN THROUGH OUR ANALYTIC FRAMEWORK

In this section we intend to examine the historical development of the English police, testing the previously developed model against generally well accepted knowledge of both English and police history. This history (greatly oversimplified) can be divided into periods dominated by four different civilizations: Celtic (600 B.C. to A.D. 43), Roman (A.D. 43 to A.D. 410), Anglo-Saxon (410 to 1066), and Norman (1066 to 1154).

Because Roman strategy called for building and living only in cities and dealing almost exclusively with the native elite, Roman influence effectively ended at the city walls (Trevelyan, 1953: 43–45). Anglo-Saxon raids recommenced in the mid-fourth century, just as Rome itself was under assault, and the Romans were forced to withdraw all their forces by A.D. 410. Within a few generations, virtually all Roman culture and influence disappeared (Priestley, 1967: 72–73; Trevelyan, 1953: 61, 65; Stubbs, 1874: 65). The earlier Celt culture was pushed west into what is now Wales and had little influence on forming English institutions (Trevelyan, 1953: 65). Therefore, we begin our study with the Anglo-Saxon incursions.

A. *The Anglo-Saxon Period*

Raids by various tribes, which Trevelyan (ibid., p. 50) designates as "Nordic," and others that were Anglo-Saxon occurred from A.D. 300 to about 1020. More than any other group, the Anglo-Saxons gave English culture its definitive character. Migrating from northern Germany and the coast of Denmark, they came not as plunderers but with their families, in search of better farmland (Priestley, 1967: 127; Whitelock, 1968: 18–19; Trevelyan, 1953: 56–57, 68).

Tacitus (1942) writes of the society in England before the migrations. Loyalty between tribal members and the chief was personal and no longer tribal. A successful chief attempted to attract to him men from several tribes (Whitelock, 1968: 29). Tacitus shows the ideological strength that had grown around this relationship:

> When they go into battle, it is a disgrace for the chief to be surpassed in valour, a disgrace for his followers not to equal the valour of the chief. And it is an infamy and a reproach for life to have survived the chief, and returned from the field. To defend, to protect him, to ascribe one's own brave deed to his renown, is the height of loyalty. The chief fights for victory; his vassals fight for their chief (1942: 715–716).

Tacitus also describes a society in which there was a division of labor between the warriors, who went to war for their chief but did no work, and the rest, who produced. Although the significance of these economic divisions was limited by the fact that the warriors were apparently able to support themselves on their own exterior plunder, it is clear that there was a social division between producers and nonproducers:

> [M]en look to the liberality of their chief for their warhorse and their blood-stained and victorious lance. Feasts and entertainments, which, though inelegant, are plentifully furnished, are their only pay. The means of this bounty come from war and rapine. Nor are they as easily persuaded to plough the earth and to wait for the year's produce as to challenge an enemy and earn the honour of wounds. Nay, they actually think it tame and stupid to acquire by the sweat of toil what they might win by their blood (ibid., p. 716).

144   ORIGIN AND EVOLUTION OF THE POLICE FUNCTION

It was left "to the women, the old men, and all the weakest
members of the family" to till the land (ibid.).

This picture is somewhat softened by the continued importance of the common peasant in the social formation of the Anglo-Saxons at the time of their arrival in Britain (Andreski,
1968: 64). By this time, their

> form of government was autocratic Kingship, exercised
> by some member of a royal family supposed to be de-
> scended from the gods, although such autocracy was
> limited by the custom of the tribe, by the temper of
> the armed tribesmen, and by the personal qualities of
> the King himself. . . . There were many grades of
> rank, wealth and freedom among them . . . (Trevelyan,
> 1953: 50).

Kingship was already associated with "legitimate authority," the "general custom" being "for the man from the royal
kin who was fittest to rule to be selected as successor" (Loyn,
1984: 14–15). Such difference did not, however, amount to class
division or state organization. These inequalities gave the
holder no claim to "social and political rights. . . . [L]ike great
age, [nobility] entitled a man to a respectful hearing in the tribal councils . . . but it confers no political privilege . . ." (Stubbs,
1874: 22).

Having established the broad outlines of the Anglo-Saxon
social structure at the time of their arrival in Britain, we are
now ready to discuss in more detail the development of their
class structure and the modifications of the police function
growing out of that structure.

B. The Development of the Police Function Out of the English Class Structure

By the sixth century the Anglo-Saxons had consolidated
their military gains sufficiently to establish kingdoms in the
western half of England while the rest remained in Celtic
hands. Significantly, because the Anglo-Saxons had no king in
their homeland, this military adventure must have had a
profound effect on any incipient aspects of societal stratification. Stubbs suggests that such "state of society in which the
causes [common tenure and cultivation] are at work" contains
the germs of a later feudal structure. He accordingly finds in
early Anglo-Saxon England

> the principle of common tenure and cultivation . . . ,
> the villages themselves, their relation to the [territo-
> rial division] . . . and the fact that they were centres or
> subdivisions for the administration of justice. . . . [W]e
> have the nobleman, we have the warlike magistrate

with his [retainers], whose services he must find some
way of rewarding, and whose energies he must even in
peace find some way of employing. The rich man too
has his great house and court, and his family of slaves
or dependents, who may be only less than free in that
they cultivate the land that belongs to another (ibid.,
pp. 36–37).

Given such a ready social mix, the leader "has but to conquer
and colonize a new territory, and reward his followers on a
plan that will keep them faithful as well as free, and feudalism
springs into existence" (ibid., p. 37). Perhaps "springs" is not
the correct word, but the Anglo-Saxon invasion of England, by
providing the territorial spoils for distribution, supplied the basis for setting this mechanism in motion.

Stubbs (ibid., pp. 87–98) further argues that in the primitive Anglo-Saxon community the tie of kindred was synonymous with the communal ownership of lands, and that as this
community was transformed into one characterized by private
and unequal ownership, the original kindred community became a township consisting of "the body of tenants of a lord
who regulates them or allows them to regulate themselves on
principles derived from" the original communal organization
(ibid., p. 91). Church parishes were often coterminous with
townships. The tithes paid to the church gave the name "tithing" to the township as a unit of local administration.

Folkright or custom was still dominant, but by the eighth
century, the king, "together with a great assembly in his chief
men of the kingdom," by degree sought to "clarify" and to set
down the "true law" (Loyn, 1984: 42–43). As part of this process, a number of laws, principles, and ideological homilies
grew up to replace the kinship-based principles of mutual aid
for collective security. Primary responsibility for a man under
the jurisdiction of a lord no longer rested with the man's kin
but with the lord. The duty to the lord came first, a vendetta
could not be carried against a man who had killed in defense of
his lord, and one who entered the priesthood gave up the right
of vengeance for the slaying of his kinsmen, thereby terminating his ties with his kindred (Whitelock, 1968: 37–43; Loyn,
1984: 77).

What the state had done was to seize, to "double institutionalize," in Bohannan's (1968) apt phrase, the kindred social
control mechanism. The further use of collective security
mechanisms to inform the king's officer, the sheriff, of the alleged offenses of kindred had the effect of turning loyalty of
men away from kindred and toward the feudal order of lords
and kings (Pollock and Maitland, 1968: 32). This trend toward

146   ORIGIN AND EVOLUTION OF THE POLICE FUNCTION

stratification was hastened by the Viking raids that began toward the end of the eighth century (Andreski, 1968: 65; Loyn,
1984: 32).

Once English kings were converted to Christianity in the
seventh century, the church developed a reciprocal power exchange with the evolving state. As laws came to be written,
only the church could provide literate persons to draft them,
while only the king could provide legal and military protection
for church property and personnel. The church in turn could
furnish the king with legitimacy (Loyn, 1984: 44–45).

Lee describes the two-tiered system of collective responsibility that existed during the reign of King Alfred the Great
(reigned 871–899). The object of the system was to place every
subject in some type of collective security arrangement (Lee,
pp. 3–4; Critchley, 1967: 2; Jeffery, 1957: 657; Reith, 1975: 26).
Under King Athelstan (reigned 924–939), this system was sanctioned by law, apparently because of the concern of large landowners over cattle theft. As feudalism and Christianity
changed the organization of Anglo-Saxon society, the blood
feud was replaced by a system of compensation as the means of
settling disputes. At the time of the Norman Conquest in 1066,
English local government was in place, controlled by three
powers: the king, the Christian bishops who composed the
king's laws, and the local lord who administered them through
the bishop-created structure. All three had the common interest of protecting their large landholdings (Loyn, 1984: 162–163,
171).

The Norman invaders accepted the Anglo-Saxon legal system in its entirety but took over and centralized the administration of the laws (ibid., p. 179; Trevelyan, 1953: 127). King
William (reigned 1066–87) promptly seized the lands of all who
stood against him and then required all landowners to buy their
lands back from him, thereby establishing the principle that all
land originated from the king. This maneuver also had the effect of increasingly concentrating economic and political power
in the hands of a few. It has been estimated that about "a quarter of the landed wealth of England in 1086 was held by no
more than twelve men, most of whom were bound to the king
by close bonds of blood or personal loyalty or both. Only about
180 more held land worth more than 100 pounds a year. Virtually all of these were Normans" (Loyn, 1984: 179–180). The
sheriff became the most powerful royal officer of the shire and
supervised the court (ibid., p. 196). By the end of the twelfth
century, the hundreds courts gave way to local manorial courts
or courts leet. The unit of responsibility thereupon became the

feudal manor. Officers were annually elected by the court leet to serve their turn as assistants to the lord on the manor in regulating the affairs of the manor community. The constable became the principal representative of the manor for making presentments to the court leet (Critchley, 1967: 3–4; Lee, 1971: 17).

Thus by the end of the thirteenth century, the constable had lost his connection to the tithing. He was at the same time the annually appointed or elected representative of the manor in making presentments to the court leet as well as an officer of the crown as Keeper of the King's Peace (Critchley, 1967: 5; Reith, 1975: 28). No longer a member and integral part of an independent community, he was now subject to a competitive struggle for his services waged by the landlord and the crown.

The role of the police in England as a regulator of class conflict is well documented. We mention only a few of the more obvious instances of statutes requiring the police to control the working class. From the twelfth century onward, the police had a special function with reference to vagabonds, vagrants, and the "sturdy, unworking poor." The Assize of Clarendon of 1166 required sheriffs to enforce restrictions against "entertainers of strangers and the harbourers of vagabonds." A statute of King Edward III (reigned 1327–77) ordered town bailiffs "to make inquiry every week of all persons lodging in the suburbs, in order that neither vagrants, nor 'people against the peace' might find shelter . . ." (Lee, 1971: 25, 33). During the reign of King Edward VI (1547–53) statutes empowered justices of the peace and constables to compel laborers to work on farms at which labor was scarce, to wake them up in time for work, and to urge them not to take too long at their meals. These laws were in addition to many other obligations placed on constables for the control of "rogues and idle persons" (ibid., pp. 116–117; Critchley, 1967: 12; Dalton, 1975: 59–63).

Under this system, the constable became subordinated first to the lord of the manor and eventually to the justice of the peace (who was frequently also the lord of the manor). As feudalism ended, capitalism developed as an economic system, and the nation-state formed. Thus, in gross, the origin of the English police in its modern form and function can be said to be consistent and coincident with the origin of the English state and with the model we have evolved.

Likewise, the process of the growth of English feudal society meant the separation of the community into thegns and serfs. The process whereby the constable was a neutral between disputants was begun at the point at which the kindred organizations were replaced by the later tithing and the consta-

148   ORIGIN AND EVOLUTION OF THE POLICE FUNCTION

ble-justice of the peace relationship. With the passage of the
Justices of the Peace Act of 1361, 34 Edw. 3 c. 1, the crown recognized a hierarchical relationship between the constable and
the justice of the peace. This system endured until the organization of the professional police in 1829. The social and economic status of the justice as the landlord and the constable as
his unpaid inferior infused the relationship and has determined
the enduring socioeconomic position of the constable-police officer to this day (Critchley, 1967: 8–9; Robinson, 1978).

V. DISCUSSION

At the very start of this essay, we summarized the notion
of the police history and function found in much traditional
English and American literature. These notions were that
(1) the police institution in England has deep historical roots
and is said to have experienced a slow but continual development from ancient to modern times; (2) the police institution
originates with the people and depends on them for support;
(3) the community is divided into a majority of good, law-abiding people and a minority of lawbreakers; and (4) one function
of the police is to protect this virtuous majority from that criminal minority. In attempting to show how the police institution
developed out of a class-structured society, we have at the same
time suggested how an ideological history of the police may
have developed side by side with the structure it was meant to
portray (Robinson, 1979). For the dominant class, this idealized
picture of history gives the best answer to the charge that
the police represent a class-dominated system. It asserts that,
on the contrary, from its very beginnings the police function
sprang from the body of the people and that its integral identity with the community has never changed. It is accordingly
argued that the police are armed "with prestige rather than
power, thus obliging them to rely on popular support" (Critchley, 1967: xiv) and that the people and the police are identical,
except that the police are paid to give their "full-time attention
to duties which are incumbent on every citizen, in the interests
of community welfare and existence" (Reith, 1975: 163). These
notions certainly run counter to our findings, which we would
argue have implications for contemporary police-community relations.

It should be noted that just because the ruling class uses
the police to maintain inequalities does not mean that the police must be a mere instrument in the hands of the elite. Such
a portrayal confuses the desires and needs of the ruling class

(that is, that the police be just such an instrument) with the desires, needs, history, and material working conditions of the police themselves, who often assert interests that are antagonistic to those of the ruling class. Even the use of the appellation the "police" to cover three different entities—the working police officer, the management, and the police institution—hides the real and separate interests of these three, and particularly those of the police officer.

Individual police officers continue to be affected by their double and split loyalty—loyalty to their ethnic and working-class identity on the one hand and loyalty to the state, which is imposed on them by virtue of their state employment, on the other (Robinson, 1978). This schizophrenic portrait is exemplified by the metaphoric depiction of the officer as at once a "philosopher, guide and friend" (Cumming *et al.*, 1965) and a soldier in an army of occupation.[12] We have tried to show that the historic roots of this conflict lie in the original collective security system of primitive society. This system resided in the very nature of that particular social formation. In destroying the integral nature of that society but at the same time saving the collective security structure for its own use, the evolving state created an institution with conflicting loyalties.

REFERENCES

ADAMS, Robert McC. (1966) *The Evolution of Urban Society: Early Mesopotamia and Prehispanic Mexico.* Chicago: Aldine.

ALTHUSSER, Louis, and Etienne BALIBAR (1968) *Reading Capital,* trans. B. Brewster. London: NLB.

ANDRESKI, Stanislav (1968) *Military Organization and Society.* Berkeley: University of California Press.

BALANDIER, Georges (1970) *Political Anthropology,* trans. A. M. Sheridan Smith. New York: Pantheon Books.

BLACK, Donald (1976) *The Behavior of Law.* New York: Academic Press.

BOHANNAN, Paul (1968) "Law and Legal Institutions," 9 *International Encyclopedia of the Social Sciences* 73.

BOPP, William T. (1972) *Police-Community Relations: An Introductory Undergraduate Reader.* Springfield, IL: Charles C. Thomas.

CAMPBELL, Joseph (1959) *The Masks of God: Primitive Mythology.* New York: Viking Press.

CARNEIRO, Robert L. (1970) "A Theory of the Origin of the State," 169 *Science* 733.

CENTER FOR RESEARCH ON CRIMINAL JUSTICE (1977) *The Iron Fist and Velvet Glove,* 2nd ed. Berkeley: Center for Research on Criminal Justice.

CLAESSEN, Henri J. M. (1978) "The Early State: A Structural Approach," in H.J.M. Claessen and P. Skalnik (eds)., *The Early State.* The Hague: Mouton.

---

[12] For a discussion of differing perceptions of police by various segments of the community, see Scaglion and Condon (1980).

150   ORIGIN AND EVOLUTION OF THE POLICE FUNCTION

CLAESSEN, Henri J. M., and Peter SKALNIK (1978a) "The Early State: Models and Reality," in H.J.M. Claessen and P. Skalnik (eds.), *The Early State*. The Hague: Mouton.

—— (1978b) "The Early State: Theories and Hypotheses," in H.J.M. Claessen and P. Skalnik (eds.), *The Early State*. The Hague: Mouton.

—— (1978c) "Limits: Beginning and End of the Early State," in H.J.M. Claessen and P. Skalnik (eds.), *The Early State*. The Hague: Mouton.

COHEN, Ronald (1978a) "State Foundations: A Controlled Comparison," in Cohen and Service, 1978.

—— (1978b) "State Origins: A Reappraisal," in H.J.M. Claessen and P. Skalnik (eds.), *The Early State*. The Hague: Mouton.

COHEN, Ronald, and Elman R. SERVICE (1978) *Origins of the State: The Anthropology of Political Evolution*. Philadelphia: Institute for the Study of Human Issues.

CRITCHLEY, T. A. (1967) *A History of Police in England and Wales, 900 to 1966*. London: Constable and Co.

CUMMING, Elaine, Ian CUMMING, and Laura EDELL (1965) "Policeman as Philosopher, Guide and Friend," 12 *Social Problems* 276.

DALTON, Michael (1975) *The Countrey Justice*. 1618. Reprint. Norwood, NJ: Walter J. Johnson.

EISENSTADT, Samuel N. (1963) *The Political Systems of Empires*. New York: Free Press of Glencoe.

ENGELS, Frederick (1972) *The Origin of the Family, Private Property and the State*. New York: International.

FALLERS, Lloyd A. (1964) "Social Stratification and Economic Processes," in M.J. Herskovits and M. Harwitz (eds.), *Economic Transition in Africa*. Evanston, IL: Northwestern University Press.

FINLEY M. I. (1973) *The Ancient Economy*. London: Hogarth Press.

FOX, Richard G. (1976) "Lineage Cells and Regional Definition in Complex Societies," in C.A. Smith (ed.), *Regional Analysis*. Vol. 2, *Social Systems*. New York: Academic Press.

—— (1971) *Kin, Clan, Raja and Rule: State-Hinterland Relations in Pre-Industrial India*. Berkeley: University of California Press.

FRIED, Morton H. (1967) *The Evolution of Political Society*. New York: Random House.

GALLIHER, John F. (1971) "Explanation of Police Behavior: A Critical Review and Analysis," 12 *Sociological Quarterly* 308.

GODELIER, Maurice (1982) *La Production des grands hommes: Pouvoir et domination masculine chez les Baruya de Nouvelle-Guinée*. Paris: Fayard.

—— (1972) *Rationality and Irrationality in Economics*, trans. B. Pearce. London: NLB.

GREENBERG, Douglas (1976) *Crime and Law Enforcement in the Colony of New York 1691–1777*. Ithaca: Cornell University Press.

HAAS, Jonathan (1982) *The Evolution of the Prehistoric State*. New York: Columbia University Press.

HARRIS, Marvin (1975) *Culture, People, Nature: An Introduction to General Anthropology*. New York: Thomas Y. Crowell.

HINDESS, Barry, and Paul Q. HIRST (1977) *Critique of Pre-Capitalist Modes of Production*. London: The Macmillan Press Ltd.

—— (1975) *Pre-Capitalist Modes of Production*. London: Routledge and Kegan Paul.

HOEBEL, E. Adamson (1954) *The Law of Primitive Man*. Cambridge, MA: Harvard University Press.

JEFFERY, C. Ray (1957) "The Development of Crime in Early English Society," 47 *Journal of Criminal Law, Criminology and Police Science* 647.

KRADER, Lawrence (1978) "The Origin of the State among the Nomads of Asia," in H.J.M. Claessen and P. Skalnik (eds.), *The Early State*. The Hague: Mouton.

—— (1976) *Dialectic of Civil Society*. Amsterdam: Van Gorcum, Assen.

—— (1968) *Formation of the State*. Englewood Cliffs, NJ: Prentice-Hall.

KURTZ, Donald V. (1978) "The Legitimation of the Aztec State," in H.J.M. Claessen and P. Skalnik (eds.), *The Early State*. The Hague: Mouton.

LANE, Roger (1967) *Policing the City*. Cambridge, MA: Harvard University Press.

LAW ENFORCEMENT ASSISTANCE ADMINISTRATION (1978) *Criminal Justice Research Solicitation: Citizen/Police Relations in Police Policy Setting.* Washington: National Institute of Law Enforcement and Criminal Justice.

LEACOCK, Eleanor B. (1972) "Introduction and Notes," in F. Engels, *The Origin of the Family, Private Property and the State.* New York: International.

LEE, Richard (1979) *The !Kungsan: Men, Women and Work in a Foraging Society.* Cambridge: Cambridge University Press.

—— (1968) "What Hunters Do for a Living, or, How to Make Out on Scarce Resources," in R. Lee and I. Devore (eds.), *Man the Hunter.* Chicago: Aldine.

LEE, W. L. Melville (1971) *A History of Police in England.* 1901. Reprint. Montclair, NJ: Patterson Smith.

LENSKI, Gerhard E. (1966) *Power and Privilege: A Theory of Social Stratification.* New York: McGraw-Hill.

LEWIS, I. M. (ed.) (1968) *History and Social Anthropology.* London: Tavistock.

LLEWELLYN, K. M., and E. Adamson HOEBEL (1941) *The Cheyenne Way: Conflict and Case Law in Primitive Jurisprudence.* Norman: University of Oklahoma Press.

LOWIE, Robert H. (1927) *The Origin of the State.* New York: Harcourt, Brace and Company.

LOYN, H.R. (1984) *The Governance of Anglo-Saxon England, 500–1087.* Stanford: Stanford University Press.

MACLEOD, William Christie (1937) "Police and Punishment among Native Americans of the Plains," 28 *Journal of the American Institute of Criminal Law and Criminology* 181.

MAIR, Lucy (1964) *Primitive Government.* Baltimore: Penguin Books.

MALINOWSKI, Bronislaw (1921) "The Primitive Economics of the Trobriand Islanders," 31 *Economic Journal* 1.

MALLON, Florencia E. (1983) "Murder in the Andes: Patrons, Clients and the Impact of Foreign Capital, 1860–1922," 27 *Radical History Review* 79.

MANDEL, Ernest (1968) *Marxist Economic Theory,* Vol. 1, trans. B. Pearce. New York: Monthly Review Press.

MANNING, Peter K. (1979) *Police Work: The Social Organization of Policing.* Cambridge, MA: MIT Press.

MEILLASSOUX, Claude (ed.) (1964) *L'Antropologie économique des Gouro des de Côte D'Ivoire.* Paris: Mouton.

MOMBOISSE, Raymond M. (1967) *Community Relations and Riot Prevention.* Springfield, IL: Charles C. Thomas.

MONKKONEN, Eric H. (1981) *Police in Urban America, 1860–1920.* Cambridge: Cambridge University Press.

MORGAN, L. H. (1877) *Ancient Society.* New York: World Publishing.

MURDOCK, G. P. (1967) Ethnographic Atlas: A Summary," 6 *Ethnology:* 109.

MURDOCK, G. P., and D. R. WHITE (1969) "Standard Cross-Cultural Sample," 8 *Ethnology* 329.

NADER, Laura, and Harry F. TODD (eds.) (1978) *The Disputing Process: Law in Ten Societies.* New York: Columbia University Press.

NATIONAL ADVISORY COMMISSION ON CRIMINAL JUSTICE STANDARDS AND GOALS (1973) *A National Strategy to Reduce Crime.* Washington, DC: Government Printing Office.

NEWMAN, Katherine S. (1983) *Law and Economic Organization: A Comparative Study of Preindustrial Societies.* Cambridge, Eng.: Cambridge University Press.

PEARCE, Frank (1976) *Crimes of the Powerful: Marxism, Crime and Deviance.* London: Pluto Press.

POLANYI, Karl (1968) "Anthropology and Economic Theory," in M. H. Fried (ed.), *Readings in Anthropology,* Vol. 1, New York: Thomas Y. Crowell.

—— (1957) *The Great Transformation: The Political and Economic Origins of Our Time.* Boston: Beacon Press.

POLLOCK, Frederick, and Frederick William MAITLAND (1968) *The History of English Law before the Time of Edward I,* Vol. 1. Cambridge: Cambridge University Press.

152   ORIGIN AND EVOLUTION OF THE POLICE FUNCTION

POSPISIL, Leopold (1971) *Anthropology of Law: A Comparative Study.* New York: Harper and Row.

PRICE, Barbara J. (1978) "Secondary State Formation: An Explanatory Model," in Cohen and Service, 1978.

PRIESTLEY, H. E. (1967) *Britain under the Romans.* London: Frederick Warne & Co.

PROVINSE, J. R. (1937) "The Underlying Sanctions of Plains Indian Culture," in F. Eggan (ed.), *Social Anthropology of North American Tribes.* Chicago: University of Chicago Press.

PRYOR, Frederic L. (1977) *The Origins of the Economy: A Comparative Study of Distribution in Primitive and Peasant Economies.* New York: Academic Press.

RADELET, Louis A. (1973) *The Police and the Community.* Beverly Hills: Glencoe.

RADZINOWICZ, Leon (1956) *A History of English Criminal Law and Its Administration from 1750.* Vol. 2. *The Clash between Private Initiative and Public Interest in the Enforcement of the Law.* London: Stevens and Sons.

REINER, Robert (1978) "The Police in the Class Structure," 5 *British Journal of Law and Society* 166.

REITH, Charles (1975) *The Blind Eye of History: A Study of the Origins of the Present Police Era.* 1952. Reprint. Montclair, NJ: Patterson Smith.

RICHARDSON, James F. (1979) "Historical Perspectives on the Police." Presented at the Academy of Criminal Justice Sciences, Cincinnati (March).

—— (1970) *The New York Police: Colonial Times to 1901.* New York: Oxford University Press.

ROBINSON, Cyril D. (1983) "Criminal Justice History in Progress in the United States," 3 *Criminal Justice History* 97.

—— (1979) "Ideology as History: A Look at the Way Some English Police Historians Look at the Police," 2 *Police Studies* 35.

—— (1978) "The Deradicalization of the Policeman: A Historical Analysis," 24 *Crime and Delinquency* 129.

ROCHER, Guy (1972) *Talcott Parsons and American Society,* trans. B. Mennell and S. Mennell. London: Nelson and Sons.

ROUNDS, J. (1979) "Lineage, Class, and Power in the Aztec State," 6 *American Ethnologist* 73.

RUYLE, Eugene E. (1976) "On the Origins of Class Rule," 1 *Thoughtlines* 21.

—— (1973) "Slavery, Surplus, and Stratification of the North West Coast: The Ethnoenergetics of an Incipient Stratification System," 14 *Current Anthropology* 603.

SACKS, Karen (1979) *Sisters and Wives: The Past and Future of Sexual Equality.* Westport, CN: Greenwood Press.

SAFFIRIO, G., and Richard SCAGLION (1982) "Hunting Efficiency in Acculturated and Unacculturated Yanomama Villages," 38 *Journal of Anthropological Research* 315.

SAHLINS, Marshall (1972) *Stone Age Economics.* Chicago: Aldine-Atherton.

SANDERS, William T., and Barbara J. PRICE (1968) *Meso America: The Evolution of a Civilization.* New York: Random House.

SAXE, Arthur A. (1977) "On the Origin of Evolutionary Processes: State Formation in the Sandwich Islands, A Systematic Approach," in J. N. Hill (ed.), *Explanation of Prehistoric Change.* Albuquerque: University of New Mexico Press.

SCAGLION, Richard, and R. G. CONDON (1980) "The Structure of Black and White Attitudes toward Police," 39 *Human Organization* 280.

SCHWARTZ, Richard D., and James C. Miller (1964) "Legal Evolution and Societal Complexity," 70 *American Journal of Sociology* 159.

SEDOV, Leonid A. (1978) "Angkor: Society and State," in H.J.M. Claessen and P. Skalnik (eds.), *The Early State.* The Hague: Mouton.

SERVICE, Elman R. (1975) *Origins of the State and Civilization: The Process of Cultural Evolution.* New York: W. W. Norton.

—— (1962) *Primitive Social Organization: An Evolutionary Perspective.* New York: Random House.

SKALNIK, Peter (1978) "The Early State As a Process," in H.J.M. Claessen and P. Skalnik (eds.), *The Early State.* The Hague: Mouton.

SMITH, Carol A. (1976) "Exchange Systems and the Spatial Distribution of Elites: The Organization of Stratification in Agrarian Societies;" in C. A. Smith (ed.), *Regional Analysis*. Vol. 2, *Social Systems*. New York: Academic Press.

STUBBS, William (1874) *The Constitutional History of England*, Vol. 1. Oxford: Clarendon Press.

TACITUS (1942) In A. J. Church and W. J. Brodribb (trans.), *The Complete Works of Tacitus*. New York: The Modern Library.

TERRAY, Emmanuel (1974) "Long Distance Exchange and Formation of the State: The Case of Abron Kingdom of Gyaman," 3 *Economy and Society* 315.

——— (1972) *Marxism and Primitive Societies: Two Studies*. New York: Monthly Review Press.

TREVELYAN, George (1953) *History of England*, Vol. 1. Garden City, NY: Anchor Books.

TUDEN, Arthur, and Catherine MARSHALL (1972) "Political Organization: Cross-Cultural Codes 4," 11 *Ethnology* 436.

VINOGRADOFF, Paul (1920) *Outlines of Historical Jurisprudence*, Vol. 1. London: Oxford Press.

WALKER, Samuel (1977) *A Critical History of Police Reform*. Lexington, MA: Lexington Books.

WALTER, Eugene V. (1969) *Terror and Resistance: A Study of Political Violence*. London and Oxford: Oxford University Press.

WEBER, Max (1976) *The Agrarian Sociology of Ancient Civilization*. London: NLB.

WHITE, Leslie (1959) *The Evolution of Culture: The Development of Civilization to the Fall of Rome*. New York: McGraw-Hill.

WHITELOCK, Dorothy (1968) *The Beginnings of English Society*, 2nd Ed., Vol. 2. London: Penguin Books.

WINKS, Robin W. (ed.) (1972) *Slavery: A Comparative Perspective: Readings on Slavery from Ancient Times to the Present*. New York: New York University Press.

WOLF, Eric (1959) *Sons of the Shaking Earth*. Chicago: University of Chicago Press.

WRIGHT, Burton, and Vernon FOX (1978) *Criminal Justice and the Social Sciences*. Philadelphia: W. B. Saunders.

WRIGHT, Henry T. (1977) "Toward an Exploration of the Origin of the State, in J. N. Hill (ed.), *Explanation of Prehistoric Change*. Albuquerque: University of New Mexico Press.

STATUTE CITED

Justices of the Peace Act of 1361. 34 Edw. 3 c. 1. Halsbury's Laws of England. Vol. XI, p. 212 (1930).

[2]

THE POLICEMAN AS DOMESTIC MISSIONARY:
URBAN DISCIPLINE AND POPULAR CULTURE
IN NORTHERN ENGLAND, 1850-1880[1]

Historians of the police, public order, and the criminal law have understandably concentrated on the role of the police in the repression of crime, public disorder, and popular political movements or have studied the police from the point of view of social administration.[2] The police had a broader mission in the nineteenth century, however — to act as an all-purpose lever of urban discipline. The imposition of the police brought the arm of municipal and state authority directly to bear upon key institutions of daily life in working-class neighborhoods, touching off a running battle with local custom and popular culture which lasted at least until the end of the century. Riots and strikes are by definition ephemeral episodes, but the monitoring and control of the streets, pubs, racecourses, wakes, and popular fêtes was a daily function of the "new police." It was in some part on this terrain that the quality of police-community relations in the second half of the nineteenth century was determined. In northern industrial towns of England these police functions must be viewed as a direct complement to the attempts of urban middle-class elites — by means of sabbath, educational, temperance, and recreational reform[3] — to mold a laboring class amenable to new disciplines of both work and leisure. The other side of the coin of middle-class voluntaristic moral and social reform (even when sheathed) was the policeman's truncheon. In this respect the policeman was perhaps every bit as important a "domestic missionary" as the earnest and often sympathetic men high-minded Unitarians dispatched into darkest Leeds or Manchester in the 1830s and 1840s.

Engels observed that "every week in Manchester policemen are beaten,"[4] a fact of Victorian social life by no means restricted to either Manchester or to the 1840s. Why were they beaten? What accounts for the suspicion and enmity the police seemed to engender? In what ways did they represent an unwelcome intrusion in working-class neighborhoods? One need not go far to discover numerous instances of police-community conflict in connection with strikes or great public disturbances.[5] Far from being sporadic, however, conflict was endemic and chronic, and it stemmed from the interventions of the police in the daily lives and recreational activities of the working classes, from their insertion into the heart of the working-class neighborhood.

At the time of their introduction in England fear of a modern, efficient police had several roots: the traditional English apprehension of a standing army, with which the police were initially identified in many quarters, fear of administrative centralization, fear of the political uses to which they might be put,[6] objections to their cost,[7] and fear of their being used as an auxiliary to the New Poor Law.[8] However, fully to assess the impact of the police after the period in which they were installed, one must go beyond these factors to an examination of their role and activities on the city streets and in those aspects of their mission which lay beyond the narrow repression of serious crime.

Some initial insight is gained when one gauges the effect of the "new police" upon unpoliced or insufficiently policed communities. Upon their introduction in the West Riding of Yorkshire in 1857, county police instantly made themselves obnoxious by imposing a more efficient supervision of pubs and beerhouses. Their firm insistence that pubs close during hours of divine service on Sunday created great bitterness among working men in the outtownships of Leeds and Huddersfield. At West Ardsley the police cracked down on footracing; at Wibsey near Bradford on cockfighting; and near Wakefield on Middlestown feast, a hitherto unpoliced affair.[9] In the wake of these novel interventions assaults on the West Riding police began: at Deighton and Lindley near Huddersfield; at Wibsey, Clayton Heights, and Halifax.[10] The appearance of the police at Middlestown feast resulted in a massive confrontation with local colliers and a considerable riot. Another random example: at Skelmanthorpe near Barnsley two constables were on duty at 1:30 A.M. when suddenly a large crowd materialized and attacked them with stones.[11]

The very look of the new police seemed to give offense. They were described near Coventry in 1840 as "well clothed and shod, with a pair of white gloves. . . and a great coat for bad weather. They go strutting about. . . armed with a bludgeon. . . with 18s per week. . . while the labourer toils from morning till night for 10s."[12] The police were at first resented in working-class districts because they were felt to be parasites. A Halifax publican remarked that "they were too idle to work, and such as he had to keep them."[13] Many of the terms used to describe the police in the popular press — "blue plagues," "blue drones," "blue idlers," "blue locusts" — were synonyms for persons who do not really work for a living. Most obnoxious to the policed perhaps was the imposition of the "move-on system." The practice of breaking up congregations of men on the streets and in front of pubs was considered novel and humiliating. Part of the background of a near antipolice riot at Ashton Under Lyne in May 1839 was to be found in working-class outrage at being moved-on;[14] similarly, it fed directly into the massive Colne antipolice riots of the spring/summer of 1840,[15] and into a large disturbance at Lees during the cotton famine.[16] The coming of the police produced what was perceived as an attack upon a traditionally sanctioned freedom — freedom of assembly in the streets — and a keenly felt sense of humiliation. Popular reaction to the policeman's refrain, "move on there!"[17] must be considered in assessing the sources of working-class resentment and resistance.

The degree to which the police were considered a daily pest no doubt varied from group to group and trade to trade, but between the police and street traders open warfare was the usual condition. Among these elements one finds a concern with the police which understandably bordered upon obsession. "Can you wonder at it sir," a coster told Henry Mayhew, "that I hate the police? They drive us about, we must move on, we can't stand here, and we can't pitch there."[18] In street trades the consciousness of being hounded was reflected in political feelings. Mayhew's coster-chartists conceived of the struggle for the People's Charter in terms of an Armageddon-like war between them and the police, and were unable to understand why they were exhorted to moral force

THE POLICEMAN AS DOMESTIC MISSIONARY   483

"when they might as well fight it out with the police at once."[19] The first appearance of county police in the Rochdale area was marked by increased pressure on peddlers, match sellers, and street vendors of all types.[20] There can be little doubt that the police were viewed with hostility and suspicion by such persons and by the unskilled generally throughout the last half of the nineteenth century. Evidence is relatively scarce regarding the attitudes of skilled workers. Thomas Wright, describing the lives of skilled London artisans in the mid-1860s, referred specifically to the elaborate precautions which had to be taken to evade police surveillance while drinking during hours of divine service on Sunday.[21] Being a skilled worker did not necessarily purchase immunity from the pressure of surveillance it seems, and this was perhaps reflected in these workers' attitudes toward the police.

The initiatives of the police authorities in these areas of course cannot be viewed apart from the attitudes, prejudices, and momentary reformist enthusiasms of the municipalities, magistrates, and local elites who employed them. This was especially the case outside of London where the police were much less independent of local control than in the metropolis. For this reason police actions must be considered as forming the cutting edge of a wider and larger effort in northern industrial towns to impose new standards of urban discipline. It was the boroughs after all who charged the police with the monitoring and suppression of popular activities and recreations considered conducive to immorality, disorder, or crime; it was the police who had to discharge that mandate as best they could or at least convince those to whom they were responsible that they were doing so. In 1843 the Manchester council formally prohibited dogfighting, cockfighting, and bull- and badger-baiting;[22] instructions to the new Leeds police by the watch committee included specific directives to suppress cruelty to animals.[23] In February 1836, the Leeds council requested the mayor to direct the police to give information "as shall lead to the conviction of all. . . persons as shall continue to prophane the Lord's day,"[24] to pay particular attention to drinking places on Saturday nights, to strictly enforce proper closing times, and to "observe those who resort to the public house or use sports in time of divine service."[25] A series of local acts over the next three decades closed chinks in the law which inhibited the functioning of the police in these areas: the Leeds Improvement Act of 1842 gave them power to enter unlicensed theaters and arrest those within, to prosecute publicans who managed houses where cocks, dogs, or other animals were fought, and to fine hawkers of indecent songs or ballads and those who performed them in the streets; and the Improvement Act of 1866 brought music and dancing saloons attached to public houses under much closer control and supervision.

In Bradford before police reform a parish vestry committee reported in December 1831 that "moral and municipal discipline is on the decline. . . and without an entire reform in the police. . . it may become questionable whether even property itself will not become deteriorated."[26] Complaints appeared frequently in the press lamenting the large numbers of "men and women [reeling] about the streets. . . but no policeman to take them into custody."[27] Fair days were nightmares for respectable townsmen when disorder and popular revelry ran unchecked. The *Bradford Observer* reported in 1845 that on the last fair day "the town was left absolutely without any police whatever," the entire

484   journal of social history

force of constables having been off attending Quarter Session at Wakefield.[28] By contrast at Leeds, at the first fair held after the new borough police came into operation, the watch committee assigned a detachment of *extra* police to monitor it.[29]

It must not be supposed that this municipal assault upon traditional working-class leisure activities met with either immediate or, for that matter, even long-term success. It was one thing to direct the police to monitor assemblies in the streets, drinking places, feasts, and fairs, or to suppress brutal sports or gambling; it was another to succeed at the task. Huddersfield at mid-century provides an interesting case study of the results of unusually intensive police attacks. Superintendent Tom Heaton, heading a group of semi-reformed parish constables, made a strenuous effort not only to monitor and control but to smash the locales of working-class recreational life by direct intervention at every opportunity. The "Huddersfield Crusade," as one Leeds newspaper called it, revealed the limits of this type of program of indiscriminate intervention. During its course an average of four to five publicans a week were prosecuted for permitting Sunday drinking, gambling, or illegal sports.[30] Heaton was able to sustain what amounted to a perpetual beerhouse sweep by providing his constables with shilling witness fees and a percentage of the fines paid on conviction. Heaton ransacked the statutes for obsolete, disused laws to enforce, attempting for example to obtain the conviction of three men for watching a cricket game on Sunday and not attending church when bidden — though here the magistrates refused to convict.[31] He brought charges against pubs which, following local custom, ignored the usual closing hours on the Feast Sunday. The magistrates convicted in this case. Heaton was an avid reader of *Sporting Life,* by means of which he kept himself abreast of all projected local activities, using this intelligence to break up numerous prizefights and other events in the area.[32] He cracked down on the widespread practice of holding sweeps or St. Leger clubs in the pubs. In short, he made himself a neighborhood pest. But what concrete results did the "Huddersfield Crusade" produce in the end? Illegal Sunday drinking did not diminish; when the new West Riding police took over in 1857 they found the offense very widespread.[33] Cockfighting, dogfighting, and gambling in the pubs and lanes probably diminished in the long run but were still reported with great frequency by the West Riding police, who launched their own crusade in the months immediately following their installation.

Quite generally, working-class recreational locales proved much less amenable to change by any means — whether through the instrumentality of educational, temperance, or sabbatarian reform movements or the policeman's truncheon — than middle-class elites of northern towns had originally hoped. The characteristic working-class response to both approaches to moral reform was evasion or resistance rather than immediate capitulation. It could not have been otherwise, for the police were unleashed upon many of the most vital popular habits and institutions — repulsive, immoral, harmful, or frightening though they may have appeared to others. In the discharge of their "domestic mission," then, the police were placed at the point of a larger attempt to transform popular culture. Let us examine this further.

Police authorities themselves often drew a direct parallel between popular leisure and crime and believed a close surveillance of key neighborhood recreation centers was essential to both the preservation of good order and the prevention of crime. "I have no doubt," wrote a Leeds Chief Constable, "that an extended closing of public houses on Sunday would lead to the promotion of good order. . . . I should not object to see *Beer Houses* entirely closed on that day as [they] harbour the lowest class of company. . . dog fanciers and the race running fraternity. . . . I am sure that so long as the working classes imbibe the. . . decoctions of Beer sellers there will not only be drunkenness and poverty but crimes of open violence amongst us."[34] For the police as well as for many Victorian moral reformers the public house was bad and the beershop infinitely worse. Chief Constable Wetherell of Leeds was positive that "so long as the present system of licensing continues many of them will remain. . . pests of society and the resort of dogfighters and racers. prizefighters and others taking part in demoralising games."[35] The monitoring of working-class drinking places and the suppression of many of the activities attached to them was taken quite seriously by the police; even a cursory examination of raw police records shows an enormous number of man-hours expended on public-house surveillance as well as a great concern with petty gambling in the streets by juveniles.[36] Leeds chief constables saw themselves as natural allies of the temperance movement, with whose local leaders they corresponded.[37] and the S.P.C.A. Wetherell actively encouraged the monitoring of popular amusements on Woodhouse Moor by the local S.P.C.A. agent and even made him a constable "to give him additional support."[38]

It must not be supposed. however, that the locales of working-class recreational life were under direct assault all the time; to attack all the activities attached to the pub would have placed absurd demands upon the resources of the police. Especially in the largest cities the police authorities quickly became quite realistic about the chances of actually suppressing public-house gambling, brutal sports, and illegal drinking. Campaigns of overt repression – as distinguished from normal surveillance – were often employed when the police were under pressure from the magistrates or from powerful individuals or groups concerned for the moment about some specific abuse, or immediately after a significant change in the law. At such times there might be a brief but intense flurry of beerhouse sweeps – the week or two before the annual Brewster Sessions was a favorite time – prostitute round-ups, penny-gaff closings, and charges of permitting gambling or illegal sports. Local policy of course varied, but in general the police were almost never either willing or able to follow strict municipal rule in these matters; Heaton's efforts in Huddersfield were thus atypical.

Sir Richard Mayne, one of the commissioners of the Metropolitan Police, perfectly illustrates the more common posture. Mayne professed that ideally all places of public entertainment should be duly licensed and under police control so that cockfights, dogfights, and so forth could be observed and stopped if necessary. In fact, however, as far as music halls and dancing saloons were concerned, the duties of the police were primarily to see that licenses of some sort were possessed and order preserved. Even if the material presented were immoral Mayne did not think the police "would consider it their duty to notice it" unless "it was very grossly immoral." Nor would he strike against the penny gaffs: "Many persons consider them. . . objectionable inasmuch as they induce boys and girls to steal the entrance money; if that be so that is beyond the knowledge of the police." He refused to engage the time of his men in attempts to suppress dancing in pubs licensed only for music: At "many of these places. . . they dance. . . . The women are not very correctly dressed, but I think it would be oversqueamish looking at the class of persons who frequent these places to find fault with them."[39] Even if known prostitutes were present he would not necessarily press for removal of a license if their behavior were "decorous." Mayne sometimes felt obliged to proceed against houses putting on unlicensed dramatic entertainments. In 1838 the Metropolitan Police carried out an extensive penny-gaff sweep in the East End,[40] and again in 1859 a number of them were raided and suppressed.[41] But where, asked Mayne, does one draw the line? Some pubs had a piano and singing "which is very near being a private entertainment," and in most cases he refused to interfere.[42] Out of sheer realism, Mayne pointed out that quashing the penny gaffs paid no permanent dividends; many would quickly reopen, offering a crude pantomime or dumb show in order to remain within the strict letter of the law. Mayne acquired a pragmatic awareness of the resiliency of these popular institutions and became quite hesitant to dissipate the energies of his force in constant open warfare with them. Licensing and decorum became the keynotes of Richard Mayne's bureaucratic style of policing in these areas.

Major J.J. Grieg, the Chief Constable of Liverpool in the mid-1860s, adopted a similar course regarding public houses sponsoring music and dancing. He was unsure whether he even possessed the legal authority to attack them, but in any case the problem was simply too overwhelming: "The tonnage of Liverpool brings in so many sailors, those dancing houses are principally where the sailors' boarding houses are; they go there, and you cannot find anything that will carry a conviction."[43] In other towns, however, where these abuses were apparently less highly concentrated the police might feel emboldened to adopt a much more repressive stance. In the mid-1860s, Sheffield seemed to have had only two dancing rooms attached to pubs. Both were shut down by the police, not on the grounds that unlicensed dancing was carried on – this was perfectly legal outside of London – but because they harbored prostitutes.[44] At Bolton the magistrates tried to drive the popular singing and dancing saloons out of business in the early 1850s by forbidding entrance to those under eighteen. No doubt both they and the police knew that dancing saloons were important components of the working-class marriage market and vital to courting, so that excluding those under eighteen was tantamount to a death sentence on these places. They were also aware that they had no real legal power to enforce this stricture, but threatened publicans with redoubled police surveillance if they refused to comply.[45]

In the early 1850s Leeds police authorities professed themselves reluctant to move against known rendezvous of prostitutes, because, as they put it, "the sons and daughters of vice *would* find a resting place [in] respectable neighbourhoods where their proximity would be deeply deplored."[46] Seventeen years later the Leeds police were willing to pursue a more active course under a new chief constable, but found themselves hampered by the courts, which had ruled that evidence had to be shown that prostitutes had assembled to practice their trade and not merely to eat or drink.[47] This question in fact created a great deal of confusion among both police and magistrates. At Preston the police thought that they were authorized to forbid prostitutes from sitting in beershops, and the local magistrates convicted; at Blackburn at the same time the magistrates were

THE POLICEMAN AS DOMESTIC MISSIONARY   487

unwilling to convict and the police stopped intervening.[48] In this matter an overall policy of vacillation and hesitation resulted, varying during the tenure of one chief constable and perhaps changing entirely during the administration of the next. This particular problem was inherently so intractable, whatever changes in administration or law occurred, that no policy could have resulted in significant suppression of the target abuses. In actually making decisions to mobilize police resources for an all-out assault on prostitution and many other lower-class activities, police authorities of necessity had to engage in a cost-effectiveness calculus, based upon disposable manpower, size of the district, and the extent of the pressure being exerted by moral-reform interest groups, magistrates, or watch committees. In large sprawling port cities like Liverpool or London, the policy employed by Sir Richard Mayne was not only calculated to preserve his own sanity, but was really the only one which could have been adopted.

Hence despite some dramatic confrontations, the police carried out their mission as "domestic missionary" in the largest cities not by pursuing a policy of overt suppression at every opportunity, but rather through the pressure of a constant surveillance of all the key institutions of working-class neighborhood and recreational life. It was no doubt hoped by the police and by those to whom they were responsible that ultimately after-hours drinking, low theaters, brutal sports, public-house gambling, and the like would dwindle under unremitting monitoring; but if they did not it would at least be a gain if a modicum of decorum resulted and a better flow of intelligence as to what was transpiring in the lanes and courts of Leeds or Manchester was secured. It was precisely the pressure of an unceasing surveillance and not the intense but sporadic episodes of active intervention and suppression which ultimately produced the main impact on working-class neighborhood life. The technique was thus well chosen, for it recognized that many popular recreational phenomena were not amenable to quick and easy suppression by any conceivable strategy. The pressure of surveillance cannot be calculated by precisely measuring police manpower per capita or per acre, interesting though it might be and however useful for answering other types of questions. As far as the policed were concerned the impression of being watched or hounded was not directly dependent on the presence of a constable on every streetcorner and at all times. What produced this effect was the knowledge that the police were always near and likely to appear at any time. This it seems was — and still is — the main function of the pressure of surveillance.

This approach of course did not eradicate the target abuses, but drove them into more covert channels. The Huddersfield example examined earlier, had hosts of parallels elsewhere. The dogfights or cockfights, once quite public affairs, were pushed behind the doors of the pub or out into the fields or moors of the surrounding countryside,[49] that is, to locales outside the normal range of the force and/or to times of the day — such as change of shift — when the vigilance of the police might be relaxed. This was duly noted even in the dialect literature:

> Jack: Well, oud lad, its all up we yer fancy dog-feighting nah; there's a act passed for preventing cruelty to animals. Wot thinks ta abaht that, my buck, eh?
> Savage: O they shant hinder us, an we'll feit em it spoit o ther teeth; *we can gooa intot woods whoile they're it Chetch.*[50]

In the mid-1870s James Greenwood was told in a Potteries beershop that it had become "as difficult. . . to 'pull off' a dog-fight all right and regular, and without any hole and corner business'. . . as it was to bring off a man-fight under the same open conditions."[51] Nonetheless, Greenwood ascertained that dog-fighting had by no means been eliminated in the district; though well hidden, it survived in a very healthy state. Greenwood incidentally got a bit more than he had bargained for during his visit to the Potteries: an opportunity to witness an extremely brutal contest between a man and a dog. A Liverpool observer reported in the mid-1850s that though dogfighting had been driven underground by the "efforts that have from time to time been made by the police to put an end to this 'manly and elevating' British pastime," it continued to employ "the leisure hours of great numbers of the working population in this as well as other towns. . . . Not a week elapses. . . in which several dogfights do not take place, some more or less openly, many, particularly those involving large sums of money, strictly private."[52] The same writer provided an excellent account of the evasive tactics engaged in to practice this sport. Before a match they

> talk in the coolest manner of fighting their dogs, but there is one thing you never hear them name publicly, "the trysting place." You never hear them state the hour. . . at which the fight will take place. This is learned in a quiet way. . . . In Liverpool the risk that landlords run in holding dogfights. . . is said to be very great, therefore the landlords. . . undertake the risk in turns. . . . The time chosen is generally early in the morning, when the police are going off duty, and we were told that Sunday was a very good time.[53]

The forcing of many of these activities into covert channels perhaps had certain virtues as far as the police were concerned. They might still gain the congratulations of local businessmen or clergy who could be allowed to believe that such abuses had been caused to vanish, a "fact" which some occasionally even reported to parliament.[54] In reality the police learned that popular recreations had remarkable resiliency — hence the general avoidance of frontal assault — and in addition, that the repression of one barbarous practice often resulted in its replacement by another objectionable one. When the Bradford police moved to shut down the beerhouse-attached brothels in Southgate in 1858, the beerhouse keepers immediately converted them into "low concert rooms."[55] The police could then have chosen to attack the concert rooms, but chose to let matters rest. In London by mid-century, public-house cockfighting and dogfighting had declined to be replaced by the craze — classically described by Mayhew — for rat killing. A few decades later an observer reported rat matches very rare, but described the current mania for the turf and the efforts of the police to stop ready money betting.[56]

From within the pub or beerhouse nexus a wide variety of evasive tactics could be resorted to in order to baffle the authorities and convince them not to spend too much time hunting down illegal or objectionable recreations. The chief constable of Wolverhampton recounted his frustration in trying to deal with the problem of illegal drinking: "The house door is shut, and to all appearance everything is quiet; at the same time parties are card-playing and drinking. . . in the back premises. . . . You knock at the door. . . . You are kept perhaps five minutes, the cards are removed. . . and the ale is got off the table. . . then you come in and find a very quiet and orderly company, and you are informed that these parties are lodgers."[57] It was equally difficult to deal with gambling. The courts had ruled that if play was not for money or moneysworth there was no offense. The police discovered many individuals who did not even attempt to remove the cards from sight; the only way to get a case was to plant a plainclothesman. Gambling for moneysworth was especially difficult to prove since what was being wagered for was not put out on the tables.[58] Sometimes the expedients resorted to were outrageously comical: at an Idle (Bradford) pub located near the River Aire patrons drinking during illegal hours were loaded onto a boat and rowed downriver when lookouts reported the police on their way;[59] occasionally a constable could be bribed to overlook irregularities;[60] and near Huddersfield beerhouse keepers figured out the police Sunday visitation schedule and closed for a short time when they were due to appear.[61]

In the case of activities which had either traditionally been centered on the pub or had been forced to migrate behind its doors, the police operated at something of a disadvantage; with little trouble gambling, illegal drinking, brutal sports, and prizefighting could be shielded from their eyes and often from their knowledge, or gradually transformed into other, still objectionable forms.[61] In the case of the traditional popular fête however, the terms of the situation were reversed, and by the same token surveillance could be shunned in favor of direct action. By definition popular celebrations were public affairs and had to occur in the open. Here the police were both willing and able to intervene actively, confident of achieving a great measure of success. In fact they had to intervene; in this area, both they and the magistrates were politically very much on the spot. Respectable citizens might have heard rumors of dogfights or other such activities, but were rarely in a position to witness them. It was easier to convince such people that the police were vigorous with regard to such matters and that the situation was under control. It was quite otherwise in the case of football through the town, stang-riding, Guy Fawkes celebrations, or other highly visible lower-class fêtes. Either the police acted to suppress them or they faced severe loss of face and were open to the charge that they were failing in one of their primary missions, the preservation of municipal order and decorum. The willingness of the police not merely to monitor these activities[63] but to attack them produced violent confrontations and, in some cases, left a legacy of bitterness long after the point of successful suppression. The police proved to be a weapon well-tuned to the task of terminating the popular fête with all its connotations of disorder, drunkenness, sexual license, and property damage. However, although the popular fête had nowhere to migrate or to hide once the authorities felt confident enough to act, the history of its suppression was often marked by riotous protest, for the popular culture involved was as deep-rooted as that expressed in activities that could be moved about.

The custom of stang-riding was particularly distasteful to Victorian respectables. It was first of all an open public affair always accompanied by disorder: marching, chanting, and shouting. In the West Riding the new county police attacked it as a breach of the peace.[64] At first some efforts were made by the participants either to compromise with the police or evade their intervention. At Honley near Huddersfield the arrival of the county police in 1857 forced local residents to resort to the novel expedient of asking police permission to ride the stang for an adulterer. In some places in the West Riding it came to be believed that if the performance were conducted within three townships before being officially noticed it acquired "legality" and the police were bound to stand aside. At Grassington in Wharfedale it was thought that marching three times around the parish church would legally protect stang-riders.[65]

Some of the traditional uses of this custom go far to explain why the authorities seemed so determined to put it down. It had been used around Newcastle against blacklegs in labor disputes, and in Sunderland against those who informed on striking keelmen and those who were instrumental in the kidnapping and impressment of sailors.[66] The Welsh wooden horse or "Ceffyl Pren," an analogous practice, greatly disturbed the Cardigan magistrates: a figure of a horse was carried

> to the door of any person whose domestic conduct may have exposed him to the censure of his neighbours or who may have rendered himself unpopular by. . . contributing to enforce the law. . . . The right. . . thus arrogated of. . . publicly animadverting on. . . another man's domestic conduct, is certainly characteristic of a rude state of society; but when the same measures are applied to. . . thwarting the operation of the laws of the land, they become of much more serious import.[67]

Because stang-riding and similar customs represented survivals of old forms of popular justice or self-policing or else were used as vehicles for social protest, because they symbolically short-circuited all modern agencies and bureaucracies of established authority, the police and magistrates were ruthless in their attempts to put them down.

Superintendent Heaton of Huddersfield achieved one notable and permanent success in his efforts to make the police a leading edge of moral reform. During his tenure the traditional Huddersfield Guy Fawkes celebration was quelled. At least since the 1820s local authorities had made sporadic efforts to prevent the customary bonfire from being lit in the town center. The reorganization of the local constables under an Improvement Act and the advent of Heaton led to a frontal assault on Guy Fawkes in 1848. A redoubled "move-on" policy was put into effect, and when that failed to stop the usual crowd of shopmen and apprentices from assembling Heaton ordered water hoses turned on them. The result of course was a serious riot in the course of which Heaton himself was felled, kicked about, and rolled in the mud. The police were put to rout and the crowd returned to its business of milling about and discharging fireworks.[68] The Huddersfield police lost the battle of 1848, but in so doing won the war over the perpetuation of Guy Fawkes. Neither in 1849 nor 1850 were attempts made to hold the traditional revels in the marketplace; in 1851 Guy Fawkes activities were reported being held on the far outskirts of town, the transfer signalling their disappearance in the customary form.[69] Popular resistance to the determination of the Huddersfield police to end the affair in 1848 was violent, but untimately quite brittle. Displaced from its customary locale in the center of the town, Guy Fawkes reappeared in the suburbs and then died away, eventually becoming what it is today in most places — a begging occasion for small children.

At Richmond and Malton, towns located in the agricultural districts of Yorkshire, riotous resistance was more prolonged, lasting at least through the 1870s.[70] At Wakefield, Guildford (Surrey), and Lewes (Sussex), Guy Fawkes in the mid- and late nineteenth century became a ritual occasion used by working-class youths to stand up for local custom and tradition while having a "legitimate" go at the police. Especially in Guildford the Fifth of November bore the character of a semi-institutionalized antipolice riot, an occasion on which one

THE POLICEMAN AS DOMESTIC MISSIONARY 491

might square a whole year's debts with the police and other local authorities. As for the authorities themselves, as one Yorkshire magistrate put it, "the celebration of the 5th of November was a most degrading practice. . . and all intelligent and thinking persons had ceased to be connected with it. To Lord Macauley we were indebted for getting rid of such things as services for the 5th of November. . . . The law and the public had agreed to let such days be forgotten, but at Ossett they must forsooth keep them up."[71] The bulk of society was expected to follow the new policies of the upper classes quickly, and if it did not the police could be employed to speed the process. By this time both the magistrates and the police authorities were often being put under intense pressure by local merchants and shopkeepers who were forced to close early, suffer the desertion of their shop assistants, lose an evening's custom, and bear the galling expense of boarding up their premises.[72] There was one other reason for the concern of the authorities: in some places in the last half of the nineteenth century, Guy Fawkes had been transmuted into a popular celebration with strong overtones of political and social protest.[73]

At Lewes — where Guy Fawkes survives even to this day — the celebrations were arranged by two societies of "Bonfire Boys." Each group presided over the building of its own bonfire, decked out a member in bishop's garb, and burned its guys. The "bishop" of each society habitually gave an oration of a quasi-political nature, always alluding to "the evils of the day."[74] At Ludlow (Shropshire) it was reported: "If any well known person in the place should happen to have excited the enmity of the populace, his effigy is substituted for or added to that of Guy Fawkes" and burnt.[75] At Guildford the proceedings were also organized by a semisecret society called "the Guys." The latter appeared in the town center dressed in grotesque disguises and armed with bludgeons to defend themselves against the police. Guildford celebrations were distinguished by systematic and "deliberate attacks on the property of selected citizens, who were usually members of the corporation or of the police."[76] At Guildford "the Guys" and their constituents were so formidable that in the 1850s the local police despaired of coping with them. They were often barricaded inside their station houses by the chief constable and plied with bread, cheese, and beer while "the Guys" went about their business.[77] Interestingly, "the Guys" might appear on other days beside November fifth; in 1865 they appeared on an election day. After the great riot of 1865 Guy Fawkes at Guildford was suppressed by a resort to the military. In 1867, though the usual crowd materialized and waited for "the Guys" to come out, they did not appear.[78] The Guildford fête, though more organized and centered more clearly upon themes of social protest than at Huddersfield, proved equally fragile once the authorities made a determined and concerted effort to mobilize the force needed to quell it.[79]

An examination of the suppression of other types of popular fetes by the magistrates and police reveals similar patterns.[80] At Leicester a number of traditional Shrovetide practices were ended in 1847 to the accompaniment of strong popular resistance. On Shrove Tuesday the "Whipping Toms," another society of disguised young men, would appear in the Newark carrying large cart whips and preceded by a bellman whose ringing was presumed to give them "legality." After 1:00 P.M. anyone of any social station was liable to be whipped below the knees unless a fee was paid to the Toms. In 1846 a clause of a

Leicester Improvement Act specifically declared the "Whipping Toms" and the rough game of folk football which usually followed their performance to be illegal and punishable by a £5 fine. At Leicester the frequent warnings of the authorities in the weeks previous to Shrove Tuesday, 1847 were enough to discourage the Toms from appearing; but their constituents, a large crowd, did come out and milled about under the eyes of the borough police and a group of special constables sworn in for the occasion. At 2:00 P.M. the crowd, cheated of the "Whipping Toms," proceeded to the customary game of football; the police attempted to stop it and a serious riot ensued. Eventually the Newark was cleared and the crowd dispersed. On Shrove Tuesday of both 1848 and 1849 all was quiet; neither the "Whipping Toms" nor the usual crowds made an appearance and the task of suppression was complete.[81]

The police were forceful in attempting to end other customary days of popular license, occasions on which the social order was symbolically inverted and the usual lines of authority and deference unilaterally suspended by the lower classes. At Chetwynd (Shropshire) the populace had traditionally enjoyed the right to pelt anyone with crab apples during the wakes celebration: nobody from the lowest to the highest was exempt from the "rules" governing the fête. In 1862 the aged rector of Newport was attacked by an apple-throwing crowd; the police were sent for and the custom was suppressed.[82]

It should be noted that in the past many of these customs and celebrations had not only been tacitly sanctioned by the upper classes but openly and sometimes even officially patronized by them. Once the latter decided to dissociate themselves from their old roles, however, it was usually not long before the police were unleashed and the fete in question placed under assault. In eighteenth-century Liverpool for example, the burgesses officially sponsored a bear-baiting through the town each October tenth to mark the annaul election of a mayor.[83] At Ludlow (Shropshire) the rope for the traditional tug of war through the town was customarily purchased out of corporation funds and thrown out by the mayor himself. In 1851 official participation was suddenly ended amidst talk of possible "dangerous accidents" and "disorderly scenes."[84] The affair was then quickly suppressed by those who had once presided over it.

Most obviously with regard to popular fêtes, but eventually even with more private recreation, police action ultimately had profound effects. Many nineteenth-century contemporaries specifically linked the coming of the police to the decline of traditional customs and amusements. A Batley (Yorkshire) observer writing in the 1880s spoke of the time when

> the first policeman came into our midst, to plant the thin edge of the wedge, which was. . . to revolutionise our manners and customs. Since he came. . . we have lost all trace of mumming; all trace of Lee Fair, . . . most of our mischief night; as nearly all the peace eggers; for what are left of the latter are of another mould to those of my own childhood days. . . . If mummers were to be seen upon the street now, the police would interfere. . . . I put a deal of this severance from ourselves of old customs down to the advent of the policeman in uniform.

Walter Rose, describing a rural district, spoke of the process by which the old mummer's play was hounded out of public by the local police towards the end of the nineteenth century: "The police made it their duty to hover on the heels of the players, keeping a watch on their conduct; so that they became fearful of making an unannounced entry to a private house. Thus it was that. . . the public

THE POLICEMAN AS DOMESTIC MISSIONARY   493

house became almost the only place where the play could be rendered correctly." Alfred Williams attributed at least part of the decline of the folksong to the
interventions of the police, who drove it even from the pubs: the "police looked
upon song-singing as a species of rowdyism. Their frequent complaints and
threats to the landlords filled them with misgivings; the result was that they were
forced, as a means of self protection, to request their customers not to sing on
the premises."[85] It would be absurd to advance any single explanation for
nineteenth-century transformations of popular culture, but there is no question
that interventions of the police and of those who directed them played a
considerable role.

Yet while almost all aspects of popular culture changed, the differential
between festival and other recreations remains vital, and this affected police-
community relations. Ironically, while suppression of festivals often caused a
riot, it was usually relatively clear-cut; lingering bitterness is hard to discern. Not
so with the pub-centered recreational nexus, where the police perforce relied on
ongoing surveillance. It was the pressure of surveillance on institutions and
activities that long eluded direct attack that maintained the police in the role the
workers of Lancashire and Yorkshire had understood at the moment of their
installation: an alien element in the community and a daily source of both major
and petty annoyance. Policemen continued to be beaten all through the nineteenth century,[86] for such reasons as interfering too closely in family or
neighborhood affairs or public-house proceedings, providing escort for strike-
breakers, engaging in brutality, or moving people on too forcefully, especially in
times of high unemployment. Vignettes such as the following were not atypical
at least up to the 1890s. In confrontation in the mid-1860s over preparations for
Guy Fawkes at Dunnington in the East Riding of Yorkshire, William Nicholls
was charged with an assault on a policeman. In court the defense argued that the
accused was engaged in gathering thorns for making a November fifth bonfire
and that the policeman said that Nicholls told him: "Thou b[ugge]r, thou
hindered us having a fire last year; thou shan't this." When they reached
Nicholls' house his mother came out and egged the men on, one of the others
exclaiming "We'll shoot the b[ugge]r before the winter's over." The policeman
followed the group of men to the common where they began unloading. At that
point he was knocked unconscious with a pitchfork. All present swore that the
policeman used his stick first, though this was not believed by the magistrate.[87]
In the winter of 1864 a group of young men beat up two constables outside the
Black Bull Inn at Pudsey near Leeds. The magistrates observed "Pudsey is well
known for this sort of thing." Near Wakefield a prizefight in Lupset Pastures was
interfered with by a Sgt. Coop and a PC Houlton of the West Riding force. Both
were "frightfully beaten" and Houlton almost died. A Leeds policeman was
assaulted for no apparent reason by a William Hezlenden. When asked why he
did it he replied he just "wanted to have a tussle with a policeman."[88]

An informant told Stephen Reynolds that the "first thing a policeman ought
to know is when to let well alone."[89] Reynolds discovered as much resentment
against the police in the early twentieth century as this writer found in Lancashire in 1840 or Yorkshire in 1857.[90] George Sturt wrote convincingly of his
turn-of-the-century Surrey folk that they were

> aware of the constraint imposed upon them by laws and prejudices which are none too friendly to people of their kind. One divines it in their treatment of the... policeman. There is probably no lonelier man in the parish.... One hears him mentioned in those same accents of grudging caution which the villagers use in speaking of unfriendly property owners, as though he belonged to that alien caste. The cottagers feel that they themselves are the people whom he is stationed in the valley to watch.... In theory, the policeman represents the general public; in practice, he stands for middle-class decorum and the rights of property.[91]

The police, Reynolds wrote, "are charged... with a whole mass of petty enactments, which are little more than social regulations bearing almost entirely on working class life.... Nor can it... be otherwise since the duties of the police have been made to tally with upper class... notions of right and wrong, so that a working man may easily render himself liable to arrest... without in the least doing what is wrong in his own eyes or in the opinion of his neighbours."[92] Writing about the same period in Salford, Robert Roberts reported strikingly similar attitudes: "Nobody in our Northern slum... ever spoke in fond regard... of the policeman as a 'social worker' and 'handyman of the streets.' Like their children, delinquent or not, the poor in general looked upon him with fear and dislike. When one arrived on a 'social' visit they watched his passing with suspicion and his disappearance with relief."[93]

If there were disputes to be settled within working class communities, the instinctive reaction of the poor was not to call upon a "handyman of the streets" but to settle things among themselves. A mid-century magistrate reported that "great scenes of outrage take place [in pubs] and violent conduct frequently occurs; when they come out the police interfere, and endeavour to stop it; and then they all set upon the police; this frequently occurs."[94] A wealth of contemporary evidence confirms Henry Pelling's observation that the English working class has always put a high premium on being left alone by the state and its agents.[95] It is difficult to get a firm line on the question of relations between the police and the working class from Victorian official sources alone. The truth was often left unsaid by magistrates and police authorities in testimony before parliamentary committees and royal commissions; the amount of sheer cant under which discussion of this issue was camouflaged was perhaps an index of its sensitivity. One is compelled to resort to the local press, to an examination of working-class epithets – "blue locusts," "rozzers," "crushers," "busy Bs," "raw lobsters" – music-hall songs, or to the analyses of sensitive contemporary observers such as Sturt or Reynolds.[96] Yet occasionally the wall of official silence lifts and a candid voice confirms what we know from other sources to be accurate. When asked by the 1908 Royal Commission what the feeling toward the police in his area was, the Chief Constable of Glasgow replied that it depended on the locality: "The feeling towards the police is decidedly good in the better class localities, and amongst the shopkeeping class. In the rougher localities the feeling is hostile and always in favour of the arrested person."[97] The issue was not only suspicion of the agencies of law enforcement but what E.P. Thompson has called "alienation from the law" itself. These were facts of nineteenth-century social life to which not enough attention has been directed, and they suggest in turn that the English working class was not as easily reconciled to the advent of a policed society and to newer standards of public order as official sources have led many to think.

THE POLICEMAN AS DOMESTIC MISSIONARY 495

It is known that the initial implantation of the police was often accompanied by episodes of violent resistance. After that period mass rioting against the police became more rare, but other forms of antipolice outbreaks occurred frequently throughout the nineteenth century in defense of popular recreations and customs, in reaction to instances of police brutality, in protest against police interference in strikes, and in a multitude of other daily-life situations.[98]

The charge of the new police with a "domestic missionary" function and the monitoring of many important facets of everyday life in working-class neighborhoods reflected a profound social change as well as a deep rupture in class relations in nineteenth-century Britain. One consequence of the creation of what political economists called "free labor" was the appearance of its concomitant, "free leisure," and of a working class by and large left to itself once it passed out through the factory gate or workshop door in the evening. By the middle of the nineteenth century — if not earlier — a profound interruption of communications had occurred between the classes: both the "language" and the objectives of urban masses were, if intelligible at all, deeply frightening. The upper classes saw "themselves threatened by agglomerations of the... rapidly multiplying poor of cities whose size had no precedent in Western history."[99] The older understanding that movements of the lower orders had rational, legitimate, or at least comprehensible ends was replaced in the first half of the nineteenth century by the feeling that they aimed at the utter unravelling of society. To some extent these fears were reflected in a concern that the lower classes had escaped from all social control except the discipline of work. The activities of workers after their release from the salubrious discipline of the workshop or factory therefore became a matter of both profound interest and apprehension. Dogfights, cockfights, gambling, popular fetes — always described in contemporary sources as both "sensual" and "barbarous" — were symbolic of the fear of social anarchy which always lay beneath the surface of early Victorian professions of optimism. It is probably true that after mid-century the English upper classes became both more discriminating and less fearful, and began to identify "dangerous classes" with casual labor or the residuum and not with the working classes as a whole. Yet we know that in the last half of the nineteenth century the pace of middle-class cultural missionizing did not slacken but rather gathered momentum. The history of the temperance movement and the annual accounts of Social Science Association gatherings in the 1870s or 1880s display ongoing concern over the demoralization and ignorance of the lower orders and the dangers to the social fabric such reformers thought this posed.[100]

In the new industrial cities whatever connections had subsisted between social classes in terms of common enjoyment had been decisively severed. This was tacitly recognized by the Dewsbury magistrate who stressed that "all intelligent and thinking persons" had divorced themselves from the celebration of the Fifth of November. The chaplain of Preston jail made a similar point:[101]

Have you any doubt that these were very common sports at Preston? – In former times I believe they were.
Before the Beer Act came into operation? – Yes.
They must have been in some place? – They were in the... Cockpit. I recollect persons being present at these cockfights, who are the highest in the land now.
The upper classes used to encourage it at one time, now the beerhouses do? – That is precisely the fact.

Flora Thompson pointed out that in her area the local gentry had by the 1870s long since left the local feast celebration entirely to the lower classes; in the 1820s Miss Lister of Shibden Hall in the Halifax area locked up both herself and her horse when fairtime came.[102]

The disintegration of a common sphere of enjoyment was of course paralleled by a physical separation of the classes — classically described by Engels — unprecedented in western history. The Victorian bourgeoisie which set the moral tone of cities like Manchester and Leeds were not likely to patronize the cockpit as the Preston gentry of the late eighteenth century had done, nor to shower coins on a Guy Fawkes crowd as Wakefield tories still felt at liberty to do at mid-century. Such gentlemen were much more inclined to either mind their own business and businesses or else to patronize temperance or rational recreation societies or mechanics' institutes. It was also they who supported the moral-reform mission assigned to the police and added to it in the language of numerous local improvement acts. The new demands for civil order in nine-teenth-century England produced a novel type of surrogate to replace older and perhaps more personal lines of authority and deference which were now con-ceived to be moribund. The police, a "bureaucracy of official morality,"[103] were produced to try to fill this vacuum and to act as a lever of moral reform on the mysterious terrain of the industrial city's inner core.

The police, as we have observed, once successfully installed confronted a number of serious problems in the discharge of their moral-reform mission. Many problems proved utterly intractable, leading some police authorities to quickly gauge the real limits of their effectiveness in these areas. Though the full measure of the charge to the police by the Victorian municipality and the state could never be fully lived up to, the nineteenth century saw the forging of a modern and generally effective technique of order-keeping: the installation of the eyes and ears of ruling elites at the very centers of working-class daily life. The free leisure activities of the urban lower classes proved much less amenable to the interventions of both middle-class reform movements and the pressure of the police than had been originally hoped; however, the basic technique of daily surveillance of the streets and recreational centers of working-class districts proved a lasting one, and would ultimately be applied not only to nineteenth-century Leeds or Manchester but — in highly sophisticated variants — to twentieth-century police work as well.

University of Wisconsin, Janesville   Robert D. Storch

FOOTNOTES

1. An earlier version of this article was presented at the Shelby Cullom Davis Center, Princeton University, in January 1975. The criticisms of the Davis seminar were invaluable, especially those of Professor Wilbur Miller. The author also wishes to thank Professors Stephen Haliczer and Richard Price of Northern Illinois University and Professor David Stafford of the University of Victoria, British Columbia, whose critical instincts he has often relied upon.

2. J.M. Hart, "Reform of the Borough Police 1835-1856," *English Historical Review* 70 (1955); F.C. Mather, *Public Order in the Age of the Chartists* (London, 1959); E.C. Midwinter, *Social Administration in Lancashire 1830-1860* (Manchester, 1969) and *Law and*

THE POLICEMAN AS DOMESTIC MISSIONARY 497

Order in Early Victorian Lancashire, Borthwick Institute Paper No. 34 (York, 1968); H. Parris, "The Home Office and the Provincial Police," *Public Law* 6 (1961); L. Radzinowicz, *A History of the English Criminal Law* 4 (London, 1968); C. Reith, *The British Police and the Democratic Ideal* (London, 1943); and *A New Study of Police History* (London, 1956); J.J. Tobias, *Crime and Industrial Society in the 19th Century* (London, 1967).

3. E.P. Thompson, "Time, Work Discipline and Industrial Capitalism," *Past and Present* 38 (1967); B. Harrison, "Religion and Recreation in Nineteenth Century England," *Past and Present* 38 (1967) and *Drink and the Victorians* (London, 1971); B. Harrison and B. Trinder, *Drink and Sobriety in an Early Victorian Town: Banbury 1830-1860, English Historical Review* Supplement No. 4 (London, 1969); B. Harrison, "Animals and the State in Nineteenth Century England," *English Historical Review* 87 (1973); R. Johnson, "Educational Policy and Social Control in Early Victorian England," *Past and Present* 49 (1970); R. Price, "The Working Men's Club Movement," *Victorian Studies* 15 (1971); R.D. Storch, "Middle Class Moral Reform Movements and the Problem of Working Class Leisure" (Unpublished paper presented to Edinburgh University Symposium on "Aspects of Class Relations in 19th Century Britain," May 1967).

4. F. Engels, "The Condition of the Working Class in England," in *Marx and Engels on Britain,* 2nd. edition (Moscow, 1964), p. 263.

5. e.g., the *Leeds Mercury,* December 20, 1859, reported the severe beating of a West Riding policeman near Barnsley. The latter had been assigned the unenviable task of escorting blacklegs to the Wharnecliffe-Silkstone colliery; Cf. for the Black Country, D. Phillips, "Riots and Public Order in the Black Country, 1835-1860," in J. Stevenson and R. Quinault, eds., *Popular Protest and Public Order* (London, 1974), p. 161; R. Roberts, *The Classic Slum. Salford Life in the First Quarter of the Century* (Manchester, 1971), p. 71; H. Hendrick, "The Leeds Gas Strike 1890," *Thorsby Society Miscellany* 16 Part I (1974), p. 87. For a much later period see N. Branson and M. Heinemann, *Britain in the Nineteen Thirties* (London, 1971), pp. 95-6, 105, 108; and W. Gallacher, *The Rolling of the Thunder* (London, 1947), pp. 117-19, 130-1.

6. E.P. Thompson, *The Making of the English Working Class* (London, 1963), p. 82; Radzinowicz, *English Criminal Law,* pp. 261-6; *Poor Man's Guardian,* November 5, 1831; *Destructive and Poor Man's Conservative,* November 2, 1833.

7. E.C. Midwinter, *Social Administration in Lancashire,* pp. 160-1; I. Prothero, "Chartism in London," *Past and Present* 44 (1969); *Northern Star,* September 12, 1840; *Northern Star,* February 20, 1841; *Lancaster Gazette,* August 1, 1840.

8. Radzinowicz, *English Criminal Law,* p. 78; *Report From His Majesty's Commissioners For Inquiring Into The Poor Laws,* Parliamentary Papers 1834 (44) XXVIII. Reports of Assistant Commissioners, Appendix A, pp. 197, 331; *Northern Star,* March 16, 1839.

9. *Leeds Mercury,* January 20, 24, February 10, June 20, 1857; *Leeds Times,* December 27, 1856, June 6, 1857; cf. Philips, "Riots and Public Order," p. 167.

10. *Leeds Mercury,* March 10, May 2, June 6, June 20, July 2, 1857.

11. *Leeds Mercury,* June 13, 1857. Perhaps the provocation was given in the previous weeks.

12. *Northern Star,* June 6, 1840.

13. *Leeds Mercury,* June 18, 1857. The theme of the "blue locust" or "idle drone" was still alive in the 1880s; cf. F. Thompson, *Lark Rise to Candleford* (Oxford, 1954), p. 554.

14. *Northern Star,* May 18, 1839.

15. R.D. Storch, "The Plague of the Blue Locusts: Police Reform and Popular Resistance in Northern England, 1840-1857," *International Review of Social History* 20 (1975): 1: pp. 79-83.

16. *Ibid.,* pp. 87-8.

17. The "move-on system" was duly noted in the broadside literature. See "Manchester's An Altered Town," in Charles Hindley ed., *Curiosities of Street Literature* (London, 1871), no pagination; J. Lawson, *Letters to the Young on Progress in Pudsey* (Stanningley, 1887), p. 133.

18. H. Mayhew, *London Labour and the London Poor* vol. 1 (London, 1851), p. 22. On Guy Fawkes Day 1876 in London the costers of Somers Town and Holborn came out with giant effegies of those police inspectors who strictly enforced the Sunday Observance Acts *(Annual Register,* 1876).

19. Mayhew, *London Labour,* p. 16.

20. *Northern Star,* June 6, 1840. For France cf. R. Cobb, *The Police and the People* (Oxford, 1970), passim.

21. [T. Wright] "A Journeyman Engineer," *Some Habits and Customs of the Working Classes* (London, 1867), pp. 225-26.

22. A. Redford, *The History of Local Government in Manchester,* vol. 3 (London, 1940), p. 212.

23. Manuscript Minutes of Leeds Watch Committee, April 22, 1836.

24. Manuscript Minutes of Leeds Town Council, vol. 4, February 5, 1836.

25. *Ibid.,* August 25, 1836; *Yorkshire Evening Post,* June 3, 1936.

26. G.H. Smith, "The Law Enforcement Agencies in Bradford in the Early Nineteenth Century" (Unpublished paper, part 5, pp. 5-6); W. Cudworth, *Historical Notes on the Bradford Corporation* (Bradford, 1882), pp. 68-69.

27. *Bradford Observer,* December 9, 1836.

28. *Ibid.,* March 6, 1845.

29. Manuscript Minutes of Leeds Watch Committee, July 22, 1836.

30. See *Leeds Times,* August 5, 1848, for a typical week's proceedings at Huddersfield during this period.

31. *Ibid.,* April 28, 1849.

32. *Ibid.,* February 1, 1851.

33. *Leeds Mercury,* February 10, 1857.

34. Chief Constable's Manuscript Letter Book (Leeds Police Headquarters). Letter to Edward Baines, April 10, 1868; *Borough of Leeds. Report of the Efficiency of the Police Force...* (Leeds, 1869), pp. 4-5, 18.

35. Chief Constable's Manuscript Letter Book. Letter to Leeds Watch Committee, December 17, 1868.

THE POLICEMAN AS DOMESTIC MISSIONARY   499

36. Manuscript Occurrence Books (1869-1884), Headingly and Beeston Police Stations (Leeds Police Headquarters), passim; cf. Roberts, *Classic Slum*, p. 129.

37. Chief Constable's Manuscript Letter Book. Letter to W. Hind Smith, January 23, 1872.

38. *Ibid.*, Letter to Secretary of S.P.C.A., undated but written in October 1868.

39. *House of Commons Select Committee on Theatrical Licenses and Regulations*, Parliamentary Papers 1866 (373) XVI.1. Evidence Sir R. Mayne, qq. 969-1144.

40. James Grant, *Sketches in London* (London, 1840), p. 192.

41. Mayhew, *London Labour*, pp. 42-43; G. Godwin, *Town Swamps and Social Bridges* (London, 1859), p. 95.

42. *House of Commons Select Committee on Theatrical Licenses*, Evidence Sir R. Mayne, q. 991.

43. *Ibid.*, Evidence J.J. Grieg, qq. 6698-99, 7012.

44. *Ibid.*, Evidence J. Jackson, q. 7236.

45. *House of Commons Select Committee on Public Houses*, Parliamentary Papers 1852-53 (855) XXXVII.1. Evidence G. Wolstenholme, qq. 4437-43, 4475.

46. *Criminal and Miscellaneous Statistical Returns of the Leeds Police Force for the Year 1852* (Leeds, 1852), p. 4.

47. Chief Constable's Manuscript Letter Book, Letter to G. Tatham, January 2, 1869.

48. *House of Commons Select Committee on Public Houses*, Evidence Rev. J. Clay, q. 6176.

49. W. Rose, *Good Neighbours* (New York, 1942), p. 135; J. Batty, *The History of Rothwell* (Rothwell, 1877), p. 227.

50. A. Bywater, *The Sheffield Dialect*, 2nd edition (London, 1854), p. 163. (My emphasis.)

51. J. Greenwood, *Low Life Deeps* (London, 1876), p. 19.

52. H. Shimmin, *Liverpool Life* (Liverpool, 1856), pp. 76-77.

53. *Ibid.*, pp. 78-79.

54. D. Philips, "Riots and Public Order," note 184 on p. 180.

55. Bradford Temperance Society, *Annual Report*, 1858.

56. G.R. Sims, *How the Poor Live and Horrible London* (London, 1889), pp. 79-81. Changes in popular recreational patterns, though often greatly affected by police attitudes, were, we should remember, conditioned as well by changes in cultural fashion.

57. *House of Commons Select Committee on Public Houses*, Evidence G. Hogg, q. 6617.

58. *Ibid.*, qq. 6617-20. In some places the magistrates were not so scrupulous about the law and convicted even when it could not be proven that play was for money or moneysworth. See *Leeds Mercury*, January 31, 1860.

59. *Leeds Mercury*, November 1, 1856.

60. [T. Wright], "A Journeyman Engineer," *Some Habits and Customs of the Working Classes*, pp. 225-26.

61. *Leeds Times*, November 1, 1851.

62. "A Modern Professor," *British Boxing* (London, n.d.), reported that rule 21 of the sport read, "In the event of. . . interference it shall be the duty of the umpires and referees to name the time and place for the next meeting, if possible, on the same day."

63. Popular fetes such as feasts and fairs which, by and large, were not earmarked for total or immediate suppression were nevertheless subjected to intense monitoring after police reform.

64. See *Leeds Mercury*, May 28, 1857, for one such incident at Oxspring near Barnsley.

65. Rev. A. Easther, *A Glossary of the Dialect of Almondbury and Huddersfield* (London, 1883), p. 129; F. Cobley, *On Foot Through Wharfedale* (Otley, n.d.), p. 262.

66. *Monthly Chronicle of North Country Lore and Legend*, May 1887; also see E.P. Thompson's interesting article on stang-riding and related phenomena, "Rough Music: Le Charivari Anglais," *Annales* 27 (1972).

67. *Report From His Majesty's Commissioners For Inquiring Into the Poor Laws*, p. 44.

68. An account appears in *Leeds Times*, November 11, 1848.

69. *Ibid.*, November 8, 1851.

70. *York Herald and General Advertiser*, November 7, 1863, November 9, 1867, November 8, 1877.

71. Speech from the bench by J.B. Greenwood, a Dewsbury magistrate, before fining a Guy Fawkes celebrator £23 for assaulting the police, *(Leeds Mercury*, November 24, 1859).

72. See [M.A. Lower] "An Old Inhabitant," *Observations on The Doings in Lewes on the Evening of the Fifth of November 1846* (Lewes, 1847). Lower argued (p. 9) that Guy Fawkes created an unhealthy climate for business; cf. a petition of thirty Lewes householders to the magistrates, undated but marked September 1847, complaining of the insufficient police establishment and demanding that Guy Fawkes be put down. My thanks to Ms. C. Connelly of the Lewes Area Library for providing me with this document.

73. In Wakefield Guy Fawkes was shielded for a short time by local tories, who courted the lower classes in the interest of preventing municipal incorporation. The tories organized a pro-Guy Fawkes/anti-incorporation demonstration, paid a band, and provided fireworks. During the ensuing riot of 1849, tory councillors cheered the crowds in their battles with the police and showered coins on them from the balcony of a local inn. All this represented a dying echo of a time when marked links (often manipulative) between urban crowds and their "betters" were a regular feature of the social and political landscape. For an account see *Leeds Times*, November 10, 17, 1849.

74. A.R. Wright, *British Calendar Customs*, vol. 3 (London, 1940), p. 156.

75. C.S. Burne (ed.), G.F. Jackson, *Shropshire Folklore*, vol. 3 (London, 1886), p. 390.

76. J.K. Green, *Fireworks, Bonfires, Illuminations and the Guy Riots* (Guildford, 1952), p. 3; cf. Professor Hobsbawm's remark that the "mob's activi.ies, whatever their ostensible object, ideology or lack of theory, were always directed against the rich and powerful. . ." *(Primitive Rebels*, New York, 1959), p. 111.

THE POLICEMAN AS DOMESTIC MISSIONARY 501

77. In the riot of 1864 four of the "Guys" were captured: two painters, a cooper, and a coachbuilder's laborer (Green, *Fireworks,* p. 5).

78. *Ibid.,* p. 5; G.C. Williamson, *Guildford in the Olden Time* (Guildford, 1904), p. 187.

79. For some connections between popular fetes and social protest see N.Z. Davis, "The Reasons of Misrule: Youth Groups and Charivaris in Sixteenth Century France," *Past and Present* 50 (1971); A.W. Smith, "Some Folklore Elements in Movements of Popular Protest," *Folklore* 77 (1967); E.P. Thompson, " 'Rough Music' "; D. Williams, *The Rebecca Riots. A Study in Agrarian Discontent* (Cardiff, 1955), passim.

80. For bull-running and football see R. Malcolmson, *Popular Recreations in England, 1700-1850* (Cambridge, 1973), passim; M. Marples, *A History of Football* (London, 1954), pp. 98-100; Harrison and Trinder, *Drink and Sobriety,* p. 47.

81. W. Kelly, *Notices of Leicester Relative to the Drama* (London, 1865), pp. 177-79; *Leicester Journal,* February 19, 1847. Note the resemblance of the Leicester "Toms" to the Guildford "Guys."

82. G. Burne, ed.,*Shropshire Folklore,* p. 390.

83. T.F.T. Dyer, *British Popular Customs Present and Past* (London, 1876), p. 385.

84. G. Burne, ed., *Shropshire Folklore,* p. 390.

85. J. Binns, *From Village to Town* (Batley, 1882), pp. 95-96; W. Rose, *Good Neighbours,* p. 135; A. Williams, *Folksongs of the Upper Thames* (London, 1923), p. 24; S. Walker, *Cuffs and Handcuffs. The Story of Rochdale Police. . .* (Rochdale, 1957), p. 44; Harrison and Trinder, *Drink and Sobriety,* p. 47. The decline in the violence of the annual Guy Fawkes town-versus-town rows at Oxford apparently began with the police reforms of the early 1870s. The change was hastened by the appearance of strong themes of economic protest on the town side during the great riot of 1867 (T.F. Plowman, *In the Days of Victoria. Some Memories of Men and Things* [London, 1918], p. 87).

86. See discussion in appendix.

87. *York Herald and General Advertiser,* November 7, 1863; cf. a similar incident near Dewsbury: the police tried to stop the lighting of a bonfire and were stoned and beaten by a crowd *(Leeds Mercury,* November 17, 1859).

88. *Leeds Mercury,* June 12, 1860, July 7, 1863, February 23, 1864.

89. S. Reynolds et al., *Seems So!* (London, 1911), p. 91; in the 1840s Exeter constables were popularly referred to as "the busy Bs of the police" (R. Newton, *Victorian Exeter* [Leicester, 1968], p. 69).

90. R.D. Storch, "Plague of the Blue Locusts," pp. 70-87; see also T.H.S. Escott, *England: Its People, Polity and Pursuits,* vol. 1 (London, 1880), p. 421, and Charles Rowley's remark that the inefficiency of the Manchester police in the 1880s was linked to "public distrust of the force" *(50 Years of Work Without Wages* [London, n.d.] p. 58).

91. "George Bourne" [George Sturt], *Change in the Village* (London, 1955), pp. 117-18; cf. Engels' remark that the "English bourgeois finds himself reproduced in his law as he does in his God." For that reason "the policeman's truncheon has for him a wonderfully soothing power. But for the working-man quite otherwise!" *(Marx and Engels on Britain,* p. 263).

92. S. Reynolds, *Seems So!,* pp. 86-87.

93. R. Roberts, *The Classic Slum,* pp. 76-77.

94. *Select Committee of House of Lords on the Sale of Beer*, Parliamentary Papers 1850 (25) XXIV. 265. Evidence W. Harris, p. 59.

95. H. Pelling, *Popular Politics and Society in Late Victorian Britain* (London, 1968), pp. 1-6, 16-18, 62-71; cf. W.A. Williams, *Gosforth: The Sociology of an English Village* (Glencoe, Ill., 1956), pp. 171-2.

96. See discussion in W. Miller, "Police Authority in London and New York City, 1830-1870," *Journal of Social History*, 8 (1975), pp. 92-3.

97. *Royal Commission on the Duties of the Metropolitan Police*, Parliamentary Papers 1908 [Cd. 4261], LI.1., vol. 3, q. 40246; Roberts, *Classic Slum*, p. 77.

98. R.D. Storch, "Blue Locusts," pp. 87-88.

99. A. Silver, "The Demand for Order in Civil Society," in D.J. Bordua, ed., *The Police. Six Sociological Essays* (New York, 1967), p. 31. This is by far the best theoretical piece to date on these matters.

100. B. Harrison, *Drink and the Victorians*, passim, and "Animals and the State in Nineteenth Century England," passim.

101. *House of Commons Select Committee on Public Houses*. Evidence Rev. J. Clay, qq. 6270-6281.

102. F. Thompson, *Lark Rise To Candleford*, p. 505; Manuscript Diary of Miss Lister of Shibden Hall (Halifax Reference Library), June 22, 1822.

103. The phrase is Jack Douglas'. See his discussion of the historical development of the concept of policing in modern society in *American Social Order. Social Rules in a Pluralistic Society* (New York, 1971), p. 49ff.

STATISTICAL APPENDIX

Though the main focus of this paper has been a consideration of the impact of a reformed police establishment upon certain aspects of popular culture and on the push-pull between the police and the policed in this area, it was inevitable that I should have found myself discussing the question of police-community relations in the Victorian period, and in a somewhat "revisionist" manner. I believe relations between the police and the working class were a good bit worse than the conventional wisdom has held them to be. Even recent works which treat this subject have attempted to reconfirm the notion that the implantation of the police was accompanied by a brief flurry of intense resistance which then "boiled down" within a few years.[1] Within that time span (two to ten years), it is argued, workers accepted new "respectable standards of order." I myself have argued elsewhere[2] that working-class attempts to drive the police away by force did in fact cease as soon as the futility of the objective was demonstrated, but this does not mean that resistance to the police disappeared. It simply took other forms, including the evasion and concealment tactics described above. Riotous resistance declined, but rioting is not the only form of resistance. Most of the purely literary evidence I have consulted and to which I refer above has confirmed these opinions.

A look at some criminal statistics in the period 1858-1891 provides supporting evidence from a different angle. Engels considered the frequency with which

THE POLICEMAN AS DOMESTIC MISSIONARY   503

the police were assaulted in Manchester to be an index of the contempt in which
they were generally held. Tilly et al.[3] have suggested that a "benchmark for the
difficulty of the transition from a non-policed to a policed society is the average
number of assaults on policemen annually in each decade." It would be much
more suggestive and accurate to reduce the number of assaults to a rate per
thousand of population in each year. We possess for England a complete set of
official statistics on the summary offense "Assault on Peace Officer" from a
portion of 1857 to the early 1890s. By the former date this offense was hardly
ever treated as an indictable one; therefore in this study I have ignored the
otherwise excellent advice of Messrs. Gattrell and Hadden[4] to include both
indictable and summary offenses in my tables. After reviewing the indictable
offense statistics, I concluded that their addition would not affect the results
significantly. Though my conclusions may be contested, the accuracy of the
statistics cannot. Since the crime in question by definition had to be committed
in the presence of a police officer, these figures are certainly among the most
accurate of all nineteenth-century criminal statistics.

I selected for study ten police districts, of which six were highly urbanized in
the nineteenth century: Manchester, Leeds, Salford, Wolverhampton, Bradford,
and the Metropolitan Police District (Fig. 2A gives a composite picture of the
situation in these urbanized areas). Four were more rural: Lancashire Co., West
Riding Co., Cheshire Co., and Derbyshire Co. Three of the ten were new
establishments at about the time the statistics commence: Derbyshire Co., West
Riding Co., and Cheshire Co. Absolute numbers of assaults on policemen in each
district have been converted to offenses per thousand of population. The
population figures have been arrived at by the crude but roughly accurate device
of spreading the increase between decennial censuses over the ten-year period.

Figure 1 provides an overall picture of antipolice violence for a good portion
of the second half of the nineteenth century. Table 1 shows the rates for each
district; Table 2 shows average rates over all ten districts. Though it could
conceivably be accomplished by returning to the raw judicial records of
1830-1858, we do not know what the rates for assaults on the police were from
the actual time of implantation of a number of the forces under study. In our
period however, it is obvious that no significant diminution takes place until
1876-1880. It appears that the rate for London was higher in the late 1850s than
at any time during the balance of the century. Of course what the situation was
in the 1830s or 1840s is not known exactly. Though the rate of antipolice
violence seems to decline in London in the late 1850s, it is the most consistent
and even of all the cities studied, proceeding in waves or cycles of an average
length of five years. In the case of Manchester we observe an enormous
long-term trend to greater violence against the police beginning around 1860,
peaking in 1869, and not permanently declining below its 1858 level until 1883.
When this occurs it is part of a nearly linear decline which lasts until the end of
our period. Again, in the case of Manchester, we cannot track the statistics back
to the point of installation of the police, and this is true of Leeds as well. Leeds
appears to be emerging from a period of rather low antipolice violence in the late
1850s. It exceeds its late 1850s rate at five separate times before 1876, peaking
in 1870-1871 and then falling off sharply until nearly 1890. The Lancashire Co.
force enters the late 1850s at a rate not to be permanently diminished until

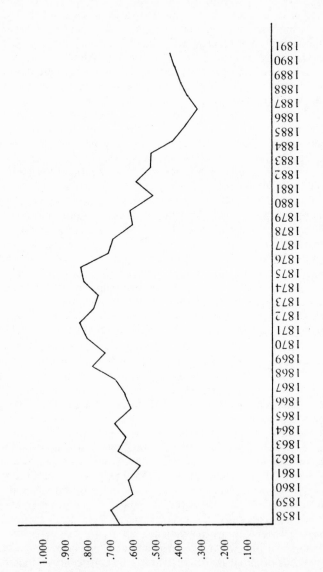

Figure 1. Assaults On Police In Ten Selected Police Districts, 1858-1891. Rate Per Mille.

SOURCE: Police Returns. *Annual Volumes of Judicial and Criminal Statistics.*

THE POLICEMAN AS DOMESTIC MISSIONARY

505

Table 1. Assaults on Police in Ten Selected Police Districts, 1858-1891. Rate per mille of population

	Bradford	Salford	Wolverhampton	Leeds	M/Chr.	London	Lancs.	W. Rid.	Derby Co.	Cheshire Co.
1858	.294	.643	.816	.813	1.162	1.460	.373	.582	.411	.272
1859	.482	.714	1.619	.839	.905	1.106	.384	.475	.406	.349
1860	.387	.653	1.070	.898	.824	.899	.370	.425	.296	.413
1861	.414	.595	1.265	.791	.957	.995	.448	.373	.289	.259
1862	.390	.697	.828	.663	1.043	.747	.526	.334	.340	.299
1863	.315	.664	1.251	.790	1.439	.873	.419	.344	.445	.351
1864	.313	1.035	.793	.475	1.467	.917	.454	.373	.261	.428
1865	.320	1.086	.971	.815	1.094	.808	.489	.425	.447	.521
1866	.476	.624	.635	.767	1.530	.726	.438	.316	.295	.468
1867	.362	.690	.352	.864	2.053	.716	.428	.334	.209	.465
1868	.463	.804	.817	.800	1.868	.767	.448	.301	.231	.434
1869	.798	.997	.569	1.032	2.333	.900	.436	.267	.260	.361
1870	.754	.987	.755	1.122	1.703	.656	.423	.303	.315	.427
1871	.631	1.682	.615	1.122	1.875	.786	.430	.345	.261	.353
1872	.548	2.201	.768	.915	1.679	.785	.380	.437	.303	.353
1873	.731	1.517	.774	.828	1.726	.702	.393	.449	.343	.334
1874	.745	1.611	.950	.525	1.707	.574	.401	.460	.322	.350
1875	.672	1.740	1.038	.927	1.679	.583	.351	.430	.355	.476
1876	.766	1.621	.875	.605	1.772	.888	.417	.478	.460	.392
1877	.601	.906	1.168	.525	1.399	.806	.429	.515	.460	.440
1878	.337	.895	1.455	.421	1.428	.730	.518	.572	.358	.268
1879	.467	.650	.943	.671	1.260	.677	.429	.403	.318	.247
1880	.513	.620	.853	.687	1.306	.679	.395	.360	.456	.268
1881	.464	.306	.607	.637	1.051	.755	.396	.382	.395	.224
1882	.553	.325	.510	.650	1.528	.842	.452	.359	.373	.362
1883	.701	.310	.557	.582	1.122	.681	.397	.368	.402	.266
1884	.798	.393	.694	.514	1.013	.672	.380	.341	.304	.256
1885	.611	.189	.408	.460	.788	.680	.343	.348	.308	.260
1886	.546	.160	.429	.387	.817	.496	.328	.241	.243	.204
1887	.448	.174	.263	.331	.779	.460	.289	.231	.211	.177
1888	.431	.407	.410	.217	.672	.617	.224	.280	.245	.207
1889	.529	.372	.628	.281	.649	.741	.226	.241	.182	.154
1890	.521	.438	.513	.464	.486	.788	.264	.276	.209	.176
1891	.573	.429	.424	.419	.627	.775	.204	.261	.322	.271

SOURCE: Police Returns, *Annual Volumes of Judicial and Criminal Statistics*.

1885, peaking in 1878. Salford does not fall below its 1858 rate — except briefly
in 1866 — until 1880. In Wolverhampton there is a nine-year period (1864-1873)
during which the rate is often below the 1858 level, though in seven of the nine
years it is either above or not very far below 1858. After 1873 it rises and stays
well above its original 1858 level until 1880-1881. Bradford never falls beneath
its 1858 rate during the entire period up to 1891.

Most interesting from our point of view however is the pattern of the three
forces under study which were implanted as a result of the County and Borough
Act of 1856 and which appear almost precisely at the opening of our period. In
these cases we have an opportunity to test the hypothesis that opposition to the
police boils down within a decade of their installation. In the West Riding
district this indeed appears to happen, but after 1869 the rate begins to rise
sharply, peaking in 1878 at just about the 1858 opening level. From then until
the end of our period the rate falls off sharply, heading downward — unlike the
other two new districts — when it leaves the charts. In Derbyshire Co., antipolice
violence slackens off from its opening level for about three years at which point
it begins an upward trend for about four years, peaking at a rate even higher
than when the force was brand new. After this the rate generally rises, peaking in
1876-1877 somewhat above the 1858 level. From 1878 on there is a steep
decline, though in the early 1890s it seems on the rise again. The rate of assaults
on the police in Derbyshire Co. exceeded the opening period — when all
researchers agree there was usually intense reaction — four separate times
between 1858 and 1891. The pattern for Cheshire Co. is even more striking.
Only once — and then briefly — in the twenty-year period 1858-1878 did the
rate of assaults on the police dip below that of the opening year, peaking in
1865 and rising again sharply in the mid-1870s. After 1877 the rate declines,
though remaining not far from the original level until around 1885. Towards
1890 assaults on the police in this district increase once again, finishing the 1891
"crime year"[5] above the level of 1858. Fig. 2B displays the pattern of antipolice
violence in the three new police districts averaged together. To test further the
hypothesis that opposition to the police boiled down within two to ten years, I
calculated the average rate of assaults in the three new districts in the first
ten-year period — when all agree they should have been very high, reflecting the
shock of initial contact — and drew a dotted line to represent the level of
violence in the initial years. It can be seen that levels of antipolice violence meet
or exceed those of the first ten years three separate times up to 1878 and that
for much of the rest of the time up to 1882, they hover not too far below them.
In the early 1890s the rate begins to rise once again, and fairly precipitously. It
would be interesting to know whether in the succeeding years of the 1890s levels
of antipolice violence converged once again on the rate of the initial base period.
Unfortunately I do not now possess this information.

There is obviously much more to be done with these data. I have not made
any attempt to correlate the statistics with the business cycle or with specific
events in the localities themselves, such as changes of command of the police.
My sole purpose here has been to try to test both the literary evidence and the
assumption that the English police received as much approbation, and as quick-

THE POLICEMAN AS DOMESTIC MISSIONARY 507

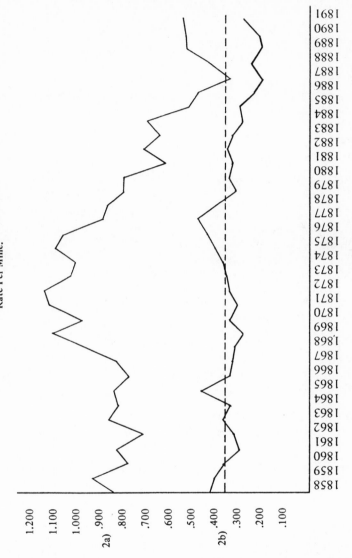

Figure 2A. Assaults On Police In Six Urban Areas, 1858-1891.
Rate Per Mille.

Figure 2B. Assaults On Police In Three New Police Districts, 1858-1891.
Rate Per Mille.

SOURCE: Police Returns, *Annual Volumes of Judicial and Criminal Statistics.*

Table 2. Assaults on Police. Average Rate in Ten Selected Police
Districts, 1858-1891.

1858−.683	1875−.825
1859−.728	1876−.827
1860−.624	1877−.725
1861−.639	1878−.698
1862−.587	1879−.607
1863−.689	1880−.614
1864−.652	1881−.522
1865−.698	1882−.595
1866−.628	1883−.539
1867−.647	1884−.537
1868−.693	1885−.440
1869−.795	1886−.385
1870−.745	1887−.336
1871−.810	1888−.371
1872−.837	1889−.400
1873−.780	1890−.414
1874−.765	1891−.431

SOURCE: Police Returns, *Annual Volumes of Judicial and Criminal Statistics.*

ly, in the communities they were installed in as has been thought. When added
to the literary evidence these statistics help us to form a more accurate and
sophisticated assessment of the problem.

Other researchers[6] have noted that in the last decades of the nineteenth
century, there was a sharp drop in *all* crimes of violence against the person. I
have nothing to contribute on the question of why this took place, except to
note that the trend we observed in the rate of assaults on the police after about
1880 is totally consistent with the larger findings, seemingly reflecting the
growth of a new docility in the English working class; but precisely because it
was part of a much more general pattern, involving all crimes of violence against
the person, perhaps even this fact does not necessarily imply any substantive
change in the *attitudes* of English workingmen towards the police after our
period.[7]

One recent researcher[8] has concluded, at least for London, that a great
cultural and political change proceeded within the working class after 1870,
reaching its full flower in the 1890s. He convincingly describes a working-class
culture − every bit as impermeable as ever, by the way − based upon "pleasure,
amusement, hospitality and sport," and combined with a kind of political
fatalism. By this period the working class was indeed described as at least
acquiescent to newer standards of order, indeed more "docile." One must be
very careful not to presume more than mere acquiescence or to assume that it
reflected some new kind of inner moral assent. Most sensitive contemporary
observers agreed that it stemmed more from fear and from concrete experience
of the manner in which the law worked and the ways in which it was enforced.[9]
The working class did change as Henry Pelling has also described in commenting
on the insularity of late Victorian working-class life; but while change must be
noted it is equally important to recognize that the transition to a "policed" society was a very long one indeed and remained complex even a century after the
new policing efforts began.

THE POLICEMAN AS DOMESTIC MISSIONARY 509

NOTES TO APPENDIX

1. See M. Thomis, *The Town Labourer and the Industrial Revolution* (London, 1974), p. 45, and D. Philips, "Riots and Public Order," pp. 167-68; A balanced view is given by W. Miller, "Police Authority in London and New York City, 1830-1870," *Journal of Social History* 8 (1975): pp. 92-93, though there is a distinct danger of generalizing from London to the provinces. A glance through the testimony presented before the 1853 *Select Committee of the House of Commons on Police* makes it quite apparent with whom the police became more popular after the initial period of suspicion and fear of exorbitant raises in the rates: "Are there any complaints on the part of ratepayers as to that. . . rate? – They were very jealous as to its being imposed upon them at first; but I think that no ratepayer would vote for the police being abolished; no *respectable man* would wish to see the police done away with." Parliamentary Papers 1853 (603) XXXVI.1, q. 440 (My emphasis); cf. qq. 209-11, 288, 735, 816, 1644-47, 1828-29. Witnesses were preoccupied primarily with "respectable" opinion, with which there had been some problems at first. On the matter of the popularity of the police with the working classes they were totally silent, apart from statements to the effect that the police *ought* to be appreciated by them: qq. 253-54, 2081-85. All Victorian specialists are aware that contemporaries often spoke in code-like phrases which require interpretation. In most cases, phrases like "public opinion" or "the ratepayers" were usually other ways of referring to "the respectable portion of the inhabitants," to use another slightly more explicit contemporary usage.

2. R.D. Storch, "The Plague of the Blue Locusts," pp. 61-90.

3. C. Tilly, A. Levett, A.Q. Lodhi, and F. Munger, "How Policing Affected the Visibility of Crime in Nineteenth Century Europe and America," University of Michigan Center for Research on Social Organization Working Paper, p. 77.

4. V.A.C. Gattrell and B. Hadden, "Criminal Statistics and their Interpretation," in E.A. Wrigley ed., *Nineteenth Century Society* (Cambridge, 1972), p. 346.

5. The statistical "crime year" was October through September in this period. Official returns dated 1858, for example, would include three months of 1857 and exclude three months of 1858.

6. Tilly et al., "Visibility of Crime," p. 82; Gattrell and Hadden, "Criminal Statistics," p. 365; cf. the tables in the *Judicial and Criminal Statistics* dated 1895 for the decline in crimes of violence against the person in Parliamentary Papers 1895 [c. 7725] CVIII.1., p. 73.

7. Tilly et al., p. 8 suggest that crimes of personal violence were in general much less sensitive to policing than other crimes. If this is so, then there are fewer grounds to conclude that a basic change in attitude occurred among the working classes after 1880.

8. G. Stedman-Jones, "Working-Class Culture and Working Class Politics in London, 1870-1900; Notes on the Remaking of a Working Class," *Journal of Social History* 7 (1974), p. 479; cf. George Sturt's observations of Surrey cottagers of the turn-of-the-century. Here we are dealing with the resignation and docility of the utterly defeated: "The people display little resentment, they accept their position. . . . Nevertheless it drives them in upon themselves. . . . Accordingly, all up and down the valley they restrict themselves. . . to their gardens and cottages, dreading few things so much as a collision with those impersonal forces which seem always to side with property and against people like them," *(Change in the Village* [London, 1955], pp. 120-21).

9. For a convincing analysis of deference as "the necessary pose of the powerless," see H. Newby, "The Deferential Dialectic," *Comparative Studies in Society and History.* 17 (1975). Newby argues that there is often a great difference between deferential behavior and inner feelings. Persons outwardly docile one day might participate in a riot – or an assault on the police – the next (pp. 142, 144).

New Society 30 August 1979

Police and people: the birth of Mr Peel's 'blue locusts'

Michael Ignatieff looks back at how the Met began, 150 years ago—amid much popular opposition.

Thinking about the history of the police requires a certain mental struggle against one's sense of their social necessity. Over the past 150 years, the London police have inserted themselves into our social subconscious as facts of life. Whether we trust them or not, we cannot imagine the city doing without them. It takes a small but appreciable stretch of the historical imagination to put oneself back into the time when there were no professional police on the streets, and when the idea of such a force seemed pregnant with danger for the "liberties of Englishmen."

The first patrols of the Metropolitan police set out on their beats on 29 September 1829, dressed in top hats, blue swallow-tail coats, heavy serge trousers and boots, and equipped with a wooden rattle and a truncheon. To us, their coming has the weight of historical inevitability, but this was not so to the Londoners of 1829. So pervasive was the resistance to their arrival that we need to ask ourselves, as we approach their 150th anniversary, how such a decisive enlargement of the powers of the state became possible at all.

The crowds who surged across Blackfriars Bridge on a November night in 1830, after listening to orator Hunt at the Rotunda, chanted, "Reform! No Wellington! No Peel! No New Police!" Next day, when the King stepped from his carriage in St James Palace Yard after opening parliament, the crowds surged against the line of blue serge protecting him and called out, "Down with the Raw Lobsters! No Martial Law! No Standing Armies!" At nightfall, abusive crowds eddied accusingly around constables who were patrolling in the West End.

The agitation against the new police was stubborn and protracted, continuing in the pages of the radical press and in meetings of parish vestries, and then bursting out into the streets again in 1833 when police used the flats of their sabres to disperse a radical meeting in Coldbath Fields. A coroner's jury, outraged by the brutality of the force, handed in a verdict of justifiable manslaughter on the body of a policeman killed in the affray. The jurymen were heroes of British fair play. Pewter mugs with their portraits were on the mantlepiece of many a radical parlour.

In London, opposition to the police passed out of the vocabulary of radical politics sometime after 1848, but a brooding residue of collective hostility remained among the London poor. This was especially so among costermongers whom, as Mayhew reported in 1851, continued to regard "serving out a copper" as a matter of honour, well worth the inevitable prison sentence. Outside

London, the introduction of the "blue locusts" brought angry crowds into the streets of many northern industrial towns during the 1840s.

There was something weightier than prejudice in the momentum of this resistance. In the cry, "No Standing Armies," there resonated an echo of the 18th century commonwealth and country party comparison between "continental despotism" (meaning standing armies, police spies, *lettres de cachet* and Bastilles) and "English liberty" meaning rule of law, balanced constitution, unpaid constables and local justices of the peace). It was this robust constitutionalism which damned Pitt's Police Bill of 1785 as "a new engine of power and authority, so enormous and extensive as to threaten a species of despotism." These arguments held the field until 1829.

The idea of a bureaucratic central force also offended against a tradition which held that social control should be a private, local and voluntary matter, best left to the master of the household, the parish beadle, and the JP. A "paid police," no longer respon-

sible to the community, would set servant spying on master and master denouncing servant. In this rhetoric, there is resistance to something we now take for granted—the right of the state to intervene in the disputes of the household.

From our vantage point today, this localism may seem an obvious anachronism in the London of the 1820s. But it was not so for many Londoners, for whom the parish still seemed a genuine boundary of administration and community. While discernibly swollen by new population, the London of the 1820s had not been ravaged by industrialism. The myth of the "dangerous classes" was not yet a waking nightmare of the propertied. The social chasm between East End and West End had still to be dug. The geographic separation of classes in the city had not yet replaced the 18th century jumble. A Londoner like the Bow Street Runner, Townshend, could still discern the lineaments of the London of his youth in the city of his old age. He could plausibly

Opposition to the Peelers took the form of satire (on the cover), humour (below) . . .

444   New Society 30 August 1979

assert that the London of the Gordon riots, the criminal "Alsatias" and the twisting corpses atop Temple Bar, was at least as turbulent and unruly as the London of the 1820s.

Certainly there were many philanthropists, police magistrates and MPs who had concluded by 1820 that the growth of the city made policing inevitable. Yet their views did not command the consensus of the powerful and the propertied. Looking back ourselves, we tend to view the London of the 1820s through the bifocals of alarmists (from Fielding through Colquhoun to Chadwick). We fail to notice that they were contending unequally against a deeply entrenched constitutionalist libertarianism as well as a more subconscious and reflexive sense of social continuity. As late as 1822, the alarmists were having the worst of the argument. The county gentlemen and urban professional men on the 1822 police committee concluded that a professional police could not be reconciled with the liberties of Englishmen.

To interpret the coming of the new police, therefore, as a "response" to crime and disorder, "caused" by urban growth—to see the force as the work of a bourgeois consensus brought together by social fear—is to rewrite history in the language of a retrospective fatalism.

The most that can be said is that Wellington convinced Peel he should set up a civilian force specialising in crowd control after witnessing the embarrassingly inept performance of the soldiery called out to control rioting after Queen Caroline's trial. This may have been the motivation of the Police Bill of 1829; but it doesn't explain how, within three generations, the force had managed to insert itself into popular awareness as a legitimate fact of London life.

The social history of the police's insertion into the warrens, courts and alleyways of St Giles, Spitalfields and Bethnal Green is usually told as a straightforward Whiggish progress from suspicion to cooperation. Yet how rapidly or easily was this progress to legitimacy achieved? Obviously, some of the skilled or regularly employed working class benefited immediately from the new police. To the extent that the washing on their lines or the tools in their boxes were now marginally more secure from theft, and they could use the police courts to secure a stay of eviction or to recover a small debt, they had some reason to believe the rhetoric proclaiming the police as "servants" of the community.

The submerged tenth

But among the "submerged tenth" who struggled to survive in the catch-as-catch-can labour market of the docks and the sweated trades, the rhetoric encountered rougher sailing. To the casual poor, the coming of the new police only meant a greater chance of being arrested for "drunkenness" "loitering," "common assault," "vagrancy" or whatever else the duty sergeant decided to write in his big book. The hackney coachmen and the street sellers, for their part, knew the police as their licensers, as the ones with whom

Mary Evans Picture Library

they waged a bickering, bantering struggle for control of a "pitch" or a profitable position on the street. For the destitute, the police were the prying inspectors of common lodging houses, the inquisitors at the entrance to the workhouse and the cloaked figures who trained the sharp light of the bulls-eye lantern on your face as you lay awake at night in the "coffins" of the night refuge.

In all these guises, the poor of London experienced the coming of the new police as a massive intensification of outside supervision over their ways of living and surviving—an intrusion which broke the casual, callous contract of disregard between rich and poor in the 18th century. A new contract between rich and poor, between police and people, had to be made.

The Police Commissioners' speeches about the necessity of securing the "cooperation" of the public were more than hollow pieties. Without poor people willing to come forward as witnesses and as prosecutors, or simply to point a breathless constable in the direction of the running figure who had just vanished down an alley, the police would have been powerless over all but the most transparent street illegal behaviour.

The history of the emerging inter-

. . . and unarmed combat

dependence between police and people has not yet been written, but we know what questions to ask. When would a fight in the street or a stairway be handled by bystanders or neighbours, and when would a child be sent running for "the constable"? When a publican or shopkeeper found his till empty, when would he go to the police, and when would he pay a visit himself to the shopboy's mother, or to a fence?

For the working poor, it must be remembered, going to the police was usually the last in a range of responses to crisis—a range which included dealing directly with the families of suspected persons, or engaging the services of the underworld network of fences, informers, enforcers, loan-sharks and debt collectors. The success of the police in securing the cooperation of the public depended less on keeping a rosy image of impartiality than on securing a near-monopoly over the market in violence and redress.

We still do not understand which range of "official" crimes were also accepted as "crimes" within different working class communities, and which were not. There were at least two, often three or four, overlapping definitions of crime competing for the al-

New Society 30 August 1979

legiances of the community. The success of
the police, both ideologically and practically, depended on convincing people to
accept the official code of illegal behaviour,
and turn to "official" channels for redress.

To win this cooperation, the police
manipulated their powers of discretion. They
often chose not to take their authority to
the letter of the law, preferring not to
"press their luck" in return for tacit compliance from the community. In each
neighbourhood, and sometimes street by
street, the police negotiated a complex,
shifting, largely unspoken "contract." They
defined the activities they would turn a blind
eye to, and those which they would suppress,
harass or control. This "tacit contract"
between normal neighbourhood activities
and police objectives, was sometimes oiled
by corruption, but more often sealed by
favours and friendships. This was the microscopic basis of police legitimacy, and it was
a fragile basis at best. A violent or unfair
eviction by the police, for example, could
bring a whole watching street together in a
hostility to be visited on policemen afterwards, in the frozen silence which would
descend when he stepped into the "local."

The bargain might also be overturned by
events outside the community. The memory
of the Trafalgar Square police charges in
1886 must have cast a pall over policemen's
beats in Poplar, Stepney and Bethnal Green.

Fair play?

In this social history, there is no clear
passage in popular behaviour from suspicion
to cooperation. Support for the police, then
as now, was inherently unstable. This was
because of the inevitable conflict between
their image as impartial embodiments of
British fair play, and their social role as
defenders of property against the propertied.

Given this conflict, such acceptance as
they could secure depended less on rhetoric
and myth, than on imperceptibly slipping
into the realm of necessary and inevitable
facts of British life. To argue that their
legitimacy rested on a massive popular consensus in the 19th century is to ignore the
depth of the opposition to their coming,
the highly sectorial character of their appeal,
and the fragility of the contract they negotiated with the urban neighbourhood.

It is worth emphasising the fragile character of public support for the police in the
last century, because our deepening economic
and social crisis is fostering a plaintive
nostalgia for a simpler, happier past. It
is widely believed that there used to be
a time, "before this crisis," "when Macmillan was Prime Minister," "before the war,"
when policemen were "respected," and police
work could count on unstinting popular support. For those of us whose memories
were formed by television, this undertow of
feeling carries us back to the mythic figure
of Dixon of Dock Green, on smiling patrol
down a leafy, eternally sunlit suburban lane.

This longing to return to a past when
"authority" was "respected" only takes us
one small step closer to the "law and order"
state. Against this use of the past, the
historically minded can plausibly object.

[4]

Ideology as History: A Look at the Way Some English Police Historians Look at the Police

Cyril D. Robinson *California State University, Long Beach, U.S.A.*

This article compares four English police historians whose writings are principally concerned with the founding of the centralized English police in 1829. A comparative study of this kind is able to reveal common ideological strains running through their writing which individual examination might overlook. Moreover, their work has contemporary importance because present rationalizations by American and English police of their relationship to the community being policed is substantially similar to that developed by these writers for the relationship of the English police to the English public.[1]

The rationalizations developed by these authors can be reduced to four themes: (1) that the need for police arises out of the division of society into good and bad citizens; (2) that one result of the growth of police power is to protect the weak against the powerful; (3) that the police is dependent for its effectiveness on public support, and (4) that historically the business of policing has been confided to the people themselves.

The four historians to be discussed are W. Melville Lee, Charles Reith, T.A. Critchley and Leon Radzinowicz. Except for Radzinowicz, who specifically limits his history of the English criminal law "from 1750," these authors begin with an inquiry into the police systems of their Anglo-Saxon forbears. Such a point of departure is in sharp contrast to American police historians who normally begin police history at the end of the eighteenth century.[2] This expansive coverage by these English authors encourages a search for historical themes and for system characteristics purportedly unique to the English people.

There has apparently been no prior attempt to analyze the writings of English police historians apart from contemporary book reviews. Works of police historians have received little notice from British historiographers.[3] Perhaps such lack of attention may be partially explained because, until recently, both English and American police historians generally tended not to be professional historians. Police history has been an avocation directly related to the author's occupation. T.A. Critchley was an Assistant Under-Secretary of State in the Home Office, in charge of a police division. Radzinowicz was Director of the Institute of Criminology at Cambridge University. Writing police history seems to have been Lee's method to prepare himself for a hoped for post of chief constable. As a "political journalist" in the 1930s "with a special concern with the international scene," Reith apparently turned to the police as a means of bringing order to what he conceived to be a world of disorder.[4]

Of the authors, only Radinowicz was attached to a university. This is not surprising if we take into consideration the relative lack of academic interest in police history until recently and the further fact that historians were not generally considered a profession nor were they connected with universities until the latter part of the nineteenth century.[5]

In surveying the works of each author I will organize my analysis around the following five questions:

1. Did the author approach his work with some organizing factor or theory of historical interpretation?
2. How does the author treat the four themes I have set forth above?
3. What developments, in his view, led to or inhibited the formation of the New Police of 1829?
4. How did the author conceive of the police

function?

5. What has been the author's contribution to police history?

In determining whether these authors employ an accepted theory of historical interpretation, I will use classifications suggested by a standard text, the *Harvard Guide to American History:*

(1) interpretations assuming a plurality of separate civilizations and dealing with the reasons for their cyclical rise and decline, such as those of Toynbee and Spengler; (2) interpretations setting forth, in systematic rules, the general principles of continuous social change applicable to all civilizations, such as those of Hegel and Marx; (3) interpretations, such as F.J. Turner's frontier thesis, which emphasize neglected factors in the historical development of a civilization, without claiming that those factors explain its whole development; (4) interpretations which deny the need for interpretation, asserting that objectivity is an attainable ideal, that the facts "speak for themselves," and that history is ultimately "scientific" . . .; (5) interpretations . . . which assert that objectivity is an unattainable ideal and rest on the frank belief that all history is contemporary history; (6) interpretations which concede that perfect objectivity is unattainable but remain hostile to rigid or dogmatic historical theories.[6]

Our first author, William Lauriston Melville Lee (1865-1955), who in 1901 published *A History of Police in England,* "came from an old distinguished family." He attended the Royal Military Academy and reached the rank of captain during his army service. Aspiring to a position of chief constable, he studied police history to prepare himself for a position that he was finally prevented from attaining by a subsequent injury. Lee calls his book "unpretentious," and he makes no claim that his is scholarly work (Lee, xxi).*

"References have been but sparingly given throughout, and in answer to those critics who may possibly object that the array of authorities quoted is too meagre, the author can only plead in extenuation that opportunities for taking full advantage of good reference libraries are often denied to dwellers in camps and barracks" (xxi).

*Citations to the works of the four Englishmen discussed in this article will be cited in brackets to avoid copious footnoting. The full citations of the writings of these authors will be found at the end of the article under References.

Lee would, I think, have denied that he was approaching the police with any theoretical framework or that the police themselves can be so explained. Like the common law, the police institution, he might have said, does not lend itself to systematic analysis for the police represents an empirical adaptation to changing conditions.

"However numerous and outrageous may be the theoretical imperfections of our method for maintaining the peace, its practical superior has yet to be discovered . . .

"English police, however, is not the creation of any theorist nor the product of any speculative school, it is the child of centuries of conflict and experiment (xxx-xxxi).

The third historical approach, that which emphasizes "neglected factors in the historical development of a civilization," would seem therefore to approximate most closely Lee's method.

Lee writes this book because "on the institution of police, we have not a single work, except perhaps the matter-of-fact publication of the late Dr. Colquhoun."

Lee will

"attempt . . . to approach this strangely neglected subject, not indeed by the avenue that a scientist would use, but simply to trace in outline the story of English police, keeping in view the underlying principles that have directed, as well as those political and other considerations that have controlled, its evolution; . . . amongst all our institutions it would be hard to find one so eminently characteristic of our race, both in its origin and in its development, or one so little modified by foreign influences . . ." (xxv-xxvi).

There are a series of themes that run through his book, common enough so that we will find all or most in the work of the other authors. Unifying all of these "themes" is the conception that England is a democracy and that the police, like her other institutions, either is identical with or is representative of her people. But if this is true, how explain the fact that the police pursue, arrest and imprison some of those people? Lee deals with this apparent paradox by citing the first of the four themes I have suggested above:

"[A]ll but a small minority of the king's subjects were . . . good citizens—and personally interested in keeping the king's peace inviolate; and that they might therefore safely be trusted to do everything in their power to preserve it, without any necessity arising for the use of coercion. Had all men been equally trustworthy in this respect no police measures would have been required and none devised; but there existed on the fringe of Anglo-Saxon society, *as will occur with all societies*, a certain number of delinquents perpetually on the look-out for opportunities of preying on their fellows . . . " (9,328. Emphasis added.)[7]

A second theme found in Lee's writing is that law and order is tied to growth of the royal power [the state] and that the general and final effect of the growth of police power is to protect the weak against the powerful. It is the constabulary which is "the primary constitutional force for the protection of individuals in the enjoyment of their legal rights [citing the Report of the Police Commissioners, 1839], designed to stand between the powerful and the weak, to prevent oppression, danger and crime . . ." (xxix-xxx)[8]

A third theme is embodied in the idea that the police in England has deep historical roots, that it is unique to the English people and dependent on them for its support, and without that support, police effectiveness, even its existence, would be in doubt.

Lee expresses this theme as follows:

"Our English police system . . . rests on foundations designed with the full approval of the people, we know not how many hundreds of years before the Norman conquest, and has been slowly moulded by the careful hand of experience, developing as a rule along the line of least resistance, now in advance of the general intelligence of the country, now lagging far behind, but always in the long run adjusting itself to the popular temper, always consistent with local self-government, and even at its worst, always, English" (xxvii, 329).

Consistent with his belief in this democratic nature of the English police, Lee fairly bristles at the notion that the police might be utilized to stop a popular rebellion:

"It has been said that if anything like an adequate police force had been available in 1381, Wat Tyler's movement [lower-class protest against a poll tax to support wars in France and Scotland] might have been arrested . . . Such may, or may not, be true of this particular rising; but happily for English liberty there has never existed in this country any police force at the disposal of the central

government, powerful enough to coerce the nation at large. Our national police has always been of the people and for the people, and obviously at no time could long be used to oppress those from whom its strength was derived, provided only that one and the same sentiment pervaded a majority of the oppressed . . .

The constitution of the general police [is] of such a nature that it was powerless to enforce any universally unpopular measure . . ." (Lee, 61-62).

The fourth theme is taken up by Lee from an earlier treatment by John Wade, published the same year, 1829, that the Metropolitan Police was organized. Wade wrote that "in England the business of police is chiefly confided to the people themselves."[9] Lee derives this principle from his "Anglo-Saxon conception of police functions."

"[T]he internal peace of the country was held by them to be of the first importance, and every free man had to bear his part in maintaining it; theoretically all men were policemen, and it was only for the sake of convenience that the headborough . . . answered for those of his neighbours . . . ."[8]

Lee's discussion of the reasons that led to the formation of the New Police are not particularly enlightening. He recounts in a clear, coherent fashion, but without systematic analysis, the development of the decline of the parish-constable system, the inefficiency of the constables, the dishonesty of the magistrates, the fear of a continental system of police, the inability of soldiers to suppress riots, and so forth. At the end of the century, considering the currents let loose by the French Revolution, he finds "the attitude assumed by the Government . . . altogether incomprehensible" in its apparent unconcern for the need of police to better maintain the peace (Lee, 174).

Lee attributes the creation of the New Police to the work and foresight of Sir Robert Peel, observing that perhaps it was fortunate that there was such a long wait "for when the inevitable change was brought about, we got a better article than we should have done if an earlier model had been adopted . . ." 230).

Lee sees the function of the police "as necessary to the welfare of society as are self-imposed moral and physical restraints to the health of the individual" (xxxix).

Police are seen to have a dual function. "[T]he object of police is not only to enforce

37

compliance with the definite law of the land, but also to encourage a general recognition of the unwritten code of manners which makes for social progress and good citizenship" (xxviii-xxiv).

The police are "not servants of any individual, of any particular class or sect, but servants of the whole community—excepting only that part of it which in setting the law at defiance, has thereby become a public enemy"[10] (328)

Perhaps, most revealingly, Lee quotes the following statement from the *Edinburgh Review* to indicate public reaction to the New Police soon after their appearance:

"The arrangements are so good, the security so general, and the complex machinery works so quietly, that the real danger which must always exist where the wealth and luxury of a nation are brought into juxtaposition with its poverty and crime, is too much forgotten: and *the people*[11] begin to think it quite a matter of course, or one of the operations of providence, that they sleep and wake in safety in the midst of hordes of starving plunderers" (Lee, 229. Emphasis added).

The sum of Lee's thoughts present a belief framework with surface coherence but with clear internal contradictions. At the same time that Lee sees the police as the protector of the *good* part of the population, he likewise sees the relationship between crime, disorder and poverty. For example, Lee perceives with acuity the economic base to transportation of prisoners[12] and sees the "prison-houses and convict establishments" as "universities of crime," (215-16) a metaphor which he may or may not have originated, but one that has endured with the conditions that provoked it.

Though Lee was obviously an extremely perceptive observer of economic injustice, he was unable to mold his individual observations into an overall theory to aid in analyzing the events about which he wrote.[13]

Nevertheless, Lee's contribution to police history is important. He has been called "the father of English police history," and his book, "the pioneer classic in the field" (Introduction by P. J. Stead, Lee x-xvi). Charles Reith is said to have found in Lee's book the "great principle which distinguished English policing— responsibility of the local community as opposed to that of the nation-state" (viii-ix). Lee can still be profitably read as a clear, concise history of the relevant economic, legal and administrative events in the development of the English police from the Anglo-Saxon period to the end of the nineteenth century.

Our next writer, Charles Reith, authored six books on police history spanning a period from 1938 to 1956. Reith worked as a tea and rubber planter in Ceylon, served as an officer in the Indian Army during the First World War, published a novel on army life, worked as a foreign correspondent and edited his own monthly publication of foreign news before writing his books on the police.[14]

Reith writes with such dedicated passion of the cause of the police and with such recurring themes throughout all his books that it is relatively easy to categorize his historical approach. He clearly falls into the first category of historical theory which conceives of the police in terms of the cyclical rise and decline of civilizations.

Reith's most comprehensive attempt to set forth a universal "history of human communities" is in his book, *Police Principles and the Problem of War*. Impressed as he was by the on-coming Second World War, he saw the application of "the preventive principles of police [as] solving the problem of recurring war among the nations" (Reith, 1940 viii).

Reith concludes that there are "certain simple and significant facts of community evolution . . . which are the common experience of all communities since the world began . . . It cannot be too strongly emphasized that a framework of rules and force in adjustment is a fundamental necessity of all community existence" (Reith, 1940:1-2). Reith thereafter attempts to show the universality of his theory to various civilizations throughout history,[15] and concludes:

"The part played by war, disease, and other similar calamities, in the disintegration of communities, is in providing circumstances in which force ceases to act in securing or compelling observance of law . . . The real cause of failure and final disintegration are inability or disinclination to repair it" (2-3).

Can we find the same themes in the work of Reith as in that of Lee? Our first theme involved the idea that the need to use force arose because of the supposed division of society into good and bad citizens. In *The Blind Eye of History*, Reith asserts that in the growth of a community

"there comes, always and inevitably, discovery or recognition of the facts that some members of the community will not keep some or all of the rules; that by their behavior in this respect they weaken and endanger the welfare and lives of other members and the existence of the community as a whole; and that to ensure its continuing welfare and survival, means must be found for compelling observance of rules" (14).

Reith also adheres to the second theme, namely that one result of the growth of police power is to protect the weak against the powerful. Reith makes this theme apparent in various forms, particularly in his oft-repeated notion that "the police have replaced the military as the use of armed force against the people . . ." (Reith, 1943:9). He points to "the sufferings endured by the working classes as the consequence of absence of police . . ." (Reith, 1956:203), and that thief-takers were of some benefit to the wealthy who could bargain back for their goods but of no benefit to the poor (Reith, 1956:204).

At numerous places in his books Reith makes the point that the police are dependent for their support and effectiveness on the people. In *A New Study of Police History*, he states:

"The power of our police is almost entirely derived from cooperation given them by the public. If this, for one reason or another is withdrawn, our police are helpless, and must cease to function"¹⁶ (265).

That the police and the people are one Reith finds embodied in the Seventh Principle adopted by the English police soon after their organization in 1829:

"To maintain at all times a relationship with the public that gives reality to the historic tradition that the police are the public and that the public are the police; the police being only members of the public who are paid to give full-time attention to duties which are incumbent on every citizen, in the interests of community welfare and existence" (Reith, 1952:163).

Reith has a rather elaborate analysis of how the Police Bill became law. In the early part of the nineteenth century there was economic dislocation due to the Napoleonic Wars, fighting between troops and "hunger-driven rioters," shock among the "educated" classes from the Peterloo Massacre, the threat of mutiny in the Guards, and increasing crime. From the standpoint of the likely success of the Police Bill in Parliament, Reith balances the foregoing threats against "growth and

hostility to the idea of establishing police: which spread to men of good-will in all classes." Reith does not, however, indicate the relative importance of these forces in the final result. Instead, he concentrates on the parliamentary skills of Peel, appointed Home Secretary in 1822. Between 1823 and 1828 Peel secured the passage of a number of criminal law reforms which "were expected to ease court and other difficulties" for the police. When Peel believed he had control of both Houses of Parliament he appointed a committee which reported back as planned, favorably recommending a Metropolitan police. According to Reith, Peel was able to secure the acquiescence of the opposing Whig Party and their allies, the City of London, by first including the City in the coverage of the Police bill and then by "compromise," dropping the City from the Bill (Reith, 1956:122, 124).

For Reith, civilization, or at least democratic civilization, literally *depends* on the establishment of the police.

". . . I submit that all means of enforcing laws comprise physical, or military, force, moral and police force, used separately or together, and that military force and moral force alone or together always fail to secure sustained observance of laws in a community unless they are provided with police force, as a medium through which they can function" (Reith, 1952:10).

If laws "are not observed, the most perfect laws which the wit of man can devise are useless, and rulers and governments are impotent" (Reith, 1952:13). Reith begins his book, *British Police and the Democratic Ideal*, with the vision of an Englishman patiently waiting in line in order to pay his taxes, picturing "the smooth and orderly collection of Income Tax in Britain" as "one of the wonders of the world." Looking to the cause of this docility, Reith sees it in the omniscient presence of the English policeman.

"It is true that individual resistance to taxation will lead, quickly and inevitably, to the appearance of a policeman, and to the setting in motion, against the individual, of the smooth-functioning and overwhelming machinery by which the most wonderful police institution in the world unobtrusively enforces the observance of order" (Reith, 1943:1).

But at this point in time, it is not only this show of force that makes him submit. It is,

rather, that his "awareness of the consequences has become subconscious," and that
"the British mind is more alive to the value of
individual contribution to public orderliness
than that of any other race on earth" (Reith,
1943:1).

"It is an unquestionable historical fact that
the appearance of public orderliness in Britain [after its disappearance for centuries],
and of individual willingness to co-operate in
securing and maintaining it coincides with
the successful establishment of the police institution . . . in 1829 . ." (Reith, 1943:3).

He concludes, therefore, that "British Police
Principles may be briefly defined as the process of transmuting crude physical force . . . into
the force of public insistence on law observance; and of activating this force by inducing,
unobtrusively, public recognition and appreciation of the personal and communal benefits
of the maintenance of public order" (Reith,
1943:4).

To Reith it follows that the function of the
police is to be found in the maintenance of this
finely balanced system, of the interplay between the police and the public, in which the
policeman is in the role of teacher of nonviolent
conduct in the school of public affairs.

This vision of the police system at work is
not inconsistent with Reith's sympathy for the
working class. It is, after all, they who had suffered by the violence of the earlier period. A
violence might then have been occasionally
necessary in order to win the political rights
that now allow them to participate in democratic government; they now benefit, at least
as much as the rest of the public, from a police
that prevents violence and permits democratic
processes to take place in a non-Wilkesian,
peaceful environment, so thought Reith.

In all Reith's books he continually pounds
away at the same idea: that the central task of
a civilized nation is to find the means of providing "authority with force which will enable
it to compel respect for its laws," concluding
that the means to attain that end is the police.
A reader of any of Reith's six books finds a
familiar echo resounding through all of his
works and leaves Reith open to the charge that
he has written but one extended book. The
failure to take his work more seriously can
probably be attributed to his over zealous and
repetitious advocacy of the police as the literal
answer to all worldly problems.

In reviewing Lee's book in 1951 for the
Police Review, Reith really describes what he

believes to be the important facets of the police
institution:

"[Lee's book] describes the prolonged inability of authority to enforce laws; its helpless-
ness and the people's sufferings in face of the
consequences; the Police remedy which was
suggested; and the fierce opposition which
this encountered, causing long delay in its
adoption. . . . It is a basic study of police
principles and duties of which it can be truly
said that, without it, no subsequently
published book on the history of the Police
could ever have been written" (Lee, x).

Reith's review reveals his own proclivity to
excessively broad statements as well as his
generosity to another author to whom he genuinely felt a debt of gratitude.

J.J. Tobias, a contemporary police historian,
regards Reith as "an invaluable if somewhat
naive and uncritical historian of the Metropolitan Police . . ."[17] I believe this statement to be a
just evaluation of Reith. Critchley credits
Reith as the source of some of his material.[18]
My view is that Reith's most significant contribution to police history is the very thing for
which he has been criticized, his attempt to set
forth a theory of the police. Naive and incomplete as it is, it is important to have this
perspective before us.

T.A. Critchley wrote three books about the
police between 1967 and 1971. The two that
principally concern us are A History of Police
in England and Wales, 900-1966, and The Conquest of Violence, Order and Liberty in Britain,
the latter being of special interest as a comparison of the way Reith and Critchley treat
the "taming" of violence. Critchley's other
book, The Maul and the Pear Tree, coauthored
with P.D. James, is a study of early nineteenth
century London police organization. This task
is accomplished by vividly describing the
police investigation of a brutal murder of two
London families. The obvious incompetence of
the magistrates and the police to adequately
investigate the crime (a matter heavily covered
by the press of the day), provoked agitation in
England for police reform.

In writing his History of Police, Critchley
sees the historical process of police development in a remarkably similar way to that of
Lee—if one disregards the professional cynicism
of the long-term public servant to accepted
police mythology.

"A central purpose of this book is to attempt
to trace the way in which this unique and
valuable system has been fashioned by the

needs and fears of society as they have been expressed from time to time in political currents. No grand design emerges, and there is no evidence of adherence to lofty constitutional principles. The empirical process about to be described gives little support to the common view that policing in England owes much of its excellence to attachment to the ideal of local responsibility for law and order, or to a mystical fusion between the policeman and the ordinary citizen. The system has never been a tidy one or logical one. It was built up with little regard to principle, but much concern, at the center, for the political expediencies of the day, and the need for popular support for the police and a measure of technical competence" (xiv).

Critchley's hostility to "rigid or dogmatic historical theories" seems to place him in the sixth category of historical interpretation.[19] This is not to say that Critchley took an unsophisticated simplistic view of police history. On the contrary, his disclaimer of a "grand design" seems to be in marked and perhaps intended contrast to the expansive approach taken by Reith.

Critchley's more critical method deprives us, however, of our theme of the division of the population into good and bad. Instead, Critchley recognizes that the confrontations he describes are between the "rulers and the ruled" (1971:201). It is this realization that ultimately the police system has a class base that leads him to reject the "mystical fusion between the policeman and the ordinary citizen." Consistent with this consciousness of class dynamics, he observes a certain identity between the unpaid working constable of Tudor times and the vagabond he was called on to ship out of town (1967:12). Nevertheless, Critchley is agreeable to the next theme, that the poor are better off for having the organized police. He notes:

"The desperate and starving mobs that characterized the latter part of the [eighteenth] century, were left to police themselves . . . After twelve hours in factory or mine, they ought, for all the law cared, to serve in rotation as night-watchmen . . .

"Meanwhile, the wealthy paid game-keepers to protect their property, slept with arms near to hand, and the middle-class tradesmen formed voluntary protection societies. The poor simply managed as best as they could until the reform of rural police was at last put in hand" (1967:24-28).

Critchley is all fours with Lee and Reith in agreeing that the English police is dependent on the public for its effectiveness. "The police," says Critchley, "represent the collective interests of the community . . ." The police "sustains our civilization; and, at the same time, promotes the freedom under a rule of law without which civilization is worthless . . . " (1967:xiii, xiv).

"The device which is most characteristically English has been to arm the police with prestige rather than power, thus obliging them to rely on popular support. Associated with this is the principle that every policeman is personally responsible to the courts for any wrongful act. These arrangements . . . are only likely to continue to work smoothly if the laws which the police enforce are themselves acceptable to public opinion" (1967:xiv, 52, 319-320).

While Critchley has pointedly rejected the "mystical fusion between the policeman and the ordinary citizen," he nevertheless substantially accepts the idea that there is a historical relationship between the police and the people. "By involving everyone in the business of keeping the peace it taught English people from early times to accept that everyone had a stake in it" (1971: 28-29, 199).

His description of the causes of the delay in the enactment of the Metropolitan Police Act and the reasons for its enactment are similar to those of Reith. He gives a good deal of credit to the strategy conceived by Peel; and he attributes more credit to the propagation of ideas on "influential public opinion" than does Reith; but with the same incredulity felt by Reith, Critchley sees the bill's passage as "one of the most remarkable facts about the history of police in England that, after three-quarters of a century of wrangling, suspicion, and hostility toward the whole idea of professional police," the Act "was passed without opposition and with scarcely any debate" (1967:50). Critchley suggests, however, that the reason that "the English upper and middle classes successfully resisted the idea of professional police for three-quarters of a century after Fielding had pointed the way . . . was because some feared the loss of liberty and most objected to the expense" (1967:320). He does not suggest, however, what might have occurred in 1829 to remove these concerns.

On the surface, Critchley's notion of the police function is quite different, if not the exact opposite, from that of Reith. While Reith believes that the "orderliness" of the English people is due to the police, Critchley states that the "gentility" of the police issues from the historical roots of the English people. The source of violence in society is the working class. Although Critchley is sympathetic to that class, it is against them that the police must be used. It is, after all "from the working classes from whom [sic] most criminals" come (quoting a Parliamentary Commission Report, Critchley, 1967:73), and while demonstrations may by peaceful, "evil" may work "its way to the fore" (1967:77). After centuries in which the British were "long habituated to violence [they were "constrained"] by a native self discipline which was rooted in antiquity, and which flowered . . . during part of the twentieth century."[20] This period of relative peace was due to a number of factors, of which the police were but one: the demands of the working-class Chartist movement were met; religious differences disappeared as a motive force in English politics and racial prejudice was absent in Britain.

"The forces of law and order were belatedly strengthened with the spread of professional police forces throughout the country; the unique character of our police (as a force of unarmed civilians, in contrast to the soldiers who had in earlier times provoked as much violence as they repressed) enabled a rapport to be established between police and troublemakers that has been of incalculable value . . . [In addition there was] the growth of trade unions and the use of strike action as a means of protest . . . finally, the spread of the franchise, together with growing literacy and the Penny Press, gave increasing numbers of men and women a sense of involvement in their own destinies that earlier generations lacked. Thus the prime causes of public violence in Britain had, by the year 1900, been largely . . . eliminated . . . (Critchley, 1971:25).

By the General Strike of 1926, "both sides in the encounter 'played the game' according to unwritten rules, as though the standards of Arnold's public schoolboys had permeated all classes" (1971:202). "The police," he says, "are used for different purposes from one generation to another."

"In the nineteenth century the main problems were poaching, vagrancy, and petty crime; during the first three decades of the twentieth, public order constituted a major

problem; now the challenge is from crime of all kinds, and road traffic" (1967:320)."

Though Critchley does not discuss which segment of society wrote the rules and delineated the problem, he writes with verve and intellectual pique. His writings are full of literary allusions, catches of song and limerick.

One reviewer of his *History* forecasts that it will be "the main historical manual for a long time," and notes that "the sources to which Mr. Critchley has had special access [as Assistant Secretary in the police department of the Home Office and as secretary of the last Royal Commission on the Police] have enabled him to trace with authority the key development of modern times, which is the bringing of the uneven and assorted police forces of the country into the standardized police service of today."[21] But it should be noted that in order to carry out his plan Critchley relegated 800 years of history to a single chapter so as to concentrate on the "next 200 years" which, he writes, "help illuminate or explain the working and problems of the police service of modern times . . ." (1967:xiv).

This is indeed an understandable decision, but in making it, Critchley obscures the crucial development of change in police function from pre- to post-state transition. Once the state has evolved, some would argue, the function of the police undergoes a qualitative change.

Of like importance is Critchley's treatment of violence in *Conquest of Violence*. In both books Critchley writes from a conservative bent, to be expected from an official of the Home Office writing about mob action. Both books involve Critchley's view of the slow elimination of mob violence (and thereby the elimination of government restriction on its policies in fear of potential violent response) through the action over the years of a series of public servants such as Critchley himself. Critchley gains his perspective on violence by examining "the causes of violence . . . and not[ing] how authority . . . responded to its threat" (1971:2).[22]

Given that mob violence has subsided, the question arises, has the working class gained or lost bargaining power as a result of giving up the "right" to shake the duke's carriage on his way to Parliament? What has been the worth of *political* gains where there is limited *economic* ability to assert these gains? These are questions historians may wish to consider when evaluating Critchley's analysis.

Sir Leon Radzinowicz, Wolfson Professor of

Criminology and Director of the Institute of Criminology at Cambridge, is the author of four volumes of *A History of English Criminal Law and its Administration from 1750*, published over a 20-year period from 1948 to 1968. Radzinowicz's series is certainly the most scholarly and detailed work[23] of the four authors considered.

The magnitude of the labor performed is described in the introduction to the first volume:

"For his chosen period from the middle of the eighteenth century down to the present day he tells us that he had to consult some 1,250 Reports of Commissions and Committees of Inquiry, 3,000 Accounts and Papers, 800 Annual Reports and 1,100 volumes of Parliamentary debates,: British as well as foreign authors, criminological, popular and historical literature so as to produce 'a full and comprehensive study of the phenomena of a great social evolution' . . ." (Radzinowicz, I:v).

Although no theory of analysis is explicitly set forth, it seems evident that Radzinowicz, both from his arrangement of material and from his own sparse comments, is heavily influenced by economic considerations. Of particular interest is his overview of his findings:

"From a study of documents—proclamations, advertisements, offers of reward, Home Office correspondence—there emerges a system by which men hoped that the public peace might be preserved and offenders brought to justice, a system which was as ingenious as it was perplexing. It was largely inspired by the creed of *laissez-faire* and to an appreciable extent was worked by private initiative, principles which were so natural to the Englishman's way of life and thought" (Radzinowicz, II:vii).

What Radzinowicz implies is that the system of criminal justice of the period is a reflection of the economic organization of the rest of the society of which it is a part, in this case, a society in the grips of a rising capitalist class struggling with a declining landed aristocracy.

Of the theories of historical interpretation, Radzinowicz seems to rely principally on the second category, "general principles of continuous historical change." It would be inconceivable for a man of Radzinowicz's erudition and European background to be unfamiliar with the writings of Hegel and Marx, the main exponents of this theory, or that he would undertake a work of this scope without a clear conceptual plan for dividing the relevant from the irrelevant.[24]

Radzinowicz seems considerably concerned with the interplay between events and ideas in the manner of Hegel. As Handlin sums up Hegel's conception of history, and social change,

"the discrepancy between ideas and social conditions reacts upon social conditions: and as ideas bring conditions up to their level, new ideas arise, and out of the ideas new conditions—until history reaches its ultimate fulfillment."[25]

Radzinowicz seems to apply this conception to the subject-matter of the criminal law:

"Child of the Common Law, nourished and moulded by Statute, the criminal law of England has always been sensitive to the needs and aspirations of the English people, and it has continuously changed under the impact of the predominant opinion of the day. Yet while it has never been static, its rate of growth has been uneven, and the main features which it presents today were built up from the movement for reform which began in the middle of the eighteenth century. To that development the forces of morality, of philosophical thought and of social consciousness all made their contribution" (I:ix).

It would not be inaccurate, therefore, to characterize the work of Radzinowicz as a social with a heavy component of intellectual history of the criminal justice system for the period covered. Therefore, in the case of Radzinowicz, in setting out themes, we will usually be setting forth his synthesis of the ideas of others rather than conceptions which purport to be his own.

We cannot, therefore, expect a statement from this author as we did from Lee and Reith, that society can be divided into good and evil men. But we do find that in Radzinowicz's description of the political affairs of the time that a belief in such a division actuated public policy. What for Lee and Reith was division of society into good and bad citizens is for the more sophisticated Radzinowicz clearly a class division. Volume III, *Reform of the Police*, begins with the following statement:

"Severe laws were held to be essential for the internal safety of the nation. Often, as in the case of the Riot Act, they were also a much

43

needed weapon in the hand of the Justice of the Peace who alone with the soldier barred the way of the riotous mob: for 'to those two it is entirely owing that they [the mob] have not long since rooted all the other orders out of the commonwealth'. The diligent and impartial execution of these laws was the honourable mission of the English police . . . ".[1]
The ruling class understands this threat only too well. A constant threat of violent mob action runs through the work of Reith and Critchley. They teach that to the police belongs the credit for the taming of the mob.

Although one finds in Radzinowicz an occasional comment concerning the law's protection of the weak from the powerful (as in the quotation from the *Quarterly Review* that because of the current wave of thefts, "The small proprietor . . . could hardly be called the owner of what he enjoys, but for the strong hand of the law" Radzinowicz, I:30), such statements are rare. Much more common is the expressed fear of the power of the mob, of the burden of the poor on the rich, or the criminality of the poor.

Radzinowicz is concerned to a greater degree with the actual arrangements made by the government to protect certain of its citizenry than in vague concepts concerning the dependence of the police on the public. In the first place, he shows in considerable detail that the pre-1829 police were totally ineffective in controlling crime. Secondly, as we will hereafter discuss in more detail, it was a time when societal organization promoted "private interest," a concept inconsistent with the notion of collective security. Thus, far from the picture of an historic idyllic continuity that our earlier writers have posited between the "people" and the police, Radzinowicz notes that:

"[W]ith the advent of the eighteenth century, this method [collective security] of stimulating local inhabitants to make better provision for the preservation of the peace ceased to be of any practical importance. Hopes were centred instead on the positive system of incentives. . . , of earning a reward . . . , of sharing in a fine" (Radzinowicz, II:167).

In fact, by the early 1800s, there was strong hostility to the proposed establishment of a new police system for the very reason that the police were regarded by some as having already departed "from those principles by which they had . . . been guided . . . " (Radzinowicz, III:335).

As to the theme that the business of policing had been confided to the people themselves, with the transformation of the constable and watchman from ordinary citizens who took their turns at service to paid substitutes from the lowest class of society, that idea lost all coherence.

Radzinowicz suggests a more complex path to the enactment of the New Police Act than that described by the other authors. There was, during the time from 1750 to the passage of the act, a series of riots, disturbances, a perceived increasing poor population and mounting crime. Yet,

"During this long period . . . there was no section of public opinion, no group in Parliament or outside, no leading newspaper or periodical which would advocate a reform in the traditional machinery for keeping the peace" (Radzinowicz, III:374).

Radzinowicz, like our other authors, is able to explain the opposition to the proposal but not its final successful passage. Until 1732 the word "police" was not even a part of the English vocabulary; it was only slowly that the concept entered public consciousness. The inefficiency of the contemporary system became apparent and was accepted; a further step was taken when it was realized that "arrangements for the maintenance of peace, as distinct from laws relating to offences against the peace, were a fit subject for a parliamentary enquiry . . . " (III:2, 63, 64). Over this whole period there were incremental changes, the effect of which was to broaden laws covering powers of arrest, and various offenses of public order and theft. Inhibiting the acceptance of such a law were the vested interests of the City of London, sheriffs, magistrates, and various other groups that either derived benefits from the old system or foresaw problems with the new (Radzinowicz, IV:167).

In addition, there was the belief among a good part of the members of Parliament and almost all reformers that a centralized police would represent a formidable threat to liberty. An important, though not the sole factor in the successful passage of the Metropolitan Police Act, was Peel's commitment to a scheme of reform of the whole criminal justice system, including earlier reforms of the criminal law. By the time, therefore, that the police bill was presented to Parliament it may no longer have seemed threatening but merely the next incremental step (Radzinowicz, I:567-589).

Radzinowicz does not himself discuss his

44

concept of the police function but he does recount that of Colquhoun "whose views on crime, poverty and police made so deep an impression on the public around the turn of the [eighteenth] century . . . " (Radzinowicz, IV:36).

To Colquhoun, "the labouring class represented the productive force of the country" but "inevitably" that class carried within it certain "noxious" elements. Thus the police would perform an important societal task in controlling this class.

"It was inevitable that its members should live in some degree of poverty, and that they might even on occasion sink into indigence or pauperism. The 'indigent and noxious classes', however, were hardly distinguishable from the elements 'supported by criminal delinquency'. Indigence 'is one of the greatest calamities which can afflict civil society, since . . . it generates every thing that is noxious, criminal and vicious in the body politic." (Radzinowicz, III:233).

Colquhoun believed that "it is a state of *indigence*, fostered by idleness, which produces a disposition to moral and criminal offenses, and they are so linked together that it will be found impracticable to ameliorate the condition of the poor without taking more effectual measures at the same time for the prevention of criminal offences" (Emphasis in original Radzinowicz, III:233).

Colquhoun would have the police

"promote the moral improvement of the labouring classes by the exercise of supervision and restraint. It would remove temptations and strengthen the moral fiber as well as the social sense of those lower orders which at present filled the ranks of the army of crime, vagrancy, dissipation and insubordination" (Radzinowicz, III:234-235).

Radzinowicz's materials argue for a more straight-forward economic analysis to better explain the conflict over the establishment of the police, the form it took and its function.

Summary and Conclusions

This article began with the statement that the relationship of the police to the community, as developed by the four English police historians discussed, could be reduced to four themes. The themes were united, it was said, by the conception that England is a democracy and that the police, being one of her institutions, is a democratic institution, either identical with or representative of her people. It was found

that these themes ran through the work of the four English police historians in amazingly similar concepts and language, leading to the conclusion that, in varying degree, we are here dealing not merely with history but with ideology serving as history.

Each of these historians accepts a consensual conception of government. For them, as Critchley put it, the English people, as a whole, have a "sense of involvement in their own destinies." The alleged "fusion" of the police and the community is part of this historical "sense." Such a view sees the police as having a historical role in the absorption of the former threatening "mob" into the political process.

It is apparent that these writers have relied heavily on the thinking of John Locke. The themes of the division of society into good and evil men, and the supposed function of the police to protect the innocent from powerful evil-doers are found in Locke's assertion that some men engage in a "state of war" against other men in an otherwise idyllic state of nature. That act of war gives a right, on the part of the man attacked, "to destroy a man who makes war upon him."[26]

Locke further argues that such a right by the injured party to use individual force may be necessary while a society is in the state of nature. But once man enters into the social contract there is a "common superior on earth to appeal to for relief." Then, says Locke, "the state of war ceases . . . because then there lies open the remedy of appeal for the past injury and to prevent future harm." A major reason "of men's putting themselves into society and quitting the state of nature" is that in society, "there is an authority, a power on earth from which relief can be had by appeal . . . "[27]

From Locke too comes the notion that the police are the public and the public are the police. Locke suggests that "every man has a power to punish the crime to prevent its being committed again, by the right he has of preserving all mankind and doing all reasonable things he can in order to that end . . . ."[28]

Even more important is his underlying philosophy of the social contract between free, independent persons to form their own government. Our historians, therefore, like Locke himself, were largely relying on a mythical state of nature out of which issued the "authority to decide between contenders"— the notion of a neutral nation-state dear to the heart of consensualists.[29] The concept of the "neutral" state is itself confused and contradictory for it is this very state, through its police, that supports one part of society against the other—the "good" against the "evil." All of our authors accept this implicit challenge to the consensus theory and apparently resolve it, in the manner of Locke, by placing evil people outside society itself.[30] Thus, the *public* identified with the police, has been purified of its evil segment. It is only in this segmental sense that the people are the police and the police the people.

Yet, each of the writers, being themselves perceptive of the social relations about which they write, cite numerous instances in which this societal division cannot be so easily disposed of, and in which the police cannot so easily be utilized as enforcer of good laws against bad men. In a particularly trenchant comment on the historical role of the police officer, Critchley states:

"The dissolution of the monasteries created a huge army of vagrants whose only alternative to starvation was plunder, and under the barbaric laws of the Tudors the parish constable was the principal agent in maiming, burning with hot irons and other refinements of torture, before whipping the vagabond, until his or her body be bloody, out of the village or town. It is surely fair to suppose that many men refused to have anything to do with such practices (1967:12).

Our authors (Lee, Reith, Critchley and Radzinowicz, quoting Colquhoun), while purportedly discussing good and evil persons, or "authority" and the "mob," were describing class and class conflict under a mystique that divided the population into those who keep and those who wilfully refuse to keep the rules. Even though each of these authors devoted a substantial part of their histories to working-class "mob" action directed against the ruling landed aristocracy and rising bourgeoisie, class was never seen as a relevant "historical question."

As a possible explanation of "patterns in men's relationships, their ideas and their institutions,"[31] class was ignored. Without such an understanding of the ongoing class struggle between the back-sliding land-owning class and the emerging bourgeoisie in the period just before the creation of the centralized police, Lee, Reith and Critchley could be only incredulous (as they were) at the prospect of "authority" refusing to adopt the remedy that seemed to them to be most obvious and efficient—the organized police.

46

But to the competing classes, replacing an "inefficient" system with an "efficient" police weapon, did not appear to be such an obvious benefit to either class until it was clear at which class this weapon might ultimately be pointed. Neither class could know that the class in power at any moment might not use the weapon against the other. Only when it became clear to leaders of both classes that the police represented a threat to neither but on the contrary could be a means of controlling the threat to both—the working class—could the centralized police become a reality.[32]

In a quotation cited earlier in this article, Critchley describes in detail how a combination of "the forces of law and order" together with a number of liberalizing political concessions by "authority" resulted in working-class "troublemakers" adhering to rules—rules, of course, made by and for the ruling class. This role of the police as teacher-carrier of good behavior from the upper class to the working population has been observed by Reith, Critchley, Colquhoun, as well as contemporary authors, Banton and Silver.[33]

These critical comments do not in any way reduce the extremely important contribution all of these authors have made to police history. It would have been extraordinary, particularly at the time at which they wrote, if they had approached their subject differently. But now it is time to ask, what should be the criteria for a proper *social* history of the police?

Rusche and Kirchheimer, in their history of the penal system, suggest one comprehensive historical approach: "It is thus necessary to investigate the origin and fate of penal systems, the use or avoidance of specific punishments, and the intensity of penal practices as they are determined by social forces, above all by economic and then fiscal forces."[34]

Marxian analysis, which Rusche and Kirchheimer employ, concerns itself with productive forces as they historically affect the configuration of most significant societal institutions.[35] With this perspective in view appropriate questions to be pursued by a social history of the police that do not seem to have been adequately examined by previous writers, English or American, include:

1. What is the origin of the police function? At what point in evolutionary development did the police function begin to appear and in what form?

2. To what extent is the development of the

police function related to changes in the nature of the community, and to resulting changes in social relations?

3. How is the incidence of the police function related to the development of a state society as compared to a stateless society, or to a class society as compared to a classless society.[36]

4. What is the historical development of the ideology necessary to support a police function? What was the process by which an élite was able to obtain and maintain police loyalty?[37]

5. How is the origin and development of the police function related to the mode of production of any particular epoch of history?

6. How do the police fit within the total system of social control?

A comment by Radzinowicz makes a fitting introduction to such an historical effort. In summing up the result of 32 years of English police history, he stated:

"By 1861 the country was covered by a network of professional police charged with the prevention of crime, the detection of offenders and the maintenance of order. Systematic enforcement of the law had replaced suspended terror as the accepted basis of control . . . Tradition, inertia, local jealousies, class distrust, fear of expense and fear of tyranny all contributed to evasions and delays. Yet the poor might engulf the country in a tide of disorder and crime, so the search continued for more acceptable expedients. Charity and relief could be used not merely to placate but to coerce the poor . . . . Of all such expedients the most far-reaching was transportation . . . . What does emerge is that its existence made it easier to relinquish reliance on the death penalty and its withdrawal clinched the argument for a general system of police.

"The nation had to live with its criminals, in or out of confinement. It could no longer eliminate them. It had arranged to police them" (Radzinowicz, IV:v).

Footnotes

1. Typical sentiments found in most American police-community relations texts may be summarized as follows: The police are agents of the people they police; the laws that the police enforce are those of a democratic society in which the people being policed participate and consent; the police do not favor one segment of society over another; all are treated fairly and equally. See L.A. Radelet, The Police and the Community (Beverly Hills: Glencoe Press, 1973) pp. vii-viii; National Advisory Commission on Criminal Justice and Goals (Washington: GPO, 1973), p. 9; D.W. McCroy, The Police and Their Public (Metuchen: N.J.: The Scarecrow Press, 1976), p. 29; R.M. Momboisse, Community Relations and Riot Prevention

(Springfield, Ill.: Charles C. Thomas, 1967), p. 4; M. Symonds, "Policeman and Psychodynamic Understanding" in A. Niederhoffer and A.S. Blumberg (eds.), The Ambivalent Force: Perspectives on the Police (Hinsdale, Ill.: Dryden Press, 1976), pp. 72-73; W.J. Bopp, Police Rebellion: A Quest for Blue Power (Springfield, Ill.: Charles C. Thomas, 1971), p. 47.

2. J. F. Richardson, Urban Police in the United States (New York: Kennikat Press, 1974) briefly mentions a few events of the late 17th century for the purpose of showing the "English background of the American police." The doctoral dissertation of S.D. Bacon, The Early Development of American Municipal Police (Ann Arbor: University Microfilms, 1966 reprint of 1939 dissertation), traces American policing from the 17th century in five American cities.

3. Police historians go unmentioned in H.J. Ausubel et al., Some Modern Historians of Britain: Essays in Honor of R.L. Schuyler (New York: Dryden Press, 1951). In R.W. Prouty, "England and Wales, 1820-1870 Recent Historiography: Selective Bibliography," in E.C. Furber (ed.), Changing Views on British History, Essays on Historical Writing since 1939 (Cambridge: Harvard University Press, 1966), C. Reith and L. Radzinowicz are mentioned. Among Reith's six books, only British Police and the Democratic Ideal is noted.

4. P.J. Stead, Introduction to C. Reith, The Blind Eye of History (1975 reprint of 1952 ed.), p. vi.

5. In England, it was 1871 before the Oxford "School of Modern History" permitted undergraduates "to study history, and history alone, for the first time, and Cambridge followed suit" in 1873. The English Historical Review, founded in 1886, was the first British periodical devoted to scholarly historical studies. J.R. Hale (ed.), The Evolution of British Historiography from Bacon to Namier (Cleveland: World Publishing Co., 1964), p. 56. The same is true for the United States, the study of history until the last decades of the 19th century being "the avocation of gentlemanly scholars and literateurs . . ." Handlin et al., Harvard Guide to American History (Cambridge: Harvard University Press, 1955), p. 5.

6. Id. at 15-16.

7. It is clear that Lee is much influenced in his argument by the thinking of John Locke. At an early point in his discussion of the origin of the police he says: "When a people emerges from the savage state its first care is the institution of some form of civil government." W.M. Lee, A History of Police in England (Montclair, N.J.: Patterson Smith, 1971 repr. of 1901 ed.), p. xx-vii. This point is elaborated hereafter.

8. Lee was not so naive as to think that there was no oppression of weak by the powerful, nor that the police always acted as a benefactor to the weak. But he believed that the overall effect was for the state to protect the weak against the strong. See page 22, where oppression of the poor is attributed to a weak king; and page 149, for his comments on police brutality; the extent of crime at the beginning of the nineteenth century and the relationship of the police thereto is treated at pp. 196-216.

9. The full quotation reads:
"In despotic countries people are accustomed to the exertions of authority in its most repulsive forms, and the police may be armed with all the powers essential to the prompt and efficient discharge of its duties; but in countries aspiring to free institutions, where the persons, property, habitations, and even amusements of the people are guarded by so many barriers, which no one with impunity can violate without legal and adequate occasion, a much more scrupulous and circuitous process is required. Consequently, in England the business of police is chiefly confided to the people themselves . . ."
J. Wade, A Treatise on the Police and Crimes of the Metropolis (Montclair, N.J.: Patterson Smith, 1972 reprint of 1829 ed.) pp. 2-3.

10. Note that this quote updates Lee's earlier statement about those who exist on the "fringe of Anglo-Saxon society."

11. The words, "people," or "society," in these quotations, can be translated to mean the middle and upper classes. Such usage is, of course, not limited to these authors but is pervasive in political science, sociology and criminal justice literature.

12. Lee notes that high prisoner mortality on ships used for transportation continued until payment to the shipowner was

English Police Historians

based on each man landed alive rather than on each man embarked (209-210).

13. Lee also observes that the "large majority" of parish constables were from the "poorer classes," were unpaid for their services, were "struggling men, who have to work hard to provide for themselves, and for their families" and therefore, he comments, it is not surprising that they are "incompetent," and the duties performed in a "purely perfunctory manner" (181). But he carries this observation no further. See C. Robinson, "The Deradicalization of the Policeman: A Historical Analysis," *Crime and Delinquency*, 1978, Volume 24 (Number 2), pp 129-151.

14. Almost nothing has been published on the life of Reith. Therefore, it will be useful to provide a biographical footnote. This information was contained in a letter to the author, dated April 6, 1976, frm Patricia Plank, Librarian of New Scotland Yard. The matter was researched by J.B. Rapkin, a former Metropolitan Police Officer. An edited version of the letter follows:

> "*Charles Edward Williams REITH* was born on November 22, 1886 in Aberdeen. His father, a doctor, sent him to schools in Stonehaven and Bridge of Allan, Scotland.
> "When he left school, Reith became a tea and rubber planter in Ceylon. With the outbreak of war in 1914 he was commissioned in the Indian Army, served with the 3rd Brahmins and later became a General's A.D.C. in Mesopotamia and Palestine. After the war he went to London and worked in the tea and rubber trades. In 1924 he married Marguerite Hannah Ellen Gordon. In 1925 his first book, a novel, was published entitled 'An Ensign of the 19th Foot'. Three years later he went to Italy but returned to London in 1933 and for a time edited his own monthly magazine. He also wrote for 'Time and Tide' magazine. It was about this time that he developed his keen interest in police matters.
> "On the outbreak of the second world war in 1939 Charles Reith went to live in Cornwall, but returned to London after two years. He was asked to lecture Polish Officers in the United Kingdom on the British constitution and way of life and this he did throughout the remainder of the war. The Polish authorities in London awarded him The Cross of Merit. He also lectured on police principles to various law societies and at Cambridge and Durham Universities.
> "In 1945 Charles Reith returned to Scotland, firstly to Stonehaven, Kincardineshire, and then, in 1950 to Edinburgh. On several occasions he lectured to students at the Scottish Police College, Tulliallan Castle, Kincardine, Alloa, Clackmannanshire. When he died on February 7, 1957, he left instructions that his books which he had used for his studies of police subjects should be given to the College. They are now recorded at Tulliallan Castle as the 'Charles Reith Bequest.'"

15. One may find many other such notions in Reith. See, for instance, *The Police Idea*, where he states:
> "The fundamental problem which confronts the nations of the world today . . . is the finding of means of providing authority with force which will enable it to compel respect for its laws and without which, as all history shows, it must inevitably and repeatedly fail to function" (vi).

16. Like statements will be found in Reith's *British Police and the Democratic Ideal* at pp. 5 and 10.

17. J.J. Tobias, "Police and Public in the United Kingdom," *Journal of Contemporary History* 1972, volume 7, 201-219.

18. In a footnote to a chapter entitled, "New Police of London, 1750-1830," in his book, *A History of Police in England and Wales*, Critchley cites Reith's *British Police and the Democratic Ideal* and *A New Study of Police History*, stating: "Mr. Reith has made valuable accounts of Home Office papers in the Public Record office and the commissioner's papers in the library of New Scotland Yard" (1967:326).

19. Although Critchley states that he has "tried to include everything . . . germane to the development of a theory about the nature and purpose of policing," he actually develops a series of observations about the "origins of the police system," the "emergence of the office of Constable," the "legal obscurity of the Constable's office," and the like. His method then is one of frequent looking back and summing up. While his insights are valuable they do not add up to a "theory." The importance

that he gives to the use of ideas arguably would place him in category two with Radzinowicz, whom he frequently quotes. This approach accentuates the interplay between ideas of the time and other social forces. The role of ideas as advocated by certain social reformers is given a particularly important role by Critchley in the enactment of the Metropolitan Police Act. See pp. 45-50.

20. Critchley admits that such an explanation "begs more questions than it answers" (1971:25).

21. *Times Literary Supplement*, Volume 617, Sept. 28, 1967, p. 921.

22. Compare this rather simple view of violence with R.P. Wolff, "Violence and the Law," in R.P. Wolff *The Rule of Law* (New York: Simon and Schuster ed. 1971), and G. Rudé, *Paris and London In The Eighteenth Century: Studies in Popular Protest* (New York: Viking Press, 1973) and G. Rudé, *Wilkes and Liberty: A Social Study of 1763 to 1774* (London, Oxford University Press, 1962).

23. Volume I, *The Movement for Reform*, undertakes to display the gradual
> "growth of public opinion which has led to the reforms brought about by modern criminal legislation . . . [H]e has been able to exhibit in the most vivid form the process of law in the making" (v).
> Volume II, *The Clash Between Private Initiative and Public Interest in the Enforcement of the Law*, concerns "the enforcement of the criminal law, as distinct from the reform of its substance, during the eighteenth and early nineteenth centuries" (vii).
> In Vol. III, *Cross-Currents in the Movement for the Reform of the Police*,
> "the movement for reform is traced through the labyrinth of trial and error, advances and regressions, theoretical anticipations, curious alternative strategems, and alarms which created a momentary readiness for change, only to give way suddenly to apathy and even hostility" (vii).
> Volume IV, *Grappling for Control*,
> "follows through to their culminating points two protracted campaigns, on one side for the reform of the capital laws, on the other for the establishment of regular police" (v).

24. Radzinowicz describes his approach as
> singling out . . . certain main sub-periods, and the examination of all the criminal problems as they appear in that sub-period . . . . It is far from being an accident that in a certain given period of its development society is confronted with certain specific problems and that it solves them in a certain way or disregards them altogether." L. Radzinowicz, "Some Sources of Modern English Criminal Legislation," *Cambridge Law Journal* 1943, volume 8 pp. 180-194.
> Radzinowicz sees the contours of criminal law then within the larger "economic, social and political structure of English political society."

25. O. Handlin et al., *Harvard Guide to American History* (Cambridge: Harvard University Press, 1955) p. 5.

26. ". . . it being reasonable and just I should have a right to destroy that which threatens me with destruction; for, by the fundamental law of nature, man being to be preserved, as much as possible when all cannot be preserved, the safety of the innocent is to be preferred; and one may destroy a man who makes war upon him . . . because such men are not under the ties of the common law of reason, have no other rule but that of force and violence, and so may be treated as beasts of prey, those dangerous and noxious creatures that will be sure to destroy him whenever he falls into their power." J. Locke, *The Second Treatise of Government* (Indianapolis: Bobbs-Merrill Co., 1952), p. 11.

27. *Id.* at pp. 13-14.

28. *Id.* at p. 8.

29. To the extent that this idea is attributable to Locke, it is a misinterpretation of Locke's meaning. While all other rights present in the state of nature are retained, it is precisely this right to enforce the law of nature that is lost by transition to a state form of social organization. *Id.* at p. xv.

30. *Id.* at pp. 6-7; *Cf.* T.H. Marshall, *Class, Citizenship, and Social Development* (New York: Doubleday and Co., 1964) pp. 80-81.

31. E.P. Thompson, *The Making of the English Working Class* (New York: Pantheon, 1964) p. 11.

English Police Historians

32. *Id.* at pp. 81-82.
33. P. Colquhoun, *A Treatise on the Police of the Metropolis* (Montclair, N.J.: Patterson Smith, 1969 reprint of 1806 ed.); M. Banton, *The Policeman in the Community* (New York: Basic Books, 1964); A. Silver, "The Demand for Order in Civil Society: A Review of Some Themes in the History of Urban Crime, Police and Riot," in David J. Bordua (ed.), *The Police: Six Sociological Essays* (New York: John Wiley & Sons, 1967).
34. G. Rusche and O. Kirchheimer, *Punishment and Social Structure* (New York: Columbia University Press, 1968 reprint of 1939 ed.).
35. M. Bober, *Karl Marx's Interpretation of History, A Study of the Central Thesis of the Marx-Engels Doctrine of Social Evolution* (New York: W.W. Norton, 1965) pp. 3-4; R. Tucker, *The Marxian Revolutionary Idea* (New York: W.W. Norton, 1969) pp. 61-62.
36. M. Fried, *The Evolution of Political Society* (New York: Random House, 1967). Each writer, with the exception of Radzinowicz, who begins his history in 1750, finds the "origin" of the police system in what Reith calls the "kin" police. But it is clear that at the time of which they write, about 900 A.D., there is already a clear-cut feudal class system, and that the vestigal kin structure is being utilized by a "higher authority" in the maintenance of order. C. Jeffery, "The Development of Crime in Early English Society," *Journal of Criminal Law and Criminology* 1957, volume 47, p. 666.
37. C. Robinson, "The Deradicalization of the Policeman: A Historical Analysis," *Crime and Delinquency* 1978, volume 24 (number 2), pp. 129-151.

References

Critchley, T.A. and P.D. James, *The Maul and the Pear Tree, the Ratcliffe Highway Murders, 1811* (London: Constable, 1971). *The Conquest of Violence, Order and Liberty in Britain.* (New York: Schocken Books, 1970).
Critchley, T.A., *A History of Police in England and Wales, 900-1966* (London: Constable, 1967).
Lee, W. Melville, *A History of Police in England* (Montclair, N.J.: Patterson Smith, 1971. Introduction by P.J. Stead.)
Radzinowicz, Leon, *A History of English Criminal Law and its Administration from 1750.* Vol. I, *The Movement for Reform* (1948); Vol. II, *The Clash Between Private Initiative and Public Interest in the Enforcement of the Law* (1956); Vol. III, *Cross-Currents in the Movement for the Reform of the Police* (1956); Vol. IV, *Grappling For Control.* (London: Stevens & Sons, 1968).
Reith, Charles, *The Police Idea, Its History and Evolution in England in the Eighteenth Century and After* (London: Oxford University Press, 1938). *Police Principles and the Problem of War* (London: Oxford University Press, 1940). *British Police and the Democratic Ideal* (London: Oxford University Press, 1943). *A Short History of the British Police* (London: Oxford University Press, 1948). *The Blind Eye of History* (Montclair, N.J.: Patterson Smith, 1975 reprint of 1952 ed. Introduction by P.J. Stead 1952). *A New Study of Police History* (Oliver and Boyd, London 1956).

[5]

Party Politics, Class Interest And Reform Of The Police, 1829-56

William Watts Miller, *University of Bristol, United Kingdom*

Abstract

The need of 19th century England to reform its police might seem obvious, whether viewed in terms of the 'public good' or the 'interests of the ruling class'. Yet even quite mild legislation ran into persistent opposition in Parliament from members of that class. Why? Detailed examination of the pattern of voting and debate shows that critics of the new police had a strong case on questions of cost, efficiency, and the interpretation of criminal statistics. They also had well-founded worries about the use of the police to attack local in favour of central government and to base the social order on coercion more than consent. Thus both right and left voted against the legislation, tories to defend the power of local elites, radicals to defend local government, but also because of the politics of reform. Support came from the middleground, readier, perhaps, to compromise, yet still solidly against the highly centralist inclinations of Peel and other frontbenchers. In conclusion, preconceptions about 'class interest' or the 'public good' are unhelpful, since people took very different views of what they were. Although reflecting social background, disagreement mainly concerned party politics and basic differences of approach underlying them.

Parliament laid the basis of a new system of police for England and Wales in the years 1829 to 1856. Professional forces were set up, under central inspection or control. An understanding of this legislation must draw heavily on the work of Critchley, Mrs. Hart, Mather and Radzinowicz. It is not hard, however, to see which side they are on. Radzinowicz finds the evidence of the 1839 Constabulary Report striking, its arguments powerful, its proposals logical.[1] Critchley writes of 1856:

To describe the buffetings which the Bill underwent during a stormy passage through the House of Commons would be tedious. The borough members outdid one another in vituperation. Bentham, Colquhoun, and Peel might never have lived; to Chadwick, the sole survivor of the early tussles, the hysteria would have an all too familiar ring.[2]

Perhaps this attitude is justified. It can be said there was an obvious need for reform. The temptation — and Critchley and the others yield to it — is to turn on critics of the new police, accusing them of dogma, prejudice and self or vested interest. The pioneers of the police idea, the account reads, had to overcome an unreasoning and unreasonable opposition, yet overcome it they did. If it is not a whig view of history, perhaps it is getting on for a tory mirror image of one.[3]

I propose to look again at the debate on the new police. My main focus will be on Parliament. But members of Parliament belonged to the elite — the 'ruling class.' Why, then, did some of them vote against measures designed to set up a more efficient system of police? Were they not conscious of the true interests of their class? From quite different standpoints, parliamentary opposition to the new police seems puzzling. That is as good a reason as any for trying to fathom it.

The Pattern of Debate

No one questioned the need for *some* system of police to uphold the law. There were, instead, three interconnected issues. What was the nature of the problem of crime and disorder? What could a police do to solve it? What system of police would be effective — or rather 'cost-effective' — yet under proper control?

Crime and Disorder

In introducing the 1829 Metropolis Police Bill, Peel emphasised the huge increase of crime in London reported by a select committee he had got up on the subject the year before.[4] The committee had taken care to relate statistics on criminal commitments to those on population, and to argue accordingly that there had been an increase not simply in the incidence but also in the rate of crime. Peel, in explaining this to the House, spoke as if the rise in commitments meant a corresponding rise in crime. Yet the committee had gone into the question and concluded:

Much may be accounted for in the more ready detection and trial of culprits, also in less disinclination to prosecute, in consequence of improved facilities afforded at the courts to prosecutors and witnesses, and of the increased allowance of costs.[5]

The point was taken up in the debate by an opponent of the Bill:

These commitments, it is obvious, are not all to be imputed to the growth of crime, though I do not deny that it has increased in a great degree, or that it is an evil of an enormous nature, and requires an enormous remedy.[6]

This may have hit on a weakness in Peel's case; it hardly exploited it. But the argument took a new turn once the Bill was passed. Commitments continued to rise. Perhaps, then, there was a continued rise in crime that the new police did nothing to prevent. Durham complained it was less efficient than the old.[7] Or perhaps the police had pushed up the rate of detection, so that the growth of crime was more apparent than real. There was just one snag. Peel had made prevention the main test of the success of a police. In 1834, a select committee offered an ingenious way out of the difficulty. It rested on the assumption that commitments measured crime before 1829, but not after.[8] Was logic saved by events?

The year after the committee's report, commitments in London and Middlesex fell, and again in 1836 and 1837. Everywhere else, except Surrey, they rose.[9] In 1838, a select committee noted, with satisfaction, the 'con-

tinuous decrease of crime' in the metropolis. Once more, crimes and commitments could be run together. Not for long. That same year, commitments started to go back up. But by then there was a standard defence. If the new police failed to stop criminals, at least it succeeded in catching them. As Sir Peter Laurie, in evidence to the committee, remarked:

When the New Police was established, it was said that the object was to prevent crime, but when a great increase of crime was found to have taken place, the answer was 'but it is all detected now.'[10]

Sir Peter was engaged in battle on another front. In 1829, Peel said he had decided not to 'meddle with' the City of London because of its 'much more perfect' police. The truth, as he admitted later, was the City did not brook meddling with.[11] The 1838 committee returned to the question, and called on the government to put the City into the hands of the metropolitan police commissioners. Hawes, its chairman, told the House, 'There was no part of the metropolis in which crime was more prevalent than in the City of London.'[12] But he had no figures to go on. Both the Home Office and the City authorities were unable or unwilling to provide him with the information he required, while Sir Peter maintained that the City police was better at detection than its metropolitan counterpart.

The committee drew another important blank in its examination of the clerk to the criminal court:

I believe... the thieves are very much driven now to those places where no police is established.

Do you think that there has been any increase in the number of thieves within the City of London, strictly such, in consequence of the better system of watching established without the City? — No, I cannot take upon myself to say that: I meant the districts beyond the metropolitan district.[13]

'Migrant criminals' have a distinguished history. Sir Richard Birnie noticed them in 1822 in evidence to a select committee.[14] In the 1829 debate they attracted the attention of

Party Politics

Peel. True, the police of some parishes was efficient, but this only drove felons to parishes
where it was inefficient. Hence the need for a
uniform system of police for the metropolis.[15]
Opponents of his Bill complained that he did
not carry the logic of the argument as far as
the City. A backbench tory peer, out of touch,
perhaps, with the government's difficulties on
the question, did the job for him:

> The efficiency of the police in the neigh-
> bouring districts will make all the thieves
> assemble in London, as an asylum. When we
> throw a dog into water, the fleas all get into
> his head to avoid drowning, and in the same
> way all the thieves will get into the City to
> avoid hanging.[16]

If the fleas were there, the 1838 committee
could not catch them. But a year later they
leapt back to life in the pages of the First
Report of the Constabulary Commissioners,
drafted by Chadwick:

> But whilst the rural districts are subjected
> to incursions of depredators from the towns,
> the towns themselves, besides incursions
> from depredators harbouring in other towns,
> are subjected to incursions from the bad
> characters who enjoy impunity in the adja-
> cent unprotected rural districts.[17]

Similar activities had been recorded in 1836
by another commission, as Lefevre, a member
of both, was no doubt aware.[18]

It is as well to understand the part of all this
in the general pattern of debate. The troop of
wandering thieves, etc., had a key role to play
in attempts to establish the need for a centralised police. Peel, we have seen, drew on
their services in pushing for a metropolitan
force. So did Lefevre and Chadwick in pushing
for a national one. So did a posse of chief constables appearing before a select commmittee
of 1853. As so did Grey, when he brought in
the County and Borough Police Bill of 1856.

The thieves were commonly put to work
alongside the figures for criminal commitments. Chadwick, however, dismissed
these as useless:

> The returns of the number of persons pros-
> ecuted or convicted which, in the reasonings

of parliament are usually assumed as correct
indications of the state of crime within any
given district, cannot be relied on for that
purpose . . . There is in general no recorded
information upon the subject on which any
reliance for exactitude can be placed.[19]

Parliament had been playing the statistics
game with the wrong rules. Only by changing
them could the full and horrifying extent of
crime be revealed:

> We have had brought before us courses of
> considerable depredation of which no traces
> have hitherto been presented to the legisla-
> ture.[20]

Chadwick's strategy was clear — to frighten
Parliament out of its wits and bring in the
police he had long set his mind on.

His plan failed. The most the government
felt it could carry was a measure allowing
magistrates to set up and control a constabulary force in their own counties or
districts. Russell deferred to the views of the
majority when, in introducing the Bill, he said
the commission's proposals 'went beyond the
necessity of the case.'[21] Some thought the same
was true of his Bill:

> There was as little crime in the rural districts
> of England as in any country in the world. In
> the rural districts, the two great classes of of-
> fences were poaching and wood cutting; but
> it was very seldom that a pheasant disap-
> peared, or a tree was cut, that the offender
> was not brought to justice.[22]

D'Israeli gave no statistics — and did not
have to, under Chadwick's new rules. Both
sides could score with them, not just the one.
But on the heads-I-win, tails-you-lose principle,
Chadwick allowed himself to use commitments
if he wanted to. As Halford noticed:

> 'We find,' say the commissioners, 'from the
> evidence that crimes of violence, whether
> originating in rapacity, or resorted to for the
> gratification of any vindictive or gross pas-
> sion, other than for money, are generally in a
> course of gradual diminution.'[23]

In fact, disagreement over the Bill did not
turn on any great feeling of alarm about crime,

44

even in counties with populous, manufacturing districts.

And the swarms of thieves put to flight by the 'efficient' new police? Mrs. Hart has questioned the argument's validity. If there was such an exodus, it was not reflected in the rate of commitments outside London.[24] What Mrs. Hart does not mention is that much the same point was made against the 1856 County and Borough Police Bill. Henley, in an important contribution to the debate, took two sets of counties, both of similar population and acreage, and both near the metropolis. Con-stabularies had been established under the 1839 Act in one but not the other:

> The police district was, it was true, almost surrounded by other police districts, but the same was true of the district not employing a rural police, so that both districts were in the same position as to thieves being driven into them by the working of the police in neighbouring counties.[25]

The figures for commitments and acquittals were:

	commitments		acquittals		% 'undetected'	
	old police	new police	old police	new police	old police	new police
1840-44:	10,321	11,094	2,883	3,380	27.9%	30.5%
1845-49:	9,796	10,028	2,490	3,074	25.4%	30.1%
1850-54:	10,316	11,038	2,531	2,934	24.5%	26.6%

If, then, the new police did not drive out criminals, it was because it was not more efficient than the old. Chadwick's objection was made, that commitments gave no idea of crime. But this, Henley pointed out, did not affect judgment of the relative success of the old and new police once cases came to trial. True, as he himself emphasised, fuller returns were needed. In Surrey, which had adopted the Act, there were 21 known instances of horse and sheep stealing in 1855, 7 arrests, 3 commitments, and no convictions. In East Sussex, according to another member, the new police failed with 54% of 1,720 larcenies in 1845-49, and 66% of 1,918 in 1850-54.[26] However, such evidence was not generally available. The evidence that was, though inadequate, was not useless — the House, Henley complained, 'had listened to opinions *usque ad nauseam.*'[27]

Critics of the new police took an informed and intelligent view of the state of crime. They were not blinded by unreasoning prejudice. It may still be they saw what they wanted to see. But the same could be said of the other side. And if crime was an excuse to disagree, we must ask what lay behind it. One answer is fear of disorder.

In the 1856 debate, Grey quoted a letter from a magistrate listing numerous disturbances of the peace which 'though called petty offences seriously affect the security of person and property.' Many would be 'entirely prevented or repressed' by the mere presence of a well-organised police.[28] What were they? If we go through the claims made over the years on behalf of the new police, we find it would clamp down on beer-houses; clear the streets of beggars and prostitutes; chase gypsies from the lanes and commons; discourage vagrants from applying for poor-relief; take up 'bad characters' *before* they did anything; stamp out prizefights, dogfights, etc.; put a stop to drinking and other amusements on the Sabbath; end 'disgraceful scenes' at fairs, races, elections; deal with strikes. The opposition was unimpressed. D'Israeli, in 1839, went over some of the evidence in Chadwick's report:

> The magistrates of Chelmsford regretted extremely that trampers, as they were called, were not exposed to be arrested for hiring beds in lodging-houses, whereas, if they only slept in the open air, they might be apprehended; but they congratulated themselves that the police, under their direction, had entered houses, and examined beds, to ascertain the character of the occupants.[29]

There were repeated allegations of brutality.[30] In 1833, Cobbett caught the new

Party Politics

police spying — even on Hume, a long-standing member of the House.[31] Although the affair embarrassed the authorities, they went on using the police to watch over political meetings. In 1842, one was broken up at Deptford, and the speaker arrested. Duncombe demanded an inquiry:

> According to the doctrine of the present day, any constable or police officer might go to any meeting and disperse it to his will and pleasure, knowing that his conduct would be supported by the magistrates, and the magistrates, in their turn, would be supported by the Home Department.[32]

What, then was at issue? The new police might, as claimed, uphold law and order more successfully than the old. But what sort of 'law and order'? Chadwick & Co. were not just in business to catch thieves. They made no secret of their plans to put down the evils that outraged them. And they were easily outraged. The opposition therefore had good reason to see in the new police an instrument of harassment, even oppression. It would be 'a Briareus, with ten thousand arms, stretching out into every village in the land.'[33]

But riot, if nothing else, breached the peace, and gave the state cause to act. The country, Grey said in 1856, needed an efficient police everywhere to meet 'sudden emergencies.' Everyone knew what he meant. Yet, his opponents claimed, the provinces had been quiet for some time, and Grey produced little evidence to the contrary.[34] Whatever prompted the Bill, it was not a visible breakdown of order.

1839 was different. Chartist mobs gave Parliament a fright, and the government an opportunity. Besides the rural police Bill, it rushed through measures to set up forces in Birmingham, Manchester and Bolton. Chadwick's fuss about crime mattered little — even to him:

> In 1835, when we were carrying out the organisation of the parishes into unions under the Poor Law Amendment Act, there were frequent riots ... I generally had to communicate with the Home Secretary to make arrangements for sending a sufficient force, generally of police, sometimes of military, or of coastguardsmen. This exper-

ience of the local deficiencies of means of preservation of the peace ... appeared to me to make it my duty to represent to Lord John Russell, who was then the Home Secretary, the importance of the issuing a Commission to inquire whether the like deficiencies prevailed throughout the country.[35]

In 1831, the administration, appalled by what had happened in Bristol, undertook to improve the police of the provincial towns 'against the occurrence of similar commotions'[36] — a promise kept in the general reform of municipal corporations four years later.

Even in 1829, although Peel talked a lot about crime, his thoughts also turned to riot. He steered clear of the subject while introducing his Bill but not in the debate itself. The old police was so defective, 'we have no other remedy than the employment of military force to repress disorder.' Lennard took him up on this:

> Other great towns, such as Bristol, Birmingham, and Manchester, will imitate the example afforded them by the metropolis, and we shall have large bodies of *gendarmerie* dispersed all over the country. I may be using, perhaps, very old-fashioned language in this House, when I say that I look with constitutional jealousy at this military force being put under the control of Government, to be employed on every occasion they think fit.[38]

Peel replied:

> I could not help smiling at the remark, recollecting, as I did, the acts of violence which had lately been committed at Manchester. I do hope that Manchester will follow the example of the metropolis in this respect, and that there will be some civil protection for the property of the great manufacturers there.[39]

The exchange is important, for it establishes that even in the 1829 debate — dismissed by Critchley and Radzinowicz as a non-event — riot entered the lists for and against the new police. It shows, too, how early the pattern of that controversy had set. Time and again, one side called for an efficient police to replace military force, while the other questioned what difference a *gendarmerie* would make — except to swell the power of Government over People. Nor was it fanciful of the opposition to warn, as it did from the outset, of a revolutionary police *en marche*. That was exactly what Peel had in mind.

The Need for a Police

Military force was too brutal and naked a way of maintaining 'order.' People got killed; an indignant public turned on the government; the army too complained, for it had little taste for the work. Peel thought his new police could do the same job, without the same risk. He even denied it would be an instrument of coercion.[40] Viscount Clements took a different view:

> If they established a police of this kind, there would be no longer any occasion for an army, for, to all intents and purposes, the police would be soldiers. He had seen the evils of an armed police in Ireland, and he had no wish to see the same system adopted in this country.[41]

It was not a far-fetched thing to say. Policemen were not put into red coats. But they wore uniform, paraded and saluted. They were usually commanded by ex-army officers, with a mania for discipline. They could be armed and were trained accordingly. Capt. Harris, chief constable of Hampshire, told the select committee of 1853:

> The men are young, energetic, and active, and patrolling for seven hours every night of their lives, are in splendid condition for marching ... The whole body is drilled to the use of the sword.[42]

Thus while some attacked the new police as 'equal to soldiers' some defended it — whatever Peel said — for the same reason:

> Mr. *Baring* highly approved of the Police, and thought it was a great advantage that it had a military character. It would be, in his opinion, a great benefit that 3,000 or 4,000 men could be assembled on any occasion accustomed to the manners of the people.[43]

The important point, however, was if the so-called 'civil force' was any better than the army at controlling disorder. People still got killed. Others were cut or beaten up. Perhaps that was their fault. The opposition thought not. The country could do without such a police.

Critchley writes:

> In a democratic state, where Parliament is supreme and the rule of law well established, a strong, highly respected police force is a condition, not a denial, of liberty within the restraints of law. This was well understood by Peel and the other pioneers of policing in England.[44]

But England was not a democracy. To Peel, the very idea was anathema. The debate on the new police involved, instead, the right of a 'constitutional' government to sustain by force an unequal social and political order.

Even in 1839, with the Chartists in full cry, the establishment claimed that the masses remained loyal — although many had been led astray by a handful of agitators and extremists.[45] It is an old tale, with an old moral. Society had to be protected against a small, but subversive minority. On the other hand, perhaps that minority was the elite.

Radicals attacked Parliament's indifference to suffering and injustice. Profit-mongers sucked the blood of the labouring classes; the poor were taxed deeply in the necessities of life; they had not the means to feed their families. What prospect, O'Connell asked, did the working classes have of finding redress, when they had no representatives and no one to look to their interests:

> You have deprived them of the franchise, and you suppose they will be contented and satisfied under that system. They would not deserve to be Englishmen if they were satisfied. They are a slave class, and you a master class; and so long as this state of things existed, it was their right and duty to be dissatisfied.[46]

Attwood summed matters up:

> If they looked to the towns, nine out of every

Party Politics

ten were Chartists. If they looked to the
villages, nine out of every ten were rick-
burners. He asserted with confidence that
the labourers of England were alienated from
that House, and that nine out of every ten
who heard of a fire felt a melancholy pleasure
at the intelligence.[47]

The dilemma is familiar. Violence, radicals
believed, was a consequence of oppression. Yet
they condemned 'physical force,' even as a last
resort. Some, like O'Connell and Hume, supported a strong police. Law was above the law.
Most opposed it. The police would be used in a
vain and costly attempt to hold back the tide
of reform. The House, Fielden warned, might
disregard the complaints of the people for a
time, but if they did they would one day have
bitter cause to regret it.[48] To secure the peace,
it was necessary to secure justice. Policemen,
'drilled to the use of the sword,' could not do
that.

Radicalism was not the only source of opposition to the police. Many convinced themselves of the essential harmony of the old
order. If a new inhumanity threatened it, that
was no reason for a new police. Gradgrinds
might demand a licence to exploit the poor, by
force if need be. Granting them it was hardly
the way to unite the nation. Raising an army of
police, D'Israeli said, amounted to a declaration of civil war.[49] If things had come to this
pass, it was time Parliament asked itself what
had gone wrong. It was time, in fact, the
privileged recognised once more their obligations towards the people. Chadwick's brave
new world was a far cry from doing that. Tories
and whigs, as well as radicals, turned from it in
disgust. It degraded everyone. Even the queen,
Buller gibed, would be imprisoned in a workhouse.[50]

Government, all agreed, should rest on consent. But that consent, the opposition felt, was
melting away. It was not just a question of
counting Chartists or fires. Even quite different tests of social and political justice threw
up evidence of the lack of it. A new police
would only make matters worse. It signalled a
decisive shift in the basis of the social order
away from consent towards force. There was
no need to accept such a change. There was
every need to resist it. The more so if, at the
same time, it upset the balance of power be-

tween one section of the ruling class and
another.

Cost, Efficiency and Control

An important part of the case against the new
police had to do with expense. This has been
caricatured by Mather, among others, as mindless pennypinching.[51] But both sides were concerned about cost. Most responsible politicians
are.

Peel promised, in 1829, that London's new
police would be as cheap as the old. In fact,
rates shot up, in some parishes well over the
limit set by Parliament. Not surprisingly, people complained. Why had they been misled?
Peel thought the new system would reduce
crime. If, then, policemen cost more, prosecutions would cost less. There might even be a
net saving.[52] Instead, commitments for trial
went up — and with them expense. Yet the
police lobby was not put out. It went on predicting commitments would go down. The
1836 report on county rates made clear why:

> The only means of relief in this branch of ex-
> penditure which could be at once legitimate
> and effectual, are those which have in view
> the prevention of crime, and a consequent
> diminution in the number of prosecutions.[53]

The new police was marketed by some with a
guarantee to slash rates — and that was not
all. Guestimates were made of the value of
property lost under the old system. This was
called the 'cost of non-protection,' on the
assumption the entry would be negligible in
the balance-sheet of an efficient force. The gain
to the public would be enormous. But the argument once again rested on the ability of the
new police to put down crime. If Chadwick
brimmed with confidence, the same could not
be said of Rowan and Mayne. The metropolitan
commissioners told the select committee of
1838 there were 'classes of crime which arise
from causes beyond the reach of the police
regulations.' These included embezzlement,
forgery, fraud, stealing from drunken persons
and carts or carriages, theft of goods exposed
for sale and of linen exposed to dry, larceny by
servants, lodgers, prostitutes . . . The list was
long and accounted for the great majority of offences against property, before 1829 and
after.[54] For a 'preventive' police, it was not

much of an advertisement. The old system cost the ratepayer far less and, the opposition added, was just as efficient.[55]

There were objections too to the funding of the new police. The trouble lay in interpreting the general principle — accepted by everyone — that those benefiting from a police ought to pay for it. Traditionally, this meant the local community, and under the 1829 Act the cost of the new system, as with the old, fell on the rates. The difference was it was pooled:

> Lord *Wharncliffe* did not see why the parish of St. George should have to pay for the wants of others; it was quite sufficient that it should be chargeable for the maintenance of its own security. The expense of the watch did not exceed 3½d. in the pound, while that of the police was 11½d.[56]

The matter was looked into but nothing was done. In 1844, Tufnell demanded a fresh inquiry:

> A uniform rate of assessment on all the metropolitan parishes had been imposed, without reference to their wants; and the consequence was, that a greatly increased expense had been entailed on many parishes, without any corresponding benefit ... In the parish of Marylebone the sum levied under the old watch-rate had been on the average of ten years 9,500*l*., and the number of men employed had been 256. The rate levied in the same parish for the New Police was 20,000*l*., and the number of men employed 211. In this parish, nothing like a corresponding advantage had been given.[57]

For the commissioners organised the new force according to their own 'professional' ideas of need. Parishes were irrelevant, except to be mulcted of cash. The City of London, high in rateable value, would have been a prize catch but escaped. Although, in 1839, it had reformed its police on metropolitan lines, that still cost only £76 a man, including superintendents, against Marylebone's assessment of £112. Rich parishes, therefore, objected to the separation of policing from payment. They were not the only ones. The 'metropolitan police district' extended far beyond the suburbs, to take in whole towns, as well as

villages and fields. Few men were stationed in the out-parishes. Why should they pay the full rate?[58] It seemed merely an expedient to subsidise London. Early on, the taxpayer was called on to help. The country at large, it was said, had an interest in preserving peace in the metropolis, and ought to contribute to maintain its police. Though this too was attacked as unfair, the government, in 1833, decided on a grant of a quarter the cost. But it would not change the single rate.

Similar difficulties over funding arose in the shires, and many refused to 'improve' their police. In 1856, the government resorted to compulsion. However, it undertook to divide counties into appropriate rating districts, while, as in London, 'efficient' forces were to have a grant of a quarter. It was a Greek gift. The Act set up an inspectorate to check on the state of the police throughout the provinces. As Home Secretary, Grey explained, he had a duty to see the taxpayer's money was well spent. This was an excuse. He turned down an amendment giving local authorities the right to do without aid, and the supervision that went with it.[59]

But feeling on the issue had always run high. Executive control of the police was 'unconstitutional.' It savoured, according to Lennard, of arbitrary power. It violated, Duncombe thought, the sacred principle of local self-government. Buller spoke of the shameful system of centralisation, Hadfield of a despicable despotism. The trouble, though, was saying where in the community responsibility should lie.

When in 1835 the whigs brought in a plan of municipal reform, the tories put up a furious opposition. They forced, in the Lords, a number of important amendments. Yet the basic principle of the Bill remained intact: town councils were to be elected on a limited franchise. They were also to have charge of the police. On this, at least, there was an agreement. The clause was not even debated. But radicals wanted all of local government opened up. Hume, in 1836, proposed the establishment of county boards elected by ratepayers. One of their functions was to be management of the police.[60] Tories and whigs voted against the idea *en masse*. They reserved authority in the shires for magistrates and gentlemen. The case was different with large unincorporated towns

4

Party Politics

and there the battle over municipal reform could be refought. Some of the local improvement commissions that provided a police were elected, others were self-nominating, and some supported the grant of borough status, others others opposed it. What mattered was if loss of control to a council meant loss of control to Liberals — the situation in Manchester and Birmingham. In 1839, the row over their police turned into a crisis. As no local force could be raised to keep the Chartists in order, the government, at Peel's suggestion, decided to set up its own. The outcry was enormous, and the councils took over three years later.

The tories used the affair to promote the idea of a police above politics. But they meant radical politics. It was not apparent to them that Conservative town councils were elected on 'mere party considerations,' and they did not press any general attack on the rights of boroughs over the police. That was left to Chadwick, who wrote:

The magistrates being tradesmen and elective as members of the municipal council are placed under considerable temptations to bid for popularity to the very lowest of the voters, and, whether justly or not, the general administration of justice is suspected and mistrusted ... Protection could be obtained only by the introduction of a well-organised police or constabulary under independent control.[61]

The select committee of 1853 pushed on with the good work. A procession of witnesses trooped in from the police lobby. Town councils were made up of 'grocers and drapers and such.'[62] Charge of even the smallest force pandered to their sense of importance. Worse, it gave them influence. In a number of boroughs, it was said, police appointments were purely and wholly political.[63] There was too the scandal of vested interest, that came between the police and the rule of law. Despite complaints from 'respectable inhabitants and the clergy,' beerhouses were allowed to stay open far into the night and on sundays during divine service. For many members of watch committees were brewers. In some towns, they were the chairmen.[64] An 'independent' police would put a stop to such abuse — and keep the 'lower

class of voters,' as Chadwick described them, in their place.

But the people, Duncombe said, ought to have control of their money, whether it was expended for the relief of the poor or for the preservation of the peace.[65] There should be no taxation, Hume reminded the House, without representation.[66] How well the police served the local community was for the ratepayer to decide. Fox, in 1856, defended the politics of accountability:

Town councils were elected; they were continually obliged to answer to their constituents; there were ready means at hand of punishing their negligence or of correcting their ignorance or stupidity; and under such circumstances the best thing that could be done was to cherish them in the exercise of their legitimate authority. The people who inhabited the boroughs must know whether they were protected; they knew they had the means of rendering those who represented them more on the alert for their protection, and no doubt they were ready to employ those means.[67]

If towns opposed amalgamation with county constabularies, it was because they would lose this check on the conduct, efficiency and expense of the police. Yet magistrates too claimed to speak for the community and act on its behalf. Self-government could be interpreted in different ways, but the general principle was agreed; local people should have care of local affairs. Inevitably, this came into conflict with the project for a new police.

A formula had been discovered, it was thought, to apply everywhere. The whole country should have a full-time, disciplined and numerous police, organised into districts that ignored inconvenient political boundaries. Although the idea made some headway, opposition remained strong. An 'efficient' system could come about only if the government imposed it. But where would that lead? Both Bright and Lennard had warned, in 1829, against a police state by instalments, and they were not the last. The cry of a *gendarmerie* was heard time and again. It may have been emotive. It was not inaccurate. The search for a new police linked centralised with irresponsible power.

50

Peel and Russell agreed, in 1839, to put the police in Manchester and Birmingham under commissioners appointed by the government. They assured the House the measure would be temporary. Yet first a whig and then a tory administration wanted to renew it. This seemed the original intention. A revealing exhange had taken place between Peel and Hume:

The right hon. Gentleman had recommended that an individual should have the management of the police in Birmingham who should be wholly independent of the corporation. (Sir *Robert Peel:* in every other corporation.)[68]

But Russell had his eye on a 'general force' run by government commissioners.[69] Neither frontbench, however, could budge Parliament from its belief in local control. In 1853, they tried again. A select committee was got up, and a year later a Bill brought in. Although it stopped short of complete centralisation, it failed to reach even a Second Reading. Proposals to draw up a set of detailed regulations and to merge county and borough forces had to be dropped, and the 'bribe' dangled of an exchequer grant, before, in 1856, an Act could be passed. This turned out to be the last attack on local autonomy, at least by way of legislation. But in the circumstances, the suspicion was entirely warranted there would be more.

Meanwhile what of London? Both whig and tory governments rejected any form of local involvement, let alone a 'Central Board chosen from all the parishes.'[70] Nor did they encourage interference by Parliament. 'The House,' Hume said in 1839, 'should have a constitutional check over the police, and, therefore, the amount of public money granted should be in the shape of an annual vote, when their conduct might be canvassed.'[71] The request was turned down. It was difficult to get an inquiry, even into the most serious of allegations.[72] If there was nothing to hide, no effective mechanism was allowed to develop to find that out. Palmerston slipped up when he spoke of the metropolitan police 'acting under the orders of Government.'[73] The Commissioners were supposed to be in charge, not the Home Secretary, who had a reserve authority. The image projected was of an 'independent' police, above politics yet under the law. Whatever the reality

of power, the doctrine held Parliament at a safe — or dangerous — distance from it.

The metropolitan police, Radzinowicz and others tell us, soon became an 'accepted institution.' This ignores continuing criticism and government attempts to stifle it. That criticism came largely from radicals. But London helped put such men into Parliament. In 1840, the City made one of them — Harvey, the member for Southwark — its commissioner of police. Although central control kept the capital in more 'reliable' hands, it is open to question if a Bill such as Peel's could have passed after 1832, or 1835, the 'Magna Charta' of local self-government. All that is certain is Parliament's refusal to accept the 'accepted institution' outside London — or Ireland.

The Pattern of Voting

Chadwick packaged a set of proposals for a new, uniform, centralised system of police. It was never put in the form of a Bill, so great was the opposition. A watered-down version, brought in by Palmerston in 1854, evaporated after a First Reading. Two years and more concessions later, a compromise acceptable to Parliament was reached. This left provincial forces largely under local control, and organised largely according to local political boundaries. But it meant an 'efficient,' professional police everywhere — except in corporate boroughs, with a population of under 5,000, that refused to amalgamate with counties. They were not to have a grant, and were not to be inspected. The deal still came under fire. Whom from?

The Metropolis Police Act passed without a division. The same happened in 1835, when town councils were given responsibility for the police. Things were different in 1839. The House voted six times on what to do about Birmingham. On each occasion save the first, the issue turned on central as against municipal control of the police. In all, 145 members supported the appointment, for two years, of a government commissioner; 34 opposed it; they rejected any tampering with the rights of a corporate town, and any questioning of Birmingham's new status as one. Almost all of them were elected by boroughs. Almost all of them were radicals or whigs. And almost all of them to vote on Attwood's motion to go into committee on the National Petition voted for it.

Party Politics

The whigs, in other words, were on the 'left' of their party. The figures are set out in Table 1.[74]

Voting on the Manchester Police Bill took a different course. Liberals, as in Birmingham, had control of the council and so claimed control of the police — something the local improvement commissions would not yield up. A whig cabal still ran the one in Birmingham. But Manchester's had just fallen to the tories.[75] Some of their parliamentary colleagues considered, therefore, the cases were unlike; Birmingham needed a government police, not Manchester. They voted against a committee on the Bill. A number of radicals did too.[76] Others let the tories have a dose of their own medicine. They voted for a committee. An amendment was then put down giving the council, instead of the government, the appointment of a commissioner. This cleared the muddle up. Of those who supported municipal control in Birmingham, only two went against it in Manchester. The tories had been found out. If they did not like the Bill, they liked the amendment less. Voting on it followed a pattern similar to that for Birmingham. Again, the figures are set out in Table 1.

The County and District Constables Bill left with magistrates the decision to set up a new system of police — under their control. Parliament, in agreeing to the measure, did not agree to much. Even so, 16 members voted against going into committee on it. Most were radicals. They tried to limit the Bill to two years and picked up more whig support. Next the tories entered the lists against it. They put down an amendment not to disqualify parish constables, even though magistrates established a full-time police. This was defeated — by a majority of two. A combination of tories, whigs and radicals then voted against a Third Reading. The figures are set out in Table 2.

The Bill as passed gave rise to a number of difficulties, and the following session the government came back with another to sort them out. One was over corporate boroughs without their own quarter sessions. Were the town councils or the county magistrates responsible for their police? The government, reluctantly, came down on the side of the councils, and 6 radicals rewarded it with their votes. Most tories, meanwhile, had gone off the original reform — a Bill brought in by a whig back-

Table 1
Voting On Birmingham And Manchester Police Bills, 1839

(a) Noes, Birmingham   (b) Noes, Manchester — committee
(c) Noes, Manchester — clause for a government commissioner

		(a)		(b)		(c)	
radicals	:	12	(15)	6	(12)	7	(10)
repealers*	:	2	(5)	0	(2)	1	(2)
whigs	:	18	(92)	2	(53)	4	(48)
tories	:	2	(67)	11	(17)	0	(19)
		34	(179)	19	(84)	12	(79)
National Petition, 1839	ayes:	19	(24)			10	(16)
	noes:	3	(96)			0	(44)
borough members	:	32	(132)	16	(65)	11	(62)

* O'Connell's 'Irish party'

Figures in parentheses give totals of ayes and noes, including tellers.

Table 2
Voting On Rural Police Bills, 1839 and 1840

(a) Noes, 1839 — committee   (b) Ayes, 1839 — 2 year limit
(c) Ayes, 1839 — not to disqualify parish constables
(d) Noes, 1839 — 3rd Reading   (e) Noes, 1840 — to proceed

	(a)	(b)	(c)	(d)	(e)
radicals :	10 (13)	9 (11)	3 (6)	6 (7)	3 (9)
repealers:	4 (6)	1 (1)	2 (3)	0 (3)	0 (9)
whigs :	2 (53)	12 (65)	5 (35)	4 (36)	2 (73)
tories :	0 (31)	1 (25)	22 (22)	5 (16)	36 (57)
	16 (103)	23 (102)	32 (66)	15 (62)	41 (148)

Figures in parentheses give totals of ayes and noes, including tellers.

bencher was more to their liking than the administration's.[77] They suggested both should be dropped, and a select committee set up to look at the matter afresh. But the government refused to bite. The tories were after a compromise that instead of doing away with the old system of police put new life into it. They turned the whigs out of office in 1842 and got a Bill through without a division. Parish constables could be part-time or full-time, as vestries decided, while magistrates, in certain circumstances, were to appoint paid superintendents over them. This appeared to seal the fate of the earlier legislation. Of the 56 counties of England and Wales, 24 set up a new police under it before 1842, only 4 after.[78]

The plan of an 'efficient,' centralised system of police foundered, as Radzinowicz and others point out, on opposition in all parties. But the picture is different if we look at the limited reforms proposed in Parliament. Feeling against them ran highest among tories and radicals.

What happened in 1856? Did Grey's Bill divide the House on similar lines? Mrs. Hart thinks not, seeing instead a 'good example of mid-nineteenth-century cross-voting.'[79] But the figures she gives are misleading, mainly because they lump Conservatives and Liberal-Conservatives together in a single political grouping. She calmly ignores the effects on the tory party of Peel's conversion to free trade. In 1852, his followers helped to turn Derby out of office, went in with the Liberals, and the coalition under Aberdeen lasted until 1855, when it was succeeded by another under Palmerston. True, most Peelites pulled out of his government shortly after, though some stayed in. Yet they hesitated to bring it down. An alliance with tories and radicals defeated it in 1857.[80] 'Liberal-Conservatives' should, therefore, be listed separately, and the result is not uninteresting. Table 3 shows they were the Bill's most enthusiastic supporters, Conservatives the least. If, however, we distinguish among the Liberals, radicals and whigs, radicals come out as the group most opposed, whigs the most in favour. Or if we compare voting on the police with voting the same year on a secret ballot at parliamentary elections, we find that 92% of Liberals against the ballot were for the Bill. But 93% of them against the Bill were for the ballot.[81] The overall impression, then, is that those at the 'centre' of the parliamentary political spectrum gave overwhelming support to the 1856 Police Bill. Opposition to it arose mainly on the 'right' and the 'left.' This repeated the pattern of 1839 and 1840.

Table 3 also shows voting according to constituency and social background.[82] The Bill applied only to provincial England and Wales and largely affected counties without a new police, as well as corporate boroughs with a

Party Politics

Table 3
Opposition To County And Borough Police Bill, 1856

(a) by party	(b) by background				(c) by constituency
(a) Liberal-Conservatives	5	(43)	—	12%	
Liberals*	56	(192)	—	29%	
Conservatives	47	(134)	—	35%	

* whigs, 10% (21); liberal/reformers, 28% (159); radicals, 83% (12)

(b) 'gentry'**	68	(283)	—	24%	
'businessmen'	38	(78)	—	49%	

** nobility, 13% (62); gentry, 25% (149); gentry-business, 32% (72)

(c) Scotland, Ireland, London	11	(69)	—	16%	
new police counties	14	(71)	—	20%	
old police counties	15	(65)	—	23%	
corporate boroughs, population 5,000 plus	68	(164)	—	41%	
	108	(369)	—	29%	

Figures in parentheses give totals of ayes and noes, including tellers.

population of 5,000 or more. Opposition to it was greatest from members of these boroughs and least from members for Scotland, Ireland and London. If we look at social background, we find that support was greatest among the nobility and least among business and professional men.

Are not party, constituency and background different ways of talking about the same sets of people? One thinks of radical millowners and large towns, of tory squires and broad acres. The reality was more complicated, and Table 4 tries to simplify it. It turns out we are able to arrange the categories of each variable so that in reading across any row, or down any column, opposition to the Bill tends to increase.[83]

Almost all Liberal-Conservatives were 'gentry,' and their support for the Bill remained high, even among those representing corporate boroughs. But the two main parties were divided, Liberals more by background, Conservatives by constituency. Conservative opposition was twice as great in counties with an old police as in counties with a new; Liberals from

both types of area were solidly behind the Bill — except for a handful of 'businessmen.' Most 'businessmen' represented corporate boroughs, and most who did were against the Bill — Conservatives more so than Liberals. Borough members of both parties were split according to background. Yet although most of the Conservative 'gentry' also voted against the Bill, most of their Liberal counterparts voted for it. The narrow majority for the Bill from the boroughs was largely the work of Liberal and Liberal-Conservative 'gentry.' So too was the substantial majority for it even in counties with an old police.

What are we to make of all this?

The Politics of Interest

The old machinery of police, we are told, was utterly inadequate, and the poor threatened to engulf the country in a tide of disorder and crime. The army was called out, workhouses brought in, trainloads of Peelers dispatched to the provinces and shiploads of convicts to the colonies. If the idea of a new police was un-

54

Table 4
Opposition To County And Borough Police Bill, 1856:
Relation of Party, Constituency And Background

(a) Scotland, Ireland and London   (b) new police counties
(c) old police counties   (d) corporate boroughs, 5,000 plus

		Liberal-Conservative		Liberal		Conservative	
(a)	'gentry' :	0% (5)		12% (32)		17% (12)	
	'business' :		—		29% (17)		—
(b)	'gentry' :	25% (8)		5% (21)		17% (36)	
	'business' :		—		57% (7)		100% (1)
(c)	'gentry' :	0% (7)		7% (14)		33% (39)	
	'business' :		—		50% (2)		0% (3)
(d)	'gentry' :	15% (20)		28% (58)		57% (35)	
	'business' :		0% (2)		55% (40)		83% (6)

Figures in parentheses give totals of ayes and noes, including tellers.

popular, so were the alternatives. The system of transportation came to an end in 1853, while by 1861, murder, almost alone, carried the death penalty. And it was in these years that Parliament, at last, came to terms with the inevitable.

The country was covered by a network of professional police charged with the prevention of crime, the detection of offenders and the maintenance of order. Systematic enforcement of the law had replaced suspended terror as the accepted basis of control.[84]

It is easy to stand Radzinowicz on his head and fit what he says into a marxist theory of the state. The ruling class, to defend capitalism against increasing attack, set up in the new police an instrument of coercion less out of keeping than others with the appearance of consent. But are we any nearer an understanding of what happened?

First let us suppose a politics based wholly on interest. Perhaps this is unrealistic. Consider, for example, the evidence Marx draws on in his discussion of the Factory Acts.[85] Much of it is a record of middle class outrage at the treatment by masters of their workforce. Marx tries to discount such sentiment in two ways.

Concessions were wrung out of the bourgeoisie by the proletariat. Or the state realised where the true interests of capital lay: labour was more productive healthy than exhausted and diseased. However if, sometimes, morality sides with interest, that does not mean it comes down to it, or is always of less weight.

Even so, let us assume a politics of interest. Let us assume too that reform of the police was in the interest of the ruling class. We must then ask why the reform was opposed in Parliament. One explanation is that it went against the interest of a section of the elite. Voting on the 1856 Bill varied, as we have seen, according to constituency and background. The 'gentry,' it could be argued, had little to lose. Westminster was as much in their grip as the shires. 'Businessmen,' on the other hand, were powerful only in the boroughs. The slightest weakening of municipal control of the police was a threat to them. True, many 'businessmen' voted for the Bill, even among borough members. But the point is that support for the interest of the ruling class as a whole was less in this segment of it.

Two difficulties, however, remain. One is that voting also varied according to political affiliation. This was still connected with background and constituency, yet only in part.

Party Politics

Liberal-Conservative opposition was consistently low. It was higher among Liberals and highest among Conservatives with otherwise similar characteristics. The second difficulty has to do with a judgment of the 'real' interests of the ruling class. Few people argue in public that the policy they favour benefits only themselves. Certainly, critics of the Bill did not. They appealed, like its supporters, to an idea of the 'common good.' It is easier said than shown that this concealed 'class interest' in one case, 'sectional interest' in the other.

Radzinowicz, for example, calls some opposition 'insincere.' Or perhaps it was just mistaken. He also talks of 'prejudice,' as though this explains the lapse. Both accounts start from the premise that Parliament was right to reform the police and would have been wrong not to. In questioning the judgment, I do not want to turn it round, still less give up hope of any. Politics, we ought to remind ourselves, are often open: good arguments exist for opposite courses of action. This mistake then is to impose a logic of closure, so that one course must be 'correct,' the alternative to it in 'error.' With the police, as with a number of other important issues, there was, I suggest, an openness of this kind. Yet if the interest of the ruling class pulled it in different directions, why did support for the 1856 Bill come from the 'centre,' opposition from the 'right' and 'left'?

The question is difficult to answer, and the trouble may be in asking it. Politics in mid-nineteenth century England had little to do with party and less with principle. The idea of a spectrum of opinion, with radicals at one end and reactionaries at the other, is a myth. There is something to be said for this view but more against.[86]

Aydelotte has examined in some detail the Parliament of 1841-47. His analysis of 110 divisions yields interesting results. As many as 72 of them form a single, cumulative scale, such that a positive vote on any issue links with a positive vote on all issues ranked 'below' it, and a negative vote with a negative vote on all issues ranked 'above' it. 28 divisions form a second scale, while 21 fit neither and 11 both. These 11 apart, the two scales are unrelated. Voting on one cuts across voting on the other. Voting on the second scale also cuts across party affiliation. This is not so of the first. In the middle of the scale, Liberals confront Con-

servatives, while at one extreme Liberals are split, at the opposite, Conservatives.[87] The impression then is of a continuum, going from 'left' to 'right.' We can base these terms on the first scale, because of its importance and its connection with party. And it is in this sense, that the second scale divides the 'left' as well as the 'right.' In 1844, for example, some radicals and tories voted for, some against, a Ten Hour Day. A few divisions — also over factory legislation — produced the alliance of 'left' and 'right' against the 'centre' that I have suggested in the case of the police.[88] But the pattern is unusual, at least for the Parliament of 1841-47, and Aydelotte is careful to confine his conclusions to it. Unfortunately for us, the issue of the police came up mainly in the Parliaments of 1837-41 and 1852-57, and a similar analysis of them is lacking. Until we have one, we must largely guess at the place of the police in the wider political context. What should the guess be, if we assume continuity of a sort between the 1830's and 50's?

A way of tackling the problem is to relate opposition to the new police to a stance associated with the 'left' that is not in conflict, or too great conflict, with a stance associated with the 'right.' For then, as one lot entered the lobby, the other would not automatically go out. Part of the puzzle seems obvious — if only we can fit it in. Let us start from there.

The Reform Bill of 1832 stirred up an enormous fuss. The row over, whigs and tories closed ranks behind the new old regime. The Act was a 'final' settlement of the representation in Parliament of the people. True, in the 1850s, Russell proposed minor adjustments but had to drop them. Change did not come until 1867, and even then against the odds. D'Israeli dished his own party as much as the whigs.[89] Meanwhile, a stand had to be made. The entry on the scene of an army of police, under government supervision, was bound to dismay the 'left.' It would stiffen resistance to reform, and the longer resistance went on, the greater repression would become. This surely is the answer to Mrs. Hart and her friends, who write off fears of a police state. Parliament avoided going too far down that road because in the end it took the other, that radicals had all along pointed out.[90]

But why did so many tories, in defending the old order, oppose the new police? The explanation seems to lie in alarm at the changing distribution of power within the ruling class. Step by step, first on this ground, then on that, central government encroached on the traditional autonomy of local elites. It was happening with the police. It had happened with public health.

The Liberals brought in a Bill in 1847. This had to be dropped. In 1848, back in office, they tried again and succeeded. A Board of Health was set up, with Chadwick a leading member. In 1854, the coalition was forced, in renewing the Act, to accept a number of changes; Chadwick & Co. were dismissed. In 1856, the same year as the Police Bill, the government's proposed 'improvements' were thrown out. And in 1858, the Board was wound up, at least in appearance — its officials moved shop to the Home Office.[91]

How did the House vote? Almost all Liberals supported the 1847 Bill. Conservatives were split, 57% for, 43% against. Opposition to it is well to the 'right' on Aydelotte's first scale.[92] The same seems to be true of 1848.[93] Although in 1854 and 1856 there was some shift of ground, the 'right' held on to its. All along, in the debate on public health, tories attacked centralisation, as they did with the police. And as with the police, Henley took a leading and effective part in their campaign. Let us listen, however, to one of his supporters:

MR. NEWDEGATE said, he hoped that, after the failure of the Board of Health . . . with its arbitrary and centralising powers — a failure which, he might remark, had been predicted by the right hon. Member for Oxfordshire (Mr. Henley) — the Government would be fully impressed with the absolute impossibility of the success of any system which was not founded on the principle of local self-government. With regard to his own constituency, he believed he might say that no greater service had ever been rendered to the great town of Birmingham than the prevention of the introduction there of the powers of the Board of Health, and the establishment of a system in lieu of them which, founded on the principle of local self-government, would be, he believed, permanent and successful.[94]

The 'left,' then, believed in extensive elec-

toral reform, the 'right' in extensive local autonomy. We must still ask why both could combine to oppose the new police, without the one putting the other off.

The 'left' too had a commitment to local self-government. If, with public health, there was cause to compromise it, that was not the case with the police. On the contrary, fear for reform reinforced fear of centralisation. The position of the 'right' was different. It was bound to be undermined by the idea, if accepted, of a new police to the rescue. But the idea was not accepted. In many parts of England, the danger to 'society' seemed remote, and where it existed, as in the large towns, under control.[95] There was no need to cover the country with a uniform system of full-time and numerous police. Circumstances varied from place to place and local authorities, not the government, could best judge what was required. Tories and radicals were thus able to make common cause.

But, radicals added, local authorities should be responsible for the police *and to the ratepayer*. The modern liberal is bound to sympathise. The police, as an institution, ought not to be independent of representative government; it cannot in this sense stand 'above politics.' All that is at issue is its degree of involvement in them. Here, the orthodox view welcomes the removal of a 'professional' police from the corrupt and incompetent grasp of local politicians. The gain was not just in efficiency but also in public respect. Miller, for example, contrasts London with New York and implies that the relative success of the English police depended on a shift from local to central control.[96] It is this I wish to question. True, evidence of 'public esteem' or the absence of it is difficult to assess, though, as I have already pointed out, continuing criticism in Parliament of the metropolitan police has been ignored. But we can compare the study of London with one of Bristol.[97] A new police was set up there in 1836. Reaction seems to have been mixed. Watch Committee records contain many glowing reports of public appreciation. The *Bristol Mercury*, on the other hand, frequently complained of wrongful arrest and assault. But its grudge was against inadequate, not local control of the police. The remedy lay in Bristol, not London. Whatever the level of 'public respect' for the police, there is nothing to suggest it was low before 1856, high after.

In conclusion, I have assumed a politics of interest and kept to the idea of a 'ruling class.' I have then asked how we are to understand opposition in Parliament to a new and more 'efficient' system of police. We can appeal to a conflict of class with sectional interest and find part of an answer. Why only part? The calculation of advantage is rarely a simple matter and depends, as much as anything, on a choice of principle. The politics of interest are filtered in this way by the politics of party. I have tried to say why 'right' and 'left' came together to oppose the new police, and why it is a mistake to think this opposition a mistake. On the contrary, it represented a realistic strategy open to the ruling class.

Perhaps my account can be fitted into marxist theory. Perhaps not. We should remember, however, that the executive of a modern state is also a committee to mismanage the affairs in common of the bourgeoisie.

Notes

1 L. Radzinowicz, *A History of English Criminal Law, Vol. 4* (London, 1968), pp. 231-2.

2 T. A. Critchley, *A History of Police in England and Wales 900-1966* (London, 1967), p. 117.

3 Mrs. Hart reduces the distinction to one of form. 'Whigs' pit good men against bad, 'tories' set impersonal social forces to work. Surely we need some notion of content. Otherwise marxists are 'tories.' Aydelotte suggests that 'tories' cast tories as the principal initiators and supporters of social reform. But this misses the point, which is the historian's commitment to certain values and assumptions. See J. Hart, 'Nineteenth-Century Social Reform: a Tory Interpretation of History,' *Past and Present, 31* (1965), 39-61, and W. O. Aydelotte, 'The Conservative and Radical Interpretations of Early Victorian Legislation,' *Victorian Studies, 11* (1967), 229, n. 13.

4 2 *Hansard*, XXI (1829), 869-71. See also Wellington, *ibid.,* 1750. For an account of the legislation, and Peel's handling of it, see N. Gash, *Mr. Secretary Peel* (London, 1961), pp. 487-503.

5 *Report from the Select Committee on the Police of the Metropolis,* P.P. 1828 (533) VI, p. 9. The same point was made in *Second Report from the Select Committee on Criminal Commitments and Convictions,* P.P. 1828 (545) VI, P. 422. I have followed contemporary usuage, which preferred 'commitment' to 'committal,' to refer to imprisonment by magistrates pending trial, on charge of an indictable offence, at Quarter Sessions or Assizes. This sense should not be confused with imprisonment on conviction.

6 Henry Bright, M.P. for Bristol, *Mirror of Parliament,* 1829, vol. 3, p. 1842.

7 3 *Hansard,* I (1831), 493. 'Radical Jack' has changed his tune:

There was no necessity for the noble duke (Wellington) to have entered into a statement of the increase of crime in the metropolis, a fact that was perfectly notorious; and it was no less notorious, that the police was quite insufficient for the purposes for which it was created.

2 *Hansard,* XXI (1829), 1752.

8 *Report from the Select Committee on the Police of the*

Metropolis, P.P. 1834 (600) XVI, p. 1. The idea was that some crimes, such as burglary, could be prevented by an efficient police; commitments for these had fallen. Others, such as common larceny, could only be detected; commitments for these had risen. Thus, the new system was a success. Radzinowicz thinks such reasoning 'plausible.' But the committee simply cooked up *ad hoc* categories of 'preventable' and 'detectable' crime to make the figures palatable. It did not try to apply the same test to show the 'failure' of the old police. It is easy to see why:

Commitments for 'preventable' crimes

	1811-17*	1821-27*	1831	1834
burglary:	63	61	133	104
housebreaking:	15	20	866	195

* average *per annum:* source, S. C. on *Police of Metropolis,* 1828, *op. cit.*

9 *Tables showing the Number of Criminal Offenders,* P.P. 1839 (177) XXXVIII, p. 243.

10 *Report from the Select Committe on Police Offices,* P.P. 1837-38 (578) XV, p. 487.

11 *Mirror of Parliament,* 1829, vol. 3, p. 1742 and 3 *Hansard,* XLV (1839), 1065.

12 Benjamin Hawes, whig, M.P. for Lambeth, *ibid.,* 1063.

13 S. C. on *Police Offices, op. cit.,* p. 493.

14 *Report from the Select Committee on the Police of the Metropolis,* P.P. 1822 (440) IV, p. 110.

15 2 *Hansard,* XXI (1829), 872-3.

16 The Earl of Malmesbury, *Mirror of Parliament,* 1829, vol. 3, p. 2052.

17 *First Report of the Commissioners appointed to inquire as to the Best Means of establishing an efficient Constabulary Force in the Counties of England and Wales,* P.P. 1839 [169] XIX, p. 15.

18 *Second Report of the Commissioners on County Rates,* P.P. 1836 [58] XXVII, p. 10. Charles Shaw Lefevre was whig M.P. for Hampshire North and became Speaker in 1839.

19 *Constabulary Report, op cit.,* p. 1.

20 *Ibid.,* p. 12.

21 3 *Hansard,* XLIX (1839), 729.

22 3 *Hansard,* L (1839), 116.

23 Henry Halford, tory, M.P. for Leicestershire South, 3 *Hansard,* LIV (1840), 1273. Chadwick also fell back on statistics to try and discredit the experimental system of police in Cheshire. At another point he claimed he could use them to show the inadequacy of commitments as a measure of the prevalence of a particular crime, forgery. But his argument depended on the assumption that the number of banknotes forged reflected the number of crimes of forgery. The Commission was said, with good reason, to have been 'packed,' and appointed to 'manufacture evidence' — see J. Toulmin Smith, *Government by Commissions Illegal and Pernicious* (London, 1849), p. 208. The best critical discussion of the Report remains S.E. Finer's, in *The Life and Times of Sir Edwin Chadwick* (London, 1952), pp. 164-80. Chadwick has a successor in Tobias, who denies official statistics are of use, then uses them, and who singles out alarmist views of crime while passing over others. See. J. J. Tobias, *Crime and Industrial Society in the 19th Century* (New York, 1967), and for an *exposé,* D. Philips, *Crime and Authority in Victorian England* (London, 1977), pp. 16-21.

24 J. Hart, 'Reform of the Borough Police, 1835-56,' *English Historical Review, 70* (1955), 413.

25 Joseph Henley, Conservative M.P. for Oxfordshire, 3 *Hansard,* CXL (1856), 2167-9, and CXLI (1856), 1567-8.

26 J. M. Cobbett, Liberal M.P. for Oldham, 3 *Hansard,* CXL (1856), 2186.

27 *Ibid.,* 2169. Henley's method still seems the best if we want to assess the impact of the new police compared with the old on criminal statistics. But it has not been followed up. Philips' study, which is extremely valuable, is limited to one area, the Black Country. Both Mrs. Hart and Gatrell and Hadden concentrate on national totals — See V.A.C. Gatrell and T. B. Hadden, 'Criminal Statistics and their Interpretation,' in E. A. Wrigley (ed.), *Nineteenth Century Society: essays in the use of quantitative methods for the study of social data* (Cambridge, 1972), pp. 336-96.

28 3 *Hansard,* CXL (1856), 2121-2.

[29] 3 *Hansard,* L (1839), 357.

[30] Thus, Lord Dudley Stuart's complaints against the metropolitan police - 3 *Hansard,* CXXVI (1853), 552, and CXXIX (1853), 1165 - echo Hunt's, 3 *Hansard,* VIII (1831), 495.

[31] William Cobbett, Radical M.P. for Oldham, 3 *Hansard,* XX (1833), 405.

[32] Thomas Duncombe, Radical M.P. for Finsbury, 3 *Hansard,* LXV (1842), 903.

[33] Thomas Attwood, Radical M.P. for Birmingham, 3 *Hansard,* XLIX (1839), 707.

[34] W. J. Fox, Liberal M.P. for Oldham, mentioned strikes and contested elections as 'the chief occasions — he believed the only ones — in which it had been necessary to invoke the aid of the military.' But there had been no strikes of the seriousness 'of late years.' Besides, putting them down by force was not the way to deal with them. Elections 'might be rendered as quiet as a Quaker's meeting' by introducing the ballot and extending the franchise. 3 *Hansard,* CXL (1856), 2163.

[35] *Second Report from the Select Committee on a more Uniform System of Police,* P.P. 1852-53 (715) XXXVI, pp. 253-4.

[36] 3 *Hansard,* IX (1831-32), 4.

[37] *Mirror of Parliament,* 1829, vol. 3, p. 1844.

[38] Thomas Lennard, whig M.P. for Maldon, *ibid.,* p. 1845.

[39] *Ibid.,* p. 1845.

[40] 3 *Hansard,* XLIX (1839), 939.

[41] Hon. W. S. Clements, Viscount Clements, whig M.P. for Leitrim, *ibid.,* 1197. There were many references to Ireland throughout the debate on the English police. In 1830, the tory administration tried but failed to get a Bill through to centralise Ireland's provincial police. Trant saw it as 'part of a settled scheme on the part of the Government to take into its own keeping, and under its own control, the police not only of Ireland, but of England.' 2 *Hansard,* XXIII (1830), 1113. The whigs succeeded in 1836 and at the same time set up a metropolitan police in Dublin on London lines. Peel, first as Chief Secretary of Ireland then as Home Secretary, had worked hard for such a development. The London reform of 1829, according to MacDonagh, applied lessons learnt in Ireland; benthamism, *pace* Mrs. Hart, had nothing to do with it. But one thing is clear. Peel spoke highly of the new Irish police. In 1839, he went as far as he dared to suggest a like one in England. So too in 1854 did Palmerston. See O. MacDonagh, *Early Victorian Government 1830-1870* (London, 1977), pp. 169-71 and 189-93, and G. Broeker, *Rural Disorder and Police Reform in Ireland, 1812-36* (London, 1970). See also below, n. 46.

[42] *First Report from the Select Committee on a more Uniform System of Police,* P.P. 1852-53 (603) XXXVI, p. 21. See also Philips, *op. cit.,* p. 77, for evidence of similar practices in Staffordshire and Wolverhampton.

[43] 3 *Hansard,* XXV (1830), 362. This could have been either Alexander or Francis Baring.

[44] Critchley, *op. cit.,* p. xiii. Silver, in describing the emergence of a 'policed society,' is more cautious. He hints at some sort of link with 'democracy,' but does not spell it out. And like Tobias, he concentrates on alarm at crime. See A. Silver, 'The Demand for Order in Civil Society: A Review of Some Themes in the History of Urban Crime, Police and Riot,' in D. J. Bordua (ed.), *The Police: Six Sociological Essays* (New York, 1967), pp. 1-24.

[45] Peel blamed reformers for hatching out revolutionaries; Russell, in reply, attacked Oastler and the 'tory radicals.' 3 *Hansard,* XLIX (1839), 703-5.

[46] Daniel O'Connell, M.P. for Dublin City and leader of the repealers (the 'Irish party'), *ibid.,* 961. Although O'Connell fell in with radical opposition to a new, centralised police in England, he was full of praise for it in Ireland. An explanation might run as follows. In Ireland, local control of the police meant control by the Protestant gentry *unless,* in the case of the towns, the corporations could be reformed on English lines. But despite the 'good offices' of the whigs, tory opposition ruled this out. O'Connell therefore settled for centralisation. It did not make the police, as he claimed, 'impartial.' Control was still with Protestants, but not with Protestant backwoodsmen. So the danger of provoking a Catholic *jacquerie* — something O'Connell dreaded — seemed less.

[47] 3 *Hansard,* XLIX (1839), 949.

[48] John Fielden, Radical M.P. for Oldham, *ibid.,* 707.

[49] *Ibid.,* 732. See also Halford, a fellow tory, 3 *Hansard,* LIV (1840), 1274:

To place at the commmand of the wealthier inhabitants of any particular district an army of strangers, in order to stifle in their birth all signs of remonstrance or discontent, so far, in his opinion, from strengthening the bonds of society would be to weaken them, alienating the minds of the poor from the rich, exempting the latter from a principal motive to the well-being of the former, and impairing the only true security for peace and order which could rest upon no other foundation than that of a reciprocity of advantage and attachment.

[50] Charles Buller, Radical M.P. for Liskeard, in a letter to Chadwick, quoted by Finer, *op. cit.,* p. 174.

[51] F. C. Mather, *Public Order in the Age of the Chartists* (Manchester, 1959), p. 140.

[52] 2 *Hansard,* XXI (1829), 878 and 880.

[53] *2nd Report on County Rates, op. cit.,* p. 8.

[54] *S. C. on Police Offices, op. cit.,* pp. 464-5. It was a variation of the 1834 committee's argument — see above, n. 8.

[55] The point was made against the metropolitan police long after the first few years of its establishment. See Tufnell, 3 *Hansard* LXIII (1844), 593-4, and Lord Dudley Stuart, 3 *Hansard,* CXXIX (1853), 1164.

[56] 3 *Hansard,* II (1831), 999.

[57] Henry Tufnell, whig, M.P. for Devonport, 3 *Hansard,* LXXIII (1844), 593.

[58] C. C. Western, whig, M.P. for Essex, 2 *Hansard,* XXV (1830), 356 and George Byng, whig M.P. for Middlesex, 3 *Hansard,* I (1831), 580.

[59] 3 *Hansard,* CXLI (1856), 1937-42, debate on clause 10; see especially Henley's comment, *ibid.,* 1940.

[60] 3 *Hansard,* XXXIV (1836), 680, 3 *Hansard,* XXXVI (1837), 415, and 3 *Hansard,* XLIII (1838), 548. Joseph Hume was a leading radical; in 1837, O'Connell installed him as M.P. for Kilkenny City.

[61] *Constabulary Report, op. cit.,* p. 75.

[62] *1st Report of S. C. on Police, op. cit.,* pp. 72 and 80.

[63] *Ibid.,* p. 132, and Martin, 3 *Hansard,* CXLII (1856), 614. The charges were vigorously denied — see 3 *Hansard,* CXLI (1856), 1932-4.

[64] *1st Report of S. C. on Police, op. cit.,* pp. 37, 103, 112, 124, 127. The only witness to defend the boroughs, an ex-mayor of Bath, was hounded by the committee on this point and on the general 'unfitness' of a town council to control the police.

[65] 3 *Hansard,* L (1839), 258.

[66] *Ibid.,* 6.

[67] 3 *Hansard,* CXL (1856), 2162.

[68] 3 *Hansard,* XLIX (1839), 957.

[69] 3 *Hansard,* LIII (1840), 21.

[70] A. W. Beauclerk, radical M.P. for Surrey East, 3 *Hansard,* XXII (1834), 129-30. See also William Ewart, radical M.P. for Liverpool, 3 *Hansard,* XXXVI (1837), 417: Peel 'would have acted more in accordance with the spirit of the age, had he, when he established the metropolitan police, placed the management and control of it under a municipal government.' The demand was revived by London radicals in the 1880s — see P. Thompson, *Socialist, Liberals and Labour, The Struggle for London 1885-1914* (London, 1967), p. 99.

[71] 3 *Hansard,* XLIX (1839), 111.

[72] After 1833, the only inquiry granted in the period was in 1855. See 3 *Hansard,* CXXXIX (1855), 369-71, 452-63, 519-35, 621-3 and 854-5, and *Report of H. M. Commissioners on the alleged disturbance of the public peace in Hyde Park,* P.P. 1856 [2016] XXIII, p. 1.

[73] 3 *Hansard,* CXXXIII (1854), 1267. It was on this occasion that he described the system of police in Ireland and in London as in principle the best. See above, n. 41.

[74] For the five division lists used on the Birmingham Police, see 3 *Hansard,* XLIX (1839), 1198-9, and L (1839), 10, 154-5, 213 and 248. Only one member cross-voted and has been omitted from both totals. H. Warburton, a whig, was teller for the noes in the first division and voted with the ayes on the second. For the division

Party Politics

lists on the Manchester Police, see 3 *Hansard*, L (1839), 259-60. For the division list on the National Petition, see 3 *Hansard*, XLIX (1839), 274-7. In this and subsequent tables, I have based party affiliation on the relevant editions of C. R. Dod's *Parliamentary Companion* (London, 1839 and 1856). I have also used M. Stenton, *Who's Who of the British Members of Parliament: vol. 1 - 1832-85* (Hassocks, 1976), which is compiled from Dod. However, Dod gave repealers as either whigs or radicals, and I have used MacIntyre's list to identify them. See A. MacIntyre, *The Liberator, Daniel O'Connell and the Irish Party, 1830-1847* (London, 1965), pp. 302-7.

75 D. Fraser, *Urban Politics in Victorian England* (Leicester, 1976), pp. 99-102. Fraser brings out the complexity of local controversy surrounding the police. It was part of a jigsaw that included gas, water, paving, poor relief.

76 For division lists, see 3 *Hansard*, L (1839), 7-8, 117-8, 355-6, 358, and 3 *Hansard*, LIV (1840), 1277-9. The defeat of the proviso, making clear that parish constables might still be appointed, did not mean they were not to be. For example, there were parish constables in Staffordshire until at least 1865. See Philips, *op. cit.*, p. 59. The old system of police, according to Philips, was not as defective as standard criticisms make out.

77 The backbencher was T. L. Hodges, M.P. for Kent West. See 3 *Hansard*, LIII (1840), 19. He did not vote with the tories but abstained.

78 Critchley, *op. cit.*, p. 89. This counts Suffolk and Sussex each as two counties, Yorkshire as three, Lincolnshire as one, and excludes the Liberty of Peterborough.

79 J. Hart, 'The County and Borough Police Act, 1856,' *Public Administration*, XXXIV (1956), p. 407.

80 To identify Liberal-Conservatives, I have used the lists of Peelites and Independent Conservatives in J. B. Conacher, *The Peelites and the Party System 1846-52* (Newton Abbot, 1972), pp. 233-5, and *The Aberdeen Coalition 1852-1855, A Study in Mid-Nineteenth-Century Party Politics* (Cambridge, 1968), pp. 556-9. See also W. D. Jones and A. B. Erickson, *The Peelites 1846-1857* (Ohio, 1972). The category, 'Liberal-Conservative,' indicates an important tendency in the politics of the time. It does not describe a hard and fast grouping. The same ought to be said of the other party labels. Three repealers voted, all for the Bill, and I have included them with the Liberals.

81 For the division list on the ballot, see 3 *Hansard*, CXLII (1856), 450-1, on the Police Bill, 3 *Hansard*, CXL (1856), 2188-90.

82 I have based the distinction between old and new police counties on Critchley's list, cited above, n. 78. 'Counties' include constituencies that did not contain or did not consist of corporate boroughs with a population of 5,000 or more according to the 1851 census. 'London' refers to the constituencies of London, Westminster, Marylebone, Tower Hamlets, Lambeth, Finsbury, Southwark, Greenwich and Middlesex. Information on population and corporate status is taken from C. R. Dod (2nd edition, 1853, reprinted, and edited with an introduction by H. J. Hanham), *Electoral Facts from 1832 to 1853* (Brighton, 1972). Information on social background is taken from Dod's *Parliamentary Companion*. The category 'gentry' is made up of (i) *nobility* - Irish peers and close agnates of U. K. peers, (ii) *gentry* - baronets, knights, landowners, army and naval officers, sons of high ranking ecclesiastics, (iii) *gentry-business* - barristers, chairman of railway companies, *etc.*, or persons with some other stated business connection, who have the characteristics of (i) or (ii) but are *not* included in them. The category 'businessmen' is made up of barristers, solicitors, chairmen of railway companies, *etc.*, without any apparent 'gentry' qualification. Obviously, both categories must be treated with caution. However, Aydelotte calculates that the 'peerage, baronetage and landed gentry' made up 71% of the Parliament of 1841-47 (or 80% on a wider definition); I calculate that of those voting on the 1856 Bill, 78% were 'gentry'. Southgate calculates that on a strict

definition 'aristocrates' made up 20% of the Liberal party in the Parliament of 1852-57; I calculate a 'noble' Liberal vote of 23%. Vincent calculates that 'businessmen' made up 30% of Liberal M.P.'s between 1859 and 1874; I calculate a 'business' Liberal vote of 26%. These figures, of course, are only straws in the wind. But at least they point in the same direction. See W. O. Aydelotte, 'The House of Commons in the 1840's,' *History*, XXXIX (1954), 254, D. Southgate, *The Passing of the Whigs 1832-1886* (London, 1962), p. 423, and J. Vincent, *The Formation of the Liberal Party 1857-1868* (London, 1966), p. 3.

83 That is, each variable has an indepenent effect on voting. This can be demonstrated by standardising relationships.

84 *Radzinowicz, op. cit.*, p. v.

85 K. Marx (ed. F. Engels, tr. S. Moore and E. Aveling), *Capital*, vol. 1 (London, 1970), Chapter X, 'The Working-Day.' Aydelotte's analysis leads him to suggest that 'economic interest, as an explanation of votes on the "ten hours" question, seems of little use.' See 'The House of Commons in the 1840's,' *op. cit.*, pp. 261-2.

86 For a summary of such arguments, see W. O. Aydelotte 'Parties and Issues in Early Victorian England,' *The Journal of British Studies*, V (1966), 95-114.

87 *Ibid.* See also Aydelotte, 'Voting Patterns in the British House of Commons in the 1840s,' *Comparative Studies in Society and History*, V (1963), 134-63, and 'The Conservative and Radical Interpretations of Early Victorian Legislation,' *op. cit.*

88 Aydelotte, 'Voting Patterns,' *op. cit.*, p. 159.

89 See M. Cowling, *1867 D'Israeli, Gladstone and Revolution, The Passing of the Second Reform Bill* (Cambridge, 1967). Still, the Act of 1867 did not go very far, while even the reform of 1884 was less radical than it seemed. This was largely due to the distribution of seats, which meant that votes in different types of constituency were of very unequal weight, and to the complicated system of franchise and registration. Thus in 1911, some 40% of all adult males were not on the electoral register. See N. Blewett, 'The franchise in the United Kingdom 1885-1918,' *Past and Present*, 32 (1965), 27-56.

90 Silver's account of a 'policed society,' although a necessary corrective to simplistic ideas of normative integration, does not give enough attention to politics. Tholfsen brings out the importance of the radical elite in harnessing popular loyalties to 'bourgeois democracy.' Radical control of the working class meant leading the campaign for reform while praying conservatives would not dig in and fight. To this we might add that radicals were to become casualties of their own success. Conservatives learnt mass politics was a game they too could play. See Silver, *op. cit.*, and T. R. Tholfsen, 'The Transition to Democracy in Victorian England,' *International Review of Social History*, VI (1961), 226-48.

91 See MacDonagh, *op. cit.*, pp. 133-61.

92 Support for the National Petition was well to the 'left,' and support for the ballot somewhat to the 'left' of the same scale. See Aydelotte, 'Parties and Issues,' *op. cit.*, p. 107.

93 Liberals voted 94% for, 6% against, Conservatives 58% for, 42% against. See the division list on going into committee on the Bill, 3 *Hansard*, XCVIII (1848), 741-3.

94 C. N. Newdegate, Conservative M.P. for Warwickshire North, 3 *Hansard*, CXXXV (1854), 1141.

95 Thus Philips writes of the Black Country:

> The evidence never suggests a society in danger of disintegrating under the strain; nor does it suggest that the maintenance of law and order was on the verge of breaking down at any point in the period under consideration.

op. cit., p.284.

96 W. R. Miller, *Cops and Bobbies: Police Authority in New York and London, 1830-1870* (Chicago, 1977), pp. 14-15.

97 R. Walters, *The Establishment of the Bristol Police Force* (Bristol, 1975).

[6]

FROM COP HISTORY TO SOCIAL HISTORY:
THE SIGNIFICANCE OF THE POLICE IN AMERICAN HISTORY

Americans have been writing about their urban police for over one hundred years. Much of the writing has been neither critical nor very deep, but the original fascination with the police runs through it all. In the past fifteen years historians have examined police with greater care and detail than ever before. Yet, though they have moved closer to a really striking analysis of the police, there remains much work of synthesis and generalization to be done. Some of the best work on the police fails to locate them within the context of urban institutions. Re-conceptualizing their organizational shape, development, and role within their urban environment assists us in better understanding both the police and the policed. This article sketches some suggestions toward forming such a synthesis and makes some empirical generalizations which are intended to stimulate and help define a provocative set of research problems. The intention is to keep the research lively and to steer the topic away from becoming a narrow specialization unrelated to broader problems in U.S. history.[1]

Section I: Recent Historiography

The historiography of U.S. urban government languished between the progressive era and the 1970s — a hiatus best symbolized by the gap between the publication of the second and third volumes of Ernest Griffith's history of U.S. city government — volume two appeared in 1928 and volume three in 1974.[2] In the interim, most exciting substantive work had been done on municipal reformers, with an emphasis on reformers rather than on municipal.[3] Literature on police often reflects the general historiographical interest in reformers and their impact by focusing on attempts to change police. This focus may best be seen in Fogelson's *Big City Police,* which is essentially an analysis of police reform, rather than of the police themselves.[4] Of course, had historians working with urban police wanted to place them more in the context of urban governmental organization, as opposed to urban reform, they would have been hard-pressed, simply because Griffith's muck-raking work did not offer much description or analysis within which to place police as an organization. But recent research in the history of the city as a municipality has begun to change the historiographic landscape, providing those interested in police organization and behavior with a perspective and the beginnings of a substantive analysis. This research starts with Frisch's work on Springfield, Massachusetts, continues through the work of Fox on urban accounting, Teaford on the legal status of cities within the various state governments, and into newer, quantiative work on urban fiscal behavior and political economy, especially that of the Hollingsworths and McDonald.[5]

This recent research in what might be called municipal history has both a perspective and substantive material to offer the historian working with police. Teaford, for instance, dramatically rejects the notion, found in writings of progressives like Griffith and perpetuated by many others, that city governments were powerless legal orphans whose prospects fluctuated at the whim of ignorant state legislators. Instead, Teaford shows that until at least the 1920s the very ignorance of the legislators worked to give the cities effective *carte blanche* in deciding those questions affected by legislation. With only a handful of exceptions, Teaford found that the legislative committees dealing with urban affairs simply followed the expert advice of urban representatives or of city officials themselves. His point makes intuitive sense: much of what cities had to request was of a detailed and technical nature, and to be actively anti-city a rural legislator would have to become an expert in each specific problem. Resistance to and limitation of city power in the legislatures came in the 1920s with the rise of suburban municipalities which no longer depended on central city government. Even with these competing municipalities, the major restriction on city-related legislation was of annexation and expansion powers which threatened adjacent municipalities. Such legislation can be read simply as mediation of inter-urban disputes.

Teaford has shown us the need to be alert to the strength and importance of city government as an actor, rather than as a prostrate victim of whim, ignorance, and prejudice. By implication, this is the way we should try to conceive the police — an organization of fiscal importance within a municipal government with rather independent power. This perspective represents a shift from that usually taken, which envisions the police as an organization active in its behavior, but passive and unimaginative in its role as an organization within city government. For in many respects, and particularly in scale, city government was an innovative actor in the changing organizational world of the nineteenth and early twentieth century. Rather than thinking only of police corruption, incompetence, participation in factional politics, brutality, and the like, we must stand at a different location and also see the police as a part of the inchoate but creative actions of city dwellers, inventing a formal and bureaucratic world of municipal services and controls hitherto unforeseen. This angle of vision will help remind us that uniformed urban police were nineteenth-century innovations, that New York City, not to mention London, had functioned without a uniformed police when it had a population of nearly a million people, apparently with no enormous crises of order.

The research of Fox on municipal accounting shows how the very way in which fiscal accounts were kept by cities and, in the twentieth century, by the federal government, mirrored the confusion of categories created by the new municipal organizations. It took a major effort of national reformers to separate fiscal accounts into capital and operating expenditures. This change is important to historians of police for two reasons. First, it demonstrated a conscious recognition that the very urban organizational forms were of a new order, one which could no longer be accounted for as had the cities of early nineteenth century. And the police were very much a part of this new form, a part, incidentally, which used mainly operating as opposed to capital expenditures. The second reason this rethinking of urban accounting is important to the historian of the police is that in creating the new system of accounting, city fiscal reformers laid the basis for the destruction of a wonderful system of police record publication, usually found in the annual reports of the chief to the mayor or city council.[6] For over a half century, police departments dutifully noted everything, or nearly everything, which they officially did, endlessly chronicling the behavior of their part of the emerging municipal government. In a literal sense, the discovery of the fiscal significance of city government took the formal record keeping out of the hands of the actors and laid the basis for the eventual nationalization of reporting on municipal topics. Thus, in the second decade of the twentieth century, the time-honored form of police reports began to disappear from city to city, often to be

FROM COP HISTORY TO SOCIAL HISTORY 577

replaced with slickly printed brochures designed to serve the same purpose as corporate annual reports and about as useful.

The annual reporting of municipal governments as fiscal entities has begun to attract the attention of historians who utilize the time series of fiscal data as an indicator of urban behavior. McDonald, for instance, uses fiscal data to ask just what the city government of San Francisco did and to compare different political regimes. The Hollingsworths use the data to develop behavioral models of middle-sized cities, trying to classify cities as different types of actors. Work of this kind should also have a substantive and methodological impact on the study of urban police. First, as more cities are analyzed, we may see expenditure patterns and typologies which will account for policing differences and developments. Second, methodologically, the analysis of fiscal time series suggests that the same kind of data can be used to analyze police, their behavior, their relative position in city government, and their variation in position between regions and over time.

Because the history of the police is so much a part of the history of the city, it is essential that the history of the city provide the first and most dominant framework within which to analyze the police. Unfortunately, until recently, much of the social history of the city did not illuminate even the basic shape of the urban container within which the police acted. However, the recent work on urban government, of which just a sample has been cited here, has begun to give us a picture of an independent, active, emerging form of organization. This picture urges us to take a broad and rather basic approach, asking how the police spent their time, comparing their fiscal status to other segments of government, and establishing simple, baseline statistics.

We must describe the broad quantitative dimension of police location, dates of emergence, the size and shape of police behavioral activities, and answer the classic and basic historical questions of where, when, how many and how much change. It may come as a surprise to some that these simple questions had not been very thoroughly answered long ago, but the general focus of prior researchers on case studies or on problems which did not lend themselves to such basic issues, such as reform, have left these questions to languish.

The case studies have established the fundamental scenarios of the creation of uniformed police in enough cities so that we may detect the modal characteristics in this urban innovation process, and these similar characteristics can be used to compare cities. Both Lane and Richardson show how the rather lengthy process which occurred before the police of Boston and New York had been transformed varied between the two cities, making it imperative to focus a national comparison on one consistent and regular part of the transformation process.[7] There are several reasons to choose the uniform as the decisive moment. The uniform finalized the unique position of the police as a semi-military presence in the city; the uniform declared the constant availability of the police; the uniform almost always came at the same time which the command hierarchy of the organization was completed; the uniform symbolized and was often coterminous with a unified police (as opposed to separate day and night police, for instance); the police themselves saw the uniform as an important, if controversial statement of their purpose; the police uniforms led to the introduction of uniforms in other civil occupations in the United States, indicating their innovative nature even outside of the police changes; finally, the switch to uniforms can be consistently, if not easily, dated.

New York City uniformed its police first, in 1853, after an earlier short-lived attempt in the 1840s. The cities of Savannah, perhaps Albany, Charleston, Jersey

City, Philadelphia, Baltimore, San Francisco, Chicago, Washington, Boston, Cincinnati, Manchester, New Hampshire, and Utica, New York, in that order, complete the list of those cities which followed in the 1850s. The 1860s and 1870s saw a deluge of smaller and smaller cities uniforming their police. Denver, for instance, uniformed its police in 1874, when its population was less than 17,000. The timing and patterns in this sequence will be pursued further below, but several preliminary observations should be made here.

Clearly the major metropolises took the initiative in the creation of the uniformed police, New York and Boston explicitly imitating London. The early innovators not in the group of leading metropolises had two or three characteristics which account for what may be termed their premature change to the uniformed police. First, some of the early innovators were virtual suburbs of New York City — Jersey City, for instance. Other cities were regional centers with many of the chracteristics of primate cities — Charleston or San Francisco, for instance. Finally, many of the early innovators were southern, slave cities, where the police were very much in the military mode of slave control. Richard Wade, for instance, has asserted that southern cities had virtual standing armies in the form of police to control slaves.[8] This thesis deserves more research, for the early uniforming of non-slaveholding San Francisco's police suggests that southern cities may have innovated more because of their roles as regional centers rather than for slave control alone. Nevertheless, this sequential list of cities suggests that the timing of innovation in urban police followed an important basic pattern in the urban network, determined primarily by size, but also heavily influenced by region. Moreover, the pattern showns the importance of a nested set of urban hierarchies, with London the central example for the largest cities, radiating from this a national American network, and within this several regional networks.[9] Thus, even in the matter of locating and dating the emergence of the uniformed police, the history of cities and their systematic relationships maintains an underlying importance.

Once we have located police in time and space, we need to describe their size and how it changed as the organizations became entrenched in city government and matured. One measure of this dimension is simply the total number of police personnel per 1,000 city population. This measure very nearly approximates an expenditure index, for salaries took up most of the police budget. Also, it has the advantage of offering comparability with modern data. Did the police get created at a modern strength, or did they grow? If they grew, when did they grow, and why?

In 1977, the mean number of police personnel per 1,000 population for all U.S. cities over 10,000 persons was 2.67.[10] This figure varied with city size in nearly linear fashion, as might be expected, with values ranging from 4.12 for central cities over a million down to 2.08 for places between 25,000 and 10,000. For comparative purposes, a better sense of police per capita distribution can be gained by controlling for metropolitan status: central cities had a mean figure of 3.02 personnel per 1,000 — as contrasted to the substantially less 2.02 for suburban cities. Over a century before, for a sample of twenty cities with populations over 50,000, the mean figure for the decade of 1860-1870 for fledgling police departments varied between a low of 1.4 and a high of 1.65. If we take the mean of these means as about 1.5, we can conclude that police personnel per capita increased somewhere between 35 to 100 percent over the past century. The amount of drama one wishes to accord this change is up to the analyst: while real, I find the difference to be rather small. The 1860s value is, for instance, virtually

FROM COP HISTORY TO SOCIAL HISTORY 579

the same as the figure for the group of cities with the lowest per capita police personnel figure for 1976, cities in the west north-central U.S. with a population between 25,000 and 50,000.[11] Moreover, the advent of these forty hour work week significantly reduced person hours on patrol, for nineteenth and early twentieth century police typically worked sixty hours or more per week.[12]

When graphed over the period 1860-1920, the shape of the mean police personnel per 1,000 in the same twenty cities shows a decline until 1882, followed by a steady rise to a 1909 peak of 2.1, and a slight decline to 1920. In other words, the graph shows a basic rise with two slight downturns. The rising trend is consistent with the somewhat larger mean size of police personnel in the 1970s compared to a century earlier. It is also consistent with and largely caused by the growth in city size over the period 1860-1920, because larger cities tend to have more officers per capita.

The mechanism of the causal sequence has not yet been explored and should prove important. Because departmental size is legislatively mandated in absolute numbers, not in per capita rates, simple maintenance of the status quo required legislative action. Were police department requests for more officers automatically granted, or was this a subject of continual political struggle? How did the great density of central cities turn into greater police per capita? Did large places have more legislative influence or was there a shared perception of the "need" for more police per capita in major cities?

When the annual change in police per 1,000,000 population is regressed against the annual change in urban population for the 1860-1920 period, the R^2 is .86, with a b coefficient of .000091.[13] This indicates that while a very high population of the police growth in strength can be accounted for by the denser policing of large cities, the actual multiple was quite low — a change of 10,000 persons yielding one more officer per million persons. The modern coefficient, which can only be roughly estimated from cross-sectional rather than change data, appears to be similar but to be distorted upward by the much more intensive policing of the five central cities over a million.[14] (Note the implication for our era as central cities lose population and independent municipalities multiply — personnel should decrease per capita, simply from the decrease in the mean size of municipalities. Or, perhaps the ages of cities offset this tendency, with older places maintaining their higher ratios.) The only other data to compare with this sample are for both urban and rural places, over the period 1910 to 1970: these data show a continuous increase in the ratio, with the exception of the depression decade of the 1930s.[15] For the whole United States, the percent increase in police officers per 1,000 population was: 19%, 1910-1920; 34%, 1920-1930; no increase, 1930-1940; 10%, 1940-1950; 10%, 1950-1960, 28%, 1960-1970. These data inflate the actual city based component of the increase, because they mask both the rapidly increasing proportion of the population in cities and the more dense policing in large central cities. Presumably, if the twentieth century increase could be adjusted to account for the growth of city size and percent of the population in the cities, we would find a much more modest increase, one even less than that of the modest increase of the twenty sample cities followed from 1860 to 1920.

Several conclusions may be drawn from these various quantitative hints. First, the major change occurred at the moment of the creation of the modern police. The transformation symbolized by the uniform was indeed a transformation, one which set an enduring precedent. Second, although police size relative to the population has increased, a large if unknown proportion of this increase can be accounted for simply because of the increased size and age of cities. Third, maintenance of the departmental status quo required constant augmentation of police departments as cities grew. Fourth, the formulation of urban police occurred within a national and even international context of change in municipal government.

The significance of the basic transformation signalled by the creation of the uniformed police leads to an examination of demands made on them. Demands on police came from elected city officials or politically powerful persons, from within the police themselves, and from the various groups and classes of the public, either acting through political representatives or autonomously. The context of demands is much more difficult to describe than the contexts of urban development or measurable components of policing, for its manifestations include public statements, private actions of political persons, that almost hidden job culture of rank and file police officers, and most nebulous, the demands of the public. Here, case studies provide clues. Miller's work comparing the London and New York police comes the closest to analyzing demands on police, for he has explored the public and private records in as much depth as possible.[16] He shows the origins of the feeling of personal responsibility for punishment, or justice, within the organization and structure of the police. Only the research of Watts on St. Louis promises to have a greater range and depth of records.[17] Watts' work should also provide insight to the job culture of early twentieth-century police, an area which has been mainly explored by Levine and Wilentz.[18] Levine's work shows that by the 1890s New York City rank and file police had a clearly defined job-consciousness which had the important consequence, even then, of creating a resistance to change and an organizational inertia, a phenomenon which has persisted for almost one hundred years. Other work, that of Johnson, Haller, Haring, and Schneider, has helped describe the impact of changing crime patterns and of governmental demands. All of this analysis suggests that from the last third of the nineteenth century on the police had strongly internalized and informally implemented demands which gave them a feeling of sole responsibility for containing crime and disorder, a feeling which structured their self-perceptions and often set them in conflict with public demands.

As the decade of the 1970s has shown, public demands on police have been difficult to voice and even more difficult to implement when they run contrary to intertia and job cultures of police departments. Not all public demands on police are so controversial as those which have motivated efforts to create civilian review boards, but even less controversial demands have run into resistance as the reference to lost children, below, will show. The major point to be made concerning public demands on police is that, whether the demands are for disarming, for civilian control, for less corruption, or for a "law and order" type of justice, no one asks for dis-establishment. The demands are for more and more fair service, for different kinds and qualities of basically the same service. This reminds us of the unqualified success of the police in establishing themselves as a fundamental municipal service.

Three more conceptual frameworks for examining the police have been developed in the recent literature. They are the social control thesis, the notions of order and disorder, and the idea that criminal behavior itself influences the development of the police. Although the social control interpretation of much social history has been misused and too often substituted for a more careful analysis, it remains exciting and an important element to consider in any history of social organizations.[20] First used to analyze varioius benevolent groups and reformers, the social control theorists discovered that underlying religious benevolence, or social welfare programs, was a conscious or semi-conscious intent to control

FROM COP HISTORY TO SOCIAL HISTORY 581

rather than to aid the afflicted. That is, the impulse to aid and assist those in need masked a deeper attempt to force them to act in ways determined by the benevolent. This discovery could account for the motives of the benevolent, explain apparent contradictions in aid programs, and show how hegemony could be subtly established and discreetly preserved.

Of course, the control goals of police are hardly discreet or subtle, and this might be why only a few historians concerned with social control have investigated the establishment and behavior of nineteenth-century police.[21] These exceptions have argued that police were established to control immigrants or workers and that they worked directly for the labor management needs of local capitalists. Although these arguments have found few direct rebuttals, many other historians have established that the police-labor-capital relationship exhibited considerable variation from place to place.[22] In certain ways, the uniformed police have proved less amenable to social control strategies in favor of one class or special group than other social organizations, for police visibility makes them somewhat open to observation and vulnerable to complaints of bias. Because their role is known, demands of fairness can be made upon them. This does not mean the police have in fact been fair, but it shows why less visible arms of city police — secret police, plain clothes operatives, or other special groups — must function as social control agents where there is conflict. Today most police activity involves consensual social control — traffic law enforcement, apprehension of felony suspects and the like — and the conflicts occur over relatively limited substantive areas — drug enforcement — or over overtly biased and wrongful activities — the Chicago convention in 1968.

In the nineteenth century the police provided a broad range of welfare services, including the provision of overnight shelter to the homeless and indigent. This range of services gave the police considerable scope for class-oriented social control activities. It is this class-oriented, if consensual, social control which is of historical interest. Although the police in every city did not necessarily act at the whims of local capitalists, they did take care of the "wandering armies" of workers. They formed an integral part of a system which saw industrial workers leave the cities in the summer for farm work and return in the winter for day labor and industrial work. The social control was often a positive rather than a negative or repressive effort on the police's part. In addition to this form of social control, Schneider's work has reinforced our understanding of how police cooperated and made emerging shopping and commercial areas attractive, as they sometimes ignored requests of neighborhoods for similar kinds of order maintenance and vice control.[24] Both of these forms of police behavior preserved the status quo and spatial separation, but in neither case was there the continuous repressive stature implied by the social control perspective. Thus, the social control perspective helps us gain an analytic tool to understand some of police activities, but it does not provide as powerful an explanatory device as one might expect.

Another conceptual framework which has some promise for examining the police and their role is that of social order and disorder. Unlike anthropologists, who mainly consider order and disorder to be perceptual categories, historians accept the concept of order as reflective of reality. Even though we use the term with often wildly different definitions, there seems to be a loosely acceptable set of observable characteristics around which these definitions hover. These include objective predictability, consensus or structured conflict, consistency in rules and behaviors, and consensually defined decorum. Subjective order includes perceptions of rationality, predictability, a modicum of fairness, and safety. These definitions are not value free and can be seen as layered — that is, a society can have deep disorder and surface order. In spite of the complexities of the notion of order, we can see that police in nineteenth-century cities, among other things, used their power to preserve or create order, particularly in public places. The actual public orderliness of cities provides the daily working context for the uniformed police.

If we have a "willing suspension of disbelief" for a moment, some arrest data for drunk and disorderly conduct can give us a powerfully suggestive insight into the order context of policing. The rate of arrests per 1,000 population by urban police between 1860 and the present decreased from over 45 to around 15.[25] With the one major exception of the brief period immediately following World War II, there has been a steady and unmistakable trend downward for the past 120 years. For whatever reason or reasons that caused this shift in arrest behavior — the rise of private drinking space, changed perceptions, use of the automobile, urban regimentation or cooling of the earth — its decline demonstrates a clearly changed context of urban policing, a decrease in urban disorder. This decrease has affected the day-to-day life of the police officer. A century ago over half of the officer's arrests were for order related offenses. Today only one arrest in five is for an order related offense. The first uniformed police officers entered a city that was a good deal less orderly than that of today. They had predictable physical contact with drunks, disorderly persons and public disorder. In other words, the daily public context for uniformed police was decidely rougher than that of today.

The causes of the increase in order are too complicated to account for here, but the increase does show that the daily priorities of policing have changed dramatically. With this change, criminal behavior has gradually assumed much greater importance. Perhaps it is because of this slowly increased public order that today we automatically associate the police with crime, a perception which obscures our basic understanding of the police. One of the explicit functions of the newly uniformed police in the 1850s was to be the prevention of crime as well as disorderliness. James W. Gerard, who studied the London police before making his well-known recommendations for creating the New York police, had a touching belief that the sight of a uniform would strike a deterrent fear into the hearts of would be criminals.[26] Thus, the uniformed police would prevent crime rather than trying to catch criminals after their offenses. Perhaps some of the contemporary resistance to the modernized police may have come from the absurdity of this argument, and the ultimate pervasiveness of the innovation may have come fron a realization of the many other benefits of a modern police organization. In any case, the concept of crime control was definitely in the heads of early police innovators: it was also behind the forming of departmental detective bureaus, and prompted the late nineteenth and early twentieth-century creation of a national identification bureau.[27] But the assessment of criminal behavior as an adequate interpretive framework within which to place the police remains elusive and difficult. Johnson has made the only major attempt to do so, and while interesting for other reasons, the actual or even implied impact of criminal behavior and its development on the police is the least successful part of his work.[28]

Implicitly, crucial aspects of criminal behavior are quantitative, yet measurement of the phenomenon presents a classic difficulty of positive social science, and the data referred to here should only be seen as suggestive. During the period 1860-1920, for the twenty largest U.S. cities, arrest rates for felony crimes declined or stayed relatively stable until the turn of the century, then begin to rise.[29] Homicide arrest rates exhibited a similar pattern, though the upturn came in the mid-1880s. Lane, in his study of violent death in Philadelphia, found the homicide rate upturn to be at a later date, in the early decades of the twentieth century.[30] Gurr's work on western Europe found a similar upturn in felony crimes in the late nineteenth century.[31] Although there is a disagreement on dates among these three studies which may come from the varying methodologies, the identified pattern is similar enough to suggest that the underlying trend has some basis in fact. Whatever the causal matrix, the amount of criminal behavior with which the police were ostensibly to deal has changed since their mid-nineteenth-century introduction. In the nineteenth century the rate seems to have been steady or declining steadily, even though urban disorder was high by modern standards. Cities were more disorderly than dangerous. In the twentieth century, on the other hand, the cities have become more orderly but also more dangerous. It is mainly this changed twentieth-century aspect of criminal behavior which has given the charge of police to deal with crime its public importance.

Section II: A Developmental Overview

By 1920 four major transformations of urban police in America had occurred. Two of these involved the spread of the innovation of the police and the unintended consequences of this innovation, and the other two involved the focus and function of police behavior. The introduction and spread of the uniformed police has been usually handled by historians in a prticularistic manner, only partly because of the case study nature of their research. Most have accepted one of three arguments for the innovation: (1) the police were created in response to rising crime; (2) the police were created in response to urban disorder and riots; (3) the police were created to control the growing immigrant and industrial working classes. The first two arguments are empirical but unverifiable — did crime or disorder increase prior to the introduction of the police? No one has tried to show this was a general situation across many cities immediately prior to their creation of the police. Instead, most case studies show that prior crimes or disorders made up a part of the arguments of the police innovators. Only Levett has approached the problem systematically, using data on changing proportions of immigrants to support his argument that cities created police to control a new immigrant population.[32] His argument, however interesting, founders on the cities which did not have even large populations yet still created uniformed police — Denver, for instance, which was hardly a city when it created its police.

An approach suggested by the basic urban perspective on policing holds more promise and is simpler. In the United States, uniformed police were simply the first of other urban services to be formalized along organizational models provided by London, the seed city for innovation in early nineteenth-century urban governance. The underlying communications pattern which determined the diffusion of other kinds of information and innovation through the urban nework determined the speed and direction of the diffusion of the police. The literature on diffusion of innovations in geography and sociology emphasizes one of two basic diffusion models, one with a constant or point source and the other where each new innovator in turn becomes a new source of information, the contagious diffusion model.[33] Had London continued to be the only model for policing, U.S. cities would have been following a point source process, but in fact each new city became a model for imitation by other cities, so the spread of uniformed police in the United States followed the contagion model.[34] In fact, the diffusion of police paralleled the mid-nineteenth century paths for the diffusion of cholera epidemics, an ironic verification of the contagion process.[35] This pattern does not

584   journal of social history

mean that the diffusion of the uniformed police innovation came about automatically or that other causal factors did not enter in. It reminds us that the police were a part of changing municipal governments and avoids an explanatory account for their spread which needlessly emphasizes vague forces or localistic explanations. As pointed out above, not all cities conformed to either model's predictions: the south got its police too early, as did some suburban cities. But the burden of analyzing these variations should be on explaining deviations from the diffusion model's predictions, those places which truly deviated meriting intense local study.

The second transformation of U.S. police came as an unintended consequence of their introduction. Never before had an urban service provided easy public access and centralized communication. Urbanites for the first time could have direct contact with easily visible, regularly available, and authoritative city workers. They immediately began to place on the police demands unrelated to crime control, but more reflective of other urban problems. As a result, police busily reported health hazards and open sewers, took censuses, gave advice to travellers, and returned lost children to their parents. This last activity gives a reasonable indicator of the quickly growing demands on police, for shortly after each city reorganized and uniformed its police, the rates of lost children returned to parents began to soar as urban people found a new ear for their demands for service and public order.[36] Whether these demands resulted in the continuing increase in public order is untestable, but it is clear that the problem of lost children found a solution unmatched by previous methods.

The third transformation was of police behavior relating to social control and crime. The new police, in providing urban services, were either formally charged with or quickly assumed the burden of temporary care for the destitute. Not only did police distribute food and coal in the winter, but they regularly took in lodgers, who sometimes slept on crude bunks, other times in cells or simply on hard hallway floors.[37] While an unintended consequence of their introduction, the police did end up actively engaged in a kind of social control, focused on the care and management of what was then called the "dangerous class." This class control did not involve indoctrination — lodgers gave police their names, ages, occupations and homes, but only so the police could identify them and keep repeaters from staying over three to five days. Lodgers slept on crude beds and the police rousted them out at daybreak, thus minimizing the time and effort they spent on lodgers. The lack of indoctrination and the lack of discrimination against "unworthy" aid recipients ended up becoming one of the main complaints against police lodging from social reformers who were more interested in social control.

The transformation of the class management of police came towards the end of the nineteenth century when the police function began to shift from class control to crime control. A multiple regression analysis of arrest rates and lodger rates as determined by police strength shows a shift in emphasis occurring in the period 1890-1920, when variation in policing no longer produced a variation in lodgers or in crimes of public order, but did begin to affect the arrest rates for felony crimes.[38] Not too surprisingly the degree of the statistical relationship declined significantly, for while police could easily control the production of public order, which included the more devious public behavior of the "dangerous class" but also an apparent upturn in felony crime, this transformation in the focus and function of the police makes sense and also helps account for the fourth transformation of policing.

The formal national communication networks established by police chiefs in the 1890s and the decline of the local management of the "dangerous class" signaled the fourth transformation of police, which came in the context of the new police focus on crime control.[39] Symbolized by the permanent formation of the organization which eventually became the International Association of Chiefs of Police (the Police Chiefs Union) in 1893, this fourth transformation responded to the need for systematic information transfer from one city to another. For several years the IACP floundered with various schemes to create a national identification program which would help one police department communicate the positive identification of one person with another department. Catching offenders outside the boundaries of one department without information coordination was difficult, and prior to the National Bureau of Identification's efforts, such publications as the *Police Gazette* had been the major source of inter-city information. The growth of the IACP, its identification system, and its continued efforts to get congressional funding created the precedent for nationally coordinated police with a focus almost completely limited to crime. The fourth transformation, like the urban network within which it was embedded, has never really been completed in a tidy fashion. Instead its complexity parallels that of the federal/municipal government relationship. One can predict that future changes in the structure of municipal government will contain or be preceded by changes in the police organization. As the previous model of urban government proved durable and flexible enough to last into the mid-nineteenth century, it may well be that the present mode of uniformed police and the municipal government within which they exist may be around a long time.

Section III: Further Research Problems

The picture sketched above is probably controversial in some aspects and is certainly incomplete. In this concluding section of the article I wish to indicate avenues in need of further exploration. The nineteenth-century decline and the twentieth-century rise of felony crime needs to be tested as an hypothesis, using more rigorous and systematic measurements than any so far.[40] Lane's use of coroner's records for Philadelphia, for instance, suggests the potential for a cross-city study of death by violence. Did it really decline in the nineteenth century? If such a curve can be established more precisely and surely, then its causal origins will also need a rigorous exploration. Several appealing but ad hoc explanations have been advanced, but none has been systematically tested. Thus, if the curve is real, the problem cries for an approach which tests the several competing hypothesis. Does the curve really chart the advent of industrialism and subsequent post-industrialism, as claimed by Lane? Or is the curve more an artifact of some other deeper (or shallower) urban change?

Or, perhaps, is a crime rate itself too dependent a variable to even try to analyze in a rigorously defined time-series? A reasonable argument can be made that there are so many independent variables whose relationships may be non-linear and inter-related in unspecified ways, variables which affect different offense rates differently, that the analysis of offense rates is bound to be speculative and untestable. When considering demographic variables, cultural variables, economic variables, opportunity variables, deterrence variables, and random perturbances with unknown effects — wars and depressions, both of which moved millions across the country, affecting both the denominators of rates and the actual number of offenses — the measurement and modeling problems may be overwhelming. Of course, if historic crime rates are not open to causal analysis, and if the criminal justice system is to a certain extent driven by the real crime rate, then the system is doubly dependent, both on crime and the multiplicity of factors that drive crime.

Even with this uncertainty, there are several problems in the history of the police in need of feasible and potentially interesting research. First and foremost, we need more series of data. While tedious to collect, the data must be developed to begin to fill in the basic context of police development and change. This is not a call for mindless data collection, but we have no reason to prolong our state of ignorance. There is no collected arrest or offense data for the period between 1920 and 1931, and the FBI considers the data it has published since 1931 to be unreliable for cross-city comparison prior to 1957. These data inconsistencies between the 1920s and the 1957 period, although not easily bridged, should yield an interesting series when it is sketched in. For example, the post-World War II burst in drunk and disorderly arrests discussed above is an hitherto unknown event discovered only by the creation of the arrest series. The major flaw of earlier data will be the absence of "offenses known to the police," long considered the most important data, but continued care and experience in dealing with these data should narrow the range of uncertainty.

We need to use more carefully articulated models with this data, and the use of advanced non-least squares based time-series statistics should be considered. The research of Blumstein and his associates provides a challenge in this regard, although it may be that advanced statistical techniques will only be useful for the more robust imprisonment data.[41] For instance, we now have the methods, historiography, and sources for detailed studies of homicide, suicide, and accidental death which should be able to confirm one of the three current impressions of crime: that "things" are falling apart, that mid-twentieth century homicide is a blip on the long decline of the crime or that the post-industrial urban crisis has made the *Clockwork Orange* come true.[42]

We must not confuse police/policy derived questions and concepts with historical/scientific ones, that the two might better and more carefully inform each other. Much work on the police answers policy related questions as asides, but the precise separation of the two should help clear up confusion and make the analysis of data more sensible. Historical data often can make significant contributions to policy and planning, but it does so best when unconfused with historical concerns. This is best exemplified by the work of Blumstein and his associates, who analyze series of imprisonment data which move through political and economic change in order to sharpen understanding of the dynamics of imprisonment, not of social change. They do not ignore historical social change, but when it seems to intrude on their material, they simply note that the unexplained variation probably came from social change, and move to other questions.[43] These footnoted variations are those of most interest to historians. For instance, by carefully separating the origins of change, Blumstein and his associates have helped identify two major eras of historical imprisonment levels, one period of relative stability from 1880 to around 1920, the other from 1920 to at least 1979. Their work shows that by proceeding with explicit policy questions, they could very carefully distinguish the kind of change which is of interest to historians from the change which attracts the attention of policy analysis. These distinctions are, finally, more than methodological. The historian wants to understand society, the policy maker to control it. But we argue that understanding is a prerequisite for control, and most of us are in favor of crime control. So as federal money works on the aim of police officers, we work on understanding their long term relationship to crime.

FROM COP HISTORY TO SOCIAL HISTORY   587

We also need more comparative work on the police: not simply work of regional and international comparison, of which Miller's remains the major example, but work comparing organizations. The obvious beginning is to compare fire and police organizations, which have similar periods of emergence and similar transitions from volunteer or volunteer-based models to uniformed and hierarchically organized city services. But other organizations will also provide useful comparisons — public schools, hospitals, and perhaps various businesses or federal bureaucracies. Only Rothman has tried such an approach, and his book, *Discovery of the Asylum,* is the stronger for it.[44] Since one of the emerging interpretations of nineteenth and early twentieth century history is known as the "organizational synthesis," the comparative analysis of the police and other organizations should improve both our understanding of the police and of organizations in history.[45]

In addition to the organizational basis of comparison, the comparison of police to other specifically governmental bureaucracies should also be illuminating. Economic historians have just begun to study the behavior of government bureaucracies as economic actors.[46] Although the main concern of the econometricians seems to be in discovering the causes of growth and estimating the overall economic impact of the growth, their work will provide financial data and economic frameworks within which to place police, or any other branch of the criminal justice system for that matter.

In a similar vein, but from a somewhat different perspective, the work in progress of political scientists Herbert Jacob and Robert Lineberry on governmental responses to crime contains two implicit challenges for historians.[47] First, as their research takes it beginning point as 1945, they have given historians a convenient end date for directly comparable work. Second, the political science perspective of the researchers invites quantitative political historians, who in large part focus on electoral politics and ignore other facets of political behavior, to shift toward thinking about the political history of public policy and crime.

We also need more straightforward descriptive legal histories of policing and crime control. Until recently, most legal history has focused on the analysis of Supreme Court decisions, and relatively little work has been done on the day-to-day operations of the lower courts, where most police originated business entered and left the judiciary.[48] The records of these lower courts do not seem to be systematically preserved, and much work on this topic will depend on luck, the aggressiveness of archives and a researcher's pluck.[49] Wunder's research on the lower courts of the northwest territory shows what can be done with the sensitive combing of statues and sporadically preserved materials. One can only hope that the Mayor's and Police Justices courts will find similar historians.

Conclusion

Police history continues to attract historians new to the field even when other forms of social and urban history are on the ascendant. It is of critical importance that the historians and other social scientists who pursue the subject stay alert to historiographic and social scientific trends in order to avoid repetition and to ask penetrating questions. The generalizations in this article should be seen as hypotheses to be tested, and the suggestions for further research should be taken as coherently related research topics, not just minor information gaps. If the field builds on previous work, becomes self-critical, and consciously works at being a part of a much larger social and political history, it promises to contribute a major component of U.S. history.

University of California, Los Angeles   Eric H. Monkkonen

588   journal of social history

FOOTNOTES

1. The research reported in this paper has been supported by grants from the Academic Senate of the University of California, Los Angeles; the Social Science Research Council, and the American Philosophical Society. Portions of the substantive analysis in Section II have been drawn from my book, *Police in Urban America, 1860-1920* (New York, 1981). An earlier version of this paper was presented at the First Conference on the History of Crime and Criminal Justice, College Park, Maryland (September 1980), sponsored by the International Association for the History of Crime and Criminal Justice. I wish to thank David Waterhouse for his research assistance. Jon Butler, Eugene Watts and Terrence J. McDonald made invaluable comments on the manuscript.

2. Ernest S. Griffith, *History of American City Government: The Colonial Period*, v. 1 (New York, 1938); *The Modern Development of City Government in the United Kingdom and the United States* (London, 1927); *A History of American City Government: The Conspicious Failure, 1870-1900* (New York, 1974); *A History of American City Government: The Progressive Years and Their Aftermath, 1900-1920* (New York, 1974).

3. Samuel P. Hays' work has stimulated much of this research. See his, *American Political History as Social Analysis: Essays by Samuel P. Hays* (Knoxville, 1980).

4. Robert M. Fogelson, *Big City Police* (Cambridge, 1977).

5. Michael H. Frisch, *Town into City: Springfield, Massachusetts, and the Meaning of Community, 1840-1880* (Cambridge, 1972); Kenneth Fox, *Better City Government: Innovation in American Urban Politics, 1850-1937* (Philadelphia, 1977); J. Rogers and Ellen Jane Hollingsworth, *Dimensions in Urban History: Historical and Social Science Perspectives on Middle-Size American Cities* (Madison, 1979); Terrence J. McDonald, "Urban Development, Political Power and Municipal Expenditure in San Francisco, 1860-1910: A Quantitative Investigation of Historical Theory,"' (Ph.D. dissertation, Stanford University, 1979).

6. For a discussion of annual reports, see Monkkonen, "Municipal Reports as an Indicator Source: The Nineteenth Century Police," *Historical Methods* (Spring, 1979), 57-75.

7. See Monkkonen, *Police in Urban America*, App. I, for complete details.

8. Richard Wade, *Slavery in the Cities: The South, 1820-1860* (New York, 1964).

9. For two examples of historical geography using a network perspective, see, Allan R. Pred, *Urban Growth and the Circulation of Information: The United States System of Cities, 1790-1840* (Cambridge, 1973), and Michael P. Conzen, "Maturing Urban Systems of the U.S., 1840-1910," *The Annals of the Association of American Geographers* (March 1977): 88-108.

10. U.S. Department of Justice, LEAA, *Sourcebook of Criminal Justice Statistics, 1978* (Washington: G.P.O., 1978), 86.

City Size	Mean Police Personnel Per 1,000 Population
1,000,000 +	4.12
500,000-999,999	2.63
250,000-499,999	2.40
100,000-249,999	2.44
50,000- 99,999	2.14
25,000- 49,999	2.06
10,000- 24,999	2.08

11. *Sourcebook*, p. 87.

FROM COP HISTORY TO SOCIAL HISTORY 589

12. Eugene Watts, "Police Priorities in Twentieth Century St. Louis," *Journal of Social History* (June, 1981): 649-674.

13. The specific first difference regression results are:
$$\text{Total Police} = 127.6 + .91\ (d - 10)\ \text{Population}^2$$
$$r^2 = .865;\ \text{D-W} = 2.5254;\ \text{DF} = 58.$$

14. *Sourcebook*, p. 86.

15. Data from U.S. Department of Commerce, Bureau of the Census, *Historical Statistics of the United States: Colonial Times to 1970* (Washington, 1976), Series D 590, 591, p. 144.

16. Wilbur R. Miller, *Cops and Bobbies: Police Authority in New York and London, 1820-1870* (Chicago, 1977).

17. Watts, "Police Priorities."

18. Jerold E. Levine, "Police, Parties and Polity: The Bureaucratization, Unionization, and Professionalization of the New York City Police, 1870-1917" (Ph.D. dissertation, University of Wisconsin, 1971); Sean Wilentz, "Crime, Poverty and the Streets of New York City: The Diary of William H. Bell, 1850-1851," *History Workshop* (Spring 1979): 126-155.

19. David R. Johnson, *Policing The Urban Underworld: The Impact of Crime on the Development of The American Police, 1800-1887* (Philadelphia, 1979); Mark H. Haller, "Illegal Enterprise: Historical Perspectives and Public Policy," in James A. Inciardi and Charles E. Faupel, eds., *History and Crime: Implications for Criminal Justice Policy* (Beverly Hills, 1980), 77-90; Sidney Harring and Lorrain McMullin, "The Buffalo Police, 1872-1900: Labor Unrest, Political Power and the Creation of The Police Institution," *Crime and Social Justice* (Fall-Winter, 1975): 5-14; John C. Schneider, *Detroit and The Problem of Order, 1830-1880: A Geography of Crime, Riot and Policing* (Lincoln, Neb., 1980).

20. For the most recent critique of the social control thesis, see David J. Rothman, "Social Control: The Uses and Abuses of the Concept in the History of Incarceration," paper presented at the First Conference on the History of Crime and Criminal Justice, College Park, Maryland (September 1980).

21. Allan E. Levett, "Centralization of City Police in the Nineteenth-Century United States" (Ph.D. dissertation, University of Michigan, 1975).

22. Bruce C. Johnson, "Taking Care of Labor: The Police in American Politics," *Theory and Society* (Spring 1976): 89-117; Samuel Walker, "The Police and the Community: Scranton, Pennsylvania, 1866-1884: A Test Case," *American Studies* (1978): 79-90; Daniel Walkowitz, *Worker City, Company Town: Iron and Cotton-Worker Protest in Troy and Cohoes, New York, 1855-1884* (Urbana, 1979), 135, 192-218, 233-239.

23. Walkowitz, *Worker City, Company Town*, 197-217, 219-238.

24. Schneider, *Detroit and The Problem of Order.*

25. Data from Monkkonen, "A Disorderly People? Urban Order in the Nineteenth and Twentieth Centuries," *Journal of American History* (Dec., 1981): 539-559.

26. James W. Gerard, *London and New York: Their Crime and Police* (New York, 1853).

27. Donald C. Dilworth, ed., *Identification Wanted: Development of the American Criminal Identification System, 1893-1943* (Gaithersburg, Md., 1977).

28. Johnson, *Policing the Urban Underworld;* see also the review by Joseph G. Woods, *Journal of American History* (June 1980): 141-142.

29. Monkkonen, *Police in Urban America*, chap. 2.

30. Lane, *Violent Death.*

31. Ted R. Gurr and Hugh D. Graham, *Violence in America: Historical and Comparative Perspectives* (Beverly Hills, 1979); see especially Gurr, "On the History of Violent Crime in Europe and America," 353-374. See also Lane, "Urban Police and Crime in Nineteenth-Century America," *Crime and Justice: An Annual Review of Research*, 2 (1980): 1-44.

32. Levett, "Centralization of City Police."

33. Gudmund Hernes, "Structural Change in Social Processes," *American Journal of Sociology* (Nov. 1976): 513-547.

34. Monkkonen, *Police in Urban America*, chap. 1, figures 1 and 2.

35. G.F. Pyle, "The Diffusion of Cholera in the U.S. in the Nineteenth Century," *Geographical Analysis* (Jan. 1969): 59-75.

36. Monkkonen, "The Consequences of Police Reform: Lost Children and Public Perceptions," Paper presented at the International Economic History Congress (Aug. 15, 1979), Edinburgh.

37. Sidney L. Harring, "Class Conflict and the Suppression of Tramps in Buffalo, 1892-1894," *Law and Society Review* (Summer 1977): 873-911.

38. See Monkkonen, *Police in Urban America*, chap. 4 and Appendix III.

39. Donald C. Dilworth, ed., *The Blue and the Brass: American Policing, 1890-1910* (Gaithersburg, Md., 1976).

40. See Ted R. Gurr, "Historical Trends in Violent Crimes: A Critical Review of Evidence," in *Crime and Justice: An Annual Review of Research*, 3 (1981): 295-353, for an example of a test of the hypothesis of the felony crime rate reversal.

41. Alfred Blumstein and Jacqueline Cohen, "A Theory of the Stability of Punishment," *Journal of Criminal Law and Criminology* (June 1973): 198-207. Also Blumstein and Soumyo Moitra, "An Analysis of the Time Series of the Imprisonment Rate in the United States: A Further Test of the Stability of Punishment Hypothesis," *Journal of Criminal Law and Criminology* (Fall 1979): 376-390.

42. Roger Lane, *Violent Death in the City: Suicide, Accident, and Murder in 19th Century Philadelphia* (Cambridge, 1979).

43. Alfred Blumstein and Soumyo Moitra, "Growing or Stable Incarceration Rates: A Comment Cahalan's 'Trends in Incarceration in the United States Since 1880'," *Crime and Delinquency* (Jan. 1980): 91-94.

44. David J. Rothman, *The Discovery of the Asylum: Social Order and Disorder in the New Republic* (Boston, 1971).

45. Robert F. Berkhofer, Jr., "The Organizational Interpretation of American History: A New Synthesis," *Prospects* (1979): 611-630.

46. Thomas E. Borcherding, ed., *Budgets and Bureaucrats: The Sources of Government Growth* (Durham, N.C., 1977); Roger L. Ransom, "In Search of Security: The Growth of Government in the United States," Department of Economics, Working Paper Number 40 (Jan. 1980), University of California, Riverside.

FROM COP HISTORY TO SOCIAL HISTORY   591

47. Herbert Jacob and Robert L. Lineberry, Governmental Responses to Crime Project, Evanston, Ill. See Jacob and Lineberry, "Governmental Responses to Cime, 1948-1978," Paper presented at Social Science History Association Annual Meeting (Nov. 1980), Rochester, New York; see also, Jacob and Michael L. Rich, "The Effects of Police on Crime: A Social Look," *Law and Society Review* (1980-81): 109-122.

48. Michael S. Hindus deals with court behavior in *Prison and Plantation: Crime, Justice and Authority in Massachusetts and South Carolina, 1767-1878* (Chapel Hill, 1980). John Wunder, *Inferior Courts, Superior Justice: A History of the Justices of the Peace on the Northwest Frontier, 1853-1889* (Westport, Conn., 1979), carefully details lower court operations and quantifies some court behavior. The important book by Lawrence M. Friedman and Robert V. Percival, *The Roots of Justice: Crime and Punishment in Alameda County, California, 1870-1910* (Chapel Hill, N.C., 1981) appeared too late to incorporate in this essay.

49. Monkkonen, "Systematic Criminal Justice History: Some Suggestions," *Journal of Interdisciplinary History* (Winter 1978): 451-464. Hindus, et al., *The Files of the Massachusetts Superior Court, 1859-1959: An Analysis and Plan for Action* (Boston, 1980), detail a systematic survey and sampling of a century of criminal court records. These data are available through the Criminal Justice Archive and Information Network, University of Michigan.

Part II
The Role of the Police
in Practice

[7]

POLICEMAN AS PHILOSOPHER, GUIDE AND FRIEND

ELAINE CUMMING, IAN CUMMING AND LAURA EDELL
Mental Health Research Unit, Syracuse, New York

This is the fourth report from a group of studies designed to throw some light upon the division of labor among the social agents whose central role is concerned with maintaining social integration by controlling various forms of deviant behavior.[1]

In earlier reports, we have adopted the convention of looking at social agents and agencies in terms of their relatively supportive or relatively controlling character. We have assumed that it is difficult for an agent to exercise both support and control at the same time and that any agent tends, therefore, to specialize in one or the other aspect of the integrative process.[2] Even when he is specialized, such an agent may be considered controlling when he is compared with some agents, and supportive when compared with others. Thus, the probation officer is more on the client's side, that is, supportive to him, than the policeman, but less so than the psychiatrist.

This research was supported in part by NIMH Grant M-4735, Principal Investigator, Elaine Cumming. Acknowledgment is made of the assistance of the staff of the Mental Health Research Unit and its Director, Dr. John Cumming. Our particular thanks are extended to the officers and men of the Syracuse Police Force whose cooperation made this study possible. At the time of the field work, Chief Harold Kelly extended his cooperation to us; since his retirement, Chief Patrick Murphy has helped us to interpret findings, although we are solely responsible for the conclusions drawn.

[1] Earlier reports include: Elaine Cumming, "Phase Movement in the Support and Control of the Psychiatric Patient," *Journal of Health and Human Behavior*, 3 (Winter, 1962), pp. 235-241; Isabel McCaffrey, Elaine Cumming and Claire Rudolph, "Mental Disorders in Socially Defined Populations," *American Journal of Public Health*, 53 (July, 1963), pp. 1025-1030; Elaine Cumming and Charles Harrington, "Clergyman as Counselor," *American Journal of Sociology*, LXIX (November, 1963), pp. 234-243.

[2] This assumption is derived in part from studies of the division of labor in small groups (see, for example, Bales' "The Equilibrium Problem in Small Groups," in T. Parsons and R. F. Bales, *Working Papers in the Theory of Action*, Glencoe: The Free Press, 1953), and upon theories of role conflict [see, for example, W. J. Goode, "A Theory of Role Strain," *American Sociological Review*, 25 (August, 1960), pp. 483-495.] At another level of analysis, of course, we all control and support one another—by showing disapproval when our expectations are not met and by friendliness, responsiveness, understanding and sympathy when they are.

Furthermore, the agent may be seen as supportive by the layman but experienced as controlling by the client, and *vice versa*. For example, the prisoner remanded by the court for psychiatric treatment may well experience his hospitalization as incarceration. Conversely, a chronic alcoholic may be grateful, in mid-winter, for a night in prison.

There is another aspect to this duality in the handling of deviance. While it is probably impossible to perform acts of support and control simultaneously, support without control is overprotection and invites passivity and dependency, while control without support is tyranny and invites rebellion. While the agent may specialize in one aspect of social control of deviance, the other must, nevertheless, be part of his repertoire.[3] Thus while physicians and clergymen are generally supportive of people in pain or trouble, such people are expected, in return, to perform appropriately the role of patient or parishioner. The support is overt, the control is latent. In general, the agent's training and professional ethics focus on the skills needed for the overt part of his role; the latent aspects are derived from and governed by general norms and values. Role conflict can be avoided in part by keeping the "contradictory" side of a role latent.

The policeman's role in an integrative system is, by definition and by law, explicitly concerned with control —keeping the law from being broken and apprehending those who break it

—and only latently with support. For example, if you break the law, you can expect to be arrested, but if you go along quietly, you can, unless there is a special circumstance, expect to be treated reasonably.[4] In the course of controlling one member of society, moreover, the policeman often provides indirect support to another. For example, when he apprehends, and thus controls a wife-beating husband, he supports the wife, just as, in a reverse situation, the doctor controls the behavior of those attending a patient when he prescribes rest and sympathy. Finally, besides latent support, the policeman often gives direct help to people in certain kinds of trouble. When he does this, the balance between support and control has shifted, and he is acting overtly as a supportive agent and only latently in his controlling role. He has, at the same time, changed from a professional to an amateur. This paper reports a study of the requests for help received by a city police department and the policeman's response to them, with special attention to what is assumed here to be the latent side of his role.

METHOD OF STUDY

Because there seems to be no systematic account of the day-to-day activities of policemen, two specific questions were posed: (1) What kinds of calls for help do policemen get, and (2) How do they answer them? Two kinds of data were collected. First, a total of 801 incoming telephone calls at the police complaint desk in a metropolitan police department were observed over a total of 82 hours. These hours were not evenly distributed around the 24 hours, for reasons connected with the field worker, not with the Police Department.

---

[3] Certain highly skilled agents, such as psychoanalysts, may be able to phase their activities so that they are supportive in certain phases of the treatment and controlling in others. It is doubtful if this is feasible in the ordinary run of events because of the ambiguity it would generate in social interaction; see, for example, Gregory Bateson, D. D. Jackson, J. Haley and J. Weakland, "Toward a Theory of Schizophrenia," *Behavioral Science*, .1 (October, 1956), pp. 251-264.

[4] For an excellent discussion of the many problems inherent in the controlling function of the police, see ed. Claude R. Sowle, *Police Power and Individual Freedom*, Chicago: Aldine, 1962.

As each complaint was received and disposed of, a description was dictated into a tape recorder. Fourteen selected prowl car calls were then observed. At the end of this phase of the study, the worker submitted field notes concerned with the general culture of the police station. Secondly, interviews were conducted with detectives concerning their special assignments. A formulation of the nature of the policeman's supporting role was then constructed from these data.

RESULTS

The Complaint Desk. Figure 1 shows that the hourly distribution of in the first part of the week from the last part of the week. The daily peak activity is between the evening hours of seven and eight o'clock excepting for Thursday, Friday and Saturday when it is between nine and ten. (Because of the gaps in the data, there is a possibility that there is a peak at about noon in the first part of the week, but on both theoretical and common-sense grounds, it seems unlikely.) The last part of the week also shows a greater volume of calls than

the first. In general, the high rate of calls in the evening and on weekends suggests that problems arise when the social pulse is beating fast—when people are coming and going, regrouping, and, of course, engaging in informal rather than formal activities.

In order to interpret these rhythms further, the 801 calls were classified according to their content, as Table I shows. One hundred and forty-nine, or 18.6 per cent of the calls, were excluded from analysis; 88 of these were call-backs on earlier complaints, 33 were requests for information only, and 28 were outside this police department's jurisdiction.[5] The remaining 652 calls were for service within the purview of these police. They are treated as independent, but the unit of analyses is the call, and not the caller, and results must be interpreted with this in mind.

The 652 calls included in the study were divided into two major groups: the first included calls for service in

_____
[5] The latter two groups (61 calls) were excluded because there was no chance of a car being sent, and therefore they could not be compared with the remainder.

Figure 1
Average Police Calls per Hour, First Part of the Week (6 a.m. Sunday - 5 a.m. Thursday) and Second Part of the Week (6 a.m. Thursday - 5 a.m. Sunday)

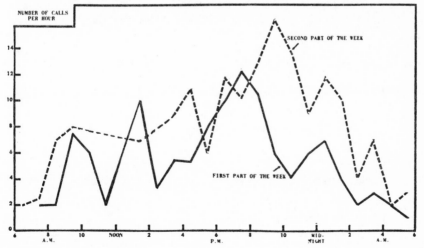

TABLE I
CLASSIFICATION OF CALLS TO THE COMPLAINT DESK OF A METROPOLITAN POLICE DEPARTMENT DURING 82 SELECTED HOURS IN JUNE AND JULY 1961

Type of call	Number of calls	Per cent of total
Total	801	100.0
Calls included in analysis	652	81.4
1. Calls about "things"	255	31.8
2. Calls for support	397	49.6
Persistent personal problems	230	28.7
a. Health services	81	10.1
b. Children's problems	83	10.4
c. Incapacitated people	33	4.1
d. Nuisances	33	4.1
Periodic personal problems	167	20.9
a. Disputes	63	7.9
b. Violence	43	5.4
c. Protection	29	3.6
d. Missing persons	11	1.4
e. Youths' behavior	21	2.6
Calls excluded from analysis	149	18.6
Information only	33	4.1
Not police business	28	3.5
Feedback calls	88	11.0

connection with things or possessions, while the second included calls for support or assistance with regard to problems of health, safety or interpersonal relationships.[6]

The first (nearly one-third of the total of 801 calls) include traffic violations, reports of losses or thefts, calls about unlocked doors, fallen power wires and so on. These are part of the regular controlling function of the police and are not the main focus of this paper. The second major group (about one-half of all calls) is concerned with personal problems and therefore may reasonably be expected to include the need or desire for some form of support. These calls were subdivided into two types: (1) persistent problems occurring throughout the week; and (2) periodic problems occurring mainly on the weekend.

As Table I shows, the first type

comprises 230 calls, of which about one-third are requests for health services, that is, ambulance escorts, investigation of accidents, suicide attempts, and so on; another third are children's problems, usually complaints about trespassing, or destructive behavior; and the remainder are divided equally between incapacitated people, usually described over the phone as drunk or "psycho," and nuisances, usually noisy behavior.

Periodic problems comprise 167 calls of which more than a third are about disputes and quarrels of all kinds, both in families and among unrelated pople. Almost half are concerned with violence or protection from potential violence[7] and the remainder are about missing persons or gangs of youths and hot-rodders.

Table II shows the distribution of the calls, by type, through the days of

---

[6] It was surprisingly easy to classify the calls on these two major dimensions and coders had no trouble getting over 90% agreement. Differences were reconciled in conferences.

[7] Most "protection" calls are for a "clothing escort," that is, for a policeman to accompany a person who has left his home, or been thrown out of it, into the house to get his clothing.

TABLE II
NUMBER OF CALLS TO THE COMPLAINT DESK OF A METROPOLITAN POLICE DEPARTMENT BY TYPE OF PROBLEM,* DAY OF WEEK, TIME OF DAY, AND HOURS OF OBSERVATION DURING 82 SELECTED HOURS IN JUNE AND JULY 1961

Time of day, hours of observation, and type of call	Total	Sun.	Mon.	Tue.	Wed.	Thur.	Fri.	Sat.
All calls	*652*	*50*	*69*	*55*	*76*	*95*	*54*	*253*
(hours observed)	(82)	(8)	(14)	(9)	(9)	(9)	(6)	(27)
12:01 a.m.-5:00 a.m.	*91*	*16*	*18*					*57*
(hours observed)	(14)	(2)	(5)	(0)	(0)	(0)	(0)	(7)
Routine	28	4	8					16
Persistent	21	4	4					13
Periodic	42	8	6					28
5:01 a.m.-noon	*52*		*9*	*19*		*17*		*7*
(hours observed)	(13)	(0)	(4)	(3)	(0)	(3)	(0)	(3)
Routine	36		6	11		15		4
Persistent	10		2	4		2		2
Periodic	6		1	4		0		1
12:01 p.m.-6:00 p.m.	*187*	*18*		*36*	*38*	*38*	*31*	*26*
(hours observed)	(26)	(4)	(0)	(6)	(5)	(3)	(4)	(4)
Routine	88	9		12	18	18	16	15
Persistent	68	6		17	11	16	12	6
Periodic	31	3		7	9	4	3	5
6:01 p.m.-midnight	*322*	*16*	*42*		*38*	*40*	*23*	*163*
(hours observed)	(29)	(2)	(5)	(0)	(4)	(3)	(2)	(13)
Routine	103	4	13		17	15	2	52
Persistent	131	5	22		18	17	7	62
Periodic	88	7	7		3	8	14	49

* Departures from uniformity:

1. Periodic interpersonal calls occur more often than chance would indicate on Friday evening ($\chi^2 = 24.1$, d.f. $= 5$, P $< .01$) and the early hours of Saturday ($\chi^2 = 8.4$, d.f. $= 2$, P $= .02$).

2. Both routine police calls and persistent interpersonal calls occur more frequently than chance would indicate on Thursday, the former in the morning ($\chi^2 = 12.3$, d.f. $= 3$, P $< .01$) and the latter in the afternoon ($\chi^2 = 13.1$, d.f. $= 5$, P $= .05$).

the week and the period of the day. It now appears that the heaping up of calls in the last part of the week is made up of two effects: first, routine police business and persistent interpersonal calls occur most frequently on Thursday, while periodic interpersonal problems heap up on Friday night. The meaning of this finding is not clear, but it may be that the tensions associated with the instrumental activity of the working week are increasing by Thursday and are then let go on Friday—payday—and on the weekend, when formal constraints are fewer. Because fewer of the other agents are available at these times, the policeman takes over many emergency health and welfare services, a kind of division of labor through time.

Almost three quarters of all 652 calls were answered by dispatch of a patrolman in a squad car to the scene, while about eight per cent received various kinds of advice or information, and about four-and-one-half per cent were referred to another source of help. Of the 29 referrals, one was to a medical service, one to a social service, 19 to other legal services and the remaining eight to commercial concerns, such as the Telephone Company. Almost 15 per cent of the calls were terminated—that is, service was withheld for reasons not determined, occasionally because no car was available.

In Table III, we see that the probability of a car being sent out is inversely related to the rate at which calls are coming in. During the six time periods in which a total of 235 calls were received at a rate of fewer than eight calls per hour, 78 per cent of them were responded to with cars. During the five time periods in which 417 calls were received at a rate of more than eight calls per hour, cars were sent only 68 per cent of the time. This difference is highly significant ($\chi^2 = 7.54$, d.f. $= 1$), and suggests that cars are sent on a simple supply-and-demand basis. Furthermore, there is no difference among the three major categories with regard to the likelihood of a car being sent. Nevertheless, certain sub-categories of complaint are more likely to get service than others. As Table IV shows, calls regarding violence (control), children and youths (support and control), and illness (support) are the most likely to be responded to with a car, although the likelihood of the law being broken —which defines the police mandate— is greater for some of these complaints than for others.

When the complainant reports a nuisance or a dispute, he has only one chance in two of getting more than advice—albeit philosophical advice. Thus, a man calls to say that he has had a fight with his girl and she hasn't come to see him, although he knows she is off duty from the hospital; the policeman says he can't make her come to his house—perhaps she doesn't want to—and goes on to advise the man that that's the way life is sometimes.

It is possible that some of the calls about violence are later stages of these unanswered dispute calls. For example, to one complaint, "My boy friend is mad at me and is going to beat me up," the answer was, "Call us again when he does."[8]

It is quite apparent that the policeman must often exercise a kind of clinical judgement about these complaints, and that this judgement reflects his own values. The field notes suggest, for example, that policemen are sincerely, if sentimentally, concerned about children, and that negligent parents are likely to find the police at their most truculent. The following example is taken from the notes:

> A call came from a very kindly-sounding Italian man at about 11 o'clock in the evening. He was reporting that he had found a little boy from next door wandering in the street . . . and he thought the police ought to know about the situation. A car was dispatched and reported that there was nobody home, and in fact, there were three smaller children in the house. . . . The captain dispatched a camera crew, child placement was notified and the children were immediately placed in a temporary placement home. A stake-out was set for the parents. Meanwhile the pictures had been developed and they showed four under-nourished, under-clothed little children lying in their own feces on a mattress on the floor. The refrigerator contained two cans of condensed milk and some rotten vegetables; the place was filthy and unheated. As the time went by, anger began to rise and when at about four o'clock in the morning the parents were brought in to the station everybody was in an ugly mood. . . . Had they been the least bit smart, glib, or said almost anything other than "yes" or "no" while they were issued tickets, they would have gotten poked.

All-out support for the children is accompanied by the barest minimum of support to the parents in the form of approval for appropriately docile behavior.

The Squad Car. Certain calls are considered serious enough to warrant a captain following the squad car to

---

8 Police Chief Murphy describes this entry as "poor police practice."

282 SOCIAL PROBLEMS

TABLE III
Per Cent of Calls to Which Cars Sent by Hours of the Day, Days of the Week and Type of Call, and Number of Calls Received per Hour 82 Selected Hours at the Complaint Desk of a Metropolitan Police Department, June and July 1961

Time of day, type of call, and calls/hr.	Total		Sun.-Wed.*		Thursday		Fri.-Sat.*	
	Calls	Per cent to which car sent	Calls	Per cent to which car sent	Calls	Per cent to which car sent	Calls	Per cent to which car sent
Total calls (Total/hr.)	652 (8.0)	72.1	250 (6.3)	72.8	95 (10.6)	71.6	307 (9.3)	70.0
12:01 a.m.-5:00 a.m. (calls/hour)	91 (6.5)	80.2	34 (4.9)	85.3			57 (8.1)	77.2
Routine	28	85.7	12	91.7			16	81.3
Persistent	21	71.4	8	87.5			13	61.5
Periodic	42	81.0	14	78.6			28	82.1
5:01 a.m.-noon (calls/hour)	52 (4.0)	86.5	28 (4.0)	89.3	17 (5.7)	88.2	7 (2.3)	71.4
Routine	36	88.9	17	94.1	15	86.7	4	75.0
Persistent	10	90.0	6	83.3	2	100.0	2	100.0
Periodic	6	66.7	5	80.0	0	—	1	—
12:01 p.m.-6:00 p.m. (calls/hour)	187 (7.2)	73.8	92 (6.1)	70.7	38 (12.7)	71.0	57 (7.1)	80.7
Routine	88	69.3	39	66.7	18	66.7	31	74.2
Persistent	68	80.9	34	76.5	16	75.0	18	94.4
Periodic	31	71.0	19	68.4	4	75.0	8	75.0
6:01 p.m.-midnight (calls/hour)	322 (11.1)	66.5	96 (8.7)	65.6	40 (13.3)	65.0	186 (12.4)	67.2
Routine	103	60.2	34	58.8	15	40.0	54	66.7
Persistent	131	72.5	45	73.3	17	76.4	69	71.0
Periodic	88	64.8	17	58.8	8	87.5	63	57.1

* Calls grouped because of similar distribution.

TABLE IV

DISPOSITION OF 397 CALLS TO THE COMPLAINT DESK OF A METROPOLITAN
POLICE DEPARTMENT REGARDING INTERPERSONAL PROBLEMS, BY SUB-
CATEGORY OF COMPLAINT

82 Selected Hours in June and July 1961

Type of call	Total calls	Per cent car sent
Total calls	397	76.8
Persistent problems	230	79.1
a. Health services	81	86.4
b. Children's problems	83	85.5
c. Incapacitated people	33	75.8
d. Nuisances	33	48.5
Periodic problems	167	73.7
a. Disputes	63	50.8
b. Violence	43	95.3
c. Protection	29	79.3
d. Missing persons	11	81.8
e. Youths' behavior	21	85.7

the scene.[9] The following thumb-nail summaries represent 14 calls made by the captains in a 23-hour period. Half of them were not considered serious, but the field worker asked the captain to go to the scene.

(1) A man, reported by his ex-wife as dangerous and perhaps mentally ill, is found asleep; his ex-wife and her mother are in an agitated state. They report that when the ex-wife came to the home the husband shook his fist under her nose and said, "I have divorced you, I want you out of this goddam house by morning." The police officer woke up the man who once again threatened his ex-wife, and the officer then told her that since it was his house and she was legally divorced from him, she and her mother should "please leave, and not cause any more trouble."

(2) A car accident severely injures a woman and the police supervise her removal to hospital.

(3) A bartender asks for, and receives, help in closing up so that there will be no problems—a routine "preventive" police service usually given by the car on the beat.

(4) A man has beaten up his female neighbor earlier in the day and she has

[9] The field worker could not go with the regular prowl car owing to a rule forbidding the officers to carry passengers. It is also possible that the captain did not want the field worker to see episodes that he did not himself monitor.

called the police and preferred charges. At the time of this call, the man's wife had threatened this woman with a knife. All are drunk and are taken to the station for further investigation.

(5) A call from a woman about neighborhood children bullying a small boy who wears glasses. The field notes read, "There was a lot of argument and a lot of screaming back and forth, nothing was particularly accomplished, the three policemen (captain and two officers from a squad car) stood around for awhile, questioned people, did a little shouting, got shouted at, then the whole thing sort of dissolved and was resolved in a manner that I don't understand."

(6) A woman complains that her husband doesn't bring home enough of his money to feed the kids. She is advised to go to Children's Court.

(7) Field notes read: "Husband destroying property at his house. He's drunk and he and his wife got in an argument over the children . . . the wife smashed the gift he had given her for Mothers' Day. This set the incident off. He fought the officers, they handcuffed him, and is taken to the station—a psycho."

(8) A slightly drunk man is an unwelcome visitor in his ex-wife's home. Police send him home in a cab.

(9) An ex-patient from a mental hospital is missing from her relative's home. They will broadcast a missing persons call.

(10) A drunk man claims he has been slugged, but cannot amplify so no action is taken. "This is a low IQ street," says the policeman.

(11) A woman in her pajamas and covered with mud says her husband threw her out. He is at home drunk with the children. As he has a police record, two cars are dispatched, one with a tear-gas gun. The house is found in a shambles. The wife is taken to hospital, children to a shelter, and the husband is booked for investigation and possible psychiatric treatment.

(12) Fight in a third floor apartment between a man and his wife. Policeman settles it in some undiscernible fashion.

(13) A man has "gone out of his mind over a girl" and has gone beserk with a gun. The man is shipped to hospital and witnesses are taken in because the gun makes the affair a felony.

(14) The call is "see if an ambulance is needed." A young Negro in a filthy, crowded house appears to be in agony. Police examine him for knife wounds and being satisfied that he has not been stabbed, and that no further investigation is needed, send him to hospital in an ambulance.

There seem to be three types of cases here. In the first, the police act as guides or conveyors to the courts and hospitals, giving indirect support meanwhile. In the second, they appear to resolve problems by giving concrete information and guidance about what is and is not possible under the law. Here both indirect and overt support are given. In the third type, they appear to settle problems through some consensual method based on mutual understanding between the police and the people involved. Here support is fairly overt but control is, of course, latent because of the policeman's representation of law and order. Occasionally, the police give outright friendly support, as in the following incident from the field notes:

> Sitting in the police station is an old man, a citizen wanderer who is on his way to Oregon, and has become dissatisfied with the Rescue Mission and walked out. He's going to spend the night out of the rain until the morning when he's going over to the Salvation Army.

It is, of course, not possible to say what proportion of the policeman's responses to citizens fall into these three types, nor indeed, to know what

other types there may be, because of the method of selecting the squad car calls.

Detectives. Four detectives of the twenty in the department, selected only because they were on duty at the time of the field worker's visit, were asked to describe their ten most recent cases. It was felt that they might be assigned the more "professional" and hence controlling tasks. Two of them were specialists in theft and forgery and so their cases were, indeed, of this character. However, fifteen out of twenty cases described by the two general detectives fell into our two personal-problem categories, and were similar to the complaint calls except that they were being further investigated because of more serious breaches of the law.

Another detective, in charge of services to alcoholics, reported that in 1956 the police department sent him to Yale for training in the handling of alcoholics. He says, "As a police officer I saw people being arrested for drunk and re-arrested for drunk and I thought it was a pretty medieval way of going about trying to help a person with a basic problem and illness that the public was just kicking in the corner and that's how I wound up here." This officer handles about 900 alcoholics a year. Of these, he takes about 150 charged persons on suspended sentence from the court and tries to arrange for some agency to carry them—an outright supportive service.

Missing persons: The sergeant in charge of this service estimates that he locates about 600 missing people from this area in a year, about half of them children. He further estimates that from three to five per cent are mentally disturbed adults. This particular officer says that he sometimes counsels with children that he has traced after they have been returned home. At the same time, he complains to the interviewer that children don't respect police officers the way they did when he was young.

Detectives in charge of homicide and those on duty with the vice squad were not interviewed, so it is impossible to say what proportion of all detective work is supportive. These data suggest that it is similar to the patrolman's.

Police Culture. The field worker reports several impressions that are relevant to our interests. Although they cannot be demonstrated from these data, some of them are similar to findings from other studies. First, poor, uneducated people appear to use the police in the way that middle-class people use family doctors and clergymen—that is, as the first port of call in time of trouble. Second, the policeman must often enforce unpopular laws among these poor people at the same time that he sees these laws being flouted by those in positions of power.[10] Third, many policemen are themselves recruited from, and sympathetic to, the class of people from whom ·most of the "interpersonal" calls for assistance come.[11]

Fourth, the police have little knowledge of, and liaion with, social or even medical agencies, and seem to feel that these agencies' activities are irrelevant to the problems they, themselves, face.

Fifth, the police appear to have a concern not only for children but also for those they define as disturbed and ill. They are tolerant, for example, about many crank calls, and will, if a car is available, help a paranoid old lady search her house for the malignant intruder she feels sure is hiding there. Nevertheless, it is possible to

see, both in episodes of prejudice against minorities, and in less dramatic ways, how their own values transcend the individual's rights. A field note says, for example, "A woman wants protection from her doctor who is trying to commit her to a mental institution; the officer replies, 'That's not police business, lady. The police cannot go against any doctor.' "[12]

Finally, many policemen are bitter about their low pay, the label "punitive" applied to them in a world that values "warmth," the conflicting demands of their jobs, and the ingratitude of the public. This bitterness is reflected, in this police force, in a catch phrase, "I hate citizens."[13]

SUMMARY AND DISCUSSION

We return now to our starting questions: What calls are made on the police and how do they respond? More than one-half of the calls coming routinely to the police complaint desk, and perhaps to detectives, appear to involve calls for help and some form of support for personal or interpersonal problems. To about three-quarters of these appeals, a car is sent. When the policeman reaches the scene, the data suggest that he either guides the complainant to someone who can solve his problem or tries to solve it himself. To do this, he must often provide support, either by friendly sympathy, by feeding authori-

---

10 This seems to be most true of the vice squad and it was not covered here. Nevertheless, a lot of police station conversation was on this topic.

11 This becomes less true, of course, as the police department becomes more professionalized, and is probably less true of this department now than it was in 1961 when these data were collected.

12 This attitude is, of course, construed by some as a denial of the basic rights of the mentally ill person. See, in this regard, Thomas Szasz, *The Myth of Mental Illness*, New York: Harper, 1961. A trickle of manifestly disturbed people may be turned down for other reasons at the complaint desk. One agitated man complained that his back yard was full of snails; the officer replied, "What do you want me to do, come and shoot them?" Even so, the field worker reports that if the complaint officer had had a car available, he would probably have sent it out.

13 It may be that the higher respect for policemen in England is related to the higher value on order and the lower value on warmth.

tative information into the troubled situation, or by helping consensual resolution to take place. We started with the assumption that these activities belonged to the latent aspect of his role, and he is certainly an amateur— these policemen have no training for this kind of service. Why, then, are they called upon to exercise their amateur talents half of the time?

The reasons are probably complex. First, the policeman has to do much of what he does because he is on duty at times of the day when no other agent is available. Second, he deals with the problems of a group of people—the poor and the ignorant—that studies of our own and others have shown no other agent to be anxious to serve[14] and, third, he has knowledge of, and access to, very few other agents. In other words, he is part of an integrative system in which the labor is divided not so much on the basis of function as on the basis of the time of day and the nature of the target population. All citizens can count on emergency help from the police when there is sudden illness at night, but only a certain kind of citizen takes his marital troubles to them.

The policeman's supportive acts are not only the latent and hence amateur part of his role, they are also latent in not being recognized and legitimated by the other agents in the integrative system. These others, our own studies show, prefer to recognize the policeman's professional controlling function, which they both need and often call upon.[15] Thus, it is as an agent of control that the policeman participates in a divided labor with social workers, doctors, clergymen, lawyers and teachers in maintaining social integration. The problems he faces appear to be a *failure of integration within the integrative system,* so that he cannot mobilize the other agents when he needs them.

Some modern advocates of "professionalization" of police work recognize that the policeman on the beat spends about half his time as an amateur social worker and they hope, instead of improving the referral process, to equip him with the skills of a professional. The policeman will then have a role containing both overtly supportive and overtly controlling elements. If our assumption that these are incompatible activities is correct, this development would lead to a division of labor within police work that would tend once more to segregate these elements. This, in turn, would result in a basic shift in the relationship of the police to the rest of the integrative system. All of this might remove the policeman's present reasons for hating citizens, but it would not guarantee that they would not be replaced with others.

---

14 See, for a discussion of this problem in this community, Claire Rudolph and John Cumming, "Where are Psychiatric Services Most Needed?" *Social Work,* 7 (July, 1962), pp. 15-20.

---

15 There is reason to believe that most social workers, clergymen, and doctors have no conception of the amount of support policemen give during a day's work. There is also reason to believe that they do not want the burden of the "unmotivated" poor and ignorant whom they believe to be increasing in number.

[8]

New Society 17 May 1973

The police: a social service

Maurice Punch and Trevor Naylor

The police have to deal with social crises as much as with law enforcement. It is time their training put more emphasis on this side of the job.

The police service of this country was born out of concern for law and order at the beginning of the last century. Priority was given to crime prevention and detection by Rowan and Mayne, the founding fathers of Peel's Metropolitan Police in 1829, and their formal definition is still learnt today by every recruit. It reads: "The primary object of an efficient police is the prevention of crime: the next that of detection and punishment of offenders if crime is committed. To these ends all efforts of the police must be directed. The protection of life and property, the preservation of public tranquillity, and the absence of crime will alone prove whether those efforts have been successful, and whether the objects for which the police were appointed have been maintained."

Because of its varied functions—covering man's social problems from birth to death—the police service has gradually, and largely unwittingly, accumulated a broad range of "welfare" functions. Indeed, the police could well be described as the only 24 hour, fully mobile, social service.

Within the police force, there is a long-standing debate as to how much of a "service" role it should play. There has been an increasingly powerful lobby arguing for more force to be used—with emphasis and resources focused on crime detection to combat a rising crime rate and meet a recurrent manpower shortage. There is little evidence to show the effect of the "service" roles because, unlike law enforcement activities, these go largely unrecorded. There is a general lack of reliable data on the police; nearly a decade has elapsed since the books on the police by Michael Banton and Ben Whitaker appeared and only now are there signs of a renewed sociological interest in the police.

Traditionally, the police themselves have given little formal emphasis to their service functions. For example, the Royal Commission on the Police in 1962 listed eight major functions of the police, of which the last was a vague duty to befriend those in need. Furthermore, the Committee on Police Extraneous Duties, in 1953, rejected the ready availability of the police outside of normal office hours as an excuse for local authorities to put a wide range of duties on to them. Perhaps more importantly, there is comparative evidence from a number of countries to suggest that policemen themselves place a low value on routine, uniformed, patrol work, with its relatively high level of involvement with the general public, compared to the more highly valued activities of criminal investigation branches. These are seen as "real" police work. Both formally and informally, then, the police tend to neglect the explicit recognition of their social functions. Yet evidence suggests that the police do, in practice, devote a good deal of their energies to service activities.

There already are specialised units within the police, such as juvenile liaison and community relations schemes, that are preeminently service activities,

Maurice Punch is Lecturer in Sociology, University of Essex; Trevor Naylor is Inspector, Essex and Southend-on-Sea Joint Constabulary

while the women's police acts largely in a welfare capacity. But this aspect scarcely comes into formal training, which emphasises the law enforcement side, coupled with para-military activities like drilling and parades. This contrasts with the reality of life led by a policeman who, after 13 weeks of training, faces the public and its many demands—which often require the most subtle of social skills to resolve.

There are four major areas of police activities that require investigation. Firstly, there are the demands that the public make on the police; secondly, there is the police response to those demands—what they actually do; thirdly, there is the nature of police inter-organisational links and cooperation with the formal social services; and, fourthly, there is the area where the police are involved in social policy, in terms of maintaining or changing the integration of society (such as in supporting marriage and the family, in supervising evictions, or in dealing with a disturbance in a supplementary benefits office). In our research, we concentrated largely on the first area, the public's demands. In an American study by E. Cummings, which looked at telephone calls from the public to the police ("The policeman as philosopher, guide, and friend"), Cummings analysed incoming calls over an 82 hour period and concluded that more than half the routine calls to the police involved demands for help and some form of support for personal and inter-personal problems.

To carry out our research, we used police records (namely the personal and telephone message books) for three smallish towns in Essex for 14 days in May 1972. Each of the towns represented a police sub-division; there was a New Town (population 66,000); an old-established market town (population 68,000); and a small county town with a rural area (population 41,000). All demands on the police are recorded in either the personal or telephone message books kept at every station. Each entry shows when and from whom the message is received, and the officer receiving it. Next come brief details of the message and action taken by the receiving officer.

Over the two week period, which was free of bank holidays or special events, some 981 calls were recorded. These were divided into two categories, "law enforcement" or "service." Law enforcement meant all reports of crime—break-ins, thefts, woundings, and so on. We also included reports suggesting that specific laws, such as parking regulations, had been broken, and reports of unnecessary obstructions or suspicious circumstances. Obviously, some calls did not fall easily into this category. For instance, family quarrels or noisy parties are potential breaches of the peace but, as they rarely result in a prosecution and often require the exercise of social skills, we put them in the service category. There were seven main groups within the service subgroup: "domestic occurrences" (family disputes, personal problems, re-

Policing I

New Society 17 May 1973

ports of annoyance or nuisance, noisy parties); "health" (physical and mental illness, attempted suicide, sudden death); "people" (missing persons, found persons, abandoned persons, concern for elderly); "animals" (lost, found, injured, stray); "errands" (messages of death or accidents, locked out, money loans); "highway incidents" (road faults, traffic control, accidents); and "property" (found, abandoned, unoccupied, escorted). In all, 59 per cent of the calls could be defined as "service" requests and the remaining 41 per cent as requests relating to law enforcement.

The results shown in table one suggest that, in urban areas, the police are more concerned with law enforcement than service problems, while in the

Table 1: Distribution of calls into law enforcement and service groups, according to area

	new town		old town		country town	
	No.	%	No.	%	No.	%
total calls	410		381		190	
law enforcement	208	50.7	148	38.9	51	27.0
service	202	49.3	233	61.1	139	73.0

more tranquil rural area, the police appear more as a general social service. This reflects the wide-ranging functions of local policemen in rural areas, where they firmly support the social structure—indeed, one Chief Constable described the village constable as being a "Holy Ghost with bicycle clips."

Table two gives the overall distribution of service calls under the seven headings. Nearly one third of the calls involved "domestic occurrences" which subdivided into domestic disputes (11 per cent); personal problems (9 per cent); creating annoyance or nuisance (7.5 per cent); and noisy parties (1 per

cent). The urban areas had the highest number of actual domestic disputes, whereas in rural areas, personal problems came up more readily. In general, the majority of service calls were received between

Table 2: Distribution of 'service' calls

	No.	%
domestic occurrences	163	28.5
highway incidents	116	20.0
property	83	14.5
people	83	14.5
errands	48	8.5
health	45	8.0
animals	36	6.0

two and six o'clock in the afternoon—when the conventional social service departments are working. Had there been a significant rise after office hours, it would have implied that people only turned to the police when the conventional services were not available, but this was not so. Why did people turn to the police and not the professional social services?

To find out some of the reasons, we interviewed 30 people who had made calls in one of the areas studied. Five people saw the police as the obvious choice when problems came up. Twelve said they were aware that some other organisation could or should have dealt with their particular incident, but either that service could not be contacted or else they did not know where to locate it. Generally, it just seemed quicker and easier to call the police than anyone else. In every case, a policeman was sent to the scene in response to the call.

A persistent theme in the interviews was that people wanted a quick remedy from a reliable, authoritative, but fatherly figure. They were less convinc-

At the moment, the social service role, and real personal contact, is more common in the countryside. Here, in north Essex, the distribution of firearms certificate application forms becomes an almost neighbourly visit

Photographs/Bryn Campbell/Magnum

360

New Society 17 May 1973

In big city life, the policeman has a social task more often than is sometimes acknowledged. But situations, as here in Brixton (to move on, or not to move on?), are inevitably more complex

ed about the effectiveness of a social worker. One woman, for example, when asked why she had called the police to a domestic dispute, replied: "I always deal with the police—the others are useless. Those youngsters come along with their airy-fairy theories but never get anything done." Another woman wanted someone to tick off her adolescent son who didn't want to go out to work and hoped that the presence of a uniformed officer might prove an incentive: "I didn't want someone giving a lot of excuses for him not working. I wanted advice on how to get him to work so I turned to the police who have the right approach." In addition, some incidents that require action by welfare agencies are probably seen initially as disturbances that need immediate action. For instance, a man phoned the station in a case where the mental welfare officer was later called in. He had been concerned because "There was all this shouting and I saw a woman in pyjamas outside in the road screaming 'let me alone, let me alone.' At the same time she was, literally, dragging a man along by his coat collar."

The evidence from the interviews, then, suggests that some of the public view the police as the first of the social services. At this initial stage, the police have a "gate-keeper" function, as they have to decide whether or not to funnel clients to the specialised services. Equally, once the other services have intervened, the police feel that they sometimes get back the hot potatoes which the welfare services—say, probation—can't handle. Here, it is as if the really hard cases filter through the mesh of the social welfare agencies, beneath which the police function as a final safety net.

On occasions, the police feel that the other services need prompting. For example, a woman was left on her own by her husband in poor housing with several children; the local authority social services department provided some material comforts for the children but apparently little else. Eventually one of the children took an overdose of tablets and the police simply forced the case into court against what they saw as the lethargy of the social services.

The police are somewhat disparaging about the other services and particularly about their non-availability in the small hours—"anyone would think that domestic crises were confined to nine to five, Monday to Friday" was how one officer expressed it. At the same time, they rather pride themselves on their ability to handle people and problems in a blunt, commonsense but humane manner. A policewoman expressed this by saying that "Parents don't need a psychiatrist to tell them that their child's got a split personality, when I tell them that I've found the girl under the bushes with a man one day, and the next day she's singing in the church choir."

In assessing these feelings, it is vital to realise that we are talking of areas of competence for which the police are not formally trained and which are not their primary function. With that in mind, here are some explicit service roles played by the police that occurred during our research. Firstly, there is the policeman as veterinary surgeon. In one incident a cat injured in a road accident was brought to a station and, with no vet available, the animal was put out of its misery with the humane killer. Secondly, there is the policeman as mental welfare officer. Shortly after midnight a man walked into a station and threatened to commit suicide unless he was taken to a mental hospital some 20 miles away. The man's doctor was reluctant to become involved, although he confirmed a history of schizophrenia, and left the police to liaise with the hospital who, in turn, refused to do anything until the morning. The officers on duty calmed down the man, who was in a very distressed condition, and only allowed him to go home when he had promised to visit the hospital later in the day. Thirdly, there is the policeman as marriage guidance counsellor. One Sunday afternoon a constable was dispatched to a domestic dispute where the husband had returned home drunk. The wife wanted a witness to her husband's condition and the officer, who suspected he was being used by the woman to gain a separation order, gave what advice he could to settle the dispute.

Then, fourthly, there is the policeman as home-help to the infirm. The police were asked to help an ambulance crew locate a bungalow in a remote area where an old lady had burst a vein. An officer knew the house to be occupied by two old ladies, one aged 80, the other 74, and he guided the ambulance to the scene. One of the ladies required hospital treatment, but this left the other lady alone and bedridden. A policewoman was called who discovered that there were no relatives and she then made numerous telephone calls to locate a social worker to care for the lady. Eventually one was traced outside the area but, as the policewoman said afterwards,

New Society 17 May 1973

"I might just as well not have bothered." The social worker had taken down the details, promising to pass on the information the following day; but, next day, she was unable to give any help and could not suggest anyone who might be able to help. At this stage, the policewoman used her own resources to find a volunteer to look after the old lady.

Fifthly, there is the policeman as welfare worker. Late on a Saturday night a recently released prisoner found himself stranded—firstly, he had got on the wrong train on the way home and, secondly, he had been turned off it because his travel voucher had expired. The nearest social security office, some ten miles away, was closed for the weekend. The police finally found a friend of the man who would help.

Sixthly, there is the policeman as accommodation officer. At a meeting for lonely people, a man who had been sleeping rough since his release from hospital was found huddled in the corner. The organisers decided to find accommodation for him and asked the police, who suggested the Samaritans, who recommended a voluntary worker, who suggested the Salvation Army. But there was no local hostel and transport could not be provided to the nearest one some 15 miles away. A doctor was contacted but, in the words of a respondent, "He was very kindly, very helpful, but adamant that he couldn't come out to see him, and equally adamant that he could not send him to an institution without first seeing him." The man was then taken to the police station so that, if necessary, he could be transported to the doctor's surgery should medical attention be required. He was allowed to spend the night there.

Seventhly, and finally, there is the policeman as friend and confidant. In one rather exceptional case, a village constable had become friend, financial adviser, legal representative, doctor and general assistant to a rather eccentric old man. This man owed about £1,600 to shopkeepers, though he was known not to be short of money. He refused the help of the social services and would listen only to the constable who arranged a meeting with a solicitor, after which the debts were paid. But some time later the man took to sleeping with the cows in the shed because he claimed it was warmer than the house. From then on, he neither washed nor changed his clothes unless directed to by the officer, who also settled his accounts. When the man became ill and the doctor advised hospital treatment, it was the policeman who had to persuade the man to enter the ambulance. The old man died shortly after ad-

mission and, at the inquest, the coroner praised the officer for the help and welfare services he gave.

One fact which our survey proved is the incredible diffuseness of the policeman's role. We expect the policeman to combat organised crime, to quell a punch-up outside a pub, to comfort people in distress, to clean up messy accidents, to be solicitous to the young and the old, and so on. In short, we demand that he be a paragon of both strength and virtue and that his actions be subject to continual public scrutiny. The point is not that we should change these expectations, but that we should clarify them. Given the multi-functional role of the police, it would not be fair to overburden them with a more positive and explicit service role without deciding how this change could take place.

Two areas suggest themselves immediately. Firstly, the training of policemen could be improved to accentuate the sociological and psychological side of the job. Training is currently being evaluated: at Hendon, the Metropolitan Police have added two weeks' instruction in the social sciences to their basic course and at Essex University there is an annual fortnightly course for serving officers. Secondly, and most vitally, cooperation and liaison between the police and the social services could be vastly improved by a clear recognition of the areas of misunderstanding, by a clarification of responsibilities, and by meetings and discussions to break down the stereotypes that each has of the other.

Finally, it may be necessary for the police to specialise more in certain areas to cope with recurring social problems. For example, the New York City Police have "family intervention units" trained to deal with domestic crises. Some policemen enjoy uniformed work and dealing with the public, and recruitment could focus more on these aspects of the job. We do not believe that it is necessary to upgrade the police as a profession by raising their academic qualifications. Basic human qualities are the essential ingredient and it would be nice to see some institutions of higher education catering specifically for the in-service training of police officers of all ranks in social science and the social services, without requiring them to take the normal entry requirements or to read for a degree. Certainly, it would be a pity if "improved" training meant the loss of that basic shrewdness and humanity in the policeman's persona which enables him to deal with short-term social crises in a blunt, effective, and even therapeutic manner.

M. Banton, *The Policeman in the Community* (Tavistock, 1964)

B. Whitaker, *The Police* (Penguin, 1964)

E. Cummings *et al*, "Policemen as philosopher, guide and friend" (*Social Problems*, vol 12, 1964)

[9]

FLORENCE NIGHTINGALE IN PURSUIT OF WILLIE SUTTON:
A THEORY OF THE POLICE

EGON BITTNER

Among the institutions of modern government the police occupies a position of special interest: it is at once the best known and the least understood. Best known, because even minimally competent members of society are aware of its existence, are able to invoke the services it provides with remarkable competence, and know how to conduct themselves in its presence. How and how well the police is known, and the ways it matters in the lives of people, vary considerably over the spectrum of social inequality. But to imagine people who are not at all touched by the police one must conjure images of virtually complete isolation or of enormous wealth and power. Least understood, because when people are called upon to explain on what terms and to what ends police service is furnished they are unable to go beyond the most superficial and misleading commonplace which, moreover, is totally unrelated to the inter-actional skill that manifestly informs their dealings with policemen. What is true of people generally is true of the police as well. Policemen have not succeeded in

AUTHOR'S NOTE: A shorter version of this paper was delivered as the August Backus Memorial Address at the University of Wisconsin Law School in 1971. I am deeply indebted to Professor Herman Goldstein for his mentorship in all matters concerning the police. But he is, of course, in no way responsible for my errors.

Florence Nightingale is the heroic protagonist of modern nursing; Willie Sutton, for those who are too young to remember, was in his days a notorious thief.

[17]

formulating a justification of their existence that would recognizably relate to what they actually do (not counting those activities the doing of which they disavow or condemn). The situation is not unlike that of a person who, asked to explain how he speaks, offers an account which, while itself linguistically in perfect order, does not even come close to doing justice to the skill involved in producing the utterance.

In this paper I propose to explain the function of the police by drawing attention to what their existence makes available in society that, all things being equal, would not be otherwise available, and by showing how all that policemen are called upon to do falls into place when considered in relationship to it. My thesis is that police are empowered and required to impose or, as the case may be, coerce a provisional solution upon emergent problems without having to brook or defer to opposition of any kind, and that further, their competence to intervene extends to every kind of emergency, without any exceptions whatever. This and this alone is what the existence of the police uniquely provides, and it is on this basis that they may be required to do the work of thief-catchers and of nurses, depending on the occasion. And while the *chances* that a policeman will recognize any problem as properly his business depend on some external regulation, on certain structured social interest, and on historically established patterns of responsiveness and responsibility, every stricture arising out of these factors is defeasible in every *specific case* of police work. This means that the appropriateness of police action is primarily determined with regard to the particular and actual nature of the case at hand, and only secondarily by general norms. The assessment whether the service the police are uniquely competent to provide is on balance desirable or not, in terms of, let us say, the aspirations of a democratic polity, is beyond the scope of the argument. But in reviewing practice and organization I will weigh what is against what ought to be, by certain criteria internal to the enterprise.

The paper is frankly argumentative and intended to furnish grist for the mills of debate. Hence, I shall not attempt to view all questions from all sides, and I will especially avoid giving consideration to mere administrative expediency or yielding to those demands of reasonableness that are connected with taking a live-and-let-live attitude. All this counts, to be sure, but I will try not to let it count in what I will have to say; and in arguing as strongly as I know how, I do not aim to dismiss polemic opponents but to pay tribute to them. My plan is to begin with a cursory review of some preliminaries—dealing mainly with the police idea—in ways I consider indispensible for what will follow. Next I shall sketch a rather ordinary and common event in police work, and use it to explain what a policeman is required to do in this situation, in such situations, and by extension, in any situation whatever. Finally, I will attempt to characterize the problems that appear to summon police intervention and to define the role force plays in these interventions. In wrapping things up I will comment about the practical significance of police work in society and about the skills that come into play, or should come into play, in this regard.

THE OFFICIAL BASIS OF
LAW ENFORCEMENT MANDATES

While we use the term Police to refer to specific corps of public officials, it bears mentioning that original usage embraced the entire field of internal government, as distinct from the conduct of foreign affairs. Sir Francis Bacon, for example, asserted that in being "civil or policied," a nation acquired the right to subdue others that were "altogether unable or indign to govern" (Bacon, 1859: 29). In time this usage gave way to one restricted to the exercise of proscriptive control in matters affecting the public interest. Blackstone stated that "public police and economy . . . mean the due regulation and domestic order of the Kingdom, whereby the individuals of the state, like members of a well governed family, are bound to conform their general behavior to the rules of propriety, good neighborhood and good manners, and to be decent, industrious and inoffensive in their respective stations" (Blackstone, n.d.: 161). This definition is located in the volume dealing with Public Wrongs, in relation to a specific class of delicts, called Offences against the Public Police and Economy. By the end of the nineteenth century this class of delicts is treated by Sir James Fitzjames Stephen as lying outside of the scope of criminal law, but is, nevertheless, explicitly related to the existence of the then existing police forces in England (Stephen, 1883: 246). Though both Blackstone and Stephen treat the category of police offenses cursorily, they do furnish *legal authority* for each item discussed. The intent at scrupulous legalization of proscriptive control also inheres in the "idiom of apologetics which belongs to the vocabulary of constitutional law," in the United States: Police Power (Hamilton and Rodee, 1937: 192), commonly invoked to justify abridgements of civil liberties in the interest of "public health, morals, and safety" (Mugler v. Kansas, 1887). Indeed, in keeping with American concepts of legality, Mr. Justice Harlan, speaking for the majority in Mugler, reserved the right of judicial review of statutes enacted in the exercise of police power.

Most of the offenses against the Public Police mentioned by Blackstone are no longer regarded as culpable. But the domain of legally sanctioned proscriptive control he discussed has expanded enormously since the Commentaries appeared, as have the provisions of criminal law. There are scarcely any human activities, any interpersonal relations, any social arrangements left that do not stand under some form of governmental regulation, to the violation of which penalties are attached. To say that modern life is thus controlled does not mean saying that it is more controlled than earlier life. Tribesmen, peasants, or citizens of colonial townships most assuredly did not live in a paradise of freedom. In fact, the most widely accepted explanation of the proliferation of formal control, which associates it with the growth of a market-oriented, industrial, and urban order, implies primarily a shift from reliance on informal mechanisms of traditional authority to reliance on legal rational means (Weber, 1947: 324).

Urbanism brought with it the need for explicitly formal regulation because the lives of the people living in cities are replete with opportunities of infringing upon one another and virtually devoid of incentives to avoid it. The former is due to the sheer congestion of very large numbers of people, the latter to the social distance between them. More importantly, perhaps, urban strangers cannot entrust their fate to the hope of somehow muddling through because of the manner in which they attend to the business of making a living, and because of the paramount significance of this interest in their lives.

Two conditions must be met to satisfy the need for formal governmental control that would bind effectively the behavior of individuals to rules of propriety. The first, already recognized in the treatment Blackstone accorded to the matter, is that all controls rest on specific authorization set forth in highly specific legal norms. The second, explicitly acknowledged by Stephen, is that the implementation of the authorizing norm must be entrusted to impersonal enforcement bureaucracies. In sum, "the due regulation and domestic order" in our times is the task of a host of law enforcement bureaucracies, each using procedures legitimized by, and incidental to, the attainment of explicitly formulated legal objectives.

Naturally, the actual interests and practices of enforcement officials are rarely as specific or explicit as the verbal formulations of their respective mandates. Hence, for example, while the formal authorization of the work of a health inspector may be clear and specific, things are apt to become a bit sticky when he undertakes to match factual realities with provisions of statutes. The amount of discretionary freedom it takes to fill the interstices of the legal formulation of law enforcement competence probably varies from one bureaucracy to the next. Agents concerned with weights and measures are probably less free than building inspectors. On the whole, however, it is safe to assume that none will busy himself, nor be permitted to busy himself, outside of the sphere of his mandate. More importantly, there is no mystery about the proper business of such law enforcement agents, and citizens are generally quite able to hold them to their limits. For example, though a truant officer's enforcement activities could be rich and varied, especially if he happens to be dedicated to his tasks, he can claim legitimate interest in the child's health, the conditions of his home, or some such matter, only insofar as they can be linked with school attendance. In practice it can be debated whether the connection he sees is defensible or not, but there is not debate about the terms on which the question must be decided. Because it is known what a truant officer is supposed to do, therefore he can be held to account for doing more or doing less than his mandate authorizes or requires him to do, and by the same token, the officer can reject demands he deems *ultra vires*.

It would seem reasonable to expect that the proper business of the police—that is, of the corps of officials who inherited the name once used to refer to the entire domain of internal, proscriptive regulation—should be determined in the manner in which the business of all other law enforcement bureaucracies is determined. That is, one would expect that their service and powers be derivative from some substantive authorizing norm. And, indeed, it is commonly assumed that the penal code contains this authorization, in addition to which the police are required to enforce other laws, in particular laws regulating vehicular traffic, and beyond that may have some responsibilities concerning such matters as the licensing of the possession of firearms or the operation of certain business enterprises, which vary greatly from place to place. All in all, however, activities relating to crime control are generally considered basic to the mandate of the police by both citizens and police officials, at least in the sense that its needs are regarded as having priority over other needs (Gorman et al., 1973; Leonard and More, 1971).[1] Though I will argue that this presumption is misguided and misleading, and that one could not possibly understand or control what policemen actually do by assuming it, it must be said that it is not without some carefully laid foundations, the import of which is difficult to overcome.

The following considerations appear to justify the presumption that the police are a law enforcement agency whose mandate is basically derivative of the provisions of penal codes. First, the police, together with many others, cultivate and propagate the image of the policeman as the vanguard fighter in the war on crime. Americans from the members of Congress to readers of tabloids are convinced that what the police do about crime is the main part of the struggle against it and that, therefore, doing something about it is the policeman's main care. Second the formal bureaucratic organization of policework stringently reinforces the view that the police are primarily dedicated to criminal law enforcement. Police training, such as it is, heavily emphasizes criminalistics, criminal law, and related matters; the internal administrative differentiation of departments tends to reflect primarily formal criminal enforcement special- izations and units are designated by names of species of offenses; and police

THE POTENTIAL FOR REFORM OF CRIMINAL JUSTICE

record keeping is almost wholly dedicated to the recording of law enforcement activity as a result of which crime control is the only *documentable* output of police work. Most importantly perhaps, career advancement in departments is heavily determined by an officer's show of initiative and ability in criminal law enforcement or, at least, an officer who has some so-called good pinches to his credit can always count that this will weigh more heavily in his favor when it comes to assessing his overall performance than any other factor. Third, the criminal process is virtually always set into motion by the police, and prosecutors, judges, and correctional personnel are heavily dependent on the police to remain occupied. Moreover, the part the police play in the administration of justice is very specific and indispensible. They are charged with the responsibility of conducting investigations leading to the identification of suspects and with securing the evidence required for successful prosecution. And they are obliged to apprehend and detain identified suspects, in the course of which they are empowered to use force if force is necessary. Fourth, the work of a certain number of policemen—the number is probably not very large but large enough to be significant—is in fact quite plainly determined by the provisions of the penal code in more or less the same manner in which the work of building inspectors is determined by building codes. These are officers assigned to various detective bureaus, whose daily routines consist of investigating crimes, arresting offenders, and of otherwise being engaged with matters related to efforts to obtain convictions.

In sum, the exercise of internal, proscriptive control by modern governments has been highly legalized, at least since the end of the eighteenth century. The exercise of this control is assigned to specifically authorized bureaucracies, each of which has a substantively limited field of enforcement competence. Even though it is allowed that officials retain a measure of discretionary freedom, the terms on which substantive decisions can be made are not in dispute. In accordance with this view the police often are viewed as one of several enforcement bureaucracies whose domain of competence is determined by penal codes and certain other statutory delegations.

THE POLICE AND CRIMINAL LAW ENFORCEMENT

With all this admitted as true, why can the police mandate not be conceived as embodying the law enforcement mandate inhering in criminal law enforcement? The answer is quite simple. Regardless of how strenuously criminal law enforcement is emphasized in the image of the policeman and in police administration, and regardless of how important police work might actually be for keeping the administration of criminal justice in business, the activity of criminal law enforcement is not at all characteristic of day-to-day, ordinary occupational practices of the vastly preponderant majority of policemen. In other words, when one looks at what policemen actually do, one finds that criminal law enforcement is something that most of them do with the frequency located somewhere between virtually never and very rarely.

Later in this paper I will address this paradox directly and try to assign to criminal law enforcement its proper place within police work. Before moving on to this, however, I must touch on some matters connected with manpower allocation, opportunity for crime control, and routine work orientation. Unfortunately the data base on which the first two observations rely is poor, partly because the information available on these matters is not as good as it could be, but in larger measure because the actuarial ratios and frequencies I shall mention are drawn from data produced to meet requirements of accountability rather than strictly factual reporting. A word of caution is in order here; it is all too easy to fall into an attitude of supercilious critique concerning the poverty of data. The fact is that neither the police nor functionaries in other practical endeavors should be expected to keep records that would make it convenient for scholars to study them. Indeed, they usually have good reasons for keeping what in the scholar's view appear to be poor records (Garfinkel and Bittner, 1967: 186-207).

According to a survey of municipal police departments of cities in the 300,000 to 1,000,000 population range which is, alas, neither exhaustive nor complete, 86.5% of all police line personnel—that is, excluding officers occupying supervisory positions from sergeant up—are assigned to uniformed patrol (Kansas City Police Department, 1971; Wilson, 1963: 293).[2] Though this figure excludes persons holding the civil service rank of patrolman while assigned to detectives' bureaus, it probably overestimates the relative size of the force of patrolmen actually working on the streets. But it would certainly seem safe to assume that four out of five members of the line personnel do the work of patrolmen, especially since patrol-sergeants, whose work is essentially of the same nature as the work of those they supervise, are not included in the 86.5%. But the importance of the uniformed patrol in the police is not altogether derivative from the preponderance of their number. They represent, in even greater measure than their numbers indicate, the police presence in society. In fact, I will argue that all the other members of the police—in particular, the various special plainclothes details—represent special refinements of police-patrol work that are best understod as derivative of the mandate of the patrol, even though their activities sometimes take on forms that are quite unlike the activities of the patrol. But I should like to make clear now that in subordinating the work of the detectives to the work of the patrol *conceptually,* I do not intend to cast doubts on the special importance the work of the former has for the prosecutors and judges. Indeed, I hope to make clear by dint of what circumstance prosecutors and judges come to be the beneficiaries of a service they ordinarily take for granted but for which—in rather rare moments of candor—they profess to lack understanding.

For the reasons I indicated, and because of reasons I hope to add as I go along, the following remarks will concern primarily the work of the uniformed patrol. But I do intend to make references to other parts of the police wherever such references are called for. In fact, the first observation about criminal law enforcement pertains equally to the work of detectives and patrolmen.

It is well known that the penal codes the police are presumed to enforce contain thousands of titles. While many of these titles are obscure, unknown, or irrelevant to existing conditions, and the administration of criminal justice is concentrated around a relatively small fraction of all proscribed acts, the police select only some, even from that sample, for enforcement. Relying mainly on my observations, I believe the police tend to avoid involvement with offenses in which it is assumed that the accused or suspected culprits will not try to evade the criminal process by flight. Characteristically, for example, they refer citizens who complain about being defrauded by businesses or landlords directly to the prosecutor. The response is also often given in cases involving other types of allegations of property crimes involving persons, real or fictional, who own substantial property. To be sure, in some of these instances it is possible that the wrong is of a civil rather than a criminal nature, and it also should be taken into account that a principle of economy is at work here, and that the police disavow responsibility for some delicts simply because of lack of resources to deal with them. It is at least reasonable to suggest, however, that police interest in criminal law enforcement is limited to those offenses in which the perpetrator needs to be *caught* and where catching him *may* involve the use of physical force. The point in all this is not that the police are simply ignorant of, and uninterested in, the majority of the provisions of the penal code, but that their selectivity follows a specific principle, namely, that they feel called upon to act only when *their* special competence is required, and that special competence is related to the possibility that force *may* have to be used to secure the appearance of a defendant in court. This restriction is certainly not impermeable, and it happens often enough that policemen are for a variety of circumstantial reasons required to proceed in cases in which the voluntary appearance of a defendant in court is not in doubt. Interestingly, however, in many of these cases the police are likely to put on a symbolic show of force by gratuitously handcuffing the arrested person.

It has become commonplace to say that patrolmen do not invoke the law often. But this is not a very good way of putting things because it could also be said that neurosurgeons do not operate often, at least not when compared with the frequency with which taxi drivers transport their fares. So it might pay to try to be a bit more specific about it. According to estimates issued by the research division of the International Association of Chiefs of Police, "the percentage of the police effort devoted to the traditional criminal law matters probably does not exceed ten per cent" (Niederhoffer, 1969: 75). Reiss, who studied the practices of the patrol in a number of American metropolitan centers, in trying to characterize a typical day's work, stated that it defies all efforts of typification "except in the sense that *the modal tour of duty does not involve an arrest* of any person" (Reiss, 1971: 19). Observations about arrest frequency are, of course, not a very good source of information about law enforcement concerns. Yet, while they must be viewed skeptically, they deserve mention. According to the Uniform Crime Reports, 97,000 detectives and patrolmen made 2,597,000 arrests, including 548,000 for Index Crimes.[3] This means that the average member of the line staff makes 26 arrests annually, of which slightly more than five involve serious crimes. Though it is admittedly no more than a rough guess, it would seem reasonable to say, allowing for the fact that detectives presumably do nothing else, that patrolmen make about one arrest per man per month, and certainly no more than three Index Crime arrests per man per year. In any case, these figures are of the same order of magnitude as reported in the draft of a report on police productivity, where it was said that patrolmen assigned to New York City's Anti-Crime Squad average about 15 felony arrests per man per year, while "a typical uniformed patrolman makes only about three felony arrests per year." In Detroit members of the Special Crime Attack Team make ten felony arrests per man per year, "considerably more than the average patrolman" (National Commission on Productivity, 1973: 39f). And the figures are also in good accord with estimates reported by the President's Commission on Law Enforcement and Administration of Justice, where it was calculated on the basis of data drawn from the operations of the Los Angeles Police Department that "an individual patrol officer can expect an opportunity to detect a burglary no more than once every three months and a robbery no more than once every 14 years" (Institute for Defense Analysis, 1967: 12).

It could be said, and should be considered, that the mere frequency of arrest does not reflect police work in the area of criminal law enforcement adequately. Two points deserve attention in this regard: first, that clearing crimes and locating suspects takes time; and second, that policemen frequently do not invoke the law where the law could be invoked and thus *are* involved in law enforcement, albeit in an unauthorized way.

In regard to the first point, it is certainly true that there are some cases that are subject to dogged and protracted investigation. It is even not unheard of that uniformed patrolmen work on some crime for long periods while attending to other duties. This, however, is not characteristic of the work of either detectives or patrolmen generally. For instance, in the majority of reported burglaries, a patrolman or a team of patrolmen are dispatched to survey the scene; this is followed by investigations done by detectives, who, after writing up a report of their investigation, in the majority of cases simply move on to the next case (Conklin and Bittner, 1973: 206-23).[4] Along these lines, Conklin reports that criminal *investigations* of robberies produce clearances only in one out of fifty cases (Conklin, 1972: 148f). And even if it were to be assumed that detectives engage in five investigations for every one they conclude successfully—no doubt a gross exaggeration—it would still remain that in the run-of-the-mill crime the kind of investigation common lore associates with detective work is not characteristic of the police, and could not be, if only because the press of new business pushes old cases into the dead file. I must add that the whole matter of crime investigation is complicated, involving activities that I did not mention. But I only intended to show that the spacing of arrests is not due to the fact that the policemen need time to work out a solution. All this means is that cases are solved, when they are solved, either at the time the offense takes place or shortly thereafter or, by and large, not at all. The information required for such solution must be mobilizable in short order, or the quest will be abandoned. In other words, either a detective knows quite clearly in the case where to turn or he will not try to pursue the matter. That he often knows where to turn is part of his craft (Bittner, 1970: 65ff).[5]

The other point, that policemen make law enforcement decisions of "low visibility," is the topic of a fairly substantial body of literature.[6] According to the prevailing view expressed in this literature, patrolmen usurp the rights of judges in a host of minor offenses and, by not invoking the law, exculpate the offender. While most authors find such practices reasonable and for the most part desirable, they also recommend that the exercise of such discretion should be placed under administrative, if not statutory, regulation (Davis, 1971). They urge that, though it appears to make good sense that policemen do not enforce statutes pertaining to gambling literally and in every applicable case, it is not right that the decision when to proceed and when to desist should be left entirely to the lights of the individual officers. Provided with more detailed instructions officers would be, presumably, on firmer grounds and, hopefully, less arbitrary. Unfortunately, underlying the approach is a presumption that begs the principal question; namely, whether in making the arrests they make, and not making the arrests they do not make, policemen are acting as the *functionaries of the law* they invoke or fail to invoke, as the case may be. All available information about the practices of patrolmen place this presumption in grave doubt, especially in regard to laws pertaining to minor offenses. I am not aware of any descriptions of police work on the streets that support the view that patrolmen walk around, respond to service demands, or intervene in situations, with the provisions of the penal code in mind, matching what they see with some title or another, and deciding whether any particular apparent infraction is serious enough to warrant being referred for further process. While it does happen occasionally that patrolmen arrest some person merely because they have probable cause to believe that he has committed crimes, this is not the way all but a small fraction of arrests come about. In the typical case the formal charge *justifies* the arrest a patrolman makes but is *not* the *reason* for it. The actual reason is located in a domain of considerations to which Professor Wilson referred as the need "to handle the situation,"[7] and invoking the law is merely a device whereby this is sometimes accomplished. Since the persons who are arrested at a backyard game of craps are not arrested because they are gambling but because of a complex of situational factors of which no mention is made in the formally filed charge, it would seem specious to try to refine the law pertaining to the charge, since any policeman worth his salt is virtually always in a position to find a *bona fide* charge of some kind when he believes the situation calls for an arrest. In sum, if criminal law enforcement means acting on the basis of, and in accordance with, the law's provisions, then this is something policemen do occasionally, but in their routine work they merely avail themselves of the provisions as a means for attaining other objectives.

In sum, the vastly preponderant number of policemen are assigned to activities in which they have virtually no opportunities for criminal law enforcement, and the available data indicate that they are engaged in it with a frequency that surely casts doubts upon the belief that this is the substance, or even the core, of their mandate. Moreover, criminal law enforcement by the police is limited to those offenses in which it is assumed that force may have to be used to bring the offender to justice. Finally, in the majority of cases in which the law is invoked, the decision to invoke it is not based on considerations of legality. Instead, policemen use the provisions of the law as a resource for handling problems of all sorts, of which *no mention* is made in the formal charge.

THE ELEMENTS OF ROUTINE POLICE PRACTICE

To explain by what conception of duty policemen feel summoned into action, and what objectives they seek to attain, I should like to use an example of ordinary practice. One of the most common experiences of urban life is the sight of a patrolman directing traffic at a busy street intersection. This service is quite expensive and the assignment is generally disliked among policemen. Nevertheless it is provided on a regular basis. The reason for this is not too difficult to divine. Aside from the private interests of citizens in maintaining safe and otherwise suitable conditions for the use of their automobiles, there is the consideration that the viability of urban life as we know it depends heavily on the mobility of vehicular traffice. No one knows, of course, how helpful police traffic control is in general, much less in the special case of a single patrolman directing traffic at a particular place and time. However uncertain the value of traffic control, the uncertainty is resolved in favor of having it simply because of the anticipated gravity of the consequences its absence might engender. In sum, traffic control is a matter of utmost seriousness. Despite its seriousness and presumed necessity, despite the fact that assignments are planned ahead and specifically funded, no assignment to a traffic control post is ever presumed to be absolutely fixed. The assigned officer is expected to be there, all things being equal, but he is also expected to have an independent grasp of the necessity of his presence. The point is not that this opens the possibility of a somewhat more casual attitude towards traffic control than the police care to admit, but rather that there exists a tacit understanding that no matter how important the post might be, it is always possible for something else to come up that can distract the patrolman's attention from it and cause him to suspend attending to the assigned task.

This understanding is not confined to traffic control assignments, but functions in all prior assigned tasks without any exceptions whatever, regardless whether the assignment involves investigating a heinous crime or feeding ice cream to a lost child, and regardless whether the prior assignment derives from the most solemn dictates of the law or whether it is based on mundane commands of immediate superiors. I am saying more than merely that patrolmen, like everybody else, will suspend the performance of an assigned task to turn to some extraordinary exigency. While everybody might respond to the call of an emergency, the policeman's vocational ear is *permanently and specifically attuned* to such calls, and his work attitude throughout is permeated by preparedness to respond to it, whatever he might happen to be doing. In the case at hand, it is virtually certain that any normally competent patrolman would abandon the traffic post to which he was assigned without a moment's hesitation and without regard for the state of the traffic he was supposed to monitor, if it came to his attention that a crime was being committed somewhere at a distance not too far for him to reach in time either to arrest the crime in its course, or to arrest its perpetrator. And it is virtually certain that all patrolmen would abandon their posts even when the probability of arresting the crime or its perpetrator was not very high, and even when the crime was of the sort which when reported to the police in the ordinary manner—that is, some time after it happened—would receive only the most cursory attention and would tend to remain unsolved in nine out of every ten reported cases. Finally, there is no doubt that the patrolman who would not respond in this manner, would thereby expose himself to the risk of an official reprimand, and to expressions of scorn from his co-workers, and from the public.

Yet there exists no law, no regulation, no formal requirement of any kind that determines that practice. Quite the contrary, it is commonly accepted that crime control cannot be total, must be selective, and that policemen cannot be expected to rush to the scene of every crime and arrest every offender. Why then should all concerned, inside and outside the police, consider it entirely proper and desirable that a patrolman abandon his post, exposing many people to serious inconvenience and the whole city to grave hazards, to pursue the dubious quest of catching a two-bit thief?

At the level of reason the patrolman himself might advance, the action merely follows the impulse to drop everything and catch a crook. And it seems perfectly reasonable that policemen should follow this impulse more readily than others, since they presumably are being paid for it. Thus considered, the action draws its justification from the public sentiment that a crime must not be allowed to pass without at least an attempt to oppose it, and from the policeman's special obligation in this regard. This sentiment is certainly a very important aspect of the policeman's frame of mind; it directs his interests, establishes priorities, furnishes justification for action, governs the expectations of reward and honor, and ultimately supplies the rhetoric with which his ready aggressiveness is explained.

But I have argued earlier that, the strength of this sentiment notwithstanding, criminal law enforcement could not possibly be the fulcrum on which the police mandate rests. How then do I explain the alacrity of the patrolman's response? Let me begin with an aside which is in its own way important but not central to the argument. For the patrolman, rushing to the scene of a crime is an opportunity to do something remarkable that will bring him to the attention of his superiors in a way that might advance his career. This aspect of his vocational interest is not rooted in the work he does but in the administrative setting within which it is done. Skolnick (1966: 231) has furnished extensive documentation for the importance of this factor in police work. Still, however important the explanation is, it fails in explaining police routines generally.

When I stated in the vignette that the patrolman will abandon his assignment to rush to the scene of a crime, I assumed without saying that the crime would

[30]   THE POTENTIAL FOR REFORM OF CRIMINAL JUSTICE

be something like an act of vandalism, an assault, or a burglary. But if the crime that came to the attention of the officer had been something like a conspiracy by a board of directors of a commercial concern to issue stock with the intention of defrauding investors, or a landlord criminally extorting payments from a tenant, or a used-car dealer culpably turning back an odometer on an automobile he was preparing for sale, the patrolman would scarcely life his gaze, let alone move into action. The real reason why the patrolman moved was not the fact that what was taking place was a crime in general terms, but because the particular crime was a member of a class of problems *the treatment of which will not abide.* In fact, the patrolman who unhesitatingly left his post to pursue an assailant would have left his post with just a little hesitation to pull a drowning person out of the water, to prevent someone from jumping off the roof of a building, to protect a severely disoriented person from harm, to save people in a burning structure, to disperse a crowd hampering the rescue mission of an ambulance, to take steps to prevent a possible disaster that might result from broken gas lines or water mains, and so on almost endlessly, and entirely without regard to the substantive nature of the problem, as long as it could be said that it involved *something-that-ought-not-to-be-happening-and-about-which-someone-had-better-do-something-now!* These extraordinary events, and the directly intuited needs for control that issue from them, are what the vocational interests of patrolmen are attuned to. And in the circumstances of such events citizens feel entitled and obliged to summon the help of the police. Naturally, in retrospect it is always possible to question whether this or that problem should or should not have become the target of police attention, but most people will agree that urban life is replete with situations in which the need for such service is not in doubt, and in which, accordingly, the service of the police is indispensible.

It is scarcely possible not to notice that the definition of the police mandate escaped Ockham's Rasor. It cannot be helped; I have seen policemen helping a tenant in arrears gain access to medication which a landlord held together with other possessions in apparently legal bailment, I have seen policemen settling disputes between parents as to whether an ill child should receive medical treatment, I have seen a patrolman adjudicating a quarrel between a priest and an organist concerning the latter's access to the church. All this suggests more than the obvious point that the duties of patrolmen are of a mind-boggling variety, it compels the stronger inference that no human problem exists, or is imaginable, about which it could be said with finality that this certainly could not become the proper business of the police.

It is fair to say that this is well-known even though police work is not thought of in these terms. It must be assumed to be well-known because in almost all instances the police service is a response to citizen demands, which must be taken as reflecting public knowledge of what is expected of the police. But evidently it is not thought of in these terms when it comes to writing books about the police, to making up budgets for the police, and to training policemen, administering departments, and rewarding performance. And even though the fact that policemen are "good" at helping people in trouble and dealing with troublesome people has received some measure of public recognition recently,[8] the plaudits are stated in ways reminiscent of "human interest stories" one finds in the back pages of the daily papers. More importantly, when it is asked on what terms this police service is made available in every conceivable kind of emergency, the usual answer is that it happens by default because policemen are the only functionaries, professionals, officials—call them what you will—who are available around the clock and who can be counted on to make house-calls. Further, it is often said that it would be altogether better if policemen were not so often called upon to do chores lying within the spheres of vocational competence of physicians, nurses, and social workers, and did not have to be all things to all men. I believe that these views are based on a profound misconception of what policemen do, and I propose to show that no matter how much police activity seems like what physicians and social workers might do, and even though what they actually have to do often could be done by physicians and social workers, the service they perform involves the exercise of a unique competence they do not share with anyone else in society. Even if physicians and social workers were to work around the clock and make house-calls, the need for the police service in their areas would remain substantial, though it certainly would decline in volume. Though policemen often do what psychologists, physicians, or social workers might be expected to do, their involvement in cases is never that of surrogate psychologists, physicians, or social workers. They are in all these cases, from the beginning, throughout, and in the last analysis, policemen, and their interest and objectives are of a radically distinct nature. Hence, saying that policemen are "good at" dealing with people in trouble and troublesome people does not mean that they are good at playing the role of other specialists. Indeed, only by assuming a distinct kind of police competence can one understand why psychologists, physicians, and social workers run into problems in *their* work for which they seek police assistance. In other words, when a social worker "calls the cops" to help him with his work, he mobilizes the kind of intervention that is characteristic of police work even when it looks like social work.

To make clear what the special and unique competence of the police consists of I should like to characterize the events containing "something-that-ought-not-to-be-happening-and-about-which-somebody-had-better-do-something-now," and the ways the police respond to them. A word of caution: I do not intend to imply that everything policemen attend to can be thus characterized. That is, the special and unique police competence comes into play about as often as practicing medicine, doing engineering, or teaching—in the narrow meanings of these terms—come into play in what physicians, engineers, and teachers do.

First, and foremost, *the need to do something* is assessed with regard for actually existing combinations of circumstances. Even though circumstances of need do become stereotyped, so that some problems appear to importune greater urgency than others, the rule *it depends* takes precedence over typification, and attention is directed to what is singular and particular to the here-and-now. Policemen often say that their work is almost entirely unpredictable; it might be more correct to say that anything unpredictable that cannot be dismissed or assimilated to the usual is *pro tanto* a proper target of police attention. That experience plays an important part in the decision-making goes without saying, but it is not the kind of experience that lends itself easily to the systematization one associates with a body of technical knowledge. Most often the knowledge upon which patrolmen draw is the acquaintance with particular persons, places, and past events. Patrolmen appear to have amazingly prodigious memories and are able to specify names, addresses, and other factual details of past experiences with remarkable precision. Indeed, it is sometimes difficult to believe that all this information could be correct. However this may be, the fact that they report their activities in this manner, and that they appear to think in such terms, may be taken as indicative of the type of knowledge they depend on in their work. It could be said that while anything at all could become properly the business of the police, the patrolman can only decide whether anything in particular is properly his business after he "gets there" and examines it.

Second, the question whether some situational need justifiably requires police attention is very often answered by persons who solicit the service. Citizen demand is a factor of extraordinary importance for the distribution of police service, and the fact that someone did "call the cops" is, in and of itself, cause for concern. To be sure, there are some false alarms in almost every tour of duty, and one reason why police departments insist on employing seasoned policemen as dispatchers is because they presumably are skilled in detecting calls which lack merit. Generally, however, the determination that some development has reached a critical stage, ripe for police interest, is related to the attitudes of persons involved, and depends on common sense reasoning. For example, in a case involving a complaint about excessive noise, it is not the volume of the noise that creates hazards for life, limb, property, and the public order, but that the people involved say and otherwise show that the problem has reached a critical stage in which something-had-better be-done-about-it. Closely connected with the feature of critical emergency is the expectation that policemen will handle the problem "then-and-there." Though it may seem obvious, it deserves stressing that police work involves no continuances and no appointments, but that its temporal structure is throughout of the "as soon as I can get to it" norm, and that its scheduling derives from the natural fall of events, and not from any externally imposed order, as is the case for almost all other kinds of occupations. Firemen too are permanently on call, but the things they are called upon to do are limited to a few technical services. A policeman is always poised to move on any contingency whatever, not knowing what it might be, but knowing that far more often than not he will be expected to *do something*. The expectation to do something is projected upon the scene, the patrolman's diagnostic instinct is heavily colored by it, and he literally sees things in the light of the expectation that he somehow *has* to handle the situation. The quick-witted and decisive activism of the police is connected with the fact that they are attuned to dealing with emergencies; and in many instances the response-readiness of the policeman rounds out the emergency character of the need to which the response was directed.

Third, though police departments are highly bureaucratized and patrolmen are enmeshed in a scheme of strict internal regulation, they are, paradoxically, quite alone and independent in their dealings with citizens. Accordingly, the obligation to do something when a patrolman confronts problems—that is, when he does police work—is something he does not share with anyone. He may call for help when there is a risk that he might be overwhelmed, and will receive it; short of such risks, however, he is on his own. He receives very little guidance and almost no supervision; he gets advice when he asks for it, but since policemen do not share information, asking for and giving advice is not built into their relations; his decisions are reviewed only when there are special reasons for review, and records are kept of what he does only when he makes arrests. Thus, in most cases, problems and needs are seen in relationship to the response capacity of an individual patrolman or teams of two patrolmen, and not of the police as an organized enterprise. Connected with the expectation that he will do what needs to be done by himself is the expectation that he will limit himself to imposing provisional solutions upon problems. Though they often express frustration at never solving anything—especially when they arrest persons and find them quickly back on the street—they do what they do with an abandon characteristic of all specialists who disregard the side-effects of their activities. As they see it, it is none of their concern that many provisional solutions have lasting consequences. In fact, it would be quite well put to say that they are totally absorbed with making arrests, in the literal sense of the term. That is, they are always trying to snatch things from the brink of disaster, to nip untoward development in the bud, and generally to arrest whatever must not be permitted to continue; and to accomplish this they sometimes arrest persons, if circumstances appear to demand it.

Fourth and finally, like everybody else, patrolmen want to succeed in what they undertake. But unlike everybody else, they never retreat. Once a policeman has defined a situation as properly his business and undertakes to do something about it, he will not desist till he prevails. That the policemen are uniquely empowered and required to carry out their decisions in the "then-and-there" of emergent problems is the structurally central feature of police work. There can be no doubt that the decisive and unremitting character of police intervention is uppermost in the minds of people who solicit it, and that persons against whom the police proceed are mindful of this feature and conduct themselves accordingly. The police duty not to retreat in the face of resistance is matched by the duty of citizens not to oppose them. While under Common Law citizens had the right to resist illegal police action, at least in principle, the recommendations contained in the Uniform Arrest Act, the adoption of which is either complete or pending before most state legislatures, provides that they must submit. To be sure, the act pertains only to arrest powers, but it takes little imagination to see that this is sufficient to back up any coercive option a policeman might elect.[9]

The observation that policemen prevail in what they undertake must be understood as a *capacity* but not a necessarily invariant practice. When, for example, a citizen is ordered to move or to refrain from what he is doing, he may actually succeed in persuading the policeman to reverse himself. But contrary to judges, policemen are not required to entertain motions, nor are they required to stay their orders while the motion receives reasoned consideration. Indeed, *even* if the citizen's objection should receive favorable consideration in *subsequent* review, it would still be said that "under the circumstances" he should have obeyed. And even if it could be proved that the policeman's action was injudicious or in violation of civil liberties, he would be held to account only if it could also be proved that he acted with malice or with wanton frivolity.[10]

In sum, what policemen do appears to consist of rushing to the scene of any crisis whatever, judging its needs in accordance with canons of common sense reasoning, and imposing solutions upon it without regard to resistance or opposition. In all this they act largely as individual practitioners of a craft.

THE SPECIFIC NATURE OF POLICE COMPETENCE

The foregoing considerations suggest the conclusion that what the existence of the police makes available in society is a unique and powerful capacity to cope with all kinds of emergencies: unique, because they are far more than anyone else permanently poised to deal with matters brooking no delay; powerful, because their capacity for dealing with them appears to be wholly unimpeded. But the notion of emergency brings a certain circularity into the definition of the mandate. This is so because, as I have indicated, the discernment of the facts of emergency relies on common sense criteria of judgment, and this makes it altogether too easy to move from saying that the police deal with emergencies, to saying that anything the police deal with is, *ipso facto*, an emergency. And so, while invoking the notion of emergency was useful to bring up certain observations, it now can be dispensed with entirely.

Situations like those involving a criminal on the lam, a person trapped in a burning building, a child in desperate need of medical care, a broken gas line, and so on, made it convenient to show why policemen move decisively in imposing constraints upon them. Having exploited this approach as far as it can take us, I now wish to suggest that the specific competence of the police is wholly contained in their capacity for decisive action. More specifically, that the feature of decisiveness derives from the authority to overpower opposition in the "then-and-there" of the situation of action. *The policeman, and the policeman alone, is equipped, entitled, and required to deal with every exigency in which force may have to be used, to meet it.* Moreover, the authorization to use force is conferred upon the policeman with the mere proviso that force will be used in amounts measured not to exceed the necessary minimum, as determined by an intuitive grasp of the situation. And only the use of deadly force is regulated somewhat more stringently.[11]

Three points must be added in explanation of the foregoing. First, I am *not* saying the police work consists of using force to solve problems, but only that police work consists of coping with problems in which force *may have to be used.* This is a distinction of extraordinary importance. Second, it could not possibly be maintained that everything policemen are actually required to do reflects this feature. For a variety of reasons—especially because of the ways in which police departments are administered—officers are often ordered to do chores that have nothing to do with police work. Interestingly, however, the fact that a policeman is quite at the beck and call of his superior and can be called upon to do menial work does not attenuate his powers vis-a-vis citizens in the least. Third, the proposed definition of police competence *fully embraces* those forms of criminal law enforcement policemen engage in. I have mentioned earlier that the special role the police play in the administration of criminal justice has to do with the circumstance that "criminals"—as distinct from respectable and propertied persons who violate the provisions of penal codes in the course of doing business—can be counted on to try to evade or oppose arrest. Because this is so, and to enable the police to deal effectively with criminals, they are said to be empowered to use force. They also engage in criminal investigations whenever such investigations might be reasonably expected to be instrumental in making arrests. But the conception of the police role in all this is upside down. It is *not* that policemen are entitled to use force because they must deal with nasty criminals. Instead, the duty of handling nasty criminals devolves on them *because* they have the more general authority to use force *as needed* to bring about desired objectives. It is, after all, no more than a matter of simple expediency that it should be so; and that is is so becomes readily apparent upon consideration that policemen show little or no interest in all those kinds of offenders about whom it is not assumed that they need to be caught, and that force may have to be used to bring them to the bar of justice.

CONCLUSIONS

There is a threefold paradox in the awesome power of the policeman to make citizens obey his command, both legitimately and effectively. First, how come such a power exists at all? Second, why has the existence of this power not received the consideration it deserves? Third, why is the exercise of this power entrusted to persons recruited from a cohort from which all those with talent and ambitions must be assumed to have gone on to college and then to other occupations? I shall attempt to answer these questions in the stated order.

The hallmark of the period of history comprising the past century and a half is a succession of vast outbreaks of internal and international violence, *incongruously combined* with an unprecedently sustained aspiration to install peace as a stable condition of social life.[12] There can be no doubt that during this period the awareness of the moral and practical necessity of peace took hold of the minds of almost all the people of our world, and while the advocacy of warfare and of violent revolution has not disappeared, it has grown progressively less frank and arguments in their favor seem to be losing ground to arguments condemning violence. The sentiments in favor of peace draw in part on humane motives, but they derive more basically from a profound shift of values, away from virtues associated with masculine prowess and combativeness, and towards virtues associated with assiduous enterprise and material progress. There is still some glamor left in being an adventurer or warrior, but true success belongs to the businessman and to the professional.[13] Resorting to violence—outside of its restricted occasions, notably warfare and recreation—is seen as a sign of immaturity or lower-class culture (Miller, 1958: 5-19; Adorno et al., 1950). The banishment of violence from the domain of private life—as compared, for instance, with its deliberate cultivation in Medieval Chivalry—is the lesser part of the story. More important is the shift in the methods of government to an almost complete civil and pacific form of administration. Physical force has either vanished or is carefully concealed in the administration of criminal justice, and the use of armed retainers to collect taxes and to recruit into the military are forgotten. Paper, not the sword, is the instrument of coercion of our day. But no matter how faithfully and how methodically the dictates of this civil culture and of the rule of law are followed, and no matter how penetrating and far-reaching the system of peaceful control and regulation might be, there must remain some mechanism for dealing with problems on a catch-as-catch-can basis. In fact, it would seem that the only practical way for banishing the use of force from life generally is to assign its residual exercise—where according to circumstances it appears unavoidable—to a specially deputized corps of officials, that is, to the police as we know it. Very simply, as long as there will be fools who can insist that their comfort and pleasure take precedence over the needs of firemen for space in fighting a fire, and who will not move to make room, so long will there be a need for policemen.

I must leave out one possible explanation for the neglect of the capacity to use force as the basis of the police mandate; namely, that I am wrong in my assessment of its fundamental importance. I have no idea why the authors of many superb studies of various aspects of police work have not reached this conclusion. Perhaps they were either too close to, or too far from, what they were researching. But I believe I know why this feature of police work has escaped general notice. Until recently the people against whom the police had cause to proceed, especially to proceed forcefully, came almost exclusively from among the blacks, the poor, the young, the Spanish speaking, and the rest of the urban proletariat, and they still come preponderantly from these segments of society. This is well-known, much talked about, and I have nothing to add to what has already been said about expressions of class- and race-bias. Instead, I should like to draw attention to a peculiar consequence of this concentration. The lives of the people I mentioned are often considered the locus of problems in which force may have to be used. Not only do most of the criminals with whom the police deal hail from among them, but they, more often than other members of society, get into all sorts of troubles, and they are less resourceful in handling their problems. And so it could be said that the police merely follow troubles into trouble's native habitat and that no further inferences can be drawn from it, except, perhaps, that policemen are somewhat too quick in resorting to force and too often resort to it for what seem to be inadequate reasons, at least in retrospect. Of course, the rise of the counter-culture, the penetration of drug use into the middle classes, the civil rights movements of the 1960s, and the student movement have proven that the police do not hesitate to act coercively against members of the rest of society. But that too has been mainly the target of critique, rather than efforts to interpret it. And the expressions of indignation we hear have approximately the effect "gesundheit" has on whatever causes a person to sneeze. The police are naturally baffled by the response; as far as they can see they did what they always did whenever they were called upon to intervene. In point of fact policemen did, *mutatis mutandis,* what physicians do under similar circumstances. Physicians are supposed to cure the sick through the practice of medicine, as everyone knows. But when they are consulted about some problem of an ambiguous nature, they define it as an illness and try to cure it. And teachers do not hesitate in treating everything as an educational problem. It is certainly possible to say that physicians and teachers are just as likely to go overboard as policemen. This does not mean, however, that one cannot find in these instances the true nature of their respective bags of tricks more clearly revealed than in the instances of more standard practice. In the case of the police, it merely obscures matters to say that they resort to force only against powerless people, either because it is more often necessary or because it is easier—even though these *are* important factors in determining frequency—for in fact, they define every summons to action as containing the possibility of the use of force.

The reasons why immense powers over the lives of citizens are assigned to men recruited with a view that they will be engaged in a low-grade occupation are extraordinarily complicated, and I can only touch on some of them briefly. Perhaps the most important factor is that the police were created as a mechanism for coping with the so-called dangerous classes (Silver, 1967: 1-24). In the struggle to contain the internal enemy and in the efforts to control violence, depredation, and evil, police work took on some of the features of its targets and became a tainted occupation. Though it may seem perverse, it is not beyond comprehension that in a society which seeks to banish the use of force, those who take it upon themselves to exercise its remaining indispensible residue should be deprecated. Moreover, in the United States the police were used blatantly as in instrument of urban machine-politics, which magnified opportunities for corrupt practices enormously. Thus, the Americam urban policeman came to be generally perceived as the dumb, brutal, and crooked cop. This image was laced by occasional human interest stories in which effective and humane police work was portrayed as the exception to the rule. The efforts of some reformers to purge the police of brutality and corruption have inadvertently strengthened the view that police work consists of doing what one is told and keeping one's nose clean. To gain the upper hand over sloth, indolence, brutality, and corruption, officials like the late Chief William Parker of Los Angeles militarized the departments under their command. But the development of stringent internal regulation only obscured the true nature of police work.

The new image of the policeman as a snappy, low-level, soldier-bureaucrat created no inducement for people who thought they could do better to elect police work as their vocation. Furthermore, the definition of police work remained associated with the least task that could be assigned to an officer. Finally, the most recent attempts to upgrade the selection of policemen have been resisted and produced disappointing results. The resistance is in large measure due to the employee interests of present personnel. It seems quite understandable that the chiefs, captains, and even veteran patrolmen would not be happy with the prospect of having to work with recruits who outrank them educationally. Furthermore, few people who have worked for college degrees would want to elect an occupation that calls only for a high school diploma. And those few will most likely be the least competent among the graduates, thereby showing that higher education is more likely to be harmful than helpful. And it is true, of course, that nothing one learns in college is particularly helpful for police work. In fact, because most college graduates come from middle-class backgrounds, while most of police work is directed towards members of the lower classes, there is a risk of a cultural gap between those who do the policing and the policed.

But if it is correct to say that the police are here to stay, at least for the foreseeable future, and that the mandate of policemen consists of dealing with all those problems in which force may have to be used, and if we further recognize that meeting this task in a socially useful way calls for the most consummate skill, then it would seem reasonable that only the most gifted, the most aspiring, and the most equipoised among us are eligible for it. It takes only three short steps to arrive at this realization. First, when policemen do those things only policemen can do, they invariably deal with matters of absolutely critical importance, at least to the people with whom they deal. True, these are generally not the people whose welfare is carefully considered. But even if democratic ideals cannot be trusted to insure that they will be treated with the same consideration accorded to the powerful, practicality should advise that those who never had a voice in the past now have spoken and succeeded in being heard. In sum, police work, at its core, involves matters of extraordinary seriousness, importance, and necessity. Second, while lawyers, physicians, teachers, social workers, and clergymen also deal with critical problems, they have bodies of technical knowledge or elaborate schemes of norms to guide them in their respective tasks. But in police work there exists little more than an inchoate lore, and most of what a policeman needs to know to do his work he has to learn on his own. Thus, what ultimately gets done depends primarily on the individual officer's perspicacity, judiciousness, and initiative. Third, the mandate to deal with problems in which force may have to be used implies the special trust that force will be used only *in extremis.* The skill involved in police work, therefore, consists of retaining recourse to force while seeking to avoid its use, and using it only in minimal amounts.

It is almost unnecessary to mention that the three points are not realized in police work. Far too many policemen are contemptuous towards the people with whom they deal and oblivious to the seriousness of their tasks. Few policemen possess the perspicacity and judiciousness their work calls for. And force is not only used often where it need not be used, but gratuitous rudeness and bullying is a widely prevalent vice in policing. While all this is true, I did not arrive at those points by speculating about what police work could be. Instead I have heard about it from policemen, and I saw it in police work. I say this not to make the obvious point that there exist, in many departments, officers whose work already embodies the ideals I mentioned. More important is that there are officers who know what police work calls for far better than I can say, and from whom I have learned what I said. As far as I could see they are practical men who have learned to do police work because they had to. No doubt they were motivated by respect for human dignity, but their foremost concern was effectiveness and craftsmanship. Perhaps I can best describe them by saying that they have in their own practices placed police work on a fully reasoned basis, moving from case to case as individual practitioners of a highly complex vocation.

Though I cannot be sure of it, I believe I have written as a spokesman of these officers because I believe one must look to them to make police work what it should be. But the chances that they will prevail are not very good. The principal obstacle to their success is the presently existing organization of police departments. I cannot go into details to show how the way police work is administratively regulated constitutes a positive impediment in the path of a responsible policeman, quite aside from the fact that most of his work is unrecognized and unrewarded.[14] But I would like to conclude by saying that, far from providing adequate disciplinary control over patent misconduct, the existing organizational structures encourage bad police work. Behind this is the ordinary dose of venality and vanity, and the inertia of the way-things-are. But the principal cause is an illusion. Believing that the real ground for his existence is the perennial pursuit of the likes of Willie Sutton—for which he lacks both opportunity and resources—the policeman feels compelled to minimize the significance of those instances of his performance in which he seems to follow the footsteps of Florence Nightingale. Fearing the role of the nurse or, worse yet, the role of the social worker, the policeman combines resentment against what he has to do day-in-day-out with the necessity of doing it. And in the course of it he misses his true vocation.

One more point remains to be touched upon. I began with a statement concerning the exercise of proscriptive control by government, commonly referred to as Law Enforcement. In all instances, except for the police, law enforcement is entrusted to special bureaucracies whose competence is limited by specific substantive authorization. There exists an understandable tendency to interpret the mandate of the police in accordance with this model. The search for a proper authorizing norm for the police led to the assumption that the criminal code provided it. I have argued that this was a mistake. Criminal law enforcement is merely an incidental and derivative part of police work. They do it simply because it falls within the scope of their larger duties—that is, it becomes part of police work exactly to the same extent as anything else in which force may have to be used, and only to that extent. Whether the police should still be considered a law enforcement agency is a purely taxonomic question of slight interest. All I intended to argue is that their mandate cannot be interpreted as resting on the substantive authorizations contained in the penal codes or any other codes. I realize that putting things this way must raise all sorts of questions in the minds of people beholden to the ideal of the Rule of Law. And I also realize that the Rule of Law has always drawn part of its strength from pretense; but I don't think pretense is entitled to immunity.

NOTES

1. Most textbooks on the police emphasize this point and enumerate the additional law enforcement obligations; see for example, A. C. Gorman, F. D. Jay and R.R.J. Gallati (1973); V. A. Leonard and H. W. More (1971).

2. Kansas City Police Department (1971). The survey contains information on 41 cities of 300,000 to 1,000,000 population. But the percentage cited in the text was computed only for Atlanta, Boston, Buffalo, Dallas, Denver, El Paso, Fort Worth, Honolulu, Kansas City, Memphis, Minneapolis, Oklahoma City, Pittsburgh, Portland, Ore., St. Paul, and San Antonio, because the data for the other cities were not detailed enough. The estimate that detectives make up 13.5 percent of line personnel comports with the estimate of O. W. Wilson (1963: 293), who stated that they make up approximately 10 percent of "sworn personnel."

3. Federal Bureau of Investigations, Uniform Crime Reports (1971). The data are for 57 cities of over 250,000 population, to make the figures correspond, at least roughly, to the data about manpower drawn from sources cited in note 2, supra. I might add that the average arrest rate in all the remaining cities is approximately of the same order as the figures I use in the argument. The so-called Index Crimes comprise homicide, forcible rape, robbery, aggravated assault, burglary, larceny, and auto theft. It should also be mentioned that arrests on Index Crime charges are not tantamount to conviction and it is far from unusual for a person to be charged, e.g., with aggravated assault, to induce him to plead guilty to simple assault, quite aside from failure to prosecute, dismissal, or exculpation by trial.

4. I have accompanied patrolmen and detectives investigating burglaries in two cities and should like to add on the basis of my observation and on the basis of interviews with officers that, in almost all of these cases, there is virtually no promise of clearance, that in most of them the cost of even a routine follow-up investigation would exceed the loss many times over, and that, in any case, the detectives always have a backlog of reported burglaries for which the reporting victims expect prompt consideration. I might also add that it seemed to me that this largely fruitless busy-work demoralizes detectives and causes them to do less work than I thought possible. See J. E. Conklin and E. Bittner (1973).

5. I have reference to the ramified information systems individual detectives cultivate, involving informants and informers, which they do not share with one another. I have touched on this topic in E. Bittner (1970).

6. The work that brought this observation into prominence is J. Goldstein (1960); a comprehensive review of the problem is contained in W. LaFave (1965).

7. J. Q. Wilson (1968: 31, and Chapter II). The observation that policemen make misdemeanor arrests most often on practical rather than legal considerations has been reported by many authors; cf., e.g., J. D. Lohman and G. E. Misner (1966: 168ff.). I have discussed this matter extensively in E. Bittner (1967a). Wistfully illuminating discussions of the topic are to be found, among others, in J. Hall (1953); J. V. Henry (1966); C. D. Robinson (1965).

8. The first expression of recognition is contained in E. Cumming, I. Cumming and L. Edell (1965); cf. also E. Bittner (1967b).

9. S. B. Warner (1942); Corpus Juris Secundum (Vol. 6: 613ff.); M. Hochnagel and H. W. Stege (1966).

10. There exists legal doctrine supporting the contention that resisting or opposing the police in an emergency situation is unlawful, see H. Kelsen (1961: 278ff.), and H.L.A. Hart (1961: 20 ff.). I cite these references to show that the police are legally authorized to do whatever is necessary, according to the nature of the circumstances.

11. "Several modern cases have imposed [a] standard of strict liability . . . upon the officer by conditioning justification of deadly force on the victim's actually having committed a felony, and a number of states have enacted statutes which appear to adopt this strict liability. However, many jurisdictions, such as California, have homicide statutes which permit the police officer to use deadly force for the arrest of a person 'charged' with a felony. It has been suggested that this requirement only indicates the necessity for reasonable belief by the officer that the victim has committed a felony." Note, Stanford Law Review (1961: 566-609).

12. The aspiration has received a brilliant formulation in one of the most influential documents of modern political philosophy. Immanuel Kant (1913); a review of the growth of the ideal of peace is contained in P. Reiwald (1944).

13. Literary glorification of violence has never disappeared entirely, as the works of authors like Nietzsche and Sorel attest. In the most recent past these views have again received eloquent expression in connection with revolutionary movements in Third World nations. The most remarkable statement along these lines is contained in the works of Franz Fanon.

14. But I have given this matter extensive consideration in E. Bittner (1970), note 5, supra.

REFERENCES

ADORNO, T. W. et al. (1950) The Authoritarian Personality. New York: Harper & Row.

BACON, F. (1859) "An Advertizement Touching an Holy War," in Collected Works. Volume 7. London: Spottiswood.

BITTNER, E. (1967a) "Police on skid row: a study of peace keeping." American Sociological Review 32: 600-715.

––– (1967b) "Police discretion in emergency apprehension of mentally ill persons." Social Problems 14: 278-292.

––– (1970) The Functions of the Police in Modern Society. Washington, D. C.: U.S. Government Printing Office.

BLACKSTONE, W. (n.d.) Commentaries on the Laws of England. Volume 4. Oxford, England: Clarendon.

CONKLIN, J. E. (1972) Robbery and the Criminal Justice System. Philadelphia: J. B. Lippincott.

––– and E. BITTNER (1973) "Burglary in a suburb." Criminology 11: 206-232.

Corpus Juris Secundum. "Arrest." Volume 6.

CUMMING, E., I. CUMMING, and L. EDELL (1965) "Policeman as philosopher, guide and friend." Social Problems 12: 276-286.

DAVIS, K. C. (1971) Discretionary Justice: A Preliminary Inquiry. Urbana, Ill.: University of Illinois Press.

Federal Bureau of Investigations (1971) Uniform Crime Reports. Washington, D. C.: U.S. Government Printing Office.

GARFINKEL, H. and E. BITTNER (1967) "Good organizational reasons for 'bad' clinic records," pp. 186-207 in H. Garfinkel, Studies in Ethnomethodology. Englewood Cliffs, N.J.: Prentice-Hall.

GOLDSTEIN, J. (1960) "Police discretion not to invoke the criminal process." Yale Law Journal 69: 543-594.

GORMAN, A. C., F. D. JAY, and R.R.J. GALLATI (1973) Introduction to Law Enforcement and Criminal Justice. Rev. 19th printing. Springfield, Ill.: C. C. Thomas.

HALL, J. (1953) "Police and the law in a democratic society." Indiana Law Journal 23: 133-177.

HAMILTON, W. H. and C. C. RODEE (1937) "Police power," in Encyclopedia of the Social Sciences. Volume 12. New York: Macmillan.

HART, H.L.A. (1961) The Concept of Law. Oxford, England: Clarendon Press.

HENRY, J. V. (1966) "Breach of peace and disorderly conduct laws: void for vagueness?" Howard Law Journal 12: 318-331.

HOCHNAGEL, M. and H. W. STEGE (1966) "The right to resist unlawful arrest: an outdated concept?" Tulsa Law Journal 3: 40-46.

Institute for Defense Analysis (1967) Task Force Report: Science and Technology. The President's Commission on Law Enforcement and Administration of Justice. Washington, D. C.: U.S. Government Printing Office.

Kansas City Police Department (1971) Survey of Municipal Police Departments. Kansas City, Mo.

KANT, I. (1913) "Zum Ewigen Frieden: Ein Philosophischer Entwurf," in Kleinere Schriften zur Geschichtsphilosophie, Ethik und Politik. Leipzig: Felix Meiner. (Originally printed in 1795.)

[44]   THE POTENTIAL FOR REFORM OF CRIMINAL JUSTICE

KELSEN, H. (1961) General Theory of Law and State. New York: Russel & Russel.

LaFAVE, W. (1965) Arrest: The Decision to Take a Suspect into Custody. Boston: Little, Brown.

LEONARD, V. A. and H. W. MORE (1971) Police Organization and Management. 3rd ed. Mineola, N. Y.: Foundation Press.

LOHMAN, J. D. and G. E. MISNER (1966) The Police and the Community. Report prepared for the President's Commission on Law Enforcement and Administration of Justice. Volume 2. Washington, D. C.: U.S. Government Printing Office.

MILLER, W. B. (1958) "Lower-class culture as a generating milieu of gang delinquency." Journal of Social Issues 14: 5-19.

National Commission on Productivity (1973) "Report of the Task Force to Study Police Productivity." Mimeo. Draft.

NIEDERHOFFER, A. (1969) Behind the Shield: The Police in Urban Society. Garden City, N. Y.: Anchor Books.

REISS, A. J., Jr. (1971) The Police and the Public. New Haven, Conn.: Yale University Press.

REIWALD, P. (1944) Eroberung des Friedens. Zurich: Europa Verlag.

ROBINSON, C. D. (1965) "Alternatives to arrest of lesser offenders." Crime and Delinquency 11: 8-21.

SILVER, A. (1967) "The demand for order in civil society: a review of some themes in the history of urban crime, police, and riot," pp. 1-24 in D. J. Bordua (ed.) The Police: Six Sociological Essays. New York: John Wiley.

SKOLNICK, J. H. (1966) Justice Without Trial: Law Enforcement in a Democratic Society. New York: John Wiley.

Stanford Law Review (1961) "Justification for the Use of Force in the Criminal Law." Volume 13: 566-609.

STEPHEN, J. F. (1883) A History of Criminal Law in England. Volume 3. London: Macmillan.

WARNER, S. B. (1942) "Uniform arrest act." Vanderbilt Law Review 28: 315-347.

WEBER, M. (1947) The Theory of Social and Economic Organization. Translation edited by T. Parsons. Glencoe, Ill.: Free Press.

WILSON, J. Q. (1968) Varieties of Police Behavior: The Management of Law and Order in Eight Communities. Cambridge, Mass.: Harvard University Press.

WILSON, O. W. (1963) Police Administration. 2nd ed. New York: McGraw-Hill.

[10]

Improving Policing:
A Problem-Oriented Approach

Herman Goldstein

The police have been particularly susceptible to the "means over ends" syndrome, placing more emphasis in their improvement efforts on organization and operating methods than on the substantive outcome of their work. This condition has been fed by the professional movement within the police field, with its concentration on the staffing, management, and organization of police agencies. More and more persons are questioning the widely held assumption that improvements in the internal management of police departments will enable the police to deal more effectively with the problems they are called upon to handle. If the police are to realize a greater return on the investment made in improving their operations, and if they are to mature as a profession, they must concern themselves more directly with the end product of their efforts.

Meeting this need requires that the police develop a more systematic process for examining and addressing the problems that the public expects them to handle. It requires identifying these problems in more precise terms, researching each problem, documenting the nature of the current police response, assessing its adequacy and the adequacy of existing authority and resources, engaging in a broad exploration of alternatives to present responses, weighing the merits of these alternatives, and choosing from among them.

Improvements in staffing, organization, and management remain important, but they should be achieved—and may, in fact, be more achievable—within the context of a more direct concern with the outcome of policing.

Complaints from passengers wishing to use the Bagnall to Greenfields bus service that "the drivers were speeding past queues of up to 30 people with a smile and a wave of a hand" have been met by a statement pointing out that "it is impossible for the drivers to keep their timetable if they have to stop for passengers."[1]

All bureaucracies risk becoming so preoccupied with running their organizations and getting so involved in their methods of operating that they lose sight

HERMAN GOLDSTEIN: Professor, Law School, University of Wisconsin at Madison. The author is indebted to the University of Wisconsin Extension Department of Law for making the time available to produce this article as part of a larger effort to reexamine the university's role in research and training for the police.

1. Newspaper report from the Midlands of England, cited in Patrick Ryan, "Get Rid of the People, and the System Runs Fine," *Smithsonian*, September 1977, p. 140.

Improving Policing   237

of the primary purposes for which they were created. The police seem un-usually susceptible to this phenomenon.

One of the most popular new developments in policing is the use of officers as decoys to apprehend offenders in high-crime areas. A speaker at a recent conference for police administrators, when asked to summarize new develop-ments in the field, reported on a sixteen-week experiment in his agency with the use of decoys, aimed at reducing street robberies.

One major value of the project, the speaker claimed, was its contribution to the police department's public image. Apparently, the public was intrigued by the clever, seductive character of the project, especially by the widely publi-cized demonstrations of the makeup artists' ability to disguise burly officers. The speaker also claimed that the project greatly increased the morale of the personnel working in the unit. The officers found the assignment exciting and challenging, a welcome change from the tedious routine that characterizes so much of regular police work, and they developed a high esprit de corps.

The effect on robberies, however, was much less clear. The methodology used and the problems in measuring crime apparently prevented the project staff from reaching any firm conclusions. But it was reported that, of the 216 persons arrested by the unit for robbery during the experiment, more than half would not have committed a robbery, in the judgment of the unit mem-bers, if they had not been tempted by the situation presented by the police decoys. Thus, while the total impact of the project remains unclear, it can be said with certainty that the experiment actually increased the number of rob-beries by over 100 in the sixteen weeks of the experiment.

The account of this particular decoy project (others have claimed greater success) is an especially poignant reminder of just how serious an imbalance there is within the police field between the interest in organizational and pro-cedural matters and the concern for the substance of policing. The assump-tion, of course, is that the two are related, that improvements in internal man-agement will eventually increase the capacity of the police to meet the objec-tives for which police agencies are created. But the relationship is not that clear and direct and is increasingly being questioned.

Perhaps the best example of such questioning relates to response time. Tre-mendous resources were invested during the past decade in personnel, vehi-cles, communications equipment, and new procedures in order to increase the speed with which the police respond to calls for assistance. Much less atten-tion was given in this same period to what the officer does in handling the variety of problems he confronts on arriving, albeit fast, where he is sum-moned. Now, ironically, even the value of a quick response is being questioned.[2]

2. The recent study in Kansas City found that the effect of response time on the capacity of the police to deal with crime was negligible, primarily because delays by citizens in reporting crimes make the minutes saved by the police insignificant. See Kansas City, Missouri, Police Department, *Response Time Analysis*, Executive Summary (Kansas City, 1977).

This article summarizes the nature of the "means over ends" syndrome in policing and explores ways of focusing greater attention on the results of policing—on the effect that police efforts have on the problems that the police are expected to handle.

THE "MEANS OVER ENDS" SYNDROME

Until the late 1960s, efforts to improve policing in this country concentrated almost exclusively on internal management: streamlining the organization, upgrading personnel, modernizing equipment, and establishing more businesslike operating procedures. All of the major commentators on the police since the beginning of the century—Leonhard F. Fuld (1909), Raymond B. Fosdick (1915), August Vollmer (1936), Bruce Smith (1940), and O. W. Wilson (1950)—stressed the need to improve the organization and management of police agencies. Indeed, the emphasis on internal management was so strong that professional policing was defined primarily as the application of modern management concepts to the running of a police department.

The sharp increase in the demands made on the police in the late 1960s (increased crime, civil rights demonstrations, and political protest) led to several national assessments of the state of policing.[3] The published findings contained some criticism of the professional model of police organization, primarily because of its impersonal character and failure to respond to legitimate pressures from within the community.[4] Many recommendations were made for introducing a greater concern for the human factors in policing, but the vast majority of the recommendations that emerged from the reassessments demonstrated a continuing belief that the way to improve the police was to improve the organization. Higher recruitment standards, college education for police personnel, reassignment and reallocation of personnel, additional training, and greater mobility were proposed. Thus the management-dominated concept of police reform spread and gained greater stature.

The emphasis on secondary goals—on improving the organization—continues to this day, reflected in the prevailing interests of police administrators, in the factors considered in the selection of police chiefs and the promotion of subordinates, in the subject matter of police periodicals and texts, in the content of recently developed educational programs for the police, and even in the focus of major research projects.

3. See President's Commission on Law Enforcement and Administration of Justice, *The Challenge of Crime in a Free Society* (Washington, D.C.: Govt. Printing Office, 1967); National Advisory Commission on Civil Disorders, *Report of the National Advisory Commission on Civil Disorders* (Washington, D.C.: Govt. Printing Office, 1968); National Commission on the Causes and Prevention of Violence, *To Establish Justice, to Insure Domestic Tranquility*, Final Report (Washington, D.C.: Govt. Printing Office, 1969); President's Commission on Campus Unrest, *Report of the President's Commission on Campus Unrest* (Washington, D.C.: Govt. Printing Office, 1970); and National Advisory Commission on Criminal Justice Standards and Goals, *Police* (Washington, D.C.: Govt. Printing Office, 1973).

4. See, for example, National Advisory Commission on Civil Disorders, *Report*, p. 158.

Improving Policing   239

At one time this emphasis was appropriate. When Vollmer, Smith, and Wilson formulated their prescriptions for improved policing, the state of the vast majority of police agencies was chaotic: Personnel were disorganized, poorly equipped, poorly trained, inefficient, lacking accountability, and often corrupt. The first priority was putting the police house in order. Otherwise, the endless crises that are produced by an organization out of control would be totally consuming. Without a minimum level of order and accountability, an agency cannot be redirected—however committed its administrators may be to addressing more substantive matters.

What is troubling is that administrators of those agencies that have succeeded in developing a high level of operating efficiency have not gone on to concern themselves with the end results of their efforts—with the actual impact that their streamlined organizations have on the problems the police are called upon to handle.

The police seem to have reached a plateau at which the highest objective to which they aspire is administrative competence. And, with some scattered exceptions, they seem reluctant to move beyond this plateau—toward creating a more systematic concern for the end product of their efforts. But strong pressures generated by several new developments may now force them to do so.

1. The Financial Crisis

The growing cost of police services and the financial plight of most city governments, especially those under threat of Proposition 13 movements, are making municipal officials increasingly reluctant to appropriate still more money for police service without greater assurance that their investment will have an impact on the problems that the police are expected to handle. Those cities that are already reducing their budgets are being forced to make some of the hard choices that must be made in weighing the impact of such cuts on the nature of the service rendered to the public.

2. Research Findings

Recently completed research questions the value of two major aspects of police operations—preventive patrol and investigations conducted by detectives.[5] Some police administrators have challenged the findings[6]; others are awaiting

5. George L. Kelling et al., *The Kansas City Preventive Patrol Experiment: A Summary Report* (Washington, D.C.: Police Foundation, 1974); and Peter W. Greenwood et al., *The Criminal Investigation Process*, 3 vols. (Santa Monica, Calif.: Rand Corporation, 1976).

6. For questioning by a police administrator of the findings of the Kansas City Preventive Patrol Project, see Edward M. Davis and Lyle Knowles, "A Critique of the Report: An Evaluation of the Kansas City Preventive Patrol Experiment," *Police Chief*, June 1975, pp. 22–27. For a review of the Rand study on detectives, see Daryl F. Gates and Lyle Knowles, "An Evaluation of the Rand Corporation's Analysis of the Criminal Investigation Process," *Police Chief*, July 1976,

240   Herman Goldstein

the results of replication.[7] But those who concur with the results have begun
to search for alternatives, aware of the need to measure the effectiveness of a
new response before making a substantial investment in it.

3. Growth of a Consumer Orientation

Policing has not yet felt the full impact of consumer advocacy. As citizens
press for improvement in police service, improvement will increasingly be
measured in terms of results. Those concerned about battered wives, for example, could not care less whether the police who respond to such calls operate with one or two officers in a car, whether the officers are short or tall, or
whether they have a college education. Their attention is on what the police
do for the battered wife.

4. Questioning the Effectiveness
of the Best-Managed Agencies

A number of police departments have carried out most, if not all, of the numerous recommendations for strengthening a police organization and enjoy a
national reputation for their efficiency, their high standards of personnel
selection and training, and their application of modern technology to their
operations. Nevertheless, their communities apparently continue to have the
same problems as do others with less advanced police agencies.[8]

5. Increased Resistance
to Organizational Change

Intended improvements that are primarily in the form of organizational
change, such as team policing, almost invariably run into resistance from
rank-and-file personnel. Stronger and more militant unions have engaged
some police administrators in bitter and prolonged fights over such changes.[9]
Because the costs in terms of disruption and discontent are so great, police

---

p. 20. Each of the two papers is followed by a response from the authors of the original studies.
In addition, for the position of the International Association of Chiefs of Police on the results of
the Kansas City project, see "IACP Position Paper on the Kansas City Preventive Patrol Experiment," *Police Chief*, September 1975. p. 16.

7. The National Institute of Law Enforcement and Criminal Justice is sponsoring a replication
of the Kansas City Preventive Patrol Experiment and is supporting further explorations of the
criminal investigation process. See National Institute of Law Enforcement and Criminal Justice,
Program Plan, Fiscal Year 1978 (Washington, D.C.: Govt. Printing Office, 1977), p. 12.

8. Admittedly, precise appraisals and comparisons are difficult. For a recent example of an
examination by the press of one department that has enjoyed a reputation for good management,
see "The LAPD: How Good Is It?" *Los Angeles Times*, Dec. 18, 1977.

9. Examples of cities in which police unions recently have fought vigorously to oppose innovations introduced by police administrators are Boston, Massachusetts, and Troy, New York.

administrators initiating change will be under increasing pressure to demonstrate in advance that the results of their efforts will make the struggle worthwhile.

Against this background, the exceptions to the dominant concern with the
police organization and its personnel take on greater significance. Although
scattered and quite modest, a number of projects and training programs carried out in recent years have focused on a single problem that the public
expects the police to handle, such as child abuse, sexual assault, arson, or the
drunk driver.[10] These projects and programs, by their very nature, subordinate the customary priorities of police reform, such as staffing, management, and equipment, to a concern about a specific problem and the police
response to it.

Some of the earliest support for this type of effort was reflected in the
crime-specific projects funded by the Law Enforcement Assistance Administration.[11] Communities—not just the police—were encouraged to direct their
attention to a specific type of crime and to make those changes in existing
operations that were deemed necessary to reduce its incidence. The widespread move to fashion a more effective police response to domestic disturbances is probably the best example of a major reform that has, as its principal objective, improvement in the quality of service delivered, and that calls
for changes in organization, staffing, and training only as these are necessary
to achieve the primary goal.

Are these scattered efforts a harbinger of things to come? Are they a natural
development in the steadily evolving search for ways to improve police operations? Or are they, like the programs dealing with sexual assault and child
abuse, simply the result of the sudden availability of funds because of intensified citizen concern about a specific problem? Whatever their origin,
those projects that do subordinate administrative considerations to the task of
improving police effectiveness in dealing with a specific problem have a re-
freshing quality to them.

WHAT IS THE END PRODUCT OF POLICING?

To urge a more direct focus on the primary objectives of a police agency
requires spelling out these objectives more clearly. But this is no easy task,
given the conglomeration of unrelated, ill-defined, and often inseparable jobs
that the police are expected to handle.

10. These programs are reflected in the training opportunities routinely listed in such publications as *Police Chief, Criminal Law Reporter, Law Enforcement News,* and *Crime Control Digest,*
and by the abstracting service of the National Criminal Justice Reference Center.

11. See, for example, National Institute of Law Enforcement and Criminal Justice, Law Enforcement Assistance Administration, "Planning Guidelines and Program to Reduce Crime,"
mimeographed (Washington, D.C., 1972), pp. vi–xiii. For a discussion of the concept, see Paul
K. Wormeli and Steve E. Kolodney, "The Crime-Specific Model: A New Criminal Justice Perspective," *Journal of Research in Crime and Delinquency,* January 1972, pp. 54–65.

The task is complicated further because so many people believe that the job of the police is, first and foremost, to enforce the law: to regulate conduct by applying the criminal law of the jurisdiction. One commentator on the police recently claimed: "We do not say to the police: 'Here is the problem. Deal with it.' We say: 'Here is a detailed code. Enforce it.'"[12] In reality, the police job is perhaps most accurately described as dealing with problems.[13] Moreover, enforcing the criminal code is itself only a means to an end—one of several that the police employ in getting their job done.[14] The emphasis on law enforcement, therefore, is nothing more than a continuing preoccupation with means.

Considerable effort has been invested in recent years in attempting to define the police function: inventorying the wide range of police responsibilities, categorizing various aspects of policing, and identifying some of the characteristics common to all police tasks.[15] This work will be of great value in refocusing attention on the end product of policing, but the fact that it is still going on is not cause to delay giving greater attention to substantive matters. It is sufficient, for our purposes here, simply to acknowledge that the police job requires that they deal with a wide range of behavioral and social problems that arise in a community—that the end product of policing consists of dealing with these *problems*.

By problems, I mean the incredibly broad range of troublesome situations that prompt citizens to turn to the police, such as street robberies, residential burglaries, battered wives, vandalism, speeding cars, runaway children, accidents, acts of terrorism, even fear. These and other similar problems are the essence of police work. They are the reason for having a police agency.

Problems of this nature are to be distinguished from those that frequently occupy police administrators, such as lack of manpower, inadequate supervision, inadequate training, or strained relations with police unions. They differ from those most often identified by operating personnel, such as lack of adequate equipment, frustrations in the prosecution of criminal cases, or inequities in working conditions. And they differ, too, from the problems that have occupied those advocating police reform, such as the multiplicity of po-

---

12. Ronald J. Allen, "The Police and Substantive Rulemaking: Reconciling Principle and Expediency," *University of Pennsylvania Law Review*, November 1976, p. 97.

13. Egon Bittner comes close to this point of view when he describes police functioning as applying immediate solutions to an endless array of problems. See Egon Bittner, "Florence Nightingale in Pursuit of Willie Sutton," in *The Potential for Reform of Criminal Justice*, Herbert Jacob, ed. (Beverly Hills, Calif.: Sage, 1974), p. 30. James Q. Wilson does also when he describes policing as handling situations. See James Q. Wilson, *Varieties of Police Behavior: The Management of Law and Order in Eight Communities* (Cambridge, Mass.: Harvard University Press, 1968), p. 31.

14. I develop this point in an earlier work. See Herman Goldstein, *Policing a Free Society* (Cambridge, Mass.: Ballinger, 1977), pp. 30, 34–35.

15. In the 1977 book I presented a brief summary of these studies. Ibid., pp. 26–28.

lice agencies, the lack of lateral entry, and the absence of effective controls over police conduct.

Many of the problems coming to the attention of the police become their responsibility because no other means has been found to solve them. They are the residual problems of society. It follows that expecting the police to solve or eliminate them is expecting too much. It is more realistic to aim at reducing their volume, preventing repetition, alleviating suffering, and minimizing the other adverse effects they produce.

DEVELOPING THE OVERALL PROCESS

To address the substantive problems of the police requires developing a commitment to a more systematic process for inquiring into these problems. Initially, this calls for identifying in precise terms the problems that citizens look to the police to handle. Once identified, each problem must be explored in great detail. What do we know about the problem? Has it been researched? If so, with what results? What more should we know? Is it a proper concern of government? What authority and resources are available for dealing with it? What is the current police response? In the broadest-ranging search for solutions, what would constitute the most intelligent response? What factors should be considered in choosing from among alternatives? If a new response is adopted, how does one go about evaluating its effectiveness? And finally, what changes, if any, does implementation of a more effective response require in the police organization?

This type of inquiry is not foreign to the police. Many departments conduct rigorous studies of administrative and operational problems. A police agency may undertake a detailed study of the relative merits of adopting one of several different types of uniforms. And it may regularly develop military-like plans for handling special events that require the assignment of large numbers of personnel.[16] However, systematic analysis and planning have rarely been applied to the specific behavioral and social problems that constitute the agency's routine business. The situation is somewhat like that of a private industry that studies the speed of its assembly line, the productivity of its employees, and the nature of its public relations program, but does not examine the quality of its product.

Perhaps the closest police agencies have come to developing a system for addressing substantive problems has been their work in crime analysis. Police routinely analyze information on reported crimes to identify patterns of criminal conduct, with the goal of enabling operating personnel to apprehend specific offenders or develop strategies to prevent similar offenses from occur-

16. For an up-to-date description of the concept of planning and research as it has evolved in police agencies, see O. W. Wilson and Roy C. McLaren, *Police Administration*, 4th ed. (New York: McGraw-Hill, 1977), pp. 157–81.

244   Herman Goldstein

ring. Some police departments have, through the use of computers, developed
sophisticated programs to analyze reported crimes.[17] Unfortunately, these
analyses are almost always put to very limited use—to apprehend a professional car thief or to deter a well-known cat burglar—rather than serving as
a basis for rethinking the overall police response to the problem of car theft
or cat burglaries. Nevertheless, the practice of planning operational responses
based on an analysis of hard data, now a familiar concept to the police, is a
helpful point of reference in advocating development of more broadly based
research and planning.

The most significant effort to use a problem orientation for improving police responses was embodied in the crime-specific concept initiated in California in 1971[18] and later promoted with LEAA funds throughout the country.
The concept was made an integral part of the anticrime program launched in
eight cities in January 1972, aimed at bringing about reductions in five crime
categories: murder, rape, assault, robbery, and burglary.[19] This would have
provided an excellent opportunity to develop and test the concept, were it not
for the commitment that this politically motivated program carried to achieving fast and dramatic results: a 5 percent reduction in each category in two
years and a 20 percent reduction in five years. These rather naive, unrealistic
goals and the emphasis on quantifying the results placed a heavy shadow over
the program from the outset. With the eventual abandonment of the projects,
the crime-specific concept seems to have lost ground as well. However, the
national evaluation of the program makes it clear that progress was made,
despite the various pressures, in planning a community's approach to the five
general crime categories. The "crime-oriented planning, implementation and
evaluation" process employed in all eight cities had many of the elements one
would want to include in a problem-oriented approach to improving police
service.[20]

DEFINING PROBLEMS WITH GREATER SPECIFICITY

The importance of defining problems more precisely becomes apparent when
one reflects on the long-standing practice of using overly broad categories to
describe police business. Attacking police problems under a categorical heading—"crime" or "disorder," "delinquency," or even "violence"—is bound to
be futile. While police business is often further subdivided by means of the

17. For examples, see National Institute of Law Enforcement and Criminal Justice, *Police
Crime Analysis Unit Handbook* (Washington, D.C.: Govt. Printing Office, 1973), pp. 90–92,
113–21.

18. For a brief description, see Joanne W. Rockwell, "Crime Specific . . . An Answer?" *Police
Chief*, September 1972, p. 38.

19. The program is described in Eleanor Chelimsky, *High Impact Anti-Crime Program*, Final
Report, vol. 2 (Washington, D.C.: Govt. Printing Office, 1976), pp. 19–38.

20. Ibid., pp. 145–50, 418–21.

labels tied to the criminal code, such as robbery, burglary, and theft, these are not adequate, for several reasons.

First, they frequently mask diverse forms of behavior. Thus, for example, incidents classified under "arson" might include fires set by teenagers as a form of vandalism, fires set by persons suffering severe psychological problems, fires set for the purpose of destroying evidence of a crime, fires set by persons (or their hired agents) to collect insurance, and fires set by organized criminal interests to intimidate. Each type of incident poses a radically different problem for the police.

Second, if police depend heavily on categories of criminal offenses to define problems of concern to them, others may be misled to believe that, if a given form of behavior is not criminal, it is of no concern to the police. This is perhaps best reflected in the proposals for decriminalizing prostitution, gambling, narcotic use, vagrancy, and public intoxication. The argument, made over and over again, is that removing the criminal label will reduce the magnitude and complexity of the police function, freeing personnel to work on more serious matters and ridding the police of some of the negative side effects, such as corruption, that these problems produce. But decriminalization does not relieve the police of responsibility. The public expects drunks to be picked up if only because they find their presence on the street annoying or because they feel that the government has an obligation to care for persons who cannot care for themselves. The public expects prostitutes who solicit openly on the streets to be stopped, because such conduct is offensive to innocent passersby, blocks pedestrian or motor traffic, and contributes to the deterioration of a neighborhood. The problem is a problem for the police whether or not it is defined as a criminal offense.

Finally, use of offense categories as descriptive of police problems implies that the police role is restricted to arresting and prosecuting offenders. In fact, the police job is much broader, extending, in the case of burglary, to encouraging citizens to lock their premises more securely, to eliminating some of the conditions that might attract potential burglars, to counseling burglary victims on ways they can avoid similar attacks in the future, and to recovering and returning burglarized property.

Until recently, the police role in regard to the crime of rape was perceived primarily as responding quickly when a report of a rape was received, determining whether a rape had really occurred (given current legal definitions), and then attempting to identify and apprehend the perpetrator. Today, the police role has been radically redefined to include teaching women how to avoid attack, organizing transit programs to provide safe movement in areas where there is a high risk of attack, dealing with the full range of sexual assault not previously covered by the narrowly drawn rape statutes, and—perhaps most important—providing needed care and support to the rape victim to minimize the physical and mental damage resulting from such an attack. Police are now concerned with sexual assault not simply because they have a direct role in the arrest and prosecution of violators, but also because sexual assault is a community problem which the police and others can affect in a variety of ways.

It seems desirable, at least initially in the development of a problem-solving approach to improved policing, to press for as detailed a breakdown of problems as possible. In addition to distinguishing different forms of behavior and the apparent motivation, as in the case of incidents commonly grouped under the heading of "arson," it is helpful to be much more precise regarding locale and time of day, the type of people involved, and the type of people victimized. Different combinations of these variables may present different problems, posing different policy questions and calling for radically different solutions.[21]

For example, most police agencies already separate the problem of purse snatching in which force is used from the various other forms of conduct commonly grouped under robbery. But an agency is likely to find it much more helpful to go further—to pinpoint, for example, the problem of teenagers snatching the purses of elderly women waiting for buses in the downtown section of the city during the hours of early darkness. Likewise, a police agency might find it helpful to isolate the robberies of grocery stores that are open all night and are typically staffed by a lone attendant; or the theft of vehicles by a highly organized group engaged in the business of transporting them for sale in another jurisdiction; or the problem posed by teenagers who gather around hamburger stands each evening to the annoyance of neighbors, customers, and management. Eventually, similar problems calling for similar responses may be grouped together, but one cannot be certain that they are similar until they have been analyzed.

In the analysis of a given problem, one may find, for example, that the concern of the citizenry is primarily fear of attack, but the fear is not warranted, given the pattern of actual offenses. Where this situation becomes apparent, the police have two quite different problems: to deal more effectively with the actual incidents where they occur, and to respond to the groundless fears. Each calls for a different response.

The importance of subdividing problems was dramatically illustrated by the recent experience of the New York City Police Department in its effort to deal more constructively with domestic disturbances. An experimental program, in which police were trained to use mediation techniques, was undertaken with obvious public support. But, in applying the mediation tech-

21. For an excellent example of what is needed, see the typology of vandalism developed by the British sociologist, Stanley Cohen, quoted in Albert M. Williams, Jr., "Vandalism," *Management Information Service Report* (Washington, D.C.: International City Management Association, May 1976), pp. 1–2. Another excellent example of an effort to break down a problem of concern to the police—in this case, heroin—is found in Mark Harrison Moore, *Buy and Bust: The Effective Regulation of an Illicit Market in Heroin* (Lexington, Mass.: Lexington Books, 1977), p. 83.

niques, the department apparently failed to distinguish sufficiently those cases in which wives were repeatedly subject to physical abuse. The aggravated nature of the latter cases resulted in a suit against the department in which the plaintiffs argued that the police are mandated to enforce the law when *any* violation comes to their attention. In the settlement, the department agreed that its personnel would not attempt to reconcile the parties or to mediate when a felony was committed.[22] However, the net effect of the suit is likely to be more far reaching. The vulnerability of the department to criticism for not having dealt more aggressively with the aggravated cases has dampened support—in New York and elsewhere—for the use of alternatives to arrest in less serious cases, even though alternatives still appear to represent the more intelligent response.

One of the major values in subdividing police business is that it gives visibility to some problems which have traditionally been given short shrift, but which warrant more careful attention. The seemingly minor problem of noise, for example, is typically buried in the mass of police business lumped together under such headings as "complaints," "miscellaneous," "noncriminal incidents," or "disturbances." Both police officers and unaffected citizens would most likely be inclined to rank it at the bottom in any list of problems. Yet the number of complaints about noise is high in many communities—in fact, noise is probably among the most common problems brought by the public to the police.[23] While some of those complaining may be petty or unreasonable, many are seriously aggrieved and justified in their appeal for relief: Sleep is lost, schedules are disrupted, mental and emotional problems are aggravated. Apartments may become uninhabitable. The elderly woman living alone, whose life has been made miserable by inconsiderate neighbors, is not easily convinced that the daily intrusion into her life of their noise is any less serious than other forms of intrusion. For this person, and for many like her, improved policing would mean a more effective response to the problem of the noise created by her neighbors.

22. See Bruno v. Codd, 90 Misc. 2d 1047, 396 N.Y.S.2d 974 (1977), finding a cause of action against the New York City Police Department for failing to protect battered wives. On June 26, 1978, the city agreed to a settlement with the plaintiffs in which it committed the police to arrest in all cases in which "there is reasonable cause to believe that a husband has committed a felony against his wife and/or has violated an Order of Protection or Temporary Order of Protection." See Consent Decree, Bruno against McGuire, New York State Supreme Court, index #21946/76. (Recognizing the consent decree, the New York Appellate Court, First Department, in July of 1978 [#3020] dismissed an appeal in the case as moot in so far as it involved the police department. From a reading of the court's reversal as to the other parts of the case, however, it appears that it would also have reversed the decision of the lower court in sustaining the action against the police department if there had not been a consent decree.)

23. It was reported that, on a recent three-day holiday weekend in Madison, Wisconsin, police handled slightly more than 1,000 calls, of which 118 were for loud parties and other types of noise disturbances. See "Over 1,000 Calls Made to Police on Weekend," *Wisconsin State Journal* (Madison, Wisc.: June 1, 1978).

248   Herman Goldstein

RESEARCHING THE PROBLEM

Without a tradition for viewing in sufficiently discrete terms the various problems making up the police job, gathering even the most basic information about a specific problem—such as complaints about noise—can be extremely difficult.

First, the magnitude of the problem and the various forms in which it surfaces must be established. One is inclined to turn initially to police reports for such information. But overgeneralization in categorizing incidents, the impossibility of separating some problems, variations in the reporting practices of the community, and inadequacies in report writing seriously limit their value for purposes of obtaining a full picture of the problem. However, if used cautiously, some of the information in police files may be helpful. Police agencies routinely collect and store large amounts of data, even though they may not use them to evaluate the effectiveness of their responses. Moreover, if needed information is not available, often it can be collected expeditiously in a well-managed department, owing to the high degree of centralized control of field operations.

How does one discover the nature of the current police response? Administrators and their immediate subordinates are not a good source. Quite naturally, they have a desire to provide an answer that reflects well on the agency, is consistent with legal requirements, and meets the formal expectations of both the public and other agencies that might have a responsibility relating to the problem. But even if these concerns did not color their answers, top administrators are often so far removed from street operations, in both distance and time, that they would have great difficulty describing current responses accurately.

Inquiry, then, must focus on the operating level. But mere questioning of line officers is not likely to be any more productive. We know from the various efforts to document police activity in the field that there is often tremendous variation in the way in which different officers respond to the same type of incident.[24] Yet the high value placed on uniformity and on adhering to formal requirements and the pressures from peers inhibit officers from candidly discussing the manner in which they respond to the multitude of problems they handle—especially if the inquiry comes from outside the agency. But one cannot afford to give up at this point, for the individualized practices of police officers and the vast amount of knowledge they acquire about the

---

24. See, for example, the detailed accounts of police functioning in Minneapolis, in Joseph M. Livermore, "Policing," *Minnesota Law Review*, March 1971, pp. 649–729. Among the works describing the police officers' varying styles in responding to similar situations are Wilson, *Varieties of Police Behavior*; Albert J. Reiss, Jr., *The Police and the Public* (New Haven, Conn.: Yale University Press, 1971); Jerome H. Skolnick, *Justice without Trial: Law Enforcement in Democratic Society* (New York: John Wiley, 1966); and Egon Bittner, *The Functions of the Police in Modern Society: A Review of Background Factors, Current Practices, and Possible Role Models* (Washington, D.C.: Govt. Printing Office, 1970).

situations they handle, taken together, are an extremely rich resource that is too often overlooked by those concerned about improving the quality of police services. Serious research into the problems police handle requires observing police officers over a period of time. This means accompanying them as they perform their regular assignments and cultivating the kind of relationship that enables them to talk candidly about the way in which they handle specific aspects of their job.

The differences in the way in which police respond, even in dealing with relatively simple matters, may be significant. When a runaway child is reported, one officer may limit himself to obtaining the basic facts. Another officer, sensing as much of a responsibility for dealing with the parents' fears as for finding the child and looking out for the child's interests, may endeavor to relieve the parents' anxiety by providing information about the runaway problem and about what they might expect. From the standpoint of the consumers—in this case, the parents—the response of the second officer is vastly superior to that of the first.

In handling more complicated matters, the need to improvise has prompted some officers to develop what appear to be unusually effective ways of dealing with specific problems. Many officers develop a unique understanding of problems that frequently come to their attention, learning to make important distinctions among different forms of the same problem and becoming familiar with the many complicating factors that are often present. And they develop a feel for what, under the circumstances, constitute the most effective responses. After careful evaluation, these types of responses might profitably be adopted as standard for an entire police agency. If the knowledge of officers at the operating level were more readily available, it might be useful to those responsible for drafting crime-related legislation. Many of the difficulties in implementing recent changes in statutes relating to sexual assault, public drunkenness, drunk driving, and child abuse could have been avoided had police expertise been tapped.

By way of example, if a police agency were to decide to explore the problem of noise, the following questions might be asked. What is the magnitude of the problem as reflected by the number of complaints received? What is the source of the complaints: industry, traffic, groups of people gathered outdoors, or neighbors? How do noise complaints from residents break down between private dwellings and apartment houses? How often are the police summoned to the same location? How often are other forms of misconduct, such as fights, attributable to conflicts over noise? What is the responsibility of a landlord or an apartment house manager regarding noise complaints? What do the police now do in responding to such complaints? How much of the police procedure has been thought through and formalized? What is the authority of the police in such situations? Is it directly applicable or must they lean on somewhat nebulous authority, such as threatening to arrest for disorderly conduct or for failure to obey a lawful order, if the parties fail to quiet down? What works in police practice and what does not work? Are specific officers recognized as more capable of handling such complaints? If so, what makes them more effective? Do factors outside the control of a police agency influence the frequency with which complaints are received? Are noise complaints from apartment dwellers related to the manner in which the buildings are constructed? And what influence, if any, does the relative effectiveness of the police in handling noise complaints have on the complaining citizen's willingness to cooperate with the police in dealing with other problems, including criminal conduct traditionally defined as much more serious?

Considerable knowledge about some of the problems with which the police struggle has been generated outside police agencies by criminologists, sociologists, psychologists, and psychiatrists. But as has been pointed out frequently, relatively few of these findings have influenced the formal policies and operating decisions of practitioners.[25] Admittedly, the quality of many such studies is poor. Often the practitioner finds it difficult to draw out from the research its significance for his operations. But most important, the police have not needed to employ these studies because they have not been expected to address specific problems in a systematic manner. If the police were pressured to examine in great detail the problems they are expected to handle, a review of the literature would become routine. If convinced that research findings had practical value, police administrators would develop into more sophisticated users of such research; their responsible criticism could, in turn, contribute to upgrading the quality and usefulness of future research efforts.

EXPLORING ALTERNATIVES

After the information assembled about a specific problem is analyzed, a fresh, uninhibited search should be made for alternative responses that might be an improvement over what is currently being done. The nature of such a search will differ from past efforts in that, presumably, the problem itself will be better defined and understood, the commitment to past approaches (such as focusing primarily on the identification and prosecution of offenders) will be shelved temporarily, and the search will be much broader, extending well beyond the present or future potential of just the police.

But caution is in order. Those intent on improving the operations of the criminal justice system (by divesting it of some of its current burdens) and those who are principally occupied with improving the operating efficiency of police agencies frequently recommend that the problem simply be shifted to

---

25. See, for example, the comments of Marvin Wolfgang in a Congressionally sponsored discussion of federal support for criminal justice research, reported in the U.S., House, Committee on the Judiciary, Subcommittee on Crime, *New Directions for Federal Involvement in Crime Control* (Washington, D.C.: Govt. Printing Office, 1977). Wolfgang claims that research in criminology and criminal justice has had little impact on the administration of justice or on major decision makers.

some other agency of government or to the private sector. Such recommendations often glibly imply that a health department or a social work agency, for
example, is better equipped to handle the problem. Experience over the past
decade, however, shows that this is rarely the case.[26] Merely shifting responsibility for the problem, without some assurance that more adequate provisions have been made for dealing with it, achieves nothing.

Police in many jurisdictions, in a commendable effort to employ alternatives to the criminal justice system, have arranged to make referrals to various social, health, and legal agencies. By tying into the services provided by
the whole range of other helping agencies in the community, the police in
these cities have taken a giant step toward improving the quality of their
response. But there is a great danger that referral will come to be an end in
itself, that the police and others advocating the use of such a system will not
concern themselves adequately with the consequences of referral. If referral
does not lead to reducing the citizens' problem, nothing will have been gained
by this change. It may even cause harm: Expectations that are raised and not
fulfilled may lead to further frustration; the original problem may, as a consequence, be compounded; and the resulting bitterness about government services may feed the tensions that develop in urban areas.

The search for alternatives obviously need not start from scratch. There is
much to build on. Crime prevention efforts of some police agencies and experiments with developing alternatives to the criminal justice system and with
diverting cases from the system should be reassessed for their impact on specific problems; those that appear to have the greatest potential should be developed and promoted.[27] Several alternatives should be explored for each
problem.

1. Physical and Technical Changes

Can the problem be reduced or eliminated through physical or technical
changes? Some refer to this as part of a program of "reducing opportunities"
or "target hardening." Extensive effort has already gone into reducing,
through urban design, factors that contribute to behavior requiring police
attention.[28] Improved locks on homes and cars, the requirement of exact fares

26. For further discussion of this point, see American Bar Association, *The Urban Police Function*, Approved Draft (Chicago: American Bar Association, 1973), pp. 41–42.

27. Many of these programs are summarized in David E. Aaronson et al., *The New Justice:
Alternatives to Conventional Criminal Adjudication* (Washington, D.C.: Govt. Printing Office,
1977); and David E. Aaronson et al., *Alternatives to Conventional Criminal Adjudication:
Guidebook for Planners and Practitioners*, Caroline S. Cooper, ed. (Washington, D.C.: Govt.
Printing Office, 1977).

28. The leading work on the subject is Oscar Newman, *Defensible Space: Crime Prevention
through Urban Design* (New York: Macmillan, 1972). See also Westinghouse National Issues
Center, *Crime Prevention through Environmental Design—A Special Report* (Washington, D.C.:
National League of Cities, 1977).

on buses,[29] and the provision for mailing social security checks directly to the recipients' banks exemplify recent efforts to control crime through this alternative.

What additional physical or technical changes might be made that would have an effect on the problem? Should such changes be mandatory, or can they be voluntary? What incentives might be offered to encourage their implementation?

2. Changes in the Provision of Government Services

Can the problem be alleviated by changes in other government services? Some of the most petty but annoying problems the police must handle originate in the policies, operating practices, and inadequacies of other public agencies: the scattering of garbage because of delays in collection, poor housing conditions because of lax code enforcement, the interference with traffic by children playing because they have not been provided with adequate playground facilities, the uncapping of hydrants on hot summer nights because available pools are closed. Most police agencies long ago developed procedures for relaying reports on such conditions to the appropriate government service. But relatively few police agencies see their role as pressing for changes in policies and operations that would eliminate the recurrence of the same problems. Yet the police are the only people who see and who must become responsible for the collective negative consequences of current policies.

3. Conveying Reliable Information

What many people want, when they turn to the police with their problems, is simply reliable information.[30] The tenant who is locked out by his landlord for failure to pay the rent wants to know his rights to his property. The car owner whose license plates are lost or stolen wants to know what reporting obligations he has, how he goes about replacing the plates, and whether he can drive his car in the meantime. The person who suspects his neighbors of abusing their child wants to know whether he is warranted in reporting the matter to

29. For a summary of a survey designed to assess the effect of this change, see Russell Grindle and Thomas Aceituno, "Innovations in Robbery Control," in *The Prevention and Control of Robbery*, vol. 1, Floyd Feeney and Adrianne Weir, eds. (Davis, Calif.: University of California, 1973), pp. 315–20.

30. In one of the most recent of a growing number of studies of how police spend their time, it was reported that, of the 18,012 calls made to the police serving a community of 24,000 people in a four-month period, 59.98 percent were requests for information. Police responded to 65 percent of the calls they received by providing information by telephone. See J. Robert Lilly, "What Are the Police Now Doing?" *Journal of Police Science and Administration*, January 1978, p. 56.

the police. And the person who receives a series of obscene telephone calls wants to know what can be done about them. Even if citizens do not ask specific questions, the best response the police can make to many requests for help is to provide accurate, concise information.

4. Developing New Skills among Police Officers

The greatest potential for improvement in the handling of some problems is in providing police officers with new forms of specialized training. This is illustrated by several recent developments. For example, the major component in the family-crisis intervention projects launched all over the country is instruction of police officers in the peculiar skills required to de-escalate highly emotional family quarrels. First aid training for police is being expanded, consistent with the current trend toward greater use of paramedics. One unpleasant task faced by the police, seldom noted by outsiders, is notifying families of the death of a family member. Often, this problem is handled poorly. In 1976, a film was made specifically to demonstrate how police should carry out this responsibility.[31] Against this background of recent developments, one should ask whether specialized training can bring about needed improvement in the handling of each specific problem.

5. New Forms of Authority

Do the police need a specific, limited form of authority which they do not now have? If the most intelligent response to a problem, such as a person causing a disturbance in a bar, is to order the person to leave, should the police be authorized to issue such an order, or should they be compelled to arrest the individual in order to stop the disturbance? The same question can be asked about the estranged husband who has returned to his wife's apartment or about the group of teenagers annoying passersby at a street corner. Police are called upon to resolve these common problems, but their authority is questionable unless the behavior constitutes a criminal offense. And even then, it may not be desirable to prosecute the offender. Another type of problem is presented by the intoxicated person who is not sufficiently incapacitated to warrant being taken into protective custody, but who apparently intends to drive his car. Should a police officer have the authority to prevent the person from driving by temporarily confiscating the car keys or, as a last resort, by taking him into protective custody? Or must the officer wait for the individual to get behind the wheel and actually attempt to drive and then make an arrest? Limited specific authority may enable the police to deal more directly and intelligently with a number of comparable situations.

31. *Death Notification* (New York: Harper & Row, 1976).

254 Herman Goldstein

6. Developing New Community Resources

Analysis of a problem may lead to the conclusion that assistance is needed from another government agency. But often the problem is not clearly within the province of an existing agency, or the agency may be unaware of the problem or, if aware, without the resources to do anything about it. In such cases, since the problem is likely to be of little concern to the community as a whole, it will probably remain the responsibility of the police, unless they themselves take the initiative, as a sort of community ombudsman, in getting others to address it.

A substantial percentage of all police business involves dealing with persons suffering from mental illness. In the most acute cases, where the individual may cause immediate harm to himself or others, the police are usually authorized to initiate an emergency commitment. Many other cases that do not warrant hospitalization nevertheless require some form of attention: The number of these situations has increased dramatically as the mental health system has begun treating more and more of its patients in the community. If the conduct of these persons, who are being taught to cope with the world around them, creates problems for others or exceeds community tolerance, should they be referred back to a mental health agency? Or, because they are being encouraged to adjust to the reality of the community, should they be arrested if their behavior constitutes a criminal offense? How are the police to distinguish between those who have never received any assistance, and who should therefore be referred to a mental health agency, and those who are in community treatment? Should a community agency establish services for these persons comparable to the crisis-intervention services now offered by specially organized units operating in some communities?

Such crisis-intervention units are among a number of new resources that have been established in the past few years for dealing with several long-neglected problems: detoxification centers for those incapacitated by alcohol, shelters and counseling for runaways, shelters for battered wives, and support services for the victims of sexual assault. Programs are now being designed to provide a better response to citizen disputes and grievances, another long-neglected problem. Variously labeled, these programs set up quasi-judicial forums that are intended to be inexpensive, easily accessible, and geared to the specific needs of their neighborhoods. LEAA has recently funded three such experimental programs, which they call Neighborhood Justice Centers.[32] These centers will receive many of their cases from the police.

---

32. The concept is described in Daniel McGillis and Joan Mullen, *Neighborhood Justice Centers: An Analysis of Potential Models* (Washington, D.C.: Govt. Printing Office, 1977). See also R. F. Conner and R. Suretta, *The Citizen Dispute Settlement Program: Resolving Disputes outside the Courts—Orlando, Florida* (Washington, D.C.: American Bar Association, 1977).

Thus, the pattern of creating new services that bear a relationship with police operations is now well established, and one would expect that problem-oriented policing will lead to more services in greater variety.

7. Increased Regulation

Can the problem be handled through a tightening of regulatory codes? Where easy access to private premises is a factor, should city building codes be amended to require improved lock systems? To reduce the noise problem, should more soundproofing be required in construction? The incidence of shoplifting is determined, in part, by the number of salespeople employed, the manner in which merchandise is displayed, and the use made of various anti-shoplifting devices. Should the police be expected to combat shoplifting without regard to the merchandising practices by a given merchant, or should merchants be required by a "merchandising code" to meet some minimum standards before they can turn to the police for assistance?

8. Increased Use of City Ordinances

Does the problem call for some community sanction less drastic than a criminal sanction? Many small communities process through their local courts, as ordinance violations, as many cases of minor misconduct as possible. Of course, this requires that the community have written ordinances, usually patterned after the state statutes, that define such misconduct. Several factors make this form of processing desirable for certain offenses: It is less formal than criminal action; physical detention is not necessary; cases may be disposed of without a court appearance; the judge may select from a wide range of alternative penalties; and the offender is spared the burden of a criminal record. Some jurisdictions now use a system of civil forfeitures in proceeding against persons found to be in possession of marijuana, though the legal status of the procedure is unclear in those states whose statutes define possession as criminal and call for a more severe fine or for imprisonment.

9. Use of Zoning

Much policing involves resolving disputes between those who have competing interests in the use made of a given sidewalk, street, park, or neighborhood. Bigger and more basic conflicts in land use were resolved long ago by zoning, a concept that is now firmly established. Recently, zoning has been used by a number of cities to limit the pornography stores and adult movie houses in a given area. And at least one city has experimented with the opposite approach, creating an adult entertainment zone with the hope of curtailing the spread of such establishments and simplifying the management of attendant problems. Much more experimentation is needed before any judgment can be made as to the value of zoning in such situations.

IMPLEMENTING THE PROCESS

A fully developed process for systematically addressing the problems that make up police business would call for more than the three steps just explored —defining the problem, researching it, and exploring alternatives. I have focused on these three because describing them may be the most effective way of communicating the nature of a problem-oriented approach to improving police service. A number of intervening steps are required to fill out the processes: methods for evaluating the effectiveness of current responses, procedures for choosing from among available alternatives, means of involving the community in the decision making, procedures for obtaining the approval of the municipal officials to whom the police are formally accountable, methods for obtaining any additional funding that may be necessary, adjustments in the organization and staffing of the agency that may be required to implement an agreed-upon change, and methods for evaluating the effectiveness of the change.

How does a police agency make the shift to problem-oriented policing? Ideally, the initiative will come from police administrators. What is needed is not a single decision implementing a specific program or a single memorandum announcing a unique way of running the organization. The concept represents a new way of looking at the process of improving police functioning. It is a way of thinking about the police and their function that, carried out over an extended period, would be reflected in all that the administrator does: in the relationship with personnel, in the priorities he sets in his own work schedule, in what he focuses on in addressing community groups, in the choice of training curriculums, and in the questions raised with local and state legislators. Once introduced, this orientation would affect subordinates, gradually filter through the rest of the organization, and reach other administrators and agencies as well.

An administrator's success will depend heavily, in particular, on the use made of planning staff, for systematic analysis of substantive problems requires developing a capacity within the organization to collect and analyze data and to conduct evaluations of the effectiveness of police operations. Police planners (now employed in significant numbers) will have to move beyond their traditional concern with operating procedures into what might best be characterized as "product research."

The police administrator who focuses on the substance of policing should be able to count on support from others in key positions in the police field. Colleges with programs especially designed for police personnel may exert considerable leadership through their choice of offerings and through the subject matter of individual courses. In an occupation in which so much deference is paid to the value of a college education, if college instructors reinforce the impression that purely administrative matters are the most important issues in policing, police personnel understandably will not develop their interests beyond this concern.

Likewise, the LEAA, its state and local offspring, and other grant-making organizations have a unique opportunity to draw the attention of operating personnel to the importance of addressing substantive problems. The manner in which these organizations invest their funds sends a strong message to the police about what is thought to be worthwhile.

EFFECT ON THE ORGANIZATION

In the context of this reordering of police priorities, efforts to improve the staffing, management, and procedures of police agencies must continue.

Those who have been strongly committed to improving policing through better administration and organization may be disturbed by any move to subordinate their interests to a broader concern with the end product of policing. However, a problem-oriented approach to police improvement may actually contribute in several important ways to achieving their objectives.

The approach calls for the police to take greater initiative in attempting to deal with problems rather than resign themselves to living with them. It calls for tapping police expertise. It calls for the police to be more aggressive partners with other public agencies. These changes, which would place the police in a much more positive light in the community, would also contribute significantly to improving the working environment within a police agency—an environment that suffers much from the tendency of the police to assume responsibility for problems which are insolvable or ignored by others. And an improved working environment increases, in turn, the potential for recruiting and keeping qualified personnel and for bringing about needed organizational change.

Focusing on problems, because it is a practical and concrete approach, is attractive to both citizens and the police. By contrast, some of the most frequent proposals for improving police operations, because they do not produce immediate and specifically identifiable results, have no such attraction. A problem-oriented approach, with its greater appeal, has the potential for becoming a vehicle through which long-sought organizational change might be more effectively and more rapidly achieved.

Administrative rule making, for example, has gained considerable support from policy makers and some police administrators as a way of structuring police discretion, with the expectation that applying the concept would improve the quality of the decisions made by the police in the field. Yet many police administrators regard administrative rule making as an idea without practical significance. By contrast, police administrators are usually enthusiastic if invited to explore the problem of car theft or vandalism. And within such exploration, there is the opportunity to demonstrate the value of structuring police discretion in responding to reports of vandalism and car theft. Approached from this practical point of view, the concept of administrative rule making is more likely to be implemented.

Long-advocated changes in the structure and operations of police agencies

Herman Goldstein

have been achieved because of a concentrated concern with a given problem: The focus on the domestic disturbance, originally in New York and now elsewhere, introduced the generalist-specialist concept that has enabled many police agencies to make more effective use of their personnel; the problem in controlling narcotics and the high mobility of drug sellers motivated police agencies in many metropolitan areas to pool their resources in special investigative units, thereby achieving in a limited way one of the objectives of those who have urged consolidation of police agencies; and the recent interest in the crime of rape has resulted in widespread backing for the establishment of victim-support programs. Probably the support for any of these changes could not have been generated without the problem-oriented context in which they have been advocated.

An important factor contributing to these successes is that a problem-oriented approach to improvement is less likely to be seen as a direct challenge to the police establishment and the prevailing police value system. As a consequence, rank-and-file personnel do not resist and subvert the resulting changes. Traditional programs to improve the police—labeled as efforts to "change," "upgrade," or "reform" the police or to "achieve minimum standards"—require that police officers openly acknowledge their own deficiencies. Rank-and-file officers are much more likely to support an innovation that is cast in the form of a new response to an old problem—a problem with which they have struggled for many years and which they would like to see handled more effectively. It may be that addressing the quality of the police product will turn out to be the most effective way of achieving the objectives that have for so long been the goal of police reform.

[11]

Contemporary Crises 6 (1982) 241–266

Elsevier Scientific Publishing Company, Amsterdam – Printed in The Netherlands

PARKING TICKETS AND CLASS REPRESSION: THE CONCEPT OF POLICING IN CRITICAL THEORIES OF CRIMINAL JUSTICE*

OTWIN MARENIN

Critical theorists [1] argue (and often merely assume) that law enforcement agencies act in the interests of the dominant groups and classes of a society; that in any social formation the state and its agents can do no other than act repressively against actual and potential challenges to the established order; and that the police (as are the other structures in the criminal justice system – legal norms, courts, corrections) are one of the main defense mechanisms, alongside welfare programs and the manipulation of consciousness, on which the safety and continuance of the state and, therefore, of the social formation rests.

Policing is defined by O'Conner as a form of guard labor. "The purpose of guard labor is not to produce something but to avoid something. Guard labor reproduces the formal structures of capitalism and maintains and reproduces capitalist production relations. Guard labor does not produce commodities, yet without guard labor commodity production would be impossible" [2]. Specifically, the police patrol the conflict among classes. "The police serve as the frontline mechanism of repression. As such, the central function of the police is to control the working class", [3] and to "enforce the class, racial, sexual and cultural oppression that has been integral to capitalist development in the United States" [4] as it serves "the interest of national and local government and the big corporations" [5]. The pre-eminent force "behind the creation of the police institution in the United States was the need of large-scale entrepreneurs to ensure the orderly control of workers during the era of capitalist industrialization", and the argument that the police served "'to accelerate the accumulation of capital by increasing the degree of exploitation of labour' is a compelling synthesis of the actual function of the police" [6].

This formulation ignores a basic point, well established by research,

Washington State University, Pullman, Washington 99164, U.S.A.

*This article was presented originally as a paper at the March 1981 meeting of the Academy of Criminal Justice Sciences Convention in Philadelphia. I wish to thank the discussant at the panel, David O. Friedrichs, as well as Ben Menke, Terry Cook, and the anonymous reviewers for *Contemporary Crises* for their encouraging and helpful comments on this earlier draft. The article would have been better had I taken all their suggestions to heart. I am, of course, responsible for not doing so.

242

namely, that not all actions of the police are repressive (e.g., providing a service such as stopping family quarrels) though some clearly are (e.g., the proverbial midnight knock at the door or dispersing demonstrations against unpopular government policy); the formulation also ignores the theoretical strictures of critical thought, namely, that actions should be concretely specified, that is, be linked to a theoretically complex and complete understanding of the state and society. The question arises — which actions of the police indicate class repression? How does one recognize those specific acts of the police which concretely show domination and exploitation and those which do not? If not all actions of the police are repressive, then some actions would seem to be in the interest of the dominated — why do these actions occur? how must they be incorporated into a theory of the role and function of the police in specific societies and into theories of the state in general? These questions — easy enough to ask — need a systematic answer, so far lacking in critical theory.

This article will extend two ideas central to recent critical thought on the nature of society and on methodology to a discussion of the police. These ideas include the concept of "relative autonomy of the state" and the argument that existing relations in society need to be understood concretely and dialectically rather than merely empirically and schematically. Both points, the substantive description of the state and the methodological question of how one is to observe and understand existing realities, can serve as a springboard to a better formulation of the role of the police than is now found in either critical thought or positivist science. I will argue that the role of the police is more complex than that of being the protector or the instrument of the powerful; that the police perform a variety of functions and protect a variety of interests; that universal and specific functions of the police can and must be kept distinct; in short, that the police are "relatively autonomous" and that their autonomy can be observed empirically and must be interpreted theoretically. The variety of interests which the police serve, and the groups whose interests these are, must be clearly specified and incorporated into a theoretical discussion of the function of the police in society.

The first section of the paper will discuss critical theories of the state and law since one cannot explain the role of the police in critical theory without first establishing the general model of the society and the role of the concept "relative autonomy of the state" in that model. The latter sections will extend the discussion of relative autonomy to the police and will argue that one cannot understand the role of policing without combining elements derived from critical thought and empirical research, that is, without developing an approach which embraces "both 'societal' and 'organizational—occupational—cultural' reference points in ways that existing

approaches have failed adequately to do" [7]. The article is not meant to
be a definitive statement on the state, class, crime, or law enforcement in
the US or other societies but hopes to open a dialogue on a topic which has
important practical and theoretical dimensions.

The Critical Model

Critical theories of society and the state are in flux. The paradigm revolution [8] against positivist social science and its supporting capitalist order
and liberal ideology has shown itself to be less complete or convincing than
initially expected. (One suspects that it has always been more a struggle
between generations of academics over control of the conceptual terrain
than a true paradigm change — that is, a different set of assumptions, methodologies, and findings in response to puzzles perceived by a community
of scholars.) The main reason the hope and promise have gone unfulfilled
has been the inability of critical theory to convincingly deal with the puzzles
it in turn has created. Critical theory has failed to develop a concept of the
state and of politics subtle enough to withstand the rigors of empirical tests
or praxis, that is, a model of the state which incorporates what is known
about the actions of the state when making and enforcing law, morality,
and order and retains, at the same time, a dialectically reflexive stance
towards its own theory. In Skocpol's words, "no self-declared neo-Marxist
theory of the capitalist state has arrived at the point of taking state structures and party organization *seriously enough*. Various ways of short-
circuiting political analyses have been too tempting" [9]. Secondly, critical
theory has not yet developed its own method, has failed to move beyond
a merely antipositivist stance to devise a methodology which remains empirical without becoming positivist [10].

Critiques of the critical model, especially its more pronounced Marxist
variants, have focused on three crucial and problematic linkages in it: first,
the connection of base to superstructure, specifically the question of the
economic base of group life and the materialistic base of consciousness
[11]; second, the connection of class structure to the state, specifically
the degree to which class determines and controls the actions of the state;
and, third, the connection of the state to policy, that is, the variety of appearances under which state policies present themselves. Critical theory
has dealt with the puzzles associated with these connections in various
ways. The materialistic base to consciousness connection has been "explained" by developing a distinction in types of consciousness (that is,
between false and true consciousness) for actors (what does class consciousness consist of?) and for the observer (when is reality correctly perceived
and interpreted?). Consciousness, false and correct, connects base to super-

244

structure and mediates the material forces which propel history [12]. The second problematical connection, that of class to the state, has been much argued recently and has been "solved" by developing the concept "the relative autonomy of the state", rejecting in the process merely instrumentalist and schematic versions of control and direction [13]. The third connection, that of the variety of appearances (how can the state do things which on their face are clearly against the interests of ruling groups?) has been "solved" by an appearance versus essence distinction which denies certain observations and "mere" facts the power to disprove established modes of interpretation [14].

Encompassing these arguments about how these linkages are to be understood is the notion of dialectical understanding as necessary for the determination of what is and is not false in consciousness; what determines the relative autonomy of the state; and what separates appearance from essence in the observable [15].

There is much disagreement among critical theorists on the "tightness" of these linkages, and arguments deal with the best holistic model of social formations which is to serve as the foundation for a new understanding, and with the question of determinism — what is meant by "ultimately" determining, by "relatively" autonomous, or by "concretely" specified.

The general effect of these solutions within the critical outlook has been a loosening of the hold of materialist base over consciousness, of class over the state, and of the state over policy. In Greenberg's words, by "loosening the functional relationship between law and economy a bit, one creates the possibility of developing a materialist approach to the sociology of law that transcends mechanical economic determinism, and which, in particular, does not try to explain every element of legislation in terms of its functional necessity for the economy" [16].

The thrust of rethinking Marxist concepts is this: to attempt to retain the critical model, yet modify it, make it more complex, so that the concepts which constitute the model — domination, class, autonomy, consciousness, legitimation, hegemony — are clearly and empirically specified. Even critics of variants of critical thought, especially its more polemical and mechanical formulations, agree that the critical model has served a useful function, has presented a "revealing counter-image which serves as a point of departure for a critical understanding of capitalist society". Yet critical theory now faces the "formidable task of systematically examining the empirical validity of its propositions" [17].

The Concept of Dialectical Understanding

The most useful methodological impact of critical thought on positivist science has been the resurrection of historical analysis [18]; the worst drawback, the rejection of comparative research. Both effects stem from a primary epistemological assumption, namely, that appearances cannot be understood in an abstracted or universalistic way but must be specifically and concretely understood as bounded by time and place and anchored in a larger whole. History reveals concepts in concrete moments; comparison is difficult since each moment is unique. For example, law enforcement or order must be understood as specific to a historical stage of a social formation and cannot be understood as order or law enforcement in general, that is, in isolation from the larger whole which gives meaning to concepts and the realities they point to. Yet critical thinkers are less persuasive here than in other areas; clearly, to argue for dialectical analysis as necessary or that concepts cannot be understood unless embedded in correct theoretical conciousness implies degrees of universality and specificity. It would seem useful for critical thought to clarify how one can be both specific and universalizing at one and the same time without losing "concreteness". The statement that "it is not a contradiction in method to speak simultaneously about roles and structures common to various capitalist states and yet avoid the notion of a 'capitalist state in general' " needs a lot more argument to make it convincing [19]. It would be useful for critical theory to apply its methods and concepts not only to the study of precapitalist and capitalist social formations (as has been the tendency) but also to non-capitalist formations of the present (i.e., the state in China or the USSR) or envisioned future formations (i.e., the expected disappearance of crime in socialist societies). Until critical theory comes to grips with comparison, it has little hope of convincing either the community of scholars who determine a paradigm or potential actors who might prove it true in action. As Spitzer argues, the persuasiveness of critical thought rests "in the final analysis on the willingness and capacity of critical criminology to provide a grounded, sophisticated, and accessible body of research findings" and, one might add, the epistemological basis for grounding these findings comparatively [20].

The call for dialectical and empirically based analyses is, in large measure, a response to critiques of schematic applications of the critical model to specific events and of the functionalist logic which infuses such applications. Statements such as: "capital required . . . ", "it became necessary for the bourgeoisie to . . . ", or "police organization is a function of . . . " mean little [21]. As explanations they are useless, since any event, even diametrically opposed ones, would have been equally necessary had they occurred. In Chambliss' words, "such a view is theoretically untenable because it is tautological and teleological. It is tautological because any solution to a problem can be interpreted as protecting ruling class interests, because the

246

ruling class survives the change. It is teleological because it attributes some kind of rationality to the system that is independent of people making decisions" [22]. The counterargument possible, that another event did not occur, would be refutation only if one also assumed that specific events are inevitable, an assumption even critical theorists do not make.

In practical terms, being dialectical and concrete has meant being selectively empirical. To describe the reality of social formations or aspects of them requires data. Critical theory cannot depend on positivist science for its methods or the data these methods create. Yet the methodology for a dialectical analysis has not yet been worked out. Doing dialectical thinking must involve more than describing the dialectic as a useful sensitizing device which can lead one to detect tendencies in social change and "empirical plausibilities", as Spitzer justifies the method [23]. Recourse to the dialectic and dialectical thinking cannot be what it is now, an invocation to "magically fill an etiological chasm [which] exists between independent and dependent variables" [24], but must begin to spell out how it can be used by people with less insight, by everybody as a means to separate appearance from essence.

The Concept of Relative Autonomy

Critical concern about the roles of the state arose from specific puzzles. The seeming failure or delay of the class struggle in advanced capitalist societies raised the question of how the natural contradictions of capitalist development are prevented from working themselves out in the expected manner. In developing countries, the problem has been the role of the state and politics in the creation and maintenance of underdevelopment, and the possibility of an autonomous state acting to overcome the constraints of underdevelopment. The problem for socialist societies has been the nonwithering away of the state. These puzzles have led to a reformulation of the concept of the state, away from Marx's often quoted notion of the state as the executive committee of the ruling class and toward the rediscovery of his arguments on the Bonapartist state and its autonomy.

Revisions for Western societies have involved the development of structuralist and phenomenological versions of the Marxist model which de-emphasize the instrumentalist goals of state activity and argue, instead, for a role for the state as defender of the capitalist class in general or of the capitalist social formation as a whole and in the long run. To achieve such goals, the state employs subtler means of control than were envisioned in the struggle version of the model — the clash of armed force and violent repression is supplemented by bribery (the welfare state) and, more importantly, by control of consciousness as the state and its agencies strive to maintain hegemonic control and ensure, thereby, the legitimacy of the existing order [25]. Cultural elements loom large in the reproduction of the capitalist state, and rationalization and liberal ideology are the fundamental mystifying devices which enshrine the power of the state in the minds of its subjects [26]. A second aspect of the revision is this: since class rule does not mean control of the state and its policies, other factors must be brought in to explain specific events. Gurr concludes, after surveying the history of state reaction to public disorder and crime, that it is "too simplistic to maintain that changing policies of public order are merely manifestations of an elite's class interests and narrow desire to retain power. . . . Since the 1850s, public order in English society generally has rarely been any more than a secondary concern for most of the elite or the public at large" [27]. Under these conditions, moral entrepreneurs or organizational interests [28] or the "cognitive processes, moral development, and personal qualities" [29] of individuals may become the dominant influences in shaping policy and law.

It also follows that the realities of the capitalist system need to be described more accurately than has been done. Critical theorists have wrestled with the question of what the class structure of capitalist society really looks like, who belongs to which class, and what becomes of individuals who find themselves classless or in contradictory class positions [30]. In sum, things have become much less simple than they used to be — the state uses a variety of means to assure its power and dominance; numerous classes, fractions and strata must be taken into account in order to explain what happened; the articulation of base to superstructure (or whether this is even a useful distinction) is perceived as complex and difficult to pin down.

The non-withering away of the state in socialist societies and its obviously repressive actions in some (i.e., the gulag experience in the USSR) have led to a number of reformulations. One, the validity of the label is denied, and it is argued that existing social formations represent state socialism rather than the true, cooperative, and participant socialism described by Marx and Engels [31]. Two, it is argued that the current stages of socialistic formations which can be observed are temporary (albeit of a long run) and that the state is also a temporary phenomenon [32]. Third, there is the argument that Marx never really meant to say that the state would wither away, but that he meant exploitation and politics would and that the state, thought of as the administrative structure necessary for the provision of a minimum of law and order and a modicum of authority and obedience to law, would continue to exist, being essential for all societies [33].

Revisions in thinking about developing societies can be found in theoretical shifts from neo-colonialism (the state as the naked agent of the exploiting capitalist power) to dependency thinking (the state as the tool for

248

incorporation of the periphery of the world system into its core) to arguments that the state can be autonomous and promote genuine development based on the capacity of indigenous classes to resist external control [34], and arguments that dependency is a condition which applies to all relations of developing countries with external powers, be they capitalist or socialist [35].

In all cases, critical theorists have found anchors in Marx's voluminous writings for theoretical positions which earlier would have been rejected as deviations. (In that sense, critical theory is coming of age.) In all cases, whether capitalist, socialist, or underdeveloped societies are analyzed, the state has emerged as a powerful and independent actor in the political economy of social formations. In the process of making the state relatively autonomous, critical theory has opened the concept of the state to empirical validation and scrutiny — when, how, to what degree, under what conditions is the state autonomous? How does it protect and express its autonomy? What is it autonomous for? The answers lie equally in what the state does as in theoretical understandings of social formations.

Once the state is relatively autonomous, can state policy be far behind? Critical thinking on one state policy, that of law, has parallelled theoretical changes in the analysis of the state itself. The instrumentalist position — that law reflects and sustains the distribution of power among ruling and exploited classes — has given way to a more complex conceptualization as effective critiques by liberal and critical scholars, that law can be genuinely equalizing, have made an impact. The main arguments against the instrumentalist position follow. One, the instrumentalist position reduces the complexity of social relations, their concrete conjunctures and dialectical dynamics, to simple cause—effect statements [36] which misrepresent the realities of crime and the creation, content, and application of laws; the specific content of laws passed by ruling classes has not always been exploitative or repressive and sometimes does infringe on the interests of the ruling class itself; the capacity of law to hurt the interests of the powerful needs to be explained [37]. Two, the instrumentalist version fails to take into account the importance of a mediating consciousness, nor does it incorporate consciousness as a theoretically valid element in the construction of a theory of the state and law. Three, instrumentalism assumes that the capitalist class possesses a clearsightedness and omnipotence to protect its short and long run interests, which goes far beyond known powers of control or knowledge [38].

Law, for these reasons, has become disconnected from the immediate interests of the ruling classes or the state and, in the latest variant derived from the writings of Pashukanis and elaborated in a number of writings [39], has become truly autonomous of people and classes and functions in the interests of the capitalist order as a whole. Law is the crucial element in the mystification process, the central legitimation device which, by converting unique individuals into juridical equals and labor into an exchange commodity, hides the differences in class, power, and life chances which exist. It is the very fact that law does treat people equally which mystifies.

Yet one can argue that, despite the frequent use of the phrase, the theoretical importance of "relative autonomy" for critical theories of law has been little appreciated or applied. In Tushnet's words, critical theorists "must proceed to give content to the idea of the relative autonomy of law," specifically by examining the actions of lawyers [40]. At the minimum, relative autonomy cannot mean less than that the state and law at times act independently of larger social forces. If the state did not, the concept would be unnecessary. Since it is not larger social forces and structures which determine what the law is and does, other factors must be brought in to explain differences in the law – obvious candidates are the values, concerns, and interests of those groups and individuals who "carry" the law. When the law steps in, as the saying goes, it does so on the feet of lawyers, policemen, judges, probation officers, and others. Autonomy means that both the underlying forms of social relations and the pervasiveness of dominant and conflicting forms of consciousness affect what the state does in policy formation and execution.

The puzzles which exist for critical theories as a whole are reflected in discussions of crime and criminal justice, and lead to these questions. How is one to understand the reaction of the state which is relatively autonomous (there is little disagreement by now among critical theorists that the state is) to crime (its definition and overall incidence) and criminality (the individual act) which are determined by the consciousness of non-determined actors? How can law, a "relatively autonomous" policy of the "relatively autonomous" state, be used effectively as a means of repression and social control and thereby ensure the reproduction of a social formation? How, in turn, is one to understand law enforcement and the role of the police within these shifting contexts?

The next sections will develop the notion of the "relative autonomy" of the police. Relative autonomy can be justified empirically – it exists – and argued theoretically – that is, accepting the idea that the police can be autonomous does not deny that they also serve the interests of the powerful or contribute toward the maintenance of the system. The aim will be further to loosen the state-to-policy linkage by arguing that critical conceptions of the role of the police are overly simplified and fail to incorporate what is known about the history and reality of law enforcement into a systematic and coherent model of policy formation in social formations.

250

The Concept of the Function of the Police

Since critical thinkers accept the notion of the relative autonomy of the state and law (and have most to lose, theoretically speaking, by doing so) one can accept that the state does act autonomously, that it routinely violates the interests of the ruling classes. Bourgeois and liberal scholars have always known this to be true. I wish to push the argument a step further. If the state and law can be autonomous, why should not law enforcement be so? To answer this question requires some conceptual distinctions, specifically, what is meant by the notions of interest, function, and policing. Equally important is the analysis of police work as performed in the past and present in all social formations.

Interests may be defined as those needs which people are authentically conscious of and which they try to meet, in the short and in the long run, through individual and group actions. The definition of interest may encompass only individual needs or include collective, trans-individual components. Collective needs arise from a common position in the social structure, similarities in religion or culture, agreement on social issues, or social affect. Classes are interested groups which arrive at a common consciousness by their experience in the process of production. All interested individuals, when organized as groups, attempt to control the state and impose their specific definitions of the "public good" as generic ones for a society.

The key word in this conception is "authentic". The important question here is not whether interests are subjective or objective [41] but who will decide both the criteria and their application to specific issues and circumstances. I accept that the people likely to be affected by an action are the best determiners of their individual and collective interests, though under certain conditions — fraud, ignorance, mystification — they may be wrongly aware. Interests are, then, defined by both subjective preference and the potential for objective judgment [42], a capacity that belongs to all [43]. The obligation to define and defend what is meant by "wrongly aware" and "falsely conscious" rests on the observer rather than the participant. It is an empirical as well as a theoretical assertion.

Function may be defined as a logical relation or as an activity. In the first sense, a function depends for its meaning on its connections to something else. A function in a social system is that activity necessary to perform a task, meet a goal, fulfill a need, or express a purpose. This conception of function presupposes an idea of a larger whole for which the function is performed, for which it is necessary, essential, vital. Most conceptions of the role of the police one finds in critical theories use this conception of function. Alternatively, function may be defined as whatever something or someone does, that is, the routine behavior of individuals and groups. This conception does not presuppose a model of some larger whole and remains basically descriptive. The two conceptions are related — one can argue that something would not be performed routinely, be descriptively correct, unless it were useful or necessary for some larger purpose. As used here, function will attempt to incorporate both meanings, but I wish to start from the notion of function as routine behavior and then extrapolate to purpose or need as this lessens the danger of assuming what should be proved. A teleological conception of function makes it difficult to discriminate among observations, makes it hard to detail the variety of specific purposes an activity may achieve [44].

Who are the police in a society? Though the core meaning of the concept policing seems clear — the use or threatened use of force by agents of the state to enforce laws — there remain exceptions which quickly muddle the edges of the concept. Should privately employed personnel be considered a police force? Should the military when it quells a riot be considered as performing a policing function? Should persons who have limited rather than generalized law enforcement powers, e.g., customs agents, be considered to be police? [45].

Most critical theories see the police as "servants of the state" [46] pure and simple, as a group which unquestioningly and consistently carries out the directives it receives from the state and those who control it. This conception of policing presumes too much, as it derives the meaning of police work by deduction from prior models of capitalist development and the class struggle embedded in it. This starting point precludes any explanation of police work which does not see it as a necessary function for the reproduction of the social formation; and it is not amenable to empirical tests. Missing from this conception is any notion of the relative autonomy of the state and far less, of course, of the relative autonomy of the police. With few exceptions [47], there is little discussion of the concrete linkages of policing to social bases; of the varieties of policing organizations; of the implications of a service orientation in police departments; of differentiations among oppressed groups; or of the needs which the powerless have in being protected in person and property. For instance, Cain's assertion that the "variations in the way policing is organized are themselves a function of a particular mode of production" [48] means little and ignores her own advice that the police should be studied concretely before arguing their function. There is, after all, a large gap between the mode of production or productions (since no social formation is pure) and the specifics of organizing an agency of the state.

Definitions of who the police are need to be based on what the police do; the police must be "defined in terms of their key practice" [49]. Bayley proposes this definition: the police "are a group authorized in the name of

252

territorial communities to utilize force within the community to handle whatever needs doing" [50]. Manning proposes a slightly different emphasis: "policing can be seen as being a presentation of coercive potential and its enactment, the application of force to everyday affairs; being backed by law and conventional institutional structures in the community; and reflecting the interests of those who control and define situations requiring the application of authority" [51]. Common to all definitions is the notion that the police are guards. The key police practice is guarding by the potential or actual application of force. There is disagreement on two key issues: what it is the police are guarding – whether order in general, the state, moral consensus, a specific class interest, the vanguard party, people, property, the capitalist system, the interests of all. Secondly, there is disagreement on whether the police are only those guardians employed by the state, that is, paid from public funds, or whether privately employed guards are policing when they work.

The first issue depends for its resolution on examinations of police work in the past and now. It requires that we develop a "theory of the state which is elaborated downwards" [52] and analyze the specifics of policing – its organization, tasks, personnel, and structural relations. Rather than asking whether the police protect order in general or a specific class, we need to ask: whose interests are protected by policing? This question does not prejudge the functions of a police force; it does not presume that the police are either defenders of a moral consensus or capitalist rule. It allows for the inclusion of all interests, including those of the police, when considering whose are served; it makes comparative work possible.

The second issue is more difficult to deal with since any definition of key practice, including the one advocated here, leads to areas of ambiguity when applied. Which aspects of public, state-directed activity which guards by the use of force are not policing, or are all? Which aspects of privately employed guarding, if they lack the legitimated right to use force, are still policing; e.g., ticket takers at the cinema? It seems reasonable to accept that both private and public guarding of interests is policing. The definition of the police which will be used, then, is this: the police are the privately and publicly employed guardians of interest who are entitled to use force to do whatever needs doing. It is the function of the police forcefully to guard interests.

Police Work

Descriptions of the police and their work can be organized under the headings of history, organization, function, ideology, personality, and control. These factors, when adequately described and taken together, constitute the concrete relative autonomy of the police; these factors define the police and policing not as an abstracted functional requirement for the reproduction of order or a social formation (whether capitalist or other) but as the working life of order, service, and repression demanded by interested groups in society and enacted by interested police forces.

Critical and other scholars agree frequently on the description of police work yet differ on the meaning to be assigned to what is observed. For instance, the drive toward professionalization of police forces in the US is seen by some as the purposive alienation of the police force from its working class roots in an effort to make class rule more effective [53], while others see this development as a "function of the changing structure of capital" from local toward monopoly capitalism [54], or as an effort by police forces for greater independence from external political influence [55]. It is obvious from these contrasting interpretations that one's conception of the function and role of the police depends more on one's theory than one's observations and, also, that the reality of police work is complex enough to make contrasting interpretations theoretically plausible. The sections which follow will describe the accepted reality of police work in a general way.

The origins of police forces vary. In general, policing as a separate activity arose in response to social complexity [56] and the extension of state power, that is, the transformation of social control from community-based to state-directed activity [57]. In Western societies, the creation of public police forces (forces working for and paid by the state or state-granted rights to collect fees) resulted from the desire by groups which controlled the state for information on potential challengers, e.g., in France and Russia during Bonapartist and Czarist rule [58]; the need to deal with problems of disorder as defined through the interactions of the powerful and the dominated. "The paramilitary form of early police bureaucracy was a response not only, or even primarily, to crime per se, but to the possibility of riotous disorder. Not crime and danger but the 'criminal' and 'dangerous classes' as part of the urban social structure led to the formation of uniformed and militarily organized police" [59]. Lastly, police forces made it possible for the emerging state to sustain itself by the collection of resources (taxes) and labor (forced labor and military draft) [60].

In former colonies, which now comprise most developing countries, police forces were established to bring law and order, to pacify the population, and to ensure the orderly administration of colonial rule as defined by colonial rulers and their local allies [61]. In socialist countries, patterns of policing which developed after the success of revolutionary activities reflected the demands of vanguard parties as they controlled the emerging state apparatus, and included normally the carry-over of existing secret police forces, the creation of small regular forces, and massive doses of popular participation

254

in and responsibility for maintaining public order [62].

The specific development of policing reflects, then, the circumstances and values of interested groups in conflict. In the USA, police forces developed under the constraints of crime and order needs [63], democratic sensibilities [64], the interactions of the police with crime and criminals [65], and, most importantly, the imperatives of local level politics as affected by underlying social, economic, and cultural relations [66]. In some instances, local politics reflected the domination of class interests in particular cities [67]; in other cases the police supported working class interests. "Today and over time," argues Johnson, "local public police have been accessible to the viewpoints and preoccupations of the American working class; many of their activities have served and do serve to defend and extend the (modest) social privileges of this class". The police "have taken care of labor". When the powerful needed to exert their influence, during periods of industrial unrest, they had to resort to private police forces or shift control of the local police toward the state level, as local forces were never reliable allies against their own class [68]. Lane concludes that the "police were never fully controlled from the outside or above. In practice, the generally decentralized governments of the nineteenth century were incapable of enforcing real direction along a hierarchical chain of command. In most cases the [police] were largely responsible for shaping their own development and tradition" [69].

It is clear from these descriptions and arguments that the police developed for numerous reasons and served numerous interests and that the police themselves are capable of shaping both the development of police work and their relations to the social formation in which they are anchored. In the USA, the fragmentation of the political system made control efforts by local and national ruling groups difficult; the working class background of members of the police force made them unreliable means of social control; police organizations, as they developed, created and shaped organizational interests and patterns of work which allowed them to resist external control and direction.

Current patterns of policing vary widely [70]. The current organizational structure of policing shows strong pressures toward horizontal and vertical fractures. Police organizations as a whole reveal different styles of policing which differ from community to community [71] and from urban to rural setting [72] — styles which reflect external and internal pressures on the organization. Chief among internal pressures are conflicts, consistently there whether openly expressed or not, between rank and file and staff, between officers on the beat and managers in the station house or city hall. The ability of management in the police organization to control its workers has always been low since much of police work is dispersed and not directly visible to management. Being on the beat is being on one's own. (There are some differences from country to country, e.g., the USA compared to Japan [73].) Open conflict can erupt over work-related issues – the right to form unions, to strike, to engage in political activity, or to form special interest groups within departments, e.g., black police alliances or gay rights cops. A second fissure stems from functional divisions in police departments – detective versus patrolman – or specific work assignment – traffic, juvenile, vice. Each division develops its own working styles and forms of management–worker interaction [74]. Special police units – intelligence, secret police, political dissent – may not even appear on organization charts yet diversify the organizational characteristics of police forces [75].

In sum, there is no typical police organization past the most generalized statement that departments tend to be organized in a paramilitary fashion – that they are uniformed, armed, disciplined, and on constant call. The reality of police organizations is a conflict of views and interests among all on how to organize and control police work.

Studies of the police at work agree on two issues: one, that police work is discretionary; and, two, that most of what the police do is not specifically concerned with crime. The decisions which police must make routinely – whether a law has been broken, whether a threat to order exists, whether an arrest should be made, how to treat citizens and accused in contact situations, how to conduct an investigation, in short, how they define their role – occur in circumstances in which discretion is part of the definition of the situation; discretion cannot be avoided. The police cannot meet all the demands placed on them nor enforce all laws, but must select what events they wish to focus their efforts on [76]. Secondly, studies of police work loads show clearly, despite some qualms about the validity of the measures which are used [77], that most of police work and attention is not related to crime but deals with the maintenance of peace and order and the provision of services [78]. The police are as much a social service agency as they are a crime fighting outfit.

The functions of the police are diverse and executed with discretion. The contributions which the police make toward the stability or change of social formations must be interpreted. For example, the services which the police provide may be seen as a legitimating device by the state to support its generally repressive rule – the state gives a little in order to take more back. Such a view makes it impossible to judge whether services may indeed be an objective short and long run benefit to all classes. The argument is like the Freudian argument for the existence of the Oedipus complex – if you are jealous of your father, you have it, and, if you are not, this only shows how well you have mystified yourself.

Policing is done by people who carry with them, as they work, a history

256

of learning and socialization, of values, beliefs, and personal ideologies which will affect their individual interpretation of the police role and their adjustment to the demands of police work. There are common elements to this adjustment — the development of police cultures which "solve" for individual police officers such questions as when and how to use force, how to relate to citizens and to criminals, how to deal with the potential for danger in their work, and how to prevent the job from disrupting their personal lives [79]. Other adjustments reflect the importance of factors unique to the individual, his education, personality [80], or race [81].

In sum, there is no typical policeman, no one 'cop personality" which the demands of police work create from a heterogeneous group of recruits. Adjustment to management demands, to the need for discretion, to having to define their role — these are shaped by individual variables.

Discussions of ideology and control in policing focus on the relations of the police to external forces. The ideology of policing contains the justifications the police make for their work and the demands they place on society for support and the right to be autonomous. The police are, and present themselves as, the effective and symbolic presence of government, law, and order in society [82]. They attempt to legitimate their mandate by appealing to the interests of groups (protection from crime and disorder) and by presenting themselves as agents of the law in general rather than specific governments or groups in power [83]. They believe that they are the frontline of social defense, the thin blue line standing between anarchy and disorder [84]. Much of the misconception of police work by outsiders stems from taking this rhetoric seriously rather than observing what the police do. Secondly, being in charge of social defense, the police argue that theirs is a profession which entitles them to autonomy and freedom from political control and class favoritism. They are willing to back these claims for autonomy by resisting attempts at external control by citizens individually [85] or as organized groups [86], and do so quite successfully. The police have become increasingly willing to carry their demands directly into the political arena to argue for a role not only in defining what law enforcement should be like but also in determining the laws and policies themselves [87].

Control of policing deals with the efforts and capacity by external groups to direct police work. A variety of means exist and have been tried — legal norms and procedural constraints, court decisions, legislative oversight, external agencies (ombudsmen, police review boards, police authorities), and internal recruitment, training, and discipline practices [88]. Studies make it pretty clear that external control efforts have not been very effective (despite the fact that the police depend on others for resources and budgets) for a number of reasons. One, the willingness of the police to resist and divert control efforts reflects a strong organizational interest in survival

257

[89]. Two, demands on the police — what they should do and whose interests they should protect — have simply not been uniform or unified. Social structures and their reflection or non-reflection in the state have been too diverse and fractured to impose consistent demands on the state and its agencies. The police are capable of choosing what interests to enforce. Three, both the powerful and the powerless have alternative forms of action which can do what the police cannot or refuse to do. The police can be by-passed or supplemented — control of the police is not necessary for the execution of the guarding function. Private security agencies are available to the powerful. Mechanisms available to the powerless are more limited yet do exist — defense committees, neighborhood watch groups — or could be created [90]. Four, policing has been done and is done largely by members of the working classes. In Wright's terminology, the police are in a "contradictory class" position, since they "share the relational characteristics of two classes. They share class interests with two different classes but have interests identical to neither." They "are objectively situated in more than one class" [91]. Their specific articulation to the class structure is problematic. They cannot, therefore, be used indiscriminately or simply as a tool for repression by one class against another or in violation of their own specific interests. A clear-thinking oppressor will think twice about when and how to use them. The easy notion that "if a large number of the controlled can be converted into a first line of defense, threats to the system of class can be transformed into resources for its support" [92] simply does not hold water, for it assumes a degree of unconsciousness on the part of working police about the nature of their work which is simplistic. The police are a problem to class rule as well as a support by the very nature of who they are and what they have the capacity to do [93].

What emerges from this description of the police at work is a powerful argument for the relative autonomy of the police. Their willingness and ability to resist control, their formal and informal powers of discretion in the enforcement of law and order, as determined by personal, organizational, and ideological factors, and their interests as an organization and as individuals all point to the need to reformulate critical conceptions of the functions of the police. The police guard interests, yet they do so on the basis of their own perceptions and interests as well as those of others. The key practice of policing is not easily described.

The practical implications of the "relative autonomy" of the police are twofold. Whether the police are oppressors or potential allies of the powerless is a question that can and needs to be asked in a serious way. The harshest oppressors of militant groups in the US have been the police, yet it is also the professionalism of the police and the procedural protections of the law which have been the strongest protection for militants. Legal

258

equality is not "mere ideology" but also an effective constraint on rule, nor do the "courts of a class state function exclusively as organs of repression against the ruled classes" [94]. The police and law do serve, perhaps unconsciously, objective interest for change; strengthening the professionalism of the police, their organizational autonomy, may be a means of promoting change. It's a question worth looking at. A second implication is this: the police as individuals may be appealed to on the basis of their class position; they may become, as Nkrumah thought it possible for the rank and file, potential allies of the powerless [95]. An analysis and call for action which automatically precludes the possibility that the police can support change ignores a potentially powerful agent for change.

The Concept of Order

The state exists to protect interests, as people are conscious of them and attempt to engage the state in actions which will protect and promote specific interests, conceived in the short or long run. A common interest of all groups in society is the maintenance of regularity and the protection of lives and property. No group in a social formation has an interest in being victimized by crime or in being fearful in public or private places. The autonomous interest of the state lies in the reproduction of ordered social relations, and the maintenance of those institutions and resources which allow for reproduction. The state's interest in ordered social relations competes with the interests of specific groups to shape ordered relations to their benefit. In Therborn's words, the "state apparatus operates simultaneously as an expression of class domination and as the executor of the rule-adjudicating, rule-enforcing, rule-defending tasks of society" [96]. (I would substitute "interested domination" for "class domination".)

The concept of ordered social relations does not mean the maintenance of existing social formations but of regularity, an irreducible minimum of confidence in the future which allows groups and individuals to engage in routine activities, including the promotion of change. What is impossible under this conception is a state which is revolutionary, or a social formation which exists without a state. There can be no state during revolutions, when interactions are based on force; there is no need for a state in anarchy, as interactions are based on cooperation. The state is a practical necessity in other periods. The state may be overthrown, but it will re-emerge as the interests of all demand regularity and order.

A concrete social formation embodies two orders: a general order and a specific order. General order, the interests of all in regularity, is denoted by the phrase the "relative autonomy of the state". General order specifies the capacity of the state to guarantee public tranquility and safety. Specific order, that is the use of state power to promote particular interests, is denoted by the phrase "domination by the state". An existing social formation incorporates both goals and exhibits a variety of reproductive mechanisms to ensure the autonomy of the state, and its interest in general order, against challenges from both ruling and ruled groups.

An existing conception of general order, what forms of regularity need protecting in the short and the long run, is itself a reflection of existing social relations and consciousness. States may define general order, the irreducible minimum, in a number of ways. The conception of general order during the cultural revolution in China is far different from that held in the Soviet Union under Stalin or from the liberal conception of the "rule of law". Despite these variations, the distinction between general and specific order, between a universal interest and interested domination, remains. In Engels' words: "on the one hand, a certain authority, no matter how delegated, and, on the other hand, a certain subordination are things which, independent of all social organization, are imposed upon us together with the material conditions under which we produce and make products circulate" [97]. The view that there is only one order in a social formation which is protected by the state is overly simplified. As Sparks puts it, critical theorists must address the distinction "between prohibitions aimed at protecting the essential conditions of organized existence, without which group life would be impossible, and prohibitions necessary for particular forms of social existence, e.g., those dependent on a particular economic system" [98].

It is the role of the police to provide one of the mechanisms for the protection of general and specific order. The police, a priori, are neither repressive nor deserving of support as defenders of a universal consensus on the public good. What the police defend depends on the concrete situation in which they work and the degree of control, through ideology or power, by the state over them. The fundamental question to ask is this: what is being enforced in specific situations and for whom are the police acting as agents — general order, specific domination or their own interests? The range of activities which the police perform is not and cannot be indicative of the same function. At what point along the spectrum of police actions — changing a tire for the stranded motorist, giving a parking ticket, stopping a family quarrel, squad car patrolling, arresting a DWI, a stop-and-frisk encounter, acting as a mugging decoy, investigating a burglary, organized crowd control, swat teams, undercover vice work, intelligence operations, police killings — do police actions indicate domination, and when not? To be persuasive, a theory of the state must possess the theoretical criteria to be able to discriminate between those actions of the state which indicate domination and those which do not. The persuasiveness of the theory will

260

rest both on its generalizing capacity and on its fit with empirically validated propositions. I have tried to suggest how an analysis of one state agency leads to a reformulation of the concepts of "function of the police", "relative autonomy", and "order" which is faithful to both the theoretical and the empirical standards and, therefore, provides a firmer guide to action.

Notes

1 By critical theories I mean Marxist inspired, derived, or flavored analyses which argue that material conditions are the ultimately determining factors of social life, that the interactions between determining material conditions and immaterial reflections need to be understood dialectically, and that currently existing systems of the production and reproduction of material and ideal life fail to meet, though to varying degrees, the needs of people organized as groups in conflict and, therefore, must be changed. Attempts to separate. clearly variants of the critical approach – radical, conflict, Marxist, class analyses – are beyond the scope of the article. A general discussion of the critical approach can be found in J. Garofalo (1978), "Radical criminology and criminal justice: points of divergence and contact", *Crime and Social Justice* 10: 51–72.

2 J. O'Conner (1975), "Productive and unproductive labor", *Politics and Society* 5: 304.

3 Center for Research on Criminal Justice (1977), *The Iron Fist and The Velvet Glove*, Rev. Ed., Berkeley: Center for Research on Criminal Justice, p. 16.

4 S. Balkan, R.J. Berger, and J. Schmidt (1980), *Crime and Deviance in America: A Critical Approach*, Belmont, CA: Wadsworth, p. 101; the phrase is cited, without acknowledgment, from Center, op. cit., p. 11.

5 Balkan, Berger, and Schmidt, op. cit., p. 113.

6 K. Marx, cited in S.L. Harring (1976), "The development of the police institution in the United States", *Crime and Social Justice* 5: 54, 58. A similar interpretation of police work is found in J.F. Galliher (1971), "Explanations of police behavior: a critical review and analysis", *The Sociological Quarterly* 12: 308–18; A. Platt and L. Cooper (eds.) (1974), *Policing America*, Englewood Cliffs: Prentice-Hall; or R.E. Quinney (1980) *Class, State and Crime*, Sec. Ed., New York: Longman.

7 T. Jefferson (1980), "Review of Simon Holdaway, ed., *The British Police*", *International Journal of the Sociology of Law* 8: 459.

8 For a description of various paradigms see R.M. Rich (1979), *The Sociology of Criminal Law*, Toronto: Butterworths; and the articles in C.E. Reasons and R.M. Rich (eds.) (1978), *The Sociology of Law: A Conflict Perspective*, Toronto: Butterworths.

9 T. Skocpol (1980), "Political response to capitalist crisis: neo-Marxist theories of the State and the case of the New Deal", *Politics and Society* 10: 199–200. The analysis which follows deals with the police, yet it is, I think, an appropriate approach to all state actions and agencies.

10 Critical theorists could argue that the epistemological basis for knowledge lies not in its empirical character but in its utility for praxis. For a further critique and discussion of this point, see O. Marenin (1981), "Essence and empiricism in African politics", *The Journal of Modern African Studies* 19: 1–30.

11 In R. Sklar's words, "the presumed economic basis of class determination is a major obstacle to the comprehension of class structures that may appear to have been reared, largely, upon non-economic foundations" and are determined by power rather than production relations (1980). "The nature of class domination in Africa", *The Journal of Modern African Studies* 17: 532.

12 B. Ollman (1972), "Toward consciousness next time: Marx and the working class", *Politics and Society* 3: 2.

13 The variety of critical "solutions" and schools of thought on this question is described by P. Beirne (1979), "Empiricism and the critique of Marxism on law and crime", *Social Problems* 26: 373–385, who distinguishes the instrumentalist, structuralist, and phenomenological approaches;

261

by B.J. Berman (1981), "Class Struggle and the Origins of the Relative Autonomy of the Capitalist State", paper presented at the 1981 Convention of the American Political Science Association, who perceives four critical schools — the instrumentalist, structuralist, capital-logic, and historical derivationist ones; and by Skocpol, op. cit., who perceives instrumentalist, political-functionalist, and class struggle versions of Marxist theory.

14 E.g., see the arguments in G. Lukacs (1971), "What is Orthodox Marxism" in G. Lukacs, *History and Class Consciousness: Studies in Marxist Dialectics,* London: Merlin Press, pp. 1–26.

15 On the dialectical method, see M. Shaw (1975), *Marxism and Social Science,* London: Pluto Press.

16 D. Greenberg (1976), "On one-dimensional Marxist criminology", *Theory and Society* 3: 617. Of course, loosening the linkages also opens the model to examination and creates the opportunity and need for empirical assessments. C. Sumner (1981) describes this process more brusquely as the "epistemological dilution of structuralist Marxism through its confrontation with the nasty business of empirical reality." "Race, crime and hegemony: a review essay", *Contemporary Crises* 5: 277–78. See also similar arguments in E. Greer (1978), "A reply to the critique", *Crime and Social Justice* 9: 70; and M. Los (1980) "Economic Crimes in Comparative Perspective", in G. Newman (ed.), *Crime and Deviance: A Comparative Perspective,* Beverly Hills; Sage, p. 254.

17 D.O. Friedrichs (1980), "Carl Klockars versus the 'Heavy Hitters': A Preliminary Critique", in J.E. Inciardi (ed.), *Radical Criminology: The Coming Crisis,* Beverly Hills: Sage, p. 153, p. 155. Yet the possibility exists and must be faced that critical theory, in the absence of an established empirical methodology of its own, will be forced to move toward an accommodation with positivist social science and some of its central assumptions. The most obvious similarity is the role of function in holistic models of society, held by both critical and positivist thinkers. The argument that holistic needs and purposes must be taken as explaining the activities one sees performed is common to Parsons and Marx. There is always the tension between a fundamentally holistic mode of thinking (where acts of the state are seen as in some sense required by the system — no matter how tenuous the connection between system and act) and the specific appearances of state forms (which lead to explanations in terms of will and choice). Critical theory will find it difficult to bridge the gap between volition and appearance and function and holistic thought, yet, unless it does so and develops a method to justify its arguments, it will lose its concepts. Unless a clear statement of how essential concepts are to be applied can be made, such concepts will be taken over by competing modes of thought and drained of their critical insight and content. E.g., see the conversion of "autonomy" into a common characteristic of the liberal democratic state in E.A. Nordlinger (1981), *On the Autonomy of the Democratic State,* Cambridge: Harvard University Press; or the reduction of the "fiscal crisis of the state" argument to a policy dilemma in M.M. Feeley and A.D. Sarat (1980), *The Policy Dilemma,* Minneapolis: University of Minnesota Press.

18 See the arguments in R.F. Sparks (1980), "A Critique of Marxist Criminology", in N. Morris and M. Tonry (eds.). *Crime and Justice: An Annual Review of Research,* vol. 2, Chicago: Chicago University Press, pp. 159–210.

19 B. Frankel (1979), "On the state of the State: Marxist theories of the State after Leninism", *Theory and Society* 7: 200. It is true, nevertheless, that some critical theorists do describe the state in general, for example, members of the "capital-logic" school; see C. Offe's (1975) description of the capitalist state in his "The Theory of the Capitalist State and the Problem of Policy Formation", in L.N. Lundberg (ed.), *Stress and Contradiction in Modern Capitalism,* Lexington: D.C. Heath, pp. 125–144.

20 S. Spitzer (1980), "'Left-Wing' Criminology — An Infantile Disorder?" in J.E. Inciardi, op. cit., p. 186; see also D.F. Greenberg, op. cit.

21 There is a charming naiveté in the writings and tone of Marxist thinkers, as they assume that their understanding of social life, correct as it must be, need merely be evoked for each new situation as it comes along; that the Marxist model provides an unwavering guide to understanding and explaining whatever it is one observes. In D. Greenberg's words, the "result is little more than science fiction, usually of a fairly unimaginative variety," (op. cit., p. 615). When W.W. Mayer

262

1978–1979) argues that recent shifts in critical thought, specifically structural and phenomenological Marxism, are, after all, only the necessary ideological expression of the monopolistic capitalist state in crisis, such faith reaches touching heights. "Science and praxis: a sociological inquiry into the epistemological foundations of structural and phenomenological Marxism", *The British Journal of Sociology* 23: 183–199.

This belief in the Marxist model ignores a central point of dispute – whether Marxism is best understood as a method or as a substantive answer. I would argue, as many critical thinkers have all along, that Marxism is best understood as a method. See the arguments in Lukacs, op. cit.; U. Melotti (1977), *Marx and the Third World*, London: MacMillan; or B. Ollman (1976), *Alienation*, Sec. Ed., Cambridge: Cambridge University Press. In A. Hunt's (1980) words, "Marxism does not constitute a 'ready-made theory' that can be simply taken up and 'applied' to law, crime or deviance", "The radical critique of law: an assessment", *International Journal of the Sociology of Law* 8: 43. The method, thinking dialectical and being concrete, means, at the very least, that one's arguments should be susceptible to straightforward empirical tests. By straightforward, I mean some statement must be made on what empirical evidence counts, what would support an argument directly – that is without recourse to intervening or mediating levels of consciousness or mystification which will allow all evidence to mean all things.

Discussions of what is critical in method, apart from the utility of knowledge for or in praxis, have moved closer and closer to abolishing explanation, thought of as a cause–effect relationship, as a useful concept. Instead, the argument runs, describing events in certain terms is in and of itself, since those terms are part of a holistic, dynamic, and dialectical understanding, equivalent to knowing why things happen and why they do not. The authentic perception of shifting patterns of tendencies and a "relational" logic, rather than the search for cause–effect linkages, constitutes correct consciousness and conveys explanation. It is difficult to think of what such a method means in practice.

22 W.J. Chambliss (1979), "Problems and Conflicts in Law Creation", in S. Spitzer (ed.), *Research in Law and Sociology*, vol. 2, Greenwich: JAI Press, p. 11.

23 S. Spitzer (1980), op. cit., pp. 180–186.

24 C. Groves (1980), "Theory and Method in Criminology: A View from the Frankfurt School", paper given at the American Society for Criminology Convention, San Francisco, p. 2.

25 See the arguments in R. Miliband (1977), *Marxism and Politics*, Oxford: Oxford University Press; J. O'Conner (1973), *The Fiscal Crises of the State*, New York: Basic Books; N. Poulantzas (1973), *Political Power and Social Class*, London: Sheed and Ward.

26 I.e., J. Habermas (1970), "Technology and Science as Ideology", in J. Habermas, *Toward a Rational Society*, Boston: Beacon Press, pp. 81–122; I. Illich (1977), "'Disabling professions': notes for a lecture", *Contemporary Crises* 1: 359–70; W. Heydebrand (1979), "The Technocratic Administration of Justice", in S. Spitzer (ed.), op. cit., pp. 29–64; S. Spitzer (1979), "The rationalization of crime control in capitalist society", *Contemporary Crises* 3: 187–206; or S. Spitzer and A.T. Scull (1977), "Social Control in Historical Perspective: From Private to Public Responses to Crime", in D.F. Greenberg (ed.), *Corrections and Punishment*, Beverly Hills: Sage, pp. 265–286.

27 T.R. Gurr (1976), *Rogues, Rebels and Reformers*, Beverly Hills: Sage, p. 94, 96.

28 W.J. Chambliss (1976), "The Law of Vagrancy," in W.J. Chambliss and M. Mankoff (eds.), *Whose Law? What Order?*, New York: Wiley, pp. 9–26.

29 B. Frankel, op. cit., p. 230.

30 E.g., see the discussion in E.O. Wright (1980), "Varieties of Marxist conceptions of class structure", *Politics and Society* 9: 323–70. Shifts in the class structure matter; in B. Frankel's words, "any theory of the state which does not take into account the employment [by the capitalist state] of about one quarter to more than one third of the labor force is useless." (op. cit., p. 213).

31 Observers may select other countries, i.e., China or Cuba or Mozambique, as better examples of socialism in action. Still, the analysis of the state in socialist societies is the largest lacuna in critical writing. The same point applies to the analysis of the criminal justice system and the police. There is, in the few descriptions that exist, much emphasis on the participatory and voluntary cooperation of the citizenry with each other and the state, while formal state agencies,

263

including the police, are little examined. I.e., see J. Brady (1981), "The Revolution Comes of Age: Justice and Social Change in Contemporary Cuba", in C. Summer (ed.), *Crime, Justice and Underdevelopment,* London: Heineman, pp. 248–310; - - - , (1977), "Political contradictions and justice policy in People's China", *Contemporary Crises* 1: 127–62; H.E. Pepinsky (1973), "The people versus the principle of legality in the People's Republic of China", *Journal of Criminal Justice* 1: 51–60; - - - (1975), "Reliance on formal written law and freedom and social control in the United States and the Poeple's Republic of China", *The British Journal of Sociology* 26: 330–42; N. Tiruchelvam (1978), "The Ideology of Popular Justice", in Reasons and Rich (eds.), op. cit., pp. 263–280. Yet, as others point out, formal agencies, their public and secret arms, function as the "second line" of social defense when participatory control breaks down. I.e., J.A. Cohen (1968), *The Criminal Process in the People's Republic of China, 1949–1963,* Cambridge: Harvard University Press; or L. Salas (1979), "The Police as a Social Control Mechanism in Post Revolutionary Cuba", in his *Social Control and Deviance in Cuba,* New York: Praeger. The interactions of informal participation and formal control with the state in socialist societies need to be incorporated into critical theories of the state.

32   I. Wallerstein (1980), "The withering away of the states", *International Journal of the Sociology of Law* 8: 369–78.

33   L. Panitch (1980), "The state and the future of Socialism", *Capital and Class* 11: 121–37.

34   I.e., K.A.A. Rana (1977), "Class formation and social conflict: a case study of Kenya", *Ufahamu* 7: 17–72; Sklar, op. cit.

35   P. Clawson (1981), "The character of Soviet economic relations with Third World countries", *Review of Radical Political Economics* 13: 76–84.

36   Beirne (1979), op. cit.

37   Beirne (1979), op. cit., pp. 378–79.

38   A. Wolfe (1977), *The Limits of Legitimacy: Political Contradictions of Contemporary Capitalism,* New York: Free Press, p. xiv.

39   I.e., I. Balbus (1978), "Commodity Form and the Legal Form", in Reasons and Rich, op. cit., pp. 73–90; P. Beirne (1975), "Marxism and the sociology of law: theory and practice", *British Journal of Law and Society* 2: 78–81; H. Steinert (1978), "The functions of criminal law", *Contemporary Crises,* 2: 166–93; D.F. Greenberg and N. Anderson (1981), "Recent Marxisant books on law: a review essay", *Contemporary Crises* 5: 293–322.

40   M. Tushnet (1978), "A Marxist analysis of American law," *Marxist Perspectives* 1: 96.

41   I. Balbus (1971), "The concept of interest in pluralist and Marxian analyses", *Politics and Society* 1: 151–177.

42   C. Bay (1968), "Needs, wants and political legitimacy", *Canadian Journal of Political Science,* 1: 246–60; W.E. Connolly (1972), "On 'interests' in politics," *Politics and Society* 2: 459–77.

43   J. Habermas (1970), *Knowledge and Human Interest,* Boston: Beacon Press.

44   Most of this discussion is taken from E. Nagel (1961), *The Structure of Science,* New York: Harcourt Brace and World, pp. 520–535.

45   D. Bayley (1979), "Police Function, Structure and Control in Western Europe and North America: Comparative and Historical Studies", in N. Morris and M. Tonry (eds.), *Crime and Justice: An Annual Review of Research,* Vol. 1, Chicago: Chicago University Press, pp. 111–13.

46   A. Platt and L. Cooper (eds.), op. cit., p. 7.

47   I.e., Center for Research on Criminal Justice, op. cit.; Harring, op. cit.; S.L. Harring (1977), "Class conflict and the suppression of tramps in Buffalo, 1892–1894," *Law and Society Review* 11: 873–911; S.L. Harring and L.M. McMullin (1975), "The Buffalo police 1872–100: labor unrest, political power and the creation of the police institution", *Crime and Social Justice* 4: 5–14.

48   M. Cain (1979), "Trends in the sociology of police work", *International Journal of the Sociology of Law* 7: 161.

49   Cain, op. cit., p. 158.

50   Bayley, op. cit., p. 113.

51   P.K. Manning (1977), *Police Work: The Social Organization of Policing,* Cambridge: MIT Press, pp. 101–102.

264

52   M. Cain (1977), "An Ironical Departure: The Dilemma of Contemporary Policing", in K. Jones
     et al. (eds.), *Yearbook of Social Policy in Britain*, 1977, London: Routledge and Kegan Paul,
     p. 164.
53   C.D. Robinson (1978). "The deradicalization of the policeman: a historical analysis", *Crime and
     Delinquency* 24: 129--51.
54   Cain (1979), op. cit., p. 158.
55   R.M. Fogelson (1977), *Big City Police*, Cambridge: Cambridge University Press.
56   R.D. Schwartz and J.S. Miller (1964), "Legal evolution and societal complexity", *The American
     Journal of Sociology* 70: 159–69.
57   S. Diamond (1971), "The Rule of Law Versus the Order of Custom", in R.P. Wolff (ed.), *The
     Rule of Law*, New York: Simon and Schuster, pp. 115–44; E.L. Parks (1975), "From Con-
     stabulary to Police Society: Implications for Social Control", in W.J. Chambliss (ed.), *Criminal
     Law in Action*, Santa Barbara: Hamilton, pp. 81–93; Spitzer and Scull, op. cit.
58   I.e., D. Bayley (1975), "The Police and Political Development in Europe", in C. Tilly (ed.), *The
     Foundation of National States in Europe*, Princeton: Princeton University Press, pp. 328–379;
     V. Chalidze (1977), *Criminal Russia*, New York: Random House; R.J. Stead (1957), *The Police
     of Paris*, London: Staples Press.
59   A. Bordua and A. Reiss, Jr. (1967), "Law Enforcement", in P.F. Lazarsfeld et al. (eds.), *The
     Uses of Sociology*, New York: Basic Books, p. 282; Gurr, op. cit., p. 123; A. Silver (1967),
     "The Demand for Order in Civil Society: A Review of Some Themes in the History of Urban
     Crime, Police and Riot", in D.J. Bordua (ed.), *The Police: Six Sociological Essays*, New York:
     Wiley and Sons, pp. 1–24.
60   Diamond, op. cit.
61   I.e., D. Bayley (1969), *The Police and Political Development in India*, Princeton: Princeton
     University Press; Sir C. Jeffries (1952), *The Colonial Police*, London: Max Parrish; T.N. Tamuno
     (1970), *The Police in Modern Nigeria*, Ibadan: University of Ibadan Press.
62   T. Bowden and D.S. Goodman (1976), *China: The Politics of Public Security*, London: Institute
     for the Study of Conflict; R. Conquest (1968), *The Soviet Police System*, New York: Praeger;
     Salas, op. cit.
63   R. Lane (1967), *Policing the City: Boston 1822--1885*, Cambridge: Harvard University Press.
64   M.H. Haller (1976), "Historical roots of police behavior: Chicago 1890–1925", *Law and Society
     Review* 10: 303–23; W. Miller (1977), *Cops and Bobbies: Police Authority in New York and
     London, 1820–1870*, Chicago: Chicago University Press.
65   D.R. Johnson (1979), *Policing the Urban Underworld: The Impact of Crime on the Develop-
     ment of the American Police, 1800–1887*, Philadelphia: Temple University Press.
66   R. Lane (1980), "Urban Police and Crime in Nineteenth Century America", in Morris and Tonry,
     op. cit., pp. 1–43; see also R.B. Fosdick (1921), *American Police Systems*, New York: The
     Century Co.; J.F. Richardson (1974), *Urban Police in the United States*, Port Washington:
     Kennikat Press; C.D. Robinson (1974), "The Mayor and the Police: The Political Role of Police
     in Society", in G.L. Mosse (ed.), *Police Forces in History*, Beverly Hills: Sage, pp. 277–315;
     B. Smith (1960), *Police Systems in the United States*, Sec. Rev. Ed., New York: Harper and
     Brothers.
67   Harring, op. cit.; Harring and McMullin, op. cit.
68   B.C. Johnson (1976), "Taking Care of Labor: The Police in American Politics", *Theory and
     Society* 3: 91, 94.
69   Lane (1980), op. cit., p. 21.
70   The discussion which follows deals primarily with local municipal forces. The existence of four
     levels of law enforcement in the USA – local, county, state and national – makes generalizations
     difficult. National forces and law enforcement related agencies operate under different con-
     straints. The demand for intelligence services, the types of problems dealt with, recent trends
     toward standardization and national control, and direct ties to national ruling groups affect the
     autonomy of these forces, yet their role in domination and control can be studied with the same
     framework as that which I advocate for local forces here.
71   J.Q. Wilson (1975), *Varieties of Police Behavior*, New York: Atheneum.
72   M. Cain (1973), *Society and the Policeman's Role*, London: Róutledge and Kegan Paul.

73 D. Bayley (1976), *Forces of Order*, Berkeley: University of California Press.
74 L. Tifft (1975), "Control systems, social bases of power and power exercise in police organizations", *Journal of Police Science and Administration* 3: 66–76.
75 T. Bunyan (1976), *The Political Police in Britain*, London: Routledge and Kegan Paul.
76 H. Goldstein (1977), *Policing a Free Society*, Cambridge: Ballinger; S. McCabe (1978), *Defining Crime: A Study of Police Decisions*, Oxford: Basil Blackwell; P.K. Manning, op. cit.; H.E. Pepinsky (1975), "Police Decision-Making", in D.M. Gottfredson (ed.), *Decision-making in the Criminal Justice System: Review and Essays*, Rockville: National Institute of Mental Health, pp. 21–52; J. Rubinstein (1973), *City Police*, New York: Ballantine.
77 G. Cordner (1979), "Police patrol work load studies: a review and critique", *Police Studies* 2: 50–60.
78 M. Banton (1964), *The Policeman in the Community*, New York: Basic Books; Bayley (1979), op. cit.; A.J. Reiss, Jr. (1971), *The Police and the Public*, New Haven: Yale University Press; P.G. Shane (1980), *Police and People: A Comparison of Five Countries*, St. Louis: Mosby.
79 J. Skolnick (1966), *Justice Without Trial*, New York: Wiley and Sons; J.M.N. Wasikhongo (1976), "The role and character of the police in Africa and Western countries: a comparative approach to police isolation", *International Journal of Criminology and Penology* 4: 383–396.
80 W.K. Muir, Jr. (1977), *Police: Streetcorner Politicians*, Chicago: University of Chicago Press; R. Reiner (1978), *The Blue Coated Worker: A Sociological Study of Police Unionism*, Cambridge: Cambridge University Press.
81 E. Greer (1978), "The class nature of the urban police during the period of Black municipal power", *Crime and Social Justice* 9: 49–61.
82 P.K. Manning (1974), "The Police: Mandate, Strategy and Appearances", in R.E. Quinney (ed.), *Criminal Justice in America*, Boston: Little, Brown and Co., pp. 170–200; Silver, op. cit.
83 R. Reiner (1980), "Review of John Alderson *Policing Freedom*", *International Journal of the Sociology of Law* 8: 449–454.
84 Professor G.L. Kirkham learned this as one of his "street lessons": "Whatever the risk to himself, every police officer understands that his ability to back up the lawful authority which he represents is the only thing which stands between civilization and the jungle of lawlessness". (1978), "A Professor's 'Street Lessons'", in J.R. Snortum and I. Hader (eds.), *Criminal Justice: Allies and Adversaries*, Pacific Palisades: Palisades Publishers, p. 31.
85 S. Box and K. Russell (1975), "The politics of discreditability: disarming complaints against the police", *Sociological Review*, New Series 23: 315–346; D.F. Regan (1971), "Complaints against the police", *Political Quarterly* 42: 402–413.
86 Fogelson, op. cit.
87 R. Reiner (1980), "Fuzzy thoughts: the police and law and order politics", *Sociological Review*, New Series 28: 377–413.
88 Bayley (1979), op. cit., pp. 130–135; G. Berkley (1969), *The Democratic Policeman*, Boston: Beacon Press.
89 W.J. Chambliss (1971), "Vice, corruption, bureaucracy and power", *Wisconsin Law Review*, 1130–1155; W.J. Chambliss and R.B. Seidman (1971), *Law, Order and Power*, Reading: Addison-Wesley.
90 The potential for change is there. Whether one wants to wait for the larger revolution or whether alternatives of more limited aims should be pursued is the crucial question for strategy.
91 Wright, op. cit., p. 331, p. 356. This formulation presents a theoretical problem for a materialist construction of reality.
92 S. Spitzer (1975), "Toward a Marxian theory of deviance", *Social Problems* 22: 649.
93 See the discussion in Greer, op. cit.; and G. Ray (1978), "Class, race and the police: a critique of 'The Class Nature of the Urban Police During the Period of Black Municipal Power'", *Crime and Social Justice* 9: 63–69.
94 G. Therborn (1978), *What Does the Ruling Class Do When It Rules? State Apparatuses and State Power under Feudalism, Capitalism and Socialism*, London: NLB, p. 228, p. 235.
95 N. Nkrumah (1970), *Class Struggle in Africa*, New York: International Publishers, pp. 42–43.
96 Therborn, op. cit., p. 47.

266

97   F. Engels (1959), "On Authority", in L.S. Feuer (ed.), *Marx and Engels: Basic Writings in Politics and Philosophy*, Garden City: Doubleday, p. 484.

98   Sparks, op. cit., p. 189.

[12]

BRIT. J. CRIMINOL. Vol. 27 No. 1 WINTER 1987

USING THE POLICE

JOANNA SHAPLAND and JON VAGG (*Oxford*)*

PUBLIC surveys about police practice show consistent and clear-cut findings: a strong request for a more visible police presence in their areas, particularly on foot; the treatment of serious crime as a priority, especially in inner-city areas; disquiet about the extent of and the manner used in stopping and searching people on the streets; and an unwillingness' to report or see prosecuted a whole range of more minor crime and nuisances, despite their undoubted problematic nature (Hough, 1985; Jones *et al.*, 1986; Kinsey, 1984; Jones and Levi, 1983).

Police managers and commentators alike see these results as unhelpful, if not contradictory. Why ask for the police to deal with crime yet remain unwilling to report victimisation? Why demand more foot patrols, except in the mistaken belief that these are likely to catch criminals? It has been suggested that the public is simply unaware of the realities of police work (see Hough, 1985; Soetenhurst, 1983). Such interpretations of the results, however, seem to be based upon the view that "policing" is something only the police do and that, in expressing a wish for the police to undertake particular tasks, the public is asking the police to take over those tasks and solve them alone in their own way. This has of course been the implied message of police and crime prevention material broadcast over many years: that if anything unusual is seen or any problem arises, the police should be called and the problem "handed over".

It is the contention of this paper that the demands and expectations of the public are neither contradictory nor necessarily unrealistic. We shall argue that members of the public (the many individuals living and working in a particular area) are themselves engaging in a great deal of "policing" work, and that they wish the police to complement and extend what they themselves are currently doing. Members of the public also choose (and wish to be able to choose) whether to involve the police. They would like to continue to have an input into any subsequent policing activity concerning "their" problems.

The Study

Our evidence comes largely from a study we conducted between 1983 and 1985 into residents' and business people's perceptions of nuisances, problems and crimes and into the ways in which these should be dealt with (Shapland and Vagg, 1985). The study took place in two rural areas: one large village (Southton) and one group of small villages (Northam), and in four small areas near the centre of a large town in the same shire county in

* Centre for Criminological Research, University of Oxford.

The research described in this paper was funded by the Home Office, but the views expressed are those of the authors.

USING THE POLICE

the Midlands (the urban areas). All these areas contained industrial premises, shops and a large number of residential dwellings. We interviewed formally 141 residents and business people in the urban areas, 94 in Northam and 87 in Southton. We spent a total of 17 months studying the areas informally, compiling a register of all the incidents that had occurred during the two years prior to and during the fieldwork, and doing more formal observations of public activity. We interviewed 53 police officers responsible for policing these areas, analysed a sample of a whole year of crime reports for the surrounding areas (2,584 crimes in all), and considered in detail a sample of 72 days of the messages received from the public and recorded by the police as making requests for police action.

The result was a mass of detailed information about occurrences in a number of small areas, together with the views of victims, offenders, witnesses, residents, business people, councillors and police officers about these incidents and about the problems affecting those areas. The results are, of course, specific to the areas and may not generalise to other parts of the same county or to other places in Britain (though there are no current research findings that would lead us to see the situation elsewhere as quite different in kind). The data do, however, enable us to flesh out the bald findings from public surveys or studies of demands on the police.

Local Problems, Local Concerns, Local Action

Our research confirmed that it was impossible to describe people's use of and attitudes concerning the police without also considering the kinds of informal social control occurring, and without setting these in the context of the kinds of problems, nuisances and crimes which were affecting residents and business people. Though the precise mix of the cocktail varied in each area, the nature of problems was very similar in all, as can be seen from the following chart:

Most commonly cited problems

Urban areas	Northam	Southton
1=damage	1 damage	1 damage
1=parked cars	2 teenagers	2 teenagers
3 crime	3 noise	3=parked cars
4 noise	4= parked cars	3=planning decisions
5 teenagers	4= children on cycles	5 litter
6 neighbours	6 suspicious people	6 noise

The precise manifestation of a particular problem, however, was very localised; to one street, or even part of a street. Cars might be scratched in one street, but the next one complain of noise from a club, or teenagers hanging around a bus stop, or a spate of burglaries. Knowlege about that problem and about any incidents used as exemplars of it was equally localised, which has important consequences for the detection of any

JOANNA SHAPLAND AND JON VAGG

suspects and for crime prevention. In general, as well, knowledge about incidents occurring on private property (including burglaries) was much less widespread than knowledge about incidents in public places: in shops, pubs, community centres and the street. Direct knowledge of, or gossip about, these latter tended to be more important than media coverage in informing people's views about the kind of area they lived or worked in and in influencing their crime prevention precautions and fear of crime. People's attitudes were related to their own personal experiences and to reports of other incidents by their friends, by local shopkeepers and by publicans. People in urban areas tended to cite a greater number of different nuisances or problems than villagers (though villagers were just as concerned about, and plagued by, certain problems, such as spates of vandalism by children or youths).

Our study, in common with others, shows the stress that individuals put on "low-grade" problems such as teenagers hanging about, or vandalism. Such things were worrying and annoying, in part because they were so frequent. Although burglary might have a much greater effect on the victim, the incidence of such crime, even in the urban area, was comparatively rare. However, one link between problems of disorder and crime was made through the individuals suspected: local youths and others who caused the nuisances were often thought also to be engaged in at least some of the burglary and other offending in the area.

The extreme localisation of problems, and the diverse nature of problem sources, imply that solutions would need to be equally local and diverse. A considerable amount of informal activity was occurring, in both rural and urban areas, to try to monitor and to check these problems. People, particularly the elderly and business people, were actively engaged in watching out for anything suspicious. This watching and noticing was, in general, considered a positive thing to do; it was caring, rather than nosiness. Some residents even "adopted" certain public spaces, as well as taking care of factories situated near their houses. The watching, however, was also quite localised: feelings of responsibility and active noticing of what was going on extended only to a handful of houses adjacent to the watcher's house or business. The street was too large a unit. Equally, large public spaces, such as parks, were too large for any individual to adopt.

A great deal of watching and communicating what was seen was focused on centres of activity: businesses and service industries. These included corner shops, newsagents, post offices, garages, spare parts dealers, secondhand shops, pubs and community centres. Such commercial centres of life, both in urban areas and in villages, appeared to be essential to the local flow of information about problems and nuisances.

Apart from watching and noting, people employed a wide range of types of informal action to deal with anything they perceived to be suspicious. Responses varied from direct action by the watcher (going out and challenging the suspicious person or watching so ostentatiously the person is aware of the watcher); through informing the owner of a property later that someone had been around: informing the police; bringing the matter

USING THE POLICE

to the notice of the council or some other body, "responsible person" or "community leader"; to just carrying on watching; or ignoring the matter completely. There were very great individual differences in people's preferred form of informal action. The option chosen in any particular situation depended upon their definition of the situation and, particularly, the kind of person being watched or suspected.

If the suspicious person was known to the watcher, then the response would be tailored to that person, rather than being a "tariff" response to "children", "youths", "strange men" and so on. Unless the suspect was feared (a member of the local "gang" of youths, for example), personal knowledge of the suspect would be more likely to promote personal involvement of the watcher in dealing with the situation, challenging the suspect, telling him off or telling his parents, where appropriate. The perceived youthfulness of the suspect was a powerful factor promoting direct intervention. So was being the direct owner of any property involved, or any feeling that there was some social obligation to protect that particular property (such as knowing the owners were away or being a member of an organisation responsible in some way for that property). The potential consequences of the action or inaction being contemplated were also important: not just in terms of possible retaliation (though this was influential in the urban area), but also including the risk of social embarrassment if the person challenged turned out to be there legitimately. The greater willingness to intervene actively to stop children doing things was due not only to their lesser powers of retaliation but also to the fact that telling a child off wrongly was thought to carry less risk of social disapproval than doing the same to an adult.

There were differences between urban and rural areas in the options favoured for informal action. People in Northam village were more prepared to rely on their own resources (as opposed to ignoring the problem or bringing in the police). People in Southton village, for whom "the police" consisted of a known, resident officer, were more likely to call in the assistance of the police (though keeping the matter to oneself was also normal). In the urban areas, informal action was rarer. People called in the police more often and to less serious incidents, but they also ignored a larger proportion of problems.

In part, this was due to the lack of informal options in the urban area. The possibility of raising the matter with the parish council did not exist (district councils were considered too remote to deal with the very localised problems); there was no effective community organisation (organisations had city-wide rather than neighbourhood-based memberships); there were few local "responsible people" to consult (such as teachers in a local school); and while there were many businesses, comparatively few functioned as centres of neighbourhood activity.

Despite these problems, informal action remained remarkably prevalent, even in the urban areas. It has, however, intrinsic limitations. People's stereotypes of suspicious people and activities were inaccurate (perhaps not surprisingly, given the inaccuracy of the images used even by official

JOANNA SHAPLAND AND JON VAGG

sources for instance, regarding burglary). People differed in their perceptions of whether something was a problem, whether something needed to
be done about it and what should be done. A concerted community
response was, and is likely to continue to be, a considerable rarity.
Informal action was primarily aimed at coping with problems, not with
deterring them, preventing them or punishing those involved. People were
usually not prepared to take on a coercive role. And, most importantly,
informal action was localised. Its strength was that it could deal sensitively
with the (equally localised) problems. Its weakness was that it could not
follow offenders who were strangers back to their houses, or deal with
widespread offending.

The Roles Allocated to the Police

Residents and business people in both urban and rural areas saw the police
as fulfilling several different roles, most of which built on the weaknesses of
the attempts at informal social control. Four roles were identified: three of
which (to respond to "real crime", to deal with problems and nuisances
which were proving otherwise intractable, and to note and collate
information about problems) had the function of extending and making
more effective people's own ideas about what should be happening in their
areas. The fourth was to provide a visible symbol of order and normality.
In each case, people brought to the issue a set of assumptions and
expectations about the kinds of cases in which the police "ought" to be
involved; the extent to which the police should take the initiative in dealing
with problems; and about acceptable and unacceptable ways for the police
to process problems and local offenders.

These roles do, of course, embody intrinsic tensions when operational-
ised. There is considerable dissension between people in every area (rural
and urban) as to what is a problem and at what point the police should be
called in. Equally, there will be discrepancies between the views of the area
and those of the police (based not only on differences between the law and
the moral beliefs of individuals, but also on the different ideas, experiences
and stereotypes of police officers about, say, local youths, compared to
those of people in the area).

The first role defined for the police was for a speedy response to crime;
not to any crime, but to what we (and many residents) called "real crime".
"Real crime" was seen as quite different in kind to nuisances, or the
"things kids do". Its compass varied greatly between individuals and to a
lesser extent between villagers and urban dwellers. It always included
serious violent assaults and woundings (but not fights in pubs or at discos),
almost all sexual assaults, robbery by a stranger, and any burglary
involving forcible entry into a dwelling house and the taking of property
(interestingly, these are also the crimes given the highest seriousness
ratings in the British Crime Survey: Hough and Mayhew, 1985). "Real
crime" might also include some instances of theft, or burglary of business
premises, or serious vandalism. The dividing line between "real crime"

58

USING THE POLICE

and other criminal activity was, however, much higher up the scale of "seriousness" than that between indictable/either way crime and the rest. The majority of crimes would not be "real crimes", they would not automatically be reported to the police, and there would be no expectation that the offenders should necessarily be prosecuted.

The police in our areas generally responded swiftly to instances of "real crime" reported to them and fulfilled people's expectations by treating such offences in the traditional manner of the criminal justice system: recording them as crimes and putting in investigative effort leading, where possible, to prosecution. The problems expressed by victims in our areas were similar to those reported elsewhere (in particular, lack of information about the progress of the investigation and such annoyances as the police missing appointments: see Shapland *et al.*, 1985). Those of our interviewees who had had some experience of this end of police work often noted, for example, that the different branches of the police appeared not to be operating in consort (an observation also made by the police we interviewed, and caused principally by CID working practice, where the notional allocation of work to officers on the basis of beats was undercut by the allocation of work according to other criteria). It appeared that the arrangements for investigation were not conducive to picking up any local knowledge or information about the crime that might exist. Moreover, information about the police investigation and any subsequent proceedings was often not fed back into the local area, so that local knowledge stopped at "and then the police arrived ...". The lack of feedback is both distancing and inefficient (public action is not encouraged). It is now being remedied to some extent by a force policy of notifying all victims in writing of the result of the incident.

The second role which residents and business people seem to be demanding was for the police to "deal with" problems and incidents of crime that did not fall into the category "real crime". This was, generally, a demand that the problem should stop, rather than any specification of any particular method that should be used. It formed the area of greatest potential disagreement between residents themselves and between residents and the police. The right to decide to call in the police was generally assigned to the victim or to those responsible for any property involved. There might be adverse comment about any matter on which the decision was seen as inappropriate, but rarely overt criticism of the victim. The methods used by the police, however, might well cause concern and annoyance, particularly if the suspects were local people.

Though this is obviously a difficult area for the police, many of the local area officers we interviewed seemed to be able to perform the juggling act required between the demands of interested parties, the constraints of the law and police opinion as to when it is necessary to invoke formal sanctions. Even though both our villages and our urban areas were policed primarily by officers assigned permanently to those beats, the visibility of local officers and the extent of their acquaintance with local people was not ideal (except in Southton, only a minority knew there was a local police

JOANNA SHAPLAND AND JON VAGG

officer and only about 20 per cent. had ever met him or her). In particular, police contact was limited to those who were involved in incidents, and did not necessarily extend to the "watchers". However, local officers did have some idea of the concerns of residents and business people and how they felt about any suspects. Problems were more likely to arise where other specialist units (such as CID) were brought in or where officers from other beats were "covering" for the local officers. In other parts of the country where most policing is by uniformed reliefs not permanently assigned to one beat (whether on foot or in cars), the potential for lack of understanding between residents, business people and police is very high.

The third role for the police was to receive information about disorder and problems, without any particular expectation on the part of the public that a solution could be found. The police were seen as the collators of that information and as those who might decide, having put together information over several small local areas, that some action might be required. It was often hoped that the results of these deliberations would be communicated back to the neighbourhood. Unfortunately, the style of police work is towards immediate response and action. A facility for sustained enquiry and, particularly, for problem solving, is only now beginning to be seen as important within the police force (see Weatheritt, 1986). Similarly, the response of police coordinators/despatchers and of local officers may tend towards immediate action or else the dismissal of information. The facility for recording, storing and processing that information is likely itself to be lacking.

The fourth, and in many ways the most important role which the public in our study wished the police to undertake, was the symbolic one of, by their very presence, proclaiming a state of order (see also Manning, 1977). This was the basis of the demands, found in many studies, for increased foot patrols. (Car patrols did not seem to provide the same reassuring presence). This demand has often been dismissed, usually on the grounds that foot patrols do not provide an "effective" use of manpower (for example, Hough, 1985). However, our residents in both urban and rural areas did not seem to be expecting concrete results from their wish for increased foot patrols. "Effectiveness", for them, was not measuring solely by deterrence. The task of the police was to be seen in the areas at least occasionally, to "show those youths they're around" and to provide an opportunity for the passing on of concerns about problems and of information about disorder.

Residents were not suggesting a mammoth increase in manpower to enable patrols to be conducted wholly by walking. In all the areas, people (even the disillusioned young) believed that the police were overstretched and had more important things to do than meet public demands; though much patrol time appears actually to be under-utilised (see, for example, Smith and Gray, 1983; Kinsey, 1985; Martin and Wilson, 1969; Comrie and Kings, 1974). What was suggested was local policing conducted by local officers walking in the area for at least part of their time: with the flexibility to spend some time talking. In less densely populated rural areas,

USING THE POLICE

in particular, it would be sufficient for local officers to walk around the
centre of each locus of population and talk to residents and, especially, to
business people, once every month or every two months. The local gossip
networks (through shops, schools, members of organisations and just
neighbours chatting) are quite strong enough to spread his or her presence
around the rest of the neighbourhood.

The Dilemmas of Local Justice

Policing cannot entirely be carried out by the public—the mechanisms of
criminal justice exist, at least in part, in order to define and enforce a
state-wide jurisdiction over criminal conduct. On the other hand, we would
emphasise that policing also cannot entirely be carried out by the police for
the public. This is not merely a problem of police resources and
manpower—it is that the public are intimately concerned with policing in
its widest sense. Their necessary involvement with the control of what they
see as social disorder also implies that the priorities and practices of
policing cannot all be set by the police or by any other part of the criminal
justice system. The methods and principles of policing are not the province
of the police alone.

We are left with two scenarios: policing by the police (using their own
principles and methods) with, separately, policing by the public (using
their own principles and methods); or policing by police and public
together (policing with the public) using a negotiated, common set of
principles and methods. Both are "ideal cases", defining the ends of the
possible spectrum for policing and its control.

The first, separate policing, is likely to be ineffective policing and to
create misunderstanding and hostility between police and public. Both
police and public would need to meet their own needs out of their own
resources. Possible results of this might be vigilante action on the part of
the public, and "military" policing (Lea and Young, 1984) on the part of
the police. Efforts are now being made through consultative committees
and the like to improve communication, but the predominant model today
seems to be separate policing (though the historically-engendered good will
on both sides over the last thirty or so years has prevented the emergence of
extreme signs of alienation; see Reiner, 1985). Separate policing does,
however, have some advantages. It will promote a common standard for
the more coercive, formal forms of policing, at least over any one divisional
area. Under such a model, policing may be decided according to the police
view of the world, but at least activity will tend to be coherent and
predictable.

We are very far from the second model of policing *with* the public; in
which public views about policing would be acknowledged to have weight
in determining the scope and manner of policing, and in which decision
making would be a joint enterprise. Insofar as local areas currently have
any influence, it is at a highly informal level: "taking account of" a
neighbourhood may be rated only as "good beatcraft" on the part of the

61

JOANNA SHAPLAND AND JON VAGG

individual constable. Certain interest groups within a subdivision may have some contact with the senior officers of that subdivision or with community relations officers from headquarters, but there is often no effective communication system by which residents' and business people's concerns can be funnelled up through the police force to those making decisions about deployment or prosecution.

It is not clear that the means for a "partnership" between police and public exist or, indeed, could exist. The police and the public operate on different scales of concern and interest about problems. Public concern is extremely localised. There is no formal or hierarchical structure at the levels of streets and neighbourhoods to promote the representation of these points of view. Any such structure would need to reach down to street level and up to the level of towns, districts and counties at which the police, many local authority services and consultative committees work. Even if it were to exist, it is doubtful that it could pay sufficient attention to street-level issues. Inter-agency consultation and subdivisional consultative committees cannot hope to gather data on local problems. In rural areas, parish councils may provide one forum. In urban areas, equivalent bodies, such as tenants' associations, are rare. Equally, the police are not currently organised for consultation and communication at the level of streets or beats, with the possibility of that consultation influencing operational deployment.

Secondly, the idea of joint policing necessarily entails the development of "local" justice. If the public are involved in decision making, then different parts of the country are likely to have different styles of policing and different levels of enforcement. Though equality of enforcement has never been seen as paramount in the development of British policing (some of the resistance to a national police force stems from its presumed inability to cope with local problems and feelings), the inequalities of enforcement that would stem from consumer-led policing are likely to be of a different order of magnitude. The question of "whose order?" becomes paramount. Even very small areas were found in our study to contain rival views about the preferred social order: between different age groups, different social classes, different racial groups. Whose order should predominate?

There is no answer to this dilemma. We do not know how to attain policing in complete harmony between police and public: in a complex society, it would, by definition, be impossible to maintain, if it were once attained. But separate policing—police and public going their own ways with no contact—is certain to produce both the mutual incomprehension we documented at the beginning of this paper and the potential for serious distrust and serious disorder.

The need for greater partnership between police and public is now apparent in the prevalent rhetoric of communication and consultation. However, the implications of a greater partnership have not been faced. If it is accepted that progress in policing and crime prevention is more likely if formal social control builds on public attempts at informal social control (rather than fights it), then this implies a concentration on local policing (a

USING THE POLICE

model is given in Shapland and Vagg, 1985). It also requires a willingness on the part of those local police both to find out what is happening in those neighbourhoods and to explain what they are doing. Most crucially of all, it implies a need for the police to give up at least some of their symbolic ownership of disorder and crime to the public and to accept and to acknowledge that they can never attempt to deal with it on their own. The implications of this are as exciting as they are uncharted.

REFERENCES

BAYLEY, D.H. and BITTNER, E. (1985). "Learning the skills of policing", in special edition of *Journal of Law and Contemporary Social Problems: "Discretion in Law Enforcement"* ed. by R.J. Allen, 35-60.

BRADLEY, D., WALKER, N. and WILKIE, R. (1986). *Managing the Police*, Brighton: Wheatsheaf.

FIELDING, N.G. (1986). "Evaluating the role of training in police socialization: a British example". *Journal of Community Psychology*.

KINSEY, R. (1985). *Survey of Merseyside Police Officers: first report*. Liverpool: Merseyside County Council.

KINSEY, R., LEA, J. and YOUNG, J. (1986). *Losing the fight against crime*. Oxford: Blackwell.

MANNING, P.K. (1982). "Modern police administration, the rise of crime-focused policing and critical incident analysis." in R. Donelan (ed.) *The Maintenance of Order in Society*. Ottawa: Ministry of Supply & Services. 56-74.

SHAPLAND, J. and VAGG, J. (1985). *Social control and policing in rural and urban areas*. Final report to the Home Office. Oxford: Centre for Criminological Research.

SMITH, D.J. (1983). *Police and People in London Vol.III: a survey of police officers*. London: P.S.I.

SMITH, D.J. and GRAY, J. (1983). *Police and People in London Vol. IV: the police in action*. London: P.S.I.

[13]

BRIT. J. CRIMINOL. Vol. 27 No. 1 WINTER 1987

BEING USED BY THE POLICE

Nigel G. Fielding (*Surrey*)*

The Issue and the Practice

Shapland and Vagg note, in the previous paper, some contradictory but compelling findings from recent surveys of the public about policing. They suggest the contradictions are neutralised if one accepts an assertion whose very unfamiliarity marks the pervasiveness of the modern police idea, the assertion that much social control is informal. It is encouraging to think that many problems allotted the police may be returned to the public, but the title Shapland and Vagg chose points to a complementary relationship. One must ask how receptive the police will be to these overtures.

Shapland and Vagg are particularly concerned with "the stress that individuals put on 'low-grade' problems such as teenagers hanging about, or vandalism". These minor nuisances are the things ordinary folk, in what is still a remarkably pacific society, become exercised about; indeed, the "public" associates these young pests with burglary, and tied to their data, Shapland and Vagg can only agree. There are certainly lessons in the lists of "commonly-cited problems" elicited in their sample areas; one might protest there can be precious little to worry about if car parking, "teenagers" and "damage" are in the top six crime-related worries. In 150 hours of patrol observation I recently spent in a polyglot inner city division, most criminal damage was indeed low-key (for example, broken windows, cut payphone wires). In most cases it was the police officers who persuaded citizens to deal with the matter informally, because they did not want to drive up insurance premiums by reporting everything a twitchy citizenry took as evidence of crime.

This is not to deny the utility to police of the avid "watching" Shapland and Vagg found the public doing, "particularly the elderly and business people". It is only to sound a note of caution before one accepts the perception of crime embraced by such people. Shapland and Vagg have one kind of data, from certain kinds of communities, and if one is really to accept the idea of microscopic local variation in pertinences and problems, one had better have a clear notion of its limits.

Shapland and Vagg's data compares urban and rural areas, but finds informal action "remarkably prevalent, even in the urban areas". Presumably the degree of stability in a community is more significant than the degree of urbanisation in evoking protectiveness towards the locale. It is critical that local action is *very* localised; in all areas it was found that people will protect their immediate vicinity but even the street was too large a unit around which to organise effective informal control. An agency with trans-local responsibility is necessary; no one is talking about

* Department of Sociology, University of Surrey. The author acknowledges the support of the Economic and Social Research Council in the research reported here.

BEING USED BY THE POLICE

replacing the police. Shapland and Vagg note that local officers knew the concerns of residents and business people, and their feelings about suspects (they do not say what the officers thought about what they knew). As they note, the problems come when CID or relief officers cover for local beat officers, or where most policing is by uniformed reliefs having no permanent beat. Since for many years over half Britain's population has been in urban areas having just that mode of policing, most of us live where "the potential for lack of understanding between residents, business people and police is very high". It may be debatable whether policing is a profession, but before asking the police to be more responsive to local definitions of disorder, and to the efforts of ordinary people to help, one must acknowledge what the police currently think of amateurs.

It is also necessary to appreciate the present organisation of policing. Street cover in divisions, typically five square miles in cities, is normally by nine constables, six in vehicles and three on foot. Walking is mainly by probationers, and, of the vehicles, at least two will have no function bringing them into sustained local contact, being a fast-response area car and a van for collecting arrested persons. They are double-manned. Since drivers tend to be the older officers, the most experienced are kept away from local contact situations. Operational officers spend 10 per cent. of their time on foot patrol; the figure rises to 29 per cent. if vehicle patrol is included. In London, only 5 per cent. of officers are permanently assigned to a beat. The officers on reliefs change from one shift to the next and do not have responsibility for a specific patch over a continuous period. Indeed, officers are seldom confined to a beat even for a particular eight hour shift, and they do not know on which function (car, communications, etc.) they will be deployed until they parade for that shift (Smith and Gray, 1983, p.18). Even if assigned a beat, it is common when given something specific to do for it to be off the beat, and to make arrests off one's patch.

Tactical planning and teamwork are rare on the reliefs. Most activity is in response to calls. Officers choosing their own activity do so on their individual initiative and with short-term objectives. The relief as a whole does not, as Smith and Gray note, decide to do something about vandalism on a particular estate. An individual may decide to have a look around the estate but is likely to be interrupted by a call before getting there (Smith and Gray, 1983, p.32). There are, of course, better opportunities for permanent beat officers to plan tactically. They are more autonomous and their role explicitly includes cultivating community contact and putting over a friendly image of the force. Yet their independence enables considerable variation; some construe their role as "P.R." while others are as crime-oriented as the reliefs and use their local contacts to uncover crime information (Smith and Gray, 1983, p.35). This information may go to CID, but CID are mainly responsive to entries in the major crime book and much of their work is clerical. The local contact they seek is notoriously not with ordinary local folk.

65

NIGEL G. FIELDING

Public and Police Roles

It is quite right that "policing" is not something only the police do, and, in calling the police out, the public help determine the present boundary between informal and formal control. Their preoccupation with civil order matters is also well-founded. Crime control is not an *objective* basis for the constable's self-image; even in the Metropolitan Police District, 43 per cent. of officers had not made a single arrest in the six weeks prior to completing the questionnaire sent out by the Policy Studies Institute team. Police have little difficulty endorsing the four roles Shapland and Vagg's respondents saw for the police: to respond to "real crime", deal with intractable nuisances, collate information, and provide a symbol of order. It is the status of the elements left after law enforcement-related activities are "subtracted" which is chiefly at issue, those matters Bradley *et al.* neatly summarise as "ensuring public tranquillity, befriending, and providing assistance" (Bradley *et al.*, 1986, p.145).

One tangible implication of the argument that the public can do more provided police will engage in a partnership is an increase in stops of suspect youths and other minority people in response to information received from suspicious citizens. It is worth noting that, while stops produce a very substantial number of total arrests, they are far more effective at detecting some kinds of offence than others, particularly theft, driving and substance abuse offences (Smith, 1983, p.88). Only 15 per cent. of arrests for violent or sexual offences arise from stops.

One must pause to consider the effect of increasing stops on norms of public civility. Where they are cognisant of local information these stops may improve on the vague hunches that often seem to motivate police-initiated stops but even so the procedure is regarded by many as an intrusive one and in many minority groups as a good deal closer to harassment than inconvenience. The Policy Studies Institute report concluded that a substantial number of stops are made "if not randomly, at any rate without there being any specific reason for making them" (Smith, 1983, p.98). Some 47 per cent. of pedestrians stopped were questioned because they were running, hurrying or loitering, "all rather vague reasons and ones that may not, in themselves, give grounds for reasonable suspicion", and 7 per cent. because of their "unconventional appearance", the category one would foresee increasing if the police were to act more on people's suspicions. Young people are already a good deal more likely to be stopped for no specified reason, and, one anticipates, this too would increase. One must consider whether one really wants to make police more responsive to the petty suspicions of the public, particularly if these emanate from the elderly and business people, groups not known for their tolerance of minorities. It is worth noting evidence from our present ethnographic study of community policing that the police take care to mediate demands arising from such suspicions when they think the net effect may be disruptive of local civil order. Like the civil liberties lobby, the police are already worried about stopping people without clearly reasonable grounds.

66

BEING USED BY THE POLICE

Another plausible consequence of a greater public contribution would be raised expectations about what police could do to solve problems identified by a more forthcoming citizenry. Were this to fall on relief officers it would most likely be dealt with in the ways to which officers are accustomed. Any "problem-solving" efforts will be very short-term; as Bayley and Bittner maintain, the patrol officer's perspective on time is radically different to that of services such as medicine and social work, which are used to long-term case assignment (Bayley and Bittner, 1983). Officers' efforts are also likely to focus on referral, either to intra-organisation specialist services or to agencies which can take the long view.

Not all of this is for self-serving reasons. The roughly three-quarters of police time not spent on patrol includes 8 per cent. of time on specific outside activities like protection of notables, 2 per cent. in court, 5 per cent. contacting witnesses, 10 per cent. running communications and front office, 19 per cent. on clerical/administrative work and 5 per cent. on training (giving or receiving it). It is hard to see how any of these could be reduced. A sustained attempt to re-direct officers' priorities would also have to confront the independence of relief officers in responding to calls, and the autonomy of the permanent beats. Assignment to calls is by a fellow constable at the communications desk. The officer assigned then has a choice whether to respond. To break this system would entail breaking a highly effective hidden scheme of shopfloor management.

In an ideal world, the work could be re-structured (and the rewards re-aligned) to counteract these problems, but in the real world the officers' predilections and crime-centred role concept could well lead to the fatal disillusionment of cooperative citizens. Further, research has not got to grips with the fiercely independent CID, and if it is anticipated that relief officers will resist greater responsiveness to low-level problems, it is plain that it would be even less likely with detectives.

Complementarity and Conflict

One cannot assume that the police are a malleable, impartial public service, mutely obedient to shifts of public opinion. At the level of local order they are meaning-creating actors with vested interests in particular modes of work (Fielding, 1986). Overtime payments encourage constables to make arrests rather than do other work, especially towards the end of a shift. Smith and Gray note "there are few activities involving 'positive' contacts with members of the public that lead to overtime" (Smith and Gray, 1983, p.80). At the level of political economy, the police institution is led by senior managers who are astute political actors, and as Manning (1982) has argued, prising them off the "crime" role concept that has worked so well in the past is immensely difficult.

Police presently define low-key "problem" calls and community-cultivating contacts as "rubbish work". It is scarcely credible that they could take up the suggestion that, where a stop has not led to discovery of an offence, they engage in an attempt to improve public confidence in the

NIGEL G. FIELDING

police by offering information, help or advice. An attempt to uncover crime that has proved fruitless is not a sound basis from which to make a positive contact. Further there is less difference in the relief and beat officers' perspective on the crime self-concept than may be thought; according to the Policy Studies Institute questionnaire, 25 per cent. of beat officers had arrested someone in the previous week compared to 40 per cent. of reliefs, while 75 per cent. of beat officers and 78 per cent. of relief officers had made a stop in the past fortnight (Smith, 1983, p.94). Beat officers may accept the assignment for instrumental reasons rather than commitment to local policing; one told me he was using his year as a permanent beat officer to bone up for the examinations for promotion to sergeant, it being a job with plenty of autonomy.

A final obstacle is the level of direct supervision (Smith, 1983, pp.141–2). Managers presently have few non-crime-related incentives with which to motivate the ranks, and the evidence is that even promotion is largely outside the line supervisor's control; the "certificate of fitness" they must supply for promotion is almost never refused (Smith 1983, p.60). Some 59 per cent. of the Policy Studies Institute respondents thought senior officers were not effective at encouraging them to do the job well. It is even possible to find units who literally do not know who is supposed to be in charge of them (Smith and Gray, 1983, p.37), and it is quite usual for officers to be unable to name most of their senior officers (Smith and Gray, 1983, p.276). Direct supervision is for probationers and, as Bradley *et al.* note, "the first-line supervisor checks that which can be definitely checked" (p.183), *i.e.* not the quality of the work but whether the constable was active. A final twist is that officers who construe their work as related to significant crime are more likely to be promotion-minded (Smith, 1983, p.64).

Nevertheless, the call for more proactive policing is welcome in contrast to the demand for more reactive policing which has lately come from some quarters (Kinsey, 1985; Young, 1986). The likelihood of reactive policing meeting crime, major or not, is doubtful. The case for public involvement must be plainly predicated on increased "proactive" contact and explicitly tackle encouraging the police to use the public. The only way the public will be "used" positively is if the police judge they have something to offer. Information is the key. Population size and mobility, and the lack of pre-gathered information, often mean officers are reduced to using the immediate cues picked up on arrival at the scene. Importantly, "what . . . emerges from an analysis of the difference between public and police-initiated crime-related contacts is that it is much easier to cope with the informational constraints, with the risks associated with uncertainty and unpredictability, in the former type of contact" (Bradley *et al.*, 1986, p.173). If for no other reason it is worth knocking one's head against the hard facts of public willingness and police suspicion.

But one must recognise that the very role definition police have embraced is at issue. There may be some potential to change it if (a) the uniform officers can be stimulated to value local contact by playing on their

68

BEING USED BY THE POLICE

rivalry with CID officers and (b) it is made to seem a way they can beat the boredom of patrol (Smith and Gray, 1983, pp.52–6). One must have such incentives, for one is asking them to foresake a symbolic reality no less real for its symbolism. While officers actually use force infrequently, the idea of authority is central to the meaning of the job, and "force . . . is for them the main *symbol* of authority and power" (Smith and Gray, 1983, p.87). If one is to stimulate closer police/community cooperation, their role definition must value the negotiational skills critical in eliciting reliable local knowledge.

REFERENCES

COMRIE, M. and KINGS, B. (1974). "Urban workloads", *Police Research Bulletin*, **23**, 32-38.
HOUGH, M. (1985). *Demand for policing and police performance: progress and pitfalls in public surveys?* Paper given to conference: "Police Research: where now?" Harrogate, December 1985 (to be published by the Police Foundation.)
HOUGH, M. and MAYHEW, P. (1985). *Taking account of crime: key findings from the British Crime Survey*. Home Office Research Study, no. 85. London: H.M.S.O.
JONES, D.J.V. (1983). "The New Police, Crime and People in England and Wales, 1829-1888." *Transactions of the Royal Historical Society*. Fifth Series, 33.
JONES, T., MACLEAN, B. and YOUNG, Y. (1986). *The Islington Crime Survey: crime, victimisation and policing in inner-city London*. Aldershot: Gower.
KINSEY, R. (1984). *The Merseyside Crime Survey: first report*. Liverpool: Merseyside County Council.
KINSEY, R. (1985). *Survey of Merseyside Police Officers: first report*. Liverpool: Merseyside County Council.
LEA, J. and YOUNG, J. (1984). *What is to be done about law and order?* Harmondsworth: Penguin.
MANNING, P.K. (1977). *Police work: the social organization of policing*. Cambridge, Mass.: M.I.T. Press.
MARTIN, J. and WILSON, G. (1969). *The Police: a study in manpower*. London: Heinemann.
REINER, R. (1985a). *The Politics of the Police*. Brighton: Wheatsheaf.
SHAPLAND, J. and VAGG, J. (1985). *Social control and policing in rural and urban areas*. Final report to the Home Office Oxford: Centre for Criminological Research.
SHAPLAND, J., WILLMORE, J. and DUFF, P. (1985). *Victims in the Criminal Justice System*. Farnborough: Gower.
SMITH, D.J. and GRAY, J. (1983). *Police and People in London Vol. IV: the police in action*. London: P.S.I.
SOETENHURST, J. (1983). "Fear of crime as a policy problem." *Victimology*, **8**, 289-295.
WEATHERITT, M. (1986). *Innovations in Policing*. London: Croom Helm.

Part III
Police and Crime Control

[14]

PRODUCTION OF CRIME RATES *

DONALD J. BLACK

Yale Law School

This paper makes problematic the situational conditions under which policemen write official crime reports in field encounters with complainants. These reports are the raw materials for official crime rates—"crimes known to the police." They also are a prerequisite of further investigation of the crime by the detective bureau and thus of apprehension of the offender. They constitute official recognition of crimes. The findings derive from a three-city observation study of routine police encounters. Among the conditions that relate to the production of official crime reports are the following: the legal seriousness of the complaint, the complainant's observable preference for police action, the relational distance between the complainant and the suspect, the complainant's degree of deference toward the police, and the complainant's social-class status. However, there is no evidence of racial discrimination in crime-reporting. We interpret these empirical patterns not only from the standpoint of crime rates as such but also from the standpoint of the relation between police work and other aspects of social organization.

SOCIOLOGICAL approaches to official crime rates generally fail to make problematic the production of the rates themselves. Theory has not directed inquiry to the principles and mechanisms by which some technically illegal acts are recorded in the official ledger of crime while others are not. Instead crime rates ordinarily are put to use as data in the service of broader investigations of deviance and control. Yet at the same time it has long been taken for granted that official statistics are not an accurate measure of all legally defined crime in the community (e.g., de Beaumont and de Tocqueville, 1964; Morrison, 1897; Sellin, 1931).

The major uses of official crime statistics have taken two forms (see Biderman and Reiss, 1967); each involves a different social epistemology, a different way of structuring knowledge about crime. One employs official statistics as an index of the "actual" or "real" volume and morphology of criminal deviance in the population. Those who follow this approach typically consider the lack of fit between official and actual rates of crime to be a methodological misfortune. Historically, measurement of crime has been the dominant function of crime rates in social science. A second major use of official statistics abandons the search for "actual" deviance. This is managed either by defining deviance with the official reactions themselves—a labeling approach—or by incorporating the official rates not as an index of deviant behavior but as an index of social control operations (e.g., Kitsuse and Cicourel, 1963; Erikson, 1966; Wilson, 1968). In effect this second range of work investigates "actual" social control rather than "actual" deviance. Hence it encounters methodological problems of its own, since, without question, social control agencies do not record all of their official attempts to counteract or contain what they and others regard as deviant conduct.[1] A striking feature of police work, for instance, is the degree to which officers operate with informal tactics, such as harassment and manipulative human-

---

* The findings in this paper derive from a larger research project under the direction of Professor Albert J. Reiss, Jr., Department of Sociology, University of Michigan. The project was supported by Grant Award 006, Office of Law Enforcement Assistance, U. S. Department of Justice, under the Law Enforcement Assistance Act of 1965. Other grants were awarded by the National Science Foundation and the Russell Sage Foundation. Preparation of this paper was facilitated by the Russell Sage Program in Law and Social Science at Yale Law School. The author is indebted to the following for their constructive suggestions: Maureen Mileski, Albert J. Reiss, Jr., Stanton Wheeler, Abraham S. Goldstein, and Sheldon Olson.

[1] An approach that operationally defines criminal deviance as that which the police record as criminal—and nothing else—is immune to these problems. This would be the most radical "labeling" approach. It would exclude from the category of crime, for example, a murder carried out so skillfully that it goes undetected. It would necessarily exclude most "police brutality," since crimes committed by policemen are seldom detected and officially recorded as such.

relations techniques, when they confront law-violative behavior (e.g., Skolnick, 1966; La-Fave, 1965; Bittner, 1967; Black, 1968; Black and Reiss, 1970). In sum, when official statistics are used as a *means* of measurement and analysis, they usually function imperfectly. This is not to deny that such methods can be highly rewarding in some contexts.

This paper follows an alternative strategy that arises from an alternative conceptual starting point. It makes official records of crime an end rather than a means of study (see Wheeler, 1967; Cicourel, 1968:26–28). It treats the crime rate as itself a social fact, an empirical phenomenon with its own existential integrity. A crime rate is not an epiphenomenon. It is part of the natural world. From this standpoint crime statistics are not evaluated as inaccurate or unreliable. They are an aspect of social organization and cannot, sociologically, be wrong. From the present perspective it nevertheless remains interesting that social control systems process more than they report in official statistics and that there is a good deal more rule-violative behavior than that which is processed. These patterns are themselves analytically relevant aspects of crime rates.

An official crime rate may be understood as a rate of *socially recognized* [2] deviant behavior; deviance rates in this sense are produced by all control systems that respond on a case-by-case basis to sanctionable conduct. This does not say that deviant behavior as a general category is synonymous with socially recognized deviant behavior. As a general category deviance may be defined as any behavior in a *class* for which there is a *probability* of negative sanction subsequent to its detection (Black and Reiss, 1970). Thus, whether or not an agent of control detects or sanctions a particular instance of rule-violative behavior is immaterial to the issue of whether or not it is deviant. Deviance is behavior that is *vul-*

nerable to social control. This approach generates three empirical types of deviance: (1) undetected deviance, (2) detected, unsanctioned deviance, and (3) sanctioned deviance. It should be apparent that, while every control system may produce a rate of socially recognized deviance, much unrecognized deviance surely resides in every social system.[3] By definition undetected deviance cannot be recognized by a control system, but, as will become apparent in this presentation, even detected deviance may not be recognized as such. The notion of sanctioned deviance, by contrast, presumes that a social recognition process has taken place. The concept of social recognition of deviance is nothing more than a short-hand, more abstract way of stating what we mean by concrete expressions such as invocation of the law, hue and cry, bringing a suit, blowing the whistle, and so forth.

The concept of deviance should be applied with reference to specific systems of social control. For example, deviance that is undetected from the standpoint of a formal, legal control system, such as the police, may be detected or even sanctioned in an informal control context, such as a business organization, neighborhood or friendship group, or family. Crime rates then are rates of deviance socially recognized by official agencies of criminal-law enforcement. They are official rates of *detection* ("crimes known to the police") and of *sanctioning* (arrest rates and conviction rates).[4] Enforce-

---

[2] In his definition of law, Hoebel (1954:28) notes that enforcement of law is a "socially recognized" privilege. In the same vein a crime rate may be understood as a socially recognized product of law enforcement work. Malinowski (1962:79–80) stresses the importance of social recognition of deviant acts for the community as well as for the deviant person.

[3] The moral and physical organization of social life into public and private places guarantees contemporary society some volume of secret deviance (Schwartz, 1968; Lofland, 1969:62–68). As far as criminal deviance is concerned, other well-known factors are the failure of citizens to report victimizations to the police and the failure of the police to report what is reported to them.

Evidence from victimization surveys suggests that underreporting of crime in official statistics is more a consequence of police discretion than of the failure of citizens to notify the police. Citizens claim that they report far more crimes to the police than the police ultimately report; this margin of unreported crime exceeds that which citizens admit they withhold from the police (Biderman, 1967).

[4] The "clearance rate" is a hybrid form of crime rate produced in American police systems. This is the proportion of "crimes known to the police" that have been solved, whether through arrest or some other means (see Skolnick, 1966:164–181).

ment agencies handle many technically illegal acts that they omit from their official records. This paper explores some of the conditions under which the police produce official rates of crime detection in field encounters with citizens.

SOCIAL ORGANIZATION OF CRIME DETECTION

Detection of deviance involves (1) the discovery of deviant *acts* or behavior and (2) the linking of *persons* or groups to those acts. Types of deviance vary widely according to the extent to which either or both of these aspects of detection are probable. Some deviant acts are unlikely to be discovered, although discovery generally is equivalent to the detection of the deviant person as well. Examples are homosexual conduct and various other forms of consensual sexual deviance. Acts of burglary and auto theft, by contrast, are readily detected, but the offending persons often are not apprehended. These differential detection probabilities stem in part from the empirical patterns by which various forms of violative behavior occur in time and social space. In part they stem as well from the uneven climate of social control.

The organization of police control lodges the primary responsibility for crime detection in the citizenry rather than in the police. The uniformed patrol division, the major line unit of modern police departments, is geared to respond to citizen calls for help via a centralized radio-communications system. Apart from traffic violations, patrol officers detect comparatively little crime through their own initiative. This is all the more true of legally serious crime. Thus crime detection may be understood as a largely *reactive* process from the standpoint of the police as a control system. Far less is it a *proactive* process. Proactive operations aimed at the discovery of criminal behavior predominate in the smaller specialized units of the large police department, particularly in the vice or morals division, including the narcotics squad, and in the traffic division. Most crimes, unlike vice offenses, are not susceptible to detection by means of undercover work or the enlistment of quasi-employed informers (see Skolnick, 1966). Unlike traffic offenses, furthermore, most crimes cannot

be discovered through the surveillance of public places. Since the typical criminal act occurs at a specifically unpredictable time and place, the police must rely upon citizens to involve them in the average case. The law of privacy is another factor that presses the police toward a reactive detection system (Stinchcombe, 1963). Even without legal limitations on police detective work, however, the unpredictability of crime itself would usually render the police ignorant in the absence of citizens. Most often the citizen who calls the police is a victim of a crime who seeks justice in the role of *complainant*.

Vice control and traffic enforcement generally operate without the assistance of complainants. It appears that most proactive police work arises when there is community pressure for police action but where, routinely, there are no complainants involved as victims in the situations of violative behavior in question. In the average case proactive detection involves a simultaneous detection of the violative act and of the violative person. Proactively produced crime rates, therefore, are nearly always rates of arrest rather than rates of known criminal acts. In effect the proactive clearance rate is 100%. Crime rates that are produced in proactive police operations, such as rates of arrest for prostitution, gambling, homosexual behavior, and narcotics violation, directly correlate with police manpower allocation. Until a point of total detection is reached and holding all else constant, these vice rates increase as the number of policemen assigned to vice control is increased. On the other hand, the more important variable in rates of "crimes known to the police," is the volume of complaints from citizens.

Nevertheless, rates of known crimes do not perfectly reflect the volume of citizen complaints. A complaint must be given official status in a formal written report before it can enter police statistics, and the report by no means automatically follows receipt of the complaint by the police. In the present investigation patrol officers wrote official reports in only 64% of the 554 crime situations where a complainant, but no suspect, was present in the field setting. The decision to give official status to a crime ordinarily is an outcome of face-to-face interaction between the police and the complainant rather than a programmed police response to a bureaucratic or legal formula. The content and contours of this interaction differentially condition the probability that an official report will be written, much as they condition, in situations where a suspect is present, the probability that an arrest will be made (Black, 1968; Black and Reiss, 1970).

Whether or not an official report is written affects not only the profile of official crime rates; it also determines whether subsequent police investigation of the crime will be undertaken at a later date. Subsequent investigation can occur only when an official report is forwarded to the detective division for further processing, which includes the possibility of an arrest of the suspect. Hence the rate of detection and sanctioning of deviant *persons* is in part contingent upon whether the detection of deviant *acts* is made official. In this respect justice demands formality in the processing of crimes. This paper considers the following conditions as they relate to the probability of an official crime report in police-complainant encounters: the legal seriousness of the alleged crime, the preference of the complainant, the relational distance between the complainant and the absentee suspect, the degree of deference the complainant extends to the police, and the race and social-class status of the complainant.

FIELD METHOD

Systematic observation of police-citizen transactions was conducted in Boston, Chicago, and Washington, D.C., during the summer of 1966. Thirty-six observers—persons with law, social science, and police administration backgrounds—recorded observations of routine encounters between uniformed patrolmen and citizens. Observers accompanied patrolmen on all work-shifts on all days of the week for seven weeks in each city. However, the times when police activity is comparatively high (evening shifts, particularly weekend evenings) were given added weight in the sample.

Police precincts were chosen as observation sites in each city. The precincts were selected so as to maximize observation in lower socioeconomic, high crime rate, racially homogeneous residential areas. This was ac-

complished through the selection of two precincts in Boston and Chicago and four precincts in Washington, D.C.

The data were recorded in "incident booklets," forms structurally similar to interview schedules. One booklet was used for each incident that the police were requested to handle or that they themselves noticed while on patrol. These booklets were not filled out in the presence of policemen. In fact the officers were told that our research was not concerned with police behavior but only with citizen behavior toward the police and the kinds of problems citizens make for the police. Thus the study partially utilized systematic deception.

A total of 5,713 incidents were observed and recorded. In what follows, however, the statistical base is only 554 cases, roughly one-in-ten of the total sample. These cases comprise nearly all of the police encounters with complainants in crime situations where no suspect was present in the field situation. They are drawn from the cases that originated with a citizen telephone call to the police, 76% of the total. Excluded are, first, encounters initiated by policemen on their own initiative (13%). Police-initiated encounters almost always involve a suspect or offender rather than a complainant; complainants usually must take the initiative to make themselves known to the police. Also excluded are encounters initiated by citizens who walk into a police to ask for help (6%) or who personally flag down the police on the street (5%). Both of these kinds of police work have peculiar situational features and should be treated separately. The great majority of citizen calls by telephone are likewise inappropriate for the present sample. In almost one-third of the cases no citizen is present when the police arrive to handle the complaint. When a citizen is present, furthermore, the incident at issue pertains to a noncriminal matter in well over one half of the cases. Even when there is a criminal matter a suspect not infrequently is present. When a suspect is present the major official outcome possible is arrest rather than a crime report. Finally, the sample excludes cases in which two or more complainants of mixed race or social-class composition participated. It may appear that, in all, much has been eliminated.

Still, perhaps surprisingly, what remains is the *majority of crime situations* that the police handle in response to citizen telephone calls for service. There is no suspect available in 77% of the felonies and in 51% of the misdemeanors that the police handle on account of a complaint by telephone. There is only a complainant. These proportions alone justify a study of police encounters with complainants. In routine police work the handling of crime is in large part the handling of complainants. Policemen see more victims than criminals.

LEGAL SERIOUSNESS OF THE CRIME

Police encounters with complainants where no suspect is present involve a disproportionately large number of felonies, the legally serious category of crime. This was true of 53% of the cases in the sample of 554. When a suspect is present, with or without a citizen complainant, the great majority of police encounters pertain only to misdemeanors (Black, 1968). In other words, the police arrive at the scene too late to apprehend a suspect more often in serious crime situations than in those of a relatively minor nature.[5] In police language, felonies more often are "cold." A moment's reflection upon the empirical patterns by which various crimes are committed reveals why this is so. Some of the more common felonies, such as burglary and auto theft, generally involve stealth and occur when the victim is absent; by the time the crime is discovered, the offender has departed. Other felonies such as robbery and rape have a hit-and-run character, such that the police rarely can be notified in time to make an arrest at the crime setting. Misdemeanors, by contrast, more often involve some form of "disturbance of the peace," such as disorderly con-

duct and drunkenness, crimes that are readily audible or visible to potential complainants and that proceed in time with comparative continuity. In short, properties of the social organization of crime make detection of felony offenders relatively difficult and detection of misdemeanor offenders relatively simple, given detection of the act.[6]

When the offender has left the scene in either felony or misdemeanor situations, however, detection and sanctioning of the offender is precluded unless an official report is written by the police. Not surprisingly, the police are more likely to write these reports in felony than in misdemeanor situations.[7] Reports were written in 72% of the

---

[5] It is interesting to note that in ancient Roman law the offender caught in the act of theft was subject to a more serious punishment than the offender apprehended some time after detection of his theft. In the *Laws of the Twelve Tables* these were called "manifest" and "non-manifest" thefts. The same legal principle is found in the early Anglo-Saxon and other Germanic codes (Maine, 1963:366–367). It could well be that a similar pattern is found in present-day law-in-action. What is formal in one legal system may be informal in another.

[6] The heavier penalties that the law provides for felonies may compensate for a loss in deterrence that could result from the relatively low rate at which felons are apprehended. Likewise, the law of arrest seemingly compensates for the social organization of crime that gives felons a head start on the police. In most jurisdictions the police need less evidence in felony than in misdemeanor situations to make a legal arrest without warrant. By a second technique, then, the legal system increases the jeopardy of felony offenders. The power of substantive law increases as procedural restrictions on legal officials are weakened. By both penalty and procedure, the law pursues the felon with a special vengeance.

[7] Crime situations were classified as felonies or misdemeanors according to legal criteria. These criteria were applied to the version of the crime that prevailed in the police-citizen transaction. The observation reports required the observer to classify the incident in a detailed list of categories as well as to write a long-hand description of the incident. The felony-misdemeanor breakdown was made during the coding stage of the investigation. The major shortcoming of this strategy is that the tabulation allows no gradations of legal seriousness within the felony and misdemeanor categories. This shortcoming was accepted in order to facilitate more elaborate statistical analysis with a minimum of attrition in the number of cases.

It should also be noted that the tabulations do not provide information pertaining to the kind of official report the police wrote for a given kind of crime situation. Occasionally, the police officially characterize the crime with a category that seems incorrect to a legally sophisticated observer. Most commonly this involves reducing the legal seriousness of the crime. However, there are cases where the officer, sometimes through sheer ignorance of the law or inattention, increases the legal seriousness of the crime. In one case, for example, a woman complained about two young men in an automobile who had made obscene remarks to her as she walked along the street near her residence. She claimed she was prepared to press charges.

312 felonies, but in only 53% of the 242 misdemeanors. It is clear that official recognition of crimes becomes more likely as the legally defined seriousness of the crime increases. Even so, it remains noteworthy that the police officially disregard one-fourth of the felonies they handle in encounters with complainants. These are not referred to the detective division for investigation; offenders in these cases thus unknowingly receive a pardon of sorts.

Now the reader might protest an analysis that treats as crimes some incidents that the police themselves do not handle as crimes. How can we call an event a law violation when a legal official ignores that very event? This is a definitional problem that plagues a sociology of law as well as a sociology of deviance and social control. How is a violation of the "law on the books" properly classified if "in practice" it is not labeled as such? It is easy enough to argue that either of these criteria, the written law or the law-in-action, should alone define the violative behavior in question. No answer to this dilemma is true or false. It is of course all a matter of the usefulness of one definition or another. Here a major aim is to learn something about the process by which the police select for official attention certain technically illegal acts while they bypass others. If we classify as crimes only those acts the police officially recognize as crimes, then what shall we call the remainder? Surely that remainder should be conceptually distinguished from acts that are technically legal and which carry no sanctions. For that reason, the present analysis operates with two working categories, crimes and officially recognized crimes, along with an implicit residual category of non-crimes. Crime differs from other behavior by dint of a probability, the probability that it will be sanctioned in a particular administrative system if it is detected. The written law usually—though not always—is a good index of whether that probability exists. "Dead let-

ter" illegal acts, i.e., those virtually never sanctioned, are not classified as crimes in this analysis. Crime as a *general category* consists in a probability of sanction; official recognition in the form of a crime report is one factor that escalates that probability for a *specific instance* of crime. It is worthwhile to have a vocabulary that distinguishes *between crimes* on the basis of how the police relate to them. Without a vocabulary of this kind police invocation of the law in the face of a law violation cannot be treated as empirically or theoretically problematic. Rather, invocation of the law would *define* a law violation and would thereby deprive sociology of an intriguing problem for analysis. Indeed, if we define a law violation *with* invocation of the law, we are left with the peculiar analytical premise that enforcement of the law is total or universal. We would definitionally destroy the possibility of police leniency or even of police discretion in law enforcement.

THE COMPLAINANT'S PREFERENCE

Upon arriving at a field setting, the police typically have very little information about what they are going to find. At best they have the crude label assigned to the incident by a dispatcher at the communications center. Over the police radio they hear such descriptions as "a B and E" (breaking and/ or entering), "family trouble," "somebody screaming," "a theft report," "a man down" (person lying in a public place, cause unknown), "outside ringer" (burglar-alarm ringing), "the boys" (trouble with juveniles), and suchlike. Not infrequently these labels prove to be inaccurate. In any case policemen find themselves highly dependent upon citizens to assist them in structuring situational reality. Complainants, biased though they may be, serve the police as primary agents of situational intelligence.

What is more, complainants not infrequently go beyond the role of providing information by seeking to influence the direction of police action. When a suspect is present the complainant may pressure the police to make an arrest or to be lenient. When there is no available suspect, it becomes a matter of whether the complainant

---

After leaving the scene the officer filled out an official report, classifying the incident as an "aggravated assault," the felonious level of assault. Before doing so he asked the observer for his opinion as to the proper category. The observer feigned ignorance.

prefers that the crime be handled as an official matter or whether he wants it handled informally. Of course many complainants are quite passive and remain behaviorally neutral. During the observation period the complainant's preference was unclear in 40% of the encounters involving a "cold" felony or misdemeanor. There were 184 felony situations in which the complainant expressed a clear preference; 78% lobbied for official action. Of the 145 misdemeanor situations where the complainant expressed a clear preference, the proportion favoring official action was 75%, roughly the same proportion as that in felony situations. It seems that complainants are, behaviorally, insensitive to the legal seriousness of crimes when they seek to direct police action.

Police action displays a striking pattern of conformity with the preferences of complainants. Indeed, in not one case did the police write an official crime report when the complainant manifested a preference for informal action. This pattern seen in legal perspective is particularly interesting given that felony complainants prefer informal action nearly as frequently as misdemeanor complainants. Police conformity with those complainants who do prefer official action, however, is not so symmetrical. In felony situations the police comply by writing an official report in 84% of the cases, whereas when the complaint involves a misdemeanor their rate of compliance drops to 64%. Thus the police follow the wishes of officially-oriented complainants in the majority of encounters, but the majority is somewhat heavier when the occasion is a legally more serious matter. In the field setting proper the citizen complainant has much to say about the official recognition of crimes, though the law seemingly screens his influence.[8]

Recall that the raw inputs for the official detection rate are generated by the citizenry who call the police. At two levels, then, the operational influence of citizens gives crime rates a peculiarly democratic character. Here the servant role of the police predominates; the guardian role recedes. Since an official report is a prerequisite for further police investigation of the crime, this pattern also implies that complainants are operationally endowed with an adjudicatory power. Their observable preferences can ultimately affect probabilities of arrest and conviction. While the structure of the process is democratic in this sense, it most certainly is not universalistic. The moral standards of complainants vary to some extent across the citizen population, thereby injecting particularism into the production of outcomes. There appears a trade-off between democratic process and universalistic enforcement in police work. This is an organizational dilemma not only of the police but of the legal system at large. When the citizenry has the power to direct the invocation of law, it has the power to discriminate among law-violators. Moral diversity in the citizen population by itself assures that some discrimination of this kind will occur. This is true regardless of the intentions of individual citizens. When a legal system organizes to follow the demands of the citizenry, it must sacrifice uniformity, since the system responds only to those who call upon it while it ignores illegality that citizens choose to ignore. A legal system that strives for universalistic application of the law, by contrast, must refuse to follow the diverse whims of its atomized citizenry. Only a society of citizens homogeneous in their legal behavior could avoid this dilemma.

---

[8] Here two general remarks about analytical strategy seem appropriate. One is that the present approach abdicates the problematics of psychological analysis. The observational study does not provide data on the motives or cognitions of the police or the citizens whose behavior is described. Still, findings on patterns of behavior make prediction of police behavior possible. They also offer opportunities for drawing inferences about the impact or implications of police work for social organization. Much can be learned about man's behavior in a social matrix without knowing how he experiences his behavior. The consequences of behavior, moreover, are indifferent to their mental origins.

Secondly, the strategy pursued in this analysis is not sensitive, except in the broadest terms, to the temporal dimension of police-citizen transactions. Thus, simply because the complainant's preference is treated prior to other variables does not mean that it is temporally prior to other aspects of police-citizen interaction. Like the other variables treated in this investigation, the complainant's preference is prior in time only to the final police response to the encounter.

RELATIONAL DISTANCE

Like any other kind of behavior, criminal behavior is located within networks of social organization. One aspect of that social organization consists in the relationship existing between the criminal offender and the complainant prior to a criminal event. They may be related by blood, marriage, friendship, neighborhood, membership in the same community, or whatever. In other words, the adversarial relation that is created by a crime may itself be viewed as it is structured within a wider social frame. The findings in this section permit the conclusion that the probability of official recognition of a crime varies with the relational network in which the crime occurs.[9] The greater the relational distance between citizen adversaries, the greater is the likelihood of official recognition.

Citizen adversaries may be classified according to three levels of relational distance: (1) fellow family members, (2) friends, neighbors, or acquaintances, and (3) strangers. The vast majority of the cases fall into the "stranger" category, though some of these probably would be reclassified into one of the other relational categories if the criminal offender were detected. The complainant's first speculation generally is that a stranger committed the offense in question.

Table 1 shows that when a complainant expresses a preference for official action the police comply most readily when the adversaries are strangers to one another. They are less likely to comply by writing an official crime report when the adversaries are friends, neighbors, or acquaintances, and they are least likely to give official recognition to the crime when the complainant and suspect are members of the same family. The small number of cases in the "fellow family members" category prohibits comparison between felony and misdemeanor situations. In the other relational categories this comparison reveals that the police follow the same pattern in the handling of both felonies and misdemeanors. With the relational distance between the adversaries held constant, however, the probability of an official report is higher for felony than for misdemeanor situations. The highest probability of an official response occurs when the crime is a felony and the adversaries are strangers to one another (91%); the lowest calculable probability is that for misdemeanors when the adversaries are related by friendship, neighborhood, or acquaintanceship (42%). On the other hand, it appears that relational distance can override the legal seriousness of crimes in conditioning police action, since the police are more likely to give official recognition to a misdemeanor involving strangers as adversaries (74%) than to a felony involving friends, neighbors, or acquaintances (62%). Here again, therefore, the law screens but does not direct the impact of an extra-legal element in the production of crime rates.

Beyond the importance of relational distance for an understanding of crime rates as such is another implication of these findings. Because a follow-up investigation of the crime report by the detective division may result in apprehension of the criminal offender, it is apparent that the probability of an official sanction for the offender lessens as the degree of social intimacy with his adversary—usually his victim—increases. When an offender victimizes a social intimate the police are most apt to let the event remain a private matter, regardless of the complainant's preference. A more general consequence of this pattern of police behavior is that the criminal law gives priority to the protection of strangers from strangers while it leaves vulnerable intimates to intimates. Indeed, victimizations of strangers by strangers may be comparatively more damaging to social order and hence, from a functional standpoint, require more attention from the forces of control. A victimization between intimates is capsulated by intimacy itself. Furthermore, as social networks are more intimate, it surely is more likely that informal systems of social control operate. Other forms of legal control

---

[9] Hall (1952:318) suggests that the relational distance between the victim and offender may influence the probability of *prosecution*. The present investigation, following Hall, seeks to predict social control responses from variations in relational distance. A different strategy is to predict community organization from the relationships between adversaries who enter the legal system, under the assumption that legal disputes bespeak a relative absence of informal control in the relational contexts where they arise (see Nader, 1964).

TABLE 1. PERCENT OF POLICE ENCOUNTERS WITH COMPLAINANTS ACCORDING TO TYPE OF CRIME AND RELATIONAL TIE BETWEEN CITIZEN ADVERSARIES, BY SITUATIONAL OUTCOME: COMPLAINANT PREFERS OFFICIAL ACTION

Situational Outcome	Type of Crime and Relational Tie between Citizen Adversaries								
	Felony			Misdemeanor			All Crimes		
	Family Members	Friends, Neighbors, Acquaintances	Strangers	Family Members	Friends, Neighbors, Acquaintances	Strangers	Family Members	Friends, Neighbors, Acquaintances	Strangers
Official Report	(4)	62	91	(3)	43	74	41	51	84
No Official Report	(5)	38	9	(5)	57	26	59	49	16
Total Percent	...	100	100	...	100	100	100	100	100
Total Number	(9)	(16)	(92)	(8)	(23)	(62)	(17)	(39)	(154)

also may become available in the more intimate social relationships. In contrast there is hardly anyone but the police to oversee relations among strangers. Seemingly the criminal law is most likely to be invoked where it is the only operable control system. The same may be said of legal control in general (see Pound, 1942; Schwartz, 1954; Nader and Metzger, 1963). Legal control melds with other aspects of social organization.

THE COMPLAINANT'S DEFERENCE

Evidence accumulates from studies of police sanctioning that the fate of suspects sometimes hangs upon the degree of deference or respect they extend to policemen in field encounters (Westley, 1953; Piliavin and Briar, 1964; Black, 1968; Black and Reiss, 1970). As a rule, the police are especially likely to sanction suspects who fail to defer to police authority whether legal grounds exist or not. Situational etiquette can weigh heavily on broader processes of social life (see Goffman, 1956 and 1963). This section offers findings showing that the complainant's deference toward the police conditions the official recognition of crime complaints.

The deference of complainants toward the police can be classified into three categories: (1) very deferential or very respectful, (2) civil, and (3) antagonistic or disrespectful. As might be expected, complainants are not often antagonistic toward policemen; it is the suspect who is more likely to be disrespectful (Black and Reiss, 1967:63–65). The number of cases of police encounters with antagonistic complainants is too few for separate analysis of felony and misdemeanor situations. When felonies and misdemeanors are combined into one statistical base, however, it becomes clear that by a large margin the probability of an official crime report is lowest when the complainant is antagonistic in the face-to-face encounter. (See Table 2.) Less than one-third of the disrespectful complainants who prefer official action see their wishes actualized in a crime report. Because of the small number of cases this finding nevertheless should be taken as tentative. The comparison between the very deferential and the civil complain-

ants, which is more firmly grounded, is equally striking. The police are somewhat more likely to comply with very deferential complainants than with those who are merely civil. In sum, then, the less deferential the complainant, the less likely are the police to comply with his manifest preference for official action in the form of an official crime report.[10]

Table 2 also shows that the complainant's degree of deference conditions crime-reporting in both felony and misdemeanor situations. In fact, it seems that the complainant's deference can predict official recognition as well, or even slightly better than the legal seriousness of the crime. The probability of a crime report in misdemeanor situations where the complainant is very deferential (85%) is as high as it is in felony situations where he is only civil toward the police (80%). Still, when we

---

[10] The findings in this section present a problem of interpretation, since no information about the police officer's behavior toward the citizen is provided apart from whether or not he wrote an official report. Therefore, nothing is known from the tabulation about whether the officer behaved in such a way as to *provoke* the citizen into one or another degree of deference. Nothing is known about the subtle exchange of cues that takes place in any instance of face-to-face interaction. Other studies of the role of deference in police work are subject to the same criticism. Here, again, no inquiry is made into the motivational dimensions of the pattern. It nevertheless should be emphasized that whatever the motivation of the complainant behavior, the motivation was not the failure of the police to write an official report. In the cities studied the complainant ordinarily did not even know whether or not an official report was written, since the police ordinarily wrote the report in the police car or at the police station after leaving the encounter with the complainant. During the encounter they recorded the relevant facts about the incident in a notebook, whether or not they intended to write an official report. As some officers say, they do this "for show" in order to lead the complainant to believe they are "doing something." Thus, in the average case, it can be assumed that the complainant's deference is not a consequence of the situational outcome. Furthermore, the observers were instructed to record only the level of citizen deference that appeared prior to the situational outcome. A separate item was provided in the observation booklet for recording the citizen's manifest level of satisfaction at the close of the encounter. It therefore remains reasonable to hold that the complainant's deference can aid in calculating the probability of an official crime report.

TABLE 2. PERCENT OF POLICE ENCOUNTERS WITH COMPLAINANTS ACCORDING TO TYPE OF CRIME AND COMPLAINANT'S DEGREE OF DEFERENCE, BY SITUATIONAL OUTCOME: COMPLAINANT PREFERS OFFICIAL ACTION

| | Type of Crime and Complainant's Degree of Deference | | | | | | | | |
| | Felony | | | Misdemeanor | | | All Crimes | | |
Situational Outcome	Very Deferential	Civil	Antagonistic	Very Deferential	Civil	Antagonistic	Very Deferential	Civil	Antagonistic
Official Report	100	80	(2)	85	65	(1)	91	73	30
No Official Report	..	20	(1)	15	35	(6)	9	26	70
Total Percent	100	100	..	100	100	..	100	99	100
Total Number	(15)	(127)	(3)	(20)	(79)	(7)	(35)	(206)	(10)

hold constant the complainant's deference, the legal seriousness of the incident looms to importance. In felony situations where the complainant is very respectful, the police satisfy his preference for official action in no less than 100% of the cases.

The findings in this section reveal that the level of citizen respect for the police in field encounters has consequences beyond those known to operate in the sanctioning of suspects. Here we see that the fate of citizens who are nominally served, as well as those who are controlled by the police, rides in part upon their etiquette. The official response to an avowed victimization in part depends upon the situational *style* in which the citizen presents his complaint to the control system. Official crime rates and the justice done through police detection of criminal offenders, therefore, reflect the politeness of victims. That sanctions are sometimes more severe for alleged offenders who are disrespectful toward the police can be understood in many ways as a possible contribution to the control function. Perhaps, for example, disrespectful offenders pose a greater threat to society, since they refuse to extend legitimacy to its legal system. Perhaps deterrence is undermined by leniency toward disrespectful suspects. Perhaps not. The point is that rationales are available for understanding this pattern as it relates to the police control function. It should be apparent that such rationales do not apply as readily to the tendency of the police to underreport the victimizations of disrespectful complainants. Surely this pattern could have only the remotest connection to deterrence of illegal behavior. Etiquette, it would seem, can belittle the criminal law.

THE COMPLAINANT'S STATUS

The literature on police work abounds in speculation but provides little observational evidence concerning the relation of social status to police outcomes. The routine policing of Negroes differs somewhat from that of whites, and the policing of blue-collar citizens differs quite massively from that of white-collar citizens. Nevertheless, there is a dearth of evidence that these differences arise from discriminatory behavior by po-

licemen. It appears that more consequential in determining these outcomes are aggregative differences between the races and classes in the kinds of incidents the police handle along with situational factors such as those the present analysis examines (e.g., Skolnick, 1966; Black, 1968; Black and Reiss, 1970). Nevertheless, the research literature remains far too scanty to permit confident generalization on these questions.

Studies in the discretionary aspects of police work focus almost solely upon police encounters with suspects. The present sample provides an opportunity to investigate the relation between a complainant's race and social-class status and the probability that the police will give official recognition to his complaint. The tabulation limits the cases to those where the complainant expresses a preference for official action and to those where he is civil toward the police. This section concludes that the race of complainants does not independently relate to the production of official crime rates, but there is some evidence that the police give preferential treatment to white-collar complainants in felony situations.

For all crimes and social-class statuses taken together, the difference between Negroes and whites in the probability of an official crime report is slight and negligible (see Table 3); it is a bit higher for whites. Table 3 also shows that this probability is the same for blue-collar Negroes and blue-collar whites in felony situations, though it is comparatively higher for blue-collar Negroes in misdemeanor situations. Evidence of racial discrimination thus appears weak and inconsistent. It should nonetheless be noted that if there were consistent evidence of a race differential it is not readily clear to whom a disadvantage could be attributed. Considered from the complainant's standpoint, a higher frequency of police failure to comply with complainants of one race could be viewed as discrimination *against* that race. But police failure to write a crime report also lowers the likelihood that the offender will be subjected to the criminal process. Since we may assume that complainants more commonly are victims of offenses committed by members of their own race than by members of another race (Reiss, 1967), then disproportionate police

TABLE 3. PERCENT OF POLICE ENCOUNTERS WITH COMPLAINANTS ACCORDING TO TYPE OF CRIME AND COMPLAINANT'S SOCIAL-CLASS STATUS AND RACE, BY SITUATIONAL OUTCOME: COMPLAINANT PREFERS OFFICIAL ACTION AND IS CIVIL TOWARD POLICE

Type of Crime and Complainant's Social-Class Status and Race

Situational Outcome	Felony Blue-Collar Negro	White	Felony White-Collar Negro	White	Felony Class Unknown Negro	White	Misd. Blue-Collar Negro	White	Misd. White-Collar Negro	White	Misd. Class Unknown Negro	White	All Crimes and Classes Negro	White
Official Report	77	77	(5)	100	(3)	90	69	55	(2)	64	(2)	80	72	76
No Official Report	23	23	...	...	(5)	10	31	45	...	36	(3)	20	28	24
Total Percent	100	100	...	100	...	100	100	100	...	100	...	100	100	100
Total Number	(64)	(22)	(5)	(18)	(8)	(10)	(26)	(22)	(2)	(14)	(5)	(10)	(110)	(96)

failure to comply with complainants could be viewed as discrimination *in favor* of that race, considered from the offender's standpoint. Race differentials in arrest rates for crimes where there is an identifiable victim necessarily pose a similar dilemma of interpretation. Definitionally, there always is a conflict of legal interests between offenders and victims. Offender-victim relationships tend to be racially homogeneous. The social organization of crime therefore complicates questions of racial discrimination in law enforcement.[11]

Along social-class lines there is some evidence of discrimination against complainants and offenders. Table 3 shows that in felony situations the police are somewhat more likely to comply with white-collar complainants than with those of blue-collar status. In fact an official crime report resulted from every encounter between the police and a white-collar felony complainant of either race. The probability of official recognition drops to about three-fourths for blue-collar felony complainants. There does not appear to be a clear social-class differential in misdemeanor situations, however.

Only in felony situations, then, does an inference of discrimination offer itself. In these encounters the police seem to discriminate against blue-collar complainants. Moreover, when both white-collar and blue-collar complainants report felonious offenses, we should be able to assume that the offenders characteristically are of blue-collar status. There is every reason to believe, after all, that white-collar citizens rarely commit the common felonies such as burglary, robbery, and aggravated assault. A possible exception is auto theft, a crime in which youths from white-collar families occasionally indulge. Since this study was conducted in predominantly blue-collar residential areas the assumption should be all the more warranted. It would follow that the police discriminate against blue-collar citizens who feloniously offend white-collar citizens by being comparatively lenient in the investigation of felonies committed by one blue-collar citizen against another. In this instance the legal system listens more attentively to the claims of higher status citizens. The pattern is recorded in the crime rate.

OVERVIEW

The foregoing analysis yields a number of empirical generalizations about the production of crime rates. For the sake of convenience they may be listed as follows:

I. The police officially recognize proportionately more legally serious crimes than legally minor crimes.
II. The complainant's manifest preference for police action has a significant effect upon official crime-reporting.
III. The greater the relational distance between the complainant and the suspect, the greater is the likelihood of official recognition.
IV. The more deferential the complainant toward the police, the greater is the likelihood of official recognition of the complaint.
V. There is no evidence of racial discrimination in crime-reporting.
VI. There is some evidence that the police discriminate in favor of white-collar complainants, but this is true only in the official recognition of legally serious crime situations.

On the surface these findings have direct methodological relevance for those who would put official statistics to use as empirical data, whether to index actual crime in the population or to index actual police practices. Crime rates, as data, systematically underrepresent much crime and much police work. To learn some of the patterns by which this selection process occurs is to acquire a means of improving the utility of crime rates as data.

It should again be emphasized that these patterns of police behavior have consequences not only for official rates of detection as such; they also result in differential

---

[11] It may seem that in criminal matters the costs are slight for the complainant when the police fail to comply with his preference for official action. However, it should be remembered that crimes frequently involve an economic loss for the victim, a loss that can sometimes be recouped if and when the offender is discovered. In other cases, discovery and punishment of the offender may net the victim nothing more than a sense of revenge or security or a sense that justice has been done—concerns that have received little attention in social science. For that matter, social scientists generally examine questions of discriminatory law enforcement *only* from the offender's standpoint. Ordinary citizens in high crime rate areas probably are more interested in questions of discrimination in police allocation of manpower for community protection.

investigation of crimes and hence differential probabilities of arrest and conviction of criminal offenders. Thus the life chances of a criminal violator may depend upon who his victim is and how his victim presents his claim to the police. The complainant's role is appreciable in the criminal process. Surely the complainant has a central place in other legal and nonlegal control contexts as well, though there is as yet little research on the topic. Complainants are the consumers of justice. They are the prime movers of every known legal system, the human mechanisms by which legal services are routed into situations where there is a felt need for law. Complainants are the most invisible and they may be the most important social force binding the law to other aspects of social organization.

REFERENCES

Biderman, Albert D.
  1967 "Surveys of population samples for estimating crime incidence." The Annals of the American Academy of Political and Social Science 374 (1967):16–33.
Biderman, Albert D. and Albert J. Reiss, Jr.
  1967 "On exploring the 'dark figure' of crime." The Annals of the American Academy of Political and Social Science 374 (1967):1–15.
Bittner, Egon
  1967 "The police on skid-row: A study of peace-keeping." American Sociological Review 32 (1967):699–715.
Black, Donald J.
  1968 Police Encounters and Social Organization: An Observation Study. Unpublished Ph.D. Dissertation, Department of Sociology, University of Michigan.
Black, Donald J. and Albert J. Reiss, Jr.
  1967 "Patterns of behavior in police and citizen transactions." Pp. 1–139 in President's Commission on Law Enforcement and Administration of Justice, Studies in Crime and Law Enforcement in Major Metropolitan Areas. Field Surveys III, Volume 2. Washington, D. C.: U.S. Government Printing Office.
  1970 "Police control of juveniles." American Sociological Review 35 (February):63–77.
Cicourel, Aaron V.
  1968 The Social Organization of Juvenile Justice. New York: John Wiley and Sons, Inc.
de Beaumont, Gustave and Alexis de Tocqueville
  1964 On the Penitentiary System in the United States and Its Application in France. Carbondale, Ill.: Southern University Press. (orig. pub. 1833)
Erikson, Kai T.

  1966 Wayward Puritans: A Study in the Sociology of Deviance. New York: John Wiley and Sons.
Goffman, Erving
  1956 "The nature of deference and demeanor." American Anthropologist 58 (1956):473–502.
  1963 Behavior in Public Places: Notes on the Social Organization of Gatherings. New York: The Free Press.
Hall, Jerome
  1952 Theft, Law and Society. Indianapolis, Ind.: The Bobbs-Merrill Company. (2nd Ed.)
Hoebel, E. Adamson
  1954 The Law of Primitive Man: A Study in Comparative Legal Dynamics. Cambridge: Harvard University Press.
Kitsuse, John I. and Aaron Cicourel
  1963 "A note on the uses of official statistics." Social Problems 11 (1963):131–139.
LaFave, Wayne R.
  1965 Arrest: The Decision to Take a Suspect into Custody. Boston: Little, Brown and Company.
Lofland, John
  1969 Deviance and Identity. Englewood Cliffs, N. J.: Prentice-Hall.
Maine, Henry Sumner
  1963 Ancient Law: Its Connection with the Early History of Society and Its Relation to Modern Ideas. Boston: Beacon Press. (orig. pub. 1861)
Malinowski, Bronislaw
  1962 Crime and Custom in Savage Society. Paterson, N. J.: Littlefield, Adams and Co. (orig. pub. 1926)
Morrison, William Douglas
  1897 "The interpretation of criminal statistics." Journal of the Royal Statistical Society 60 (1897):1–24.
Nader, Laura
  1964 "An analysis of Zapotec Law cases." Ethnology 3 (1964):404–419.
Nader, Laura and Duane Metzger
  1963 "Conflict resolution in two Mexican communities." American Anthropologist 65 (1963):584–592.
Piliavin, Irving and Scott Briar
  1964 "Police encounters with juveniles." American Journal of Sociology 70 (1964):206–214.
Pound, Roscoe
  1942 Social Control Through Law. New Haven: Yale University Press.
Reiss, Albert J., Jr.
  1967 "Measurement of the nature and amount of crime." Pp. 1–183 in President's Commission on Law Enforcement and Administration of Justice, Studies in Crime and Law Enforcement in Major Metropolitan Areas. Field Surveys III, Volume 1. Washington, D.C.: U.S. Government Printing Office.
Schwartz, Barry
  1968 "The social psychology of privacy." Ameri-

can Journal of Sociology 73 (1968):741–752.

Schwartz, Richard D.
1954 "Social factors in the development of legal control: A case study of two Israeli settlements." Yale Law Journal 63 (1954):471–491.

Sellin, Thorsten
1931 "Crime." Pp. 563–569 in Edwin R. A. Seligman (ed.), Encyclopaedia of the Social Sciences, Volume 4. New York: The Macmillan Company.

Skolnick, Jerome H.
1966 Justice Without Trial: Law Enforcement in Democratic Society. New York: John Wiley and Sons.

Stinchcombe, Arthur L.

1963 "Institutions of privacy in the determination of police administrative practice." American Journal of Sociology 69(1963): 150–160.

Westley, William A.
1953 "Violence and the police." American Journal of Sociology 59 (1955):34–41.

Wheeler, Stanton
1967 "Criminal statistics: A reformulation of the problem." Journal of Criminal Law, Criminology and Police Science 58 (1967):317–324.

Wilson, James Q.
1968 Varieties of Police Behavior: The Management of Law and Order in Eight Communities. Cambridge, Mass.: Harvard University Press.

[15]

Police Field Services and Crime: The Presumed Effects of a Capacity

George L. Kelling

Research into the police function, police activities—preventive patrol, rapid response to calls for service, team policing, and investigations—and technology suggests that the emphasis on crime-related activities has failed to achieve crime reduction goals and may have exacerbated problems of police-citizen alienation and citizen fear of crime. Even at best, the police can have only a limited effect on crime. In the future, police must abandon strategies which prevent extensive contact with citizens. They must direct their attention to improving the quality of police-citizen interaction and to developing approaches to policing that reduce citizen fear.

During the past fifteen years, policing has been recognized by the public and its leaders as a major social institution—one in need of great political and financial support. While some have perhaps overstated the importance of the police in problems occurring during the last two decades (e.g., Godfrey Hodgson has asserted that the police were largely responsible for most of the riots in the sixties[1]), it is fair to say that the police contribute significantly to both the solution and the exacerbation of social problems.

This period will also be noted in the history of policing as the time when the remarkable insularity of the police ended. The police began to collaborate —at first begrudgingly but finally with enthusiasm—with other major institutions such as universities, foundations, and research institutes.

Other changes occurred as well. Salaries for police increased greatly. The size of police departments doubled and tripled. Major investments were made in technology. Women and minorities were slowly admitted into police service. University programs developed to educate the police, and officers entered these programs on both a preservice and a postservice basis. Entrance requirements were modified in light of this emphasis on education. Many police benevolent associations became powerful unions, forcing police managers to adjust to a new force in police policy making. Finally, the police and police services were probably more thoroughly scrutinized and evaluated than almost any other part of the criminal justice system.

GEORGE L. KELLING is Evaluation Field Staff Director, Police Foundation, Madison, Wisconsin.

This paper was adapted from a speech delivered at the 24th National Institute on Crime and Delinquency, June 1977, Salt Lake City, Utah.

1. Godfrey Hodgson, *America in Our Time* (Garden City, N.Y.: Doubleday, 1976).

George L. Kelling

It is not hard for many of us to remember those days when police agencies were almost totally inaccessible to researchers. Police business was considered to be just that—police business. However, during the past fifteen-year period, researchers and police have developed interorganizational and interprofessional strategies and techniques which allow for successful collaboration. The police have learned that they can become successfully involved in research and that research can contribute significantly to the improvement of public service.

The purpose of this paper is to review research related to the changing police role to determine what this suggests about the future of police tactics. On the surface, much of the research seems contradictory and confusing, but I believe that consistent themes do emerge. These themes provide the basis for continued research, development, and innovation.

THE POLICE AS A PUBLIC SERVICE AGENCY

The myth of the police as primarily a crime-fighting, deterring, and investigating agency is deeply engrained in our society. This view is reinforced each day by the media, which portray the police as going from critical event to critical event, constantly dealing with crime, and often resorting to weapons. The effect of this is considerable. Young persons are drawn toward policing as a career because of the excitement of such activities. The police themselves cite crises in their attempt to get public, financial, and moral support. Even today, some police chiefs go beyond the title "law enforcement officers" and describe themselves as "crime fighters enforcing the law."

However, considerable research done since 1950 has shown this image to be inaccurate.[2] The police have been found to spend a relatively low percentage of their time on crime-related matters (less than 20 percent); most of their time is spent in activities related to public service—settling family fights, handling drunks, dealing with teenagers, maintaining order, and so on.

The consequences of this knowledge are not inconsequential. If it is true—and every bit of evidence suggests it is—almost every aspect of present police organization is affected. As Herman Goldstein has pointed out, this awareness of the multiple functions of the police has significant implications for recruitment, training, and organization.[3] Thus, if service activities do dominate over crime-fighting activities, the police will have to recruit different kinds of

---

2. W. A. Westley, *Violence and the Police* (Cambridge, Mass.: MIT Press, 1970); E. Cumming, I. Cumming, and L. Edell, "Policeman as Philosopher, Guide and Friend," *Social Problems*, Winter 1965; James Q. Wilson, *Varieties of Police Behavior* (Cambridge, Mass.: Harvard University Press, 1968); A. J. Reiss, Jr., *The Police and the Public* (New Haven, Conn.: Yale University Press, 1971); American Bar Association, *The Urban Police Function* (Chicago: American Bar Association Project on Standards for Criminal Justice, 1971).

3. Herman Goldstein, *Policing a Free Society* (Cambridge, Mass.: Ballinger, 1977).

Police Services and Crime   **175**

people than those attracted to the stereotypical crime-fighting functions. Training will have to focus less on legal and crime-related matters and more on conflict management and social relations. Less organizational emphasis need be placed on command, control, and on technological systems to get police to the scenes of crime quickly. More can be placed on developing quality relations with citizens. Further, people tend to concentrate on performing well in those activities for which they receive rewards—both financial reimbursement and promotions. Unless organizations reward non-crime-related activities, successful performance in these functions will remain less crucial.

But the most important consequence of this mistaken conception of the police function is its impact on patrol. By defining themselves as crime fighters the police have developed crime-prevention strategies that emphasize patrol; allocation for patrol, in turn, is almost entirely based on police functions that relate directly to crime. We are only now beginning to understand that this strategy has been at the expense of other important activities.

PREVENTIVE PATROL AS THE PRIMARY MEANS OF POLICE SERVICE DELIVERY[4]

O. W. Wilson has best described—and best justified—the concept of preventive patrol, as we know it today.[5] According to Wilson, the automobile was first used to increase the patrol range of foot beat officers by enabling them to move quickly from one beat to another.[6] While cars could be used to pursue offenders, their primary function was to increase the number of beats officers could handle. The theory of preventive patrol developed only after cars had been used for some time transporting officers between stations and between beats. Wilson theorized that, by moving police vehicles rapidly through beats and unpredictably past likely crime targets, police could create the feeling of police omnipresence. The benefits of this omnipresence were to be decreased crime, increased apprehensions, reduced citizen fear, and increased citizen satisfaction. Coupled with rapid response to calls for service, this police omnipresence would dramatically and effectively reduce crime.

With some variations, this attempt to affect crime through preventive patrol became the dominant mode of delivering police service. Beats were structured to facilitate this proposed impact. As allocation models became more complex, it became apparent that, although the police had multiple functions, patrol came to be organized around the presumed effects of police on crime.

4. For a wider discussion of this and the following section, see George L. Kelling and David Fogel, "The Future of Policing," in *Sage Criminal Justice Annuals*, vol. 9, Alvin W. Cohn, ed. (Beverly Hills, Calif.: Sage Publications, Spring 1978).

5. O. W. Wilson and Roy Clinton McLaren, *Police Administration*, 3d ed. (New York: McGraw-Hill, 1963).

6. Ibid.

Some persons called for "getting rid of" the non-crime-related functions[7]; others developed models for "interception patrol,"[8] a form of rapid patrol with the goal of intercepting crimes in action. Still others advocated covert patrol,[9] a form of inconspicuous patrol in which the police force would "blend into" a community.

As practice and theory developed, the use of the car substantially changed. Whether intentional or not, that change in the use of the car brought a substantial skew in the activities of the police. Wilson continued to advocate police-citizen interaction,[10] but the trend was away from this personal contact. Modeling theorists such as J. Elliot and Richard Larson provided a justification for police officers' remaining *in* their police vehicles rather than using them as a means of getting from place to place.[11] Police came to describe themselves as being "in-service" when they were cruising in their cars—attempting to create the effect of police omnipresence—and "out-of-service" when outside their vehicles actually dealing with citizens. To be patrolling was to be "in the action"—or at least apparently available for "action." The goal of police action was to "bust criminals." Obviously, contact with citizens diminished in importance.

This rationale behind the creation of police omnipresence was logical. In many respects, it made sense. But were the effects as predicted?

The theory of preventive patrol was first challenged in the early 1960s. Albert Reiss found that the time spent in preventive patrol was remarkably unproductive, contradicting the idea that the self-initiated, proactive (interception) activities of the police would increase apprehensions.[12] James Press found mixed effects of markedly increasing manpower.[13] The Institute for Defense Analysis reported that interviews with prison inmates suggested fear of police was not a significant deterrent.[14] Donald Fisk studied the Indianapolis Fleet Car Plan, an effort to simulate police presence by having police officers use their police vehicles off duty, and essentially found no positive

7. William J. Bayer, "Service-Oriented Functional Management in Patrol," *The Police Chief*, April 1975, pp. 42-45.

8. J. F. Elliot, *Interception Patrol* (Springfield, Ill.: Charles C Thomas, 1973).

9. James D. Bannon, "Foot Patrol: The Litany of Law Enforcement," *The Police Chief*, April 1972, pp. 44-45.

10. O. W. Wilson, "Put the Cop Back on the Beat," *Public Management*, June 1953.

11. Elliot, *Interception Patrol*; and Richard C. Larson, *Urban Police Patrol Analysis* (Cambridge, Mass.: MIT Press, 1972).

12. Reiss, *The Police and the Public*.

13. J. S. Press, Some Effects of an Increase in Police Manpower in the 20th Precinct of New York City, Report R704-NYC (New York: New York City Rand Institute, October 1971).

14. "Part III: Analysis of Response to Police Deterrence," unpublished study cited with permission (Washington, D.C.: Institute for Defense Analysis, 1966).

effects.[15] In the Kansas City Preventive Patrol Experiment, preventive patrol once again failed to demonstrate its proposed effect.[16]

Other, nonempirical challenges to preventive patrol can be inferred from the report by the President's Commission of 1967 on Law Enforcement and Administration of Justice[17] and from researchers studying the problem of police-citizen alienation.[18] The commission report, while backing preventive patrol because of its assumed crime-preventive effectiveness, conceded that the strategy may create serious community relations problems. Others have suggested that the tactic of preventive patrol has contributed to police officers' image as an alien force that is remote from the community. In minority communities, police vehicles have grown to symbolize the establishment's repression and occupation. The result has been a mutual withdrawal—the police from the citizens, and the citizens from the police. Proposals for community relations programs and public service officers can now be seen as attempts to make up for some of the problems created by preventive patrol. However, since preventive patrol has failed to demonstrate its effectiveness, it becomes clear that such proposals were misplaced attempts to change image rather than improve service.

If police critics are correct, the strategy of preventive patrol has not only failed to demonstrate its effectiveness but has also created the worst possible situation: an ineffectiveness which alienates citizens.

RESPONSE TIME

As preventive patrol strategy developed it was linked with a second and, in many respects, complementary tactic—rapid response to calls for service. If police could reduce the time between commission of a crime and the arrival of the police on the scene, increased apprehension of offenders, deterrence, increased citizen satisfaction, and decreased fear should result. The goal of most police departments became a response time of three minutes. Evaluators became so convinced that there would be a causal link between response time and police effectiveness (apprehensions, deterrence, etc.) that response time itself became an outcome variable, an indicator of police effectiveness.

Two recently published studies measured the effects of response time. Studying data from the Kansas City Police Department, Deborah Bertram and

15. D. Fisk, *The Indianapolis Police Fleet Plan* (Washington, D.C.: Urban Institute, October 1970).

16. George L. Kelling et al., *The Kansas City Preventive Patrol Experiment* (Washington, D.C.: Police Foundation, 1974).

17. President's Commission on Law Enforcement and Administration of Justice, *Task Force Report: The Police* (Washington, D.C.: U.S. Govt. Printing Office, 1967).

18. Irving Piliavin, "Police-Community Alienation: Its Structural Roots and a Proposed Remedy" (Andover, Mass.: Warner Modular Publications, Module 14, 1973), pp. 1-25.

Alexander Vargo found that response time had no effect on apprehensions for the crime of robbery.[19] They also learned that citizens who have experienced serious crimes allow considerable periods of time to elapse before contacting the police. Pate et al. correlated response time with levels of citizen satisfaction and found that response time was not the critical variable in determining citizen satisfaction.[20] What was important was the *expectation* of how long it would take the police to arrive. If police response time exceeded the citizen's expectation, he tended to be dissatisfied; if, however, response time was shorter than anticipated, the citizen was generally satisfied. The authors suggest that dispatchers could play an important role in controlling citizens' expectations about the police arrival.

As in the case of effects of preventive patrol, it appears logical that police response time should make a difference in effectiveness. But this strategy lacks empirical support. It was assumed that citizens called the police immediately. In fact, citizens called someone else first and considerable time elapsed.

Here we have a police strategy that is expensive to develop and maintain. To reduce response time, multimillion-dollar automatic vehicle locator systems have been developed. Yet evaluations of the strategy have bypassed the question of whether it affected apprehensions, only measuring the extent to which it reduced response time.[21] But it has been a tremendous expense in terms of its effect on police allocation plans, in the way it confines police in their automobiles, and in its impact on police supervison and organization.

TEAM POLICING

One of the most promising developments in the past several decades has been the concept of team policing. There is much about it that seems "right": Team policing encourages close interactions between citizens and police; it emphasizes a decentralized decision making by police officers and supervisors actually working in the prescribed area; it acknowledges the multipurpose functions of the police and often provides general *and* special training for police; and it encourages police officer familiarity with community agencies and other resources.

Yet the implementation of this promising form of policing has been an elusive goal. Team policing has been tried in Detroit, New York, Dallas, Cincinnati, and many other cities, but no large city has been able to implement or maintain it on a city-wide basis.

19. D. K. Bertram and A. Vargo, "Response Time Analysis Study: Preliminary Finding on Robbery in Kansas City," *The Police Chief*, May 1976, pp. 74-77.
20. Pate et al., *Police Response Time: Its Determinants and Effects* (Washington, D.C.: Police Foundation, 1976).
21. Richard C. Larson, Kent W. Colton, and Gilbert C. Larson, "Evaluating a Police-Implemented AVM System: The St. Louis Experience," Phase I (unpublished paper).

Police Services and Crime 179

A recent evaluation of team policing in Cincinnati may best illustrate this point.[22] Team policing was begun on an experimental basis with great enthusiasm. After the first year, citizen satisfaction had increased, crime had decreased, and officers remained enthusiastic about the project. The program appeared to be a truly amazing success. However, at the end of year two, citizen satisfaction had returned to levels comparable with other areas of the city, crime had returned to comparable levels, and officer satisfaction had diminished. Team policing simply expired. Police officers went back to "business as usual," and authority was recentralized.

Two interpretations are possible. The first is that an "innovator effect" was operating during the first year; in other words, programs tend to start with flourish and promise because of factors such as participants' enthusiasm and publicity. This might well explain Cincinnati's initial success.

However, there is a second interpretation which I find more plausible since the Cincinnati experience followed the pattern of almost every other team policing effort. Team policing can start with enthusiasm, commitment, and great promise and then either remain confined to one or two districts or, as in Cincinnati, simply be terminated.

Two factors seem to operate. First, team policing represents a real threat to police departments' formal and informal power distribution. While officers can mobilize considerable enthusiasm for such attempts, organizational decentralization threatens established and entrenched interest groups which have considerable power inside the organization, often control employee organizations, and, in the case of detectives, often have important ties with the press and politicians.[23]

The second factor is that the present police orientation around rapid response to service calls is essentially incompatible not only with team policing but also with almost every other approach which emphasizes planning of "out-of-service" activities. Meetings with citizens' groups and with individual citizens involve considerable out-of-service time. Regardless of what a sergeant or team leader may plan for police officers during any tour of duty, as long as the primary goal of the police department revolves around rapid response to calls for service, that will have priority over almost every other activity.

The conflict between supervisory and dispatch goals may well have contributed to the failure of innovations such as team policing. Yet the role of supervision has received little attention. So far as I know, there is not one good study examining the impact of the sergeant on the police force. Jonathan

---

22. Alfred I. Schwartz and Sumner N. Clarren, *Evaluation of Team Policing in Cincinnati (after 30 months of Experimentation)* (Washington, D.C.: Police Foundation, in press).

23. A forthcoming evaluation of the attempt in Dallas to decentralize operations and develop generalist/specialist police officers will describe this resistance in detailed and stark terms.

Rubinstein suggests both sergeants and dispatchers may significantly control police activities,[24] but we have little understanding of how this operates.

INFORMATION

At least five studies suggest that, to the extent that police can affect crime, availability of information and the management of that information seem to be of critical importance. These findings, though still tentative, run counter to the present police concern with interception of crimes or rapid response to calls for service. The Rochester program, which studied case management to identify factors contributing to the solution of a crime,[25] the Rand study of investigative effectiveness,[26] the Police Foundation's evaluation of the Criminal Information Center in Kansas City,[27] the San Diego program of field interrogations,[28] and the San Diego community profile program[29] are exploratory studies, but they suggest that continued research and program development in the gathering and managing of information may be useful.

These findings lead to the following questions. How can we improve the quality and quantity of police-citizen contacts so that citizens report more crime, give police information—both formally and informally—about crime patterns, and discuss their community concerns? How can we improve the ability of the individual police officer and the organization to gather that information, store it, and bring it to bear on appropriate events and issues? How can we improve the police officer's and the police organization's ability to understand their community so that they can better interpret the information they receive? How can we modify the reward structures of police organizations so that sharing, not retaining, information is properly encouraged and rewarded? These questions combine issues of police organization, police strategy, and police technology.

Organizational issues pertinent to effectively obtaining information include supervision, training, and incentives for gathering and sharing useful information. Strategy issues include how to maximize police-citizen contacts so that they can be most productive of relevant information. The technological issue is how to properly arrange for the easy storage and retrieval of information.

24. Jonathan Rubinstein, *City Police* (New York: Farrar, Straus and Giroux, 1973), pp. 73-87.

25. Peter B. Bloch and James Bell, *Managing Investigation: The Rochester System* (Washington, D.C.: Police Foundation, 1976).

26. Peter W. Greenwood et al., *The Criminal Investigation Process,* 3 vols. (Santa Monica, Calif.: Rand Corporation, 1976).

27. Tony Pate, Robert A. Bowers, and Ron Parks, *Three Approaches to Criminal Apprehension in Kansas City: An Evaluation Report* (Washington, D.C.: Police Foundation, 1976).

28. John E. Boydstun, *San Diego Field Interrogation: Final Report* (Washington, D.C.: Police Foundation, 1975).

29. John E. Boydstun and Michael E. Sherry, *San Diego Community Profile: Final Report* (Washington, D.C.: Police Foundation, 1975).

Police Services and Crime 181

INVESTIGATIONS

The myths about investigative work are perhaps best summarized by Goldstein:

> Part of the mystique of detective operations is the impression that a detective has difficult-to-come-by qualifications and skills; that investigating crime is a real science; that a detective does much more important work than other police officers; that all detective work is exciting; and that a good detective can solve any crime. It borders on heresy to point out that, in fact, much of what detectives do consists of very routine and rather elementary chores, including much paper processing; that a good deal of their work is not only not exciting, it is downright boring; that the situations they confront are often less challenging and less demanding than those handled by patrolling police officers; that it is arguable whether special skills and knowledge are required for detective work; that a considerable amount of detective work is actually undertaken on a hit-or-miss basis; and that the capacity of detectives to solve crimes is greatly exaggerated.[30]

Both the Rand study and the Rochester study underline this issue. The Rand study, which has been the subject of much controversy, suggests that the role played by investigators in crime solution has been overrated. The study is exploratory, but the authors' findings and recommendations are highly plausible. The Rochester study demonstrated that one problem in investigations is case management. Thus, investigators found that their time could be spent more efficiently if they concentrated on those cases which had a high probability of success. Further, it was found that patrol officers could provide the necessary information for that screening process by identifying "solvability factors."

Clearly, much research is still needed. Only preliminary studies of the relationship between patrol and investigation are available. However, the combined findings of the Rand study and the Rochester study identify significant problems in investigation and suggest means of using patrol officers to improve investigative effectiveness.

TECHNOLOGY

There have always been high hopes that technology would greatly enhance police effectiveness or would at least give officers an "edge" over the criminals. In 1929, when the radio was first installed in police vehicles, some predicted that radios would enable police to eliminate city crime altogether.[31] While we may not be as enthusiastic today, we continue to invest heavily in devices such as helicopters, computers, new weapon systems, and surveillance systems, with the expectation that new technology will significantly improve police functioning.

30. Goldstein, *Policing A Free Society*.
31. Rubinstein, *City Police*.

Certainly, innovations such as the personal radios have great utility for police agencies. Radios—especially personal radios—can be used to both protect the officer and increase his effectiveness. Yet one might argue that they are more important as management devices than as crime-fighting instruments, for there is little evidence that radios have given police any "edge" over criminal offenders. Recent lightweight bullet protection devices are useful and should be available; however, they are warm, uncomfortable, and restrictive. It is unlikely that more than a few officers are willing to wear them routinely.

With these possible exceptions, there is no evidence that any technological devices have significantly improved the effectiveness of police service. Helicopters may have been useful as ambulances, but their effectiveness in patrol remains hypothetical. And the cost of use has not been analyzed.

Computer-aided dispatch and automatic vehicle locator systems have failed to demonstrate that they can reduce response time.[32] Besides, there is no evidence that reduced response time achieves anything. This is not meant to imply that computers and other instruments cannot be used effectively in police departments. I have no doubt that they have great potential in efficient management. But their impact on the multiple police services remains to be seen.

Critics of technological innovation generally see new devices as being, at worst, expensive, useless "toys." But this criticism does not go far enough. The "worst" is not the wasting of money but the deterioration in the quality of service. The radio, for example, has been used to decrease police response time. The beneficial effect of rapid response to calls for service was presumed, not proved. Nevertheless, the radio created a priority, spawning other hardware such as computer-aided dispatch and automatic vehicle locator systems. All this came as a result of a capacity to achieve a *presumed effect*.

Technology does not, "at worst," create wasteful expensive toys; technology used in organizations can lead to goal displacement, the dominance of one function over another because of presumed effects, and a substantial change not only in how services are delivered but also in what those services are.

In discussing technology and the military, Joseph Lewis has suggested that when people have money and are facing difficult problems, they are easily diverted to the technology which seems to be related to those problems (capacity for presumed effect).[33] It is much more fun to play with computers (be scientific) than to solve hard problems. You can prove that you are "doing something about the problem" by spending large sums of money in dignified, scientifically respectable, socially acceptable ways.

The problem can also be stated quite briefly in this way. What we have been saying is that there is not a firm bridge in the area of command and control

---

32. Joseph H. Lewis, "Evaluation of Systems Effectiveness," unpublished paper (Washington, D.C.: Police Foundation, 1964).
33. Ibid.

Police Services and Crime 183

between scientific and technical capabilities and operational utility. In most areas of application of science and technology, it is easy to see the connection between the scientific or technical ability to do something and the use that can be made of doing that something. That is not true here. There is technology lying around in heaps that we have not the remotest idea how to employ usefully. There is technology lying around in heaps that we know something about employing but have no valid way to establish what it is worth, or how much we should pay for it."[34]

The question in policing is, technology for what purpose? That question simply has not been answered.

CONCLUSION

The police have developed strategies oriented around just one of their many functions. These strategies have not only failed to obtain their desired results but have also led the police to ignore other important functions and have alienated citizens, whose support is vital in effective police performance.

Except for the period between World War I and World War II, our cities and countryside have probably never been safer. Those who respond hysterically to our present crime problems and claim that we are experiencing a complete breakdown in law and order should read about crime in the past.[35] Cities have always been unsafe places. And, not long ago, those leaving the city to travel in the countryside were hardly better off. Unless they hired protection, travelers were lucky to arrive at their destination with their horse (if they had a horse) and their boots. Even with protection, it was essential that they reach their destination—or stop in a city or at an inn—before nightfall. Today, one can travel throughout the countryside with little fear of crime. Campers can sleep outside with little risk of losing their equipment. A person can safely walk in most city neighborhoods during the day with relatively little fear. If one is reasonably prudent, the probability of becoming a victim is really quite low.

I do not mean to suggest that crime is not a serious problem. It is. But our fear far exceeds the danger and is seriously affecting our lives in the cities.

At this time, it appears that the police officer's impact on crime must remain relatively limited. This is not only because of the kind of open society in which we live but also because of the nature of particular kinds of crime. Most assaults and murders are hard to control because they involve friends, neighbors, relatives, or lovers. Subtract these from the total number of murders and assaults and the number of potentially suppressible crimes is greatly reduced. Subtract those crimes committed indoors or in places inaccessible to police, and those committed by professionals, and the number decreases further.

34. Douglas Hay et al., *Albion's Fatal Tree* (New York: Pantheon, 1975).
35. See, for example, Christopher Hibbert, *London: The Biography of a City* (London: Longmans, Green and Co., 1969).

Consider armed robbery, a threatening, potentially violent crime. If the Vera Institute study is correct, fully one-third of all armed robberies are committed by people who are known by their victims.[36] Here too, if one subtracts those robberies committed in inaccessible places and those committed by professionals, the number that actually may be suppressible is reduced to an extremely low level.

Consider child molestation, most of which occurs in the home. How do the police mobilize to deal with this?

Certainly there are murders, assaults, armed robberies, and child molestations that are potentially suppressible. However, it is likely that a "floor effect" is operating—that the remaining cases are at such a low level that massively mobilizing the police to deal with those problems can have only a very marginal effect and at *enormous cost*. And that cost probably includes undesirable police-citizen relations.

Acute problems or a threatening series of crimes may demand mobilization, but as a routine policy this seems to have a limited effect and be enforced at enormous financial cost and at the expense of other functions.

What does this mean for the development of future plans, styles of policing, strategies, and research innovation? Briefly, the critical need is to improve the quality and quantity of police-citizen interaction. This must be a central task, not for the purpose of improving the police image but rather to encourage the normal social control exercised by a healthy community. The police must be seen as only an aid to the community, as the community itself deals with social problems. The police certainly are essential, but *policing* is too important to be left to the police alone.

Police methods must reflect the entire police task. We must examine how information is handled and how officers are rewarded for sharing it. The focus on rapid response time must be modified in part by changing citizens' expectations about police service. Police must see reduction of fear as an important part of their purpose. Citizens must be encouraged to use streets prudently but comfortably. We have never tested the hypothesis that it is the extent to which the police provide the full range of police services—in a civil and helpful way—that determines the degree to which *citizens* fully exploit and mobilize the police to deal with crime. The time has come when we should test that hypothesis. As Lewis has suggested with the military,[37] we should declare a ten-year moratorium on technology and concentrate hard on learning just what it is that the police should—and can—do.

---

36. Vera Institute, "Felony Arrests: Their Prosecution and Disposition in New York City's Courts," monograph published by Vera Institute of Justice, 1977.

37. Joseph H. Lewis, "Evaluation of Systems Effectiveness" (Lecture sponsored by the University of California, 1964); shortened version published in *Operational Research and the Social Sciences*, J. K. Lawrence, ed. (London: Tavistock, 1966), p. 46.

[16]

The police and neighborhood safety

BROKEN WINDOWS

BY JAMES Q. WILSON AND GEORGE L. KELLING

I N THE MID-1970S, THE STATE OF NEW JERSEY AN-
nounced a "Safe and Clean Neighborhoods Program,"
designed to improve the quality of community life in
twenty-eight cities. As part of that program, the state provided money to help cities take police officers out of their
patrol cars and assign them to walking beats. The governor and other state officials were enthusiastic about using
foot patrol as a way of cutting crime, but many police
chiefs were skeptical. Foot patrol, in their eyes, had been
pretty much discredited. It reduced the mobility of the police, who thus had difficulty responding to citizen calls for
service, and it weakened headquarters control over patrol
officers.

Many police officers also disliked foot patrol, but for different reasons: it was hard work, it kept them outside on
cold, rainy nights, and it reduced their chances for making
a "good pinch." In some departments, assigning officers to
foot patrol had been used as a form of punishment. And
academic experts on policing doubted that foot patrol
would have any impact on crime rates; it was, in the opinion of most, little more than a sop to public opinion. But
since the state was paying for it, the local authorities were
willing to go along.

Five years after the program started, the Police Foundation, in Washington, D.C., published an evaluation of
the foot-patrol project. Based on its analysis of a carefully
controlled experiment carried out chiefly in Newark, the
foundation concluded, to the surprise of hardly anyone,
that foot patrol had not reduced crime rates. But residents
of the foot-patrolled neighborhoods seemed to feel more
secure than persons in other areas, tended to believe that
crime had been reduced, and seemed to take fewer steps to
protect themselves from crime (staying at home with the
doors locked, for example). Moreover, citizens in the foot-
patrol areas had a more favorable opinion of the police than
did those living elsewhere. And officers walking beats had
higher morale, greater job satisfaction, and a more favorable attitude toward citizens in their neighborhoods than
did officers assigned to patrol cars.

These findings may be taken as evidence that the skep-

*James Q. Wilson is Shattuck Professor of Government at Harvard
and author of* Thinking About Crime. *George L. Kelling, formerly
director of the evaluation field staff of the Police Foundation, is currently a research fellow at the John F. Kennedy School of Government
at Harvard.*

tics were right—foot patrol has no effect on crime; it merely fools the citizens into thinking that they are safer. But in
our view, and in the view of the authors of the Police Foundation study (of whom Kelling was one), the citizens of
Newark were not fooled at all. They knew what the foot-
patrol officers were doing, they knew it was different from
what motorized officers do, and they knew that having officers walk beats did in fact make their neighborhoods
safer.

But how can a neighborhood be "safer" when the crime
rate has not gone down—in fact, may have gone up? Finding the answer requires first that we understand what
most often frightens people in public places. Many citizens,
of course, are primarily frightened by crime, especially
crime involving a sudden, violent attack by a stranger.
This risk is very real, in Newark as in many large cities.
But we tend to overlook or forget another source of fear—

ILLUSTRATIONS BY SEYMOUR CHWAST

PAGE 30   THE ATLANTIC MONTHLY   MARCH 1982

the fear of being bothered by disorderly people. Not violent people, nor, necessarily, criminals, but disreputable or obstreperous or unpredictable people: panhandlers, drunks, addicts, rowdy teenagers, prostitutes, loiterers, the mentally disturbed.

What foot-patrol officers did was to elevate, to the extent they could, the level of public order in these neighborhoods. Though the neighborhoods were predominantly black and the foot patrolmen were mostly white, this "order-maintenance" function of the police was performed to the general satisfaction of both parties.

One of us (Kelling) spent many hours walking with Newark foot-patrol officers to see how they defined "order" and what they did to maintain it. One beat was typical: a busy but dilapidated area in the heart of Newark, with many abandoned buildings, marginal shops (several of which prominently displayed knives and straight-edged razors in their windows), one large department store, and, most important, a train station and several major bus stops. Though the area was run-down, its streets were filled with people, because it was a major transportation center. The good order of this area was important not only to those who lived and worked there but also to many others, who had to move through it on their way home, to supermarkets, or to factories.

The people on the street were primarily black; the officer who walked the street was white. The people were made up of "regulars" and "strangers." Regulars included both "decent folk" and some drunks and derelicts who were always there but who "knew their place." Strangers were, well, strangers, and viewed suspiciously, sometimes apprehensively. The officer—call him Kelly—knew who the regulars were, and they knew him. As he saw his job, he was to keep an eye on strangers, and make certain that the disreputable regulars observed some informal but widely understood rules. Drunks and addicts could sit on the stoops, but could not lie down. People could drink on side streets, but not at the main intersection. Bottles had to be in paper bags. Talking to, bothering, or begging from people waiting at the bus stop was strictly forbidden. If a dispute erupted between a businessman and a customer, the businessman was assumed to be right, especially if the customer was a stranger. If a stranger loitered, Kelly would ask him if he had any means of support and what his business was; if he gave unsatisfactory answers, he was sent on his way. Persons who broke the informal rules, especially those who bothered people waiting at bus stops, were arrested for vagrancy. Noisy teenagers were told to keep quiet.

These rules were defined and enforced in collaboration with the "regulars" on the street. Another neighborhood might have different rules, but these, everybody understood, were the rules for *this* neighborhood. If someone violated them, the regulars not only turned to Kelly for

MARCH 1982   THE ATLANTIC MONTHLY   PAGE 31

help but also ridiculed the violator. Sometimes what Kelly did could be described as "enforcing the law," but just as often it involved taking informal or extralegal steps to help protect what the neighborhood had decided was the appropriate level of public order. Some of the things he did probably would not withstand a legal challenge.

A determined skeptic might acknowledge that a skilled foot-patrol officer can maintain order but still insist that this sort of "order" has little to do with the real sources of community fear—that is, with violent crime. To a degree, that is true. But two things must be borne in mind. First, outside observers should not assume that they know how much of the anxiety now endemic in many big-city neighborhoods stems from a fear of "real" crime and how much from a sense that the street is disorderly, a source of distasteful, worrisome encounters. The people of Newark, to judge from their behavior and their remarks to interviewers, apparently assign a high value to public order, and feel relieved and reassured when the police help them maintain that order.

SECOND, AT THE COMMUNITY LEVEL, DISORDER AND crime are usually inextricably linked, in a kind of developmental sequence. Social psychologists and police officers tend to agree that if a window in a building is broken *and is left unrepaired*, all the rest of the windows will soon be broken. This is as true in nice neighborhoods as in run-down ones. Window-breaking does not necessarily occur on a large scale because some areas are inhabited by determined window-breakers whereas others are populated by window-lovers; rather, one unrepaired broken window is a signal that no one cares, and so breaking more windows costs nothing. (It has always been fun.)

Philip Zimbardo, a Stanford psychologist, reported in 1969 on some experiments testing the broken-window theory. He arranged to have an automobile without license plates parked with its hood up on a street in the Bronx and a comparable automobile on a street in Palo Alto, California. The car in the Bronx was attacked by "vandals" within ten minutes of its "abandonment." The first to arrive were a family—father, mother, and young son—who removed the radiator and battery. Within twenty-four hours, virtually everything of value had been removed. Then random destruction began—windows were smashed, parts torn off, upholstery ripped. Children began to use the car as a playground. Most of the adult "vandals" were well-dressed, apparently clean-cut whites. The car in Palo Alto sat untouched for more than a week. Then Zimbardo smashed part of it with a sledgehammer. Soon, passersby were joining in. Within a few hours, the car had been turned upside down and utterly destroyed. Again, the "vandals" appeared to be primarily respectable whites.

Untended property becomes fair game for people out for fun or plunder, and even for people who ordinarily would not dream of doing such things and who probably consider

themselves law-abiding. Because of the nature of community life in the Bronx—its anonymity, the frequency with which cars are abandoned and things are stolen or broken, the past experience of "no one caring"—vandalism begins much more quickly than it does in staid Palo Alto, where people have come to believe that private possessions are cared for, and that mischievous behavior is costly. But vandalism can occur anywhere once communal barriers—the sense of mutual regard and the obligations of civility—are lowered by actions that seem to signal that "no one cares."

We suggest that "untended" behavior also leads to the breakdown of community controls. A stable neighborhood of families who care for their homes, mind each other's children, and confidently frown on unwanted intruders can change, in a few years or even a few months, to an inhospi-

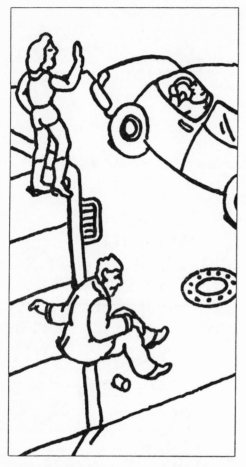

table and frightening jungle. A piece of property is abandoned, weeds grow up, a window is smashed. Adults stop scolding rowdy children; the children, emboldened, become more rowdy. Families move out, unattached adults move in. Teenagers gather in front of the corner store. The merchant asks them to move; they refuse. Fights occur. Litter accumulates. People start drinking in front of the grocery; in time, an inebriate slumps to the sidewalk and is allowed to sleep it off. Pedestrians are approached by panhandlers.

At this point it is not inevitable that serious crime will flourish or violent attacks on strangers will occur. But many residents will think that crime, especially violent crime, is on the rise, and they will modify their behavior accordingly. They will use the streets less often, and when on the streets will stay apart from their fellows, moving with averted eyes, silent lips, and hurried steps. "Don't get involved." For some residents, this growing atomization will matter little, because the neighborhood is not their "home" but "the place where they live." Their interests are elsewhere; they are cosmopolitans. But it will matter greatly to other people, whose lives derive meaning and satisfaction from local attachments rather than worldly involvement; for them, the neighborhood will cease to exist except for a few reliable friends whom they arrange to meet.

Such an area is vulnerable to criminal invasion. Though it is not inevitable, it is more likely that here, rather than in places where people are confident they can regulate public behavior by informal controls, drugs will change hands, prostitutes will solicit, and cars will be stripped. That the drunks will be robbed by boys who do it as a lark, and the prostitutes' customers will be robbed by men who do it purposefully and perhaps violently. That muggings will occur.

Among those who often find it difficult to move away from this are the elderly. Surveys of citizens suggest that the elderly are much less likely to be the victims of crime than younger persons, and some have inferred from this that the well-known fear of crime voiced by the elderly is an exaggeration: perhaps we ought not to design special programs to protect older persons; perhaps we should even try to talk them out of their mistaken fears. This argument misses the point. The prospect of a confrontation with an obstreperous teenager or a drunken panhandler can be as fear-inducing for defenseless persons as the prospect of meeting an actual robber; indeed, to a defenseless person, the two kinds of confrontation are often indistinguishable. Moreover, the lower rate at which the elderly are victimized is a measure of the steps they have already taken—chiefly, staying behind locked doors—to minimize the risks they face. Young men are more frequently attacked than older women, not because they are easier or more lucrative targets but because they are on the streets more.

Nor is the connection between disorderliness and fear made only by the elderly. Susan Estrich, of the Harvard Law School, has recently gathered together a number of surveys on the sources of public fear. One, done in Portland, Oregon, indicated that three fourths of the adults interviewed cross to the other side of a street when they see a gang of teenagers; another survey, in Baltimore, discovered that nearly half would cross the street to avoid even a single strange youth. When an interviewer asked people in a housing project where the most dangerous spot was, they mentioned a place where young persons gathered to drink and play music, despite the fact that not a single crime had occurred there. In Boston public housing projects, the greatest fear was expressed by persons living in the buildings where disorderliness and incivility, not crime, were the greatest. Knowing this helps one understand the significance of such otherwise harmless displays

MARCH 1982   THE ATLANTIC MONTHLY   PAGE 33

as subway graffiti. As Nathan Glazer has written, the proliferation of graffiti, even when not obscene, confronts the
subway rider with the "inescapable knowledge that the environment he must endure for an hour or more a day is
uncontrolled and uncontrollable, and that anyone can invade it to do whatever damage and mischief the mind
suggests."

In response to fear, people avoid one another, weakening
controls. Sometimes they call the police. Patrol cars arrive, an occasional arrest occurs, but crime continues and
disorder is not abated. Citizens complain to the police
chief, but he explains that his department is low on personnel and that the courts do not punish petty or first-time
offenders. To the residents, the police who arrive in squad
cars are either ineffective or uncaring; to the police, the
residents are animals who deserve each other. The citizens
may soon stop calling the police, because "they can't do
anything."

The process we call urban decay has occurred for centuries in every city. But what is happening today is different
in at least two important respects. First, in the period before, say, World War II, city dwellers—because of money
costs, transportation difficulties, familial and church connections—could rarely move away from neighborhood
problems. When movement did occur, it tended to be along
public-transit routes. Now mobility has become exceptionally easy for all but the poorest or those who are blocked
by racial prejudice. Earlier crime waves had a kind of
built-in self-correcting mechanism: the determination of a
neighborhood or community to reassert control over its
turf. Areas in Chicago, New York, and Boston would experience crime and gang wars, and then normalcy would
return, as the families for whom no alternative residences were possible reclaimed their authority over the
streets.

Second, the police in this earlier period assisted in that
reassertion of authority by acting, sometimes violently, on
behalf of the community. Young toughs were roughed up,
people were arrested "on suspicion" or for vagrancy, and
prostitutes and petty thieves were routed. "Rights" were
something enjoyed by decent folk, and perhaps also by the
serious professional criminal, who avoided violence and
could afford a lawyer.

This pattern of policing was not an aberration or the
result of occasional excess. From the earliest days of the
nation, the police function was seen primarily as that of a
night watchman: to maintain order against the chief
threats to order—fire, wild animals, and disreputable behavior. Solving crimes was viewed not as a police responsibility but as a private one. In the March, 1969, *Atlantic*,
one of us (Wilson) wrote a brief account of how the police
role had slowly changed from maintaining order to fighting
crimes. The change began with the creation of private detectives (often ex-criminals), who worked on a contin-
gency-fee basis for individuals who had suffered losses. In
time, the detectives were absorbed into municipal police

agencies and paid a regular salary; simultaneously, the responsibility for prosecuting thieves was shifted from the
aggrieved private citizen to the professional prosecutor.
This process was not complete in most places until the
twentieth century.

In the 1960s, when urban riots were a major problem,
social scientists began to explore carefully the order-maintenance function of the police, and to suggest ways of improving it—not to make streets safer (its original function)
but to reduce the incidence of mass violence. Order-maintenance became, to a degree, coterminous with "community relations." But, as the crime wave that began in the
early 1960s continued without abatement throughout the
decade and into the 1970s, attention shifted to the role of
the police as crime-fighters. Studies of police behavior
ceased, by and large, to be accounts of the order-maintenance function and became, instead, efforts to propose and
test ways whereby the police could solve more crimes,
make more arrests, and gather better evidence. If these
things could be done, social scientists assumed, citizens
would be less fearful.

A GREAT DEAL WAS ACCOMPLISHED DURING THIS transition, as both police chiefs and outside experts emphasized the crime-fighting function in their plans, in the allocation of resources, and in deployment of personnel. The police may well have become better crime-fighters as a result. And doubtless they remained aware of their responsibility for order. But the link between order-maintenance and crime-prevention, so obvious to earlier generations, was forgotten.

That link is similar to the process whereby one broken window becomes many. The citizen who fears the ill-smelling drunk, the rowdy teenager, or the importuning beggar is not merely expressing his distaste for unseemly behavior; he is also giving voice to a bit of folk wisdom that happens to be a correct generalization—namely, that serious street crime flourishes in areas in which disorderly behavior goes unchecked. The unchecked panhandler is, in effect, the first broken window. Muggers and robbers, whether opportunistic or professional, believe they reduce their chances of being caught or even identified if they operate on streets where potential victims are already intimidated by prevailing conditions. If the neighborhood cannot keep a bothersome panhandler from annoying passersby, the thief may reason, it is even less likely to call the police to identify a potential mugger or to interfere if the mugging actually takes place.

Some police administrators concede that this process occurs, but argue that motorized-patrol officers can deal with it as effectively as foot-patrol officers. We are not so sure. In theory, an officer in a squad car can observe as much as an officer on foot; in theory, the former can talk to as many people as the latter. But the reality of police–citizen encounters is powerfully altered by the automobile. An officer on foot cannot separate himself from the street people; if he is approached, only his uniform and his personality can help him manage whatever is about to happen. And he can never be certain what that will be—a request for directions, a plea for help, an angry denunciation, a teasing remark, a confused babble, a threatening gesture.

In a car, an officer is more likely to deal with street people by rolling down the window and looking at them. The door and the window exclude the approaching citizen; they are a barrier. Some officers take advantage of this barrier, perhaps unconsciously, by acting differently if in the car than they would on foot. We have seen this countless times. The police car pulls up to a corner where teenagers are gathered. The window is rolled down. The officer stares at the youths. They stare back. The officer says to one, "C'mere." He saunters over, conveying to his friends by his elaborately casual style the idea that he is not intimidated by authority. "What's your name?" "Chuck." "Chuck who?" "Chuck Jones." "What'ya doing, Chuck?" "Nothin'." "Got a P.O. [parole officer]?" "Nah." "Sure?" "Yeah." "Stay out of trouble, Chuckie." Meanwhile, the other boys laugh and exchange comments among themselves, probably at the officer's expense. The officer stares

harder. He cannot be certain what is being said, nor can he join in and, by displaying his own skill at street banter, prove that he cannot be "put down." In the process, the officer has learned almost nothing, and the boys have decided the officer is an alien force who can safely be disregarded, even mocked.

Our experience is that most citizens like to talk to a police officer. Such exchanges give them a sense of importance, provide them with the basis for gossip, and allow them to explain to the authorities what is worrying them (whereby they gain a modest but significant sense of having "done something" about the problem). You approach a person on foot more easily, and talk to him more readily, than you do a person in a car. Moreover, you can more easily retain some anonymity if you draw an officer aside for a private chat. Suppose you want to pass on a tip about who is stealing handbags, or who offered to sell you a stolen TV. In the inner city, the culprit, in all likelihood, lives nearby. To walk up to a marked patrol car and lean in the window is to convey a visible signal that you are a "fink."

The essence of the police role in maintaining order is to reinforce the informal control mechanisms of the community itself. The police cannot, without committing extraordinary resources, provide a substitute for that informal control. On the other hand, to reinforce those natural forces the police must accommodate them. And therein lies the problem.

S HOULD POLICE ACTIVITY ON THE STREET BE SHAPED, in important ways, by the standards of the neighborhood rather than by the rules of the state? Over the past two decades, the shift of police from order-maintenance to law-enforcement has brought them increasingly under the influence of legal restrictions, provoked by media complaints and enforced by court decisions and departmental orders. As a consequence, the order-maintenance functions of the police are now governed by rules developed to control police relations with suspected criminals. This is, we think, an entirely new development. For centuries, the role of the police as watchmen was judged primarily not in terms of its compliance with appropriate procedures but rather in terms of its attaining a desired objective. The objective was order, an inherently ambiguous term but a condition that people in a given community recognized when they saw it. The means were the same as those the community itself would employ, if its members were sufficiently determined, courageous, and authoritative. Detecting and apprehending criminals, by contrast, was a means to an end, not an end in itself; a judicial determination of guilt or innocence was the hoped-for result of the law-enforcement mode. From the first, the police were expected to follow rules defining that process, though states differed in how stringent the rules should be. The criminal-apprehension process was always understood to involve individual rights, the violation of which was unac-

MARCH 1982   THE ATLANTIC MONTHLY   PAGE 35

ceptable because it meant that the violating officer would be acting as a judge and jury—and that was not his job. Guilt or innocence was to be determined by universal standards under special procedures.

Ordinarily, no judge or jury ever sees the persons caught up in a dispute over the appropriate level of neighborhood order. That is true not only because most cases are handled informally on the street but also because no universal standards are available to settle arguments over disorder, and thus a judge may not be any wiser or more effective than a police officer. Until quite recently in many states, and even today in some places, the police make arrests on such charges as "suspicious person" or "vagrancy" or "public drunkenness"—charges with scarcely any legal meaning. These charges exist not because society wants judges to punish vagrants or drunks but because it wants an officer to have the legal tools to remove undesirable persons from a neighborhood when informal efforts to preserve order in the streets have failed.

Once we begin to think of all aspects of police work as involving the application of universal rules under special procedures, we inevitably ask what constitutes an "undesirable person" and why we should "criminalize" vagrancy or drunkenness. A strong and commendable desire to see that people are treated fairly makes us worry about allowing the police to rout persons who are undesirable by some vague or parochial standard. A growing and not-so-commendable utilitarianism leads us to doubt that any behavior that does not "hurt" another person should be made illegal. And thus many of us who watch over the police are reluctant to allow them to perform, in the only way they can, a function that every neighborhood desperately wants them to perform.

This wish to "decriminalize" disreputable behavior that "harms no one"—and thus remove the ultimate sanction the police can employ to maintain neighborhood order—is, we think, a mistake. Arresting a single drunk or a single vagrant who has harmed no identifiable person seems unjust, and in a sense it is. But failing to do anything about a score of drunks or a hundred vagrants may destroy an entire community. A particular rule that seems to make sense in the individual case makes no sense when it is made a universal rule and applied to all cases. It makes no sense because it fails to take into account the connection between one broken window left untended and a thousand broken windows. Of course, agencies other than the police could attend to the problems posed by drunks or the mentally ill, but in most communities—especially where the "deinstitutionalization" movement has been strong—they do not.

The concern about equity is more serious. We might agree that certain behavior makes one person more undesirable than another, but how do we ensure that age or skin color or national origin or harmless mannerisms will not also become the basis for distinguishing the undesirable from the desirable? How do we ensure, in short, that

the police do not become the agents of neighborhood bigotry?

We can offer no wholly satisfactory answer to this important question. We are not confident that there *is* a satisfactory answer, except to hope that by their selection, training, and supervision, the police will be inculcated with a clear sense of the outer limit of their discretionary authority. That limit, roughly, is this—the police exist to help regulate behavior, not to maintain the racial or ethnic purity of a neighborhood.

Consider the case of the Robert Taylor Homes in Chicago, one of the largest public-housing projects in the country. It is home for nearly 20,000 people, all black, and extends over ninety-two acres along South State Street. It was named after a distinguished black who had been, during the 1940s, chairman of the Chicago Housing Authority. Not long after it opened, in 1962, relations between project residents and the police deteriorated badly. The citizens felt that the police were insensitive or brutal; the police, in turn, complained of unprovoked attacks on them. Some Chicago officers tell of times when they were afraid to enter the Homes. Crime rates soared.

Today, the atmosphere has changed. Police–citizen relations have improved—apparently, both sides learned something from the earlier experience. Recently, a boy stole a purse and ran off. Several young persons who saw the theft voluntarily passed along to the police information on the identity and residence of the thief, and they did this publicly, with friends and neighbors looking on. But problems persist, chief among them the presence of youth gangs that terrorize residents and recruit members in the project. The people expect the police to "do something" about this, and the police are determined to do just that.

But do what? Though the police can obviously make arrests whenever a gang member breaks the law, a gang can form, recruit, and congregate without breaking the law. And only a tiny fraction of gang-related crimes can be solved by an arrest; thus, if an arrest is the only recourse for the police, the residents' fears will go unassuaged. The police will soon feel helpless, and the residents will again believe that the police "do nothing." What the police in fact do is to chase known gang members out of the project. In the words of one officer, "We kick ass." Project residents both know and approve of this. The tacit police–citizen alliance in the project is reinforced by the police view that the cops and the gangs are the two rival sources of power in the area, and that the gangs are not going to win.

None of this is easily reconciled with any conception of due process or fair treatment. Since both residents and gang members are black, race is not a factor. But it could be. Suppose a white project confronted a black gang, or vice versa. We would be apprehensive about the police taking sides. But the substantive problem remains the same: how can the police strengthen the informal social-control mechanisms of natural communities in order to minimize fear in public places? Law enforcement, per se, is no answer. A gang can weaken or destroy a community by standing about in a menacing fashion and speaking rudely to passersby without breaking the law.

WE HAVE DIFFICULTY THINKING ABOUT SUCH MATters, not simply because the ethical and legal issues are so complex but because we have become accustomed to thinking of the law in essentially individualistic terms. The law defines *my* rights, punishes *his* behavior, and is applied by *that* officer because of *this* harm. We assume, in thinking this way, that what is good for the individual will be good for the community, and what doesn't matter when it happens to one person won't matter if it happens to many. Ordinarily, those are plausible assumptions. But in cases where behavior that is tolerable to one person is intolerable to many others, the reactions of the others—fear, withdrawal, flight—may ultimately make matters worse for everyone, including the individual who first professed his indifference.

It may be their greater sensitivity to communal as opposed to individual needs that helps explain why the residents of small communities are more satisfied with their police than are the residents of similar neighborhoods in big cities. Elinor Ostrom and her co-workers at Indiana University compared the perception of police services in two poor, all-black Illinois towns—Phoenix and East Chicago Heights—with those of three comparable all-black neighborhoods in Chicago. The level of criminal victimization and the quality of police–community relations appeared to be about the same in the towns and the Chicago neighborhoods. But the citizens living in their own villages were much more likely than those living in the Chicago neighborhoods to say that they do not stay at home for fear of crime, to agree that the local police have "the right to take any action necessary" to deal with problems, and to agree that the police "look out for the needs of the average citizen." It is possible that the residents and the police of the small towns saw themselves as engaged in a collaborative effort to maintain a certain standard of communal life, whereas those of the big city felt themselves to be simply requesting and supplying particular services on an individual basis.

If this is true, how should a wise police chief deploy his meager forces? The first answer is that nobody knows for certain, and the most prudent course of action would be to try further variations on the Newark experiment, to see more precisely what works in what kinds of neighborhoods. The second answer is also a hedge—many aspects of order-maintenance in neighborhoods can probably best be handled in ways that involve the police minimally, if at all. A busy, bustling shopping center and a quiet, well-tended suburb may need almost no visible police presence. In both cases, the ratio of respectable to disreputable people is ordinarily so high as to make informal social control effective.

Even in areas that are in jeopardy from disorderly elements, citizen action without substantial police involvement may be sufficient. Meetings between teenagers who like to hang out on a particular corner and adults who want to use that corner might well lead to an amicable agreement on a set of rules about how many people can be allowed to congregate, where, and when.

Where no understanding is possible—or if possible, not observed—citizen patrols may be a sufficient response. There are two traditions of communal involvement in maintaining order. One, that of the "community watchmen," is as old as the first settlement of the New World. Until well into the nineteenth century, volunteer watchmen, not policemen, patrolled their communities to keep order. They did so, by and large, without taking the law into their own hands—without, that is, punishing persons or using force. Their presence deterred disorder or alerted the community to disorder that could not be deterred. There are hundreds of such efforts today in communities all across the nation. Perhaps the best known is that of the Guardian Angels, a group of unarmed young persons in distinctive berets and T-shirts, who first came to public attention when they began patrolling the New York City subways but who claim now to have chapters in more than thirty American cities. Unfortunately, we have little information about the effect of these groups on crime. It is possible, however, that whatever their effect on crime, citizens find their presence reassuring, and that they thus contribute to maintaining a sense of order and civility.

The second tradition is that of the "vigilante." Rarely a feature of the settled communities of the East, it was primarily to be found in those frontier towns that grew up in advance of the reach of government. More than 350 vigilante groups are known to have existed; their distinctive feature was that their members did take the law into their own hands, by acting as judge, jury, and often executioner as well as policeman. Today, the vigilante movement is conspicuous by its rarity, despite the great fear expressed by citizens that the older cities are becoming "urban frontiers." But some community-watchmen groups have skirted the line, and others may cross it in the future. An ambiguous case, reported in *The Wall Street Journal*, involved a citizens' patrol in the Silver Lake area of Belleville, New Jersey. A leader told the reporter, "We look for outsiders." If a few teenagers from outside the neighborhood enter it, "we ask them their business," he said. "If they say they're going down the street to see Mrs. Jones, fine, we let them pass. But then we follow them down the block to make sure they're really going to see Mrs. Jones."

THOUGH CITIZENS CAN DO A GREAT DEAL, THE POLICE are plainly the key to order-maintenance. For one thing, many communities, such as the Robert Taylor Homes, cannot do the job by themselves. For another, no citizen in a neighborhood, even an organized one, is likely to feel the sense of responsibility that wearing a badge confers. Psychologists have done many studies on why people fail to go to the aid of persons being attacked or seeking help, and they have learned that the cause is not "apathy" or "selfishness" but the absence of some plausible grounds for feeling that one must personally accept responsibility. Ironically, avoiding responsibility is easier when a lot of people are standing about. On streets and in public places, where order is so important, many people are likely to be "around," a fact that reduces the chance of any one person acting as the agent of the community. The police officer's uniform singles him out as a person who must accept responsibility if asked. In addition, officers, more easily than their fellow citizens, can be expected to distinguish between what is necessary to protect the safety of the street and what merely protects its ethnic purity.

But the police forces of America are losing, not gaining, members. Some cities have suffered substantial cuts in the number of officers available for duty. These cuts are not likely to be reversed in the near future. Therefore, each department must assign its existing officers with great care. Some neighborhoods are so demoralized and crime-ridden as to make foot patrol useless; the best the police can do with limited resources is respond to the enormous number of calls for service. Other neighborhoods are so stable and serene as to make foot patrol unnecessary. The key is to identify neighborhoods at the tipping point—where the public order is deteriorating but not unreclaimable, where the streets are used frequently but by apprehensive people, where a window is likely to be broken at any time, and must quickly be fixed if all are not to be shattered.

Most police departments do not have ways of systematically identifying such areas and assigning officers to them. Officers are assigned on the basis of crime rates (meaning that marginally threatened areas are often stripped so that police can investigate crimes in areas where the situation is hopeless) or on the basis of calls for service (despite the fact that most citizens do not call the police when they are merely frightened or annoyed). To allocate patrol wisely, the department must look at the neighborhoods and decide, from first-hand evidence, where an additional officer will make the greatest difference in promoting a sense of safety.

One way to stretch limited police resources is being tried in some public-housing projects. Tenant organizations hire off-duty police officers for patrol work in their buildings. The costs are not high (at least not per resident), the officer likes the additional income, and the residents feel safer. Such arrangements are probably more successful than hiring private watchmen, and the Newark experiment helps us understand why. A private security guard may deter crime or misconduct by his presence, and he may go to the aid of persons needing help, but he may well not intervene—that is, control or drive away—someone challenging community standards. Being a sworn officer—a "real cop"—seems to give one the confidence, the sense of duty, and the aura of authority necessary to perform this difficult task.

Patrol officers might be encouraged to go to and from duty stations on public transportation and, while on the bus or subway car, enforce rules about smoking, drinking, disorderly conduct, and the like. The enforcement need involve nothing more than ejecting the offender (the offense, after all, is not one with which a booking officer or a judge wishes to be bothered). Perhaps the random but relentless maintenance of standards on buses would lead to conditions on buses that approximate the level of civility we now take for granted on airplanes.

But the most important requirement is to think that to maintain order in precarious situations is a vital job. The police know this is one of their functions, and they also believe, correctly, that it cannot be done to the exclusion of criminal investigation and responding to calls. We may have encouraged them to suppose, however, on the basis of our oft-repeated concerns about serious, violent crime, that they will be judged exclusively on their capacity as crime-fighters. To the extent that this is the case, police administrators will continue to concentrate police personnel in the highest-crime areas (though not necessarily in the areas most vulnerable to criminal invasion), emphasize their training in the law and criminal apprehension (and not their training in managing street life), and join too quickly in campaigns to decriminalize "harmless" behavior (though public drunkenness, street prostitution, and pornographic displays can destroy a community more quickly than any team of professional burglars).

Above all, we must return to our long-abandoned view that the police ought to protect communities as well as individuals. Our crime statistics and victimization surveys measure individual losses, but they do not measure communal losses. Just as physicians now recognize the importance of fostering health rather than simply treating illness, so the police—and the rest of us—ought to recognize the importance of maintaining, intact, communities without broken windows. ⊔

[17]

BRIT. J. CRIMINOL. Vol. 27 No. 1 WINTER 1987

THINKING ABOUT EFFECTIVENESS

MIKE HOUGH (*London*)*

AT one level, everyone recognises that the remit of the police is a broad one. The 1962 Royal Commission on the Police identified very general duties, such as "maintaining law and order" and "preventing crime"; more specific ones, such as detection, prosecution, traffic control; and others which were stated only vaguely, such as "coping with major or minor emergencies". That there can be conflict between these different functions is also well recognised. Lord Scarman (1981), for example, and the Commissioner of the Metropolitan Police (Metropolitan Police, 1984) have both offered statements of principle about the balance to be struck between law enforcement and order maintenance. More prosaically, there is the clichéd complaint of the motorist stopped for traffic offences: "Why waste time on me when you could be out catching criminals?"

But when it is effectiveness that is at issue, the police are too often judged by criteria which are one-dimensional and narrow. "Effective" tends to be used to mean "effective in dealing with crime"; statistics of recorded crime and clear-up are still the staple indicators used in, for example, parliamentary debate, the media and even some Chief Constables' annual reports. Management technology has so far been premised on crime-fighting goals (see Hough, 1980). And certainly the man-in-the-street would say that effective policing means getting to grips with crime, and would subscribe to the commonsense theory that this can be done through strategies of deterrence. People would offer a variety of reasons for the failure of the police to get to grips with crime, but the most common of these would be that the police force is undermanned.

However, a now quite substantial body of research suggests only limited scope for the police either to catch more offenders or, more generally, to deter people from crime. The research implies that the police have a more limited *capability* for crime control than is generally assumed, and raises the possibility that they are being held responsible for objectives beyond their control. The first part of this paper summarises research on conventional crime control; and the second part examines some of the implications of this research: the ways in which conceptions of police function and police effectiveness could be adjusted to take the research into account.

But first, some definitional ground-clearing is needed. In this paper, "crime" refers to offences at the more serious end of the spectrum, ranging from burglary and mugging to bank robbery, serious wounding, rape and murder. Vandalism, rowdyism, brawling and other behaviour at the margins of criminality are not embraced by the definition. The "conventional methods" to deal with crime are routine uniformed patrol, on foot or in cars, and routine detective work; the definition excludes largely

* Principal Research Officer, Research and Planning Unit, Home Office.

THINKING ABOUT EFFECTIVENESS

unresearched innovations, which are discussed in the second part of the paper. Forbearance is asked of those readers who feel that "conventional crime control" is too much of an Aunt Sally; the target has been set up in this way because the most favoured solutions for rising crime include its key elements: more patrols back on the beat and more detective effort.

Research on Crime Control

Work on police effectiveness in dealing with crime was energised in America by the President's Crime Commission (1967), which led to a decade and a half of vigorous research sponsorship. Work in Britain has proceeded on a much smaller scale and has been heavily influenced by American research. Findings are reviewed in Morris and Heal (1981), Clarke and Hough (1984) and Burrows and Tarling (forthcoming). The summary below deals first with the scope for catching more offenders and goes on to discuss the deterrent impact of policing strategies.

1. *Catching offenders*

Offenders can be caught red-handed or detected after the event. A small proportion are apprehended by the police whilst committing their crime; for example, Bottomley and Coleman (1981) estimated that only 6 per cent. of recorded crimes were discovered in this way by uniformed patrols (though officers can determine quite largely how many arrests they make for motoring offences and "regulatory offences" involving drunkeness or disorderly conduct). Nor can uniformed patrols improve arrest rates significantly by strategies of fast response to calls for assistance (Bieck, 1977; Spelman and Brown, 1981; Ekblom and Heal, 1982). Whilst a proportion of incidents require emergency response, few of these are unequivocally criminal. Burglaries, robberies, rapes and woundings are usually reported well after the event by victims or witnesses, leaving the police with the task of detection.

The measure most often used to assess detective effectiveness is the clear-up rate. At present, the police can put an offender's name to a crime in a third of recorded cases. Clear-up rates can be determined by factors other than detective success. The proportion of burglaries finding their way into police records has grown since the early 1970s (Hough and Mayhew, 1985) and the same may be true for other crimes. The effect of this will have been to depress the clear-up rate by enlarging its denominator, recorded crime. By the same token, comparison of clear-up rates across areas can also mislead, as different forces record different proportions of crime (Farrington and Dowds, 1985). Setting aside measurement problems of this sort, Burrows and Tarling (1982) and Burrows (1986) have shown that some areas devote much more effort than others to strategies of "secondary detections" (T.I.C.s, prison write-offs and so forth), in contrast to "primary detections", which generally lead to prosecution or cautioning; the higher clear-up rates which secondary detections achieve do not as a result reflect higher arrest rates.

71

MIKE HOUGH

Research suggests that the scope for increasing rates of *primary* detections seems limited. In most primary detections, the offender's identity is plain from the outset: victims or witnesses can say who did it, or else the offender is detained at the scene of the crime or is clearly implicated in some other way. If such information is not readily available,the prospects for detection are in most cases bleak, until or unless the crime turns up later on a list of T.I.C.s. Of course, crimes can be solved even where there are no immediate leads; with enough time, effort and (sometimes) luck, the police have been successful in tracking down notorious offenders.

In other words, most crimes fall into two categories: the readily detectable and those which are solvable only at considerable cost and effort. The proportion falling into the middle category, where extra effort could bring improvements in clear-up rates, is probably small, though precisely how small is unclear. Crust (1975) argued that the cost of the additional manpower that would be needed to make significant inroads into the clear-up rate was unrealistic. An American study estimated that only 3 per cent. of primary detections arose from "investigative effort where organisation, training or skill could make any conceivable difference" (Greenwood *et al.*, 1977). And Burrows (1986) found that the amount of investigative time devoted to cases of burglary in six different localities was unrelated to arrest rates.

On the other hand, experiments where detectives have shared their investigative duties with uniformed officers have shown improvements in clear-up rates (Bloch and Bell, 1976; Elliot, 1978). There is some evidence that case-screening pays off (Eck, 1979). Tarling and Burrows (1982) found a small but positive relationship between manpower levels and clear-up. Thus there may be *some* scope for improving primary detection rates; just how much scope is unknown, but the likelihood is that it is marginal, at least within realistic levels of investment.

2. *Deterring people from crime*

Common-sense theories of the impact of the police on crime are premised on deterrence: people are deterred from crime by the threat of being caught by the police; more police (either patrolling or investigating crimes) should increase the level of threat and thus reduce crime. The durability of such ideas depends partly on their intuitive appeal and partly on their resistance to empirical test: outside of experimental settings, the failure of extra manpower to curb crime can always be attributed to extraneous factors such as inadequate amenities, unemployment, declining standards, and so on.

However, experimental studies of both mobile and foot patrol have rarely found any relationship between patrol levels and crime, except when patrol density is maintained at saturation levels. The best known is the Kansas City Preventive Patrol Experiment (Kelling *et al.*, 1974), which showed that a two- or three-fold increase in the level of vehicle patrol had no measurable impact on crime. Whilst there is some question whether the experimental conditions were successfully maintained, the most probable

THINKING ABOUT EFFECTIVENESS

explanation of the findings is that people simply failed to notice increases of this size. Similar findings for foot patrol were found in a British study (Bright, 1969); provided there was *some* level of patrol, the precise patrol level seemed not to affect crime rates. The Newark Foot Patrol Experiment (Police Foundation, 1981) also found that introducing or withdrawing foot patrols from an area did not affect crime levels—though in contrast to the Kansas study, residents were aware of changes: foot patrols appeared to reduce people's fear of crime.

Of course there must be a threshold of police presence above which crime is reduced; several experiments of saturation policing, and rather more anecdotes, support this view (see, for example, Chaiken *et al.*, 1974; Schnelle *et al.*, 1977; Wilson, 1975). However, high patrol density can only be maintained in localised areas and at considerable cost; with the likelihood of displacement to adjacent areas.

Experimental research has paid no attention to the preventive effects of increased detection rates, presumably because, on the one hand, improvements in investigative performance are hard to achieve, and, on the other, an area's detection rates cannot be depressed for experimental purposes. However, it is hard to see how offenders would learn of the marginal changes in clear-up rates which lie within the bounds of the possible. And even if they knew that the chances of detection had increased, it is unclear that they would act on this.

In addition to the rather piecemeal approach of experimental research, there is a growing body of econometric studies which attempt to model the impact of changes in police manpower on reported crime rates and clear-up rates, and the impact of changes in clear-up rate on crime rates. These analyses are limited by the absence of any valid indicator of the extent of crime, relying instead on measures of recorded crime. They have yielded no consistent relationships between manpower and recorded crime levels, suggesting, if nothing else, that this is neither simple nor invariant. They usually show that areas with high clear-up rates have low crime rates, but are unable to say whether this is a causal relationship (Carr-Hill and Stern, 1979; Joyce, 1985).

Responding to the Research

It would be wrong to conclude from these studies that the police are without impact on crime. When the police have been removed from the streets, as in police strikes, for example, widespread crime and disorder can result. But the weight of research evidence is that further expenditure on conventional deterrent strategies will secure only small gains at the margin. One response to this message is simply to "shoot the messenger". This can be done by challenging either the generalisability or the methodology of a piece of work. Certainly one must be alive to the risks of importing wholesale to Britain the results of American research. Certainly, too, social research deploys blunt instruments, which may not be sensitive to small changes. Social policy often sets its sights at only marginal improvements,

MIKE HOUGH

and there is a world of difference between "nothing works" and "nothing works very well". But if the research commands any credence, it calls into question the extent to which the remit of the police should be thought of in terms of crime control. The less the capacity of the police to affect crime rates and clear ups, the less reasonable it is to hold them responsible for crime control and to judge their effectiveness in these terms.

It is one thing to say that conventional methods of crime control do not achieve much impact, another thing to sketch the nature and limits of their real capabilities or competences. The remainder of this paper discusses under five headings some of the possible responses to the limitations of conventional methods of crime control. Of course, it is not the logic of research findings alone that has driven people to adopt these positions; set against the other factors which shape policing politics, the voice of research is small (see Weatheritt, 1986). And the classification is only a heuristic device: subtle and complex ideas have been caricatured to make them fit into one of the five categories below.

1. *The technological "fix"*

The most obvious position to adopt in the face of these negative research findings is to call for better deterrent strategies. Existing ones may have limited impact, but this does not mean that every deterrent approach is doomed to failure; it would be surprising if there were no room for technological solutions to detection. The pursuit of the technological fix leaves unchallenged both the goals of crime control and the means of achieving these—deterrent threat; it aims to extend the capabilities of the police in producing this.

New techniques may well improve clear-up rates. There are, for example, promising methods for analysing physical evidence such as computerised fingerprint searches ("automatic fingerprint retrieval" or A.F.R.) and D.N.A. "fingerprinting". Information technology also has obvious potential. Computerised information systems should allow effective crime analysis: sifting clues, locating shared features of crimes, identifying patterns of offending and pools of suspects. Such applications are being explored through the Police National Computer system, using crime analysis conducted with local information systems, and by means of H.O.L.M.E.S. (the Home Office (Large) Major Enquiry System for the investigation of major and serial crimes).

Measured in terms of research and development budgets, the search for technological solutions commands considerable priority. The investment could pay off by significantly altering the ratio between crimes which can be solved through detective effort and those which are (barring good luck and T.I.C.s) insoluble. Against this, pessimists would anticipate an expensive game of "technological leapfrog", whereby offenders learn to defeat each new method as it is introduced.

2. *Encouraging the flow of information from the public*

If technological solutions are a way of amplifying information which is

74

THINKING ABOUT EFFECTIVENESS

available to the police, a related approach is to try to stimulate the flow of information about crime from the public. A tenet of Community Policing (Alderson, 1979, 1984) has been that better relations between police and public will yield improved intelligence about crime. It is also a central part of the Metropolitan Police strategy. Team policing and neighbourhood policing also embrace this concept.

The idea in slightly different clothes also has the support of "realist criminologists" (Kinsey *et al.*, 1986; Jones *et al.*, 1986). In Community Policing, the police set out to coopt the community into *their* fight against crime; for the "realist criminologists", the community must coopt the police into *their* fight against crime. The "realist" argument is that the public expect a crime control role from the police, and police effectiveness should be measured in these terms; the primary indicator of performance should be the proportion of crimes committed (rather than recorded) which are cleared up. A more accountable and controlled style of policing, it is argued, should improve public confidence in the police; this should yield a better flow of information to the police and consequent improvements in the clear-up rate.

Improving the perceived legitimacy of police authority is an undeniably valuable goal—arguably, the key to policing. But it is questionable how much this would actually release usable criminal intelligence currently withheld from the police. Certainly the Broadwater Farm Inquiry (1986) found that as many as 37 per cent. of residents on the estate said they would be unwilling to help identify a mugger and half would be unprepared to give evidence in court. But it is unclear how often people actually find themselves in possession of information which forces these choices on them. Nor has research examined whether *primary* clear-up rates vary according to the temperature of relations between police and public; if anything, it would seem that areas with high clear-up rates are distinguished from others by the ability of their police to obtain evidence not from the public but from interrogation and lengthier investigative methods (see Burrows, 1986).

3. *Strengthening informal social control*

This position assumes, uncontroversially, that mechanisms of informal social control play a far greater part than formal policing in determining crime levels, and, more controversially, that the police should extend their role in supporting and strengthening such mechanisms. A wide range of strategies can be placed under this umbrella: schools liaison work to promote positive attitudes to the law and the police among the young; youth work in more informal settings but with the same aims; schemes to resuscitate a sense of community; more specific schemes to mobilize "defensive" behaviour among residents, such as Neighbourhood Watch and crime prevention programmes; coordinating local authority planning and design against crime; and coopting shops, businesses and other organisations in crime prevention. Position 3 overlaps with Position 2 insofar as it calls not for a specific set of activities to be pursued by

MIKE HOUGH

designated officers, but for an overall style of policing aimed at achieving good relations between police and public. The difference is to be found in the goals: Position 2 sees good relations as a lever for criminal intelligence, whilst Position 3 is in pursuit of "hearts and minds": increasing people's commitment to law-abiding norms.

As a package, such strategies are most associated with Community Policing, which ascribes to the police a catalytic function in supporting community action through leadership, education and coordination (see, for example, Alderson, 1984). "Situational prevention" can also be linked with Position 3, insofar as it ascribes to the police a more interventionist role in encouraging crime prevention (see Clarke and Mayhew, 1980). And the need for policing strategies to be dove-tailed with informal methods of control has been identified by Shapland and Vagg (1985).

Where Position 3 tactics are clearly defined and are expected to work over short timescales, their effectiveness can be monitored as readily as deterrent strategies: it is possible but not simple to do so. Some tactics, however, offer benefits only in the long term: work with school children, for example, or attempts to regenerate a sense of community. Plausible though they may be, monitoring these latter is a researcher's, and manager's, nightmare (see Weatheritt, 1983). It would be overoptimistic to quantify a causal link between the intervention and a fall in crime, even if such a link exists. Whether it is for the police to try to regulate informal mechanisms of social control raises questions not simply about their competence to achieve the desired effect, but also about the appropriateness of so doing. When crime-control through enforcement and deterrence is seen as the primary police task, the criminal law fairly clearly defines the boundaries of police responsibilities; but the more that their task is defined in Position 3 terms, the more open-ended it becomes.

4. *"Broken windows"*

As questions have been raised about the crime-fighting capabilities of the police, more attention has focused on the task of order maintenance: the role of "peace officer" identified by Banton (1964). The right balance between law enforcement and order maintenance has, of course, been debated for years. Recently, however, a justification for extending or consolidating the order-maintenance function has been offered in terms of the long-term gain in crime control: the so-called "Broken windows" hypothesis which took its name from the title of an article by J. Q. Wilson and George Kelling (1982).

Wilson and Kelling suggested that certain levels of disorderly behaviour (on the part of drunks, tramps, rowdy youths, prostitutes and other disreputables) can trigger a spiral of neighbourhood decline, with increased fear of crime, migration of the law-abiding from the area, weakening of informal social control and, ultimately, increases in serious crime. According to this view, beat policemen should be assigned long term to areas at risk to break the spiral, clamping down on the "incivilities" which lead to decline. The "Broken Windows" hypothesis thus shares with

76

THINKING ABOUT EFFECTIVENESS

Position 2 the aim of nurturing informal control mechanisms, but offers a distinctive set of means for doing this. Whether informal control mechanisms are responsive to the policing of disorder is unclear. Research has certainly shown correlations between crime and both fear of crime and the presence of "incivilities" (for example, Skogan, 1983; Hope and Hough, 1986), but the causal sequence specified by Wilson and Kelling has yet to be established. In the only experimental evaluation carried out to date, aggressive policing of incivilities was not found to reduce fear (Pate *et al.*, 1986).

Other factors may limit the viability of the approach. Wilson and Kelling have always recognised that this style of policing is a recipe for corruption and for abuse of power (Kelling, 1985). (Many of the pre- and post-war reforms in American policing aimed precisely to disentangle the police and local communities from relationships which were too close and consequently too venal and too inequitable). And some of the appealing images of order maintenance: street-wise yet avuncular cops called Kelly (or Dixon) keeping their "regulars" in line, mask the scope for spiralling distrust and conflict between police and policed. Especially in heterogeneous urban communities, which lack firm consensus about the nature of disorder, aggressive beat policing could be a recipe for disaster.

5. *Shifting the focus from crime*

The four positions sketched out so far have all retained crime control as the core function of the police, and have varied only in the type of strategy they advocate. A final option is to reformulate police functions so as to give a less central place to crime control.

It has long been recognised that the police not only deal with crime, but also handle non-criminal disorder (large and small) and provide emergency services to people other than victims of crime. Many researchers have documented the extent to which police time is taken up by incidents of disorder and a variety of other demands which bear at least a passing resemblance to the work of the welfare or social services. In general, this work can be criticised for classifying incidents not according to their intrinsic characteristics, but according to the means used by the police to deal with them—a highly contingent affair (Reiner, 1985). This has distracted attention away from the characteristics shared by these incidents which make them a matter for the police.

The ideas of Egon Bittner (1970, 1974) have been influential, especially over the last five years, in offering a perspective which simultaneously de-emphasises crime control and integrates the diverse elements of policing. He stresses not "disorder" or "service" but "emergency" as the unifying aspect of police work: the police characteristically deal with "*Something that ought not to be happening and about which someone had better do something now*". Bittner's dictum setting out what it is that makes this work for the police is much quoted. The specific competence of the police is contained in their capacity for decisive action, which

MIKE HOUGH

"... derives from the authority to overpower opposition in the 'there-and-then' of the situation of action. The policeman, and the policeman alone, is equipped, entitled, and required to deal with every exigency in which force may have to be used to meet it". (Bittner, 1974, p.35).

This sort of analysis entails a considerable broadening of perspective on effectiveness. From the crime control perspective, police work can be seen as a process of signalling and gathering *information* (Manning, 1977); police are trying simultaneously to identify people who already have committed crimes and to communicate a persuasive threat to potential offenders. Most calls for service, according to this view, are a distraction from the task in hand.

From the "emergency" perspective, by contrast, the encounters between police and public are the stuff of effectiveness, and the use of police powers becomes central in assessing this. Whether they perform effectively turns on their success in handling incidents which contain a potential for violence. The perspective thus draws into sharper focus the fact that coercive force, power and authority are concepts central to the assessment of effectiveness; something which is rendered invisible when the core police function is seen as crime control. This is not to say that the police should abandon crime control objectives; on the contrary, the task of detection falls to the police precisely because at its heart, the point of arrest, lies the potential for violence. If this were not so, criminal investigation could readily be hived off to private security firms.

Empirical research has only secured a toe-hold in this area so far (see Muir, 1977; Bayley and Bittner, 1985; Southgate, 1986). One set of questions concerns the effectiveness of *tactics* in handling encounters, what works and what doesn't in achieving a satisfactory outcome. The focus on crime fighting tactics has tended to distract attention away from fundamental questions about the "craft" of policing: styles of handling power and authority, and standards by which one can judge good or effective police work. Then there are issues at a more strategic level: what boundaries are to be drawn to delimit the range of incidents in which the police ought to become involved? what constitutes a satisfactory outcome in dealing with different types of incident—domestic disputes, for example, or bar fights or rowdiness? no repeats that evening? or that week? or that month? and what balance should be struck between *reactive* and *proactive* intervention?

Policing Futures

This paper has summarised research suggesting that the capacity of the police to control crime through conventional methods is limited and has set out a variety of responses to this message. The first four retain the centrality of crime control as a police function, either refining deterrent strategies or offering alternatives to deterrence. The fifth position involves not refining crime-fighting strategies but re-conceptualising police function, so that crime control becomes a less central objective.

THINKING ABOUT EFFECTIVENESS

None of the five options can be discarded at present; all hold out a degree of promise, as well as risks. But to this author, at least, the need seems pressing for *some* adjustment in the way that people think about policing objectives. We should not continue to set unrealistic goals of crime control for the police service. In the first place, it is dangerous to hold the police to account for objectives which are impossible within legal constraints. Secondly, judging police performance in terms of crime control will deflect the energies of managers from those functions which are within the capacity of the police. And finally, pinning misplaced hopes for crime control on the police will distract people from the search for effective strategies for dealing with the problem.

To be pessimistic, there is not a great likelihood of change. Certainly there have been a number of recent attempts to inject a more purposive managerial style into policing, such as the Home Office Circular on Efficiency and Effectiveness, and the "policing by objectives" movement (Lubans and Edgar, 1979; Goldstein, 1979; Butler, 1984). But these have not in themselves been prescriptive about police functions, and the emphasis they place on rendering objectives explicit may by default make objectives of crime control even more salient. For the pressures to define police functions in terms of crime control are considerable. The crime-fighting role meets with least opposition across the spectrum of policing politics. It promises accountability, measurable output and popular consent. It offers clarity of purpose, which carries a greater premium than precision in both political and media discussion of policing. And finally, there is the inexorable demand from the public that the police get to grips with crime; people have for years been encouraged to regard this as a reasonable expectation, and they will not readily change their minds.

REFERENCES

ALDERSON, J. (1979). *Policing Freedom*. Plymouth: McDonald and Evans.

ALDERSON, J. (1984). *Law and Disorder*. London: Hamish Hamilton.

BANTON, M. (1964). *The Policeman in the Community*. London: Tavistock.

BAYLEY, D.H. and BITTNER, E. (1985). "Learning the skills of policing", in special edition of *Journal of Law and Contemporary Social Problems*: "Discretion in Law Enforcement" ed. by R.J. Allen, 35-60.

BIECK, W. (1977). *Response Time Analysis*. Kansas City Police Department.

BITTNER, E. (1970). *The Function of the Police in Modern Society*. Washington: U.S. G.P.O. (Republished 1975 by James Ronson, N.Y.).

BITTNER, E. (1974). "Florence Nightingale in Pursuit of Willie Sutton: a theory of the police", in Jacob, H. (ed.) *The Potential for Reform in Criminal Justice*. Beverly Hills: Sage. 17-44.

MIKE HOUGH

BLOCH, P.B. and BELL, J. (1976). *Managing Investigations: the Rochester System.* Washington D.C.: Police Foundation.

BOTTOMLEY, K. and COLEMAN, C. (1981). *Understanding Crime Rates.* Farnborough, England: Gower.

BRIGHT, J.A. (1969). *The Beat Patrol Experiment.* Home Office Police Research and Development Branch. (Unpublished).

BROADWATER FARM INQUIRY. (1986). *The Broadwater Farm Inquiry: report of the Independent Inquiry into disturbance of October 1985 at the Broadwater Farm Estate, Tottenham.* London: Eagle House Press.

BURROWS, J. (1986). *Investigating Burglary: the measurement of police performance.* Home Office Research Study Number 88. London: H.M.S.O.

BURROWS, J. (1986). *Burglary: Police Actions and Victim Views.* Home Office Research and Planning Unit Paper.

BURROWS, J. and TARLING, R. (1982). *Clearing Up Crime.* Home Office Research Study No. 73. London: H.M.S.O.

BURROWS, J. and TARLING, R. (forthcoming). *The Investigation of Crime in England and Wales.* London: Home Office Research Unit.

BUTLER, A. (1984). *Police Management.* Farnborough: Gower.

CARR-HILL, N.A. and STERN, N.H. (1979). *Crime, the Police and Criminal Statistics.* London: Academic Press.

CHAIKEN, J.M., LAWLESS, M.A. and STEVENSON, K.A. (1974). *The Impact of Police Activities on Crime: robberies in the New York City Subway System.* Santa Monica, California: The Rand Corporation.

CLARKE, R.V.G. and HOUGH, J.M. (1984). *Crime and Police Effectiveness.* Home Office Research Study Number 79. London: H.M.S.O.

CLARKE, R.V.G. and MAYHEW, P. (eds.) (1980). *Designing Out Crime.* London: H.M.S.O.

CRUST, P.E. (1975). *Criminal Investigation Project.* Home Office Police Research Services Unit (unpublished).

ECK, J.E. (1979). *Managing Case Assignment: the burglary investigation decision model replication.* Washington, D.C.: Police Executive Research Forum.

EKBLOM, P. and HEAL, K. (1982). *The Police Response to Calls from the Public.* Research and Planning Unit Paper 9. London: Home Office.

ELLIOTT, J.E. (1978). "Crime Control teams: an alternative to the conventional operational procedure of investigating crimes". *Journal of Criminal Justice,* **6**, 1, 11-23.

FARRINGTON, D.P. and DOWDS, A. (1985). "Disentangling criminal behaviour and police reaction". In Farrington, D.P. and Gunn, J. (Eds.) *Reactions to Crime: the public, the police, courts and prisons.* Chichester: John Wiley.

GOLDSTEIN, H. (1979). "Improving policing: a problem-oriented approach". *Crime and Delinquency,* 25 April, 236-258.

GREENWOOD, P.W., CHAIKEN, J.M. and PETERSILIA, J. (1977). *The Criminal Investigation Process.* Lexington, Mass: D.C. Heath.

HOPE, T. and HOUGH, M. (forthcoming) "Area, crime and incivilities: findings from the British Crime Survey." In Hope, T. (Ed.). *Communities and Crime Reduction,* Proceedings of conference at Cambridge, July 1986.

HOUGH, M. (1980). "Managing with less technology: the impact of information technology on police management." *British Journal of Criminology,* **20**, 4, 344-357.

HOUGH, M. and MAYHEW, P. (1985). *Taking account of crime: key findings from the British Crime Survey.* Home Office Research Study, no. 85. London: H.M.S.O.

JONES, T., MACLEAN, B. and YOUNG, Y. (1986). *The Islington Crime Survey: crime, victimisation and policing in inner-city London.* Aldershot: Gower.

JOYCE, M.A.S. (1985). *Spending on law and order: the Police Service in England and Wales.* N.I.E.S.R. Discussion Paper No. 104.

KELLING, G. (1985). "Order maintenance, the quality of urban life, and the police: a line of argument." in Geller, W. (ed.) *Police Leadership in America.* New York: Praeger. 296-308.

THINKING ABOUT EFFECTIVENESS

KELLING, G., PATE, T., DIECKMAN, D. and BROWN, C. (1974). *The Kansas City Preventive Patrol Experiment.* Washington, D.C.: Police Foundation.

KINSEY, R., LEA, J. and YOUNG, J. (1986). *Losing the fight against crime.* Oxford: Blackwell.

LUBANS, V.A. and EDGAR. J.M. (1979). *Policing by Objectives.* Hartford, Conn: Social Development Corporation.

MANNING, P.K. (1977). *Police work: the social organization of policing.* Cambridge, Mass.: M.I.T. Press.

METROPOLITAN POLICE (1984). *The Policing Principles of the Metropolitan Police.* London: Metropolitan Police.

MORRIS, P. and HEAL, K. (1981). *Crime Control and the Police.* Home Office Research Study No 67. London: H.M.S.O.

MUIR, W.K. (1977). *Police: Streetcorner Politicians.* Chicago: University of Chicago Press.

PATE, T., WYCOFF, M., SKOGAN, W. and SHERMAN, L. (1986). *Reducing Crime in Houston and Newark: a summary report.* Washington: Police Foundation.

POLICE FOUNDATION. (1981). *The Newark Foot Patrol Experiment.* Washington D.C.: Police Foundation.

PRESIDENT'S COMMISSION ON LAW ENFORCEMENT AND THE ADMINISTRATION OF JUSTICE (1967). *The Challenge of Crime in a Free Society.* Washington D.C.: U.S. Government Printing Office.

REINER, R. (1985a). *The Politics of the Police.* Brighton: Wheatsheaf.

REINER, R. (1985b). "Policing strikes." *Policing.* Vol 1, no 3, 138-48.

REINER, R. (1985c). "Retrospect on the riots." *New Society.* October 25.

SCARMAN, THE RT. HON. THE LORD, OBE (1975). *The Red Lion Square Disorders of 15 June 1974.* London: H.M.S.O.

SCHNELLE, J.E., KIRCHNER, R.E., CASEY, J.D., USELTOR, P.H. and MCNEES, M.P. (1977). "Patrol evaluation research: a multiple baseline analysis of saturation police patrolling during day and night hours." *Journal of Applied Behaviour Analysis,* **10**, 33-40.

SCHAPLAND, J. and VAGG, J. (1985). *Social control and policing in rural and urban areas.* Final report to the Home Office. Oxford: Centre for Criminological Research.

SKOGAN, W. (1983). "Disorder, crime and community deterioration: a test of the Wilson-Kelling hypothesis." Paper presented at IXth International Congress on Criminology, Vienna.

SOUTHGATE, P. (1986). *Police-Public Encounters.* Home Office Research Study No. 90. London: H.M.S.O.

SPELMAN, W. and BROWN, D. (1981). *Calling the Police: Citizen Reporting of Serious Crime.* Washington, D.C.: Police Executive Research Forum.

TARLING, R. and BURROWS, J. (1986 in press). "The Work of Detectives." *Police Journal.*

WEATHERITT, M. (1983). "Community policing: does it work and how do we know? A review of research. " in Bennett, T. (ed.) *The Future of Policing: papers presented to 15th Cropwood Round-Table Conference December 1982.* Cropwood Conference Series No. 15. Cambridge: Institute of Criminology. 127-45.

WEATHERITT, M. (1986). *Innovations in Policing.* London: Croom helm.

WILSON, J.Q. (1975). *Thinking about Crime.* New York: Basic Books.

WILSON, J.Q. and KELLING, G.L. (1982). "Broken windows" *The Atlantic Monthly*, March, 29-38.

[18]

BRIT. J. CRIMINOL. Vol. 27 No. 1 WINTER 1987

ASSESSING POLICE EFFECTIVENESS – FUTURE PROSPECTS

MICHAEL CHATTERTON (*Manchester*)*

Introduction

AT the present time, our knowledge about police work is extremely limited. We know even less about police effectiveness. It would be unreasonable to draw any other conclusions about police effectiveness at this stage (Engstad and Evans, 1980; Kelling *et al.*, 1980).

It is for this reason that I consider the conclusions stated in the previous article about the effectiveness of the police in the apprehension of offenders and the prevention of crime to be premature. I do not dispute them *a priori* because the possibility must be left open that they may subsequently *be proved* to be valid. What this article does challenge is the claim that it is possible to support them on the basis of the evidence currently available to us.

This does not amount to "shooting the messenger" as Hough suggests, but rather an unwillingness to accept the message at face value. The approach advocated in this article is one which leads us to interview "the messenger" at length, and to ascertain the quality of his evidence—most importantly, to ask him why he considers the battle was lost and how it might have been won. Could the strategies and tactics have worked successfully if used differently? Did other factors affect the result?

I shall argue that this is the type of investigation that needs to be carried out into police effectiveness. There are not enough studies which *explain* the level of output achieved by police units. Insufficient time has been spent on *analysis of data* to establish whether different results might have been achieved if the organisation and parts of its environment had been managed in a different way. The instances are far and few between where this kind of data-based enquiry has prompted a piece of *action research* where an attempt was made to eliminate or reduce the effects of the factors which obtruded on the previous occasion, together with the careful monitoring of the change process (Greenwood, 1980).

The debates about the British Government's Financial Management Initiative, the Home Office Circular 114/1983, the feasibility of policing by objectives and other rational management models, have thrown up a number of propositions about policing which are drawn from earlier research and which can be interrogated in a similar fashion (Butler, 1985; 1986; Sinclair and Miller, 1984; Waddington, 1986; Weatheritt, 1986). We must ask whether the influence of these features of policing is as constant and universal as we might be encouraged to believe? Can their influence be mitigated if other factors are altered?

* Senior Lecturer, Department of Social Administration, University of Manchester.

ASSESSING POLICE EFFECTIVENESS – FUTURE PROSPECTS

There will not be space here to discuss in detail all such propositions but a number will be addressed which relate to issues of whether the police can ever be effective, whether their effectiveness can be measured, and whether police managers can identify prospectively, and stand any reasonable chance of attaining, specified objectives. These issues are often fused in discussions of police effectiveness.

Problems of Evaluation

There are several problems particular to the evaluation of policing, which make this a more complicated task than the evaluation of the effectiveness of some other organisations:

1) The police organisation has a multiple goal structure. Resource deployment is hence a complex task, since effectiveness in one area may mean ineffectiveness in another. The link between ends and means is correspondingly complex. The means to attain one end, even if used successfully, may make effective achievement of another more unlikely. In what way can the organisation then be described as "effective" (Bunyard, 1978)?

2) Generalised statements of objectives such as "keeping the peace" are so broad they can be used to legitimise courses of action which conflict. For example, strategies of strict and lenient law enforcement can both be justified by appeal to the aim of "keeping the peace". Against which situational derivation from these abstract prescriptions should effectiveness then be assessed (Bradley *et al.*, 1986)?

3) The public regard the police as an available resource to call upon in any crisis situation. This makes resource allocation and prioritisation difficult. There may be no alternative to investing huge resources of manpower into activities considered unlikely to produce the desired result, such as murder hunts. Such activities remind us that policing has a symbolic as well as an instrumental significance (Bittner, 1970; Manning, 1977; Punch, 1979). Some politicians aggravate the conflict between goals by their uncompromising demands for police effectiveness in apprehending criminals, less expenditure on policing and more legal restrictions on the police (Boateng, 1984; Kinsey *et al.*, 1986).

4) To an often unappreciated extent, the activities of police personnel are frequently directed by persons outside the police organisation. For example, procedures subsequent to the initial response often necessitate officers crossing boundaries into other organisations. The timetables of these organisations are meant to accommodate to their central partici-pants, not the police (for example, the courts) (Chatterton, 1985). When their deployment capabilities are thus restricted, can police managers be held accountable for effective and efficient use of "their" personnel?

5) In policing, the link between motives and acts and outcomes is a tenuous one. Specific targets can be identified, sophisticated plans developed, substantial resources committed, but the objective may not be realised. This loose coupling can result in police officers focussing on less

MICHAEL CHATTERTON

difficult targets in order to control their work and produce small but measurable successes (Manning, 1980).

6) Information is power. The lower ranks have acquired a level of autonomy by controlling the information about their work received by the higher-ups. Assessment of police work is threatening if the information retrieval systems introduced for this purpose endanger these strategies and the autonomy they protect. If this also entails an increase in the amount of paper work required from lower rank officers then their well-documented negative attitudes towards such assessment will increase the chances of resistance and subversive strategies (Chatterton, 1976; 1979; 1983; Holdaway, 1983; Manning, 1977).

7) Performance measures are resented by the lower ranks. They are regarded with suspicion, as being irrelevant to the realities of the work and counter-productive. Many sergeants in a recent study, for example, considered that the higher ranks placed too much importance on self-initiated work, and neglected to take other relevant skills and achievements into account (Manning, 1980; Chatterton, 1986).

8) Segments within the organisation develop their own sub-system goals. These may interfere with those of other agents. "Good housekeeping" and tidy administration detract from the performance of the main producers. In the study mentioned above, administrative units and other segments used the patrol sergeants to act as errand boys running messages and correcting for administrative over-sights. The time limits imposed for the completion of paper work also limited the capacity of operational personnel and their supervisors to plan their duties (Manning, 1977; Punch, 1983).

Such propositions should not be treated as unqualifiable statements of what is inevitable or inherent in policing; as the termination points of research enquiry and policy debate. They state *facts* that need *explanation*. They can be used constructively to *generate* a large number of additional *questions* about police activities and their effectiveness, such as: under what circumstances might the conflict between goals be reduced, leading to greater effectiveness in achieving each one? Will graded response systems moderate the disruptive effects of public demands? If managers in future calculate the amount of time personnel spend servicing other organisations, will this not provide a useful backcloth to review their achievements the rest of the time? Could policy statements, which research tells us chief officers are unprepared to make, encourage their officers to aim at more ambitious targets? Success is not the only indicator of endeavour; carefully planned and skilfully executed operations deserve merit. Is the suspicion of the lower ranks of existing appraisal and performance measures justified? *Are* they too divorced from reality? If they documented good practice would they be resisted?

Goals, Means and Results: Conclusions as Question-Originators

There are signs that this approach is beginning to take hold. Reiner has

82

ASSESSING POLICE EFFECTIVENESS – FUTURE PROSPECTS

recently challenged the message received from structuralist accounts that formal rules have no impact and that anything goes. "Which rules, in which circumstances, may be bent, and in what ways?", he asks (Reiner, 1985, p.176).

Manning's study of narcotics agents elaborates upon Skolnick's classic work, showing how the conflict between crime control and due process and the resultant organisational deviance can be mediated by organisational policies, types of reward and supervision systems, etc. His investigator-centred/organisation-centred models are worthy of further exploration (Skolnick, 1966; Manning, 1980).

Burrows' excellent research on burglary investigation serves as another good example of how questions can be produced which owe their sharpened focus to the conceptual apparatus and findings of an earlier study (Burrows, 1986). Burrows reports that explanations for variations in the detection rates in six force areas lie in the variable use made of 'secondary' detections, notably prison visits and offences taken into consideration at court (rather than charged). These are distinguished from "primary" detections which relate to offences for which the suspect was first picked up. Another interesting finding is that the chance of a burglary being cleared up is *not* determined simply by the ability of the police to put sufficient time into its investigation. Several directions for investigating effectiveness are indicated by this study.

First, has use of the detection rate as the traditional measure of police performance had the unintended consequence of leading police to concentrate on obtaining "secondary" detections? Have the traditional methods of "primary" investigation, of which earlier studies are so critical because of their modest contribution to the apprehension of offenders, consequently been under-utilised and under-developed? Does this apply also to arrests and detections for other types of offences?

Secondly, in view of the separate types of processes distinguished by this important conceptual refinement, will they be used in future by Chief Constables and Inspectors of Constabulary in their annual reports, and with what effects?

Thirdly, will different Chief Constables adopt different policies on whether officers should concentrate on "primary" or "secondary" detections? The consequences of this should be monitored. Will we witness the focus of attention turning upon primary means of detection, leading to systematic reviews of conventional methods and strategies which we may learn have been prematurely written off as ineffective?

Fourthly, bearing in mind the old adage that it is not the hours put in but also what is put into the hours, do we need to push the analysis of effectiveness further to enquire more closely into how investigators fill their time and use their skills?

According to some writers, certain primary methods of detection are dangerously self-perpetuating. In essence this thesis states that an alleged break-down of consensus policing, police failure to control crime and to detect criminals, and riotous behaviour results from the use of proactive

MICHAEL CHATTERTON

strategies (Cowell *et al.*, 1982; Kinsey *et al.*, 1986). The chain of causality presented by these "messengers" warrants much closer examination than I can afford here. Whole communities are supposed, apparently, to respond to the use of proactive strategies by denying to the police information about who is responsible for crime. This is postulated to lead to enforced reliance on proactive strategies, resulting in an increase in public disorder and unsolved crime.

However, traditionally, members of the public who provided the police with information which culminated in the apprehension of offenders have been victims or people connected to them (Chatterton, 1976; 1983; Mawby, 1979). If they are no longer prepared to give this information is this perhaps because they fear reprisals? Secondly, one may ask what has been the quality of the information provided by members of the public in the past? How frequently has it enabled the police to take the accused to court without further investigation? If the police have then to follow up such information in many cases because it does not justify a charge or prosecution and the complainant will not make a statement or enter the witness box, do the police then call upon their powers to interrogate and use the additional information to build a case or clear the suspect? (Softley, 1980). Has then the Police and Criminal Evidence Act 1984 restricted the police to the extent that they consider that they can no longer follow through in this manner the information provided by the public? And, finally, will this lead to a reduction in public confidence in the police?

We can extrapolate from the reasons given for not reporting crime that if the public consider the police do nothing with the information they provide about offenders then they will lose confidence and not offer any in future. The link between "the mobilisation of by-standers", riots and victims' unwillingness to inform on criminals they know, suggests that students of police effectiveness should turn their attention to the effectiveness of police tactics and strategies in dealing with small-scale outbursts of public disorder. The frequency and duration of such incidents may provide an indication of how much control the police have in an area. Moreover, if citizens believe that the price of informing may be a riot, leading to the burning of their businesses and houses, then it is important that the police develop the resource capability and strategical deployments to ensure arrests can be achieved effectively and the rowdy by-standers dispersed before they intervene or riot.

It is also true that proactive measures, such as use of the power to stop and search, do contribute significantly to the total of persons arrested for offences against property (Chatterton, 1976; Smith, 1983). Another neglected factor which may explain why these tactics are attractive to patrolling officers is the fact that the amount of discretionary "own" time available to them to attempt other, more prolonged methods is very limited. In a recent study of patrolling on 66 tours of duty, on only 62 occasions did the constables have periods of one·hour or more to use for such work (Chatterton and Ellis, 1986).

84

ASSESSING POLICE EFFECTIVENESS – FUTURE PROSPECTS

Circular 114/1983 and the Evaluation of Change

As anyone in close touch with the police service would confirm, since the use of Home Office Circular 114/83, we have witnessed an unprecedented amount of effort invested in reviews of operational policies, force structure and training, in internal and externally-funded research projects and in promoting organisational change. Whether these developments will have any effect upon the quality of the service delivered to the public will depend to a large extent upon how well the evaluations are conducted and on how police managers use the results of those assessments.

Although the Circular emphasises the need for explicit statements of objectives and of the plans for achieving them, it attaches particular importance to research, research skills and internal reviews (Collins, 1985). Rigorous, critical and objective evaluation of any initiatives introduced to promote greater effectiveness is presented as the hall-mark of good managerial practice.

The police manager envisaged by the rational management approach espoused in the Circular would not equate a result with the successful achievement of the objective. The results of some initiatives for change may indicate that the objectives were not achieved, but used constructively they may also indicate why not and what might be tried next time to increase the probability of success. In this sense, accounts of "failures" can be as useful as those of successes. By encouraging managers to examine in retrospect the consequences of the initiatives they have taken and to project forward by designing new initiatives that build upon previous knowledge, the rational management model seems to reconcile the opposed views of two recent protagonists on the feasibility of this approach (Butler, 1985; 1986; Waddington, 1986). The approach also presents police forces with a different conception of change from the one that has prevailed previously. It moves from the idea of the "one-off" innovation to the idea of a change-sequence comprising innovation, evaluation and redesign. It may take members of the service some time to appreciate that the first round of evaluation may produce more questions than it answers!

There is no guarantee, of course, that the new spirit of enquiry will alter significantly evaluative practices and introduce new conceptions of the change proces. Old habits die hard. Commenting upon 'the rigging' of data, Farmer states: "Those who do not understand the pervasiveness of misrepresentation in police life fail to understand policing" (Farmer, 1980, p.28). From Weatheritt's penetrating review of several "innovations" and "experiments" in the British police service, we can expect that the temptation will exist to gloss over the need for evaluation. Her work demonstrates that in the past, the incidence of policing successes has tended to be in inverse proportion to the rigour with which policing schemes were evaluated. She also alludes to the change sequence and to the role which evaluation must play in that process: "one of the notable features of most of the available documentation of policing initiatives is how little it has to say about change as a process with all its attendent

MICHAEL CHATTERTON

irritations, compromises and back-tracking; *about how change is managed and about how and why it can fail"*. (Weatheritt, 1986, italics supplied).

Perhaps the kind of personnel appraisal which has been advocated by Bittner and, more recently, Waddington, will be necessary to encourage police managers to be more systematic in their evaluations in the future (Waddington, 1986). Evidence of workmanship, which is the criterion, they argue, against which managerial competence can be judged, would require that the manager can demonstrate that he has used knowledge, skill and judgement to account for both successes and failures and attempted to design out the conditions of failure next time.

REFERENCES

BITTNER, E. (1970). *The Function of the Police in Modern Society.* Washington: U.S. G.P.O. (Republished 1975 by James Ronson, N.Y.).

BOATENG, P. (1984). The Police, the Community and Accountability. 152-9. In Benyon, J., *Scarman and After.* London: Pergamon Press.

BRADLEY, D., WALKER, N. and WILKIE, R. (1986). *Merging the Police,* Brighton: Wheatsheaf.

BUNYARD, R.S. (1978). *Police: Organisation and Command.* McDonald & Evans: Plymouth.

BURROWS, J. (1986). *Investigating Burglary: the measurement of police performance.* Home Office Research Study Number 88. London: H.M.S.O.

BUTLER, A. (1985). *Objectives and Accountability in Policing. Policing,* Vol. 1 No. 3. 174-86.

BUTLER, A. (1986). "Purpose and Process", *Policing,* Vol. 2, No. 2, pp. 160-166.

CHATTERTON, M. (1976). "Police in Social Control". In King, J., (ed.) *Control Without Custody.* Cropwood Papers, University of Cambridge Institute of Criminology. pp 104-22.

CHATTERTON, M. (1979). "The Supervision of Patrol Work under the Fixed Points System." In Holdaway, S., *The British Police.* London: Edward Arnold.

CHATTERTON, M. (1983). "Police Work and Assault Charges". In Punch, M. (ed.) *Control in the Police Organisation.* Cambridge, Mass: M.I.T. Press.

CHATTERTON, M. (1985). Resource Controls: Issues and Prospects. *Policing,* Vol. 1, No. 4, 226-35.

CHATTERTON, M. and ELLIS, T. (1986). *An Investigation of the Feasibility of a Focussed Patrolling System.* (Unpublished: Manchester University, Department of Social Administration).

COLLINS, K. (1985). "Efficiency Revisited", *Policing,* Vol. 1, No. 2, 70-76.

COWELL, D., JONES, T. and YOUNG, J. (1982). "The Riots in Britain, 1981: Urban Violence & Political Marginalisation." In Lea & Young (eds.) *Policing the Riots.* Junction Books, 5-20.

ENGSTAD, P. and EVANS, S. (1980). "Responsibility, Competence and Police Effectiveness in Crime Control". In Clarke, R.V.G. and Hough, J.M., *The Effectiveness of Policing.* Farnborough: Gower 139-162.

FARMER, D. (1980). "Out of hugger-mugger: the case of police field services". In Clarke, R. and Hough, M. (Eds.) *The Effectievness of Policing.* Farnborough: Gower 17-34.

GREENWOOD, P. (1980). "The Random Study of Criminal Investigation: the Findings and its Impact to Date". In Clarke, R.V.G. and Hough, J.M. (Eds.), *The Effectiveness of Policing.* Gower.

ASSESSING POLICE EFFECTIVENESS - FUTURE PROSPECTS

HOLDAWAY, S. (1983). *Inside the British police*, Oxford: Blackwell.

KELLING, E., WYCOFF, M.A., PATE, T. "Policing: a Research Agenda for Rational Police Making." In Clarke, R.V.G., and Hough, J.M. *The Effectiveness of Policing.* Gower. 44-69.

KINSEY, R., LEA, J. and YOUNG, J. (1986). *Losing the fight against crime.* Oxford: Blackwell.

MANNING, P.K. (1977). *Police work: the social organization of policing.* Cambridge, Mass.: M.I.T. Press.

MANNING, P.K. (1980). *The Narcs' Game.* Cambridge, Mass.: M.I.T. Press.

MAWBY, R. (1979). *Policing the City.* Farnborough: Gower.

PUNCH, M. (1979). "The Secret Social Service. " In Holdaway, S. (ed.) *The British Police.* London: Edward Arnold, pp.102-117.

PUNCH. M. (1983). "Officers and Men." In Punch, M. *Control in the Police Organisation.* Cambridge, Mass.: MIT Press.

REINER, R. (1985a). *The Politics of the Police.* Brighton: Wheatsheaf.

REINER, R. (1985b). "Policing strikes. *Policing.* Vol 1, no 3, 138-48.

REINER, R. (1985c). "Retrospect on the riots." *New Society.* October 25.

SINCLAIR, I. and ,MILLER, C. (1984). *Measures of Police Effectiveness and Efficiency.* Research & Planning Unit Paper, 25. London: Home Office.

SKOLNICK, J. (1966). *Justice Without Trial.* New York: Wiley.

SOFTLEY, P. (1980). *Police Interrogation: An Observational Study in Four Police Stations.* Royal Commission on Criminal Procedure: Research Paper No. 4.

WADDINGTON, P.A.J. (1986). "Defining Objectives: A Response to Tony Butler." *Policing*, Vol. 2, No. 1 17-25.

WADDINGTON, P.A.J. (1986). "Policing the pickets." *Police.* Vol XVIII, June, 34.

WEATHERITT, M. (1986). *Innovations in Policing.* London: Croom Helm.

[19]

Lawrence W. Sherman

Attacking Crime: Police and Crime Control

ABSTRACT

Growing experimental evidence suggests police actions can reduce crime,
increase it, or make no difference, depending on a wide range of
conditions. Growing epidemiological evidence suggests police can focus
their crime-control efforts much more sharply on high-risk places, times,
offenders, and (to a lesser extent) victims. These twin findings suggest the
value of a more intensive and sustained program of research and
development for testing current and innovative police efforts to control
crime. Less than 3 percent of street addresses and 3 percent of the
population in a city produce over half the crime and arrests. There has
been little testing of alternative police tactics for addressing these high-risk
targets. Improving police strategy and tactics for crime control requires
much more empirical evidence to specify the conditions under which they
succeed or fail. It also requires hard choices about resource allocation and
more ideas for how to attack specific crime targets.

Can police efforts reduce crime? The answer is in the eye of the beholder. In the "get-tough" climate of the 1980s, victims' advocates and
their lawsuits increasingly demanded more of the police actions they
were certain would help reduce specific types of crime, such as more
arrests for drunk driving (Jacobs 1988, p. 173) and domestic violence

Lawrence W. Sherman is professor of criminology, University of Maryland, and
president of the Crime Control Institute. Appreciation is expressed for the work of
Dennis Rogan, Janell Schmidt, Robert Velke, and Nancy Beatty, and for the comments
of David H. Bayley, Alfred Blumstein, Gary T. Marx, Sheldon Messinger, Mark H.
Moore, Norval Morris, Albert J. Reiss, Jr., Michael Tonry, and Franklin E. Zimring
on an earlier draft of this essay. Parts of the research discussed in this essay were
supported by grants 89-IJ-CX-0033 and 89-IJ-CX-0058 from the National Institute of
Justice to the Crime Control Institute.

(Lempert 1984; Sherman and Cohn 1989). At the same time, sociologists and social reformers reacted with increasing stridency about the inability of police to control crime in the face of the "root causes" of crime: family structure, unemployment, and poverty (Currie 1985; Gottfredson and Hirschi 1990). Police themselves partially embraced that view, placing renewed emphasis on the importance of voluntary action by citizens to supplement police efforts at crime control (Brown 1989). A 1989 Gallup poll reported 48 percent of the respondents confident and 50 percent not confident of the ability of the police to protect them from violent crime (Flanagan and Maguire 1990, p. 133).

Within this contentious historical context, police research on crime control has moved forward rapidly. Police have cooperated with unprecedented and powerful research methods, developed massive data bases revealing new insights, and brought research results more explicitly into policy-making. While the sum of the research is no more than a drop in an ocean of unanswered questions, it has provoked major strides in police thinking about crime control. Most important, it has fostered debate on major questions of police strategy, stimulating new ideas and innovations in police attempts to control crime.

The new research has made two specific contributions. One is to focus more attention on the *epidemiology* of specific crime problems, especially the concentrations of problems in small proportions of offenders, places, and victims. This has stimulated new ideas about strategies for setting police priorities among potential targets for crime-control efforts. The other contribution of the research is to probe more precisely the *results* of police work in relation to specific crime-control objectives. This has stimulated new debate about police tactics in reacting to crime and attacking crime problems.

What the research has not done is to settle the debate about the possibility of police efforts reducing crime. Those predisposed against that possibility read the mixed results of this research as evidence for their position. Those predisposed in support of it read the same results as proving the need for more policing. Those employed in doing the research, like most employees, argue that their work has value and should be continued, if only to discover when police work can *increase* crime as well as reduce it. But all would agree that the results so far are scant in relation to the complexity of the questions. If research is ever to make any contribution to crime control, it will come from a painfully slow process of accumulating and replicating results from hundreds of policy experiments and epidemiological studies, the way of the tortoise and not the hare (Zimring 1976). For police policy research after two decades, the race has only just begun.

This essay examines what has been learned so far about the epidemiology of crime-control targets and the crime-control results of police work. Section I considers the strengths and weaknesses of the primary methods of police research on crime control, as viewed from the perspectives of opposing camps in the crime-control debate. Section II examines the new choices of *strategy* in attacking crime raised by crime-control research. It then considers those strategic options, with appropriate tactics, in a crime-specific manner with four kinds of targets: offenders, places, times, and victims.[1] Section III examines police efforts to control stranger violence, finding diverse evidence that field interrogations and directed patrol may reduce robbery, but that place-oriented and victim-oriented problem solving remains underdeveloped. Section IV reviews the evidence on police control of soft crime, with more specific findings about the conditions of deterrence versus escalation in offender-oriented strategies. Section V reviews recent research on the prediction and control of domestic violence. Early evidence of the predictability of domestic homicide by place was seriously flawed; and such homicides appear unpredictable from currently available police data. Minor domestic battery, in contrast, is highly predictable among chronically violent couples, but reactive arrest has not deterred it in most experiments and has even made unemployed suspects more violent in one. Section VI provides briefer overviews of police efforts to control street-level drug marketplaces, burglary, auto theft, and drunk driving. Section VII concludes by suggesting how further research could help identify harmful, helpful, and wasteful police practices in their efforts to control crime.

I. Crime-Control Research: Methods and Perspectives

Three methods dominate modern crime-control research. One is essentially epidemiological, examining the variations, distributions, and concentrations of crime problems in the population. A second is quasi-experimental, examining the before-after differences in crime rates in a target population subjected to a new policy intervention. The third method is fully experimental, randomly assigning alternate tactics or

---

[1] Police strategies for a fifth kind of target, communities, are reviewed in Sherman (1986) and (1990a). The major crime-control evaluations of policing communities published since the 1986 review are found in Rosenbaum (1986); Skogan (1988, 1990); Pate (1989); and Uchida, Forst, and Sampson (1990).

162   Lawrence W. Sherman

sanctions across a large sample of equivalent units.[2] Each of these methods has different uses, strengths, and weaknesses. All of them make
certain philosophical, empirical, and theoretical assumptions about the
police role in crime control and what can realistically be expected from
research at this stage in its development.

A. Methods—Epidemiology

The epidemiological method helps identify crime-control targets
with the greatest potential yield, by showing where the risk of future
crime is greatest. Many credit Wolfgang, Figlio, and Sellin (1972) with
establishing the model for this kind of criminal epidemiology, by showing that a small proportion of all young males and a somewhat larger
proportion of male offenders in a birth cohort produced the majority
of all official police contacts. But the approach goes back at least two
centuries, to Fielding (1751) and Colquhoun (1795), both of whom
identified high-risk locations, victims, and offenders. Fielding stressed
gambling houses and gin parlors and proposed to prevent crime more
effectively by tighter regulation of those establishments. Colquhoun
(p. 25) proposed the creation of a comprehensive registry of criminals
as a tool for selecting the most dangerous for ongoing surveillance.

The strength of this method is that it helps distinguish between
low-risk and high-risk units in the jurisdiction, whether people, places,
or activities. It points, in theory, to targets yielding the "biggest bang
for the buck," or the highest return on an investment of resources. It
provides a more rational alternative to equal allocation of police resources across the community, without regard to extreme variations in
risk. In a military analogy, it identifies key military targets for precision
bombing as an alternative to indiscriminate bombing of an entire city.

One major difficulty with using epidemiological data for policy purposes is the risk of false positives, or incorrect predictions of future
criminality. A National Academy of Sciences report on criminal careers, for example, shows the dangers of using this method to determine the length of prison sentences (Blumstein et al. 1986). Yet this

---

[2] A fourth method, cross-sectional correlations among large samples of cities, has
been used very little in recent policy research, with the exceptions of Wilson and Boland
(1978) and Sampson and Cohen (1988) discussed below (see Phillips and Votey 1972;
Tittle and Rowe 1974; Logan 1975). Most of that research, however, fails to adjust for
interactions between crime levels and measures of police activity that are hypothesized
to affect crime levels (Nagin 1978; Sampson and Cohen 1988). Continuing difficulties of
interpreting such models have limited their use and impact, and they are not considered
further here.

problem is less severe where the costs of error are also less severe. It is remarkable, for example, how little difficulty false positives pose for public health policy. When the prediction is the basis for telling people to use condoms or to stop smoking cigarettes, few critics object that most unprotected sexual encounters do not transmit AIDS or that most smokers never contract "smoking-related" illnesses. When the prediction is the basis for sentencing people to longer prison terms, the problem of false positives becomes far more serious. Since most police strategies are far less intrusive than prison, however, it can be argued that false positives with crime-risk targets are not a serious problem. Performing surveillance and conducting investigations, for example, should not cause irreparable harm to individual liberty, as long as they are done legally and properly.

A more serious difficulty is that the crime distributions do not really identify targets very efficiently. High-risk units often cannot be identified in advance, especially those in the highest risk levels. This objection, where true, is sound, but the evidence presented below shows it is hardly universal. A second problem is that the distributions are not always skewed enough to make high-risk targeting strategies very profitable. If the top 2 percent of the units only account for 10 percent of the crime, then why bother? The answer, of course, is that a successful strategy could reduce crime by 10 percent, a substantial achievement by our current modest standards of success.

The most serious difficulty has been the cost of examining vast amounts of data on large populations. But recent technological advances in police record keeping have diminished this problem in most communities. Where offense and arrest reports were once kept on paper records and filed chronologically, they are now entered directly on computers. While few police departments have used these data sets to conduct their own epidemiological analyses, it is now relatively easy for them to do so.

B. Methods—Quasi Experiments

Police culture thrives on anecdotal evidence, with an epistemology driven by case-by-case analysis. Quasi experiments fit this mold perfectly but offer considerably more rigor for interpretations of cause and effect. Their major tool is a standard list of alternative hypotheses to examine whenever someone claims that "x" made crime go down. The archetype is the Campbell and Ross (1968) analysis of a Connecticut police crackdown on speeding. This analysis examined whether the decline in traffic accidents immediately after the crackdown could have been due to regression to the mean, general changes in weather or road conditions, changes in methods of recording accident statistics, or other factors besides deterrence of speeding from stricter enforcement. These analyses can be made more rigorous by comparing the target jurisdiction to a similar jurisdiction subject to the same historical trends but lacking the specific policy intervention—such as other New England states.

The strengths of such quasi experiments include their relatively low cost and the speed with which they can indicate the success or failure of a new policy. Moreover, accumulations of similar cases over time provide a basis for beginning to draw more general policy conclusions, such as in the case of uniformed patrol crackdowns (Sherman 1990*a*). The limitations include their vulnerability to misinterpretation or misrepresentation. Klockars (1980), for example, shows how a quasi-experimental analysis misrepresented the effects of sting operations in reducing crime. Sherman (1991) suggests that failure to consider rival hypotheses in general will limit police efforts to solve crime problems, allowing self-deception about police effectiveness. Most important, because each quasi experiment is still essentially an anecdote, it is not possible to generalize very far from the results. Yet policymakers unschooled in the cautions required of such research are sorely tempted to draw fairly broad conclusions from a single anecdote, as the state of Florida is now considering doing with statewide regulation of convenience stores based on one quasi experiment in robbery preventions in a single city (Clifton 1987). Quasi experiments are not nearly as powerful a basis for drawing conclusions as are randomized experiments with large samples, yet they are often given equal weight in policy deliberations as having "proven" something does or does not work.

C. Methods—Large-Sample Randomized Experiments

This most powerful method in police research merits special consideration since it has provided more concrete answers about the effects of policing on crime than any other method. It assesses evidence of cause and effect from equal probability (random) assignment of alternative treatments to a large sample of target units (Pocock 1983). The logic is elegantly simple: equalizing most characteristics of two groups prior to giving them different treatments creates high *internal validity* (whether a change in one variable really caused a change in another) by eliminating most rival hypotheses about the cause of any differences in outcomes (Farrington 1983, p. 260). In this respect the method stands far above quasi experiments, which may always suffer unknown and undetected validity threats from rival hypotheses (Cook and Campbell 1979).

Randomized experiments were invented for testing agricultural strategies and quickly spread to medicine (Fisher 1935). They were first applied to criminal justice policy in the Cambridge-Somerville project, which found (thirty years later) that assigning a "big brother" social worker to high-risk youth had many negative effects on their future lives (McCord 1978). Their first major policy impact came from the Vera Institute's release on recognizance experiment, the Manhattan Bail Project (Ares, Rankin, and Sturz 1963; Botein 1965), an unreplicated 730-case study that became the basis for national adoption of pretrial release without bail on the basis of community ties.

The bail experiment model heavily influenced the board of directors of the Police Foundation, established by the Ford Foundation in 1970 to foster innovation and improvement in American policing. After some initial battles over how best to accomplish that mission, the board decided to spend most of its initial funding of $30 million on a series of what it called policy experiments. The most visible of these was the Kansas City Preventive Patrol Experiment (Kelling et al. 1974), which found no difference in crime from assigning increased and reduced patrol to fifteen different patrol beats. But there were other Police Foundation policy experiments: the San Diego Field Interrogation Experiment (Boydstun 1975), the Cincinnati Team Policing Experiment (Schwartz and Clarren 1977), the San Diego one- versus two-officer patrol car experiment (Boydstun, Sherry, and Moelter 1977), and the Newark Foot Patrol Experiment (Police Foundation 1981). These experiments created a strong model for federal research funding, especially by the National Institute of Justice.

These experiments were not, however, large-sample randomized experiments (Farrington 1983). They were really small-sample quasi experiments, with some attempt to build randomization into the samples of two to fifteen units, usually patrol beats or districts. The randomization did little to improve on the internal validity problems from the many rival hypotheses associated with before-and-after case studies. Nor did it help to increase the weak statistical power associated with the small sample sizes. Not until the Minneapolis Domestic Violence Experiment (Sherman and Berk 1984) did the Police Foundation conduct a medical-style, large-sample randomized experiment in police

crime-control tactics, by randomly assigning arrest and no arrest in
314 cases of minor domestic assault. The finding that arrest produced
the lowest recidivism was widely publicized, contributing to policy
changes and support for further research (Sherman and Cohn 1989).

Randomized experiments in police crime control had actually been
pioneered (Dennis 1988) in 1974, with National Institute of Mental
Health funding, by Klein (1986); 306 moderately serious juvenile offenders were randomly assigned to postarrest release versus three other
increasingly serious dispositions. That the experiment remained unpublished for so long limited its influence on police policy research,
despite its striking finding that released juveniles had the lowest official
recidivism rate (with no difference in self-reported delinquency). The
lack of national publicity about the study may also have limited its
impact on police policy in juvenile arrests and its likelihood of replication.

As the first randomized experiment in arrest, it is fortunate that the
Minneapolis Domestic Violence Experiment was replicated in six other
cities, with varying degrees of similarity to the original experiment.
Three of those experiments have reported findings at this writing
(Dunford, Huizinga, and Elliott 1990; Hirschel et al. 1990; Sherman
et al. 1991). None of them found a deterrent effect of arrest in the main
experimental analyses. This pattern raises major substantive questions
about arrest policies addressed in Section V. Equally important is the
effect of these mixed results on the future of police policy experiments.

The issue of replication constitutes the major difficulty with policy
experiments. In most cases, results go unreplicated, which leaves unad-
dressed the question of *external validity*, or generalizability to other
populations beyond the experimental sample. Randomized experiments are valued for strong *internal* validity; external validity is largely
unexplored, even in medical research. For example, a drug found effective in treating AIDS among white males may not be effective among
blacks and Hispanics (Kolata 1991). Similarly, arrests for domestic
violence in Minneapolis appear to be more effective than arrests for
domestic violence in Omaha.

The consequences of this first and only program of replications of a
promising result in police crime-control research are still unknown.
But the pattern of inconsistent replication results has predictably exposed the methods of policy experiments and crime-control research
for police to some attack. These attacks derive not just from the method

but from more basic perspectives and assumptions about the roles of police and research in crime control.

D. *Perspectives on Crime Control and Research*

Police research on crime control has two basic premises. One is that it is a good thing for police to try to control crime. The other is that research results are in some sense portable from the setting in which they are produced to other settings where they can be applied. Both premises provoke considerable debate.

In recent years, many scholars and police executives have suggested that it is not, in fact, a good thing for police to try to control crime, as distinct from apprehension of offenders and provision of reactive peacekeeping services. They suggest that the police *can*, *do*, and *should do* little about reducing crime. Many crime victims and their advocates, however, claim that police have great powers, opportunity, and moral duty to prevent crime but often fail to do so out of negligence or ill-chosen priorities. These arguments, then, are respectively theoretical, empirical, and philosophical, with views on the replicability of crime-control programs as a corollary.

1. *Theoretical Perspectives.* The theoretical argument against police controlling crime is that the causes of routine "street" crime—interpersonal violence, property offenses, and illegal vices—are far too complex for an agency like the police to address. More basic institutions of social bonding, such as the economy, family, schools, and churches, are the primary crime-control forces in society. The effects of police on crime are only marginal in relation to these master institutions, the argument suggests. These institutions, not punishment, control the "root causes" of crime (Currie 1985). This sensible assessment of the relative capacity of social and governmental institutions breaks down, however, when it gets to the subject of the police. It leads otherwise careful scholars into extreme and dogmatic claims about what "cannot be" (Klockars 1991, p. 542). As Gottfredson and Hirschi (1990, p. 270) conclude: "no evidence exists that augmentation of police forces or equipment, differential patrol strategies, or differential intensities of surveillance have an effect on crime rates." This claim is made without even discussing or citing the relevant literature (except to miscite Sherman [1983], which actually discusses three separate experiments showing police effects on crime control).

In making the same point, but with more emphasis on the "demystification" of crime control as mere police marketing rhetoric, Klockars (1991, p. 537) claims that "despite the fact that for the past 50 years police have been promoting themselves as crime fighters . . . the best evidence to date is that no matter what they do they can only make marginal differences in it." The use of the term "marginal" provides ample room for debate. A 10 percent reduction in robbery, for example, would be marginal to some, but substantial to others. Nonetheless, the thrust of the theoretical argument that police methods are essentially irrelevant to the crime rate is that research on such methods is pointless.

2. *Empirical Perspective.*   Until recently, the preceding argument was bolstered by the empirical claim that police actually spend very little time on crime (Cumming, Cumming, and Edell 1965; Wilson 1968; Goldstein 1977). This claim arose from descriptions of police calls for service and observations of police activities, using categories that define much police work as unrelated to crime. This led many others to the conclusion that the "real" role of the police is provision of a wide range of community services rather than primarily the control of crime. An agency committed to helping people who lock their keys inside their cars cannot accurately claim to be engaged solely, or even primarily, in crime control. The unstated corollary was that that is how it is, so that is how it must be.

As Greene and Klockars (1991) observe, these descriptions were somewhat misleading and may now be very out of date. They were somewhat misleading because they only examined patrol work and not other police units. They also classified events that could potentially turn into violence, such as "disturbances," as not crime related. They are out of date because they preceded the adoption of 911 and computer-aided dispatch (CAD) systems around the United States, both of which appear to have expanded the volume of calls for service handled by patrol officers on a typical tour of duty. Analyzing CAD data for the city of Wilmington for a one year period ending May 31, 1986, Greene and Klockars (1991, p. 281) concluded that patrol officers "spend nearly half the time they are doing police work in dealing with criminal activity." Similarly, Sherman (1989) found over half the dispatched calls for service in Minneapolis in 1986 to be clearly crime related. While most of the work they actually do in relation to crime may have little connection to its control, the best evidence is that urban police actually do deal with crime, and not cats up in trees, most of the time.

3. *Philosophical Perspective.* Underlying these theoretical and empirical arguments may be a more basic philosophical distaste for coercive institutions and punishment as a tool of social policy. Police policy research is inescapably linked to values and perspectives on core issues of authority, liberty, democracy, and order. The old joke about the greatest safeguard of American liberty being the incompetence of the police summarizes one position. The joke about America's internationally high crime rate making it the land of the brave, if not necessarily of the free, suggests another. The view that crime control and liberty (or at least legality) are mutually exclusive values has dominated much of the debate about the police. Packer (1968) is the most influential writer on that view, posing crime control and due process as polar opposites. Periodic scandals over police excesses tend to reinforce that view, such as the nationally broadcast videotape of California police brutally beating a restrained suspect in early 1991 (Mydans 1991).

This view leads to a preference not to develop research on more effective crime-control strategies, for fear that police may adopt them. This view is attractive to both left-wing and right-wing libertarians, who distrust the authority of the state. It may also be attractive to those who see the police as an important institution of social service and fear the effects of a crime-control focus in limiting police service activities (Goldstein 1977, 1990; Sparrow, Moore, and Kennedy 1990).

4. *Program Replication.* These three arguments lead critics to oppose more police efforts at crime control and more research to evaluate those efforts. This conclusion easily leads to a second premise: that what works in one experiment is not very portable to other populations. The complexity of social life is too great for positivistic methods to discover any general laws of behavior, especially across the great diversity of American cities (Marx 1990). And if the external validity of police research is so poor, then policy experiments may be the wrong method to use. Clinical case studies of police practices seeking wisdom, not quantification (cf. Marx 1988), may be more appropriate. The failure of the Minneapolis replications to confirm the initial results seems to support this view.

A more sensitive position is that policy experiments are important but should be carefully replicated before their results are publicized (Lempert 1984, 1989). This position holds that, because the question of external validity is unanswered, it is better not to have police change what they are doing until at least some replications have been completed.

170   Lawrence W. Sherman

5. *Crime Victims' Perspective.* Crime victim advocates, in contrast, offer many counterarguments. They take on faith the proposition that police can control crime if they want to and that they have many opportunities to do so. Advocates have a strong philosophical preference for policing and punishment as a tool of social policy, fusing retributivist demands for just deserts to offenders with empirical claims that punishment deters. Through legislation, litigation, and lobbying, they have pressed police for almost two decades to take a more punitive approach to crime or at least to make crime control a higher priority. Advocates for victims of drunk drivers and domestic violence have been particularly effective in redirecting police resources toward those offenses and in provoking more punitive action. They have also argued that the results of police experiments are highly portable, at least where they support the more punitive position. Some domestic violence victims' advocates, for example, opposed the replications of the Minneapolis experiment on the grounds that it was unethical to create new control groups after arrest had already been found to be effective in one site—a position consistent with much medical research practice (Sherman and Cohn 1989).

6. *Policy Research Perspective.* Police policy research takes a different view on each of these arguments. *Theoretically*, it views the police as a central social institution, less powerful than the family and economy but perhaps as powerful as schools. While no reasonable theory would claim police alone determine crime rates, it is just as unreasonable to write police off as irrelevant without better evidence than we have now. *Empirically*, most work of urban police is already devoted to crime prevention and reaction, including the management of drunks (as potential robbery victims), noise and disputes (as potential assaults), and traffic violators (as potential suspects—see Wilson and Boland 1978, 1981–82). The nature of the work is all in the eyes of the beholder, and most of it can be justified as crime related. *Philosophically*, it is not necessary to like punishment or disvalue due process to value the development and testing of police crime-control strategies. Many of the most innovative police approaches to crime control (Goldstein 1990) employ methods other than punishment, and even police tactics implying the threat of punishment carry no obligation or inherent propensity to violate due process (but see Sherman 1990a, p. 41).

Most complex is the question of portability and replications. The research position on this is that it is indeed a matter for research. It is not a matter to be resolved by theoretical fiat or philosophies of science. The extent to which findings from one jurisdiction, or one offense, or one type of offender can be generalized to others is simply unknown. Only hundreds of experiments and replications with diverse samples can even begin to answer that question. Where results differ from one type of sample (such as cities or offender types) to another, that is not reason to give up the effort to test police strategies. It is merely a challenge to discover what specific aspects of the differences in the samples (or methods) may account for differences in the results. When such characteristics can be specified, the results may appear to be more robust than they first appear. The proposition that "arrest deters spouse abusers in high-employment neighborhoods but not in low-employment neighborhoods," for example, may be far more robust than the less precise proposition that "arrest deters domestic violence."

The question of whether to publicize research results without replication is more difficult, given the concerns about external validity. Three factors argue in favor of doing so. One is that not announcing results creates a bias for the status quo in police practices, for which there is usually no empirical support; one experiment is arguably better than none. A second factor is that a steady stream of these results will only help make police more sophisticated consumers of research, rather than treating policymakers as if they cannot be trusted until findings have received a scientific seal of approval. Policymakers in all fields misuse research to comport with their biases, which is no argument to stop doing research. The most important factor, however, is that publicizing policy experiments helps to foster their replication, the essential but usually ignored step in the process. There is little reason to believe, for example, that the Minneapolis Domestic Violence Experiment (Sherman and Berk 1984) would have been replicated had it not received substantial publicity (Sherman and Cohn 1989).

The basic questions are what to expect from police crime-control research and how quickly it can be produced. For some, this research is little more than "rearranging the deck chairs on the Titanic" as center-city violence becomes more terrible (Marx 1990). For others, the central problem is that insufficient funds have been invested to speed the process along (U.S. Attorney General's Task Force on Violent Crime 1981, p. 73; Zimring 1990). Inconsistent results are an inherent part of scientific investigation. It is impossible to cite any field that made major breakthroughs in curing a social problem within two decades after starting from scratch. From any perspective, however, research has clearly succeeded in stimulating police debate and innovations in crime-control strategy (Goldstein 1990), for better or worse.

II. Crime-Control Strategy: Hard Choices

The past two decades of research have sharpened several key questions. What is the optimal balance of proactive and reactive police effort? Should police strategies focus on specific crimes or on crime in general? Should police target offenders, victims, times, or places? Should priorities be set within or across types of crime? Every police department answers each of these questions on a daily basis. The answers are often shaped by organizational and political factors. Less often, perhaps, they are also shaped by a concern for crime-control effectiveness.

A. Balancing Proactive and Reactive Strategies

In the quarter-century since Reiss and Bordua (1967) first raised the question of who mobilizes police in any given action, the terms "reactive" and "proactive" have achieved widespread use. The language has helped clarify the hardest strategic choice police face. The choice concerns both philosophical questions of how police can best serve democratic values (Black 1973) and empirical questions about how police can most effectively control crime.

When police action is self-initiated, or proactive, police select their own targets. When police mobilization is initiated by a specific citizen demand, or reactive, police allow citizens to select police targets. All municipal police agencies use both forms of mobilization. The difficult choice is how to allocate personnel time between the two strategies.

Most police patrol time is devoted to reactive mobilizations (Reiss 1971). In recent years, however, there is increasing evidence of new emphasis on proactive strategies, such as decoy units to catch robbers (Wycoff, Susmilch, and Brown 1981), sting operations to catch burglars (Marx 1988), special units to watch repeat offenders (Martin and Sherman 1986), problem-solving strategies to attack high burglary locations (Eck and Spelman 1987), and intensified patrol crackdowns in retail drug marketplaces (Sherman 1990a). There is also more evidence that police agencies vary widely in the extent of their proactivity in patrol tactics generating citizen encounters (Wilson and Boland 1978; Sampson and Cohen 1988). Scholars are increasingly pressed to consider whether a far more proactive police would be good for both democracy and crime control.

1. *Democratic Philosophy.* The philosophical choice is deceptively simple, with reactive policing appearing to be far more democratic than proactive policing. What could be more egalitarian than to give all citizens an equal right to pick the targets of police crime control? Yet absent an equal willingness to use that right, reactive policing becomes anything but egalitarian.

Enormous "selection bias," as statisticians call it, afflicts every choice of police targets by citizens. Many crime victims never call the police, for example, for reasons ranging from fear of retaliation to lack of homeowner's insurance (Flanagan and Maguire 1990, p. 226). Other people falsely accuse enemies and relatives, using police as a tool for private disputes. Reactive policing is completely vulnerable to racial, class, religious, sexual, and ethnic prejudices in citizen decisions to complain about other citizens (Black 1973).

Proactive policing is equally vulnerable to such prejudices on the part of the police. It has the added disadvantage of potentially systematic discrimination against certain ethnic or political groups. Such biases, when they occur, are compounded by the imprimatur of state action. Yet unlike reactive policing, proactive policing has great potential for controlling such selection bias. Using objective criteria for target selection, proactive strategy can come far closer to egalitarian policing, giving all similarly situated individuals equal odds of being selected as targets. Whether using the principles of random selection from a list of congressmen for corruption investigations (Sherman 1983), rank-order targeting of street addresses by frequency of prior police problems (Sherman, Gartin, and Buerger 1989), or some other logic, police can attempt to reduce bias in target selection. While research shows some persistence of selection bias even with fairly objective targeting criteria (Martin and Sherman 1986; Sherman et al. 1989), the result is arguably less biased than purely reactive target selection.

More troubling to democratic philosophy may be any attempt to eliminate citizen power to mobilize police about certain problems. Even if proactive target selection is more egalitarian, it may do less to defuse citizen conflict that may cause crime. Shifting resources from reactive to proactive policing could foster increased vigilantism or "self-help" (Black 1983; Weisburd 1989), which can in turn cause a breakdown of democracy.

Democracy may also break down, however, with the anarchy of high crime rates. Crime control is merely another aspect of serving democratic values, rather than a contradiction of those values. While control of "street" crime may appear to be easier in nondemocratic regimes, there is little systematic evidence supporting that proposition (but see Greenhouse 1990). Even dictatorships must decide how proactive police should be and answer the same questions about crime-control effectiveness.

2. *Crime-Control Effectiveness.* Is proactive policing more effective than reactive policing in controlling crime? The available evidence permits no definitive answer. Each distinct type of crime may be more or less susceptible to proactive crime attacks, depending in large measure on how predictable in time and space the crime may be. Police have historically used proactive strategies most often with the most obviously predictable crimes, such as street prostitution, public intoxication, drunk driving, gambling, and (recently) street-level drug dealing. More recent analyses in the spirit of Goldstein's (1979) problem-oriented policing have revealed less obvious patterns of predictability in a wider range of offenses, such as burglary concentrated in a single apartment complex (Eck and Spelman 1987) and robbery concentrated in less than 2 percent of all addresses in a city (Sherman, Gartin, and Buerger 1989).

Predictability alone, however, does not necessarily make a proactive strategy more effective than a reactive one. It is also necessary to have tested and effective tactics available for attacking predictable crime. When confronted by 125 commercial addresses with highly predictable crime problems, for example, a specially selected group of five Minneapolis police officers (the Repeat Call Address Policing [RECAP] unit) was unable to develop effective ways to reduce repeat calls for service at those addresses (Sherman et al. 1989). They succeeded in closing down two high-crime taverns, reorganized security at a bus station, had fences built around a high-crime parking garage, and tried to install better access control at a YMCA. But overall, they could not reduce total calls compared to a control group. The team was more successful at reducing multifamily residential calls for service by working with the property managers on tenant problems (including evictions), but only temporarily; after six months of reduced calls, the effects of proactive intervention withered away.

To the extent that experiments in proactive strategy employ a wide range of tactics (Wycoff, Susmilch, and Brown 1981; Martin and Sherman 1986; Sherman et al. 1989), they may obscure a key point. Effectiveness at crime control may depend more on specific tactics than on general strategy. There may be a substantial crime-control difference between two proactive tactics, such as robbery stakeouts and target hardening with bulletproof enclosures. There may also be great differences between two reactive tactics, such as hidden robbery alarms or use of 911. Yet there is no difference between two ineffective tactics, regardless of whether they are reactive or proactive.

On empirical grounds, then, the balance between proactive and reactive strategies should depend on the availability of proven specific tactics. If more tactics are proven effective, then more proactive effort may become justified. And the evidence of effectiveness may become even clearer when specific tactics are linked to specific offenses.

B. Specific or General Strategies?

Police strategies are usually expressed in general terms. One strategy is often presumed to work for all offenses. The threat and delivery of apprehension and charging of criminals is implicitly applied across the board. Uniformed patrol and postcrime investigation are the master strategies—both reactive—for every crime from noise to homicide (Colquhoun 1795; Wilson 1963). Just as criminological theory makes few distinctions among types of crimes in explanations of crime (Wilson and Herrnstein 1985; Gottfredson and Hirschi 1990), police have historically made few distinctions among offenses in strategies for controlling crime.

To some, crime-general strategies may be justified by the apparent lack of offense specialization among offenders (Blumstein et al. 1986). To others, police could control crime better if they targeted the specific situations creating opportunities for specific offense types to occur (Clarke 1983). The judgment hinges in part on the choice between a "hydraulic" pressure model of crime causation or an opportunity model (Clarke and Mayhew 1988). Hydraulic models presume that the supply of offenses is determined largely by the supply of offenders and their innate rates of offending (e.g., Merton 1968, chap. 6). Opportunity models presume that the supply of offenders (given their predisposed rates of offending) is only one factor determining crime rates, with the supply of suitable victims and capable guardianship also necessary elements (Cohen and Felson 1979). Hydraulic models logically imply a need for general strategies. Opportunity models imply a need for specific strategies. This strategic choice relates, in turn, to the choice of targets for police strategy.

176   Lawrence W. Sherman

C. *Offenders, Places, Times, or Victims as Targets*

Reactive policing deals with incidents, which generally feature victims and offenders intersecting in time and place (Cohen and Felson 1979). It makes little strategic distinction among types of incidents, although this is changing. "Differential police responses" to calls for service are increasingly being used, such as taking a telephone report of a crime or making an appointment for a police car to visit the next day on a low-priority call. These responses explicitly vary by call type and are accepted by callers when they are clearly told what to expect (McEwen, Connors, and Cohen 1986). Such call-screening only delays or rechannels, however, a single strategy of response (investigation), regardless of the elements of the offense. Proactive policing, in contrast, can target any element of a given *pattern* of incidents, especially the most predictable ones (Eck and Spelman 1987). The question then becomes which elements are most predictable.

1. *Places.* Police have long focused on offenders as the most predictable element in any incident. Yet the places—defined as street addresses or intersections—where crime occurs may be far more predictable than the people who commit crimes. In Minneapolis, for example, our analysis of 323,000 calls to the police in 1986 found that a small number of hot spots produced most of the crime in the city (Sherman, Gartin, and Buerger 1989). Only 3 percent of the places produced 50 percent of the calls to which police were dispatched. This concentration was even greater for the predatory crimes of robbery, criminal sexual conduct, and auto theft. Only 5 percent of the 115,000 street addresses and intersections in the city produced 100 percent of the calls for those usually stranger offenses. These findings have subsequently been replicated in Kansas City (Sherman, Rogan, and Velke 1991; see also Pierce, Spaar, and Briggs 1988).

One cause of that concentration, of course, is the small number of those crimes relative to the large number of places. Even without any repeat locations, for example, all of the robberies could only have occurred at 3.6 percent of all places. But the fact is that with repeat occurrences, they occurred at only 2.2 percent of all places, a 40 percent reduction from the hypothetical number with no repeat locations. If the analysis were restricted to commercial establishments or other high-risk places, the concentration would not be as great, but the identification of targets would still be just as clear. Only 297 addresses, for example, produced over half of all dispatched calls to the Minneapolis police in 1986.

Domestic violence is even more concentrated by place of occurrence than robbery. While 21 percent of the places in Minneapolis could have had a domestic disturbance call if no place had more than one, only 8.6 percent of addresses actually produced one or more calls—a 59 percent reduction. While it is probably true that multifamily housing units comprised the bulk of those locations, and that much of the city (such as industrial areas) would be unlikely to have such calls, the identification of the 161 addresses with fifteen or more calls per year might stimulate some useful ideas for a proactive strategy against such violence.

Further examination reveals possible routine activities heavily implicated in causing hot spots (Sherman, Rogan, and Velke 1991). For example, analyses of taverns and surrounding areas in Milwaukee and Kansas City shows that, in 1986–89 in Milwaukee, 4 percent of homicides, 5 percent of aggravated assaults, 3 percent of robberies, and 3 percent of all serious violent offenses combined occurred in taverns—which constituted only 0.5 percent of all places in the city. Kansas City showed a similar pattern, with 3 percent of homicide, 6 percent of robbery, 4 percent of aggravated assaults, and 4 percent of total serious violence in its taverns, which constituted 0.3 percent of the places. These crime risks are also connected to violent crime on the block. In Milwaukee, *the location of a tavern on a block increases the relative risk of the block being violent (defined as 20 or more such offenses in four years) by a factor of 3*. Only 15 percent of 5,672 blocks without taverns met the criteria for violent blocks. Some 29 percent of the 625 blocks with nonviolent taverns were violent blocks, but 51 percent of the 170 blocks with at least one violent tavern (defined as four or more violent offenses in four years) were violent blocks. In Kansas City, the comparable ratios for the same time period were 11 percent for no-tavern blocks, 24 percent for nonviolent tavern blocks, and 44 percent for violent tavern blocks.

The fact that most taverns do not have these risks, however, shows the importance of analyzing all factors in each hot spot. Only 12 percent (132) of Milwaukee taverns produced over half of all 2,019 violent offenses in 1986–89, with 40 percent of taverns reporting no violence at all and 85 percent with one or less violent offense per year. The maximum was twenty-three violent offenses in four years. In Kansas City, only 10 percent of the taverns produced half of the 2,757 violent offenses in 1985–89, with 31 percent of the taverns reporting no violence and 68 percent with one or less violent offense annually. The maximum was seventy-five violent offenses in five years.

Police once gave substantial attention to high-crime bars, with frequent field interrogations of customers. Current practices appear more limited to answering calls for service. The continuing connection of some taverns to concentrations of violent crime suggests they should be a central part of any proactive crime-control strategy.

2. *Offenders.*   Annual distributions similar to those for places can be found among all arrestees in a city as an indicator of the active offender population. In Kansas City, Missouri, for example, the 2.7 percent of the estimated 500,000 city-user (as distinct from resident only) population that was arrested two or more times in 1990 produced over 60 percent of all arrests that year (Sherman, Rogan, and Velke 1991). The most frequently arrested 642 persons produced over 10 percent of all 71,461 "body arrests," defined as each event of taking a person into custody regardless of the number of charges, victims, or co-offenders. One hundred persons were arrested fifteen or more times that year, and ten persons were arrested thirty-two times or more. The distributions for nontraffic arrests only are virtually identical.

More important is the predictability of these offenders' levels of activity, assuming that their frequency of arrests has something to do with their frequency of crime commission. Once a nontraffic offender was arrested three times in 1990 (as over 5,000 persons were), the conditional probability (odds) of yet another arrest hit 55 percent. After seven arrests, the 751 offenders who qualified had a 71 percent chance of a further arrest. The curve of the probability of recidivism rises to 93 percent at the nineteenth arrest that year, with an unstable plateau thereafter as the available time at risk to be arrested declines (because most of the year has been used up by the time one has been arrested nineteen times). On a year-to-year basis, the 426 (less than 1 percent of total) offenders who had ten or more arrests (7 percent of all arrests) in 1989 had, as a group, an 82 percent likelihood of being arrested at least once in 1990. Whether this is a high level of predictive accuracy or a high level of false positives depends, of course, on what kind of proactive policing program is being considered. Nonintrusive surveillance, for example, or listing the person on a "most active" list to be considered by investigators would seem to entail little or no cost for false positives or suffering needlessly inflicted on a person from an inaccurate prediction.

Epidemiological analysis of this type can produce startling results. In 1989, for example, Kansas City police arrested by citation one individual 345 times for false alarm violations. While one could discount this problem as a false indicator of repeat criminality, one can also ask the question of why 345 separate citations were written without the problem being solved. The case is similar to a Philadelphia noise problem generating over 500 police calls in six months (Goldstein 1990, p. 81). Both examples indicate the inherent lack of coordination of reactive effort across the hundreds of patrol officers who can be assigned to each call and the value of proactive strategy based on epidemiological data solely from the standpoint of conserving police resources.

For all the emphasis police have placed on serious offenders, however, there have been remarkably few efforts to develop strategies targeting them. Incidents still drive police actions far more than any analysis of the offenders repeatedly involved in those incidents. Even a unit explicitly aimed at repeat offenders, like the Washington, D.C., Repeat Offender Project (ROP) was highly subjective, and minimally analytical, in its procedures for target selection (Martin and Sherman 1986). Prior to the Kansas City analysis cited above (Sherman, Rogan, and Velke 1991), no police agency ever (to my knowledge) rank ordered all offenders arrested in the past year by total or crime-specific arrest frequency. While such a ranking alone may not be sufficient as a targeting strategy, it would at least provide a check on the subjective tips and leads. This would help insure that targets selected for proactive investigation, or even extra reactive investigation, would be "worth" that effort in potential reduction of offenses.

3. *Times.*   Both places and offenders are highly time-sensitive targets. The concentration of all criminal events by time of day (Barr and Pease 1990, p. 296) may be even more marked within specific targets. For example, a recent analysis of some 1,200 violent crimes over four years in the Georgetown area of Washington, D.C., found that 65 percent of them occurred within a 1,000 foot radius of the "hot spot" intersection of Wisconsin and M Streets, a small portion of the total area. Of those crimes, however, fully half, or about one-third of the total violent crimes in the area, were reported to have occurred between midnight and 3:00 A.M. (Sherman et al. 1991c). Other hot spots, however, are not quite so time sensitive. A one-year analysis of all calls for service in 100 Minneapolis hot spot address clusters (with an average of over 100 calls for service each) found that they were all quite inactive between 3:00 A.M. and 11:00 A.M. Their prime times of high activity in the remaining sixteen hours, however, varied widely across locations.

Places may also become temporarily "hot," as in the immediate aftermath of a burglary. Canadian evidence cited by Barr and Pease (1990,

p. 297), for example, shows that the expected rate of burglary of an address during the first month after it has been burglarized is twelve times the rate without the first burglary. Bars and the immediate vicinity around them are typically hottest around closing time.

Time may also be important for specific offenders. Any offender with ten or more arrests can be analyzed for prime times of day for criminal activity. The times may vary widely across individuals, but that may be irrelevant once a specific person has been targeted for investigation.

The strategic question is the use to which police are willing or able to put these facts. The concentration of calls for service from 7:00 P.M. to 3:00 A.M. is widely known, for example, yet few police departments match that peak load period with peak assignments of personnel. The obvious inconvenience of these hours for police officers leads their unions to fight against making a standard shift to match them. Most agencies persist in using the traditional three eight-hour shifts starting at 7:00 or 8:00 A.M., many with equal numbers of personnel on each shift. This strategy would seem to be impossible to justify on a crime-control basis.

4. *Victims.* Compared to places and offenders, the individual victims of crime are substantially less predictable. In Kansas City in the five-year period 1985–89, for example, 3 percent of the city "user" population produced only 20 percent of all 231,714 victimizations of persons, as distinct from businesses (counting each person as victimized separately by each crime event, even with multiple victims, offenses, or offenders for a single event). All of the individuals with two or more victimizations in that period contributed only 38 percent of the total, in contrast to all persons with two or more *arrests* producing 62 percent of total arrests (Sherman, Rogan, and Velke 1991).

The fact that victims are not as predictable as arrestees does not rule them out as viable targets for crime prevention efforts, however. If the 3,452 people with an average of one or more Kansas City victimizations per year could be successfully "cured" of victimization, for example, it would reduce the number of victimizations by 7 percent. While this gain may appear "marginal" in percentage terms, it would still prevent 22,314 victimizations over a five-year period, or almost 4,500 victimizations per year. The 269 people with ten or more victimizations alone produced 3,372 of those problems, each of which may involve medical costs, lost days at work, and police investigative time (Sherman, Rogan, and Velke 1991).

We know little about how police might intervene effectively with repeat victims. But there is good reason to believe that victimizations are strongly related to "lifestyle." This perspective on routine activities (Hindelang, Gottfredson, and Garofalo 1978) suggests that some people manage their lives in ways that place them at much higher risk of being victimized. The number one victim in Kansas City in 1985–89, for example, suffered thirty-five offenses in 3.5 years: ten burglaries, ten larcenies, four robberies, two assaults, and nine other offenses, including attempted suicide. A white male in his 60s living in a poor black area, he had six home addresses and fourteen arrests (all minor) in the same time period. One of the arrests was for soliciting for prostitution, one for carrying a weapon, and several for violation of the animal leash law. This pattern may be consistent with any of the five reasons Sparks (1981) offered for multiple victimization: victim provocation, victim inability to defend, victim provision of criminal opportunities, victim attractiveness, or criminal impunity because victims are themselves breaking the law.

One of the helpful aspects of an official records repeat victim analysis (which police can now easily do), as distinct from national victimization surveys (which is all scholars have analyzed in the past), is the insight it offers into particular aspects of the victim's lifestyle. The overlap with the victim's arrest record is one example. A more surprising result is that eleven of the top fifty repeat victims in Kansas City for a five-year period were police officers, primarily victimized by assaults presumably committed by persons they were arresting. This may lead some to discount the value of the analysis. But if these officers are in fact suffering at least three (or more) assaults a year for five years, that should be an important flag for a personnel inquiry. Even in a high-crime area, this seems to suggest some problem in the officers' conduct (Toch 1975).

While there is no precedent for police targeting of high-risk victims, the computer systems needed to identify them are rapidly spreading throughout American policing. Once a citywide ranking of victims by frequency can be produced, as Kansas City has done, the only bar to effective intervention strategies will be inadequate ingenuity and lack of resources for testing them with controlled experiments.

D. Priorities Within or Across Crime Types?

The enormous overreach of the criminal law (Morris and Hawkins 1970) beyond the resources available for its enforcement always requires some triage among offenses: discretion not to invoke the criminal justice process. But the conventional triage criterion of offense seriousness has substantial limitations. Police may well achieve better crime control by setting priorities within, rather than across, offense types.

The main limitation with using only a seriousness criterion is that it can virtually legalize less serious offenses. Such de facto legalization can have serious consequences, possibly undermining any general deterrence of the problem. The maintenance of at least token levels for every type of offense may help to make some deterrence a part of a rational choice to commit the offense. How much enforcement is sufficient to accomplish that goal is an empirical question. But it is clearly possible to provide some enforcement for both homicide and minor assaults, speeding and parking violations, shootings and unscooped dog feces, and burglary and jaywalking. With limited enforcement efforts for the less serious offenses, the question becomes how to set priorities within those offense types.

Seriousness alone may also be a bad guide to setting priorities within offense types. Consider the value-of-goods-lost criterion for burglary investigations, which some departments employ. The not unprecedented threshold of $5,000 value may have the effect of decriminalizing burglary in poorer areas. Yet the arrest of a burglar for a $5,000 theft may have no better crime-control effect than arresting a burglar for a $50 theft. If burglary rates are higher in poorer areas already, then a crime-control perspective might concentrate burglary investigation among low-value theft losses, where greater crime control may be possible from each arrest.

Discretion to make arrests—or not—both within and across offense types has been left largely to street officers as individuals, with little structuring of that discretion by management. But there is no reason why guidelines could not be used to set criteria for high- and low-priority arrests. The same logic could even be used to *limit* arrests, especially where arrests compete with patrol presence. Until we know that arrests are better for crime control than police patrol presence in hot spots, it may be quite important to seek nonarrest alternatives to curbing minor disorder. In agencies with substantial time costs for booking each offender, too many arrests can deplete the street of patrol and possibly encourage more offenses than the arrests deter. The evidence reviewed below suggests all the more reason to have management attempt to structure discretion far more clearly, using criteria based on crime-control effectiveness as well as offense seriousness.

Police managers could, for example, establish an annual arrest "budget," projecting and limiting the number of arrests to be made for each offense type in each area on each watch (Sherman 1990*b*). Officers would then be given goals, limits, and standards for arrests to use whenever there is an evidentiary basis for making an arrest. Such budgeting would help to reveal tradeoffs between offense types, as well as resource choices between preventive patrol and enforcement. Patrol officers, of course, would certainly resist such attempts to restrict their discretion, but they might come to support the idea if they were given some power in the planning process.

III. Controlling Stranger Violence

There is good reason to apply these strategic perspectives first to stranger violence. Citizen rankings of crime severity (Rossi et al. 1974) suggest that stranger violence is the top priority for crime control. It is also the problem police may be least able to control. It is far rarer than other kinds of crimes and therefore much less predictable. The specific chains of causation are harder to identify, and vulnerable links are harder to find. While stranger violence offenders may be deemed most worthy of long-term incapacitation, very few offenders can actually be controlled by that strategy.

Stranger violence encompasses some, but not all, of the legal categories of homicide, rape, robbery, assault, and arson. Applying the estimates of the proportions of each offense committed by strangers (Flanagan and Maguire 1990, p. 247) to the FBI data on the relative frequency of these offenses (Federal Bureau of Investigation 1989), we can estimate the proportion of stranger violence each offense type produces (table 1). The majority of the problem is aggravated assault, which is fairly difficult to predict by place of occurrence, victims, or offenders. Only 24 percent of all 1989 assaults in Kansas City occurred at the 336 addresses with more than one assault, for example. Almost half of all stranger violence is robbery, which is somewhat (but not much) more predictable by place of occurrence. Almost half (44 percent) of the 1989 Kansas City robberies occurred at the 503 addresses (0.31 percent of all addresses) with two or more robberies. These epidemiological data suggest the potential, if modest, value of proactive police strategies aimed at places as targets. Other data suggest the potential

184   Lawrence W. Sherman

TABLE 1

Distribution of Stranger Violence by Offense Type, 1988

Offense	Total	Crime by Stranger (in Percent)	Stranger Violence (in Percent)
Robbery	542,968	77	40
Rape	92,486	42	4
Aggravated assault	910,092	63	55
Homicide	20,675	12	1
Total	1,566,221		

Sources.—Federal Bureau of Investigation (1989); Flanagan and Maguire (1990).

value of field interrogations aimed generally at all "suspicious" persons on the streets. Perhaps the most effective strategy would be a combination of the two, with strict attention paid to proper methods of field interrogation.

A. *Offender-oriented Strategies*

A major issue in criminology is the extent to which offenders specialize. Whatever the evidence over a criminal career, it is relatively hard for police to identify currently active robbers from current year arrest data. Only seventy-nine persons had two or more robbery arrests in Kansas City in 1990. Those seventy-nine, in contrast, accounted for 20 percent (173) of all 879 robbery arrests and may have accounted for even more than that proportion of all robberies (for which the clearance rate is only about 10 percent). The question is what effects on crime would result from giving *legal* special attention to such offenders. Previous efforts have not always met that standard.

In the 1930s, when automobiles were still relatively rare, New York police operated "Strong Arm Squads" against violent criminals (Behan 1990), just as other jurisdictions operated "Goon Squads." The target "goons," or offenders, were probably contract workers who committed stranger violence against people who had broken business deals or failed to pay extortion money. They were a very different type of offender from the modern robber or rapist, if only because they were more readily identifiable through criminal networks. Their known faces allowed police squads to roam the streets by the carful, stopping to jump out if they passed by a known goon. The preventive action consisted of beating the goon up, taking his gun away, and telling him to leave town or at least watch his step. By some accounts, this was an effective way to attack stranger violence.

Detroit maintained a similar tradition well into the 1960s with the "Cruiser" unit (Reiss 1990), also a car full of uniformed officers. Its demise was followed shortly by the creation of the STRESS unit (Stop the Robberies—Enjoy Safe Streets), a group of plainclothes officers that attempted to put stress onto robbery suspects. Its record of killing black suspects (and nonsuspects), if not of reducing crime, made the unit a central issue in the next mayoral campaign (Milton et al. 1977). The results included the election of Detroit's first black mayor and abolition of the unit.

Contemporary attacks on suspected active stranger assailants suggest they are relatively hard to find. The seventy-officer Washington, D.C., Repeat Offender Project began with the goal of focusing constant surveillance on stranger robbers but could not identify enough of them to stay busy. The ones they did identify had the unfortunate habit of going home at night and staying there for 12 to 16 hours, which made surveillance extremely expensive and very boring. ROP officers wound up making more "serendipitous" arrests while watching their targets than actual arrests of the targets. Citing the theory of frequent offense switching among repeat offenders, the unit eventually concentrated on making arrests of reportedly active property offenders, on any charges they could find. The target selection was based almost entirely on tips, with no systematic analysis of repeat arrest patterns like those described for Kansas City. Using informants to lure offenders into burglarizing locations where the officers were waiting, or raiding a home full of stolen property, the Washington ROP unit arrested about half of its targets within one week of being targeted (Martin and Sherman 1986). Whether the active offenders they arrested for property crimes were also the highest risk offenders for robbery and rape, however, is unknown.

One major problem with offender-oriented strategies may be the failure to recognize important patterns of co-offending. While the lone offender model may be generally correct for adult robbers, juvenile robberies are more often committed by groups of two or more (Reiss 1988). Locking up one offender who participates in one or several groups may do nothing to reduce the total number of crimes, given the continuation of the co-offending groups. The one offender, one crime assumption is clearly inadequate as a causal model for stranger violence.

Both juveniles and adults may also be vulnerable to the suggestive influence of "Typhoid Marys," or people who accumulate high numbers of co-offenders (Reiss 1988). These "carriers" are not ringleaders of an ongoing group as much as idea men in a social network, people whose presence in any particular group may tip the balance of action toward committing a violent offense. While the evidence for the existence of these spreaders of criminality is not strong, it can be readily assembled in any police agency with computer systems linking individual rap sheets to arrest reports naming co-arrestees. Rank ordering of all rap sheet subjects by total numbers of co-offenders could reveal enormous disparity, with a small number of offenders being linked to over half of all other offenders. Such persons could just as easily be the unlucky ones who are always talked into crimes resulting in arrests by smarter ringleaders who do not get caught. But the possibility of their being true recruiters warrants closer examination.

If a police department could identify Typhoid Marys of stranger violence in this fashion, they would clearly become a high priority target for proactive investigation. Given the same number of offenses by two different offenders, one a lone wolf and the other a Typhoid Mary, there could be far greater crime reduction from incarcerating the latter. This could occur from the spinoff effects of the carrier's recruitment of new offenders into a first offense of stranger violence. Given that experience, the co-offender could go on to commit other offenses without the carrier, with or without other co-offenders. The lone wolf, in contrast, does not seem to spread crime around, making less contribution to the total volume of stranger violence.

Field Interrogations.   Not all offender-oriented strategies that reduce robbery are focused on specific names or even on that specific crime of stranger violence. Indeed, there is substantial evidence that a police department's level of proactive traffic and disorderly conduct enforcement can affect its robbery rate. Wilson and Boland (1978), using a simultaneous equation model across thirty-five U.S. cities, first reported an inverse relation between the number of moving violations per officer and the rate of robbery victimizations per capita. They theorized that aggressive traffic enforcement was an indicator of the general level of active surveillance with which police patrolled the streets in any given city, which in turn was a function of municipal culture and predictable by various characteristics of local government.

They hypothesized that more intensive watchfulness by police on the streets was an effective deterrent to robbery, either indirectly by apprehending more actual or would-be robbers, or directly by affecting community perceptions of the likelihood of arrest. While admitting their evidence was not as conclusive as a randomized experiment, Wilson and Boland still found strong support for the theory.

Further research has refined and extended the conclusion. Jacob and Rich (1981) challenged the conclusion on the grounds that it could not be replicated with longitudinal data *within* cities on traffic citations and robbery rates. Wilson and Boland (1981–82) replied that, among other things, changes over time within cities did not approximate the differences across cities in patrol style and that Jacob and Rich failed to use the traffic citations per officer as a measure of proactive patrol. More important was the replication and extension of Wilson and Boland by Sampson and Cohen (1988), using a more complex design with the much larger sample of 171 cities. They combined traffic enforcement and disorderly conduct enforcement per officer as a single indicator of "aggressive policing," defined as a tendency to invoke the law even for minor offenses. They also employed elaborate controls on the urban social structural characteristics most highly correlated with street crime rates—the only cross-sectional police and crime study to do so. Police aggressiveness was inversely related to both robbery offenses per capita (but not burglary) and the prevalence of robbery offenders in the cities. Police behavior was almost as powerful an influence on crime as the city's divorce rate.

Sampson and Cohen (1988) also found complex effects of police aggressiveness on robbery offending rates by age and race. Citywide aggressiveness had more powerful effects in reducing black robbery rates than white rates, for both juveniles and adults. Yet further analysis showed that police aggressiveness toward whites (drunk driving and disorder enforcement rates per capita whites), who comprise the majority population in most of the cities, had an independent effect in reducing both white and black adult robbery offending rates. Similarly, police aggressiveness toward blacks had an independent negative effect on adult robbery offending rates among whites and blacks. But black adult robbery rates are more strongly associated with proactive policing of *whites* than of blacks. Thus police aggressiveness has a "pervasive effect" in reducing robbery rates, at least among adults. The effects are generally weaker among juveniles but show more impact on black juveniles than on whites.

The troublesome aspect of these findings is that they run directly contrary to the "friendly policing" thrust of current police innovations (Skolnick and Bayley 1986), designed in part to counteract the kind of aggressive policing Sampson and Cohen find to be so effective in reducing robbery. Proactive field encounters with suspicious persons received very bad press in the 1960s and early 1970s, in large part because of overtones and evidence of racial discrimination and harassment (Rossi, Berk, and Eidson 1974). Field interrogations and traffic stops clearly have a high potential for officer rudeness and racial slurs. Even worse, the police culture associated with proactive patrol has been blamed for causing extreme cases of brutality (Nazario and Jefferson 1991).

Yet there is no reason why legalistic traffic and disorder enforcement needs to be offensive or insensitive to persons stopped and questioned. With proper training and supervision in a community relations–conscious police culture, field interrogations need not provoke community hostility, as the San Diego Field Interrogation Experiment suggests (Boydstun 1975, pp. 54–55). This 1973–74 quasi experiment compared three patrol areas: one area where all field interrogations were suspended for nine months and then reinstated, one area where field interrogations were only conducted by officers specially trained to reduce friction with citizens they stop, and one area where there was no change in field interrogation practices only. Total reported crime was virtually unchanged in the two areas retaining field interrogation, but it rose significantly from seventy-five "suppressible" crimes a month in the baseline period to 104 per month in the experimental period, dropping again to eighty-one crimes per month in the follow-up period. Suppressible crimes were defined as those in theory most sensitive to field stops: robbery, burglary, theft and auto theft, assault, sex crimes, malicious mischief, and disturbances. Citizen surveys in the three areas found that reducing field interrogations had no effect on community attitudes toward police. Interviews with interrogation subjects found most favorable attitudes toward officers who had been given special training in field interrogations, although observations of trained and untrained officers found no differences in their behavior.

The results suggest that, with proper organizational development, it should be possible to do proactive field stops without alienating those persons stopped, with the benefit of controlling suppressible crime by a margin of about 20 percent. The cost of doing so is about 5 percent of a patrol officer's time. The difference across areas in dosage, as reported in police logs, was 22 minutes of field interrogations per officer per shift in the control area compared to 0 minutes in the experimental area. There may also be community relations costs in such a practice. The U.S. Supreme Court's subsequent ruling (*Kolender v. Lawson*, 46 U.S. 352 [1983]) that the San Diego Police had collectively and discriminatorily harassed a black man with a "dreadlock" hair style who liked to walk around town suggests the potential difficulty with any proactive policy aimed at "suspicious" persons as targets. But this is again a problem that might be solved with more specific guidelines, especially if they are race-neutral in design and effect.

An unmeasured aspect of the experiment was the kinds of places in which the field interrogations were conducted. Any guidelines for the selection of a "suspicious" person must entail a judgment about persons in relation to the places where they are found. In that sense, field interrogations may also be seen as a place-oriented strategy for crime control.

B. Place-oriented Strategies

Some stranger robberies are highly predictable by place over a one-year period, but most robbery locations have had no recent prior robberies. Even where robbery is predictable, it is impossible to predict when, in the short run, robbery will occur, absent an informant's tip. Of the 161 addresses with three to six robberies in Kansas City in 1988, for example, 116 of them (72 percent) had at least one robbery in 1989. This compares, however, to 1,947 addresses robbed in 1989 that had no robberies in 1988. While the latter group was only 1 percent of the places with no 1988 robbery, it was also 77 percent of all 1989 robbery locations. Thus, only 5 percent of those locations were highly predictable as robbery targets.

The most common place-oriented antirobbery strategy has been stakeout units, which were discredited in many cities for the high rate of shootouts with and deaths of robbers they produced (Milton et al. 1977). They also seem fairly inefficient in their consumption of police time, even with informant tips, although this question has not been examined systematically; epidemiological data alone are clearly inadequate, with a one-year time period covered by the prediction. One unintended consequence of stakeout units was to reveal an unknown portion of the robbery rate as fraudulent cover-up of employee theft. On several occasions in Kansas City in the 1970s, for example, off-site stakeouts of commercial premises were conducted without notification

of the store clerks. While plainclothes police sat observing no one go
into the store, the clerk phoned in a robbery at the premises. When
the uniformed officers responded to investigate, the stakeout squad
came in. Searches of the clerks revealed the money missing from the
register (Joiner 1990). Similar discoveries were made in Washington,
D.C., with robberies of both convenience stores and dry-cleaning delivery trucks (Wilson 1990*a*).

This phenomenon is important to interpreting the effects of more
recent innovations in robbery control through situational crime prevention. Cash control devices in stores, bulletproof barriers for lone gas
station attendants, and the requirement of two clerks after dark in
certain stores may all defeat *fraudulent* robbery as well as real robbery.
Where unwitnessed robbery is at stake, it will be difficult to determine
how much of it is real or fraudulent. But where environmental design
makes it much harder to lie credibly about the occurrence of a robbery,
any reduction in reported robbery should not be uncritically accepted
as evidence of control of stranger violence.

One of the most influential recent place-oriented strategies to reduce
robbery (Goldstein 1990, p. 80; Moore, in this volume) falls victim to
this kind of interpretive problem, among others. In Gainesville, Florida, police attacked a rapid rise in convenience store robberies in the
mid-1980s by a thorough analysis of the epidemiology of the problem,
including its prevalence and frequency across all stores in the community. They analyzed the situational features of the crime and concluded
that robbers prefer to wait until they are alone with a clerk before
committing the robbery. This conclusion, of course, was based on lone
clerks' accounts of how the robberies occurred. It was also supported
by a University of Florida survey of imprisoned convenience store
robbers the police department commissioned, which found that robbers took the number of clerks (as well as their size and gender, even
if alone) to be very important factors in their decision to rob a store.

The police chief used this extensive analysis (Clifton 1987) to support
a recommendation to the city council for requiring convenience stores
to employ two clerks in each store open after dark. After it was passed,
the department claimed a 65 percent reduction in convenience store
robberies was attributable to the law. Problem-oriented police officers
in other cities, such as Minneapolis, accepted the results as valid, and
the *New York Times* cited it on the editorial page as a success story
(Anderson 1990). The Florida Legislature was scheduled in 1991 to
consider adopting a statewide two-clerk requirement, and other juris-

dictions have considered adopting the law based on the success of the Gainesville results (Richman 1990).

Unfortunately, closer inspection by a former Washington police chief retained by the National Association of Convenience Stores (Wilson 1990*b*) found little compelling evidence for the effectiveness of a two-clerk rule, which took effect four months *after* the robberies had already dropped precipitously. He also found several plausible rival hypotheses explaining the reduction in convenience store robberies. Chief among these is an almost identical pattern of rise and fall in convenience store robberies in the Alachua County Sheriff's jurisdiction surrounding Gainesville, even though the county passed no requirement for using two clerks. County police do report, however, that three convenience store robbers, highly active in both the city and county, were apprehended and continuously incarcerated four months prior to and long after the two-clerk rule took effect. The date of their arrests corresponds exactly to the sudden drop in convenience store robberies in both jurisdictions. The robberies merely continued at the same low rate in both areas after the two-clerk rule took effect, with no additional drop in rate.

Additional rival theories for the drop include legislative requirements for a set of additional security features, such as cameras and cash control, which went into effect the same month the robbers were apprehended (by stakeout methods) and robberies declined. The difficulty of concocting a fraudulent robbery claim with a co-employee present is another rival theory, as is simple regression to the mean after a sudden eighteen-month peak (Campbell and Ross 1968).

A more effective place-oriented approach to robbery reduction may be bulletproof booths, which have been widely adopted in gas stations, subway change booths, banks, and liquor stores. In 1987, the Maryland legislature enacted a law requiring their use at all gas stations. The governor vetoed the law, however, and appointed a task force on retail security to study the matter. The task force could find no evidence that the booths were effective and did uncover evidence of pouring and igniting gasoline in the cash hole as a technique for injuring clerks. Examples of robbers taking customers hostage have also been found. The question awaits careful experimentation for resolution.

1. *Preventive Patrol.* The most basic police strategy against public stranger violence has been preventive patrol. This strategy has been given little credence since the Kansas City Preventive Patrol Experiment found increases in patrol ineffective at reducing crime (Kelling

et al. 1974). This quasi experiment in a relatively low-crime area attempted to double patrol car presence in five patrol beats, eliminate it
altogether (except for answering calls) in another five, and hold it constant in a third group of five beats. No *statistically significant* changes
were observed in crime rates, although there were ample differences
of magnitude that the small sample size lacked statistical power to test
(Sherman 1986). Moreover, Larson (1976) has suggested that the volume of calls answered in the no-patrol area gave it virtually as much
patrol presence as the regular patrol area. Hence the frequent conclusion that "it makes about as much sense to have police patrol routinely
in cars to fight crime as it does to have firemen patrol routinely in fire
trucks to fight fire" (Klockars and Mastrofski 1991) is not supported
by the Kansas City experiment and is contradicted by numerous other
quasi-experimental results (Sherman 1990*a*).

Perhaps the most compelling evidence for the preventive effects of
patrol on stranger violence is the increase in such crime during the
major police strikes for which good data are available. The mayhem
during the Liverpool (Sellwood 1978) and Boston (Russell 1975) police
strikes in the late summer of 1919 included looting, armed robbery,
and (in Boston) numerous rapes and gang rapes (Russell 1975, p. 137).

Admittedly, this increase might be written off to the general political
instability of that period rather than to a loss of deterrence from police
patrol. Yet, the political instability argument is weaker when used to
explain away the crime increase during the seventeen-hour Montreal
police strike of October 7, 1969 (Clark 1969): 13.5 times the normal
hourly rate of burglaries, 50 times the normal hourly rate of bank
robberies, and widespread looting by "ordinarily disciplined, peaceful
citizens," although there were no reported rapes (Clark 1969, p.176).

The political instability argument completely fails to explain away
the 50 percent increase in store robberies and 42 percent increase in
hospital admissions for violent injuries at a large Helsinki clinic during
the seventeen-day Finnish police strike of February 1976 (Makinen and
Takala 1980). The Finnish "experiment," in an era of long-term political stability, is even more compelling because of very cold weather, a
major national fixation on the televised Winter Olympics, and the fact
that the data evaluating crime rate changes came from sources independent of the police. Even without the looting and collective behavior of
the more famous strikes, Finland's loss of 86 percent of its police force
and virtually all of its uniformed patrol force was accompanied by a

clearly documented increase in the rate of violence and stranger violence. Similarly, the Nazi arrest of the entire Copenhagen police force in 1944 was followed by a tenfold increase in both robberies and larcenies reported to insurance companies (Andenaes 1974, p. 51).

Drawing conclusions from Kansas City is also inappropriate because traditional preventive patrol in automobiles has been widely dispersed, even along the main commercial arteries police prefer to frequent. Yet as I noted earlier, stranger violence and crime in general are highly concentrated in a small number of addresses (Sherman, Gartin, and Buerger 1989). The odds of a widely dispersed police patrol encountering stranger violence in progress are so low that it appears unreasonable to expect it to have much deterrent effect. Over 6,000 hours of evening observations of high-crime intersections in Minneapolis, for example, found a mean frequency of patrol cars driving by only once in every 23 hours (Sherman and Weisburd 1990).

2. *Hot Spots Patrol.*   Given the concentration of stranger violence in hot spots of crime, the same dosage of patrol can be applied much more intensely where it may do the most good. Police have increasingly employed such a "directed patrol" strategy over the past two decades, with open-air drug markets providing a wealth of targets in recent years. Privately owned premises have also expanded their use of such patrols by off-duty police officers, in such locations as shopping center parking lots, fast-food restaurants, and garden apartment complexes. Until recently, however, there has been little systematic evidence on the effects of such focused patrols at deterring stranger violence, or any other kind of crime.

The Minneapolis Hot Spots Patrol Experiment (Sherman and Weisburd 1990) begins to fill that gap. From December 1988 through November 1989, the Minneapolis Police Department, Crime Control Institute, and Rutgers School of Criminal Justice conducted a randomized experiment in directed patrol in marked automobiles by uniformed police at 110 specially selected hot spots of crime. These locations were clusters of an average of fifteen street addresses selected on the basis of high frequencies of calls for police service for "hard," or predatory, crimes, as well as high volumes of calls about "soft" crime and disorder. Only hot spots that were highly active two years in succession were eligible, to minimize regression to the mean. The average number of calls about both types of crime in the baseline year before the experiment was 188, or about one every forty-six hours. The typical hot spot

extended for several addresses, or up to half a block, in all four directions from an intersection, while others were centered on multiple
dwellings. All of them were visually independent of the others, so that
a police car in one hot spot could not be seen in another.

The 110 address clusters were randomly assigned to two groups of
fifty-five (in five statistical "blocks" based on call frequency), one of
which was designated to receive increased patrol. The goal was to
provide three hours per day of intermittent patrol presence between
11:00 A.M. and 3:00 A.M., the highest crime period. Officers left the
hot spots to answer radio calls, but returned at unpredictable intervals
to write reports, talk with pedestrians, or just (in their words) "sit on
the hot spot." The actual dosage over the year was about 2.5 hours per
day according to official police logs. Some 6,500 hours of independent
observations in both the experimental and control groups during the
evening hours (7:00 P.M. to 2:30 A.M.) showed that police cars were
present in the hot spots for 12.8 percent of the observation time of the
experimental group, but only 4.5 percent in the control group. This
patrol dosage ratio of 2.83 to 1 does not count police car drive throughs,
the addition of which drops the ratio slightly to 2.6 to 1. Patrol time
was fairly evenly distributed within each group, with only 9 percent
of the addresses overall receiving dosage levels close to the mean of the
other group. The greater inconsistency was across groups over seasons.
When total calls were down, there was less (reactive) patrol presence
in the control group and more (proactive) presence in the experimental
group. When calls were up, the pattern reversed. The ratio of observed
police presence time between the experimental and control group varied from almost 6 to 1 in March to 1.2 to 1 in August, but exceeded
2 to 1 in all months but August.

David Weisburd's preliminary analysis of the call data for stranger
violence suggests that directed patrol had a modest deterrent effect on
robbery in the hot spots, although there was no significant deterrence
of hard crime calls generally (Sherman and Weisburd 1990). Subsequent analyses will explore the extent to which any crime reduction
in the experimental hot spots was attributable to displacement to other
locations (Cornish and Clarke 1987; Barr and Pease 1990). Scholars
will also need time to reflect on the findings and their implications,
just as they have on past experiments. But if displacement and other
problems are found to be minor, then directed public (though perhaps
not private) police patrol in hot spots may be a viable, if expensive,
robbery-control strategy.

C. Victim-oriented Strategies

Police have attempted relatively few victim-oriented strategies against stranger violence, apparently with good reason. There is very little repeat victimization for robbery (including larceny purse snatch) found in official crime reports. Over the period 1985–89 in Kansas City, only 2.72 percent of the robbery victimizations were accounted for by the 127 victims who were robbed three times or more. However, those people had seven times the risk of further robberies of people who had not been robbed before. While it makes sense to devote some attention to such a high-risk group, the crime-control payoff citywide would be very marginal indeed.

The most common victim-oriented strategy for stranger violence is police lectures to concerned groups. Subjects include how to prevent crimes through simple precautions, many of which reflect common sense (such as looking in the back of a car before entering it, and always locking a parked car). More problematic topics include how to respond to a criminal attack once it begins: what to do if a rapist attacks, or if you hear a burglar in your home, or if a gun is pointed at you.

One problem with such lectures is that they are based on questionable beliefs about the consequences of taking the various options recommended or described. Victims of would-be rapists are more likely to escape if they offer nonforceful resistance, for example, but only if they live to answer the survey questionnaire (Skogan and Block 1983). The relative rate of death for resistance and cooperation remains unknown. The consequences of forcefully resisting armed robbers, however, are somewhat clearer, in that it increases risks of physical attack and injury (Skogan and Block 1986), and standard police advice is to cooperate. More subtle points about tone of voice, eye contact, speed of movements, and so on are also made in these lectures, but with questionable empirical foundation.

The major problem with this line of strategy is that it remains virtually unevaluated. No one has any idea whether these lessons reduce injury rates or increase them, and both possibilities are quite plausible. The major obstacle to evaluation, fortunately, is that the base rates of stranger violence victimization after receiving this instruction are so low. Reliable estimates of the impact of such instruction, even with a randomized design, would require a very large sample to be observed for many years.

More controversial, but also better evaluated, is the practice of police in some communities of recommending that potential victims—

especially women—buy guns. Recent public health research (reviewed in Cook 1991) suggests that the presence of guns in a home is a strong factor in firearms deaths, including accidents and suicides. But this does not alter the view many hold about the need for guns in self-protection, as well as the evidence some researchers have mustered to support the hypothesis (see Cook 1991). While police executives are increasingly in favor of regulating gun sales to bar access to criminals, many are of mixed minds about the virtues of honest citizens possessing guns to fight criminals.

As long as there is no strong message from police professionals against keeping guns for self-defense, purchases for that reason seem likely to increase. And as gun density grows, the overall homicide rate goes up, according to increasing evidence (Cook 1991). It should follow that police could fight serious violence by actively discouraging most private ownership of guns as merely throwing oil on the fire, even if the effect is that some crimes cannot be rebuffed by armed citizens.

IV. Controlling Soft Crime

Stranger violence dominates the headlines, but the far more frequently occurring "soft" or minor crimes (Reiss 1985) dominate police workloads. They also have a dominant role in generating public fear of crime and contributing to residential and large corporate flight from center cities (Skogan and Maxfield 1981). Soft crime may also attract hard crime, by communicating to potential assailants that an area is "out of control" (Wilson and Kelling 1982). One of the strongest correlates of calls about robbery in Minneapolis hot spots is calls about drunks (Weisburd, Maher, and Sherman 1991).

Soft crime embraces a wide range of behavior with similar community consequences. Car break-ins leave shattered glass for all passersby to see. Drunks use foul language, urinate in public, or collapse on the sidewalk. Teenagers use "boom boxes" to disturb a quiet residential block as they walk by late at night. A man beats his wife in a parking lot. Each of these events suggests that anarchy is around the corner and underlines the continuing threat of crime in the local environment.

Police strategies against soft crime are often not explicit because most of the offense categories at stake are not serious enough for priority treatment. Soft crimes are often good examples of how some offenses have been effectively decriminalized, with virtually no police attention. Yet there are some things police do already that can have effects on soft crime.

A. *Offender-oriented Strategies*

Field interrogations, for example, appear to have substantial impact on soft crime. Boydstun (1975, p. 33) found significant increases in a range of soft crime in the San Diego quasi-experimental comparison of one area where field interrogations were suspended for nine months, compared to two comparison areas where they were continued. The soft crimes deterred during the baseline and follow-up periods, but that increased when interrogations were suspended, included petty theft, grand theft, sex crimes, malicious mischief, and disturbances.

Antiloitering "sweeps," invoking ordinances against obstructing pedestrian traffic, produced a decline in recorded crime (but not surveyed victimization) in an experimental area in Newark, New Jersey (Pate et al. 1986). The procedure of ordering young males to clear the sidewalk, then arresting them minutes later if they fail to leave, has been attacked as unconstitutional by scholarly observers (Skolnick and Bayley 1986, p. 199) but not by the courts. Other police procedures employed in this area during the experimental year, which may also have contributed to the measured crime-reduction effect, included automobile checkpoints, random police inspections of public transit buses, and foot patrol. Which of these, if any, was more important than the others in producing the effect is impossible to tell from the design. But it is instructive that the same crime-reduction effect was achieved with much more positive citizen attitudes in a similar area that received a "community policing" program of a storefront, door-to-door police visits, and a neighborhood cleanup as well as street sweeps and other intensive enforcement (Skogan 1990, p. 119).

Newark was also the site of an unevaluated police effort to combat predominantly soft youth crime through truancy enforcement (Williams 1983). Working in the early 1980s with specially powered truancy officers and a school bus, police officers cruised the city during school hours looking for school-aged children. Those picked up were taken to a special detention center—study hall and kept until school hours ended. Parents were also contacted, although without much optimism. The primary objective was to incapacitate the truants from daytime burglary and shoplifting.

Another youth-focused but unevaluated strategy against soft crime was the Minneapolis RECAP unit's enforcement of the state curfew law. Plagued by frequent soft crime calls at 7-Eleven's and other youthful gathering places, the RECAP unit organized a "sweep" of the entire neighborhood surrounding these locations looking for underage people after 10:00 P.M. While it is not clear that the sweeps reduced calls for service at the repeat call locations, over two-thirds of the apprehended juveniles had prior arrests. It seems plausible that sustained curfew enforcement pressure, where legal, could incapacitate the youths from being out at night, perhaps reducing a wide range of soft crime as well as drug abuse and other evening activities (Buerger 1991).

Foot patrol officers have long used a variety of techniques for managing panhandlers, drunks, the homeless, and the mentally ill on their beats. As Bittner (1970) and Wilson and Kelling (1982) have shown, police effectiveness in controlling the potential for soft crime by these marginal populations depends heavily on knowing them as persons. With verbal orders or persuasion based on trial and error with each local "character" in the officer's repertoire, a great deal can be prevented with minimal effort and very rare use of force or arrest. The conventional strategy of wide-ranging automobile patrol, however, greatly limits the capacity of officers to gain this depth of experience with specific individuals.

The use of arrest and prosecution for soft crime may have different consequences than patrol does and different consequences for individuals than for communities. While Boydstun (1975) and Sampson and Cohen (1988) find deterrent community effects from legalistic policing of soft crime, Klein (1986) found crime-*increasing* effects from legalistic treatment of juveniles arrested for primarily soft crimes. This three-month experiment in 1974 was conducted in nine of the eighteen police stations in an unnamed West Coast metropolis, randomly assigning 306 arrested juveniles to four conditions in the juvenile division office: release with no further action, referral to social services, referral with subsidies to cover the costs of social services, and petition (prosecution) to juvenile court. Initial cheating by police on the random assignment procedures was detected and apparently overcome. Follow-up interviews with the juveniles were conducted nine months later with a 59 percent completion rate. Official data on repeat crime were collected for 100 percent of the sample for twenty-seven months after random assignment.

The more complete data set showed the more startling results. While there were no significant differences across the groups in subsequent self-reported crime, there were significant differences in official recidivism. The prevalence of recidivism at fifteen months varied directly with the formality of the treatment, from 37 percent among those juveniles released to 63 percent among those prosecuted. While this experiment does not show that the *arrests* had a crime-escalating effect, it did show that police decisions to treat juveniles legalistically had a clear effect of increasing crime.

Clearly much more needs to be learned about the effects of offender-oriented patrol and arrest strategies on soft crime, preferably through additional randomized experiments. The possibility that police may be increasing crime or hurting community relations with these methods is too serious to ignore.

B. Place-oriented Strategies

Just as there is more soft than hard crime overall, the frequencies of soft crime in specific locations are much higher than frequencies of hard crime. Targeting police resources at hot spots of soft crime is thus even more efficient than targeting at hot spots of hard crime, although they often turn out to be the same places. Two of the most popular place-oriented strategies are problem solving and directed patrol (Moore, in this volume).

1. *Problem Solving.* Eck and Spelman (1987) describe the Newport News experience with the general approach of "problem-oriented policing" that has been used in many cities to deal with disorderly places (Goldstein 1990). Based on the concepts of Goldstein (1979), and using a strategy similar to the RECAP model (Sherman 1986), problem-oriented policing tries to diagnose the causes of soft crime concentrations at specific locations, do something about them, and then follow up to see if the strategy has been effective.

In Newport News, for example, the approach was used with prostitution as a cause of the problem of robbery in a four block area of downtown. Diagnosis showed that about half the robberies were linked to the persistent prostitution problem with twenty-eight "regulars" in the same area. The multiple-tactic solution began with showing the local judges the connection between prostitution and robbery and obtaining their agreement to increase the sentence for prostitution to two months. In addition, they agreed to suspend ten more months with the condition that the prostitutes stay away from that area or else go back to jail. Police also put enforcement pressure on area bars and rooming houses, using regulatory statutes aimed at control of prostitution. After six months, only six of the twenty-eight regulars were still found in the area, and robberies (of an unspecified frequency) had dropped by 43 percent (Eck and Spelman 1987, p. 80).

In Houston, problem-oriented policing led to the diagnosis of a park as an open-air drug market due to lax supervision at night (Brown 1989). Mobilizing sufficient resources to close down the park at night, police were able to dry up the local drug market.

In Minneapolis, problem-oriented policing led the RECAP unit to a diagnosis of two taverns as disorderly from serving intoxicated patrons, as well as encouraging drug sales. The solution was to have their liquor licenses suspended; both were later torn down for urban renewal, with no new liquor license granted for another location (Buerger 1991).

All of these examples constitute quasi experiments in problem solving for soft crime. Unfortunately, they suffer from strong selection biases, both in picking the problems to begin with and then in reporting success in the literature. Buerger (1991) reports detailed case studies of about 100 attempts by the Minneapolis RECAP unit to solve soft crime problems at specific addresses selected solely on the basis of high total call volume. There are as many failures as successes in the casebook, with opportunities to reflect on what might have been done differently to insure greater success. Perhaps the leading critique is that there were too many diverse problems and individuals at each address, and too many addresses for each officer (about sixty over one year) to take on successfully, even as a full-time assignment (Buerger 1991).

Whatever the reason, the first controlled experiment in problem solving at high-call locations showed no effect on calls in the experimental group for commercial addresses. This conclusion from the RECAP experiment suggests that "problem solving" as a strategy is probably too general for a meaningful experimental test. More useful may be controlled experiments on homogeneous kinds of places with similar problems, testing identical tactics at all experimental sites. The RECAP experiment in strategy, in contrast, targeted widely diverse kinds of places with widely diverse tactics and levels of police attention. The statistical power of any experiment under such conditions of heterogeneity is understandably quite weak. More important, perhaps, is the weakness of the knowledge base from which police can draw to diagnose and solve soft crime problems. Until there is a better literature to guide them in seeking chains of causation, problem-solving officers may be better off selecting problems subjectively on the criterion of a sound hypothesis for solving the problem.

2. *Directed Patrol.*   The evidence on directed patrol shows consistent effects in reducing soft crime. The Oakland experience of the

early 1980s (Reiss 1985), for example, is a striking quasi-experimental success in police control of soft crime through directed uniformed patrol presence. In committing themselves to a complete rebuilding of downtown Oakland, a group of developers wanted to insure that its skid row atmosphere and problems would disappear with the old pawnshops and flophouses. Their solution was to offer $1 million per year to the Oakland Police Department (OPD) for additional patrol officers to be directed to the several block "new" downtown, patrolling on foot, horseback, and scooters. The department accepted the offer on certain conditions guaranteeing total control over the officers to the OPD. The additional presence of some twenty-five police officers was multiplied by fairly close collaboration with many more office building security guards.

The destruction of the skid row physical environment, of course, may have been sufficient to displace large portions of the potential soft crime offenders. Adding the directed patrol at the same time as the environmental change makes it impossible to assess directly the effects of police alone. But the joint result insured the economic viability of the new office center. To the extent that reported crime statistics are a valid indicator of the change, they support the conclusion of a reduction in soft crime (Reiss 1985). Considering the substantial population increase in the area as an increase in the supply of potential victims, soft crime could have increased dramatically, but did not.

The conclusion that uniformed police presence can deter soft crime is strongly supported by the experience of police strikes. In the Boston police strike of 1919, for example, the first widespread lawbreaking to start and the last to end was public dice games (Russell 1975, p. 131). In Finland in 1976, systematic observation by researchers independent of police showed clear increases in public drinking and the size of groups of young males (Makinen and Takala 1980, p. 103), as well as a 50 percent increase in phone booth coin burglaries compared to the periods before and after the strike. To the extent that smashing store windows for looting constitutes "soft" crime, the Liverpool, Boston, Montreal, and Baltimore (1974) strikes all experienced that phenomenon (Russell 1975, p. 242; Sellwood 1978), although some other police strikes have not.

The most systematic evidence for this proposition comes from the Minneapolis Hot Spots Patrol Experiment (Sherman and Weisburd 1990). David Weisburd's preliminary analysis of that experiment found that a 250 percent increase in patrol presence at target hot spots produced a 13 percent reduction (or displacement) in total calls for service about crime, most of which were soft crimes. This effect lasted from the beginning of the experiment on December 1, 1988, until August 1, 1989, six weeks after directed patrol was reduced for the summer. In 300,000 minutes of observations of the hot spots during that period, the controls had disorderly events during 4 percent of the time and the experimentals had disorder for only 2 percent of the time. Measurement thereafter was unfortunately confounded by a change in the CAD system on October 1.

Two interesting observations stand out from Weisburd's preliminary results. One is that the effects of directed patrol were largely consistent at 100 crime calls deterred per month as long as the observed patrol time ratio between experimental and control spots remained in excess of 2 to 1. As soon as this ratio dropped, the deterrent (or displacement) effect disappeared. The other striking finding, consistent with the theory of residual deterrence from police crackdowns (Sherman 1990*a*), is that the deterrent effect lasted for six weeks after the directed patrol time in the experimental group was officially cut back by 33 percent. From the perspective of the department, this was a free bonus of crime control without the full price of patrol.

The price of patrol, of course, is a key issue in using directed patrol against soft crime. It is often said that directed patrol is effective but too expensive to use on a wide scale (e.g., Schnelle et al. 1977). The Hot Spots experiment provides the first experimentally based estimates of crime-control costs per crime. The price of $1,000 per prevented crime (assuming no displacement) is relatively high, at least compared to responding to a call after a crime occurs.[3] The value of preventing

---

[3] Assuming no displacement, hot spots patrol deterred 101 crime calls per month through July 31. At 2.5 hours per day × 55 hot spots × 30 days per month, the cost of this patrol in one officer cars is 4,125 patrol car/police officer hours. The gross cost per crime call deterred (or displaced) is therefore 41 car/officer hours. The cost of answering 101 crime calls, with an average of two cars per call (a low estimate, given usual backup patterns) for 15 minutes per call (also low) is at least 50 hours. Assuming twice as many officers per call answered, or twice the average length of time involved (more realistic for arrests), the cost to answer 101 calls could be 100 officer hours. For every 41 hours invested in hot spot patrol, the benefit to the city was therefore 1 crime call prevented (or displaced) and 30–60 minutes of officer time saved. Every hour on hot spots patrol saves (or displaces) 1.3–8.8 minutes in patrol officer time. There was no net cost increase per crime prevented (or displaced) by directing existing patrol personnel to target hot spots, with an annualized crime reduction benefit of 1,200 crime calls. The cost per crime call prevented of hiring additional officers to perform hot spots patrol, at $25 per hour cost to the city, is $1,000. Put another way, each officer working 2,080 hours per year would be expected to prevent 51 crime calls per year if permanently assigned to directed patrol at hot spots, and if—a very big if—there was no displacement.

the crime, of course, may be worth the higher price. Depending on how the medical costs, lost wages, and property losses from soft crimes are estimated, the cost of each crime prevented could exceed the $1,000 prevention cost. This analysis depends heavily, however, on the assumption of no displacement, an assumption that still awaits testing.

C. Victim-oriented Strategies

Virtually nothing has been done to identify patterns of repeat victimization in soft crime. The area is ripe for computerized records analysis and a problem-solving strategy (Goldstein 1990). Some repeat victim problems may be alcohol related, while others may be chronic and intractable in other respects. But there may be obvious solutions suggested by other patterns, from improved physical security to changing jobs. The first step is to identify and interview any high rate repeat victims.

V. Controlling Domestic Violence

While police can do more to control hard and soft crime than many believe, they can probably do less to control domestic violence. They can certainly do less than many victims' advocates and attorneys have claimed. The irony is that minor domestic violence is among the more predictable offenses, by places, offenders, and victims. The problem is that serious domestic violence, particularly homicide, is virtually unpredictable, despite preliminary findings suggesting the contrary.

Police may be able to do more proactively than they have done before, although our political culture makes it unlikely. Reactive arrests of on-scene offenders, however, may not be as effective as many had concluded from the Minneapolis Domestic Violence Experiment (Sherman and Berk 1984).

A. Reactive Strategies

Given our cultural preference for reactive policing of domestic violence, it is not surprising that we have embraced a reactive strategy so readily. In the period 1970 to 1980, several states loosened the evidentiary requirements for police to make arrests in cases of minor domestic violence they had not witnessed. From 1984 to 1986, there was a fourfold increase in the proportion of urban police agencies encouraging police to make such arrests; several states made such arrests mandatory (Sherman and Cohn 1989). At least part of this increase may have been due to the findings of the Minneapolis Domestic Violence Experiment (Sherman and Berk 1984).

The 1981–82 randomized experiment in Minneapolis encompassed misdemeanor domestic violence cases within four hours of occurrence in three high-crime areas of the city. Forty-four officers were given prerandomized forms for determining which of three treatments to follow: arrest, ordering the suspect to leave the home for eight hours on pain of arrest, or "advising"—essentially doing neither of the other two responses. Of the 314 valid cases, 82 percent were treated as randomized. The other 18 percent received a different treatment from the random assignment, usually arrest, under procedures agreed to at the outset for such reasons as imminent threat of violence, assault on a police officer, or the suspect's refusal to leave the premises. Follow-up measures included official crime reports and interviews with victims, although the response rate to the interviews was very poor; fewer than a third of victims completed the planned six months of interviews.

The analysis consistently found deterrent effects from arrest using a variety of different models (Sherman and Berk 1984; Berk and Sherman 1988). Both official records and victim interviews indicated that arrest had the lowest prevalence of repeat violence for the same couple over a six-month follow-up period, although the rank order of the two nonarrest treatments was different for the two measures. Linear and logistic regression and time-to-failure models all confirmed the deterrent effect of arrest. The results were the same when analyzed by treatment as randomly assigned as well as in an adjusted model of treatment as actually received (Berk and Sherman 1988).

Numerous questions have been raised about the experiment concerning both its external and internal validity. As Sherman and Berk (1984) and Sherman and Cohn (1989) point out, among other things, the sample size was too small to examine interaction effects: the question of whether the rates of repeat violence varied by suspect or victim characteristics. They also note the lack of control on the screening of cases for eligibility, with the officers knowing what the treatment would be at the time they made the eligibility decision. Finally, they suggest that the effects of arrest could be quite different in cities with different cultures or employment rates.

A central recommendation of the final report, however, was that the experiment should be replicated in other sites, in order to address these questions. A second recommendation was that neither police nor state legislatures should adopt mandatory arrest policies, given the potential for diverse individual reaction to arrest (Sherman and Berk 1984). If arrest would increase violence among some persons, even while deterring it among others, it would make little sense to order arrest in all cases where police discretion had previously employed arrest very rarely.

The second recommendation was widely ignored, in part because of the publicity about the experiment generated by the principal investigator (Sherman and Cohn 1989). But the National Institute of Justice accepted the recommendation to replicate the experiment. Police departments and state legislatures adopted mandatory arrest policies in many states, thereby making replication of the Minneapolis experiment impossible in some locales. But the National Institute of Justice did fund six replications, three of which have now been completed. The replications address the separate questions of reactive strategy when the offender is present at the scene and when the offender has departed on police arrival.

1. *Offender Present.* None of the three replications to date has reported a deterrent effect, but one (Milwaukee) has reported significant interaction effects. These results begin to show how the effects of arrest may be highly conditioned on the ecological context or offender characteristics, with arrest increasing violence under some conditions and not under others. The Omaha replication (Dunford, Huizinga, and Elliott 1990) was the most similar of all six replications to the original Minneapolis design. Its sample size (330), eligibility, treatments, and measurement closely followed Minneapolis, with improvements in randomization procedures. All patrol officers in the department were asked to screen for eligible cases without knowing the treatment that would be assigned. When they had an eligible case, they called the dispatcher for a randomly assigned disposition generated on the spot by a computer program. The three treatments were then implemented as assigned in 92 percent of the cases, in part because the more troublesome cases were not subjected to random assignment. Follow-up measures included initial and six-month victim interviews with a 73 percent completion rate overall. Both official and victim data were restricted to same-couple violence, as opposed to violence outside the relationship.

The Omaha experiment found no specific deterrent effect of on-scene arrest and no differences at all across the three treatments. This result was robust across the same range of models as in the Minneapolis analysis. A longer-term follow up, with one-year victim interviews, is still in progress.

The Charlotte replication (Hirschel et al. 1990) also found no deterrent effect of arrest, although with a different design and sample. Unlike the Minneapolis and Omaha experiments, the Charlotte sample had a strong majority (73 percent) of blacks. Unlike the Milwaukee sample, which also had a majority (75 percent) of blacks, the Charlotte sample had a majority of employed suspects. Its 686 cases were randomly assigned to three treatments, with 83 percent compliance with the design: arrest, arrest by citation without taking into custody, and no arrest. Six-month victim interviews were completed for 47 percent of the sample. No deterrent effects of arrest were found with any of the now standard models of analysis.

The Milwaukee Domestic Violence Experiment (Sherman et al. 1991*b*) greatly expanded the sample size (1,200 cases); altered the treatments (arrest with three hours in jail, arrest with overnight in jail unless bond is posted, and a warning of arrest if more trouble occurs); and provided direct experimental control over the randomization procedures by Crime Control Institute staff who were always on duty while the experiment was in operation. The misassignment rate was 2 percent, the six-month victim interview rate was 79 percent, and a systematic measure of prevalence and frequency of violence covered periods both before and after the randomized intervention. The sample was predominantly black males with very high unemployment rates, living in high unemployment neighborhoods.

The experiment found no consistent differences in recidivism across the three randomized treatments. There was some evidence, however, of an initial deterrent effect followed by a long-term escalation in the frequency of violence among those assigned to short custody arrest (Sherman et al. 1991*b*). More important, there was very powerful and consistent evidence of an interaction effect with suspects' unemployment (Sherman and Smith 1991). For employed suspects, arrest reduced the frequency rate of repeat violence by 16 percent. But for unemployed suspects, arrest *increased* the frequency of repeat violence by 44 percent. It is not clear, however, whether this effect is due to individual characteristics or the ecology of their neighborhoods and the differential shame or stigma those neighborhoods attach to arrest (Braithwaite 1989).

These mixed results suggest that arrest is certainly no proven panacea and that mandatory arrest may not be justifiable on the grounds of crime control. This may not disturb its proponents, who may be more persuaded by a policy argument in favor of vigorous state action in response to alleged domestic violence incidents. But it should concern police agencies not required by state law to make arrests when probable cause is found. Mandatory arrest policies for underclass areas with chronic unemployment, similar to Milwaukee's, may be increasing violent crime and should probably be abandoned (Sherman 1992).

Many issues must be addressed in drawing conclusions across sites, a task best left until the completion of all six replications. A central issue in comparing results across sites, however, is the threshold of seriousness necessary to have a case qualify for the experiment. Observations in different experimenting cities suggest very different interpretations of this question by experimenting officers. If that is the case, the differences in results may reflect different effects of arrest on different kinds of offenses or offenders. If that is not the case, a likely explanation for the differences is that similar police actions have different effects in different cities due to differences in demographics, local culture, and the local context of crime and criminal justice. These are all factors that must be addressed in developing systematic knowledge about the effects of the police on crime.

Moreover, these experiments are limited to the individual effects of arrest on those arrested. No analysis to date has addressed the *general* deterrent effects of a mandatory arrest policy in a jurisdiction. No quasi-experimental analyses of domestic assault reports, for example, have been performed to determine any before-after impact. Nor has the most powerful design of all, a random assignment of mandatory arrest to some cities or areas and not others, even been contemplated. But without such analyses, our understanding of the effects of arrest on minor domestic violence will be incomplete.

2. *Offender Absent.* An additional strategy for improving knowledge about this problem is the development and testing of innovative responses. One extension of reactive strategy tested in the Omaha experiment is the seeking of an arrest warrant when the offender is absent. A 247 case randomized experiment in use of this tactic, backed by a very high rate of issuance and prosecution, produced a clear deterrent effect on repeat violence (Dunford, Huizinga, and Elliott 1989). It is curious that a warrant should have more effect than actual incarceration (from arrest) in the same city. But if that result is replicated elsewhere, it would address a large portion of all domestic violence cases—up to half in some jurisdictions. Its value is enhanced by its relatively low consumption of police time.

Police time poses a larger question about policing domestic violence, however, in the relative priority it merits in relation to the cost. Mandatory arrest laws have been extraordinarily costly to some cities. In Milwaukee, for example, there were over 7,000 reports a year under a mandatory arrest policy. Under a 1989 state law mandating arrest, the net was widened to include intimidation, and reports almost doubled to around 14,000. The arrests consume at least three to four hours of police time (using two officer cars), or as much time as it would take to prevent (or displace) 1,200 crime calls in hot spots of crime.

This is a prime example of how an arrest "budget" could limit the amount of resources expended on each crime, while still avoiding decriminalization of the offense. If, for example, mandatory arrest were employed on selected days on a random sequence basis, the number of arrests could be cut substantially without, perhaps, losing the general deterrent effects of such arrests. The residual deterrence of arrests from one day carrying over to other days may be another consequence of rotating crackdowns (Sherman 1990*b*).

B. Proactive Strategies

All domestic violence control by U.S. police is now reactive. Nowhere, to my knowledge, do police identify high-risk couples and undertake proactive interventions. Such a strategy could pay off in the reduction of minor domestic violence. But it is unlikely to succeed in preventing domestic homicide, as many scholars had long hoped. It is also unlikely that any American police agency would develop proactive strategies to detect hidden domestic violence, especially among the middle and upper classes.

1. *Predicting Domestic Homicide.* The epidemiological analysis of domestic homicide is a case study in the methodological pitfalls such analysis entails. One of the most influential studies of the police role in crime control is the Police Foundation–sponsored Kansas City Police Department analysis of the precursors of domestic homicide and aggravated assault (Breedlove et al. 1977). The widely cited study, which sparked the design of the Minneapolis Domestic Violence Experiment, reported that in about 90 percent of the domestic homicides police had responded to at least one call for service at the address of the domestic homicide victim or suspect in the two years preceding the homicide and to five or more calls in about 50 percent of the cases (Breedlove et al. 1977, p. 23). Similar findings were reported for domestic aggravated assault. Wilson (1977, p. iv) concluded from these results that, at least in Kansas City, "the police can obtain some early warning of assaults

and homicides" since "any given homicide arrest is likely to be the culmination of a series of police interventions."

A follow-up study conducted by the Kansas City Police Department under a National Institute of Mental Health grant reached a similar conclusion about assaults, if not homicides: "The premise that we may have some kind of 'early warning system' embedded in the relationship of disturbances and assaults is substantiated" (Meyer and Lorimor 1977, p. V-2). No data on risk levels in relation to prior frequency of calls, however, were displayed.

Taken in conjunction with the Kansas City homicide findings, these data have suggested a pattern of escalating frequency of police interventions in domestic violence that might describe a high-risk profile for homicide. The findings raised the possibility of proactive police interventions for preventing domestic homicide, which accounts for anywhere from 8 to 21 percent of all murders nationally (Federal Bureau of Investigation 1989), and even more in specific cities. They also raised expectations about police ability to prevent domestic homicide, including numerous lawsuits when police failed to do so.

These expectations were unrealistic, however, given the major limitations of the research: units of analysis and sample sizes and selection. On the units of analysis, the research confused the criminology of *places* with the criminology of *people*. None of the findings cited above measures the prior behavior of the persons involved in the homicide. All of them merely involve police CAD records of police cars dispatched to events at certain addresses, without any record of the identities of the individuals involved. The first Kansas City study was somewhat sensitive to this issue and therefore decided to omit homicides occurring in "apartment buildings with many tenants" (Breedlove et al. 1977, p. 23). This exclusion implies, however, that two- and three-family houses, not uncommon in Kansas City, were left in the analysis. The question then becomes what percentage of the prior calls involved one of the parties involved in the subsequent homicide. Given the nameless CAD data, there was no way to tell.

On the issue of sample size, it is striking that the published version of the Kansas City study, apparently based on 1970–71 homicides (Police Foundation 1977, p. 5), did not report the exact numbers of homicides included in the analysis. We can, however, estimate the number at less than fifty and no more than seventy-three (Sherman et al. 1991a). The small number of homicides suggests that there are

probably far more *buildings* with high frequency of domestic calls than
there are domestic *homicides*. In Minneapolis, for example, a city then
of two-thirds Kansas City's population, there were 1,197 buildings
with five or more disturbance calls in 1986. If we assume there were
twice as many buildings with that many calls in Kansas City, with no
more than one homicide in any one building over two years, we have
a predictive ratio of only 73 homicides in 2,394, or only 3 percent of
high-risk buildings with a homicide. Predicting domestic homicide on
the basis of five or more calls would therefore lead to a 97 percent false
positive rate, and that is only at the level of buildings. If we multiply
the number of buildings by the number of couples in them, the false
positive rate would substantially exceed 99 percent. When cases (and
buildings) deleted for multiple tenancy are taken into account, the error
rate could be even higher.

A similar analysis in Minneapolis (Sherman et al. 1991*a*) shows that
knowing the prior number of domestic calls at an address provides
little increase in ability to predict where domestic homicides will occur,
even if it does reduce the number of candidates to about 1,000 buildings. Attempts to intervene for prevention of those homicides would
clearly produce substantial overprediction and much wasted effort.

Several of the problems described above can be overcome with data
from the Milwaukee Domestic Violence Experiment (Sherman et al.
1991*b*), one of the six replications of the Minneapolis experiment
funded by the National Institute of Justice. These data show that out
of 15,537 police reports of domestic battery among named couples
citywide from April 7, 1987, to February 8, 1989, only in one couple
did a homicide later occur (Sherman et al. 1991*a*). Even more surprising was that thirty-two of the thirty-three domestic homicide victims
during that period had no prior police record of domestic battery. Of
the 110 batteries involving guns and threat of death, none led to any
serious injury.

It thus appears unlikely that homicides are more likely to occur at
the extreme end of a distribution of repeated reports to police of less
serious violence, falsifying the "escalating violence" theory of prediction at least in terms of official data if not undetected events. The
evidence against this thesis is even more compelling with the 1,113
couples in the experiment, with a twenty-two month surveillance period and a mean follow-up period of 15.8 months from the first report.
Seventy couples had five or more reported batteries, but no homicides.

In the absence of the "early warning system" ability to make accurate predictions, there seems to be little hope for a proactive police strategy against domestic homicide.

2. *Controlling High-Risk Couples.*   The ability to predict which couples will have additional minor violence is greater, but still limited. In Minneapolis over a one-year period, 9.1 percent of the addresses with any domestic calls accounted for 39.5 percent of all domestic calls, while *9 percent of all addresses accounted for 100 percent of all domestic disturbance calls* (Sherman et al. 1991*a*). The Minneapolis analysis of crime hot spot addresses also found that domestic disturbance calls had the greatest concentration by address of any of six types of calls examined (including robbery, auto theft, burglary, assault, and criminal sexual conduct). Compared to the number of addresses at which domestic calls would be expected to occur without any repeat call addresses, the actual number of addresses with domestic calls was 59 percent lower than expected due to repeat calls—the largest reduction among call types examined (Sherman, Gartin, and Buerger 1989, p. 41). The building addresses at which domestic disturbance calls occur are fairly predictable, with better than two-thirds accuracy of predicting an additional call at some time within the year once there have already been three such calls.

Nonetheless, police predictions of specific couples likely to experience more minor batteries, or the places likely to have more domestic calls, must suffer some false positives (Sherman et al. 1991*a*). The best prediction Milwaukee Police could make about repeat batteries over an almost three-year period, for example, is that couples with seven or more prior reports will have another one during that time period. This prediction will be wrong in one out of four cases. While this error rate is low for purposes of scientific analysis, it may be too high for intrusive (as distinct from more passive) policing. Depending on the intrusiveness of any prevention measure suggested, it could be fiscally or ethically unacceptable to impose a measure that turns out to be unnecessary in such a large proportion of the cases.

If some powerful "inoculation" against domestic violence were possible, it could certainly be applied to the seven-or-more police-report couples. The problem is imagining what could work. A prosecutorial threat to invoke more serious penalties for recurrence sent by mail or delivered by police is one possibility and could be tested experimentally on this high-risk population. Other low cost ideas might also be

212   Lawrence W. Sherman

tried. The point is to continue to address a pervasive problem in a spirit of trial and error rather than concluding it is "impossible" for police to do anything constructive.

VI. Policing Other Crimes

The development of police research has hardly been systematic enough to test the control of all types of crime. This section considers several of the many remaining types of crime that offer either important research results or promising strategies for crime control: drug markets, burglary, auto theft, and drunk driving.

A. *Policing Drug Marketplaces*

Policing drug crime has been one of the most innovative areas of American law enforcement in the last decade. It is also one of the most confused areas of strategy, with entirely unclear objectives. The longstanding concern with reducing supply has gradually been supplemented with a desire to restrict demand. In the wake of the crack epidemic, however, both goals took second place to reduction of violence and disorder in the immediate vicinity of drug marketplaces.

The central strategic choice in drug enforcement has been between wholesale and retail level dealers. Through most of the 1970s and 1980s, police focused drug enforcement on drug wholesalers. Drug enforcement was limited to special units conducting fairly complex undercover investigations. But the advent of crack created highly visible street markets and crack houses, putting tremendous pressure on police to control retail-level dealers.

From 1985 to 1989, the national arrest rate for homicide doubled among persons under age eighteen (Federal Bureau of Investigation 1986–90; U.S. Bureau of the Census 1986–90). Much of that increase undoubtedly occurred in center cities near retail drug marketplaces, as it did in Washington, D.C., where the homicide rate rose by over 300 percent (Federal Bureau of Investigation 1986–90). The sounds of gunfire became a daily occurrence in some neighborhoods, and the quality of life deteriorated rapidly (Kotlowitz 1991).

Police responded with crackdowns (Chaiken 1988; Sherman 1990*b*) of massive numbers of uniformed officers on patrol, raids of crack houses, and innovative tactics: "jump-out" squads intercepting observed drug transactions, condemnation of buildings and landlord fines over drug deals in residential settings, and even using front-end loaders to assault a well-fortified crack house. Kansas City police in early 1989 began raiding about one crack house every day, and local taxpayers approved a referendum for an increase in the sales tax to hire more police and prosecutors dedicated solely to drug enforcement.

Evaluation results on drug crackdowns to date have been mixed (Kleiman and Smith 1990). A Lynn, Massachusetts, crackdown on an open-air drug market reportedly reduced the robbery and burglary rates for two years, without discernible displacement (Kleiman 1988). The Lynn crackdown's use of observation-of-sale arrests was apparently more effective than the warrant arrests made in Lawrence, Massachusetts, where the crackdown resulted in no reduced drug use and an *increase* in violent crime. A massive crackdown in New York's lower east side, "Operation Pressure Point," succeeded in reducing drug use, robbery, and homicide, but the reductions decayed after the first year—a typical pattern found in most crackdowns (Sherman 1990*a*, p. 21).

Uchida, Forst, and Annan (1990) compared intensive drug enforcement alone to intensive drug enforcement plus community oriented "door-to-door" police visits to residences in Birmingham, Alabama, and Oakland, California. The intensive enforcement consisted of street corner buy-and-bust tactics, as well as raids and sweeps. In both cities, the door-to-door tactics were not fully implemented as planned, due to police resistance. But in both cities the only reductions in violent crime were found in the areas where door-to-door visits supplemented the intensive enforcement. Combined with the positive results of door-to-door visits in Houston and Newark (Pate et al. 1986; Skogan 1990), these results suggest that visits may be a far more powerful strategy than most police imagine.

On balance, we still know very little about dealing with the quality of life and soft crime problems surrounding drug marketplaces. But the continuing war on drugs creates both opportunities and a demand for more evaluations. To make further progress, the next stage of drug enforcement evaluations will require large-sample randomized experiments using marketplaces as the unit of analysis.

B. *Controlling Burglary*

Police strategies for controlling burglary have been highly burglar oriented, minimally victim oriented, and rarely fence oriented (Shover 1991). The burglar-oriented strategies include traditional use of informants and witnesses, as well as two newer strategies. The early 1970s Robert Redford movie, "The Sting," apparently prompted similar methods against burglars. Police set up fake fencing operations and bought stolen goods from burglars to get evidence for prosecution. Despite some favorable evaluations, however, Klockars (1980) found no evidence of a crime-reduction effect. Marx (1988, p. 126) offers strong suggestive arguments that stings can simply increase the supply of burglars by raising the level of demand for stolen goods.

If Marx is correct, then Reiss (1990) may correctly hypothesize that a fence-oriented strategy could do more to reduce burglary than a burglar-oriented strategy. Police have rarely incapacitated major fences, in part because of their skill in avoiding an evidentiary trail. But a thorough diagnosis of the local market structure for stolen goods (which may vary widely by type of goods, from art to computers) could reveal a number of potential fences as targets for proactive, undercover enforcement.

A more valuable burglar-oriented strategy may be police monitoring of previously convicted burglars, in cooperation with correctional authorities. Under a National Institute of Justice grant, for example, Indianapolis police are participating in an experiment to supplement electronically monitored house arrests of juvenile burglars. One comparison is between burglars on house arrest without police surveillance and burglars visited daily at unpredictable times by the local beat car. The theory is that burglars will be less likely to cheat on their house arrest (by going out to commit burglaries, among other things) if they know police may catch them—a testament to the weak technology and correctional follow up of electronic monitoring. An added virtue of this program should be building up police information networks among burglars, which could help to identify more fences.

The advent of automatic fingerprint identification systems may also dramatically increase police capacity to apprehend, and perhaps to deter, burglars. In the past, police had to have a suspect in mind in order to check fingerprint records. In recent years, however, many states have implemented a computerized search process requiring only one good print to produce a match with any prints already in the local system. This development has produced many anecdotal accounts of improved apprehension rates, but no systematic evaluations.

One reason burglar-oriented strategies may not work, however, is the low rate of repeat burglary arrests in any given year, at least in Kansas City (Sherman, Rogan, and Velke 1991). The maximum number of repeat burglary arrests in 1990 was only four. In contrast, only 134 persons had two or more burglary arrests, collectively generating

29 percent of all burglary arrests. Assuming that they commit many burglaries besides those for which they are arrested, it would seem that those people bear watching.

The victim-oriented strategy of the 1970s focused on target hardening. Police became virtual public relations agents for lock manufacturers, alarm companies, and hardware stores. But the evidence that hardware reduced burglary risks was quite mixed. Waller and Okihiro (1978) found no evidence that hardware made a difference, although having someone in the home did. Yet hardware-encouraging community-organizing programs in both Seattle (Lindsay and McGillis 1986) and Portland (Schneider 1986) reported substantial crime-reduction effects. One reason they may have been so successful, however, is the selection bias built into the choice of neighborhoods. Attempting to mount similar neighborhood watch programs in Chicago and Minneapolis neighborhoods that were less eager to implement the programs met with no measured crime-reduction effect (Skogan 1990, chap. 6).

Marking identification on personal property, or "Operation Identification," also shows mixed results. While it has not been found to increase the likelihood of property being recovered, both U.S. (Schneider 1986) and Welsh (Laycock 1986) evaluations have found that it reduces the rate at which homes are burglarized. It is possible, of course, that the act of marking goods creates some greater level of watchfulness by families or that visible stickers indicating participation in the program displace burglars to other locations. But in the absence of any better evidence, the police effort expended in getting the property marked appears to be cost-effective (Laycock 1986).

High-risk victims could also be the focus of special police programs, with a potentially greater crime-reduction effect. In Kansas City in 1985–89, only 1 percent of the population (5,423 people) produced 26 percent of the burglary victimizations (Sherman, Rogan, and Velke 1991). There were 751 people burglarized at the rate of one per year or higher, and one victim reported thirty-six burglaries in five years. These people could be targeted for problem-solving efforts to diagnose the causes of the repeat burglaries and the possible solutions to each individual set of circumstances.

C. Controlling Auto Theft

Big-city auto theft enforcement is often focused on professional "chop shops" for breaking up cars and on professional gangs of car

216   Lawrence W. Sherman

thieves. And in Kansas City, a small number of auto thieves—who may or may not be very "professional"— are repeatedly arrested. In 1990, 209 persons accounted for 502 auto theft arrests, or 32 percent of all such arrests (Sherman, Rogan, and Velke 1991). But the offender-oriented focus has been problematic in the late 1980s, as increased auto theft rates appear to be connected to drug shipments and subsequent abandonment of cars. The problem might be better controlled by increased technology and potential fraud analysis.

The primary new technological solution is the Lo-Jack car locator system, which has been tested in Massachusetts since 1986 (Grable 1991). The commercially marketed system, based in Needham, Massachusetts, works by having a radio transmitter installed in a hidden location in the car by company personnel. If the owner reports the car stolen, duly equipped police agencies are then able to pinpoint the location of the car within a twenty-five mile square, after they activate the transmission device from police headquarters. In the first five years of operation, Massachusetts police recovered 95 percent of the vehicles reported stolen. The average recovery time is two hours, and the fastest was seven minutes. Arrest rates average 20 percent, compared to the national auto theft clearance rate of 5 percent.

The cost of the system to private citizens is about $600. A more expensive system ($1,500) activates a central station alarm if the car is moved without proper authorization codes. The Michigan-based Code-Alarm system avoids the possible delay in reporting associated with Lo-Jack since the owner does not need to discover the theft for the system to be activated. Code-Alarm also gives police a device that enables them to turn off the engine of the stolen car once they are in pursuit of it, avoiding the possible damage of a high-speed chase (Grable 1991).

If either commercial system were universally adopted by police agencies, police could track and arrest a car thief at any time until the car is disassembled and the locator destroyed. This capacity would not create a deterrent effect, however, until the prevalence of the system was so high that thieves would calculate the risk to be unattractive. This could happen more readily with mandatory installation in all new cars, which in the long run could make a big dent in car theft rates. In the short run, however, it would probably just displace theft on to older cars made before the new requirements. That is exactly what happened in England, for example, after the introduction of steering column locks on all new cars (Mayhew et al. 1976). In Germany in

1963, however, auto theft went down 60 percent across the board when all cars—old and new—were required to install steering column locks (Mayhew et al. 1976).

A mandatory locator system would also help to deter insurance fraud in car theft reporting, although smart con artists might still find ways around it. What will be harder to escape is a regional or national registry of car theft victims, which would identify repeat victims by social security number or drivers' licenses. Unusually high levels of car theft would either expose victims as frauds or restrict their access to further car insurance as plain bad risks. In Kansas City, for example, in 1985–89, there were 386 people who reported three or more car thefts in five years, and eighteen people who reported five or more (Sherman, Rogan, and Velke 1991). Whether careless or fraudulent, these people are worth some special attention.

D. *Controlling Drunk Driving*

Police control of drunk driving has probably been more successful than critics have claimed. H. Laurence Ross (1982), the leading student of drunk driving enforcement, has found fairly consistent evidence of actual or threatened police crackdowns producing immediate deterrent effects on single-vehicle nighttime fatal accidents. But he also finds these effects to wear off, sooner or later. He therefore concludes pessimistically that "deterrence-based policies are questionable in the long run" (Ross 1982, p. 111). As Jacobs (1988, p. 212) points out, this conclusion may be unjustified by the data, which may tap only a small subset of the potential drunk driving population. It also unduly discounts the value of the short-term deterrent effects he so consistently observes in different nations, in different decades, with different police enforcement methods.

As Sherman (1990*a*) suggests, Ross's consistent finding can be put to more strategic use. The key is the common finding of the short-term crackdowns that the measured deterrent effects persisted after the police efforts had ended. This "residual" deterrent effect lasted in some cases as long as the crackdown itself. In order to obtain twice the deterrence for the same amount of personnel time, police might continually alter targets and tactics of drunk driving crackdowns. Since there are more areas in most jurisdictions than police can cover intensively, constant shifts in geographic targets makes sense in any case.

The difficulty in evaluating some of the newer tactics, like checkpoints, is that few state laws require alcohol testing of drivers involved

in accidents, even fatal ones. Most drunk-driving data are based on
dead drivers or inferences from overall accident rates. Until wider
testing of drivers in fatal accidents is required, even the U.S. Department of Transportation's national FARS (Fatal Accident Reporting
System) data on trends in alcohol-related deaths will remain highly
speculative. At the local level, it will be difficult to examine the effects
of any geographically focused enforcement efforts on drunk driving in
the immediate vicinity of those efforts.

These strategies are primarily across-the-board, general deterrent
strategies. Relatively little problem-oriented policing has been focused
on the more persistent problem of chronic recidivists at high risk of
injuring themselves or their passengers in an accident. The situational
epidemiology of DWI-related accidents, for example, has not been
widely discussed. But a few police agencies have recognized the high
prevalence of drunk drivers who have just come from a tavern or pool
hall, over 50 percent in one California study of DWI arrestees (Yoder
and Moore 1973). Some agencies have responded to this by staking out
bars and following cars as they depart, watching for erratic driving.
Shaw (1989) suggests that police lobby for barring convicted drunk
drivers from even visiting public drinking places as a condition of probation or parole.

Reactive strategies for drunk driving enforcement take on new dimensions with the car phone. While it was once almost impossible for
good citizens to call police with the exact whereabouts of a drunk
driver, car phones allow citizens to tail the driver until police come.
Public relations campaigns to encourage such actions could stimulate
them, even with the predictable cost of some rate of false alarms.

VII. Future Prospects

What can police do about crime? One answer to the question might
be that we do not know because they never really tried. That judgment
would be overly harsh, for despite the preoccupation with answering
911 calls there is much that police do that has some effect on crime.
The important question is *what effect* since police efforts can sometimes
increase crime as well as control it. A related question is *what else* could
they do that they are not now doing, and should it be substituted for
some current activities? As little as we know about the effects of current activities, there are probably more legal, constitutional, and mor-
ally proper tactics that have not been tried than have been. Therein
lies the lesson for future prospects.

It is unlikely that police will achieve anything like medicine's spectacular successes in virtually eliminating certain diseases. There have been some such precedents in crime control: robberies of buses eliminated by eliminating cash, domestic skyjackings almost eliminated by metal detectors. But the police have not yet directly accomplished such results. Nor, given the intractability of most crime problems, are they likely to.

What seems more likely to work is a steady accumulation of results, searching for some with modest success. While this process is necessarily plagued by a "theory gap" in frameworks for organizing and understanding diverse results (Zimring 1978), that problem seems likely to be solved more quickly with more data rather than more dataless theory. Police are more than willing to step up the pace of experimentation with specific tactics against specific crime problems. The major problem is a lack of trained and willing social scientists available to work with them, a shortage linked directly to the dearth of federal and foundation support for research and development for crime control.

This pace will remain sluggish if it is wholly or primarily dependent on federal sources of funding. While police chiefs have called for more research and development on drug enforcement, Congress has ignored their pleas. What may be more feasible is a combination of city and foundation funds for conducting local experiments, with technical support from the national research organizations. The New York City Police, for example, have funded research by the Vera Institute of Justice. But American foundations in the 1990s are almost uniformly uninterested in crime, and the continuing decline of most big cities makes city funding unlikely.

No matter how research is funded, the key resource will still be imagination. Without creative ideas for diagnosing and treating a crime problem with policing, there will be nothing to evaluate. Academics tend to scorn the process of idea generation and to respect rigorous tests. But rigorous tests of bad ideas will make little progress. Police professionals should be emboldened by their own detailed knowledge of the crime problems they face and encouraged to gather even more systematic data on them. There are only 500 active research criminologists in the United States and over 500,000 police. The odds should support more ideas from the rank and file. Anything national and local organizations can do to encourage the "suggestion box" for crime control will increase the stockpile of hypotheses.

Innovative crime-control tests could also revive the office of chief of police, a position now slowly being strangled by police unions, red tape, and 911 calls. Modern police chiefs have relatively little opportunity to exercise leadership in crime control except for bold initiatives, which can be even more valuable if properly evaluated. For despite the quasi-military symbolism of police rank structure, the jurisprudence of policing assumes more of a hospital model. Officers, like doctors, deal with cases and take the primary responsibility for the decisions they make. The police department, like the hospital, is merely a source of organizational support and personnel resources for those decisions, but not the decision maker itself. Police chiefs have become hospital administrators rather than generals.

This essay's reliance on the military concepts of strategy and tactics may seem inappropriate for the hospital model of police work. But it is the hospital model itself that is inappropriate to crime control. Hospitals are reactive organizations, relying on people to come to them when they are sick. The goal of the hospital is to heal the sick, not to control disease. Public health organizations, by contrast, take no patients, but seek to control disease. They employ many doctors, but decision making is an organizational, not individual, responsibility. The strategies and tactics for fighting epidemics like AIDS, or chronic sources of mortality like heart disease, are determined in truly quasi-military fashion. It is no accident that the federal Centers for Disease Control is an arm of the U.S. Public Health Service, which is a uniformed service commanded by a (surgeon) general.

A police chief as "surgeon general" would be far more concerned with crime analysis, especially chains of causation and emerging epidemiological trends. A crime-control chief would strike at those causal chains wherever there is a vulnerable link. Just as the surgeon general speaks out against smoking, a police chief could speak out against divorce and other individual choices that may contribute to community crime rates—even while respecting the rights of people to make such choices. And just as the local health department closes down restaurants for operating unclean kitchens, a crime-control police department can close down taverns or entertainment facilities for operating high-crime establishments.

Police departments cannot escape their responsibilities as "hospitals," of course. But they already do refuse to deal with many kinds of cases, through the exercise of officer discretion. This precedent opens the door to the addition of the public health model to the traditional hospital model of police organization, paying for "disease control" by cutting back on the costs of "patient care" (McEwen, Connors, and Cohen 1986). Indeed, the merger of the two approaches may allow joint strategies that are unheard of in disease control. Hospitals play relatively little role in providing preventive medicine, despite the enormous opportunity they have through direct contact with the sick. Police can use their contacts with victims, places, and offenders to attack causal chains as well as to treat the specific cases.

Given this perspective on the possible future—and to some extent, current—directions for police departments, there is every reason to talk about strategic and tactical choices for crime control. Police chiefs can become both surgeons general and hospital administrators. There is no major legal obstacle to clearer organizational direction of officers' time, including discretion to arrest. This does not mean that the direction must be top-down since policies can be made just as well through bottom-up initiatives and participation. But it does mean that the organization can make coordinated and systematic choices rather than letting the choices emerge topsy-turvy from the individual decisions of each officer.

Approaching strategic choices in this manner can also breathe new life into the concept of community policing (Skolnick and Bayley 1986). In making explicit choices about priorities, strategy, and tactics, police agencies can seek citizen comment before the choices become final. They can also make different choices for different communities, in reflection of local preferences. Interest group pressure can also be dealt with more rationally through clear choices. Rather than seeing the police department as a bottomless well, interest groups could be educated to see it as an organization of finite resources. If there is to be increased attention to one problem, attention to something else must be cut. Getting interest groups to see the broader public interest, rather than making unilateral assaults on police executives, would be much better for democratic policing. It might even foster more effective crime control.

REFERENCES

Andenaes, Johannes. 1974. *Punishment and Deterrence.* Ann Arbor: University of Michigan Press.
Anderson, David C. 1990. "Editorial Notebook: The Tyranny of 911." *New York Times* (September 17, eastern ed.).

222   Lawrence W. Sherman

Ares, C. E., Anne Rankin, and Herbert Sturz. 1963. "The Manhattan Bail
    Project: An Interim Report on the Use of Pre-trial Parole." *New York Univer-
    sity Law Review* 38:67–95.
Barr, Robert, and Ken Pease. 1990. "Crime Placement, Displacement, and
    Deflection." In *Crime and Justice: A Review of Research*, vol. 12, edited by
    Michael Tonry and Norval Morris. Chicago: University of Chicago Press.
Behan, Cornelius J. 1990. Personal communication with author.
Berk, Richard E., and Lawrence W. Sherman. 1988. "Police Responses to
    Family Violence Incidents: An Analysis of an Experimental Design with
    Incomplete Randomization." *Journal of the American Statistical Association*
    83:70–76.
Bittner, Egon. 1970. *The Functions of the Police in Modern Society: Background
    Factors, Current Practices, and Possible Role Models*. Chevy Chase, Md.: Na-
    tional Institute of Mental Health.
Black, Donald. 1973. "The Mobilization of Law." *Journal of Legal Studies*
    2:125–49.
———. 1983. "Crime as Social Control." *American Sociological Review* 48:34–45.
Blumstein, Alfred, Jacqueline Cohen, Jeffrey Roth, and Christy Visher. 1986.
    Criminal Careers and "Career Criminals." Washington, D.C.: National Acad-
    emy Press.
Botein, Bernard. 1965. "The Manhattan Bail Project: Its Impact in Criminol-
    ogy and the Criminal Law Process." *Texas Law Review* 43:319–31.
Boydstun, John. 1975. "San Diego Field Interrogation: Final Report." Wash-
    ington, D.C.: Police Foundation.
Boydstun, John, Michael E. Sherry, and Nicholas P. Moelter. 1977. *Patrol
    Staffing in San Diego: One- Or Two-Officer Units*. Washington, D.C.: Police
    Foundation.
Braithwaite, John. 1989. *Crime, Shame, and Reintegration*. Cambridge: Cam-
    bridge University Press.
Breedlove, Ronald K., John W. Kennish, Donald M. Sandker, and Robert K.
    Sawtell. 1977. "Domestic Violence and the Police: Kansas City." In *Domestic
    Violence and the Police: Studies in Detroit and Kansas City*. Washington, D.C.:
    Police Foundation.
Brown, Lee P. 1989. "Community Policing: A Practical Guide for Police Offi-
    cials." *Police Chief*, August, pp. 72–82.
Buerger, Michael. 1991. *Repeat Call Policing: The RECAP Casebook*. Washington,
    D.C.: Crime Control Institute.
Campbell, Donald T., and H. Laurence Ross. 1968. "The Connecticut Crack-
    down on Speeding: Time-Series Data in Quasi-experimental Analysis." *Law
    and Society Review* 3:33–53.
Chaiken, Marcia R., ed. 1988. *Street-Level Drug Enforcement: Examining the
    Issues*. Washington, D.C.: National Institute of Justice.
Clark, Gerald. 1969. "What Happens When the Police Strike." *New York Times
    Magazine* (November 16), sec. 6, pp. 45, 176–85, 187, 194–95.
Clarke, Ronald V. 1983. "Situational Crime Prevention: Its Theoretical Basis
    and Practical Scope." In *Crime and Justice: An Annual Review of Research*, vol.
    4, edited by Michael Tonry and Norval Morris. Chicago: University of
    Chicago Press.

Clarke, Ronald V., and Patricia Mayhew. 1988. "The British Gas Suicide Story and Its Criminological Implications." In *Crime and Justice: A Review of Research*, vol. 10, edited by Michael Tonry and Norval Morris. Chicago: University of Chicago Press.

Clifton, Wayland, Jr. 1987. "Convenience Store Robberies in Gainesville, Florida: An Intervention Strategy by the Gainesville Police Department." Photocopy. Gainesville, Fla.: Gainesville Police Department.

Cohen, Lawrence E., and Marcus Felson. 1979. "Social Change and Crime Rate Trends: A Routine Activity Approach." *American Sociological Review* 44:588–608.

Colquhoun, Patrick. 1795. *A Treatise on the Police of The Metropolis*. London. 7th ed. enlarged 1806, reprinted at Montclair, N.J.: Patterson-Smith, 1969.

Cook, Philip. 1991. "The Technology of Personal Violence." In *Crime and Justice: A Review of Research*, vol. 14, edited by Michael Tonry. Chicago: University of Chicago Press.

Cook, Thomas, and Donald T. Campbell. 1979. *Quasi-experimentation: Design and Analysis Issues for Field Settings*. Chicago: Rand-McNally.

Cornish, Derek, and Ronald V. Clarke. 1987. "Understanding Crime Displacement: An Application of Rational Choice Theory." *Criminology* 25:933–47.

Cumming, Elaine, I. Cumming, and Laura Edell. 1965. "Policeman as Philosopher, Friend and Guide." *Social Problems* 12:276–86.

Currie, Elliott. 1985. "Crimes of Violence and Public Policy: Changing Directions." In *American Violence and Public Policy*, edited by Lynn A. Curtis. New Haven, Conn.: Yale University Press.

Dennis, Michael L. 1988. "Implementing Randomized Field Experiments: An Analysis of Criminal and Civil Justice Research." Ph.D. dissertation, Northwestern University, Department of Psychology.

Dunford, Franklyn W., David Huizinga, and Delbert S. Elliott. 1989. "The Omaha Domestic Violence Police Experiments: Final Report to the National Institute of Justice." Washington, D.C.: U.S. Department of Justice, National Institute of Justice.

Dunford, Franklyn W., David Huizinga, and Delbert S. Elliott. 1990. "The Role of Arrest in Domestic Assault: The Omaha Police Experiment." *Criminology* 28:183–206.

Eck, John, and William Spelman. 1987. *Problem Solving: Problem-oriented Policing in Newport News*. Washington, D.C.: Police Executive Research Forum.

Farrington, David. 1983. "Randomized Experiments on Crime and Justice." In *Crime and Justice: An Annual Review of Research*, vol. 4, edited by Michael Tonry and Norval Morris. Chicago: University of Chicago Press.

Federal Bureau of Investigation. 1986–90. *Crime in the United States*. Washington, D.C.: U.S. Government Printing Office.

Fielding, Henry. 1751. *An Enquiry Into the Causes of the Late Increase of Robbers*. London. Reprinted 1977 at Montclair, N.J.: Patterson-Smith.

Fisher, R. A. 1935. *The Design of Experiments*. Edinburgh: Oliver & Boyd.

Flanagan, Timothy J., and Kathleen Maguire. 1990. *Sourcebook of Criminal Justice Statistics—1989*. Washington, D.C.: Government Printing Office.

Goldstein, Herman. 1977. *Policing a Free Society*. Cambridge, Mass.: Ballinger.

224   Lawrence W. Sherman

———. 1979. "Improving Policing: A Problem-oriented Approach." *Crime and Delinquency* 25:236–58.

———. 1990. *Problem-oriented Policing*. New York: McGraw-Hill.

Gottfredson, Michael R., and Travis Hirschi. 1990. *A General Theory of Crime*. Stanford, Calif.: Stanford University Press.

Grable, Ron. 1991. "Stolen Car Retrieval Systems." *Motor Trend* (January), p. 106.

Greene, Jack R., and Carl B. Klockars. 1991. "What Police Do." In *Thinking about Police*, edited by Carl B. Klockars and Stephen D. Mastrofski. 2d ed. New York: McGraw-Hill.

Greenhouse, Steven. 1990. "Poles Find Crime Replacing Police State." *New York Times* (March 4, eastern ed.), p. 20.

Hindelang, Michael, Michael R. Gottfredson, and James Garofalo. 1978. *Victims of Personal Crime*. Cambridge, Mass.: Ballinger.

Hirschel, J. David, Ira W. Hutchison III, Charles W. Dean, Joseph J. Kelley, and Carolyn E. Pesackis. 1990. "Charlotte Spouse Assault Replication Project: Final Report." Washington, D.C.: U.S. Department of Justice, National Institute of Justice.

Jacob, Herbert, and Michael J. Rich. 1981. "The Effects of the Police on Crime: A Second Look." *Law and Society Review* 15:109–15.

Jacobs, James B. 1988. "The Law and Criminology of Drunk Driving." In *Crime and Justice: A Review of Research*, vol. 10, edited by Michael Tonry and Norval Morris. Chicago: University of Chicago Press.

Joiner, Larry. 1990. Personal communication with author (former chief of police, Kansas City, Missouri).

Kelling, George L., Tony Pate, Duane Dieckman, and Charles Brown. 1974. *The Kansas City Preventive Patrol Experiment: A Summary Report*. Washington, D.C.: Police Foundation.

Kleiman, Mark. 1988. "Crackdowns: The Effects of Intensive Enforcement on Retail Heroin Dealing." In *Street-Level Drug Enforcement: Examining the Issues*, edited by Marcia Chaiken. Washington, D.C.: U.S. Department of Justice, National Institute of Justice.

Kleiman, Mark, and Kerry Smith. 1990. "State and Local Drug Enforcement: In Search of a Strategy." In *Drugs and Crime*, edited by Michael Tonry and James Q. Wilson. Vol. 13 of *Crime and Justice: A Review of Research*, edited by Michael Tonry and Norval Morris. Chicago: University of Chicago Press.

Klein, Malcolm W. 1986. "Labeling Theory and Delinquency Policy: An Experimental Test." *Criminal Justice and Behavior* 13:47–79.

Klockars, Carl B. 1980. "Jonathan Wild and the Modern Sting." In *History and Crime: Implications for Criminal Justice Policy*, edited by James Inciardi and Charles E. Faupel. Beverly Hills, Calif.: Sage.

———. 1991. "The Rhetoric of Community Policing." In *Thinking about Police*, edited by Carl B. Klockars and Stephen D. Mastrofski. 2d ed. New York: McGraw-Hill.

Klockars, Carl B., and Stephen Mastrofski, eds. 1991. *Thinking about Police*. 2d ed. New York: McGraw-Hill.

Kolata, Gina. 1991. "In Medical Research, Equal Opportunity Doesn't Always Apply." *New York Times* (March 10, eastern ed.), p. E16.

Kotlowitz, Alex. 1991. *There Are No Children Here*. New York: Doubleday.

Larson, Richard C. 1976. "What Happened to Patrol Operations in Kansas City." *Evaluation* 3:117–23.

Laycock, Gloria. 1986. "Property Marking as a Deterrent to Domestic Burglary." In *Situational Crime Prevention*, edited by Kevin Heal and Gloria Laycock. London: H.M. Stationery Office.

Lempert, Richard. 1984. "From the Editor." *Law and Society Review* 18:505–10.

———. 1989. "Humility Is a Virtue: On the Publicization of Policy-relevant Research." *Law and Society Review* 23:145–61.

Lindsay, Betsy, and Daniel McGillis. 1986. "Citywide Community Crime Prevention: An Assessment of the Seattle Program." In *Community Crime Prevention: Does It Work?* edited by Dennis P. Rosenbaum. Beverly Hills, Calif.: Sage.

Logan, Charles. 1975. "Arrest Rates and Deterrence." *Social Science Quarterly* 56:376–89.

McCord, Joan. 1978. "A Thirty Year Follow-up of Treatment Effects." *American Psychologist* 33:284–89.

McEwen, J. Thomas, Edward F. Connors III, and Marcia I. Cohen. 1986. *Evaluation of the Differential Police Response Field Test*. Washington, D.C.: U.S. Department of Justice, National Institute of Justice.

Makinen, Tuija, and Hannu Takala. 1980. "The 1976 Police Strike in Finland." *Scandinavian Studies in Criminology* 7:87–106.

Martin, Susan, and Lawrence W. Sherman. 1986. "Selective Apprehension: A Police Strategy for Repeat Offenders." *Criminology* 24:155–73.

Marx, Gary T. 1988. *Undercover: Police Surveillance in America*. Berkeley and Los Angeles: University of California Press.

———. 1990. Personal communication with author.

Mayhew, Patricia, Ronald V. G. Clarke, Andrew Sturman, and J. Michael Hough. 1976. *Crime as Opportunity*. Home Office Research Study no. 34. London: H.M. Stationery Office.

Merton, Robert K. 1968. *Social Theory and Social Structure*. New York: Free Press.

Meyer, Jeanie Keeny, and Theron D. Lorimor. 1977. "Police Intervention Data and Domestic Violence: Exploratory Development and Validation of Prediction Models." Report prepared under grant Ro1MH27918 from National Institute of Mental Health to Kansas City, Missouri, Police Department.

Milton, Catherine H., Jeanne Halleck, James Lardner, and Gary Abrecht. 1977. *Police Use of Deadly Force*. Washington, D.C.: Police Foundation.

Moore, Mark. In this volume. "Problem-solving and Community Policing."

Morris, Norval, and Gordon Hawkins. 1970. *The Honest Politician's Guide to Crime Control*. Chicago: University of Chicago Press.

Mydans, Seth. 1991. "Tape of Beating by Police Revives Charges of Racism." *New York Times* (March 7, eastern ed.), p. A 18.

Nagin, Daniel. 1978. "General Deterrence: A Review of the Empirical Evidence." In *Deterrence and Incapacitation: Estimating the Effects of Criminal Sanction on Crime Rates*, edited by Alfred Blumstein, Jacqueline Cohen, and Daniel Nagin. Washington, D.C.: National Academy Press.

226   Lawrence W. Sherman

Nazario, Sonia, and David Jefferson. 1991. "L.A. Law: A Videotaped Beating Highlights Problems of Los Angeles Police." *Wall Street Journal* (March 12), p. 1.
Packer, Herbert S. 1968. *The Limits of the Criminal Sanction.* Stanford, Calif.: Stanford University Press.
Pate, Antony Michael. 1989. "Community Policing in Baltimore." In *Police and Policing: Contemporary Issues,* edited by Dennis Jay Kenny. New York: Praeger.
Pate, Tony, Mary Ann Wycoff, Wesley Skogan, and Lawrence W. Sherman. 1986. *Reducing Fear of Crime in Houston and Newark: A Summary Report.* Washington, D.C.: Police Foundation.
Phillips, Llad, and Harold Votey. 1972. "An Economic Analysis of the Deterrent Effect of Law Enforcement on Criminal Activity." *Journal of Criminal Law, Criminology and Police Science* 63:336–42.
Pierce, Glen L., Susan A. Spaar, and LeBaron R. Briggs IV. 1988. "The Character of Police Work: Strategic and Tactical Implications." Report to the National Institute of Justice. Boston: Northeastern University, Center for Applied Social Research.
Pocock, Stuart J. 1983. *Clinical Trials: A Practical Approach.* New York: Wiley.
Police Foundation. 1977. *Domestic Violence and the Police: Studies in Detroit and Kansas City.* Washington, D.C.: Police Foundation.
———. 1981. *The Newark Foot Patrol Experiment.* Washington, D.C.: Police Foundation.
Reiss, Albert J., Jr. 1971. *The Police and the Public.* New Haven, Conn.: Yale University Press.
———. 1985. *Policing a City's Central District: The Oakland Story.* Washington, D.C.: U.S. Government Printing Office.
———. 1988. "Co-offending and Criminal Careers." In *Crime and Justice: A Review of Research,* vol. 10, edited by Michael Tonry and Norval Morris. Chicago: University of Chicago Press.
———. 1990. Personal communication with author.
Reiss, Albert J., Jr., and David J. Bordua. 1967. "Environment and Organization: A Perspective on the Police." In *The Police: Six Sociological Essays,* edited by David J. Bordua. New York: Wiley.
Richman, Teri. 1990. Personal communication with author (vice president, National Association of Convenience Stores).
Rosenbaum, Dennis P., ed. 1986. *Community Crime Prevention: Does It Work?* Beverly Hills, Calif.: Sage.
Ross, H. Laurence. 1982. *Deterring the Drinking Driver: Legal Policy and Social Control.* Lexington, Mass.: D. C. Heath.
Rossi, Peter, Richard E. Berk, and Bettye K. Eidson. 1974. *The Roots of Urban Discontent.* New York: Wiley.
Rossi, Peter H., Emily Waite, Christine E. Bose, and Richard E. Berk. 1974. "The Seriousness of Crimes: Normative Structure and Individual Differences." *American Sociological Review* 39:224–38.
Russell, Francis. 1975. *A City in Terror: 1919—the Boston Police Strike.* New York: Viking.
Sampson, Robert J., and Jacqueline Cohen. 1988. "Deterrent Effects of Police

on Crime: A Replication and Theoretical Extension." *Law and Society Review* 22:163–89.

Schneider, Anne L. 1986. "Neighborhood-based Anti-burglary Strategies: An Analysis of Public and Private Benefits from the Portland Program." In *Community Crime Prevention: Does It Work?* edited by Dennis P. Rosenbaum. Beverly Hills, Calif.: Sage.

Schnelle, J. F., R. E. Kirchner, J. D. Casey, P. H. Uselton, and M. P. McNees. 1977. "Patrol Evaluation Research: A Multiple-Baseline Analysis of Saturation Police Patrolling during Day and Night Hours." *Journal of Applied Behavioral Research* 10:33–40.

Schwartz, Alfred I., and Sumner N. Clarren. 1977. *The Cincinnati Team Policing Experiment: A Summary Report.* Washington, D.C.: Police Foundation.

Sellwood, A. V. 1978. *Police Strike—1919.* London: W. H. Allen.

Shaw, James. 1989. "Reinventing the Police: A New Tactic for Dealing with Driving while Intoxicated Offenders." Unpublished manuscript. University of Maryland, Institute of Criminal Justice and Criminology.

Sherman, Lawrence W. 1983. "From Whodunit to Who Does It: Fairness and Target Selection in Deceptive Investigations." In *Abscam Ethics: Moral Issues and Deception in Law Enforcement,* edited by Gerald M. Caplan. Cambridge, Mass.: Ballinger.

———. 1986. "Policing Communities: What Works." In *Communities and Crime,* edited by Albert J. Reiss, Jr. and Michael Tonry. Vol. 8 of *Crime and Justice: A Review of Research,* edited by Michael Tonry and Norval Morris. Chicago: University of Chicago Press.

———. 1989. "Repeat Calls for Service: Policing the 'Hot Spots.'" In *Police and Policing: Contemporary Issues,* edited by Dennis J. Kenny. New York: Praeger.

———. 1990*a.* "Police Crackdowns: Initial and Residual Deterrence." In *Crime and Justice: A Review of Research,* vol. 12, edited by Michael Tonry and Norval Morris. Chicago: University of Chicago Press.

———. 1990*b.* "An Arrest Budget?" Address before the National Conference on Crime, John Jay College of Criminal Justice, New York, March 6.

———. 1991. "The Results of Police Work: Review of *Problem-oriented Policing,* by Herman Goldstein." *Journal of Criminal Law and Criminology* (forthcoming).

———. 1992. *Policing Domestic Violence: Experiments and Policy Dilemmas.* New York: Free Press.

Sherman, Lawrence, and Richard A. Berk. 1984. "The Specific Deterrent Effects of Arrest for Domestic Assault." *American Sociological Review* 49:261–72.

Sherman, Lawrence, Michael E. Buerger, Patrick R. Gartin, Robert Dell'Erba, and Kinley Larntz. 1989. "Beyond Dial-a-Cop: Repeat Call Address Policing." Report to the National Institute of Justice. Washington, D.C.: Crime Control Institute.

Sherman, Lawrence, and Ellen G. Cohn. 1989. "The Impact of Research on Legal Policy: The Minneapolis Domestic Violence Experiment." *Law and Society Review* 23:117–44.

Sherman, Lawrence, Patrick Gartin, and Michael E. Buerger. 1989. "Hot Spots of Predatory Crime: Routine Activities and the Criminology of Place." *Criminology* 27:27–55.

Sherman, Lawrence, Dennis Rogan, and Robert Velke. 1991. "The Menagerie of Crime: Targets for Police Crime Control Strategies." Unpublished manuscript. Washington, D.C.: Crime Control Institute.

Sherman, Lawrence, Janell D. Schmidt, Dennis Rogan, and Christine DeRiso. 1991a. "Predicting Domestic Homicide: Prior Police Contact and Gun Threats." In *Woman Battering: Policy Responses*, edited by Michael Steinman. Cincinnati, Ohio: Anderson.

Sherman, Lawrence, Janell D. Schmidt, Dennis P. Rogan, Patrick R. Gartin, Ellen G. Cohn, Dean J. Collins, and Anthony R. Bacich. 1991b. "From Initial Deterrence to Long-Term Escalation: Short Custody Arrest for Underclass Domestic Violence." *Criminology* (forthcoming).

Sherman, Lawrence, and Douglas A. Smith. 1991. "Ghetto Poverty, Crime, and Punishment: Formal and Informal Control of Domestic Violence." Unpublished manuscript. University of Maryland, Institute of Criminal Justice and Criminology.

Sherman, Lawrence, Robert Velke, Carol Bridgeforth, and Danee Gaines. 1991c. *Violent Crime in Georgetown: High-Risk Places and Times*. Washington, D.C.: Crime Control Institute.

Sherman, Lawrence, and David Weisburd. 1990. "The General Deterrent Effects of Increased Police Patrol in Hot Spots of Crime." Paper presented to the Academy of Criminal Justice Sciences, Denver, March.

Shover, Neal. 1991. "Burglary." In *Crime and Justice: A Review of Research*, vol. 14, edited by Michael Tonry. Chicago: University of Chicago Press.

Skogan, Wesley G. 1988. "Community Organizations and Crime." In *Crime and Justice: A Review of Research*, vol. 10, edited by Michael Tonry and Norval Morris. Chicago: University of Chicago Press.

———. 1990. *Disorder and Decline: Crime and the Spiral of Decay in America's Neighborhoods*. New York: Free Press.

Skogan, Wesley, and Richard Block. 1983. "Resistance and Injury in Non-fatal Assaultive Violence." *Victimology* 8:215–26.

———. 1986. "Resistance and Nonfatal Outcomes in Stranger-to-Stranger Predatory Crime." *Violence and Victims* 1:241–53.

Skogan, Wesley, and Michael Maxfield. 1981. *Coping with Crime: Individual and Neighborhood Reactions*. Beverly Hills, Calif.: Sage.

Skolnick, Jerome, and David Bayley. 1986. *The New Blue Line: Police Innovation in Six American Cities*. New York: Free Press.

Sparks, Richard F. 1981. "Multiple Victimization: Evidence, Theory and Future Research." *Journal of Criminal Law and Criminology* 72:762–78.

Sparrow, Malcolm K., Mark H. Moore, and David Kennedy. 1990. *Beyond 911: A New Era for Policing*. New York: Basic.

Tittle, Charles R., and Alan R. Rowe. 1974. "Certainty of Arrest and Crime Rates: A Further Test of the Deterrence Hypothesis." *Social Forces* 52:455–62.

Toch, Hans. 1975. *Agents of Change: A Study in Police Reform*. Cambridge: Schenkman.

Uchida, Craig D., Brian Forst, and Sampson Annan. 1990. *Modern Policing and the Control of Illegal Drugs: Testing New Strategies in Two American Cities: Draft Executive Summary*. Washington, D.C.: National Institute of Justice.

U.S. Attorney General's Task Force on Violent Crime. 1981. *Final Report*. Washington, D.C.: U.S. Government Printing Office.

U.S. Bureau of the Census. 1986–90. *Current Population Reports*. Washington, D.C.: U.S. Government Printing Office.

Waller, Irwin, and Norma Okihiro. 1978. *Burglary: The Victim and the Public*. Toronto: University of Toronto Press.

Weisburd, David. 1989. *Jewish Settler Violence*. State College: Pennsylvania State University Press.

Weisburd, David, Lisa Maher, and Lawrence W. Sherman. 1991. "Contrasting Crime-general and Crime-specific Theory: The Case of Hot Spots of Crime." In *Advances in Criminological Theory*, vol. 5. New Brunswick, N.J.: Transaction Press.

Williams, Hubert. 1983. Personal communication with author (former police director, city of Newark).

Wilson, James Q. 1968. *Varieties of Police Behavior*. Cambridge, Mass.: Harvard University Press.

———. 1977. "Foreword." In *Domestic Violence and the Police: Studies in Detroit and Kansas City*. Washington, D.C.: Police Foundation.

Wilson, James Q., and Barbara Boland. 1978. "The Effect of the Police on Crime." *Law and Society Review* 12:367–90.

———. 1981–82. "The Effects of the Police on Crime: A Rejoinder." *Law and Society Review* 16:163–69.

Wilson, James Q., and Richard Herrnstein. 1985. *Crime and Human Nature*. New York: Simon & Schuster.

Wilson, James Q., and George Kelling. 1982. "Broken Windows: The Police and Neighborhood Safety." *Atlantic Monthly* (March), pp. 29–38.

Wilson, Jerry V. 1990a. Personal communication with author (former chief of police, Washington, D.C.).

———. 1990b. *Gainesville Convenience Store Ordinance: Findings of Fact, Conclusions and Recommendations*. Report prepared for the National Association of Convenience Stores. Washington, D.C.: Crime Control Research Corporation.

Wilson, Orlando W. 1963. *Police Administration*. 2d ed. New York: McGraw-Hill.

Wolfgang, Marvin, Robert Figlio, and Thorsten Sellin. 1972. *Delinquency in a Birth Cohort*. Chicago: University of Chicago Press.

Wycoff, Mary Ann, Charles Susmilch, and Charles Brown. 1981. "The Birmingham Anti-robbery Experiment." Draft report. Washington, D.C.: Police Foundation.

Yoder, Richard, and Robert Moore. 1973. "Characteristics of Convicted Drunken Drivers." *Quarterly Journal of Studies on Alcohol* 34:927–36.

230   Lawrence W. Sherman

Zimring, Franklin E. 1976. "Field Experiments in General Deterrence: Preferring the Tortoise to the Hare." *Evaluation* 3:132–35.
———. 1978. "Policy Experiments in General Deterrence: 1970–1975." In *Deterrence and Incapacitation: Estimating the Effects of Criminal Sanctions on Crime Rates*, edited by Alfred Blumstein, Jacqueline Cohen, and Daniel Nagin. Washington, D.C.: National Academy of Sciences.
———. 1990. Personal communication with author.

Part IV
Police and Order-Maintenance

20

AMERICAN SOCIOLOGICAL REVIEW

October 1967   Volume 32, No. 5

THE POLICE ON SKID-ROW: A STUDY OF PEACE KEEPING *

EGON BITTNER

Langley Porter Neuropsychiatric Institute

Following the distinction proposed by Banton, police work consists of two relatively different activities: "law enforcement" and "keeping the peace." The latter is not determined by a clear legal mandate and does not stand under any system of external control. Instead, it developed as a craft in response to a variety of demand conditions. One such condition is created by the concentration of certain types of persons on skid-row. Patrolmen have a particular conception of the social order of skid-row life that determines the procedures of control they employ. The most conspicuous features of the peace keeping methods used are an aggressively personalized approach to residents, an attenuated regard for questions of culpability, and the use of coercion, mainly in the interest of managing situations rather than persons.

THE prototype of modern police organization, the Metropolitan Police of London, was created to replace an antiquated and corrupt system of law enforcement. The early planners were motivated by the mixture of hardheaded business rationality and humane sentiment that characterized liberal British thought of the first half of the nineteenth century.[1] Partly to meet the objections of a parliamentary committee, which was opposed to the establishment of the police in England, and partly because it was in line with their own thinking, the planners sought to produce an instrument that could not readily be used in the play of internal power politics but which would, instead, advance and protect conditions favorable to industry and commerce and to urban civil life in general. These intentions were not very specific and had to be reconciled with the existing structures of governing, administering justice, and keeping the peace. Consequently, the locus and mandate of the police in the modern polity were ill-defined at the outset. On the one hand, the new institution was to be a part of the executive branch of government, organized, funded, and staffed in accordance with standards that were typical for the entire system of the executive. On the other hand, the duties that were given to the police organization brought it under direct control of the judiciary in its day-to-day operation.

The dual patronage of the police by the executive and the judiciary is characteristic for all democratically governed countries. Moreover, it is generally the case, or at least it is deemed desirable, that judges *rather than* executive officials have control over police use and procedure.[2] This preference is based

---
* This research was supported in part by Grant 64-1-35 from the California Department of Mental Hygiene. I gratefully acknowledge the help I received from Fred Davis, Sheldon Messinger, Leonard Schatzman, and Anselm Strauss in the preparation of this paper.

[1] The bill for a Metropolitan Police was actually enacted under the sponsorship of Robert Peel, the Home Secretary in the Tory Government of the Duke of Wellington. There is, however, no doubt that it was one of the several reform tendencies that Peel assimilated into Tory politics in his long career. Cf. J. L. Lyman, "The Metropolitan Police Act of 1829," *Journal of Criminal Law, Criminology and Police Science,* 55 (1964), 141–154.

[2] Jerome Hall, "Police and Law in a Democratic Society," *Indiana Law Journal,* 28 (1953), 133–177. Though other authors are less emphatic on this point, judicial control is generally taken for granted. The point has been made, however, that in modern times judicial control over the police has been asserted mainly because of the default of any other general controlling authority, cf. E. L. Barrett, Jr.,

on two considerations. First, in the tenets of the democratic creed, the possibility of direct control of the police by a government in power is repugnant.[3] Even when the specter of the police state in its more ominous forms is not a concern, close ties between those who govern and those who police are viewed as a sign of political corruption.[4] Hence, mayors, governors, and cabinet officers—although the nominal superiors of the police—tend to maintain, or to pretend, a hands-off policy. Second, it is commonly understood that the main function of the police is the control of crime. Since the concept of crime belongs wholly to the law, and its treatment is exhaustively based on considerations of legality, police procedure automatically stands under the same system of review that controls the administration of justice in general.

By nature, judicial control encompasses only those aspects of police activity that are directly related to full-dress legal prosecution of offenders. The judiciary has neither the authority nor the means to direct, supervise, and review those activities of the police that do not result in prosecution. Yet such other activities are unavoidable, frequent, and largely within the realm of public expectations. It might be assumed that in this domain of practice the police are under executive control. This is not the case, however, except in a marginal sense.[5] Not only are police departments generally free to determine what need be done and how, but

aside from informal pressures they are given scant direction in these matters. Thus, there appear to exist two relatively independent domains of police activity. In one, their methods are constrained by the prospect of the future disposition of a case in the courts; in the other, they operate under some other consideration and largely with no structured and continuous outside constraint. Following the terminology suggested by Michael Banton, they may be said to function in the first instance as "law officers" and in the second instance as "peace officers." [6] It must be emphasized that the designation "peace officer" is a residual term, with only some vaguely presumptive content. The role, as Banton speaks of it, is supposed to encompass all occupational routines not directly related to making arrests, without, however, specifying what determines the limits of competence and availability of the police in such actions.

Efforts to characterize a large domain of activities of an important public agency have so far yielded only negative definitions. We know that they do not involve arrests; we also know that they do not stand under judicial control, and that they are not, in any important sense, determined by specific executive or legislative mandates. In police textbooks and manuals, these activities receive only casual attention, and the role of the "peace officer" is typically stated in terms suggesting that his work is governed mainly by the individual officer's personal wisdom, integrity, and altruism.[7] Police departments generally keep no records of procedures that do not involve making arrests. Policemen, when asked, insist that they merely use common sense when acting as "peace officers," though they tend to emphasize the elements of experience and practice in discharging the role adequately. All this ambiguity is the more remarkable for the fact that peace keeping tasks, i.e., procedures not involving the formal legal remedy of arrest, were explicitly built into the program of the modern police from the outset.[8]

"Police Practice and the Law," *California Law Review*, 50 (1962), 11–55.

[3] A. C. German, F. D. Day and R. R. J. Gallati, *Introduction to Law Enforcement*, Springfield, Ill.: C. C Thomas, 1966; "One concept, in particular, should be kept in mind. A dictatorship can never exist unless the police system of the country is under the absolute control of the dictator. There is no other way to uphold a dictatorship except by terror, and the instrument of this total terror is the secret police, whatever its name. In every country where freedom has been lost, law enforcement has been a dominant instrument in destroying it" (p. 80).

[4] The point is frequently made; cf. Raymond B. Fosdick, *American Police Systems*, New York: Century Company, 1920; Bruce Smith, *Police Systems in the United States*, 2nd rev. ed., New York: Harper, 1960.

[5] The executive margin of control is set mainly in terms of budgetary determinations and the mapping of some formal aspects of the organization of departments.

[6] Michael Banton, *The Policeman in the Community*, New York: Basic Books, 1964, pp. 6–7 and 127 ff.

[7] R. Bruce Holmgren, *Primary Police Functions*, New York: William C. Copp, 1962.

[8] Cf. Lyman, *op. cit.*, p. 153; F. C. Mather, *Public Order in the Age of the Chartists*, Manchester: Manchester University Press, 1959, chap-

The early executives of the London police saw with great clarity that their organization had a dual function. While it was to be an arm of the administration of justice, in respect of which it developed certain techniques for bringing offenders to trial, it was also expected to function apart from, and at times in lieu of, the employment of full-dress legal procedure. Despite its early origin, despite a great deal of public knowledge about it, despite the fact that it is routinely done by policemen, no one can say with any clarity what it means to do a good job of keeping the peace. To be sure, there is vague consensus that when policemen direct, aid, inform, pacify, warn, discipline, roust, and do whatever else they do without making arrests, they do this with some reference to the circumstances of the occasion and, thus, somehow contribute to the maintenance of the peace and order. Peace keeping appears to be a solution to an unknown problem arrived at by unknown means.

The following is an attempt to clarify conceptually the mandate and the practice of keeping the peace. The effort will be directed not to the formulation of a comprehensive solution of the problem but to a detailed consideration of some aspects of it. Only in order to place the particular into the overall domain to which it belongs will the structural determinants of keeping the peace in general be discussed. By structural determinants are meant the typical situations that policemen perceive as *demand conditions* for action without arrest. This will be followed by a description of peace keeping in skid-row districts, with the object of identifying those aspects of it that constitute a *practical skill*.

Since the major object of this paper is to elucidate peace keeping practice as a skilled performance, it is necessary to make clear how the use of the term is intended.

Practical skill will be used to refer to those methods of doing certain things, and to the information that underlies the use of the methods, that *practitioners themselves* view as proper and efficient. Skill is, therefore, a stable orientation to work tasks that is relatively independent of the personal feel-

ings and judgments of those who employ it. Whether the exercise of this skilled performance is desirable or not, and whether it is based on correct information or not, are specifically outside the scope of interest of this presentation. The following is deliberately confined to a description of what police patrolmen consider to be the reality of their work circumstances, what they do, and what they feel they must do to do a good job. That the practice is thought to be determined by normative standards of skill minimizes but does not eliminate the factors of personal interest or inclination. Moreover, the distribution of skill varies among practitioners in the very standards they set for themselves. For example, we will show that patrolmen view a measure of rough informality as good practice vis-a-vis skid-row inhabitants. By this standard, patrolmen who are "not rough enough," or who are "too rough," or whose roughness is determined by personal feelings rather than by situational exigencies, are judged to be poor craftsmen.

The description and analysis are based on twelve months of field work with the police departments of two large cities west of the Mississippi. Eleven weeks of this time were spent in skid-row and skid-row-like districts. The observations were augmented by approximately one hundred interviews with police officers of all ranks. The formulations that will be proposed were discussed in these interviews. They were recognized by the respondents as elements of standard practice. The respondents' recognition was often accompanied by remarks indicating that they had never thought about things in this way and that they were not aware how standardized police work was.

STRUCTURAL DEMAND CONDITIONS OF PEACE KEEPING

There exist at least five types of relatively distinct circumstances that produce police activities that do not involve invoking the law and that are only in a trivial sense determined by those considerations of legality that determine law enforcement. This does not mean that these activities are illegal but merely that there is no legal directive that informs the acting policeman whether what he does must be done or how it is to be done. In these circumstances, policemen act

ter IV. See also Robert H. Bremer, "Police, Penal and Parole Policies in Cleveland and Toledo," *American Journal of Economics and Sociology,* 14 (1955), 387–398, for similar recognition in the United States at about the turn of this century.

as all-purpose and terminal remedial agents, and the confronted problem is solved in the field. If these practices stand under any kind of review at all, and typically they do not, it is only through internal police department control.

1. Although the executive branch of government generally refrains from exercising a controlling influence over the direction of police interest, it manages to extract certain performances from it. Two important examples of this are the supervision of certain licensed services and premises and the regulation of traffic.[9] With respect to the first, the police tend to concentrate on what might be called the moral aspects of establishments rather than on questions relating to the technical adequacy of the service. This orientation is based on the assumption that certain types of businesses lend themselves to exploitation for undesirable and illegal purposes. Since this tendency cannot be fully controlled, it is only natural that the police will be inclined to favor licensees who are at least cooperative. This, however, transforms the task from the mere scrutiny of credentials and the passing of judgments, to the creation and maintenance of a network of connections that conveys influence, pressure, and information. The duty to inspect is the background of this network, but the resulting contacts acquire additional value for solving crimes and maintaining public order. Bartenders, shopkeepers, and hotel clerks become, for patrolmen, a resource that must be continuously serviced by visits and exchanges of favors. While it is apparent that this condition lends itself to corrupt exploitation by individual officers, even the most flawlessly honest policeman must participate in this network of exchanges if he is to function adequately. Thus, engaging in such exchanges becomes an occupational task that demands attention and time.

Regulation of traffic is considerably less complex. More than anything else, traffic control symbolizes the autonomous authority of policemen. Their commands generally are met with unquestioned compliance. Even when they issue citations, which seemingly refer the case to the courts, it is common practice for the accused to view the allegation as a finding against him and to pay the

fine. Police officials emphasize that it is more important to be circumspect than legalistic in traffic control. Officers are often reminded that a large segment of the public has no other contacts with the police, and that the field lends itself to public relations work by the line personnel.[10]

2. Policemen often do not arrest persons who have committed minor offences in circumstances in which the arrest is technically possible. This practice has recently received considerable attention in legal and sociological literature. The studies were motivated by the realization that "police decisions not to invoke the criminal process determine the outer limits of law enforcement." [11] From these researches, it was learned that the police tend to impose more stringent criteria of law enforcement on certain segments of the community than on others.[12] It was also learned that, from the perspective of the administration of justice, the decisions not to make arrests often are based on compelling reasons.[13] It is less well appreciated that policemen often not only refrain from invoking the law formally but also employ alternative sanctions. For example, it is standard practice that violators are warned not to repeat the offense. This often leads to patrolmen's "keeping an eye" on certain persons. Less frequent, though not unusual, is the practice of direct disciplining of offenders, especially when they are juveniles, which occasionally involves inducing them to repair the damage occasioned by their misconduct.[14]

The power to arrest and the freedom not to arrest can be used in cases that do not involve patent offenses. An officer can say to a person whose behavior he wishes to control, "I'll let you go this time!" without

---

[9] Smith, op. cit., pp. 15 ff.

[10] Orlando W. Wilson, "Police Authority in a Free Society," Journal of Criminal Law, Criminology and Police Science, 54 (1964), 175–177.

[11] Joseph Goldstein, "Police Discretion Not to Invoke the Criminal Process," Yale Law Journal, 69 (1960), 543.

[12] Jerome Skolnick, Justice Without Trial, New York: Wiley, 1966.

[13] Wayne LaFave, "The Police and Nonenforcement of the Law," Wisconsin Law Review (1962), 104–137 and 179–239.

[14] Nathan Goldman, The Differential Selection of Juvenile Offenders for Court Appearance, National Research and Information Center, National Council on Crime and Delinquency, 1963, pp. 114 ff.

indicating to him that he could not have been arrested in any case. Nor is this always deliberate misrepresentation, for in many cases the law is sufficiently ambiguous to allow alternative interpretations. In short, not to make an arrest is rarely, if ever, merely a decision not to act; it is most often a decision to act alternatively. In the case of minor offenses, to make an arrest often is merely one of several possible proper actions.

3. There exists a public demand for police intervention in matters that contain no criminal and often no legal aspects.[15] For example, it is commonly assumed that officers will be available to arbitrate quarrels, to pacify the unruly, and to help in keeping order. They are supposed also to aid people in trouble, and there is scarcely a human predicament imaginable for which police aid has not been solicited and obtained at one time or another. Most authors writing about the police consider such activities only marginally related to the police mandate. This view fails to reckon with the fact that the availability of these performances is taken for granted and the police assign a substantial amount of their resources to such work. Although this work cannot be subsumed under the concept of legal action, it does involve the exercise of a form of authority that most people associate with the police. In fact, no matter how trivial the occasion, the device of "calling the cops" transforms any problem. It implies that a situation is, or is getting, out of hand. Police responses to public demands are always oriented to this implication, and the risk of proliferation of troubles makes every call a potentially serious matter.[16]

4. Certain mass phenomena of either a regular or a spontaneous nature require direct monitoring. Most important is the controlling of crowds in incipient stages of disorder. The specter of mob violence frequently calls for measures that involve coercion, including the

use of physical force. Legal theory allows, of course, that public officials are empowered to use coercion in situations of imminent danger.[17] Unfortunately, the doctrine is not sufficiently specific to be of much help as a rule of practice. It is based on the assumption of the adventitiousness of danger, and thus does not lend itself readily to elaborations that could direct the routines of early detection and prevention of untoward developments. It is interesting that the objective of preventing riots by informal means posed one of the central organizational problems for the police in England during the era of the Chartists.[18]

5. The police have certain special duties with respect to persons who are viewed as less than fully accountable for their actions. Examples of those eligible for special consideration are those who are under age [19] and those who are mentally ill.[20] Although it is virtually never acknowledged explicitly, those receiving special treatment include people who do not lead "normal" lives and who occupy a pariah status in society. This group includes residents of ethnic ghettos, certain types of bohemians and vagabonds, and persons of known criminal background. The special treatment of children and of sick persons is permissively sanctioned by the law, but the special treatment of others is, in principle, opposed by the leading theme of legality and the tenets of the democratic faith.[21] The important point is not that such persons are arrested more often than others, which is quite true, but that they are per-

[15] Elaine Cumming, Ian Cumming and Laura Edell, "Policeman as Philosopher, Guide and Friend," *Social Problems*, 12 (1965), 276–286.

[16] There is little doubt that many requests for service are turned down by the police, especially when they are made over the telephone or by mail, cf. LaFave, *op. cit.*, p. 212, n. 124. The uniformed patrolman, however, finds it virtually impossible to leave the scene without becoming involved in some way or another.

[17] Hans Kelsen, *General Theory of Law and State*, New York: Russell & Russell, 1961, pp. 278–279; H. L. A. Hart, *The Concept of Law*, Oxford: Clarendon Press, 1961, pp. 20–21.

[18] Mather, *op. cit.;* see also, Jenifer Hart, "Reform of the Borough Police, 1835–1856," *English History Review*, 70 (1955), 411–427.

[19] Francis A. Allen, *The Borderland of Criminal Justice*, Chicago: University of Chicago Press, 1964.

[20] Egon Bittner, "Police Discretion in Emergency Apprehension of Mentally Ill Persons," *Social Problems*, 14 (1967), 278–292.

[21] It bears mentioning, however, that differential treatment is not unique with the police, but is also in many ways representative for the administration of justice in general; cf. J. E. Carlin, Jan Howard and S. L. Messinger, "Civil Justice and the Poor," *Law and Society*, 1 (1966), 9–89; Jacobus tenBroek (ed.) *The Law of the Poor*, San Francisco: Chandler Publishing Co., 1966.

704 AMERICAN SOCIOLOGICAL REVIEW

ceived by the police as producing a special problem that necessitates continuous attention and the use of special procedures.

The five types of demand conditions do not exclude the possibility of invoking the criminal process. Indeed, arrests do occur quite frequently in all these circumstances. But the concerns generated in these areas cause activities that usually do not terminate in an arrest. When arrests are made, there exist, at least in the ideal, certain criteria by reference to which the arrest can be judged as having been made more or less properly, and there are some persons who, in the natural course of events, actually judge the performance.[22] But for actions not resulting in arrest there are no such criteria and no such judges. How, then, can one speak of such actions as necessary and proper? Since there does not exist any official answer to this query, and since policemen act in the role of "peace officers" pretty much without external direction or constraint, the question comes down to asking how the policeman himself knows whether he has any business with a person he does not arrest, and if so, what that business might be. Furthermore, if there exists a domain of concerns and activities that is largely independent of the law enforcement mandate, it is reasonable to assume that it will exercise some degree of influence on how and to what ends the law is invoked in cases of arrests.

Skid-row presents one excellent opportunity to study these problems. The area contains a heavy concentration of persons who do not live "normal" lives in terms of prevailing standards of middle-class morality. Since the police respond to this situation by intensive patrolling, the structure of peace keeping should be readily observable. Needless to say, the findings and conclusions will not be necessarily generalizable to other types of demand conditions.

THE PROBLEM OF KEEPING THE PEACE
IN SKID-ROW

Skid-row has always occupied a special place among the various forms of urban life.

While other areas are perceived as being different in many ways, skid-row is seen as completely different. Though it is located in the heart of civilization, it is viewed as containing aspects of the primordial jungle, calling for missionary activities and offering opportunities for exotic adventure. While each inhabitant individually can be seen as tragically linked to the vicissitudes of "normal" life, allowing others to say "here but for the Grace of God go I," those who live there are believed to have repudiated the entire role-casting scheme of the majority and to live apart from normalcy. Accordingly, the traditional attitude of civic-mindedness toward skid-row has been dominated by the desire to contain it and to salvage souls from its clutches.[23] The specific task of containment has been left to the police. That this task pressed upon the police some rather special duties has never come under explicit consideration, either from the government that expects control or from the police departments that implement it. Instead, the prevailing method of carrying out the task is to assign patrolmen to the area on a fairly permanent basis and to allow them to work out their own ways of running things. External influence is confined largely to the supply of support and facilities, on the one hand, and to occasional expressions of criticism about the overall conditions, on the other. Within the limits of available resources and general expectations, patrolmen are supposed to know what to do and are free to do it.[24]

[22] This is, however, true only in the ideal. It is well known that a substantial number of persons who are arrested are subsequently released without ever being charged and tried, cf. Barret, *op. cit.*

[23] The literature on skid-row is voluminous. The classic in the field is Nels Anderson, *The Hobo,* Chicago: University of Chicago Press, 1923. Samuel E. Wallace, *Skid-Row as a Way of Life,* Totowa, New Jersey: The Bedminster Press, 1965, is a more recent descriptive account and contains a useful bibliography. Donald A. Bogue, *Skid-Row in American Cities,* Chicago: Community and Family Center, University of Chicago, 1963, contains an exhaustive quantitative survey of Chicago skid-row.

[24] One of the two cities described in this paper also employed the procedure of the "round-up" of drunks. In this, the police van toured the skid-row area twice daily, during the mid-afternoon and early evening hours, and the officers who manned it picked up drunks they sighted. A similar procedure is used in New York's Bowery and the officers who do it are called "condition men." Cf. *Bowery Project,* Bureau of Applied Social Research, Columbia University, Summary Report of a Study Undertaken under Contract Approved by the Board of Estimates, 1963, mimeo., p. 11.

POLICE ON SKID-ROW 705

Patrolmen who are more or less permanently assigned to skid-row districts tend to develop a conception of the nature of their "domain" that is surprisingly uniform. Individual officers differ in many aspects of practice, emphasize different concerns, and maintain different contacts, but they are in fundamental agreement about the structure of skid-row life. This relatively uniform conception includes an implicit formulation of the problem of keeping the peace in skid-row.

In the view of experienced patrolmen, life on skid-row is fundamentally different from life in other parts of society. To be sure, they say, around its geographic limits the area tends to blend into the surrounding environment, and its population always encompasses some persons who are only transitionally associated with it. Basically, however, skid-row is perceived as the natural habitat of people who lack the capacities and commitments to live "normal" lives on a sustained basis. The presence of these people defines the nature of social reality in the area. In general, and especially in casual encounters, the presumption of incompetence and of the disinclination to be "normal" is the leading theme for the interpretation of all actions and relations. Not only do people approach one another in this manner, but presumably they also expect to be approached in this way, and they conduct themselves accordingly.

In practice, the restriction of interactional possibilities that is based on the patrolman's stereotyped conception of skid-row residents is always subject to revision and modification toward particular individuals. Thus, it is entirely possible, and not unusual, for patrolmen to view certain skid-row inhabitants in terms that involve non-skid-row aspects of normality. Instances of such approaches and relationships invariably involve personal acquaintance and the knowledge of a good deal of individually qualifying information. Such instances are seen, despite their relative frequency, as exceptions to the rule. The awareness of the possibility of breakdown, frustration, and betrayal is ever-present, basic wariness is never wholly dissipated, and undaunted trust can never be fully reconciled with presence on skid-row.

What patrolmen view as normal on skid-row—and what they also think is taken for granted as "life as usual" by the inhabitants—is not easily summarized. It seems to focus on the idea that the dominant consideration governing all enterprise and association is directed to the occasion of the moment. Nothing is thought of as having a background that might have led up to the present in terms of some compelling moral or practical necessity. There are some exceptions to this rule, of course: the police themselves, and those who run certain establishments, are perceived as engaged in important and necessary activities. But in order to carry them out they, too, must be geared to the overall atmosphere of fortuitousness. In this atmosphere, the range of control that persons have over one another is exceedingly narrow. Good faith, even where it is valued, is seen merely as a personal matter. Its violations are the victim's own hard luck, rather than demonstrable violations of property. There is only a private sense of irony at having been victimized. The overall air is not so much one of active distrust as it is one of irrelevance of trust; as patrolmen often emphasize, the situation does not necessarily cause all relations to be predatory, but the possibility of exploitation is not checked by the expectation that it will not happen.

Just as the past is seen by the policeman as having only the most attenuated relevance to the present, so the future implications of present situations are said to be generally devoid of prospective coherence. No venture, especially no joint venture, can be said to have a strongly predictable future in line with its initial objectives. It is a matter of adventitious circumstance whether or not matters go as anticipated. That which is not within the grasp of momentary control is outside of practical social reality.

Though patrolmen see the temporal framework of the occasion of the moment mainly as a lack of trustworthiness, they also recognize that it involves more than merely the personal motives of individuals. In addition to the fact that everybody *feels* that things matter only at the moment, irresponsibility takes an *objectified* form on skid-row. The places the residents occupy, the social relations they entertain, and the activities that engage them are not meaningfully connected over time. Thus, for example, address, occupation, marital status, etc., matter much less on skid-row than in any other part of society. The fact that present whereabouts, activities, and affiliations imply neither continuity nor direction means that life on skid-row lacks a socially structured background of accountability. Of course, everybody's life contains some sequential incongruities, but in the life of a skid-row inhabitant every moment is an accident. That a man has no "address" in the future that could be in some way inferred from where he is and what he does makes him a person of *radically reduced visibility*. If he disappears from sight and one wishes to locate him, it is virtually impossible to systematize the search. All one can know with relative certainty is that he will be somewhere on some skid-row and the only thing one can do is to trace the factual contiguities of his whereabouts.

It is commonly known that the police are expert in finding people and that they have developed an exquisite technology involving special facilities and procedures of sleuthing. It is less well appreciated that all this technology builds upon those socially structured features of everyday life that render persons findable in the first place.

Under ordinary conditions, the query as to where a person is can be addressed, from the outset, to a restricted realm of possibilities that can be further narrowed by looking into certain places and asking certain persons. The map of whereabouts that normally competent persons use whenever they wish to locate someone is constituted by the basic facts of membership in society. Insofar as membership consists of status incumbencies, each of which has an adumbrated future that substantially reduces unpredictability, it is itself a guarantee of the order within which it is quite difficult to get lost. Membership is thus visible not only now but also as its own projection into the future. It is in terms of this prospective availability that the skid-row inhabitant is a person of reduced visibility. His membership is viewed as extraordinary because its extension into the future is *not* reduced to a restricted realm of possibilities. Neither his subjective dispositions, nor his circumstances, indicate that he is oriented to any particular long-range interests. But, as he may claim every contingent opportunity, his claims are always seen as based on slight

merit or right, at least to the extent that interfering with them does not constitute a substantial denial of his freedom.

This, then, constitutes the problem of keeping the peace on skid-row. Considerations of momentary expediency are seen as having unqualified priority as maxims of conduct; consequently, the controlling influences of the pursuit of sustained interests are presumed to be absent.

THE PRACTICES OF KEEPING THE PEACE IN SKID-ROW

From the perspective of society as a whole, skid-row inhabitants appear troublesome in a variety of ways. The uncommitted life attributed to them is perceived as inherently offensive; its very existence arouses indignation and contempt. More important, however, is the feeling that persons who have repudiated the entire role-status casting system of society, persons whose lives forever collapse into a succession of random moments, are seen as constituting a practical risk. As they have nothing to foresake, nothing is thought safe from them.[25]

The skid-row patrolman's concept of his mandate includes an awareness of this presumed risk. He is constantly attuned to the possibility of violence, and he is convinced that things to which the inhabitants have free access are as good as lost. But his concern is directed toward the continuous condition of peril *in the area* rather than *for society in general*. While he is obviously conscious of the presence of many persons who have committed crimes outside of skid-row and will arrest them when they come to his attention, this is a peripheral part of his routine activities. In general, the skid-row patrolman and his superiors take for granted that his main business is to keep the peace

---

[25] An illuminating parallel to the perception of skid-row can be found in the more traditional concept of vagabondage. Cf. Alexandre Vexliard, *Introduction a la Sociologie du Vagabondage*, Paris: Libraire Marcel Riviere, 1956, and "La Disparition du Vagabondage comme Fleau Social Universel," *Revue de L'Instut de Sociologie* (1963), 53–79. The classic account of English conditions up to the 19th century is C. J. Ribton-Turner, *A History of Vagrants and Vagrancy and Beggars and Begging*, London: Chapman and Hall, 1887.

and enforce the laws *on skid-row*, and that he is involved only incidentally in protecting society at large. Thus, his task is formulated basically as the protection of putative predators from one another. The maintenance of peace and safety is difficult because everyday life on skid-row is viewed as an open field for reciprocal exploitation. As the lives of the inhabitants lack the prospective coherence associated with status incumbency, the realization of self-interest does not produce order. Hence, mechanisms that control risk must work primarily from without.

External containment, to be effective, must be oriented to the realities of existence. Thus, the skid-row patrolman employs an approach that he views as appropriate to the *ad hoc* nature of skid-row life. The following are the three most prominent elements of this approach. First, the seasoned patrolman seeks to acquire a richly particularized knowledge of people and places in the area. Second, he gives the consideration of strict culpability a subordinate status among grounds for remedial sanction. Third, his use and choice of coercive interventions is determined mainly by exigencies of situations and with little regard for possible long range effects on individual persons.

The Particularization of Knowledge. The patrolman's orientation to people on skid-row is structured basically by the presupposition that if he does not know a man personally there is very little that he can assume about him. This rule determines his interaction with people who live on skid-row. Since the area also contains other types of persons, however, its applicability is not universal. To some such persons it does not apply at all, and it has a somewhat mitigated significance with certain others. For example, some persons encountered on skid-row can be recognized immediately as outsiders. Among them are workers who are employed in commercial and industrial enterprises that abut the area, persons who come for the purpose of adventurous "slumming," and some patrons of second-hand stores and pawn shops. Even with very little experience, it is relatively easy to identify these people by appearance, demeanor, and the time and place of their presence. The patrolman maintains an impersonal attitude toward them,

and they are, under ordinary circumstances, not the objects of his attention.[26]

Clearly set off from these outsiders are the residents and the entire corps of personnel that services skid-row. It would be fair to say that one of the main routine activities of patrolmen is the establishment and maintenance of familiar relationships with individual members of these groups. Officers emphasize their interest in this, and they maintain that their grasp of and control over skid-row is precisely commensurate with the extent to which they "know the people." By this they do not mean having a quasi-theoretical understanding of human nature but rather the common practice of individualized and reciprocal recognition. As this group encompasses both those who render services on skid-row and those who are serviced, individualized interest is not always based on the desire to overcome uncertainty. Instead, relations with service personnel become absorbed into the network of particularized attention. Ties between patrolmen, on the one hand, and businessmen, managers, and workers, on the other hand, are often defined in terms of shared or similar interests. It bears mentioning that many persons live *and* work on skid-row. Thus, the distinction between those who service and those who are serviced is not a clearcut dichotomy but a spectrum of affiliations.

As a general rule, the skid-row patrolman possesses an immensely detailed factual knowledge of his beat. He knows, and knows a great deal about, a large number of residents. He is likely to know every person who manages or works in the local bars, hotels, shops, stores, and missions. Moreover, he probably knows every public and private place inside and out. Finally, he ordinarily remembers countless events of the past which he can recount by citing names, dates and places with remarkable precision. Though there are always some threads missing in the fabric of information, it is continuously woven and mended even as it is being used. New facts, however, are added to the texture,

---

[26] Several patrolmen complained about the influx of "tourists" into skid-row. Since such "tourists" are perceived as seeking illicit adventure, they receive little sympathy from patrolmen when they complain about being victimized.

not in terms of structured categories but in terms of adjoining known realities. In other words, the content and organization of the patrolman's knowledge is primarily ideographic and only vestigially, if at all, nomothetic.

Individual patrolmen vary in the extent to which they make themselves available or actively pursue personal acquaintances. But even the most aloof are continuously greeted and engaged in conversations that indicate a background of individualistic associations. While this scarcely has the appearance of work, because of its casual character, patrolmen do not view it as an optional activity. In the course of making their rounds, patrolmen seem to have access to every place, and their entry causes no surprise or consternation. Instead, the entry tends to lead to informal exchanges of small talk. At times the rounds include entering hotels and gaining access to rooms or dormitories, often for no other purpose than asking the occupants how things are going. In all this, patrolmen address innumerable persons by name and are in turn addressed by name. The conversational style that characterizes these exchanges is casual to an extent that by non-skid-row standards might suggest intimacy. Not only does the officer himself avoid all terms of deference and respect but he does not seem to expect or demand them. For example, a patrolman said to a man radiating an alcoholic glow on the street, "You've got enough of a heat on now; I'll give you ten minutes to get your ass off the street!" Without stopping, the man answered, "Oh, why don't you go and piss in your own pot!" The officer's only response was, "All right, in ten minutes you're either in bed or on your way to the can."

This kind of expressive freedom is an intricately limited privilege. Persons of acquaintance are entitled to it and appear to exercise it mainly in routinized encounters. But strangers, too, can use it with impunity. The safe way of gaining the privilege is to respond to the patrolman in ways that do not challenge his right to ask questions and issue commands. Once the concession is made that the officer is entitled to inquire into a man's background, business, and intentions, and that he is entitled to obedience, there opens a field of colloquial license. A patrolman

seems to grant expressive freedom in recognition of a person's acceptance of his access to areas of life ordinarily defined as private and subject to coercive control only under special circumstances. While patrolmen accept and seemingly even cultivate the rough *quid pro quo* of informality, and while they do not expect sincerity, candor, or obedience in their dealings with the inhabitants, they do not allow the rejection of their approach.

The explicit refusal to answer questions of a personal nature and the demand to know why the questions are asked significantly enhances a person's chances of being arrested on some minor charge. While most patrolmen tend to be personally indignant about this kind of response and use the arrest to compose their own hurt feelings, this is merely a case of affect being in line with the method. There are other officers who proceed in the same manner without taking offense, or even with feelings of regret. Such patrolmen often maintain that their colleagues' affective involvement is a corruption of an essentially valid technique. The technique is oriented to the goal of maintaining operational control. The patrolman's conception of this goal places him hierarchically above whomever he approaches, and makes him the sole judge of the propriety of the occasion. As he alone is oriented to this goal, and as he seeks to attain it by means of individualized access to persons, those who frustrate him are seen as motivated at best by the desire to "give him a hard time" and at worst by some darkly devious purpose.

Officers are quite aware that the directness of their approach and the demands they make are difficult to reconcile with the doctrines of civil liberties, but they maintain that they are in accord with the general freedom of access that persons living on skid-row normally grant one another. That is, they believe that the imposition of personalized and far-reaching control is in tune with standard expectancies. In terms of these expectancies, people are not so much denied the right to privacy as they are seen as not having any privacy. Thus, officers seek to install themselves in the center of people's lives and let the consciousness of their presence play the part of conscience.

When talking about the practical necessity of an aggressively personal approach, officers

POLICE ON SKID-ROW

do not refer merely to the need for maintaining control over lives that are open in the direction of the untoward. They also see it as the basis for the supply of certain valued services to inhabitants of skid-row. The coerced or conceded access to persons often imposes on the patrolman tasks that are, in the main, in line with these persons' expressed or implied interest. In asserting this connection, patrolmen note that they frequently help people to obtain meals, lodging, employment, that they direct them to welfare and health services, and that they aid them in various other ways. Though patrolmen tend to describe such services mainly as the product of their own altruism, they also say that their colleagues who avoid them are simply doing a poor job of patrolling. The acceptance of the need to help people is based on the realization that the hungry, the sick, and the troubled are a potential source of problems. Moreover, that patrolmen will help people is part of the background expectancies of life on skid-row. Hotel clerks normally call policemen when someone gets so sick as to need attention; merchants expect to be taxed, in a manner of speaking, to meet the pressing needs of certain persons; and the inhabitants do not hesitate to accept, solicit, and demand every kind of aid. The domain of the patrolman's service activity is virtually limitless, and it is no exaggeration to say that the solution of every conceivable problem has at one time or another been attempted by a police officer. In one observed instance, a patrolman unceremoniously entered the room of a man he had never seen before. The man, who gave no indication that he regarded the officer's entry and questions as anything but part of life as usual, related a story of having had his dentures stolen by his wife. In the course of the subsequent rounds, the patrolman sought to locate the woman and the dentures. This did not become the evening's project but was attended to while doing other things. In the densely matted activities of the patrolman, the questioning became one more strand, not so much to be pursued to its solution as a theme that organized the memory of one more man known individually. In all this, the officer followed the precept formulated by a somewhat more articulate patrolman: "If I want to be in control of my work and keep the

street relatively peaceful, I have to know the people. To know them I must gain their trust, which means that I have to be involved in their lives. But I can't be soft like a social worker because unlike him I cannot call the cops when things go wrong. I am the cops!"[27]

The Restricted Relevance of Culpability. It is well known that policemen exercise discretionary freedom in invoking the law. It is also conceded that, in some measure, the practice is unavoidable. This being so, the outstanding problem is whether or not the decisions are in line with the intent of the law. On skid-row, patrolmen often make decisions based on reasons that the law probably does not recognize as valid. The problem can best be introduced by citing an example.

A man in a relatively mild state of intoxication (by skid-row standards) approached a patrolman to tell him that he had a room in a hotel, to which the officer responded by urging him to go to bed instead of getting drunk. As the man walked off, the officer related the following thoughts: Here is a completely lost soul. Though he probably is no more than thirty-five years old, he looks to be in his fifties. He never works and he hardly ever has a place to stay. He has been on the street for several years and is known as "Dakota." During the past few days, "Dakota" has been seen in the company of "Big Jim." The latter is an invalid living on some sort of pension with which he pays for a room in the hotel to which "Dakota" referred and for four weekly meal tickets in one of the restaurants on the street. Whatever is left he spends on wine and beer. Occasionally, "Big Jim" goes on drinking sprees in the company of someone like "Dakota." Leaving aside the consideration that there is probably a homosexual background to the association, and that it is not right that "Big Jim" should have to support the drinking habit of someone else, there is the more important risk that if "Dakota" moves in with "Big Jim" he will

---

[27] The same officer commented further, "If a man looks for something, I might help him. But I don't stay with him till he finds what he is looking for. If I did, I would never get to do anything else. In the last analysis, I really never solve any problems. The best I can hope for is to keep things from getting worse."

very likely walk off with whatever the latter keeps in his room. "Big Jim" would never dream of reporting the theft; he would just beat the hell out of "Dakota" after he sobered up. When asked what could be done to prevent the theft and the subsequent recriminations, the patrolman proposed that in this particular case he would throw "Big Jim" into jail if he found him tonight and then tell the hotel clerk to throw "Dakota" out of the room. When asked why he did not arrest "Dakota," who was, after all, drunk enough to warrant an arrest, the officer explained that this would not solve anything. While "Dakota" was in jail "Big Jim" would continue drinking and would either strike up another liaison or embrace his old buddy after he had been released. The only thing to do was to get "Big Jim" to sober up, and the only sure way of doing this was to arrest him.

As it turned out, "Big Jim" was not located that evening. But had he been located and arrested on a drunk charge, the fact that he was intoxicated would not have been the real reason for proceeding against him, but merely the pretext. The point of the example is not that it illustrates the tendency of skid-row patrolmen to arrest persons who would not be arrested under conditions of full respect for their legal rights. To be sure, this too happens. In the majority of minor arrest cases, however, the criteria the law specifies are met. But it is the rare exception that the law is invoked merely because the specifications of the law are met. That is, compliance with the law is merely the outward appearance of an intervention that is actually based on altogether different considerations. Thus, it could be said that patrolmen do not really enforce the law, even when they do invoke it, but merely use it as a resource to solve certain pressing practical problems in keeping the peace. This observation goes beyond the conclusion that many of the lesser norms of the criminal law are treated as defeasible in police work. It is patently not the case that skid-row patrolmen apply the legal norms while recognizing many exceptions to their applicability. Instead, the observation leads to the conclusion that in keeping the peace on skid-row, patrolmen encounter certain matters they attend to by means of coercive action, e.g., arrests. In doing this,

they invoke legal norms that are available, and with some regard for substantive appropriateness. Hence, the problem patrolmen confront is not which drunks, beggars, or disturbers of the peace should be arrested and which can be let go as exceptions to the rule. Rather, the problem is whether, when someone "needs" to be arrested, he should be charged with drunkeness, begging, or disturbing the peace. Speculating further, one is almost compelled to infer that virtually any set of norms could be used in this manner, provided that they sanction relatively common forms of behavior.

The reduced relevance of culpability in peace keeping practice on skid-row is not readily visible. As mentioned, most arrested persons were actually found in the act, or in the state, alleged in the arrest record. It becomes partly visible when one views the treatment of persons who are not arrested even though all the legal grounds for an arrest are present. Whenever such persons are encountered and can be induced to leave, or taken to some shelter, or remanded to someone's care, then patrolmen feel, or at least maintain, that an arrest would serve no useful purpose. That is, whenever there exist means for controlling the troublesome aspects of some person's presence in some way alternative to an arrest, such means are preferentially employed, provided, of course, that the case at hand involves only a minor offense.[28]

The attenuation of the relevance of culpability is most visible when the presence of legal grounds for an arrest could be questioned, i.e., in cases that sometimes are euphemistically called "preventive arrests." In one observed instance, a man who attempted to trade a pocket knife came to the attention of a patrolman. The initial encounter was attended by a good deal of levity

---

[28] When evidence is present to indicate that a serious crime has been committed, considerations of culpability acquire a position of priority. Two such arrests were observed, both involving check-passers. The first offender was caught *in flagrante delicto*. In the second instance, the suspect attracted the attention of the patrolman because of his sickly appearance. In the ensuing conversation the man made some remarks that led the officer to place a call with the Warrant Division of his department. According to the information that was obtained by checking records, the man was a wanted checkpasser and was immediately arrested.

and the man willingly responded to the officer's inquiries about his identity and business. The man laughingly acknowledged that he needed some money to get drunk. In the course of the exchange it came to light that he had just arrived in town, traveling in his automobile. When confronted with the demand to lead the officer to the car, the man's expression became serious and he pointedly stated that he would not comply because this was none of the officer's business. After a bit more prodding, which the patrolman initially kept in the light mood, the man was arrested on a charge involving begging. In subsequent conversation the patrolman acknowledged that the charge was only speciously appropriate and mainly a pretext. Having committed himself to demanding information he could not accept defeat. When this incident was discussed with another patrolman, the second officer found fault not with the fact that the arrest was made on a pretext but with the first officer's own contribution to the creation of conditions that made it unavoidable. "You see," he continued, "there is always the risk that the man is testing you and you must let him know what is what. The best among us can usually keep the upper hand in such situations without making arrests. But when it comes down to the wire, then you can't let them get away with it."

Finally, it must be mentioned that the reduction of the significance of culpability is built into the normal order of skid-row life, as patrolmen see it. Officers almost unfailingly say, pointing to some particular person, "I know that he knows that I know that some of the things he 'owns' are stolen, and that nothing can be done about it." In saying this, they often claim to have knowledge of such a degree of certainty as would normally be sufficient for virtually any kind of action except legal proceedings. Against this background, patrolmen adopt the view that the law is not merely imperfect and difficult to implement, but that on skid-row, at least, the association between delict and sanction is distinctly occasional. Thus, to implement the law naively, i.e., to arrest someone *merely* because he committed some minor offense, is perceived as containing elements of injustice.

Moreover, patrolmen often deal with situations in which questions of culpability are profoundly ambiguous. For example, an officer was called to help in settling a violent dispute in a hotel room. The object of the quarrel was a supposedly stolen pair of trousers. As the story unfolded in the conflicting versions of the participants, it was not possible to decide who was the complainant and who was alleged to be the thief, nor did it come to light who occupied the room in which the fracas took place, or whether the trousers were taken from the room or to the room. Though the officer did ask some questions, it seemed, and was confirmed in later conversation, that he was there not to solve the puzzle of the missing trousers but to keep the situation from getting out of hand. In the end, the exhausted participants dispersed, and this was the conclusion of the case. The patrolman maintained that no one could unravel mysteries of this sort because "these people take things from each' other so often that no one could tell what 'belongs' to whom." In fact, he suggested, the terms owning, stealing, and swindling, in their strict sense, do not really belong on skid-row, and all efforts to distribute guilt and innocence according to some rational formula of justice are doomed to failure.

It could be said that the term "curb-stone justice" that is sometimes applied to the procedures of patrolmen in skid-rows contains a double irony. Not only is the procedure not legally authorized, which is the intended irony in the expression, but it does not even pretend to distribute deserts. The best among the patrolmen, according to their own standards, use the law to keep skid-row inhabitants from sinking deeper into the misery they already experience. The worst, in terms of these same standards, exploit the practice for personal aggrandizement or gain. Leaving motives aside, however, it is easy to see that if culpability is not the salient consideration leading to an arrest in cases where it is patently obvious, then the practical patrolman may not view it as being wholly out of line to make arrests lacking in formal legal justification. Conversely, he will come to view minor offense arrests made solely because legal standards are met as poor craftsmanship.

The Background of Ad Hoc *Decision Making.* When skid-row patrolmen are pressed to explain their reasons for minor offense arrests, they most often mention that it is done for the protection of the arrested person. This, they maintain, is the case in virtually all drunk arrests, in the majority of arrests involving begging and other nuisance offenses, and in many cases involving acts of violence. When they are asked to explain further such arrests as the one cited earlier involving the man attempting to sell the pocket knife, who was certainly not arrested for his own protection, they cite the consideration that belligerent persons constitute a much greater menace on skid-row than any place else in the city. The reasons for this are twofold. First, many of the inhabitants are old, feeble, and not too smart, all of which makes them relatively defenseless. Second, many of the inhabitants are involved in illegal activities and are known as persons of bad character, which does not make them credible victims or witnesses. Potential predators realize that the resources society has mobilized to minimize the risk of criminal victimization do not protect the predator himself. Thus, reciprocal exploitation constitutes a preferred risk. The high vulnerability of everybody on skid-row is public knowledge and causes every seemingly aggressive act to be seen as a potentially grave risk.

When, in response to all this, patrolmen are confronted with the observation that many minor offense arrests they make do not seem to involve a careful evaluation of facts before acting, they give the following explanations: First, the two reasons of protection and prevention represent a global background, and in individual cases it may sometimes not be possible to produce adequate justification on these grounds. Nor is it thought to be a problem of great moment to estimate precisely whether someone is more likely to come to grief or to cause grief when the objective is to prevent the proliferation of troubles. Second, patrolmen maintain that some of the seemingly spur-of-the-moment decisions are actually made against a background of knowledge of facts that are not readily apparent in the situations. Since experience not only contains this information but also causes it to come to mind, patrolmen claim to have developed a special sensitivity for qualities of appearances that allow an

intuitive grasp of probable tendencies. In this context, little things are said to have high informational value and lead to conclusions without the intervention of explicitly reasoned chains of inferences. Third, patrolmen readily admit that they do not adhere to high standards of adequacy of justification. They do not seek to defend the adequacy of their method against some abstract criteria of merit. Instead, when questioned, they assess their methods against the background of a whole system of *ad hoc* decision making, a system that encompasses the courts, correction facilities, the welfare establishment, and medical services. In fact, policemen generally maintain that their own procedures not only measure up to the workings of this system but exceed them in the attitude of carefulness.

In addition to these recognized reasons, there are two additional background factors that play a significant part in decisions to employ coercion. One has to do with the relevance of situational factors, and the other with the evaluation of coercion as relatively insignificant in the lives of the inhabitants.

There is no doubt that the nature of the circumstances often has decisive influence on what will be done. For example, the same patrolman who arrested the man trying to sell his pocket knife was observed dealing with a young couple. Though the officer was clearly angered by what he perceived as insolence and threatened the man with arrest, he merely ordered him and his companion to leave the street. He saw them walking away in a deliberately slow manner and when he noticed them a while later, still standing only a short distance away from the place of encounter, he did not respond to their presence. The difference between the two cases was that in the first there was a crowd of amused bystanders, while the latter case was not witnessed by anyone. In another instance, the patrolman was directed to a hotel and found a father and son fighting about money. The father occupied a room in the hotel and the son occasionally shared his quarters. There were two other men present, and they made it clear that their sympathies were with the older man. The son was whisked off to jail without much study of the relative merits of the conflicting claims. In yet another case, a middle-aged woman was forcefully evacuated from a bar even after the bartender explained that her loud behavior was merely a response to goading by some foul-mouth youth.

In all such circumstances, coercive control is exercised as a means of coming to grips with situational exigencies. Force is used against particular persons but is incidental to the task. An ideal of "economy of intervention" dictates in these and similar cases that the person whose presence is most likely to perpetuate the troublesome development be removed. Moreover, the decision as to who is to be removed is arrived at very quickly. Officers feel considerable pressure to act unhesitatingly, and many give accounts of situations that got out of hand because of desires to handle cases with careful consideration. However, even when there is no apparent risk of rapid proliferation of trouble, the tactic of removing one or two persons is used to control an undesirable situation. Thus, when a patrolman ran into a group of four men sharing a bottle of wine in an alley, he emptied the remaining contents of the bottle into the gutter, arrested one man— who was no more and no less drunk than the others—and let the others disperse in various directions.

The exigential nature of control is also evident in the handling of isolated drunks. Men are arrested because of where they happen to be encountered. In this, it matters not only whether a man is found in a conspicuous place or not, but also how far away he is from his domicile. The further away he is, the less likely it is that he will make it to his room, and the more likely the arrest. Sometimes drunk arrests are made mainly because the police van is available. In one case a patrolman summoned the van to pick up an arrested man. As the van was pulling away from the curb the officer stopped the driver because he sighted another drunk stumbling across the street. The second man protested saying that he "wasn't even half drunk yet." The patrolman's response was "OK, I'll owe you half a drunk." In sum, the basic routine of keeping the peace on skid-row involves a process of matching the resources of control with situational exigencies. The overall objective is to reduce the total amount of risk in the area. In this,

practicality plays a considerably more important role than legal norms. Precisely because patrolmen see legal reasons for coercive action much more widely distributed on skid-row than could ever be matched by interventions, they intervene not in the interest of law enforcement but in the interest of producing relative tranquility and order on the street.

Taking the perspective of the victim of coercive measures, one could ask why he, in particular, has to bear the cost of keeping the aggregate of troubles down while others, who are equally or perhaps even more implicated, go scot-free. Patrolmen maintain that the *ad hoc* selection of persons for attention must be viewed in the light of the following consideration: Arresting a person on skid-row on some minor charge may save him and others a lot of trouble, but it does not work any real hardships on the arrested person. It is difficult to overestimate the skid-row patrolman's feeling of certainty that his coercive and disciplinary actions toward the inhabitants have but the most passing significance in their lives. Sending a man to jail on some charge that will hold him for a couple of days is seen as a matter of such slight importance to the affected person that it could hardly give rise to scruples. Thus, every indication that a coercive measure should be taken is accompanied by the realization "I might as well, for all it matters to him." Certain realities of life on skid-row furnish the context for this belief in the attenuated relevance of coercion in the lives of the inhabitants. Foremost among them is that the use of police authority is seen as totally unremarkable by everybody on skid-row. Persons who live or work there are continuously exposed to it and take its existence for granted. Shopkeepers, hotel clerks, and bartenders call patrolmen to rid themselves of unwanted and troublesome patrons. Residents expect patrolmen to arbitrate their quarrels authoritatively. Men who receive orders, whether they obey them or not, treat them as part of life as usual. Moreover, patrolmen find that disciplinary and coercive actions apparently do not affect their friendly relations with the persons against whom these actions are taken. Those who greet and chat with them are the very same men who have been disciplined, arrested, and ordered around in the past, and who expect to be thus treated again in the future. From all this, officers gather that though the people on skid-row seek to evade police authority, they do not really object to it. Indeed, it happens quite frequently that officers encounter men who welcome being arrested and even actively ask for it. Finally, officers point out that sending someone to jail from skid-row does not upset his relatives or his family life, does not cause him to miss work or lose a job, does not lead to his being reproached by friends and associates, does not lead to failure to meet commitments or protect investments, and does not conflict with any but the most passing intentions of the arrested person. Seasoned patrolmen are not oblivious to the irony of the fact that measures intended as mechanisms for distributing deserts can be used freely because these measures are relatively impotent in their effects.

SUMMARY AND CONCLUSIONS

It was the purpose of this paper to render an account of a domain of police practice that does not seem subject to any system of external control. Following the terminology suggested by Michael Banton, this practice was called keeping the peace. The procedures employed in keeping the peace are not determined by legal mandates but are, instead, responses to certain demand conditions. From among several demand conditions, we concentrated on the one produced by the concentration of certain types of persons in districts known as skid-row. Patrolmen maintain that the lives of the inhabitants of the area are lacking in prospective coherence. The consequent reduction in the temporal horizon of predictability constitutes the main problem of keeping the peace on skid-row.

Peace keeping procedure on skid-row consists of three elements. Patrolmen seek to acquire a rich body of concrete knowledge about people by cultivating personal acquaintance with as many residents as possible. They tend to proceed against persons mainly on the basis of perceived risk, rather than on the basis of culpability. And they are more interested in reducing the aggregate total of troubles in the area than in evaluating individual cases according to merit.

There may seem to be a discrepancy between the skid-row patrolman's objective of preventing disorder and his efforts to maintain personal acquaintance with as many persons as possible. But these efforts are principally a tactical device. By knowing someone individually the patrolman reduces ambiguity, extends trust and favors, but does not grant immunity. The informality of interaction on skid-row always contains some indications of the hierarchical superiority of the patrolman and the reality of his potential power lurks in the background of every encounter.

Though our interest was focused initially on those police procedures that did not involve invoking the law, we found that the two cannot be separated. The reason for the connection is not given in the circumstance that the roles of the "law officer" and of the "peace officer" are enacted by the same person and thus are contiguous. According to our observations, patrolmen do not act alternatively as one or the other, with certain actions being determined by the intended objective of keeping the peace and others being determined by the duty to enforce the law. Instead, we have found that *peace keeping occasionally acquires the external aspects of law enforcement*. This makes it specious to inquire whether or not police discretion in invoking the law conforms with the intention of some specific legal formula. The real reason behind an arrest is virtually always the actual state of particular social situations, or of the skid-row area in general.

We have concentrated on those procedures and considerations that skid-row patrolmen regard as necessary, proper, and efficient relative to the circumstances in which they are employed. In this way, we attempted to disclose the conception of the mandate to which the police feel summoned. It was entirely outside the scope of the presentation to review the merits of this conception and of the methods used to meet it. Only insofar as patrolmen themselves recognized instances and patterns of malpractice did we take note of them. Most of the criticism voiced by officers had to do with the use of undue harshness and with the indiscriminate use of arrest powers when these were based on personal feelings rather than the requirements of the situation. According to prevailing opinion, patrolmen guilty of such abuses make life unnecessarily difficult for themselves and for their co-workers. Despite disapproval of harshness, officers tend to be defensive about it. For example, one sergeant who was outspokenly critical of brutality, said that though in general brutal men create more problems than they solve, "they do a good job in some situations for which the better men have no stomach." Moreover, supevisory personnel exhibit a strong reluctance to direct their subordinates in the particulars of their work performance. According to our observations, control is exercised mainly through consultation with superiors, and directives take the form of requests rather than orders. In the background of all this is the belief that patrol work on skid-row requires a great deal of discretionary freedom. In the words of the same sergeant quoted above, "a good man has things worked out in his own ways on his beat and he doesn't need anybody to tell him what to do."

The virtual absence of disciplinary control and the demand for discretionary freedom are related to the idea that patrol work involves "playing by ear." For if it is true that peace keeping cannot be systematically generalized, then, of course, it cannot be organizationally constrained. What the seasoned patrolman means, however, in saying that he "plays by ear" is that he is making his decisions while being attuned to the realities of complex situations about which he has immensely detailed knowledge. This studied aspect of peace keeping generally is not made explicit, nor is the tyro or the outsider made aware of it. Quite to the contrary, the ability to discharge the duties associated with keeping the peace is viewed as a reflection of an innate talent of "getting along with people." Thus, the same demands are made of barely initiated officers as are made of experienced practitioners. Correspondingly, beginners tend to think that they can do as well as their more knowledgeable peers. As this leads to inevitable frustrations, they find themselves in a situation that is conducive to the development of a particular sense of "touchiness." Personal dispositions of individual officers are, of course, of great relevance. But the license of discretionary freedom and the expectation of success under conditions of autonomy, without any indication that the work of the successful craftsman is based on an acquired preparedness for the task, is ready-made for failure and malpractice. Moreover, it leads to slipshod practices of patrol that also infect the standards of the careful craftsman.

The uniformed patrol, and especially the foot patrol, has a low preferential value in the division of labor of police work. This is, in part, at least, due to the belief that "anyone could do it." In fact, this belief is thoroughly mistaken. At present, however, the recognition that the practice requires preparation, and the process of obtaining the preparation itself, is left entirely to the practitioner.

21

BRIT. J. CRIMINOL. VOL. 33 NO. 3 SUMMER 1993

THE CASE AGAINST PARAMILITARY POLICING CONSIDERED

P. A. J. WADDINGTON*

Tony Jefferson's recent book, The Case against Paramilitary Policing *(Jefferson 1990) deserves serious consideration not only because it takes issue at length with a brief article written by me, but, more importantly, because it represents a powerful polemic against modern methods of police riot control. However, this polemic fails to convince for several reasons, both analytical and factual.*

This article will challenge Jefferson's thesis on four grounds: the definition of 'paramilitary' that is employed; the factual basis for the alleged 'strong correlation' between paramilitary policing and ensuing violence; the stance of viewing paramilitary policing 'from below'; and, finally, his criticism of the supposedly idealistic emphasis in my prescription of impartiality and restraint.

Defining Paramilitarism

The central issue that divides Jefferson and me is the meaning of the word 'paramilitary'. This has become something of a term of abuse in recent commentaries on policing (see, for example. Scraton 1985; Stephens 1988; Fielding 1990). It has several connotations: police wearing protective clothing and carrying shields; the existence of specialist public order units, like the SPG (Special Patrol Group) or TSG (Territorial Support Group); the deployment of police in squad formations; and the willingness to use force. It was the central contention of my original article (Waddington 1987) that there was an additional, and potentially valuable, connotation of the term that was largely ignored, namely *co-ordination through superior command and control*. Instead of leaving individual officers to take uncoordinated action at their own discretion, a paramilitaristic approach deploys squads of officers under the direction and control of their superiors. This allows for a more disciplined response to disorderly and violent situations than is possible by traditional methods.

Helmets and shields

Although Jefferson does not make too much of the appearance of officers equipped for riot control, this factor is clearly just beneath the surface of his analysis and uppermost in the minds of many other commentators. For example, one definition of paramilitarism that he uses is policing comprising 'large numbers, military organization, *protective clothing and equipment* and so on' (Jefferson 1990: 109, emphasis added). It is obviously an unwelcome sight to see police officers equipped with visored helmets and flame-retardant overalls, carrying shields, and conveyed in vehicles with window-grilles; at the same time, however, it should be acknowledged that all this equipment is merely *defensive*. Police officers are also employees, and it is no more acceptable to expose them to a hazardous working environment without adequate protection than it is so to

---

* Director, Criminal Justice Studies, University of Reading.

P. A. J. WADDINGTON

expose any other group of workers. Those who complain of the 'militaristic' appearance of police officers engaged in riot control rarely, if ever, complain of the fact that ambulance crews sent to riot areas are sometimes equipped with visored helmets *identical* to those worn by police, or that at Orgreave they used a field ambulance borrowed from the army.

Specialized squads

In practice Jefferson equates paramilitary policing with public order policing *per se* (1990: 52); 'aggressive' police tactics undertaken by whomsoever (p. 55); but most persistently with the activities of SPG-type units (chs. 3, 4, and 6). Now, there are valid criticisms that can be made of this kind of specialist squad and Jefferson makes some of them, but it is surely incorrect to equate them with paramilitarism *per se*.[1]

First, specialization, even in the use of force, is not distinctively militaristic, nor a modern feature of policing. Many police forces have traditionally deployed specialized mounted officers in public order situations—certainly they have been a conspicuous feature of the Metropolitan Police since its inception. Military forces, it is true, have their specialized components: artillery, sappers, signals, armoured divisions, infantry, and so on. However, they would win, or even effectively fight, very few conflicts if simply left to roam the battlefield fighting their opponents in whatever way seemed expedient at the time. What is crucial to military operations is not that soldiers are armed, specially trained, and operate in squads, but that their actions are *co-ordinated* in accordance with the strategy and tactics taken by those in *command*.[2]

Second, many of the tasks performed by members of SPG-like squads are indistinguishable from those undertaken by ordinary uniformed patrol officers. For example, Jefferson describes an arrest made by a pair of SPG officers at a football match, which could just as readily have been made by any pair of officers. Tuck's observations of policing disorderly young people in Gravesham (Tuck 1989: 33–5) suggest that patrol officers can be just as aggressive with boisterous crowds of youngsters as the officers cited by Jefferson. Surely, anyone who has observed officers on routine patrol can recite such episodes. Indeed, Jefferson admits as much, for not only did he observe the SPG officers being aggressive, but at the same football match also reports seeing 'a *divisional officer* on traffic patrol manhandle a child and tell him to go' (1990: 57, emphasis added).

The use of such force is ubiquitous among the police, whether deployed as members of the SPG-like units or not. What distinguishes SPG-type squads is that they are trained in *how* to use force, if it becomes necessary. By contrast, as the Policy Studies Institute report on the Metropolitan Police (1983) noted, the ordinary constable has

---

[1] At least Jefferson avoids the error committed elsewhere (Fielding 1990) of equating all PSUs with such squads. For the record, a 'PSU' is a collection of officers, comprising eighteen constables, three sergeants, and an inspector, plus drivers where appropriate. They may be permanently constituted specialist units trained in advanced public order tactics (Level I). They may be a more or less *ad hoc* collection of individuals who have no permanent unity aside from the period when they are deployed for public order training and duty and who are either (a) equipped with protective clothing and trained in basic shield manoeuvres (Level II) or almost entirely untrained in public order tactics (Level III). However, what unites specialist squads (Level I) with Levels II and III is that they are all officers deployed, *not individually*, but in *squads* under superior command.

[2] Of course, this does not extend only to battle. One of the reasons why military forces are deployed for the purposes of disaster relief is that their superior command and control increases their effectiveness.

little more training in techniques of restraint and arrest than that acquired in school playground brawls. This means not only that the latter are vulnerable to assault, but that they are not able to use a judicious measure of force to overcome resistance. Being trained in how to use force can mean using less with equal effectiveness.

Violence and weaponry

This brings us to the next connotation of 'paramilitary'—its association with un-restrained violence against an enemy. Put bluntly, if officers are trained to use force, will they use it in preference to other means? Certainly, many paramilitary police forces worldwide have reputations for violence. However, excessive violence is not the preserve of paramilitary forces. Both the Walker report into the violence that accompanied the 1968 Democratic Party Convention in Chicago (Walker 1968) and the Kerner report on the 1967 Detroit riot (Kerner 1967) drew invidious comparisons between the disciplined restraint shown by militarized units compared to the excessive and punitive force used by the civil police. The fear and anxiety generated in ordinary police officers by unruly or disorderly crowds is likely to increase violence and arbitrary arrest. Only to the extent that such officers are kept under close command can restraint be maintained. The lesson to be drawn from Stark's rather partial analysis of 'police riots' (Stark 1972) is that poorly organized police forces, unable to gather sufficient intelligence, overreacted to events. Far from exemplifying 'paramilitarism', the police described by Stark were its very antithesis. The reason why members of the regular army showed more restraint during the Detroit riot than did the police or National Guard was because they were ordered by their commanders to remove live rounds from their rifle magazines (Kerner 1967). They did not do this out of *self*-discipline and restraint, but because they were told to do so by those in command.

When force becomes necessary it is at least arguable that traditional methods of policing are *more* likely to inflict serious injury on arbitrarily selected members of a disorderly crowd than would paramilitary weapons and tactics. The use of para-military-style weapons, such as CS smoke and water cannon, may inflict *less* serious injury than the traditional method of crowd dispersal used in Britain, the baton or mounted charge (Waddington 1991). When Jefferson complains of police 'clearing the street' he is referring not to some modern, paramilitary innovation, but a method employed since 1830 (Palmer 1988). This is not to commend or even excuse such methods: Jefferson is quite correct in pointing to how supervison and control break down once such a manoeuvre is commenced. Under such conditions, frightened, angry, and possibly vengeful officers are unleashed upon the crowd. Officers no longer do as they are commanded, because there is no opportunity to exert command over dispersed individuals. However, to describe such a manoeuvre as 'paramilitary terror' (1990: 99) is simply derogatory rhetoric which aids neither description nor analysis.

Command and control

If force is to be used with *restraint* against crowds, it is crucial that command and control be maintained by superior officers. Jefferson's own analysis suggests that this is so, for when officers are deployed to 'clear the street', it is the breakdown of supervision (he suggests) that allows for confrontations and exacerbates tension.

P. A. J. WADDINGTON

What distinguishes modern methods of public order policing, and justifies the description 'paramilitary', is precisely the co-ordination and integration of all officers deployed as squads under centralized command and control. It is this that is the essence of the application of '(quasi-)military training, equipment, *philosophy and organization* to questions of policing' (Jefferson 1990: 16, emphasis added). It is also paramilitary 'philosophy and organization' which are singularly absent from Jefferson's discussion of paramilitarism. Indeed, he suggests—probably quite justifiably—that in the police force in which he conducted fieldwork during the early 1980s policy was conspicuous by its absence (1990: 70), which, if true, is the very antithesis of military 'philosophy and organization'. It is this that has been traditionally absent from policing and which genuine paramilitarism promises to inject.

Of course, the police have not been wholly transformed in their approach to public order, which is why they can only be described as moving '*towards* paramilitarism' (Waddington 1987). However, gradually there is a growing recognition that in order to police public order situations effectively officers must act in a co-ordinated fashion under higher command and not be left to 'do their own thing' as in the past. Instead of 'flying by the seat of their pants', senior officers now convene strategy meetings to consider the 'What ifs' of an operation and how they might respond to them. There is a growing recognition of the need for effective briefing and debriefing.[3] All of this is moving the policing of public disorder towards a more militaristic command structure, not only of the SPG-type squads, but of all PSUs (whether protected or unprotected), which are increasingly deployed in accordance with predetermined tactics. This applies to the policing of large orderly gatherings as well as disorder, for the Hillsborough tragedy (Taylor 1989) shows what can happen when command and control is lost and officers act as isolated individuals at their own discretion.

It is through the means of command and control that paramilitary organization enhances discipline. Such discipline is not a characteristic with which individuals in specialist squads have to be imbued, it is a structure which is *imposed* upon them. TSG units do not decide on their own initiative to hold back and move in only when disorder erupts, but do so because they are instructed so to act. The fact that the police subculture glorifies 'action and excitement' (Holdaway 1983) makes it all the more imperative that officers are *not* allowed to act on their own initiative in public order situations. Paramilitary command and control over ordinary PSUs is just as imperative as it is in relation to SPG-type squads, in order to ensure that they perform the role assigned to them by senior officers in accordance with the strategy.

Paramilitary command suppresses the discretion of individual officers and undermines the influence of subcultural values which Jefferson believes to be responsible for excessive violence once officers are freed from close supervision (1990: 54–5). Instead of leading to police officers being unleashed upon a crowd to 'make arrests' and 'clear the street', paramilitary developments maintain and enhance supervision and control in aspects of public order policing that were previously beyond the scope of commanders. For example, evidence gatherers and intelligence cells, working in co-ordination with arrest squads, target particular offenders in an unruly crowd and direct officers

---

[3] The latter is something that Jefferson himself advocates (1990: 117) without appearing to appreciate its paramilitary overtones; for it is a military characteristic to brief and debrief, and the terms themselves have strong military connotations.

selectively to arrest those individuals for specific offences for which evidence exists. This stands in stark contrast to the indiscriminately heavy-handed arrests which have traditionally occurred in public order situations and are described by Jefferson.

There is, it is true, the danger that my earlier association of paramilitarism with disciplined restraint (Waddington 1987) allows for any act of indiscipline to be disowned as not genuinely paramilitary (Jefferson 1990: 83), but equally there is the danger that ignoring the centrality of paramilitary command and equating paramilitarism with the actions of the SPG-like units or with public order policing *per se* is simply to use the word 'paramilitary' as a synonym for violence and aggression.

In sum, one of the defining characteristics of militarism—the co-ordination of squads under superior command—offers the prospect of policing public disorder with restrained discipline. Paramilitary organization is not a sufficient condition for ensuring restraint, but it is a necessary condition: disciplined co-ordination is simply not possible by traditional means.

Paramilitary Amplification of Disorder

So far, I have been concerned with the definition of 'paramilitarism' and its implications *in principle*. Jefferson goes on to argue that *in practice* paramilitary policing entails an inevitable *amplification of disorder*, creating what he describes as a 'strong positive correlation between the amount of paramilitary force applied and the degree of violence ensuing' (1990: 103).

It is important to appreciate that Jefferson's model avoids the simplistic association between the police deployment of protected officers and the occurrence of disorder. Such a hypothesis would be practically untestable, since the police would maintain that any such deployment was always in response to crowd violence and not its cause, whereas members of the crowd would probably claim the contrary. In the unavoidably confused and fluid circumstances of crowd behaviour arbitrating between these contradictory accounts would always prove hazardous.

Jefferson's theory is more sophisticated and complex. He suggests that disorder arises from a four-stage sequence involving 'preparation for the "worse case" scenario [which] contains the germ of a self-fulfilling prophecy'; 'controlling space' and 'controlling the ground', both of which create resentment among, followed by the resistance of, the crowd; resulting, inevitably it seems, in aggressive 'clearance' or dispersal. Jefferson seems tacitly to accept that the appearance of officers clad in riot gear is unlikely to occur until the final stage. However, the fact that they are held in reserve, pent up in personnel carriers, is itself a step in the amplificatory process. Like war, it seems, paramilitary policing has its own logic that leads to confrontation and violence.

Evidence

To support this hypothesis, Jefferson offers a partial reading of various unofficial reports regarding the riot at Broadwater Farm estate on 6 October 1985, the disorder at the Manchester University Students' Union on 1 March 1985, the violent picket at Orgreave on 18 June 1984, and general discussions about events in the USA and Australia.

P. A. J. WADDINGTON

Inevitably, evidence concerning the policing of demonstrations and riots will tend to be anecdotal and contestable. Nevertheless, allow me to offer a somewhat lengthier list of anecdotes gathered since February 1990 while conducting research with the Metropolitan Police into the policing of political marches and demonstrations. I have observed every major event since that time.[4] By a 'major event' I mean those occasions when the force's special operations room has opened. This occurs when a march or demonstration is either so large or has, in the estimation of police, such potential for disorder, that it is regarded as problematic. 'Opening' the control room is a step in the chain of 'preparation' which Jefferson presumably considers 'self-fulfilling'. Therefore, in so far as this non-random sample is biased, it is towards including those events thought by the police most likely to occasion disorder. Unlike most other analyses of crowd violence, it does not rely upon a sample of those rare events where violence occurs.[5] Thus it enables us to correlate, to a limited extent, features of the police operation with the occurrence or non-occurrence of disorder.

This period of observation has, at the time of writing, included all three major anti-poll tax demonstrations in London, plus the demonstration at Lambeth against the setting of a poll tax in 1990; all the anti-Gulf War marches; two NUS marches opposing government policies on higher education; two Remembrance Sundays (when National Front marchers attend the Cenotaph and are invariably opposed by anti-fascist groups); a march by the National Front and a subsequent protest by the Rolan Adams Campaign protesting at fascist violence, both in south-east London; two 'Gay Pride' marches and a march of the Lesbian and Gay Coalition protesting about the Criminal Justice Bill; plus marches by the National Anti-Vivisection Society, the 'Troops Out of Ireland' movement's annual commemoration of Bloody Sunday on the particularly sensitive occasion of the twentieth anniversary in 1992, and the 'Anti-Election Alliance' protesting against the holding of the 1992 general election. I also observed the 1991 Notting Hill Carnival, an event associated with disorder in the past. As well as accompanying a senior officer during the operation, I have witnessed the planning and other preparations for these events.[6]

In addition, I have attended three other Notting Hill Carnivals, in 1987, 1988, and 1991; the operation to forestall any disorder that might have arisen at Broadwater Farm following the conviction of Winston Silcott and others for the murder of PC Keith Blakelock; a large reggae concert on Clapham Common in 1987; and 'Operation Kingfisher'—the drugs raid on Broadwater Farm in September 1989.

An inevitable amplificatory spiral?

These observations refute Jefferson's hypothesized amplificatory spiral simply because the conditions for amplification are *normally present*, but confrontation, disorder, and violence are thankfully rare.

---

[4] Many minor operations have also been observed, but this article will rely upon the major operations in which the paramilitary style of policing is most evident. See the methodological appendix for details.
[5] In this respect it is comparable to the research conducted by David Waddington and his colleagues (Waddington *et al.* 1989).
[6] See the methodological appendix for details of all operations observed.

THE CASE AGAINST PARAMILITARY POLICING CONSIDERED

Preparation for the 'worst case' scenario   The assertion of a self-fulfilling 'preparation as provocation' (Jefferson 1990: 103) is simply false, since, as mentioned previously, every major public order operation entails considerable preparation. A constant cannot explain a variable, and a constant feature, for example, at the Notting Hill Carnival, is preparation for disorder. TSG units are held in reserve, equipped in riot gear and available for immediate deployment. They practise shield manoeuvres at the Public Order Training Centre at Hounslow during the weeks preceding the Carnival. Yet, despite this, violence flares only on some occasions, as it did in 1987 and 1989, but not on others, as in 1988, 1990, and 1991. One has to look for factors other than police preparedness to explain disorder at the Notting Hill Carnival.

Nor is Notting Hill the exception: large-scale preparations involving large numbers of officers, some of whom were deployed as shield reserves, were mounted for the end of the Silcott trial in 1987, the second NUS anti-loans demonstration in 1990, successive protests about war in the Gulf throughout the autumn of 1990 and winter of 1991, and the march of the 'Anti-Election Alliance' during the 1992 election campaign, at *none* of which was there any significant disorder. In *none* of these cases was this because the protest was overwhelmed by the strength of police: reserves remained on stand-by but out of sight of protestors.

Controlling space and the crowd   Certainly, it is true that the police seek to control space. They do this habitually by placing barriers, cordoning off junctions, and using other means to demarcate areas in which the public can assemble from those where they cannot. Most commonly, this demarcation is achieved by devices such as 'tape and winker'—white tape strung between yellow boxes with an amber flashing light on top which marks the assembly area and/or the route to be followed.

Even when space and the crowd are controlled more overtly by a police presence, disorder does *not* habitually occur. David Waddington *et al.*'s (1987, 1989) analysis shows *inter alia* that there is not the simple association that Jefferson supposes. The 'Thatcher Unwelcoming' demonstration at Sheffield in 1983 had all the hallmarks of paramilitary policing without a riot. Police rigorously controlled space and the crowd, with mounted officers and cordons of officers several rows deep being deployed, but no violence ensued.

In one of the examples chosen by Jefferson to support the escalatory hypothesis—the demonstration at Manchester Students' Union in 1985—space was not controlled prior to the assembly of the demonstrators and then was fought for with violent results. At the so-called 'Battle of the Beanfield' near Stonehenge in 1985, police did not have control of the space in which vehicles careered around before being violently brought to a halt by officers smashing windscreens. It is in an attempt to avoid such confrontations that police 'take the ground' well before a crowd assembles. This is why the police whom Jefferson observed arrived at the football stadium an hour and a half before the kick-off (1990: 56).

It is not clear why Jefferson takes such objection to police controlling space when the book opens with a tacit endorsement of precisely this approach: ' "dense cordons of police to restrict movement"—neatly captures the essence of the *traditional* approach to public order policing' (1990: 1, emphasis in original). Just five pages later this 'relatively static and defensive human shield' is described as provoking anger, frustration, and missile-throwing. By the end of the book it is credited as an inevitable

P. A. J. WADDINGTON

stage in amplifying violence: 'Crowd anger will almost certainly follow such containment' (1990: 87).[7]

Nor does 'controlling the crowd', even coercively, necessitate a dive into the spiral of violence imagined by Jefferson, not even when all the paraphernalia of paramilitary policing are readily available. On the evening following the commencement of the Gulf bombing campaign in January 1991 an illegal march from Trafalgar Square to Parliament Square was mounted by opponents of the war in defiance of the Sessional Order of Parliament.[8] Police were prepared to allow the demonstrators to walk along the footpath to Parliament Square, but felt that they could not allow a full-blown march along the highway. To prevent the latter a cordon was placed at an angle across Whitehall in an attempt to funnel the marchers on to the footpath. When the marchers came into contact with the cordon there was vigorous 'pushing and shoving' and TSG reserves were deployed in support. This lasted for some minutes before the protestors were successfully diverted on to the footpath. Thereafter not only was there no increase in disorder, tension actually declined as police shepherded protestors on to the central area of Parliament Square, stopping the traffic in order to do so.

Even when TSG officers are employed to control the crowd the situation does not inevitably escalate. During a protest demonstration on the evening when the UN Gulf deadline expired, protestors staged a sit-down in Parliament Square. TSG officers were deployed to arrest them and did so without further incident. Nor was there an escalation of violence when TSG officers removed and then arrested protestors trying to block the entrance and exit to the Palace of Westminster during a similar protest a month later. Indeed, the specialized training of TSG officers enabled them to remove sit-down demonstrators without the struggling scrum of officers that is all too common on such occasions and often exacerbates tension. At the Lambeth poll tax demonstration in March 1990, officers from PT18 (shield training instructors deployed as a highly specialist public order unit) were deployed as an arrest squad.[9] During the evening they made a number of arrests of individuals identified committing specific offences, but did so with such speed, competence, and minimal force that on no occasion did tension increase more than momentarily.

Clearing the street Jefferson's notion of 'clearance' is also too crude (1990: 89–90). Officers often 'clear the street' with little or no violence, simply by ushering people along. The occasions when police do so aggressively seem greatly outweighed by other occasions when aggression is absent. Even when officers *are* deployed in protective equipment to disperse unruly people, violence is not a necessary corollary, as a dispersal at the Clapham Common reggae concert illustrates. A crowd of around 200 youths broke away from the main group of concert-goers and attacked officers at the edge of

---

[7] It should also be remembered that controlling space is necessary for public safety: the Taylor Inquiry into the Hillsborough disaster criticized police for their failure to control space effectively, as did the inquiry into the Heysel stadium disaster when the Belgian police failed adequately to segregate supporters.

[8] Each session, both Houses of Parliament direct the Commissioner of the Metropolitan Police to ensure unimpeded access to the Palace of Westminster and prevent disorder in the precincts of Parliament. This is technically enforced under s. 52 of the Metropolitan Police Act 1839, which prohibits marches, processions, and demonstrations within one mile of the Palace of Westminster while the House is sitting. This is known as the 'sessional area' subject to the 'sessional order'.

[9] PT 18 has since been redesignated TO18.

THE CASE AGAINST PARAMILITARY POLICING CONSIDERED

the common. Officers with shields and mounted officers were deployed to disperse them, which they did in full view of the crowd without further disorder.

A 'strong correlation'?

Even if it is conceded, for the purpose of this argument, that Jefferson's characterization of events at Orgreave and Manchester Students' Union is accurate, it does not establish a correlation between violence and paramilitary policing, still less a 'strong correlation'. To do so requires not only that violence should occur when paramilitary deployments are present, but that it should be avoided when such deployments are absent.

The non-existence of such a correlation is testified to most instructively, perhaps, by the comparison of the three anti-poll tax marches of 31 March 1990, 20 October 1990, and 23 March 1991. On the first march just over 2,000 officers were deployed to control a crowd eventually estimated by police as 40,000 strong. A total of twenty mobile reserve PSUs plus ten mounted officers were available, but shields were not deployed until two hours after the unprotected officers at Downing Street came under missile attack. Violence escalated, not from the deployment of officers in protective equipment, but from an attempt by officers in ordinary uniform to move a missile-throwing crowd up Whitehall away from Downing Street. As the official report notes (Metcalfe 1991), TSG officers in protected carriers, *responding* to calls for assistance from those policing the march, became entrapped within the crowd and were attacked, leading to a significant rise in tension. There was a breakdown of effective command and control by senior officers. The result was reputedly the worst riot in central London since the 'Bloody Sunday' riot of 1887, in which 1,985 crimes were reported, 408 people were arrested at the time and 123 subsequently, 42 complaints against police were received, 542 police were injured, and the cost was £9 million in riot damages alone (Metcalfe 1991).

The following October a crowd estimated by police at 5,000 marched from Kennington Park to Brockwell Park in conditions very different from those appertaining the previous March. First, they had been served with a prescribed route under s. 12 of the Public Order Act 1986, requiring that the marchers should take a route other than that the organizers had wished. Second, they were policed by just over 3,000 officers, including eleven PSUs of TSG officers, plus one PSU comprising shield instructors from PT18 (the Public Order Training Branch), and a further fifteen PSUs of Level II shield-trained officers were deployed as mobile reserves along with three PSUs of mounted officers. Third, the TSG shield reserves each spent two days at the Metropolitan Police's public order training centre at Hounslow, practising their tactics in the event of a shield deployment. Fourth, as the march progressed, TSGs were stationed along the route, leapfrogging to keep abreast of it as it made its way towards the Park. Fifth, senior officers spent many hours discussing contingencies they might face and the strategy to be employed in the event that trouble occurred. All three of the initial amplificatory conditions were thus satisfied: the police undoubtedly planned for a 'worst case scenario'; and they controlled both space and the crowd, both legally, and physically by huge numbers of officers. In the event *there was no trouble at all during the main march,* despite a number of occasions when marchers acted in ways that might have justified a forceful police response, such as blocking the entire width of Denmark Hill.

361

P. A. J. WADDINGTON

It was later that violence erupted, when a subsidiary march of 2,000 people went to picket Brixton prison when only 200 had been expected to do so. This additional event was notified to police quite late in the planning and it had not received the 'worst case scenario' treatment that the rest of the march had. It was here that disorder did ensue and shield officers were deployed to disperse the picket after missiles had been thrown and officers assaulted. The disorder lasted less than an hour and a half, and the entire afternoon saw 105 arrests and very few casualties.

On the occasion of the third anti-poll tax march, a crowd estimated at 11,500 was policed by almost 5,000 officers, including reserves of twenty-six TSGs, sixteen Level II PSUs and four PSUs of mounted officers on standby, all attired in protective clothing, albeit out of sight. Over 700 officers were deployed in Trafalgar Square alone. Again the march was required to follow a route prescribed under the Public Order Act. The senior officers spent several days preparing for the event, including a one-day exercise in which they worked out tactics in response to situations envisaged by PT18. There was no disorder *at all* in the area of the greatest concentration of police. Despite provocative acts by some marchers as they proceeded through the less heavily policed streets—including an assault on a woman officer, the knocking over of 'winkers' marking the route, and throwing missiles on several occasions—*no serious disorder* occurred. Only two arrests were made and one injury recorded.[10]

In sum, contrary to Jefferson's 'strong positive correlation', this set of events suggests the contrary relationship. When the police were not deployed in paramilitary strength serious disorder, indeed a fully-fledged riot, occurred; when significant numbers of police, including specialists in riot control, were deployed there was progressively less violence. The *more* the police planned for the 'worst case scenario' the *less* disorder there was; when control of space and the crowd was at its *greatest*, violence was at its *lowest*.

As the second and third anti-poll tax marches illustrate, preparation allows for effective planning to prevent and avoid disorder, for example by formulating contingency plans and rehearsing the necessary tactics. It is those incidents for which there has been least preparation, such as the unexpected arrival of 2,000 people at Brixton prison after the second anti-poll tax demonstration, that are more likely to cause problems. It is unplanned-for contingencies, like personnel carriers becoming surrounded by a mob, as they did during the first anti-poll tax march, that raise the tension.

Perhaps the one occasion which, when taken as a whole, refutes the thesis of a causal link between paramilitarism (however defined) and disorder was the drugs raid on Broadwater Farm in September 1989, for this was a paramilitary operation in virtually every respect.[11] Not only were 400 officers deployed to raid the 'deck' area of the Tangmere block in September 1990, the event was meticulously planned as a quasi-military operation. Almost every conceivable 'worst case scenario' was catered for. There was detailed covert surveillance, secret planning of the raid by a group of senior

---

[10] Incidentally, the protestors also held their march despite strong political pressure from Westminster City Council to ban it for fear of a repetition of the previous year's violence and damage to property.

[11] My observation of this event was circumscribed by the secrecy that surrounded its planning. I observed the full briefing given to all officers of the rank of sergeant and above and followed the 'first wave' of officers on to the 'deck' of the Tangmere block, where I remained for the duration of the operation, leaving shortly before midnight. I subsequently viewed the evidence-gathering video showing drug-dealing on the deck in the weeks prior to the raid and the raid itself. After the trials arising from the raid were complete, I was given full access to police documentation and interviewed the senior officers commanding the operation.

THE CASE AGAINST PARAMILITARY POLICING CONSIDERED

officers, and the assemblage of large numbers of officers, each with a specialized role. The raid was initiated by a pre-emptive use of force, led by officers in protective equipment, who subdued and arrested all suspects at the scene, forcibly entered premises, and took control of the 'deck' and surrounding area. Additional officers were on standby to deal with any outbreak of disorder, but despite this explicitly paramilitary operation, *no disorder occurred*. Indeed, tension declined so swiftly that, only an hour after the commencement of the raid, officers in ordinary uniform replaced those who had staged the initial 'assault'. Protected officers held on reserve were not deployed either during the raid or, according to police records, at any time during the following weekend. Senior police officers report that tension on the estate has declined since the raid and liaison with the local council and community groups has greatly improved.[12] Twenty people were charged with various drugs-related offences, all of whom were convicted.

The Broadwater Farm riot

Thus, even if Jefferson's *post hoc* analysis of events at Orgreave and the Manchester Students' Union is accepted as accurate for the purposes of this discussion, there are many other examples which contradict the proposed relationship between a paramilitary approach and the occurrence of disorder.

What cannot be allowed to pass without challenge is the description of, and explanation for, the events surrounding the Broadwater Farm riot of 1985. Jefferson contrasts the restraint shown by officers on the picket outside Tottenham police station on the afternoon preceding the riot with the aggressive response of a DSU (District Support Unit) which encountered youths leaving the estate after an angry meeting in the Youth Association.[13] The policing of the picket, Jefferson tells us, quoting the Gifford report, 'was restrained and sensible. They blocked off the High Road in both directions to give room for the demonstration. They policed the demonstration with a thin line of officers in ordinary uniform with special units well out of sight. They stood while the crowd shouted angrily and made intimidating gestures, without reacting or making arrests.' This is approvingly described by Jefferson as a 'traditional response'. 'Meanwhile', he adds, again citing Gifford, 'among the paramilitary reserves on standby "the atmosphere must have been charged with anticipation of trouble"' (1990: 87).[14]

Jefferson's invidious comparison between the officers at the picket and the 'paramilitary reserves on standby' is erroneous on two counts. First, he is simply wrong to imply that the officers at the picket were different from those on standby—they were *all* DSUs (Couch, private communication). The DSU deployed at the picket did not withstand the taunts and insults of the protestors simply out of individual self-discipline, but because they acted as a disciplined body under the *orders* of Chief Superintendent Couch. Second, the reason why youths encountered a DSU as they left

[12] Indeed, one local commentator regards the consultation between police and local community leaders and the invitation for them to 'police the police' during the raid as a 'spectacular' implementation of 'cooperative policing in a multi-racial society' (Craig 1992).

[13] DSUs (District Support Units) were effectively the successors to the SPG as a public order reserve in London and have since been replaced by the TSG.

[14] Note that there is *no evidence* to support this; it is merely conjecture.

P. A. J. WADDINGTON

the estate was because an inspector in plain clothes and driving an unmarked car had a full milk bottle thrown through the driver's door window, spraying glass into his face, and more particularly into his eyes. He was at the time making a reconnaissance to ascertain whether the large number of emergency calls being received by police from callers at Broadwater Farm were genuine or hoaxes. The DSU carrier went to the estate in reply to the inspector's urgent call for assistance (Richards 1986). The police maintain that the officers on board that carrier and others called to the estate were not 'riot-clad'—why else would they need to retreat before the youths leaving the estate? Photographs of the carrier taken shortly after the incident show that it was subjected to a ferocious attack.

Historical myopia?

The specifics of the Broadwater Farm riot aside, Jefferson tries to persuade us that recent developments in public order policing are responsible for violent confrontations between police and various sections of the underclass. Observations from my research and other evidence suggest that things are not nearly so simple. But perhaps it is historical myopia exclusively to concentrate attention upon the contemporary scene, because there is nothing particularly novel about confrontations between police and the underclass. Long before the development of paramilitary methods the police acted in very aggressive and violent ways towards unruly crowds. This is testified to by Critchley (1970), Geary (1985), Dunning *et al.* (1987), and Morgan (1987), all of whom cite many historical examples of police charging crowds and breaking heads. Within such a longer time-frame any supposed correlation between paramilitarism and crowd violence surely disappears and obliges us to look elsewhere for explanations of disorder.

The 'View from Below'

Jefferson's selective account of the Broadwater Farm riot reflects the self-conscious adoption of what he calls the 'view from below'. But it is a very selective perspective, adopted to decry the growth of an authoritarian 'law and order' society. The downtrodden masses seem largely to comprise pickets, racial minorities, and students— although it must be admitted that he also shows sympathy for football hooligans and 'lager louts'. However, those 'below', whose vision we are invited to adopt, cannot be so easily limited: they must also include white fascists who, more than anyone else, were subjected to banning orders under the 1936 Public Order Act.[15] It also includes religious fundamentalists, like those who sought to prevent the publication of the *Satanic Verses*.

This selectivity is particularly relevant to the Northern Ireland context, the discussion of which (Jefferson 1990: 35–6) makes no mention of the destruction of the one .significant attempt to reach consensus—the Power Sharing Executive of Prime Minister Brian Faulker—by the Loyalist strike, backed by intimidation. There is also a deafening silence about the violent opposition to the Anglo-Irish Agreement and a

---

[15] Adopting a more comparative perspective, it also includes the racist rioters of various eastern German cities who, in the summer of 1992, attacked hostels for refugees and asylum-seekers.

THE CASE AGAINST PARAMILITARY POLICING CONSIDERED

failure to record the RUC's protection of the Catholic enclaves of Castlewellan and Portadown from provocative, and ultimately violent, Loyalist marches in 1985.

When discussing Northern Ireland Jefferson sees only the oppression of the nationalist/Republican minority. But his analysis is a two-edged sword, for the complaint that all violence is denuded of political significance and treated as simply 'criminal' (1990: 36) could apply as much to the UVF, the UFF, or the Red Hand Commando as to Republican terrorism. It is unlikely that Jefferson would wish sectarian murderers, such as the 'Shankhill Butchers', to be regarded as anything other than a bunch of 'criminally motivated thugs'. Likewise, how else do we describe and respond to racist attackers and wife batterers? The 'bottom up' perspective, if applied universally, incorporates some very unsavoury bottoms!

The 'bottom up' approach also contains a comforting, but implausible, view of the relationship between the perpetrators and the victims of riot and disorder. Like a collection of latter-day Robin Hoods, downtrodden rioters wreak revenge upon oppressive Sheriff of Nottingham lookalikes. The reality is not nearly so comforting. When football hooligans run amok it is usually other football supporters and hapless passers-by who are their victims. It was two Asian sub-postmasters who were burned to death during the Handsworth riot; an Asian-owned mini-supermarket that was destroyed by arson during the Broadwater Farm riot. Rioters in Cardiff during September 1991 claimed that they were protesting about the actions of a local Asian shopkeeper (*The Times*, 3 September 1991). National Front demonstrators are rarely drawn from the dominant social strata: they are more frequently one group at the bottom of society protesting against others who are similarly situated.

Restraint and Impartiality

Northern Ireland poses in its acutest form an issue that Jefferson seems unwilling to confront: should the police be given or denied the means effectively to suppress dissent by force, whatever the circumstances? His final chapter gives the impression that the police should be denied the means, since this would allow those adversely affected by or opposed to government policy to make their protest effective. For example, had the miners in 1984–5 not confronted the nationally co-ordinated power of the police, they might have succeeded in bringing economic activity to a virtual halt, as they did in 1972 and 1974, and thereby prevented the wholesale closure of collieries in pursuit of economic viability. But, as noted above, this is a two-way street: Ulster Loyalists also frustrated government policy in the mid-1970s by much the same means. Fundamentalist Muslims might succeed in preventing the publication or sale of the *Satanic Verses* and other texts of which they disapprove if the police were powerless to prevent them. Nor do the social divisions and conflicts that produce disorder and violence on the streets of Britain necessarily originate here. Conflicts between Greek and Turkish Cypriots, Indians and Pakistanis, Kurds and their various oppressors, and within the Sikh community have all erupted on the streets of Britain.

Certainly, it is preferable that violent conflict should be avoided where possible. The avoidance in Britain of major disorders, comparable to those that occurred elsewhere in the industrializing and industrialized world throughout the nineteenth century and the first half of the twentieth, is attributable not mainly to British policing methods, but to the successful incorporation of the working class into institutionalized politics. The

P. A. J. WADDINGTON

uncompromising stance taken by the Thatcher government during the 1980s reversed this process and undoubtedly exacerbated tension and conflict. Regrettable though this reversal has been, it does not mean that every conflict can or should be avoided. There are times when standing up for something means standing up against someone. There are few, I suspect, who would not wish to oppose, by force if necessary, attempts to prevent the publication of the *Satanic Verses*. In circumstances such as these, the use of coercion to suppress violent protest is surely justified.

If disorder is ever to be prevented by force, it is better that it be done effectively and with only as much force as is necessary. The achievement of both effectiveness and 'minimum force' is, I maintain, more likely under paramilitary organization comprising effective intelligence and trained personnel operating under hierarchical command in accordance with a formulated strategy and tactics. If this is an 'idealistic', 'top-down' view, then so be it. It is certainly no less 'idealistic' than Jefferson's own stance, for to propose that the view 'from below' should dictate, or even strongly influence, police policy is clearly utopian (1990: 140). The point of view of what Jefferson calls the 'new lumpen' (1990: 40–1) is unlikely ever to be taken seriously, for if it were they would no longer be 'below' but have acquired power and risen nearer to the top. It would seem that his prescription for 'non-discriminatory' and 'trouble free' policing (1990: 144) is indistinguishable from 'impartial' and 'restrained' policing. At the very least 'impartiality' and 'restraint' serve the same purpose in my analysis as 'socialist justice' and 'democracy' do for Jefferson (1990: 141)—as ideals to aim at.

Conclusion

Jefferson's adoption of the 'view from below' and the idealism of 'socialist justice' suggest that what he is actually registering is not the empirical connection between certain methods of policing and the likelihood of disorder, but a *distaste* for those methods and what they represent. The use of force is never palatable, but the reality is, as Bittner (1970, 1975) so keenly observed, that the police *are* monopolists of force in civil society. It is inevitable that when social, political, and economic conflict increases, that force becomes more conspicuous. But if police coercion is intrinsically unpalatable, it is all the *more* necessary that it be used with circumspection. The application of force without effective command and control is the proverbial loose cannon. Paramilitary organization brings that 'loose cannon' under a greater measure of control than would otherwise be possible. It allows force to be used more accountably, because those who command and control must be responsible for those whom they command. If paramilitary force is used with unwarranted aggression, then it is not the means that should be questioned, but the end. Provided that the end is the minimum use of force for the achievement of publicly acceptable purposes, then paramilitary methods hold out the prospect of achieving them more effectively than traditional alternatives.

REFERENCES

BITTNER, E. (1970), *The Functions of the Police in a Modern Society*. Washington, DC: US Government Printing Office.
—— (1975), 'A Theory of the Police', in H. Jacob, ed., *Potential for Reform of Criminal Justice*. Beverly Hills: Sage.

THE CASE AGAINST PARAMILITARY POLICING CONSIDERED

CRAIG, E. (1992), 'Policing the Poor: Conciliation or Confrontation? A Preliminary Comparative Study of Policing Poor White and Black Communities', in T. F. Marshall, ed., *Community Disorders and Policing*. London: Whiting and Birch.

CRITCHLEY, T. (1970), *The Conquest of Violence*. London: Constable.

DUNNING, E. *et al*. (1987), 'Violent disorders in 20th century Britain', in G. Gaskell and R. Benewick, eds, *The Crowd in Contemporary Britain*. London: Sage.

FIELDING, N. (1990), *The Police and Social Conflict*. London: Athlone.

GEARY, R. (1985), *Policing Industrial Disputes: 1893 to 1985*. Cambridge: Cambridge University Press.

HOLDAWAY, S. (1983), *Inside the British Police*. Oxford: Blackwell.

JEFFERSON, T. (1990), *The Case against Paramilitary Policing*. Milton Keynes: Open University Press.

KERNER, O. (1967), *The Report of the National Advisory Commission on Civil Disorders*. Washington, DC: US Government Printing Office.

METCALFE, J. (1991), 'Trafalgar Square Riot Debriefing, Saturday, 31 March 1990'. London: Metropolitan Police.

MORGAN, J. (1987), *Conflict and Order*. Oxford: Clarendon Press.

PALMER, S. H. (1988), *Police and Protest in England and Ireland, 1780–1850*. Cambridge: Cambridge University Press.

RICHARDS, M. D. (1986), 'Public Disorder in Tottenham, 6th October 1985'. London: Metropolitan Police.

SCRATON, P. (1985), *The State of the Police*. London: Pluto Press.

STEPHENS, M. (1988), *Policing: the Critical Issues*. London: Wheatsheaf.

STARK, R. (1972), *Police Riots: Collective Violence and Law Enforcement*. Belmont, Ca.: Wadsworth Press.

TAYLOR, LORD JUSTICE (1989), *The Hillsborough Stadium Disaster 15 April 1989, Inquiry by Rt Hon. Lord Justice Taylor, Interim Report*, Cmnd. 765. London: HMSO.

TUCK, M. (1989), *Drinking and Disorder: A Study of Non-Metropolitan Violence*, Home Office Research Study no. 108. London: HMSO.

WADDINGTON, D., JONES, K., and CRITCHER, C. (1987), 'Flashpoints of Public Disorder', in G. Gaskell and R. Benewick, eds., *The Crowd in Contemporary Britain*. London: Sage.

—— (1989), *Flashpoints: Studies in Public Disorder*. London: Routledge.

WADDINGTON, P. A. J. (1987), 'Towards Paramilitarism? Dilemmas in the Policing of Public Order', *British Journal of Criminology*, 27: 37–46.

—— (1991), *The Strong Arm of the Law*. Oxford: Clarendon Press.

WALKER, D. (1968), *Rights in Conflict*. New York: Banton.

METHODOLOGICAL APPENDIX

The research in progress referred to in this article consists of a participant observation of public order policing in London. When possible, I attend all the meetings in connection with a forthcoming public order event. I observe any meetings between police representatives and the organizers of events; strategy meetings; briefings; and any debriefings. I am supplied with copies of minutes of meetings, operation orders (detailing the deployments of officers), and any other relevant documentation. I accompany the most senior ground commander at the scene, equipped with a police radio with which to monitor broadcasts. This provides an unrivalled opportunity to observe the policing operation, since the senior ground commander would be

367

P. A. J. WADDINGTON

informed of any trouble, would probably attend any incident likely to escalate into disorder, and needs to approve the deployment of specialist units, such as mounted officers or TSG.

I have also interviewed senior officers who command public order events, but these data are not utilized in this article.

A detailed list of the observations relied on for this article is provided below.

National Union of Students march, 15 February 1990

Observation of march and rally

Anti-poll tax demonstration, Lambeth Town Hall, 29 March 1990

Observation of protest outside Lambeth Town Hall

Anti-poll tax march and demonstration, 31 March 1990

Observations at Trafalgar Square, Haymarket, and Piccadilly Circus

Muslims in Britain and Socialist Workers' Party marches, Saturday 1 September 1990

Planning meeting, 29 August 1990
Briefing, Scotland Yard, 30 August 1990
Observation of marches, 1 September 1990

Hands Off the Middle East Committee march, 8 September 1990

Strategy meeting and briefing, 6 September 1990
Observation of march, 8 September 1990

Campaign against War in the Gulf march, 15 September 1990

Meeting with organizer, 3 September 1990
Strategy meeting and briefing, New Scotland Yard, 13 September 1990
Observation of the march, 15 September 1990

Anti-Poll Tax Federation march, Brockwell Park, 20 October 1990

Meeting with London Anti-Poll Tax Federation, 2 September 1990
Meeting with London Anti-Poll Tax Federation, 6 September 1990
Meeting with London Anti-Poll Tax Federation, 11 September 1990
Meeting with London Anti-Poll Tax Federation and Officials of Lambeth Council, New Scotland Yard, 17 September 1990
Strategy meeting, Brixton Police Station, 28 September 1990
Meeting with National Federation organizers, New Scotland Yard, 3 September 1990
Meeting, Assistant Commissioner, 3 October 1990
Training at Public Order Training Centre, Hounslow, 8 October 1990
Strategy meeting, New Scotland Yard, 10 October 1990
Meeting with London Anti-Poll Tax Federation, New Scotland Yard, 15 October 1990
Strategy Meeting, Brixton, 15 October 1990

THE CASE AGAINST PARAMILITARY POLICING CONSIDERED

Briefing, New Scotland Yard, 18 October 1990
Meeting with London Anti-Poll Tax Federation and Trafalgar Square Defence Campaign and
    Public Order Branch, New Scotland Yard, 19 October 1990
Observation of Anti-Poll Tax march, the Defence Campaign picket and march, 20 October
    1990

Remembrance Sunday, 11 November 1990

Briefing, New Scotland Yard, 8 November 1990
Observations in Whitehall, 11 November 1990

Committee to Stop War in the Gulf march and rally, 24 November 1990

Strategy meeting, 8 Area HQ, 22 October 1990
Strategy meeting, 8 Area HQ, 19 November 1990
Briefing, New Scotland Yard, 21 November 1990
Observation of march and rally, 24 October 1990

Committee to Stop War in the Gulf march and rally, 15 January 1991

Strategy meeting, Cannon Row, 13 December 1990
Briefing, New Scotland Yard, 10 January 1991
Ad hoc meeting, Public Order Branch, New Scotland Yard, 10 January 1991
Observation of march and rally, 12 January 1991

Various events connected with the Gulf crisis, 15 January 1991

Informal discussion, Public Order Branch, New Scotland Yard, 10 January 1991
Briefing for senior officers, Cannon Row, 14 January 1991
Observation of events in Trafalgar Square, Whitehall and Parliament Square, 15 January 1991
Debriefing, Cannon Row, 16 January 1991

Events following the outbreak of war in the Gulf

Strategy meeting, Cannon Row, 16 January 1991

Events in Westminster protesting at the outbreak of hostilities in the Gulf, 17 January 1991

Strategy briefing, Cannon Row, 18 January 1991
Observation of events in Westminster, 17 January 1991

Campaign to Stop War in the Gulf march and rally, 19 January 1991

Senior officers' briefing, Cannon Row, 18 January 1991
Observation of march and rally, 19 January 1991

Campaign to Stop War in the Gulf march and rally, 27 January 1991

Briefing, New Scotland Yard, 25 January 1991
Observation of march and rally, 26 January 1991

369

P. A. J. WADDINGTON

Campaign to Stop War in the Gulf march and rally, 2 February 1991

Strategy meeting, Cannon Row, 28 January 1991
Meeting between Public Order Branch, New Scotland Yard and Campaign to Stop War in the
    Gulf and CND organizers, Public Order Branch, New Scotland Yard, 28 January 1991
Briefing, New Scotland Yard, 1 February 1991
Observation of march and rally, 2 February 1991

Anti-war protests in and around Trafalgar and Parliament Squares, 15 February 1991

Briefing, New Scotland Yard, 15 February 1991
Observation of events in Trafalgar Square, Whitehall, and Parliament Square, 15 February
    1991

Lesbian and Gay Coalition march and rally, 16 February 1991

Briefing, New Scotland Yard, 15 February 1991
Observation of march, 16 February 1991

International Islamic Front march, 24 February 1991

Briefing, New Scotland Yard, 22 February 1991
Observation of march, 24 February 1991

Campaign to Stop War in the Gulf march and rally, 2 March 1991

Meeting at Cannon Row to discuss the third anti-poll tax march, 6 February 1991
Meeting with organizers from Campaign to Stop War in the Gulf, New Scotland Yard, 25
    February 1991
Meeting with DoE officials, 25 February 1991
Meeting with 'Internationalists' organizer, 25 February 1991
Ad hoc meeting with officials from the DoE, 25 February 1991
Briefing, New Scotland Yard, 1 March 1991
Observation of march and rally, 2 March 1991

Women's March for Peace march and rally, 9 March 1991

Meeting with organizers from Campaign to Stop War in the Gulf, New Scotland Yard, 25
    February 1991
Briefing, New Scotland Yard, 2 March 1991

All England Anti-Poll Tax Federation march and rally, 23 March 1991

Meeting, Assistant Commissioner, New Scotland Yard, 28 January 1991
Meeting, Cannon Row, 6 February 1991
Meeting, Cannon Row, to plan presentation to public meeting, 25 February 1991
Meeting with Anti-Poll Tax Federation organizers, Public Order Branch, New Scotland Yard,
    8 March 1991
Public meeting on the anti-poll tax march, Westminster City Council Town Hall, 11 March
    1991

THE CASE AGAINST PARAMILITARY POLICING CONSIDERED

Strategy meeting, New Scotland Yard, 12 March 1991
Meeting with organizers, New Scotland Yard, 15 March 1991
Meeting with organizers, New Scotland Yard, 18 March 1991
Briefing, New Scotland Yard, 18 March 1991
Observation of Trafalgar Square, 23 March 1990
Debriefing, Cannon Row, 8 April 1991

Iraqi People's Solidarity Committee march, 13 April 1991

Meeting with organizer, Cannon Row, 10 April 1991
Briefing and observation of march, 13 April 1991

Islamic Students march and rally, 20 April 1991

Meeting with organizer, 18 April 1991
Briefing and observation of march, 20 April 1991

National Anti-Vivisection Society march and rally, 27 April 1991

Strategy meeting, 18 March 1991
Strategy meeting, 25 April 1991
Briefing, New Scotland Yard, 25 April 1991
Observation of march, 27 April 1991

British National Party march and rally, Thamesmead, 25 May 1991

Strategy meeting, Plumstead, 16 May 1991
Strategy meeting, Plumstead, 23 May 1991

'Gay Pride' march and rally, 29 June 1991

Strategy meeting, Brixton, 3 May 1991
Meeting with organizers, Public Order Branch, New Scotland Yard, 27 June 1991
Briefing, New Scotland Yard, 27 June 1991
Observation of march, 29 June 1991
Debriefing, Kennington Police Station, 3 July 1991

Cancel the Debt march and rally, Saturday 13 July 1991

Meeting with organizer, Wednesday 19 June 1991
Meeting with organizer, Public Order Branch, New Scotland Yard, 11 July 1991
Briefing, New Scotland Yard, 11 July 1991
Observation of march, 13 July 1991

Notting Hill Carnival, 24–6 August 1991

Sector Commanders' meeting, Notting Dale, 5 March 1991
Notting Hill Support Group meeting, Kensington and Chelsea Town Hall, 12 March 1991
Sector Commanders' meeting, Notting Dale, 14 March 1991
Notting Hill Carnival 'seminar', Kensington and Chelsea Town Hall, 15 March 1991

P. A. J. WADDINGTON

Working Party meeting, Notting Hill, 27 March 1991
Support Group meeting, Kensington and Chelsea Town Hall, 10 April 1991
Sector Commanders' meeting, 17 April 1991
Working Party meeting, Notting Dale, 24 April 1991
Pre-Support Group meeting, 7 May 1991
Support Group meeting, Kensington and Chelsea Town Hall, 8 May 1991
Sector Commanders' meeting, Notting Dale, 15 May 1991
Strategy meeting, Notting Dale, 11 June 1991
Sector Commanders' meeting, 19 June 1991
Working Party meeting, Notting Dale, 26 June 1991
'Training Day', Public Order Training Centre, Hounslow, 5 July 1991
Strategy meeting, Notting Dale, 9 July 1991
Support Group, Kensington Town Hall, 10 July 1991
Training Day, Public Order Training Centre, Hounslow, 12 July 1991
Sector Commanders' meeting, 16 July 1991
Sector Three briefing, New Scotland Yard, 12 August 1991
Strategy meeting, 13 August 1991
Support Group, Kensington Town Hall, 14 August 1991
Sector Commanders' meeting, 15 August 1991
Observation of *Panorama*, 24 August 1991
Observation of Notting Hill Carnival, Sector Two, 25 August 1991
Observation of Notting Hill Carnival, Sector Three, Monday, 26 August 1991
Support Group, Kensington Town Hall, 8 October 1991
Debriefing, 6 November 1991

Remembrance Sunday, 10 November 1991

Strategy meeting, Cannon Row, 5 September 1991
Strategy briefing, Cannon Row, 9 October 1991
Briefing, New Scotland Yard, 7 November 1991
Observation of events in Whitehall and Victoria, 10 November 1991
Debriefing, 19 November 1991

Campaign for British Withdrawal from Ireland march and rally, 25 January 1992

Meeting with organizers, Public Order Branch, New Scotland Yard, 18 December 1991
Informal strategy meeting, following meeting with organizers
Briefing, 7 Area HQ, 21 January 1992
Observation of march and rally, 25 January 1992

'SIMBA' march and rally, 22 February 1992

Strategy meeting, Plumstead, 17 January 1992
Strategy meeting, Morris Drummond Section House, 20 February 1992
Briefing, Morris Drummond Section House, 20 February 1992
Observation of march and rally, 22 February 1992

THE CASE AGAINST PARAMILITARY POLICING CONSIDERED

Anti-Election Alliance march and rally, 5 April 1992

Meeting with organizers, 26 February 1992
Meeting with organizers, Cannon Row, 21 March 1992
Strategy meeting, Cannon Row, 26 March 1992
Briefing, Public Order Branch, New Scotland Yard, 3 April 1992
Observation of march and rally, 4 April 1992

'Gay Pride' march and festival, 26 June 1992

Meeting with organizer, 4 February 1992
Meeting with organizer, Public Order Branch, New Scotland Yard, 8 May 1992
Strategy meeting, Public Order Branch, New Scotland Yard, 15 May 1992
Meeting with organizer, Public Order Branch, New Scotland Yard, 5 June 1992
Meeting with organizer, Public Order Branch, New Scotland Yard, 22 June 1992
Briefing, Public Order Branch, New Scotland Yard, 22 June 1992
Observation of march, 26 June 1992

Lesbian and Gay Coalition, march and rally

Meeting with organizers, Public Order Branch, New Scotland Yard, 12 June 1992
Strategy briefing, Cannon Row, 1 October 1992

22

BRIT. J. CRIMINOL. VOL. 33 NO. 3 SUMMER 1993

PONDERING PARAMILITARISM:

A Question of Standpoints?

TONY JEFFERSON*

The exchange in this issue of the British Journal of Criminology *between the author and P. A. J. Waddington constitutes the second round of a debate begun in 1987 with the publication in this journal of an article by each writer on the subject of 'paramilitarism' in the British police. The present writer attempts in this article to show how the dispute between himself and Professor Waddington on this subject is rooted in a difference of standpoint rather than in a failure to engage with each other's arguments. He addresses Waddington's four challenges in the order they are presented in the latter's article in this issue, namely, definitions, facts, the 'viewpoint from below', and the question of idealism.*

I doubt Waddington and I will ever agree about paramilitary policing. Though each of us is obviously attempting to convince the reader of the rightness of his own position, the ultimate issue is less that of who is right and who is wrong about particular points, and more about standpoints. That is to say, from our different 'standpoints'—a term currently fashionable in feminist epistemology—we may both be right (or wrong) at least some of the time. Thus, our disagreements stem less from missing each other's points—Waddington's painstakingly considered reply shows he has all the relevant points clearly in his sights—and more from seeing the same points differently, from a different standpoint. This reply is undertaken, therefore, in an attempt to clarify the nature of our differences and the different standpoints from which they stem rather than in the hope of resolving them. I will deal with Waddington's four challenges in the order he has selected, namely, definitions, facts, the viewpoint from below and the question of idealism.

Defining Paramilitarism

Waddington is absolutely correct to state (1993: 353) that the 'central issue' dividing us is the meaning of 'paramilitary'. I would go further: most of our other differences stem from this. I need, therefore, to unravel these differences with particular care, since they are pivotal to an understanding of the others.

My definition of paramilitary policing, 'namely, the application of (quasi)-military training, equipment, philosophy and organization to questions of policing (whether under centralized control or not)' (Jefferson 1990: 16) is avowedly a *profane* one based on what is, for me, the contemporary reality of 'actually existing' paramilitary policing. Waddington stresses as the 'largely ignored' essence of his definition '*co-ordination through superior command and control*' (1993: 353), something he admits is often missing in actually existing paramilitary policing. It is this particular absence that prompted the title to his

* Reader in Criminology, University of Sheffield.
The author thanks Wendy Hollway for her sharp editorial eye.

PONDERING PARAMILITARISM

original article, 'Towards Paramilitarism?' (1993: 356). In terms of opposing stand-points, mine is a definition from the standpoint of 'now', i.e. paramilitary policing as presently practised; Waddington's a definition from the standpoint of a desirable future, i.e. paramilitary policing as it *ought* to be practised (from his perspective).

This distinction might suggest that we are talking of two very different sorts of situations: (1) ones where co-ordinated command and control is lacking (where, therefore, my definition holds sway), and (2) ones where such command and control is operative, and where, therefore, Waddington's definition is the relevant one. Indeed, Waddington seems to support this interpretation because he does appear to concede that, at least so far as the 1984 Orgreave picket and the 1985 Manchester Students' Union demonstration are concerned, my characterization of events might be accurate (1993: 361). But I think this conclusion would be a mistake, since it oversimplifies the nature of this difference between us.

The key to understanding this difference is to be found in our readings of Rodney Stark's book *Police Riots* (Stark 1972), especially of the police handling of the Detroit riot in 1967. Waddington and I agree that it was the police and the National Guard who overreacted and the regular army who 'showed more restraint' (Waddington 1993: 355; see also Jefferson 1990: 101–2). We disagree on how these facts should be read. He concludes that these facts demonstrate his point about the superiority of paramilitary discipline, since the army's restraint was a result of its following orders—orders co-ordinated through its command and control system. It was precisely the lack of an effective system of command and control that led to police overreaction (Waddington 1993: 355). But what this conclusion fails to emphasize is that this military discipline *cannot simply be transferred to policing without altering the nature of policing* (Jefferson 1990: 102). Why? Because civil policing, with its notion of independently liable, unarmed officers, was originally introduced precisely in order to counter the *provocative* nature of military-style policing—exemplified most dramatically by the behaviour of the Yeomanry scything down innocent protesters at Peterloo Fields in Manchester in 1822.

It could be argued that it was the lack of discipline displayed by the Yeomanry at Peterloo (a result, in Waddington's terms, of a failure of command and control) that was provocative, not the military nature of the intervention. I would argue that it was *both*; and that however the military actually behaves in a given situation, its very presence to deal with *internal* strife always connotes some failure of democracy, always signals that the deployment of force has become necessary to maintain order and harmony, that there has been some failure to secure consent from some section of the population. It is to that extent inherently provocative—a provocation, at base, to the democratic aspirations of a people. This was as true of the long-standing British fear of a standing army following the Cromwellian interregnum as it is today in any society in which the military is in command. It is this feature of the military that underpins the constant concern to secure and maintain the image of police as citizen peace-keepers operating with the consent of the people. This desired image is the very antithesis of the provocative image of the military. So, if reverting to a 'military-style' solution to problems of public order policing represents a gain in terms of more co-ordinated discipline, it is always bought at the expense of an increase in provocation. That is the paradox I point to.

If this paradox represents the theoretical heart of my argument, its practical lungs reside in the concrete reality that results from combining (provocative) military and

TONY JEFFERSON

(undisciplined) police discretion within one institution. This, surely, is the proper meaning of the phrase 'paramilitary policing'. It is a combination that gives us the 'worst of all possible worlds—provocation minus collective discipline' (Jefferson 1990: 102). Once again, this difference can be traced to two different standpoints: mine, which is the standpoint of the policed, those upon whom the maintenance of order is to be imposed; and Waddington's, which is the standpoint of order maintenance. From this standpoint, 'military-style' operations can be more disciplined, efficient, and effective. They cannot help also being provocative, even if the response to that provocation can be effectively silenced for a long while.

There are two further, related points that need emphasizing. The first is the association of the military with superior discipline. In the Detroit riot of 1967 the regular army was more disciplined than either the police or the National Guard. But this is not axiomatic. There are plenty of examples of military discipline breaking down in the actual horrors of war or civil peace-keeping. The second point to be made concerns the relationship of the military to the law. In a democracy the rule of law is sacrosanct; citizens and soldiers alike are ultimately subject to it, in principle. But when it is deemed necessary to deploy military force to counter some perceived threat to a democracy, democratic values, including the rule of law, can paradoxically become subsumed under a higher principle—the survival of the state itself. I write this having recently watched *Panorama* (BBC 1, 23 July 1991) raise serious questions about what would appear to be a 'shoot-to-kill'—in some instances one might say 'summary execution'—policy in Northern Ireland which has claimed the lives of 'joy-riders' and 'ordinary' criminals, as well as suspected terrorists. It is unclear whether this 'above the law' approach to the maintenance of the law is a result of poor discipline, a military philosophy that the ends (of the state paymaster) justify the means, or state policy—or all three. But it adds a further reason for scepticism towards Waddington's reliance on military-style 'discipline' as the professional solution to policing public order.

Interpreting the Facts

My reading of a selected number of public order events led me to conclude 'that paramilitary policing has an inherent tendency to exacerbate or amplify problems of violence and disorder (which is not to suggest that amplification is an inevitable feature of such policing, merely that there is a constant tendency towards it)' (Jefferson 1990; 82); Waddington's reading of a 'somewhat lengthier list' (Waddington 1993: 358) observed while conducting research into the Metropolitan Police leads him to the opposite conclusion: 'when the police were not deployed in paramilitary strength serious disorder . . . occurred; when significant numbers of police, including specialists in riot control, were deployed there was progressively less violence' (1993: 362). What then are we to make of this difference? The answer, once again, needs to be sought in our different standpoints.

Part of the answer lies in the slippage Waddington allows to take place in depicting my argument. In the first place, he admits that my model 'avoids the simplistic association between the police deployment of protected officers and the occurrence of disorder' (1993: 357); that it is a probabilistic not an absolute model. So far, so good. Had he maintained that position, there need not have been any discrepancy in our readings. But he quickly slips into judging my model from his own correlational/causal standpoint,

PONDERING PARAMILITARISM

which I judge to be simplistic. Because he observed a number of public order events where the correlation between paramilitary policing and disorder was negative, not positive as my model suggests is likely, he wishes to suggest that my model should be turned on its head. So, my own model is first rendered simplistic (that is, a matter of correlation) and, from that standpoint, judged and found wanting.

Lest this be considered too harsh, let me elaborate further Waddington's tendency to slip into a simplified reading of my argument—from which standpoint it is easy to discredit it. At one stage he used the Sheffield-based research of David Waddington and colleagues (Waddington *et al.* 1989) to discredit the 'simple association' allegedly supposed to obtain between overt police control of space and crowds, and disorder (Waddington 1993: 359). (Note that the important term 'paramilitary' has been dropped here.) Two things need to be said about this. In the first place, I would argue that, though different, my model is in substantial accord with that of David Waddington *et al.* Having looked at many public order events in detail, they posit a six-level model for theorizing the outbreak of disorder, ranging through the structural, political/ideological, cultural, and contextual to the situational and the interactional (Waddington *et al.* 1989: 156–67). At each of these levels numerous order-provoking or order-preventing factors are operative. Disorder (or order) is the outcome of the whole host of 'order-relevant' factors operating at these various levels. Thus, certain contingent, interactional factors can act to pre-empt disorder, even when factors operating at other levels seem to point towards a disorderly outcome, and vice versa (Waddington *et al.* 1989: 167). I would remind the reader of my starting-point: that is, the need to contextualize the emergence of paramilitary policing within the collapse of consensus and the rise of Thatcherism (Jefferson 1990: 25–43). This brief contemporary history covered the levels David Waddington and his colleagues refer to as structural, political/ideological, cultural, and contextual. My general conclusion was that this historical moment was not a propitious one for order maintenance. My later detailed look at the actual paramilitary policing of disorder covered the final two levels: the situational and interactional. My conclusion here was that the paramilitary style of policing tended to make things worse. Using the terms of David Waddington *et al.*: the relevant order-maintaining factors at the macro levels were not encouraging; the adoption of paramilitary tactics *in situ* seemed usually to worsen matters. That I ended by stressing the general tendencies (towards disorder) implicit in this historical moment which paramilitary policing has a tendency to exacerbate and David Waddington *et al.* ended by developing an overall model designed to explain all outcomes—disorderly or otherwise—does not render our accounts contradictory.

More concretely, Waddington uses David Waddington *et al.*'s account of the 1983 'Thatcher Unwelcoming' demonstration in Sheffield to demonstrate the inadequacy of my model. On this occasion, he claims, policing was paramilitary in style but there was no disorder. As a participant in that demonstration, and having reviewed David Waddington *et al.*'s account of it (Waddington *et al.* 1989: 27–37; presumably Waddington's source), I have to say that it was *not* policed paramilitary-style. Though space was confined and cordons of officers were present, certain key provocative elements were absent. The general tenor of policing was 'low-key' (Waddington *et al.* 1989: 37). Indeed I had to check the account of David Waddington *et al.* to remind myself that there were ranks of officers in front of the crowds. Only a few officers, in pairs, were in the crowd (Waddington *et al.* 1989: 36). There were no charges by the mounted

TONY JEFFERSON

police, nor were snatch squads operative. In short, if there were elements of a paramilitary presence, the policing operation generally was a very traditional one. Once again, Waddington has succeeded in simplifying my model by abstracting elements, rather than regarding it as a dynamic process in which a spiral of violence can be unleashed by a series of paramilitary-style interventions. But it follows that the absence of certain of these interventions (key 'interactional' factors in the terms of David Waddington *et al.*) can prevent the unwinding of the spiral. My model talked in terms of tendencies and spelled out the conditions for these tendencies to run their disorderly course. Many of these provocative conditions were simply absent from the 'Thatcher Unwelcoming' demonstration.

However, and here I must concede a point, there is one important factor that David Waddington *et al.* stress and about which I say very little: that is the crowd. I tend to talk as if the crowd response to provocation will always tend towards anger and resistance (Jefferson 1990: 84–5). What I do not spell out, and they do, are the conditions which will make this outcome more or less likely. This is an omission, occasioned by my research focus on the police and their specific contribution to precipitating disorder. It is quite true that the composition, solidarity, organization, etc. of the crowd are influential contingent factors (Waddington *et al.* 1989: 158–9). Thus crowd factors, as well as police factors, will determine whether outcomes are disorderly. This may well account, at least in part, for some of the orderliness accompanying paramilitary policing that Waddington observed.

However, having conceded this point, I would not want the reader to rush to the conclusion that this is sufficient to reconcile our differences. Reading Waddington's accounts of successful (i.e. orderly) paramilitary policing of certain public order events in London, I had the distinct impression that the reason some of them were successful was because, from my chosen standpoint, they were overpoliced. The third anti-poll tax demonstration with a crowd of 11,500 was policed by 5,000 officers and 'there was no disorder *at all* in the area of the greatest concentration of police' (Waddington 1993: 362; emphasis in original). The 400 officers used in a drugs raid on Broadwater Farm—'a paramilitary operation in virtually every respect'—encountered no resistance: '*no disorder occurred*' (Waddington 1993: 362, 363; emphasis in original). Waddington uses these examples, among others, to make his point that my model must be wrong. But I explicitly address this issue. In looking at three different styles of policing the annual Bathurst bike races in Australia, I conclude that it is possible, via 'tough' saturation policing, to prevent disorder. However, the corollary is that such an approach 'to all intents and purposes [prevents] the event itself' (Jefferson 1990: 108). In other words, the deployment of superior force can almost always prevent disorder. But the implications for subsequent events should be obvious.

Waddington could be said unwittingly to endorse this. The second anti-poll tax demonstration of 5,000 was policed by just over 3,000 officers (Waddington 1993: 361). No trouble occurred. But trouble did ensue when a subsidiary march of 2,000 unexpectedly went to picket Brixton police station, which was less well prepared (Waddington 1993: 362). My suspicion is that the frustrations incurred by the former 'over-policing' were a factor in the subsequent trouble. Such policing is also counter-productive in a more general sense since it disrupts the delicate balance between a people's 'right' to protest and the police role of keeping such activities within acceptable bounds.

PONDERING PARAMILITARISM

One final point. In all Waddington's observed accounts, the voices of the policed are absent. The standpoint, as I observed in the first section of this article, is one of order maintenance: did disorder occur or was it prevented? My more general reading of the anti-poll tax demonstrations, and conversations with participants, suggests that from the standpoint of the policed, paramilitary policing was perceived as provocative *whether disorder actually ensued at the time or not*. This, from the standpoint of the policed, seems to me the key issue, since perceived provocations which cannot be dealt with at the time do not disappear but linger on in collective folk memory (on David Waddington *et al.*'s contextual level; 1989: 163–4), the backcloth against which future protests will take place and which will, in part, determine their outcome.

Selectivity and the 'Viewpoint from Below'

Perhaps I misunderstand Waddington's criticism of my self-conscious adoption of the standpoint of the policed: the 'view from below'. He seems to be suggesting that my 'below' is a selective one largely comprising pickets, racial minorities, and students (though he adds that I show 'sympathy for football hooligans and "lager louts" '; 1993: 364). However, he reminds us that a view from below must also include white fascists, religious fundamentalists, sectarian murderers, and a whole host of other—in his memorable phrase—'unsavoury bottoms'. So, the nub of the criticism seems to be that my 'bottom-up' approach is premissed upon adopting the standpoint of groups towards which I am sympathetic and ignores that of others towards which, he assumes, I would be unsympathetic.

Waddington is here conflating political and analytical standpoints. In terms of a political standpoint, it is far too simple to suggest that my 'selection' of students, racial minorities, and pickets to demonstrate my thesis can be read in terms of my sympathies. And the same applies to 'football hooligans' and 'lager louts' (Waddington's terms, not mine). Does the fact that I find racial inequalities and discrimination obscene mean that I approve of the petrol bomb and the 'riot'? Matters are not that simple, even with my 'selected' minorities. The plain fact is that my selection has been made on analytical, not political, grounds: by which I mean the public order events discussed are analysed from the standpoint of the policed. I argued that from their standpoint paramilitary-style policing has a tendency to promote the very disorder it seeks to prevent. And had I examples to hand of paramilitary policing of demonstrations by religious fundamentalists, or whoever, I would have been happy to use them too. My analyses, which are of policing methods, imply nothing about my sympathy or otherwise for particular forms of protest, nor for particular types of protester. Of course, politically my sympathies rest more with some groups than others. But I was concerned solely to expose the counter-productive paradox at the heart of the concept and practice of paramilitary policing, and this paradox would be as worthy of exposure whether the policed happened to have savoury or unsavoury bottoms.

Democracy, Coercion, and the Question of Idealism

Waddington's criticism here is twofold: he thinks, on the one hand, that my conclusion amounts to denying the police 'the means effectively to suppress dissent by force' (1993: 365); on the other, that my notion that the view from below should be taken seriously is at least as idealistic as his own 'top-down' idea of effective, minimum force, paramilit-

TONY JEFFERSON

ary policing (1993: 366). The first point I find problematic on two counts. If he means that the police should be the agency for suppressing dissent by force—that is, that the police should become a sort of internal agency of coercion directed against certain groups—I strongly dissent. As I argued earlier, that would be a signal that democratic government had effectively collapsed. And we all know what happens in such cases. Ironically, Waddington takes the Northern Ireland example to be the Achilles' heel of my argument. It seems obvious to him that certain forms of dissent in Northern Ireland should be coercively restrained. In contrast, I would argue that Northern Ireland acutely illustrates what happens when military and paramilitary force, plainly perceived as undemocratic interventions by those aggrieved, is added to already existing grievances. The collapse of the pre-1989 regimes in eastern Europe surely demonstrates the point that democratic values are fundamentally opposed to the use of coercion against dissenters.

The second reason for objecting to Waddington's first point is much more prosaic: it is simply (and at the risk of repetitiousness) that the chosen (paramilitary) means to suppress dissent is counter-productive because it often ends up fuelling it.

As for who is more idealistic, perhaps we can end on a note of agreement. He is probably right that his 'top-down' idealism is matched by my 'bottom-up' utopianism. In the foreseeable future it is unlikely that the views of the 'new lumpen' will be taken seriously, or that 'socialist justice' will inform policing policies (Waddington 1993: 366). However, my analysis of what is happening *now*—the substance of the book—is based on a *realistic* appraisal of paramilitary policing when viewed from below. And I do end by suggesting that the prospects for radical changes 'are not good' (Jefferson 1990: 144). But one is duty bound to sketch out what one would like to see attempted—my 'ideal' outcome.

Conclusion

I shall finish on a second point of accord. Tucked away in Waddington's piece is a little paragraph accusing me of historical myopia (1993: 364). The suggestion is that my focus on recent developments in policing disorder, and my linking of these to crowd violence, is caused by academic myopia—a failure to see that historically 'there is nothing particularly novel about confrontations between police and the underclass' (1993: 364). Ironically, the whole of my chapter 2 ('Minimum Force: A Contingent Historical View from Below') uses a historical look at policing disorder from below to mount a critique of Waddington's notion of the 'restrained' use of force. In terms of standpoints, I argued that Waddington's notion of minimum force was a 'top-down' one and hence idealistic from the viewpoint of those 'below'. I offered a 'realistic' historical approach, suggesting that a contingent approach to modern policing rendered the notions of restraint and minimum force far more problematic, judged from the experience of the policed. Now Waddington seems to agree with me—or, for once, we are adopting the same standpoint. I welcome that. Perhaps, in time, he will shift standpoints on the rest of his arguments too.

REFERENCES

JEFFERSON, T. (1987), 'Beyond Paramilitarism', *British Journal of Criminology*, 27/1: 47–53.
—— (1990), *The Case against Paramilitary Policing* (Milton Keynes: Open University Press).

PONDERING PARAMILITARISM

STARK, R. (1972), *Police Riots: Collective Violence and Law Enforcement*. Belmont, Ca.: Wadsworth Press.

WADDINGTON, D., JONES, K., and CRITCHER, C. (1989), *Flashpoints: Studies in Public Disorder* (London: Routledge).

WADDINGTON, P. A. J. (1987), 'Towards Paramilitarism? Dilemmas in the Policing of Public Order', *British Journal of Criminology*, 27/1: 37–46.

—— (1993), '*The Case against Paramilitary Policing* Considered', *British Journal of Criminology*, 33/3: 353–73.

Part V
Futures of Policing

[23]

British Journal of Sociology   Volume *28 Number 2   June 1977*

Simon Holdaway

Changes in urban policing

ABSTRACT

Using data from a covert participant observation study, the author evaluates the effects of the professionalization of the British Police Service, and the linked introduction of Unit Beat Policing, on the occupational culture of urban policing.

Cain's research is re-examined in the light of these changes and it is argued that the dominant values and strategies of control which she found have been strengthened, despite contrary definitions of policing which are contained within the three principles of professional policing.

An explanation is sought in the managerial orientation of the professionalization of the service and in the centrality of features of the occupational culture which Cain does not emphasize but which add resistance to change.

Two definitions of professional policing exist within the British Police Service; these are the 'managerial professionalism' of supervisory officers and the 'practical professionalism' of the work force. The professionalization of the service and the introduction of Unit Beat Policing aid the continuing separation of these two conflicting definitions of urban policing.

Although completed nearly ten years ago, Cain's comparative analysis of rural and urban policing remains the most recent, major contribution to the sociology of the British Police.[1] Unlike their American counterparts, British sociologists have largely neglected the most central agents of social control within the whole of the legal process, as well as one of the most important instruments of 'unofficial' social work in Britain.[2]

In this paper Cain's analysis of urban policing is discussed in terms of the effects of two important and linked innovations in the British Police Service, which have taken place since the completion of her study. These are the professionalization of the police service and the related introduction of a new system of policing, Unit Beat Policing, which took place during the 1960s. The specific focus is upon changes in the definition of urban police work held by constables and sergeants and the strategies they use to practise the task of policing their area.

The data for the paper were gathered during a period of two years' covert participant observation of an urban police sub-division, Hilton, during which time the author was a serving police officer of supervisory rank.[3]

CAIN'S RESEARCH

Cain found that the constables who worked in the urban sub-division she studied were primarily oriented to crime-fighting, a task which formed a very minor part of their working day. The act of making an arrest for a criminal offence was the central act of policing and the primary example of proper police work. However, because this was an infrequent occurrence, drunks tended to be arrested to foster the partial experience of authentic policing.

The primacy of arrest was related to the need for action which the constables expressed, the chase and capture, the fight and scuffle before an arrest, being equally central to the constables' definition of 'real police work'. Such acts maintained their self-identity, reinforcing their definition of themselves as police officers who performed what they understood to be 'real police work'.

Time between bursts of action, defined by the officers as boring times, led the men to seek places where they could get a cup of tea, sleep or chat. Cain called such behaviour 'easing'.[4] Because 'easing' was contrary to the internal disciplinary code of the force, the constables were dependent upon each other for the retention of secrecy. 'Easing behaviour' increased the interdependency of the work group.

Secrecy was necessary to protect individual officers from the possibility of internal discipline and also to shield them from public accountability. The ability to circumvent formal legal rules was thought to be desirable and in order to retain the importance of this attribute, the protective secrecy of the work group was secured. Cain argues that this definition of police work resulted in a poverty of accountable relationships between the police and the community which was policed; the work group provided the primary source of role definition.

This definition of policing and its associated strategies for action constitutes the occupational culture of urban policing.[5] It is the effects of professionalization and Unit Beat Policing on this culture which are to be assessed.

PROFESSIONALIZATION

The history of the British Police Service during the 1960s and 1970s is primarily the history of an occupation striving for professional status.[6] Spurred by the 1962 Royal Commission on the Police[7] and the foundation of a National Police College,[8] the British Police Service was to be based on a well-qualified body of police managers who controlled a less well-educated but internally accountable work force.

The cessation of the Trenchard Scheme, which provided direct entry into senior rank, and the increasing retirement of senior officers who had held rank in the armed services, meant that senior police officers were not retaining a parity of status with the leaders of organizations with whom they had to liaise.

Direct entry at a supervisory rank was resisted; all entrants, including those who joined as graduates, being required to work as constables for at least two years. The claim for professionalism shifted emphasis from an investment in criteria achieved by senior officers prior to their entry into the police, towards characteristics which could be achieved within the service itself.

This process consisted of the establishment of some of the traits which sociologists have identified as features of a profession; for example, a body of knowledge intrinsic to the theory and practice of policing.[9] An equally important point is that it also represented a substantive attempt to retain influence in and control over areas of police work which were increasingly affected, appropriated or challenged by other agencies of State control.[10] At hte level of both central and local government, social service, race relations and traffic control policy was making a new and direct impact upon police decision-making. The professionalization of the police was a reclaiming of authority and control in these and allied areas.[11]

The hallmark of police professionalism was founded in three interrelated principles. First, the acquisition of specialist knowledge of particular aspects of policing and the restructuring of the organization into specialist units, in order to provide a framework for practice. Secondly, to a significant extent, specialist knowledge was based in the use of technology. Knowledge of vehicular policing, telecommunications and computerization became relevant to the development of systems of policing. Thirdly, although discretion has always been an integral feature of policing, the development of professionalization lead to the principle of 'informed discretion'.[12] A stress was placed on the collection of evidence prior to, rather than after, arrest.

Following a number of public inquiries which were held during the early 1960s,[13] senior officers were anxious to diminish the possibility of investigating-officers breaching the legal rules governing the securing of evidence by questioning after arrest. The ideal model of policing by 'informed discretion' is the slow build up of evidence of such overwhelming conviction that arrest becomes inevitable. The sober, informational aspects of pre-arrest judgment would not require any breach of the formal rules.

On the one hand, criminal intelligence units were established at national and local level. These were briefed to collate specialist information on known and suspected criminals, using technical aids to achieve that purpose. Fingerprint and scene-of-crime facilities were expanded to increase the possibility of gaining forensic evidence. Professional policing embraced the scientific and biographical skills required to enhance the credibility of the service.

On the other hand, the notion of 'informed discretion' was not limited to criminal detection in a direct sense. The police recognized that many of the problems they dealt with were 'social problems' and it was argued that police officers were as informed as, for example, social workers and probation officers.[14] This aspect also challenged the view that the police service was a closed, largely unaccountable organization. The claim to specialist knowledge enhanced their status, the practice of police work being more than 'commonsense'. Professional policing was now rooted in sound, specialist knowledge.

These principles of professional policing—specialization, the use of technology and informed discretion—were never subject to direct translation into practical strategies for law enforcement and peace-keeping. Their successful adaptation was initially incorporated in the training of officers of senior and intermediate rank who attended the National Police College, as well as in the duties of those officers employed in specialist units.

The important point is that the thrust of professionalization was first directed at officers whose primary task was the administration and supervision of the police service, rather than those who were engaged in the practical activity of law enforcement. 'Managerial professionalism' would change the practice of practical policing by supervisory persuasion rather than authoritative direction, by training rather than legislative prescription.

Because they are unstated, the intended consequences of professionalization on the occupational culture are difficult to assess. However, it is possible to outline some changes which could be expected and these can be compared with the definition of police work held by the constables and sergeants Cain researched.

First, the stress on 'informed discretion' and the necessity of working within the legal rules governing the collection of evidence could reduce the action orientation of urban policing. The importance of chasing suspects, the fight and the 'know-how' concerning the handling of extra-legal situations would give way to a more sober, considered practice of policing.

Secondly, because professional policing emphasizes a more accountable organization and the fostering of broad links with the community which is policed, one would expect easing behaviour to change from being a strategy designed to while away time, to one means of increased contact with the public. The chat in the local shop, a cup of tea with a nightwatchman—part of Cain's findings—would be understood as possible sources of information and part of a building of consensus, necessary for effective and accountable policing. At the very least, the development of strong relationships between the local police and the population it serves could be expected.

Thirdly, an emphasis on increased accountability and a related building of a 'consensus of consent' should reduce the interdependency of the work group. The protective secrecy which Cain found should be replaced by a greater understanding of legal rights, as well as an appreciation of the value of a police service based on a system of public accountability.

Fourthly, the criteria for assessing the success or failure of police work should shift from an emphasis on crime detection to a more broadly based notion which covers the whole of the police mandate. The crime and arrest orientation of urban policemen should decrease.

Cain's general finding that under the police system she researched strong resistance to formal authority developed would be expected to change. Resistance would be replaced by a more open, accountable, legally bound and sober orientation to urban policing.

UNIT BEAT POLICING

The intended consequences of professionalization were not just left to the whim of senior and intermediate ranked officers. Following the publication of a Home Office Report in 1967,[15] a new system of policing which enshrined some of the principles of professional policing was introduced in all forces.

Unit Beat Policing represents the change which Cain mentions[16] as a significant departure from the context within which she completed her research. She studied a system of patrolling where each constable was posted to a beat for eight hours.[17] His contact with the station was maintained by scheduled telephone calls and meetings with his supervisory officers. This basic form of policing was supplemented by a van and car patrol which had radio contact with the main force radio system. The work of each constable was therefore as broad as the police mandate itself.

Unit Beat Policing requires each police sub-division to be divided into 'Home Beats'. A Home Beat is policed on foot by a Home Beat constable whose special responsibility is liaison with local schools, social service agencies and other organized groups based on his beat. Through the building up of links within 'the community', the Home Beat officer has a specialism in what has been termed 'community relations'.[18] Furthermore, he is an integral element in the collection of information on known and suspected criminals, as well as being a person who builds up a wide range of contacts with members of the public who might provide information of diverse interest. The Home Beat officer symbolizes the principles of specialization and informed discretion.

During each shift of eight hours, Panda cars, small vehicles manned by a constable, patrol the sub-division. Each car is in contact with the sub-divisional station via a personal radio system (P.R. system). Requests for police assistance are relayed to the Panda units via this system. The principle of specialization is emphasized, Panda drivers tending to be involved in a series of incidents at which police attendance is requested.

Panda vehicles are supplemented by other vehicular patrols which are in contact with both the local station via the P.R. and the force headquarters via the 999 system. The system of specialization is also present here, the officers who man these vehicles dealing with calls for police assistance from members of the public through the emergency telephone system.

A number of constables patrol beats on foot, their work combining the work of Panda patrols and that of Home Beat officers.

All officers carry a personal radio and are in constant contact with their station. Technology and specialization are therefore central to Unit Beat Policing. The notion of 'informed discretion' is found in a more general sense in that Unit Beat Policing has been developed at a time when senior police officers have articulated their understanding of the importance of the role of the police within Britain, stressing the requirements of public accountability.[19]

It is the development of 'managerial professionalism' and Unit Beat Policing which marks the change in the policing of urban Britain since Cain completed her research.

THE PRESENT RESEARCH—HILTON SUB-DIVISION

The police sub-division, Hilton, is situated in an inner area of one of Britain's major cities. Having been policed for many years by the system studied by Cain, at the time of the present research the policing of Hilton and its neighbouring sectional station, Bluecoat, reflected the new system of Unit Beat policing which was introduced during the 1960s. The principles of professional policing were therefore central to the policing of Hilton.

The formal organization of the force was highly specialized, the commitment of most senior officers to an open and accountable police service was well known. Their commitment to 'community relations' and the use of technology was also common knowledge. The formal leadership and orientation of the force was therefore firmly based in professional policing.

At Hilton the policing was organized on the Unit Beat System. Two Panda cars, supplemented by R/T and other vehicles, patrolled during each shift.[20] A few men patrolled on foot, supplementing the six Home Beat constables who worked independently, deciding their own hours of duty and being under the direct command of the Home Beat sergeant. All officers were in contact with Hilton and Bluecoat stations through the personal radio system, which could be linked to the force radio. This meant that foot patrols and all vehicular patrols could be interlinked.

Hilton sub-division was therefore representative of a change from the beat policing studied by Cain to the new Unit Beat System. Furthermore, the training of officers employed in the force and the attitudes of senior officers demonstrated their commitment to the notion of professional policing. The effects of these changes on the occupational culture can therefore be explored.

THE POLICING OF HILTON

That's another old chestnut. The blokes here don't know how to walk a beat, they never get out and meet anybody. I think it's terrible. There is a proper way to walk a beat you know, there's a proper way to do it but do they know? No, they don't. They want to ride around in Panda cars and they don't want to get out and walk around and meet people and talk to people. They just haven't got a clue.
(Home Beat P.C. chatting to colleague about the P.C.s on the reliefs.)

Most of the P.C.s at Hilton, and certainly those on my own shift, joined the Police Service after the introduction of Panda cars and personal radios. The Home Beat P.C. was accurate in his summary of the dominant style of policing performed at Hilton—I could find only two P.C.s on my shift of nineteen men who deviated from this style.[21] However, although one implication of Panda policing is a reluctance to get out of the car and meet people, there are other implications, notably a change in patterns of easing behaviour and an increased interdependency within the work group.

EASING BEHAVIOUR

Because the basic policing was done by Panda drivers and it was commonly thought that it was possible to carry out 'proper policing' only with the use of a motor vehicle, it was likely that a P.C. who was posted to a foot beat would be given a ride during cold, rainy or quiet times. There were three official tea breaks during each shift, as well as a scheduled refreshment period, which meant that the P.C.s could stay in the station for considerable periods of time without fear of rebuke by a supervisory officer.

If it wasn't time for 'ninety-nine'[22] or if one couldn't get a ride in a motor vehicle, P.C.s tended to adopt a number of strategies to remain in the station. In short, if a P.C. was not in the station or in a car, he was on his way to an assigned task, knowing that an official break was within his immediate time schedule. There was little need to engage in easing behaviour.

Apart from a couple of constables who had been at Hilton for a considerable number of years, a large number of them did not know how to go about easing. The early turn shift (6.0 a.m. to 2.0 p.m.) was the most quiet and therefore the shift which would, on Cain's terms, engender the need for easing. However, having just 'tipped the P.C.s out of the nick at 6.30 a.m.', a fellow sergeant expressed his belief in the changing nature of easing as he passed the P.C.s walking to their patrols. He compared Hilton with a neighbouring station at which he had served. 'When I was at Queens Square and it was early turn we had a full breakfast and a couple of cups before eight and it was then time for tea at the nick. Our blokes don't even know where to go; Tom might but he's the only one.'

Although a sergeant, and to a certain extent shielded from the P.C.s' activities, this lack of knowledge by the P.C.s was highlighted during an interview by the chief superintendent with one of the probationary P.C.s who had been at the station for eighteen months. The chief superintendent had been so surprised at the information he gained that he informed the inspector of what had been said. The inspector related this conversation to me. 'I don't know what these blokes think they are up to. The guv'nor had been interviewing P.C. Brown and somewhere along the line he called the writing room the tea room, thought it was the tea room. I ask you, didn't even know it was an operational room; thought it was for tea drinking; all right, eh?'[23] The clear implication is that easing was understood by the P.C.s as a legitimate activity within the confines of the station.

This changed pattern of easing had two important consequences. First, the P.C.s at Hilton had a diminishing number of contacts with the population policed, apart from contacts within the context of official police work. Secondly, if, as Cain suggests and my research verifies, easing is a means of stimulating an interesting situation between bursts of 'real police work', at Hilton such interest was constructed through the technology of Panda policing. Fun and excitement, generated by the use of cars and radios, has replaced the cup of tea and chat in the local shop. The contacts between the police and the population policed which Cain found have diminished rather than increased; this is a change which is contrary to the principles of professional policing.

ACTION

Action, fun and excitement were at the heart of the policing of Hilton. However, as Cain points out, the police world is one of long periods of quiet, interspersed by brief moments of action—fun and excitement are socially constructed and at Hilton part of this construction was related to the use of motor vehicles and personal radios.[24]

The first and obvious point is that driving at speed, no matter what is at the end of the journey, is a stimulating experience. The ability to drive with skill, but more frequently at risk and at speed, was a position of considerable status. During tea breaks conversations about cars provided a constant source of interest; stories of chases were commonplace. During patrolling time no opportunity was missed to drive at high speed.

One night duty a Panda driver asked for directions to the location of a call where some suspects were believed to be breaking-in. This request was made over the P.R. system, meaning that all officers on the sub-division could hear it. A voice came from one of the other P.C.s, 'You want to learn your ground.' He replied. 'I bet I get there first.' Similarly, a dog handler who worked with the shift patrolled in a van. He was called to search an insecure premises and arrived after a short period of time, stopping with a squeal of brakes. As he got out of the van he said to one of the P.C.s present, 'That made them get out of the way at German House [a roundabout several miles away]. We were over there you know when we got your call. Not bad, eh?' There was a wry smile on his face. German House was too far away for the distance to be covered in the time and his banter merely reflects the value of the fast drive.

Although some sergeants disliked their constables driving at high speed because it could mean vehicular accidents, over-reaction at trivial incidents and work in 'clearing up their arrests', given the opportunity they engaged in fast driving themselves. After a fast and at times dangerous drive to an emergency call, the location of which was so far from us that it did not warrant our attention, I said to my colleague who was driving, 'The only reason you drove like that was because you wanted a fast drive'. He replied, 'Yes, well it's a bit of fun, isn't it? It all makes for a bit of excitement and gets rid of headaches. It's all very exciting. Anyway, a fight is really a good call, isn't it?'

Vehicular patrolling has heightened the fun of policing and replaced the interest previously generated by easing activities. Furthermore, it has increased the importance of the work group; satisfaction gained from police work is now confined to the official work context rather than both the official and unofficial work context. The action orientation of urban policing remains and the development of an improved consensus between police and public through the cultivation of a broad range of contacts has been retarded by Unit Beat Policing.

PERSONAL RADIOS

The personal radio system also functioned as a means of enhancing the hedonism of policing. All officers carried a personal radio with them when they patrolled; the 'talk-through' facility meant that when he transmitted, each officer could be heard by the whole sub-division. During a shift of eight hours a great deal of information was passed from officer to officer, as well as from Hilton station to individual officers. If a particular officer wanted a vehicle stopped, if he wanted some advice or, more importantly, if he wanted some assistance at a situation he thought he could not manage, he would ask a colleague to come to his aid. Furthermore, if a message sounded exciting, a fight for example, it could be passed from those officers who had R/T sets in their vehicles to those who did not. The tendency was for all officers to broadcast potentially exciting calls or to call for assistance at the slightest hint of trouble. Hedonism and interdependence were closely related.

On one occasion I was the station officer during a late shift. The communications officers, including a civilian telephonist who had worked at Hilton for many years, were also situated in my office. A call was broadcast to all P.C.s via the P.R. system, by the P.C. who was operator on the R/T car. 'All units Hilton, call to outside . . . woman being assaulted.' From my previous knowledge of policing, I could find no reason for this broadcast and at the time I thought the incident trivial, expecting it to be over by the time any vehicles arrived at the location. There would soon be another call to turn units away. I said to a constable who was in the office, 'How the hell did policemen manage when they were without cars and radios? It's crazy asking people to go to such a call.' The P.C. replied, 'So you would prefer to see a policeman get a hiding, would you, Sarge?' I replied, 'No, but he won't get a hiding, will he? All these technical aids make for bad policing.' He said, 'Well, there wasn't the crime before we had them.' The telephonist had been listening and butted in, 'No, but policemen had just as much to do and they didn't get assaulted.' At this point another message was broadcast calling for other units to cancel.

Following an incident during which a P.C. had hit a coloured youth with his truncheon, another telephonist who had also worked at the station for a considerable number of years related the following comments to me: 'Since the old personal radio came in, I think that instead of talking their way out of trouble like the old coppers did and getting by that way, they just pull their truncheons out and shout for assistance on the P.R. They don't talk their way out of it at all. They just ask for assistance and get their truncheons out.'

Both these incidents illustrate the enhanced hedonism and interdependence which personal radio communication has assisted. They also show that a more sober, consensual notion of practical policing has not resulted from professionalization and the introduction of Unit Beat Policing. The most minor of incidents is still dealt with within a perception of the world as a place of danger and hostility.[25]

THE FIGHT

Like Cain's urban policemen, the policemen of Hilton enjoyed a fight.[26] Indeed, there were times when the chance to be involved in violence was fun; it was something to seek out.

A Home Beat officer was relating an incident during which some gypsies were asked to leave a building site needed for development. Another P.C. was in the room and was listening. 'We went up there and saw the appointed leader and he said, "We will go quietly if we have got to go. If you bring your cops up here there will be trouble."' The P.C. who had been listening and who had been on reserve whilst the negotiations had been taking place, said, 'We should have gone up there then, shouldn't we?' The fight remains an activity of central importance.

A youth club which catered for young black teenagers turned out at about 10.00 p.m. every Friday night. Large numbers, probably in excess of 150 people, spilled out into the roadway but dispersed quickly. There had been very little indication that any police supervision of the club was needed. However, on one particular Friday night, a night on which a television programme dealing with the situation of young blacks in Britain had been shown, it seemed that supervision was necessary.

As the relief drank tea before going out on patrol, one of the probationary constables had mentioned the club and said that he thought that it should be supervised. At that stage I walked into the 'tea room' and heard the inspector say, 'Right, we'll go down there tonight and turn a few of them over; if they are shouting and mucking about we will nick a few.' A sergeant who had been out of the room entered and one of the P.C.s said to him, 'We've got permission to beat up niggers tonight, Sarge; have a few tonight, Sarge.'[27]

There is an element of revenge, a dislike of 'niggers' here, but there is also the chance to get involved in a fight, a tussle. The hedonism of the fight is as important as the policing of a particular racial grouping and certainly more important than a quiet, informed approach to policing.

From this preliminary discussion, it is argued that the definitions of police work held by the urban policemen Cain studied remain; indeed, they have been strengthened. However, the resistance to change which has been found may be explained by extending Cain's analysis of the occupational culture of policing to include features which she failed to emphasize.

THE ECONOMY OF ARREST AND FIGURES

If the fun of the fight, the fast drive and the pursuit are important to urban policemen, so are the economics of arrest. There is a sense in which an economy of trouble is managed; Cain refers to a reluctance to 'over-work a patch'.[28] This was present at Hilton but another, more basic economy was also found.

During the period of my research, the national economy was running at about 25 per cent inflation; all workers, policemen included, were experiencing a decline in purchasing power. One way of adding to one's basic wage was by incurring overtime. Overtime could be taken as extra time off but there was an alternative provision for immediate payment at a handsome level of remuneration. There were means of maximizing overtime.[29] For example, if one arrested and had to go to court on a rest day, overtime would be calculated at a higher rate than if one went to court on any other day. There was always a diligent search for arrests on the Monday following a week on night duty, Tuesday being the rest day. Remand dates were organized to fall on rest days or when the officer was on night duty, another opportunity to increase overtime calculations.

Arrests meant money. After the announcement of what was considered an inadequate pay rise, a P.C. commented to a group of his colleagues, 'I'll have to do a Brown now.' Another P.C. continued, 'Yes, I think that the villains had better watch out now. I've got to get rid of my overdraft and my mortgage will be finished in one more year's pay. So I think the villains had better be watching out.' P.C. Brown was the officer whose arrest work centred around a carefully calculated maximization of overtime.

The economics of arrest were enhanced when a specialist squad was formed. For example, the squad which dealt with football fans at the local First Division ground had a reputation for adequate overtime payments. The following conversation was overheard at a court after some arrests had been made at a match: 'I hear that they are going to remand this lot. *Ching!* [makes noise of cash till]. The old money comes rolling in, doesn't it? I'm rest day today; I'm doing football tonight so that means fourteen hours. Great!' The other P.C. comments, 'All you think of is money. You're like the rest of us, you just think of the money. I'm getting a fair bit of overtime out of this as well.'

Although the fiddling of overtime was contrary to force regulations and occasionally curbed by supervisory officers when abuse became too noticeable to their superiors, the production of arrests in this manner was compatible with the 'figures orientation' of the supervisory officers.

The figures of the number of charges taken at each station provide the indication of success or failure. Introducing me to the station, a fellow sergeant said, 'This is quite a good relief, really.' He went to the charge book and opened it. 'You can see that they do quite well—we've had a lot of crime arrests this night duty.' One night duty I was suddenly bombarded with a series of drunks whom I had to charge. The inspector later said to me, 'Sorry about that but I gave them a bit of a roasting on parade about not doing any work.'

Figures and crime arrests interrelate closely and the indication is that the definition of successful policing, reflected in the figures of recorded arrests, has not been broadened to incorporate the whole of the police mandate. Indeed, arrests which result in profitable overtime payments have tended to advance rather than retard the 'figures orientation' of urban policing.[30]

CONTROL—THE GROUND AND THE CHARGE ROOM

Our knowledge of British policing does not really extend beyond the station canteen or the public inquiry office into the charge room and interviewing rooms of the police station. If the arrest orientation of urban policemen is important so is the place where arrested persons are questioned and charged. The notion of 'personal control' is central to the urban policeman's perspective.[31]

To state that a policeman is an agent of social control is to state the obvious. The feeling of control over his spatial territory and inter-personal encounters is of considerable importance to the constable. The sub-division, the spatial territory policed, belongs to those who police it; officers from neighbouring stations who arrest on it or take a break from their own territory by driving around it are accused of 'poaching' by the rightful claimants to control. Commenting over the P.R. to a P.C. from Bluecoat who had strayed onto Hilton's section, an R/T driver said, 'Get off our ground, Smith, what are you doing on our ground?' The reply came that, 'If you had enough policemen to police it, I would.'

Regulations prescribe that persons arrested for further questioning or charging are to be taken to the police station on whose area they are taken into custody. In practice, the P.C.s would return a prisoner to Hilton if they made an arrest which required investigation and which was just outside the official boundary lines.

After arresting two youths on Bluecoat section for taking a motor vehicle from that same section, the following conversation took place over the P.R. system. The driver of the police vehicle said, 'Two bodies coming to Hilton.' A C.I.D. constable said, 'They nicked it from Hall Road so they might as well go to Bluecoat, then it's a straight red-inker.' (Arrest recorded.) A Hilton P.C. interjected, 'If they come to Hilton we can both have one.' The prisoners were brought to Hilton even though this meant increased administrative work.

There are two reasons for this procedure. First, figures are increased by bringing prisoners to Hilton; prisoners belong to Hilton. Secondly, and of equal importance, control over the questioning and charging process is maximized if one's immediate superiors are dealing with the matter. The 'team work'[32] orientation of policing requires trust and interdependence. One knows the preferences and limits of tolerance of one's supervisory staff; control can be maximized amongst 'the relief'.

'The prisoner' is the personal property of the arresting officer. After arresting a suspect for rape, a P.C. related the following incident to me. 'I found them and put them in the back of my Panda, then John comes up, leaps out of his Panda and gets in the passenger seat of mine. He

turns round to them and says, "I'm arresting you for rape". And that
was it, he wasn't anywhere near.' A short time later a discussion took
place between the two officers. 'Right, decision time; who takes what?'
The imbalance was redressed, 'I take the rapist and you take the other
one.'

The personal investment which arresting officers held in their
prisoners could be violated by another P.C. if he was called to assist in
questioning—a division of labour existed for such purposes. Furthermore, possession could be mortgaged or freely given to those who
wanted to go to court to get overtime or to those who 'needed the
figures'. The notion of personal control and possession remains.

One statutory means of intervention existed for the supervisory
officers whose job it was to ensure proper conduct whilst the prisoner
was in the station. There were many official rules surrounding the
supervision of prisoners in police stations—there is one central unofficial
rule and that is that the person arrested must co-operate. The primary
sign of co-operation is verbal admission of guilt and a willingness to
submit to the control of the investigation officers. Tone of voice,
demeanour, the rejection of evidence, refusal to be searched without
question—these are negative signs which require management.[33]

The rank structure which exists within the police service can result
in a contest for control between the arresting officer and the station
officer. A newly promoted sergeant illustrated the point when discussing
the problems of controlling the charge room. 'I dislike having to go in
the charge room and find about five police officers around one prisoner,
asking questions. You have to get in and ask if they mind you asking
one. I like to try and make sure that I am in the charge room as soon
as the prisoner comes in.'

Control must remain with the sergeant, even if he agrees with the
prisoner's view, against that of the arresting officer. A squatter had been
arrested by two C.I.D. constables and a uniform P.C. for possession of
a controlled drug—a minute trace of an unknown substance in a used
syringe. The sergeant turned to the officers, all being in the visual and
verbal presence of the prisoner, and said, 'What's all this shit? You're
not interested in that are you? You're not seriously interested in that?'
One of the detectives said, 'No, I'm not interested in it at all but it
was found there and we have to find out what is going on.' Another
constable said that he would complete the administration of the charge.
The sergeant looks at them in disgust and begins to leave the charge
room when the prisoner says to him, 'Now, you're surely not going to
do me for that? I'm trying to get off the stuff and you won't help me
at all if you do me for that. It's as offensive to me as it is to you.' The
sergeant said, 'I don't know what I'm going to do but I'll make my own
mind up, thank you.' The prisoner should not attempt to control the
situation in the charge room.

The centrality of personal control lends resistance to attempts to

break into the protective bonds of the work group and therefore prohibits the creation of a more accountable and legally bound police
service.

VIOLENCE

To some police officers co-operation means an admission of guilt,
despite sufficient evidence to substantiate an offence without such an
admission.

If a prisoner was to be charged with a criminal offence during night
duty, the C.I.D. had to be informed. The night duty C.I.D. usually
consisted of about five officers, under the leadership of a detective
sergeant who, when informed of an arrest, would visit to ensure that
the matter had been fully investigated. On some occasions, this officer
would interview the prisoner.

During one night duty the C.I.D. sergeant had been called and was
interviewing a prisoner arrested for attempted burglary. He went to
the cells with two temporary detective constables (T.D.C.). The two
T.D.C.s came from the cells and said to the uniformed station officer,
'He did that to one of mine; they were admitting it and he started and
they pleaded not guilty.' This comment intimated violence to me. The
C.I.D. sergeant soon appeared from the cell and said, 'He's going to
make a statement under caution admitting that he went to the flat and
if anything had been there he would have stolen it.' A T.D.C. went to
the cell and I saw him begin to write a statement.

I went to the station office and suggested to the station officer that
the detective sergeant had used violence. He replied, 'Yes, he hit one
of my prisoners not long ago; it's always best if you only hit your own
prisoner. Mind you, I had a bloke here at that time and I didn't lay
a finger on him because I had had a few investigations against me and I
didn't want any trouble. You see, the slags around here expect a bit of
a rough time when they come in here; they expect it. They don't admit
anything unless they get it.'

Within the police station, one use of violence is the gaining of evidence
of admission and as such is an important element of the occupational
culture.[34] The 'extra-legal' remedy remains as crucial to urban policing
under professionalization and Unit Beat Policing as it was at the time
of Cain's research.

CONCLUSION

The professionalization of the British Police Service was initially based
in the training and practice of supervisory and specialist officers rather
than in the values and strategies of control found in the occupational
culture of constables and sergeants.[35] 'Managerial professionalism' has
been separated from the practical policing carried out by constables

and sergeants who fulfil the total police mandate in face-to-face encounters.

My research in an urban police sub-division, Hilton, reveals the continuing dominance of the primary occupational values which Cain found prior to the professionalization of the service and the introduction of Unit Beat Policing. Indeed, it has been established that when the principles of professionalism are coupled to this new system of policing, the 'practical professionalism'[36] of the work force is enhanced rather than curtailed.

Apart from those features which are discussed by Cain, resistance to change is strengthened by elements of the occupational culture which have been neglected by sociologists of the British police. The experience of control over both the geographical area and population which is policed, the use of violence in achieving this experience and the importance of monetary as well as occupational success by the making of arrests, prevent the development of greater accountability and a more open definition of policing in which broad links between the police and the local population are stressed.

Two notions of professional policing can be found in the British police service. Managerial professionalism is represented by the specialist function of, for example, community liaison, training and administrative officers, as well as in the theory of police management and the policy statements of chief officers. This is the public image of policing which is fostered by senior officers and the Home Office. Practical professionalism remains a series of hedonistic, protective and highly practical activities and values which are largely opposed to those of managerial professionalism. Practical professionalism represents the routine policing of urban Britain.

These two notions of professionalism are separated within the system Unit Beat Policing, which has been adapted by constables and sergeants to retain the dominant orientation of practical professionalism. Vehicular policing has enhanced the hedonism of policing and the technology of radio communications has increased the interdependency of the work group. Most importantly, the specialization of the work force which is contained within this system of policing has restricted the broadening of links between the police and the community which is policed, as well as the creation of a more accountable and sensitive police service.

Foot patrols and Panda drivers are specialists who practice the practical professionalism of 'real police work'. It is the Home Beat constables who specialize in the retention of links between the police and the local community; but Home Beat constables are not defined as 'real policemen' by their colleagues. I return to the initial conversation between two Home Beat constables at Hilton who are overheard by a foot patrol as they discuss the policing of the area. 'I gave a young officer here a lift yesterday and he was going on about niggers this and

Changes in urban policing 135

niggers that and niggers the other. It was disgraceful, I can tell you, terrible. I told him, "Well, look, we get rough stuff here, 'course we do, we get some rubbish and we get some white rubbish as well." Yes, that's what I said. You've got to live here and you've got to understand that when you get kiddies who live in rotten slums with a rat infested piss-hole in the backyard and Dad comes home and thumps Mum around, what chance have you got? You've got to understand that that's how they live and you've got to get out on the ground to understand that. These youngsters just don't understand that.' The constable from my shift who had overheard these remarks left the room and retorted, 'Bloody social worker'.

Simon Holdaway B.A.
Lecturer in Sociology
University of Sheffield

Notes

1. Maureen Cain, *Society and the Policeman's Role*, Routledge & Kegan Paul, 1973. Reference should also be made to Michael Banton, *The Policeman in the Community*, Tavistock, 1964, John Lambert, *Crime, Police and Race Relations*, Oxford University Press, 1970, and Ben Whitaker, *The Police*, Penguin, 1964. Useful discussions of the police can be found in Steven Box, *Deviance, Reality and Society*, Holt, Rinehart and Winston, 1971, and Paul Rock, *Deviant Behaviour*, Hutchinson, 1973. Also see Peter K. Manning, 'Rules, Colleagues and Situationally Justified Action' in R. Blankenship (ed.), *Colleagues in Organisations: the Social Construction of Professional Work*, New York, John Wiley, forthcoming; 'Dramatic Aspects of Policing: Selected Propositions', *Sociology and Soc. Res.*, vol. 59, no. 1 (October 1974), pp. 21–9; and 'Police Lying', *Urban Life and Culture*, vol. 3, no. 3 (October 1974), pp. 283–306. This paper is concerned with the British police and in the main body of the text no attempt is made to draw parallels with the American police, which poses some largely unexplored comparative problems.

2. For research on 'social work' and 'service' aspects of policing see Maurice Punch and Trevor Naylor, 'The police: a social service', *New Society*, vol. 24, 17 (May 1973), pp. 358–61; E. Cumming et al., 'Policeman as Philosopher, Friend and Guide', *Social Problems*, vol. 12, no. 3 (Winter 1964), pp. 277–286 reports the American context.

3. The evidence from participant observation is given in a series of 'central statements' which sum up the dominant themes found during the research. All names used are fictional and provide no suggestion of the identity of persons and places cited in the text.

4. Cain, op. cit., pp. 46–75 and 190–2.

5. The notion of an 'occupational culture of American Policing' is discussed in Peter K. Manning, 'The Police: Mandate, Strategies and Appearances' in J. D. Douglas (ed.), *Crime and Justice in American Society*, Indianapolis, Bobbs Merrill, 1971.

6. E. C. Hughes, *Men and their Work*, The Free Press, 1958, pp. 42–55 and 131–44.

7. Royal Commission on the Police, *Final Report*, Cmnd 1728, H.M.S.O. 1962.

8. The National Police College trains officers of supervisory rank for the most senior posts within the Police Service. For an account of the development of the college see Philip John Stead, 'The Idea of Police College' in J. C. Alderson and Philip John Stead (eds.), *The Police We Deserve*, Wolfe, 1973.

9. For example, see E. Greenwood, 'Attributes of a Profession', *Social Work*, vol. 2 (July 1957), pp. 44–55.

10. For a useful criticism of the 'trait approach' see Terence Johnson, *Profession and Power*, Macmillan, 1972; also Hughes, op. cit.

11. See Manning, in Douglas op. cit., 1971, for a discussion of the professionalization of the American police, which, interestingly, would seem to have some similarity to the British context.

12. This is not a term taken from the writings of police officers. The manner in which the term is used sums up a number of themes which can be found in, for example, J. C. Alderson and Philip John Stead, op. cit., and John Brown and Graham Howe (eds.), *The Police and the Community*, Saxon House, 1976. However, it does relate closely to the notion of the 'due process' model of the criminal process. Herbert Packer, 'Two Models of the Criminal Process', *University of Pennsylvania Law Review*, vol. 113 (November 1964), pp. 1–68. For a discussion on the inevitability of discretionary enforcement see A. Keith Bottomley, *Decisions in the Penal Process*, Martin Robertson, 1973, pp. 37–43.

13. Two inquiries are of particular importance: the inquiry into the action of Detective Sergeant Challenor, *Report of Enquiry by Mr A. E. James, Q.C.*, Cmnd 2735, H.M.S.O., 1965, and that into the the use of violence against prisoners by Sheffield Police, *Sheffield Police Appeal Enquiry*, Cmnd 2176, H.M.S.O., 1963.

14. See J. C. Alderson, 'The principles and practice of the British police', in J. C. Alderson and Philip John Stead, op. cit., for a police officer's statement. A sociologist has discussed this emphasis but the exact relevance of senior officers' definitions of policing to the work of constables is not considered. See Keith Macdonald, 'A Police State in Britain', *New Society*, 8 January 1976.

15. Home Office, *Police Manpower, Equipment and Efficiency;* Reports of three working parties, H.M.S.O., 1967. Links between new systems of policing and the training of supervisory officers in 'management techniques' are mentioned in this report.

16. Cain, op. cit., pp. 238–46.

17. Mike Chatterton, 'Images of Police Work and the Uses of Rules: Super-

vision and Patrol Work under the Fixed Points System', unpublished manuscript presented at the Third Bristol Conference on the Sociology of the Police, 1975, also discusses such a system of policing.

18. 'Community Relations' should be distinguished from race relations. The former covers the range of police contact with the whole of the community which is policed. Most forces have appointed Community Liaison Officers on a divisional basis and in the force which is described later a Community Liaison Officer of intermediate rank worked on the division of which Hilton was a part.

19. Of course, there are disagreements amongst chief officers on the nature of such accountability. The main issue is the introduction of an independent element into the procedure for the investigation of complaints against the police.

20. The working day was divided into three shifts of eight hours: 6 a.m.–2 p.m., 2 p.m.–10 p.m., and 10 p.m.–6 a.m.

21. J. Q. Wilson, *Varieties of Police Behaviour*, Cambridge, Mass., Harvard University Press, 1968, represents an American text which is yet to be related to the British police. The Home Beat officers' summary is, of course, not particularly relevant to Wilson's typology.

22. This was the message which was broadcast over the P.R. system to signify a tea break.

23. This was not an indication of a lack of knowledge concerning 'easing'. This officer showed considerable prowess in many aspects of the occupational culture, despite his short length of service.

24. Jonathan Rubenstein, *City Police*, Ballantine Books, 1973, is an ethnography of American policing in which the use of radio communication and its implication for policing is considered.

25. The relevance of 'danger' and 'hostility' to the occupational culture has been noted by students of American police work. See especially, J. Skolnick, *Justice Without Trial*, New York, John Wiley, 1966, and William Westley, *Violence and the Police: A Sociological*

Changes in urban policing

Study of Law, Custom and Morality, Cambridge, Mass., M.I.T. Press, 1970.

26. Cain, op. cit., pp. 64–65.

27. In fact, other commitments prevented special attention being given to the club on this night. The author has evidence which suggests that 'blacks' were not subjected to 'special policing' and that this illustration would also be representative of a group of white youths.

28. Cain, op. cit., p. 65.

29. Jonathan Rubenstein, op cit., p. 167 refers to the use of arrest to increase overtime in his study of American policing.

30. This factor is relevant to the debate concerning the construction of official statistics. For a discussion of research in this area see A. Keith Bottomley, op. cit., esp. 43–77.

31. Paul Rock op. cit., p. 182, and Egon Bittner, 'The police and Skid Row' *Amer. Soc. Rev.*, vol. 32, no. 5, 1967, pp. 699–715.

32. Erving Goffman, *The Presentation of Self in Everyday Life*, Penguin, 1959, pp. 83–108.

33. I. Piliavin and S. Briar, 'Police encounters with juveniles', *Amer. J.*

Sociol. vol. 70 (1964), pp. 206–14, has implications for a wider 'clientele' and is relevant to the questioning procedure conducted in police stations.

34. William Westley, op. cit., deals with the American police but further research completed by the present author indicates that Westley's analysis requires revision when related to the British police; the present paper prevents discussion of the issues involved.

35. There have been a number of recent examples of managerial professionalism being practised in situations where armed offenders have held hostages. In each example the senior officer in command has had total supervision of every strategy of control used and the constables and sergeants employed have no freedom to use their discretion.

36. 'Practical professionalism' is a notion which deviates from the usual, range of applications of the sociological concept of 'a profession'. Its introduction is intended to emphasize the importance of 'appropriate practice' to be found in the policing of Hilton by the officers observed and therefore its relationship to 'managerial professionalism'.

[24]

SOCIAL PROBLEMS, Vol. 30, No. 5, June 1983

PRIVATE SECURITY: IMPLICATIONS FOR SOCIAL CONTROL*

CLIFFORD D. SHEARING
PHILIP C. STENNING
University of Toronto

Private security has become a pervasive feature of modern North American policing, both because of its rapid growth since 1960 and because it has invaded the traditional domain of the public police. Because this development has been viewed as an addendum to the criminal justice system, its significance for social control has not been recognized. This paper traces the development of private security in Canada and the United States since 1960, examines the reasons for its present pervasiveness, and explores its essential features: it is non-specialized, victim-oriented, and relies on organizational resources as sanctions. We conclude that private security is having a major impact on the nature of social control.

One of the most striking features of social control in North America is the pervasive presence of private security, which embraces a wide variety of services from security guards to computer fraud investigators, from home burglar alarms to sophisticated industrial and commercial surveillance systems, from anti-bugging devices to anti-terrorist "executive protection" courses. Private security offers protection for both persons and property which is often more comprehensive than that provided by public police forces. Internal security—so-called "in-house security"—has traditionally been provided by "corporate entities" (Coleman, 1974) such as profit-making corporations, and public institutions such as schools. Since the early 1960s there has been an enormous growth in "contract security," which provides police services on a fee-for-service basis to anyone willing to pay.

Private security is not a new phenomenon. Self-help and the sale of protection as a commodity have a long history (Becker, 1974; Radzinowicz, 1956). Even after the state sought to monopolize public protection through the establishment of public police forces in the 19th century, private interests continued to provide additional protection for themselves through private security (Spitzer and Scull, 1977). What is new about modern private security is its pervasiveness and the extent to which its activities have expanded into public, rather than purely private, places. In urban environments at least, private security is now ubiquitous and is likely to be encountered by city dwellers at home (especially if they live in an apartment building or on a condominium estate), at work, when shopping or banking, when using public transit, or when going to a sports stadium, university, or hospital.

In this paper we consider the extent and nature of modern private security in Canada and the United States and its implications for social control. In doing so, we draw on the findings of research which we and our colleagues have undertaken since the early 1970s in Canada. This has included a series of studies of the legal context within which private security operates (Freedman and Stenning, 1977; Stenning, 1981; Stenning and Cornish, 1975; Stenning and Shearing, 1979); a major survey of the contract security industry—guard and investigative agencies—in the province of Ontario during 1976, which involved interviews with security agency executives and the administration of a questionnaire to their employees (Shearing et al., 1980); a similar, but less extensive, survey of "in-house" security organizations in Ontario in 1974 (Jeffries, 1977); an examination of the available national statistics on the size and growth of private security in

* This is a revised version of a paper presented at the 33rd annual meeting of the American Society of Criminology in Washington, D.C., November, 1981. The authors thank John Gilmore and the anonymous *Social Problems* reviewers for their comments. Correspondence to: Centre of Criminology, University of Toronto, 8th Floor, John Robarts Library, 130 St. George Street, Toronto, Ontario M5S 1A1, Canada.

494   SHEARING AND STENNING

Canada between 1961 and 1971 (Farnell and Shearing, 1977); and three related studies of police, client, and public perceptions of private security, focussing primarily on the province of Ontario, using both interviews and questionaires during 1982.

Most studies of formal social control within sociology have focused on systems of state control. They view law, justice, and the maintenance of public order as having been virtual state monopolies since early in the 19th century. Even those studies focusing on private forms have typically examined those instances in which state functions have been contracted out to private organizations (Scull, 1977), thus implicitly reinforcing the notion of a state monopoly over such functions (Cohen, 1979).[1]

The few sociologists who have studied the modern development of private security (Becker, 1974; Bunyan, 1977; Kakalik and Wildhorn, 1977) have, with few exceptions (Spitzer and Scull, 1977), broadly followed this tradition and have treated private security as little more than a private adjunct to the public criminal justice system. They assume that private security is essentially a private form of public policing, and that it can be understood in the same way as the public police.

We argue that this approach to understanding private security is inadequate because it fails to account for some of the most important differences between private security and public police and, more importantly, between the contexts within which each operates. The context in which private security functions is not public law and the criminal justice system, but what Henry (1978:123) has called "private justice." We follow the view of legal pluralists who maintain that "in any given society there will be as many legal systems as there are functioning social units" (Pospisil, 1967:24).

We begin by examining the size and growth of private security in Canada and the United States. Then we look at changes in the urban environment which have been associated with the involvement of private security in maintaining public order. Finally we consider various features of private security: who supports it, its authority, its organizational features, and its relationship to the public police.

THE SIZE AND GROWTH OF PRIVATE SECURITY[2]

While private security has probably existed in one form or another in North America since the continent was first settled by Europeans, little is known about its practice prior to the mid-19th century. Older accounts contain no reliable information about the size and growth of private security (Horan, 1967; Johnson, 1976; Lipson, 1975.) It was not until 1969 that the first major study of contract security was undertaken in the United States (Kakalik and Wildhorn, 1971), and not until these researchers revised their findings in 1977, in the light of 1970 census data, that a reasonably complete picture of size and growth trends became available. For Canada, the available statistical information is even less adequate.

Table 1 provides a summary of the statistics available for the United States and Canada respectively. We emphasize, however, that because of definitional difficulties and unreliable record-keeping practices, these figures are at best approximate. Table 1 shows that in the United States in 1960, private security almost equalled the public police in number. By 1970, both sectors had experienced substantial growth, with public police outdistancing private security. The early 1970s show a significant slowdown in the growth of public police, but a continued escalation in the growth of private security, especially in the contract security sector; by 1975,

---

1. An exception to this is the research on dispute resolution, especially that done by anthropologists (Nader, 1980; Pospisil, 1978; Snyder, 1981).
2. For a more detailed analysis of current statistics on the size and growth of private security see Shearing and Stenning (1981:198).

Private Security

495

TABLE 1

Public Police and Private Security Personnel, in Thousands (Rounded)

	Police		Security						Ratio of Police to Security	Ratio of In-house to Contract
		% Increase	In-house	% Increase	Contract	% Increase	Total	% Increase		
UNITED STATES										
1960[a]	258		192		30		222		1.2:1	6:1
		51		15		103		27		
1970[a]	390		220		61		281		1.4:1	3.5:1
		5		18		187		55		
1975[b]	411		260		175		435		0.9:1	1.5:1
CANADA										
1971[c]	40		25		11.5		36.5		1.1:1	2.2:1
		30		14		65		32		
1975[d]	51		29		19		48		1.1:1	1.5:1

Sources:

a. Adapted from table 2.11 "Security Employment Trends by Type of Employer" (Kakalik and Wildhorn, 1977:43).

b. Police strength figure derived from U.S. Department of Justice, Federal Bureau of Investigation (1976:26). Private security figures, which are estimates only, adapted from Predicasts, Inc. (1974:26).

c. Adapted from Farnell and Shearing (1977).

d. Adapted from Friendly (1980).

private security outnumbered public police. Between 1960 and 1975 the ratio of in-house to contract security diminished from 6:1 to 1.5:1, indicating a major restructuring of the organization of private security.[3]

Directly comparable data on the growth of private security in Canada from 1960 to 1970 are not available.[4] Census data suggest, however, that growth rates within the contract security sector may have been as high as 700 percent (Farnell and Shearing, 1977:113). By 1971, however, there were almost as many private security as public police in Canada, but in-house personnel still outnumbered contract security by more than 2 to 1. Within the next four years, both public police and private security personnel continued to increase, at approximately the same rate (30 percent). Within private security, however, contract security increased 65 percent, a rate almost five times that of the rate of growth of in-house security.

While reliable national statistics since 1975 are not available, statistics for the province of Ontario (which have in the past proved a good indicator of national trends) indicate a levelling off of contract security growth during the latter half of the 1970s. Overall, contract security in Ontario appears to have increased 90 percent from 1971 to 1980, while the growth rate of public police during the same period was 29 percent (Waldie et al., 1982:8). Assuming that there has been no absolute numerical decline in in-house security, this almost certainly means that in Ontario (and probably the rest of Canada) private security now outnumbers the public police. Furthermore, contract security alone now rivals the public police numerically. In Ontario, by 1980, there were three contract security personnel for every four public police officers—15,000 contract security, and just under 20,000 public police officers (Waldie et al., 1982:9).

3. Reliable data for the United States since 1975 are not yet available.

4. Although 1961 and 1971 census data are available they cannot be compared to establish growth rates due to changes in category definitions (Farnell and Shearing, 1977:39).

These findings indicate that in Canada and the United States the public police have for some time shared the task of policing with private organizations, and that private security probably now outnumber public police in both countries. The major change has been the rapid growth, since the early 1960s, of policing provided on a contract basis, for profit, by private enterprise (Spitzer and Scull, 1977). This has established private security as a readily available alternative to public police for those with the means to afford it, and has made private security a much more visible contributor to policing than it has been hitherto. The result has been an unobtrusive but significant restructuring of our institutions for the maintenance of order, and a substantial erosion by the private sector of the state's assumed monopoly over policing and, by implication, justice.

MASS PRIVATE PROPERTY

To understand the locus of private security it is necessary to examine the changes that have taken place, particularly since the early 1950s, in the organization of private property and public space. In North America many public activities now take place within huge, privately owned facilities, which we call "mass private property." Examples include shopping centers with hundreds of individual retail establishments, enormous residential estates with hundreds, if not thousands, of housing units, equally large office, recreational, industrial, and manufacturing complexes, and many university campuses. While evidence of these developments surrounds every city dweller, there is little data on how much public space in urban areas is under private control (Bourne and Harper, 1974:213, Lorimer, 1972:21). However, the available data does indicate an enormous increase in mass private property.

Spurr (1975:18) surveyed 60 major companies producing new urban residential accommodation in 24 Canadian metropolitan centers:

> Forty-seven firms hold 119,192 acres (186 square miles) of land, including 34 firms which each own more than one square mile. . . . Forty-two firms hold 95,174 apartment units including 13 firms with 123 apartment buildings. Twenty-nine firms have 223 office and other commercial buildings, while 23 firms have nearly 26,000,000 square feet of commercial space. While these commercial and apartment figures may appear large, the survey is particularly incomplete in these areas. Finally, twenty-seven firms have 185 shopping centres and sixteen firms own 38 hotels.

Gertler and Crowley (1977:289) used data collected by Punter (1974) to study four townships within 40 miles of Toronto, from 1954 to 1971. They identified

> . . . two striking changes in the ownership patterns. Absentee ownership by individuals increased from less than 5 per cent of total area to about 20 per cent; and corporate ownership of the land which was negligible in 1954 increased to more than 20 per cent in 1971, with increases occurring particularly in the investment-developer category.

Martin (1975:21), in a study of the north-east Toronto fringe, found that corporations represented 22 per cent of all buyers and 16 per cent of all sellers. He argued that these transactions represented "the nucleus of land dealer activities in the study area between 1968 and 1974" (1975:27). Gertler and Crowley (1977:290) comment on these findings:

> Land development has changed from an activity carried out by a large number of small builder/developers in the 1950s to a process in the seventies which is increasingly shaped by large public companies. These firms are vertically integrated, that is, organized to handle the entire development package from land assembly to planning and design, construction, property management, and marketing.

The modern development of mass private property has meant that more and more public life now takes place on property which is privately owned. Yet the policing needs of such privately owned public places have not been met by the public police for two reasons. First, the routine "beat" of the public police has traditionally been confined to publicly owned property such as streets and parks (Stinchcombe, 1963). Therefore, even when they have had the resources to police privately owned public places—and typically they have not—they have been philosophically disinclined to do so. Second, those who own and control mass private property have commonly preferred to retain and exercise their traditional right to preserve order on their own property and to maintain control over the policing of it, rather than calling upon the public police to perform this function.

Because more and more public places are now located on private property, the protection of property—which lies at the heart of private security's function—has increasingly come to include the maintenance of public order, a matter which was, hitherto, regarded as the more or less exclusive prerogative of the public police. With the growth of mass private property, private security has been steadily encroaching upon the traditional beat of the public police. In so doing, it has brought areas of public life that were formerly under state control under the control of private corporations.

LEGITIMATION OF PRIVATE SECURITY AUTHORITY

The close association between private security and private property provides its most important source of social legitimation as an alternative to systems of public justice, and helps to explain why its development has proceeded with so little opposition. Because the development of modern institutions of public justice (during the early 19th century) necessarily involved the conferring of exceptional authority, such as police powers, on public officials, it has required legislative action and all the public debate which that engenders (Baldwin and Kinsey, 1980). By contrast, the development of private security has required virtually no legislation and has generated little public interest. This is because the authority of private security derives not so much from exceptional powers as from the ordinary powers and privileges of private property owners to control access to, use of, and conduct on, their property. While modern private security guards enjoy few or no exceptional law enforcement powers, their status as agents of property allows them to exercise a degree of legal authority which in practice far exceeds that of their counterparts in the public police. They may insist that persons submit to random searches of their property or persons as a condition of entry to, or exit from, the premises. They may even require clients to surrender their property while remaining on the premises, and during this time they may lawfully keep them under more or less constant visual or electronic surveillance. Before allowing clients to use the premises (or property such as a credit card) they may insist that clients provide detailed information about themselves, and authorize them to seek personal information from others with whom they have dealings. Private security may use such information for almost any purpose, and even pass it on, or sell it, to others.

In theory, the public can avoid the exercise of such private security authority by declining to use the facilities, as either customers or employees. In practice, however, realistic alternatives are often not available; for example, airport security applies to all airlines. This is a function of both the modern trend toward mass private property, and the fact that more and more public places are now situated on private property. Between them, these trends result in a situation in which the choices available to consumers are often severely limited. Employees and customers alike must submit to the authority of property owners and their agents as a condition of use. Thus, because private security is so pervasive, and because it is found in so many services and facilities essential to modern living (employment, credit, accommodation, education, health, transportation), it is practically impossible to avoid.

The fact that private security derives so much of its legitimacy from the institution of private property involves a profound historical irony. In the United States and Canada, state power has historically been perceived as posing the greatest threat to individual liberty. The legal institutions of private property and privacy arguably evolved as a means of guaranteeing individuals a measure of security against external intrusions, especially intrusions by the state (Reich, 1964; Stinchcombe, 1963). These institutions defined an area of privacy to which the state was denied access without consent, other than in exceptional circumstances. On private property, therefore, the authority of the property owner was recognized as being paramount — a philosophy most clearly reflected in the adage, "a man's home is his castle."

The validity of this notion, however, requires a reasonable congruence between private property and private places: a man's home was his castle, not because it was private property as such, but because it was a private place. However, as more and more private property has become, in effect, public, this congruence has been eroded. The emergence of mass private property, in fact, has given to private corporations a sphere of independence and authority which in practice has been far greater than that enjoyed by individual citizens and which has rivaled that of the state. The legal authority originally conceded to private property owners has increasingly become the authority for massive and continuous intrusions upon the privacy of citizens (as customers and employees) by those who own and control the mass private property on which so much public life takes place. Nevertheless, the traditional association between the institution of private property and the protection of liberty has historically been such a powerful source of legitimacy that, despite these important changes in the nature of private property, the exercise of private security authority is rarely questioned or challenged.

What little resistance has occured has been mainly in the workplace, and has taken one or both of two forms — one an "underground" movement, and the other a more open and organized phenomenon. The underground movment is apparent in a "hidden economy" (Henry, 1978) of systematic pilfering, unofficial "perks," "padding" of claims for sickness benefits and other forms of compensation, as means of circumventing the formal structures and procedures established to protect corporate assets and profits. While such resistance sometimes occurs on a grand scale, it is mostly informal and individualistic.

Labor unions have posed a more formal and openly organized challenge to the unrestricted exercise of private security authority. They have fought private security processes and procedures through industrial action, collective bargaining, and arbitration. For example, in our research we have encountered collective agreements containing clauses specifying in detail the occasions on which employees may be searched, the procedures to be used in such searches, and the processes to be followed in the event that employees come under suspicion (Stenning and Shearing, 1979:179). Indeed, the growing body of so-called "arbitral jurisprudence" suggests there may be a trend toward a greater degree of accountability within private justice in the industrial and commercial sectors, just as the growing body of administrative law suggests a similar trend in the public domain (Arthurs, 1979).

To regard such developments simply as resistance to the growth of private security, however, is obviously overly simplistic, since in an important way they serve to institutionalize and legitimate it. When private security has been negotiated rather than imposed, its legitimacy is enhanced, co-opting the unions in the process. Furthermore, as private security procedures become more formalized and institutionalized they are often abandoned in favour of newer, less formal, and more flexible ones. An example of this is the replacement of formal arbitration by informal on-site mediation processes. Other researchers have noted similar reactions in the fields of administrative and labor law (Arthurs, 1980; Zack, 1978).

THE NATURE OF PRIVATE SECURITY

Three characteristics of private security reveal its essential nature: (1) its non-specialized character; (2) its client-defined mandate; and (3) the character of the sanctions it employs. We discuss each of these in turn.

Non-Specialized Character

The criminal justice system is divided into many specialized divisions and employs people in distinct roles, such as police, prosecutors, defence counsel, judiciary, and correctional officers. In contrast, we have found that private security is often integrated with other organizational functions, as the following example illustrates.

One of the companies which we studied operated a chain of retain outlets selling fashionable clothing for teenagers and young adults. Officials of the company emphasized that security was one of their principal concerns, because the company operated in a competitive market with slender profit margins. The company tried to improve its competitive position by reducing its losses, and boasted that it had one of the lowest loss-to-sales ratios in the industry. In accounting for this, officials pointed to the success of their security measures. Yet the company employed only one specialized security officer; security was not organizationally separated into discrete occupational roles. Rather, officials attributed responsibility for security to every employee. Moreover, employees typically did not undertake security activities distinct from their other occupational activities. Security functions were regarded as most effective when they were embedded in other functions. For example, officials believed that good sales strategies made good security strategies: if sales persons were properly attentive to customers, they would not only advance sales but simultaneously limit opportunities for theft. The security function was thus seen as embedded in the sales function.

What, then, is the role of specialized persons such as security guards? Our survey of contract security guards indicated that, while they frequently engaged in such specialized security functions as controlling access to commercial facilities (26 percent), they were employed mainly to supervise the performance of security functions by non-specialized personnel (Shearing *et al.*, 1980). Thus 48 percent reported that the problem most frequently encountered was the carelessness of other employees. An important element of the security function, therefore, was to check on employees after hours, to see whether they had kept up with their security responsibilities by seeing whether doors had been left unlocked or valuable goods or confidential papers had been left in the open. When they discovered such failings, security guards would inform the employee's supervisor, using strategies such as the one described by Luzon (1978:41):

> In support of the project drive for theft reduction, Atlantic Richfield security instituted an evening patrol, still in effect. For each risk found, the patrolling officer fills out and leaves a courteous form, called a "snowflake," which gives the particular insecure condition found, such as personal valuable property left out, unlocked doors, and valuable portable calculators on desks. A duplicate of each snowflake is filed by floor and location, and habitual violators are interviewed. As a last resort, compliance is sought through the violator's department manager.

This feature of private security is reminiscent of the pre-industrial, feudal policing system in Britain known as "frankpledge," in which policing was the responsibility of all community members, was integrated with their other functions, and was supervised by a small number of specialized security persons — sheriffs and constables — designated to ensure that community members were exercising their security responsibilities properly (Critchley, 1978). This non-specialized character of private security, however, creates particular difficulties in numerically comparing private security with public police and in attempting to measure the extent of the shift in policing from public to private hands.

Client-Defined Mandate

The mandate and objectives of private security, we found, were typically defined in terms of the particular interests and objectives of those who employed them. Table 2 presents results from our study of contract security in Ontario, which show that the employers of private security are

TABLE 2

Classification of Five Largest Clients

Client	Type of Contract Security Agency					
	Guard (N = 19)		Investigator (N = 26)		G. & I. (N = 47)	
	%[a]	Rank	%[a]	Rank	%[a]	Rank
Industrial	42	1	31	5	70	1
Lawyers	5	c	92	1	28	c
Construction	32	2		b	55	2
Shopping Mall	21	5	35	4	36	4
Offices	32	2		b	45	3
Hospitals	10	c		b	30	5
Education	32	2		b	21	c
Insurance		b	69	2	17	c
Citizens	5	c	54	3	19	c
Government	21	5	15	c	28	c

Notes:
  a. As a result of multiple responses, percentages do not total 100.
  b. Client type not mentioned.
  c. Client type mentioned but not ranked within first five.
Source:
  Adapted from Shearing *et al.*, (1980).

most commonly private industrial and commercial corporations. Furthermore, we found that contract security agencies, in their advertising, appeared to assume that their major audience was made up of executives of private corporations, and that they typically promoted their services on the basis that they would increase profits by reducing losses (Shearing, *et al.*, 1980:163). While we do not have exactly comparable data revealing the distribution of in-house security, there is every reason to believe that here too private industrial and commercial corporations are the major users.

Private security is most typically a form of "policing for profit" (Spitzer and Scull, 1977:27) — that is, policing which is tailored to the profit-making objectives and its corporate clients. In those cases in which the principal objective of the clients is not the making of profit (e.g. where the client's principal objective is to provide health services, education, or entertainment) it will be that objective which will shape and determine the mandate and activities of private security.

This client orientation has important implications for the nature of policing undertaken by private security, and serves to distinguish it from public policing. In the criminal justice system, the state is nominally impartial and individuals are judged in terms of crimes against the public interest. By contrast, private security defines problems in purely instrumental terms; behavior is judged not according to whether it offends some externally defined moral standards, but whether it threatens the interests (whatever they may be) of the client. This establishes a definition of social order which is both more extensive and more limited than that defined by the state; more extensive because it is concerned with matters such as absenteeism or breaches of confidentiality (Gorrill, 1974:98) which may threaten the interests of the client but are not violations of the law; more limited because it is not normally concerned with violations of the law — such as some victimless crimes — which are not perceived as threatening the interests of the client.

In this sense, policing by private security is essentially victim-controlled policing. Corporate victims can maintain order without having to rely exclusively, or even primarily, on the criminal justice system. By establishing their own private security organizations directed to maintaining their own definitions of social order, corporate landlords and entrepreneurs not only ensure that their interests as potential victims are given priority in policing, but also avoid "the difficulty of proving matters in a formal system of justice arising from the extension of individual rights (Reiss, forthcoming). With private security, conflict remains the property of victims (Christie, 1977). As one of the security managers we interviewed put it:

> See those *Criminal Codes*? I got a whole set of them, updated every year. I've never used one. I could fire the whole set in the garbage, all of them. Security is prevention; you look at the entire operation and you see the natural choke points to apply the rules and regulations. The police, they don't understand the operation of a business. They don't come on the property unless we invite them.

Just as the social order enforced by private security is defined in terms of the interests of the client, so are the resources which are allocated for enforcement and the means which are employed. Thus, a retail organization which sells clothes will usually not install surveillance systems in changing rooms; this is not because such systems are ineffective in catching thieves, but because they might deter too many honest shoppers. The inevitable result of such instrumental policing is, of course, that a certain amount of known or suspected deviance will often be tolerated because the costs or the means of controlling it would threaten the interests of the client more than the deviance itself. There is little room for retribution within this instrumental approach. Social control exists solely to reduce threats to the interests of the client and the focus of attention shifts from discovering and blaming wrongdoers to eliminating sources of such threats in the future. This shifts the emphasis of social control from a judicial to a police function, and from detection to prevention. As one steel company security director expressed it:

> . . . The name of the game is steel. We don't want to be robbed blind, but we aren't interested in hammering people. . . . I'm not responsible for enforcing the *Criminal Code*; my basic responsibility is to reduce theft, minimize disruption to the orderly operation of the plant.

In our study of contract security we found that both security guards and private investigators focused attention primarily on identifying and rectifying security loopholes rather than on apprehending or punishing individuals who actually stole goods (Shearing *et al.*, 1980:178). This focus generates a new class of "offenders"—those who create opportunities for threats against the interests of the client. For example, a major Canadian bank launched an internal investigation into the loss of several thousands of dollars from one of its branches. The emphasis of the investigation was not on identifying the thief, but on discovering what breach of security had allowed the loss to occur and who was responsible for this breach, so that steps could be taken to reduce the risk of it recurring. The police were not involved in the investigation, despite the obvious suspicions of theft, and its results were the tightening up of security rules within the branch and the disciplining of the head teller who had breached them (*Freeborn v. Canadian Imperial Bank of Commerce*, 1981).

Even when a traditional offender is caught by private security, the client's best interest will often dictate a course of action other than invoking the criminal justice system. In 1982 in Calgary, Alberta, a bank succeeded in tracking down someone who had stolen over $14,000 from its automatic tellers. Instead of calling the police, the bank tried to persuade the offender to sign for the amount as a loan. Only when he refused to agree to this resolution of the matter was the case turned over to the police (*Globe and Mail*, 1982).

The Character of Sanctions

The fact that private security emphasizes loss prevention rather than retribution does not mean that sanctions are never employed. When they are invoked, however, they usually draw on private and corporate power, rather than state power.

The sanctions available within the criminal justice system rest ultimately on the state's access to physical force, over which it has a legal monopoly (Bittner, 1970). Private security's use of force is legally limited to cases in which they act as agents of the state, using citizen powers of

502   SHEARING AND STENNING

arrest, detention, and search (Stenning and Shearing, 1979). This does not mean that private security lacks powerful sanctions; on the contrary, as the agents of private authorities they have available a range of sanctions which are in many respects more potent than those of the criminal justice system, and which they perceive as being far more effective (Scott and McPherson, 1971: 272; Shearing *et al.*, 1980:232). One of the corporate security executives whom we interviewed said:

> [In a court] a different degree of proof is required; if the judge decides that there is insufficient evidence, you might be reinstated, because of some *legal* reason; in the disciplining process, I can get rid of you. If he's charged, we may have to continue him with benefits. To charge a person is a very serious thing, a very complicated process. We have to ask ourselves, do we just want to get rid of him, or do we want to throw the book at him? Maybe he's not a crook, he's just a dope.

As this example illustrates, foremost among the sanctions available to private security is the ability of corporations to restrict access to private property and to deny the resources which such access provides. Thus, private security can deny persons access to recreational and shopping facilities, housing, employment, and credit.

The essentially economic character of private security's sanctions does not mean that physical force has no bearing on what happens. When organizations want a legally imposed resolution to their problem, they can involve the police or initiate a civil suit. In drawing upon state power to support their legal rights to control access to property, organizations effectively expand the range of sanctions available to them.

PRIVATE SECURITY AND THE CRIMINAL JUSTICE SYSTEM

While many writers have suggested that private security is a mere adjunct to the criminal justice system—the so-called "junior partner" theory (Kakalik and Wildhorn, 1977)—our research suggests that many of those who control private security view the relationship quite differently. They saw the criminal justice system as an adjunct to their own private systems, and reported invoking the former only when the latter were incapable of resolving problems in a way which suited their interests.

Nevertheless, private security executives as well as senior public police officers preferred in public statements to characterize private security as the "junior partner" of the criminal justice system. For private security, this characterization minimized public fears that private security was "taking over" and that "private armies" were being created. It also carried the welcome implication that private security shared in the legitimacy and accepted status of the public police. The "junior partner" theory was attractive to the public police because it downplayed suggestions that they were losing their dominant role, while allowing them to take advantage of the interdependence of the private and public security systems.

The "junior partner" theory significantly distorts the relationship between the public police and private security in at least three ways. First, the theory implies that private security is concerned only with minor cases, thereby freeing the public police to deal with more serious matters (Harrington, 1982). Yet this proved to be *not* true for property "crime"; in fact, the reverse was probably the case. Private security routinely dealt with almost all employee theft, even those cases involving hundreds of thousands of dollars. Security directors told us that they typically reported only relatively petty cases of theft to the public police and one Canadian automative manufacturer reported that it was their policy never to refer employee theft to the public police. Even serious assaults, such as employee fights involving personal injury, were sometimes handled internally. Furthermore, while most serious personal injuries resulting from crimes were reported to the police, most so-called "industrial accidents" were dealt with internally (Carson, 1981).

A second, unfounded implication of the "junior partner" theory is that the public police direct the operations of private security. While the public police sometimes attempt such direction by establishing crime prevention squads and acting as consultants, private security personnel often mocked what they saw as presumptuous police officials who set themselves up as "crime prevention experts." Furthermore, because private security are usually the first to encounter a problem, they effectively direct the police by determining what will and what will not be brought to their attention (Black, 1980:52; Feuerverger and Shearing, 1982). On those occasions where the public police and private security work together — for example, police fraud squads with bank security personnel — it cannot be assumed that the public police play the leading role, either in terms of investigative expertise or in terms of direction of the investigation.

Third, private security is by no means a "junior partner" to the public police in the resources it draws upon, such as mechanical hardware or information systems. Private security not only frequently has access to sophisticated weapons and electronic surveillance systems, but is well equipped with standard security hardware including patrol cars and armored vehicles (Hougan, 1978; Scott and McPherson, 1971).

What, then, is the relationship between the public police and private security? Our research left little doubt that it was a co-operative one, based principally on the exchange of information and services. This was facilitated by the movement of personnel from public police to private security (Shearing *et al.*, 1980:195). This movement was particularly prevalent at the management level. Thirty-eight percent of the contract security executives we interviewed (Shearing *et al.*, 1980:118) and 32 percent of the in-house executives (Jeffries, 1977:38) were ex-police officers. Furthermore, many organizations reported relying on ex-police officers to gain access, through the "old boy network," to confidential police information. This was particularly common within private investigation agencies (Ontario Royal Commission, 1980:166). A private investigator summed up the exchange of information between private investigators and the public police this way:

> There are approximately a hundred private investigators in Toronto who can literally get any information they want whether it is from the Police Department, Workmen's Compensation records, O.H.I.P. [Ontario Health Insurance Plan], insurance records, or whatever. In the space of a ten-minute telephone conversation I can get what it would take me perhaps three weeks to discover. With experience and contacts, a well-established investigator can provide a better quality of information and can do so at a much lower cost to his client even though his hourly rates might be twice as much as a new investigator might charge.

The extent of this cooperation with the public police was summed up by the director of security we interviewed at a large commercial shopping mall in Toronto. After noting how easy it was for him to obtain the support of the local public police, he described his relationship with them as "one big police force." Yet there was no doubt in his mind that it was *he* who effectively controlled this force, through his control over access to the private property under his jurisdiction.

SUMMARY AND CONCLUSIONS

Private organizations, and in particular large corporations, have since 1960, and probably earlier, exercised direct power over policing the public through systems of private security. The growth of mass private property has facilitated an ongoing privatization of social control characterized by non-specialized security. As a result, North America is experiencing a "new feudalism": huge tracts of property and associated public spaces are controlled — and policed — by private corporations. To undertake this responsibility, these corporations have developed an extensive security apparatus, of which uniformed security personnel are only the supervisory tip of the iceberg.

The shift from public to private systems of policing has brought with it a shift in the character of social control. First, private security defines deviance in instrumental rather than moral terms: protecting corporate interests becomes more important than fighting crime, and sanctions are applied more often against those who create opportunities for loss rather than those who

504   SHEARING AND STENNING

capitalize on the opportunity – the traditional offenders. Thus, the reach of social control has been extended. Second, in the private realm, policing has largely disappeared from view as it has become integrated with other organizational functions and goals, at both the conceptual and behavioral levels. With private security, control is not an external force acting on individuals; now it operates from within the fabric of social interaction, and members of the communities in which it operates are simultaneously watchers and the watched. They are the bearers of their own control. Third, this integration is expressed in the sanctioning system, in which private security draws upon organizational resources to enforce compliance. Together these three features of private security create a form of social control that Foucault (1977) has termed discipline: control is at once pervasive and minute; it takes the form of small, seemingly insignificant observations and remedies that take place everywhere (Melossi, 1979:91; Shearing and Stenning, 1982).

Is private security here to stay? We think this depends less on the fiscal resources of the state, as some writers have suggested (Kakalik and Wildhorn, 1977), and more on the future structure of property ownership and the law related to it. There is little reason to believe that mass private property will not continue to develop, thereby permitting corporations to secure control over "relationships that were once exclusively in the public realm" (Spitzer and Scull, 1977:25). Thus, we believe private security will continue to develop as an increasingly significant feature of North American social life.

To the extent that control over policing is an essential component of sovereignty (Gerth and Mills, 1958:78), the development of modern private security raises the possibility of sovereignty shifting from the state directly to private corporations in both their national and, more significantly, their international guises. This in turn raises questions about the limitations of state control over private security and the validity of claims that the state is becoming more dominant in capitalistic societies (Boehringer, 1982; Cohen, 1979). Indeed, the evidence of direct control by capital over important aspects of policing points to the necessity of a thorough re-examination of conventional theoretical statements – be they instrumentalist or structural (Beirne, 1979) – about the relationship between the state and capital under modern capitalism.

REFERENCES

Arthurs, Harry W.
  1979   "Rethinking administrative law: A slightly dicey business." Osgoode Hall Law Journal 17(1):1–45.
  1980   "Jonah and the whale: The appearance, disappearance, and reappearance of administrative law."
          University of Toronto Law Journal 30:225–239.
Baldwin, Robert, and Richard Kinsey
  1980   "Behind the politics of police powers." British Journal of Law and Society 7(2):242–265.
Becker, Theodore M.
  1974   "The place of private police in society. An area of research for the social sciences." Social Problems
          21(3):438–453.
Beirne, Piers
  1979   "Empiricism and the critique of Marxism on law and crime." Social Problems 26(4):273–385.
Bittner, Egon
  1970   The Functions of the Police in Modern Society. Chevy Chase, Maryland: National Institute of
          Mental Health, Centre for Studies in Crime and Delinquency.
Black, Donald
  1980   The Manners and Customs of the Police. New York: Academic Press.
Boehringer, Gill
  1982   "The strong state and the surveillance society: Changing modes of control." Paper presented at the
          Australian and New Zealand Association for the Advancement of Science Congress, Macquarie
          University, New South Wales, Australia, May 1982.
Bourne, Larry S., and Peter D. Harper
  1974   "Trends in future urban land use." Pp. 213–236 in Larry S. Bourne, Ross D. MacKinnon, Jay
          Siegel, and James W. Simmons (eds.), Urban Futures for Central Canada: Perspectives on Fore-
          casting Urban Growth and Form. Toronto: University of Toronto Press.
Bunyan, Tony
  1977   The History and Practice of Political Police in Britain. London: Quartet Books.

Carson, W.G.
 1981 The Other Price of Britain's Oil: Safety and Control in the North Sea. Oxford: Martin Robertson.
Christie, Nils
 1977 "Conflicts as property." British Journal of Criminology 17(1):1–15.
Cohen, Stanley
 1979 "The punitive city: Notes on the dispersal of social control." Contemporary Crisis 3(4):339–364.
Coleman, James
 1974 Power and the Structure of Society. New York: Norton.
Critchley, Thomas A.
 1978 A History of Police in England and Wales: 900–1966. London: Constable.
Farnell, Margaret B., and Clifford D. Shearing
 1977 Private Security: An Examination of Canadian Statistics, 1961–1971. Toronto: Centre of Criminology, University of Toronto.
Feuerverger, Andrey, and Clifford D. Shearing
 1982 "An Analysis of the Prosecution of Shoplifters." Criminology 20(2):273–289.
Foucault, Michel
 1977 Discipline and Punish: The Birth of the Prison. New York: Pantheon Books.
Freedman, David J., and Philip C. Stenning
 1977 Private Security, Police, and the Law in Canada. Toronto: Centre of Criminology, University of Toronto.
Friendly, John Ashley
 1980 "Harbinger." Unpublished paper. Osgoode Hall Law School, Toronto.
Gerth, Hans H., and C. Wright Mills (eds.)
 1958 From Max Weber: Essays in Sociology. New York: Oxford University Press.
Gertler, Leonard O., and Ronald W. Crowley
 1977 Changing Canadian Cities: The Next Twenty-Five Years. Toronto: McClelland and Stewart.
Globe and Mail (Toronto)
 1982 "Bank scolded over theft." October 16:11.
Gorrill, B. E.
 1974 Effective Personnel Security Procedures. Homewood, Illinois: Dow Jones–Irwin.
Harrington, Christine B.
 1982 "Delegalization reform movements: A historical analysis." Pp. 35–71 in Richard L. Abel (ed.), The Politics of Informal Justice. Volume 2. New York: Academic Press.
Henry, Stuart
 1978 The Hidden Economy: The Context and Control of Borderline Crime. London: Martin Robertson.
Horan, James D.
 1967 The Pinkertons: The Detective Dynasty that Made History. New York: Crown Publishers.
Hougan, Jim
 1978 Spooks: The Haunting of America: The Private Use of Secret Agents. New York: Bantam.
Jeffries, Fern
 1977 Private Policing: An Examination of In-House Security Operations. Toronto: Centre of Criminology, University of Toronto.
Johnson, Bruce C.
 1976 "Taking care of labor: The police in American politics." Theory and Society 3(1):89–117.
Kakalik, James S., and Sorrel Wildhorn
 1971 Private Policing in the United States. Five volumes. Santa Monica, Calif.: Rand Corporation.
 1977 The Private Police: Security and Danger. New York: Crone Russak.
Lipson, Milton
 1975 On Guard: The Business of Private Security. New York: Quandrangle/New York Times Book Co.
Lorimer, James
 1972 A Citizen's Guide to City Politics. Toronto: James Lewis and Samuel.
Luzon, Jack
 1978 "Corporate headquarters security." The Police Chief 45(6):39–42.
Martin, Larry R.G.
 1975 "Structure, conduct, and performance of land dealers and land developers in the land industry." Mimeographed. School of Urban and Regional Planning, University of Waterloo.
Melossi, Dario
 1979 "Institutions of control and the capitalist organization of work." Pp. 90–99 in Bob Fine, Richard Kinsey, John Lea, Sol Picciotto, and Jock Young (eds.), Capitalism and the Rule of Law: From Deviance Theory to Marxism. London: Hutchinson.
Nader, Laura
 1980 No Access to Law: Alternatives to the American Judicial System. New York: Academic Press.
Ontario Royal Commission of Inquiry into the Confidentiality of Health Records in Ontario
 1980 Report of the Commission of Inquiry into the Confidentiality of Health Information. Volume 1. Toronto: Queen's Printer.

506 SHEARING AND STENNING

Pospisil, Leopold
 1967 "Legal levels and the multiplicity of legal systems in human societies." Journal of Conflict Resolution 11(1):2–26.
 1978 The Ethnology of Law. Menlo Park, Ca.: Cummings.
Predicasts, Inc.
 1974 Private Security Systems. Cleveland, Ohio: Predicasts Inc.
Punter, John V.
 1974 The Impact of Ex-Urban Development on Land and Landscapes in the Toronto Central Region, 1954–1971. Ottawa: Central Mortgage and Housing Corporation.
Radzinowicz, Leon A.
 1956 A History of English Law and Its Administration from 1750: The Clash Between Private Initiatives and Public Interest in the Enforcement of the Law. Volume 2. London: Stevens and Sons, Ltd.
Reich, Charles A.
 1964 "The new property." Yale Law Journal 73(5):733–787.
Reiss, Albert J.
 forth "Selecting strategies of control over organizational life." In Keith Hawkins and John Thomas (eds.),
 coming Enforcing Regulation. Boston: Kluwer-Nijhoff.
Scott, Thomas M., and Marlys McPherson
 1971 "The development of the private sector of the criminal justice system." Law and Society Review 6(2):267–288.
Scull, Andrew T.
 1977 Decarceration: Community Treatment and the Deviant – A Radical View. Englewood Cliffs, N.J.: Prentice Hall.
Shearing, Clifford D., and Philip C. Stenning
 1981 "Private security: Its growth and implications." Pp. 193–245 in Michael Tonry and Norval Morris (eds.), Crime and Justice – An Annual Review of Research. Volume 3. Chicago: University of Chicago Press.
 1982 "Snowflakes or good pinches? Private security's contribution to modern policing," Pp. 96–105 in Rita Donelan (ed.), The Maintenance of Order in Society. Ottawa: Canadian Police College.
Shearing, Clifford D., Margaret Farnell, and Philip C. Stenning
 1980 Contract Security in Ontario. Toronto: Centre of Criminology, University of Toronto.
Snyder, Francis G.
 1981 "Anthropology, dispute processes, and law: A critical introduction." British Journal of Law and Society 8(2):141–180.
Spitzer, Stephen, and Andrew T. Scull
 1977 "Privatization and capitalist development: The case of the private police." Social Problems 25(1):18–29.
Spurr, Peter
 1975 "Urban land monopoly." City Magazine (Toronto) 1:17–31.
Stenning, Philip C.
 1981 Postal Security and Mail Opening: A Review of the Law. Toronto: Centre of Criminology, University of Toronto.
Stenning, Philip C., and Mary F. Cornish
 1975 The Legal Regulation and Control of Private Policing in Canada. Toronto: Centre of Criminology, University of Toronto.
Stenning, Philip C., and Clifford D. Shearing
 1979 "Search and seizure: Powers of private security personnel." Study paper prepared for the Law Reform Commission of Canada. Ministry of Supply and Services Canada, Ottawa.
Stinchcombe, Arthur L.
 1963 "Institutions of privacy in the determination of police administrative practice." American Journal of Sociology 69:150–160.
U.S. Department of Justice, Federal Bureau of Investigation
 1976 Uniform Crime Reports for the United States: 1975. Washington, D.C.: U.S. Government Printing Office.
Waldie, Brennan, and Associates
 1982 "Beyond the law: The strikebreaking industry in Ontario – Report to the Director, District 6, United Steelworkers of America." Mimeographed. United Steel Workers of America, Toronto.
Zack, Arnold M.
 1978 "Suggested new approaches to grievance arbitration." Pp. 105–117 in Arbitration – 1977. Proceedings of the 30th annual meeting of the National Academy of Arbitrators. Washington, D.C.: Bureau of National Affairs, Inc.

Case Cited

Freeborn v. Canadian Imperial Bank of Commerce, 5(9) Arbitration Services Reporter 1 (Baum), 1981.

25

Policing and Society, 1990, Vol. 1, pp. 3–22
Reprints available directly from the publisher
Photocopying permitted by license only

CRIME PREVENTION FACING THE 1990s*

ANTHONY E. BOTTOMS

Institute of Criminology, Cambridge, UK

Crime prevention projects assumed an enhanced importance during the 1980s in a number of countries. This paper assesses the experience of crime prevention projects to date, and argues for a mixed strategy of situational, social and developmental crime prevention for the future. Additionally, potential problems in inter-agency co-operation in local crime prevention projects need to be more honestly faced, and evolving policies in the crime prevention field should be appropriately evaluated by adequately rigorous research. Attention should be paid to the relationship between crime prevention and wider social trends and policies.

KEY WORDS: Crime prevention, criminal policy, social policy, inter-agency co-operation, evaluation, police crime prevention.

INTRODUCTION

During the 1980s, crime prevention began to occupy a much more prominent place in public policy and in public consciousness than it did in earlier decades. The beginning of a new decade is a good time not only to look back upon what has been achieved, and on the lessons that have been learned, but also to look forward to some of the challenges that may be faced as crime prevention moves on into its next phase.

Let me first briefly rehearse some of the significant events of the 1980s for crime prevention policy in Great Britain. In 1983, a Crime Prevention Unit was set up in the Home Office. In 1984, a landmark was reached with the publication by the Home Office, and other government departments with responsibilities for England and Wales, of an interdepartmental circular on Crime Prevention;† this initiative was followed six months later by a similar circular for Scotland (Scottish Office, 1984). These circulars may properly be regarded as the cornerstone of most subsequent official policies on crime prevention in the two countries. Among their messages perhaps the most important were the expressed views that crime prevention was not

---

* This paper is a slightly amended version of the 1989 James Smart Lecture, delivered at the Lothian and Borders Police Headquarters, Edinburgh, on 3 November 1989. It is published here by kind permission of the Council of the James Smart Lecture Fund.

† See Home Office *et al.* (1984), reproduced in Waller (1988, Appendix C). The other government departments involved in the issue of the circular were the Department of Education and Science, the Department of Environment, the Department of Health and Social Security, and the Welsh Office.

4 A. E. BOTTOMS

simply a matter for the police,† and that inter-agency co-operation as between the police and other local agencies was of great importance in the successful delivery of effective crime prevention. As the Scottish circular put it:

The prevention of crime has always been a primary objective of the police. But some of the factors affecting crime lie outside the control or direct influence of the police, and so crime prevention cannot be left to them alone. Just as the incidence of crime can affect the whole community, so too its prevention is a task for the community. It is a task to which the public at large, and all the bodies and organisations whose policies can influence the extent of crime, can make a contribution. This circular seeks to emphasise the importance of crime prevention measures and to promote a greater awareness of their potential; it draws attention also to the relevance that the activities of agencies other than the police can have to crime prevention; and it stresses the need for a locally co-ordinated approach to these matters (Scottish Office, 1984, para.1).

Two years after the publication of the 1984 circulars, the subject of crime prevention was given a very high political profile by the holding of a special seminar in 10 Downing Street, chaired by the Prime Minister, at which the Home Secretary, the Secretaries of State for Scotland and for Wales and other ministers were present, and a particular emphasis was placed upon the role of the business community in developing relevant crime prevention measures. This seminar led directly to the creation of a Ministerial Group on Crime Prevention which is still in existence (see further, for England and Wales only, Laycock and Heal, 1989).

Also in early 1986, the Home Office Crime Prevention Unit launched the so-called "Five Towns Initiative", which was essentially a kind of demonstration project for the policies of the 1984 circular. The towns of Bolton, Croydon, North Tyneside, Swansea and Wellingborough agreed to collaborate in what were initially 18-month pilot programmes, for which the Home Office met the costs of a co-ordinator, but not the costs of actual crime prevention schemes or local running expenses. A variety of local developments took place in these five towns (see Home Office, 1988a); and in four of the towns, the projects were then carried on beyond the initial funding period.

Then in 1988 the Government launched a more ambitious scheme, the "Safer Cities Programme": it has been officially stated that the programme, "draws on the lessons learned and experience gained from a number of successful Home Office crime prevention initiatives", including "the recently completed Five Towns demonstration projects" (Home Office, 1988c). The Safer Cities programme is being established over a three-year period in a range of high-crime urban areas, twenty in England and Wales and four in Scotland.

The most recent major official initiative on crime prevention in England has been the establishment of Crime Concern, a registered charity whose aim is, "to stimulate, develop and support local crime prevention activity ... working in particular with local government, the business sector, and the police" (Crime Concern, 1989). This new organization has received initial funding for three years from the Home Office, but its aim is to be independently financed by the end of that period. A similar organization, Crime Concern Scotland, has also been established north of the border.

Crime prevention developments in the 1980s have by no means been confined to these Government-led initiatives. For example, some local police services have developed various kinds of innovative crime prevention projects. An early leader in

---

† This message acquired an additional importance from the dissemination of research findings questioning the extent to which increasing the number or frequency of police foot or car patrols would have a crime reductive effect: see, for example, Clarke and Hough (1984).

this respect was the Northumbria Police, whose Chief Constable in 1978 initiated an experiment to find whether enhanced security of dwellings in a high-crime area would have an impact on burglary rates and the fear of crime (Allatt, 1984a p. 100); more recently the same police force has been instrumental in launching the Northumbria Coalition against Crime, the first of its kind in the United Kingdom, which brings together local and national industrialists, local authorities and others, "who have the common desire to reduce crime and improve the quality of life by promoting crime prevention measures" (Northumbria Police 1989, p. 63). In addition, the neighbourhood watch movement has mushroomed during the 1980s, largely owing to the initiatives taken and the support offered by local police services all over the country. The first neighbourhood watch scheme was established in Cheshire in 1982; there are now 66 500 such schemes in England and Wales (*Good Neighbour*, Summer 1989, p.1), and 1000 schemes established or in the process of being established in Scotland (private communication from Scottish Home and Health Department, September 1989). The latest British Crime Survey shows that nationally, in England and Wales, some 14% of households are members of neighbourhood watch schemes, though this figure varies a good deal by region (Mayhew *et al.*, 1989, pp. 52–3, 80).

The voluntary agency most active in crime prevention during the period has been NACRO; after a successful pilot project in Cheshire in the 1970s (Hedges *et al.*, 1980), NACRO has steadily developed its work on community safety in housing estates, with over 80 local projects being run at one time or another (Laycock and Heal, 1989, p. 324; NACRO, 1989). Additionally, academics have had an influence on crime prevention developments in the 1980s: three very different examples are the Windsor consultation on business and crime organised by the University of Sheffield with Crime Concern (Shapland and Wiles, 1989); the work of the "left–realist" school at Middlesex Polytechnic which has, amongst other things, argued for the importance of a democratic base and close local consultation in crime prevention initiatives (see Lea *et al.*, 1988), and has also pioneered research on lighting and crime prevention (Painter, 1988), the findings of which have been taken up by a Parliamentary group; and the research of Professor Alice Coleman (1985; 1989) of King's College, London on design and crime in housing estates, which has already led a number of local authorities to make design modifications in their housing areas, and is now to be taken further, with generous Department of Environment funding, in the 1990s.

By any standards, this is a formidable list of developments. The 1980s, we can safely assert, has put crime prevention firmly on the map: a conclusion which is true not only in Britain, but certainly also, at a minimum, in France, in the Netherlands and within the Council of Europe (see generally Waller, 1988). But the key question now is: where should crime prevention go in the 1990s?

In tackling this question let us consider first, the substance of crime prevention initiatives; secondly, issues of inter-agency co-operation; thirdly, the question of evaluation; and finally, the relationship between crime prevention and broader social developments.

CRIME PREVENTION INITIATIVES

It is impossible to tackle seriously the substance of crime prevention programmes without discussing what is usually called the issue of situational versus social crime prevention.

6   A. E. BOTTOMS

In the early 1980s, in England, the concept of situational crime prevention was much emphasised, and was the subject of two important books published from the Home Office Research and Planning Unit (Clarke and Mayhew 1980; Heal and Laycock 1986). The first of these books usefully and succinctly defined situational crime prevention measures as:

(i)   measures directed at highly specific forms of crime;

(ii) which involve the management, design or manipulation of the immediate environment in which these crimes occur;

(iii) in as systematic and permanent a way as possible;

(iv) so as to reduce the opportunities for these crimes (Clarke and Mayhew 1980, p.1).

These "opportunity-reducing" situational crime prevention measures can include target hardening (more secure windows and doors on houses); target removal (the removal of cash meters for domestic gas and electricity payments); removing the means to crime (the installation of screening devices at airports to prevent weapons being taken aboard); or increasing surveillance (more caretakers in housing developments; CCTV on the London underground). (For fuller lists, see Clarke and Mayhew, 1980, ch.1; Clarke, 1983). In the late 1970s, when measures of this sort were systematically recommended for the first time as an integrated approach to crime prevention, there was a tendency in some quarters to scoff at the proposals as commonsensical, and of only trivial importance for the true prevention of crime. Such a view can no longer be sustained, for the situational approach can point to a number of successful implementations. For example:

- the Post Office in the late 1960s replaced vulnerable aluminium coin receptacles with stronger steel ones, and in doing so virtually eliminated thefts from public call boxes (Clarke 1983, p.241).

- the installation of token-operated and magnetic card-operated fuel meters in domestic premises, to replace coin meters, has led to a reduction in burglaries and thefts from dwellings (Home Office 1988b, p.60; Forrester et al., 1988).

- increasing the level of inspection in the Dutch tram and metro system (by the employment of unemployed young people to tackle fare-dodging and vandalism, and to improve the level of information and service available to passengers) led to a sharp reduction in fare-dodging and an improvement in vandalism, although not to any reduction in feelings of insecurity (van Andel 1989).†

- Northumbria Police's pioneering domestic target-hardening project (see above) led to a reduction both in burglary and in the fear of crime (Allatt 1984a, 1984b).

One important issue raised by situational crime prevention measures is that of *displacement*: that is to say, the possibility that one particular crime will be prevented, but only at the cost of the offender committing the same crime somewhere else (*spatial displacement*), or at a different time on the same target (*temporal displacement*), or committing a different crime instead (attempted burglary rather than burglary because the premises were too difficult to get into; alternatively, switching from burglary to robbery for the same reason: *offence displacement*). We know from various

---

† The experiments in The Netherlands also involved a change in the boarding procedure on buses, requiring passengers to show tickets to the driver: this also led to a reduction in fare-dodging (van Andel, 1989).

CRIME PREVENTION—1990s   7

researches that displacement of these various kinds sometimes occurs, and it is possible to speculate about the circumstances in which it is most likely to occur (see Heal and Laycock, 1988, p.240). An important question to ask when considering displacement is whether the new or displaced crime or crimes is less serious, more serious, or of the same seriousness as the prevented crime(s) (see Barr and Pease, 1990); and it is certainly reasonable to conclude, on the existing evidence, that taking seriousness into account there "have been many instances of crime prevention programmes in which displacement has not been total" (Barr and Pease, 1990). A good example of this is to be found in Patricia Allatt's (1984a) evaluation of the Northumbria Police target-hardening project. She found evidence of some spatial displacement of burglaries from the experimental area to two adjacent areas, and to a few privately-owned houses on the experimental estate itself (which, being privately owned, were not part of the security enhancement programme). There was also evidence of some offence displacement, because non-domestic burglaries, thefts of and from vehicles and other crimes went up disproportionately on the experimental estate. However, even when all this displacement was taken into account, there was still a small overall reduction in crime, and of course many of the displacement offences on the estate itself could be regarded as being less serious than the domestic burglaries that they had apparently replaced. Thus, overall, displacement was far from total.

Summing up, then, we can reasonably conclude that certain situational crime prevention measures can have a noticeable crime-reducing effect, and, while displacement may be a real limitation on the overall effectiveness of a given project, it should not necessarily be assumed that the existence of some displacement renders the whole project unsuccessful. The experience of the 1980s is clearly that we should regard situational crime prevention as an important part of a future crime prevention strategy.

It will be apparent from some of the examples I have given—such as that of the Dutch transport experiments—that situational crime prevention is not just about improving security hardware, or physically removing the targets of theft. It can also have a social dimension: in the Dutch case, that of surveillance of public transport vehicles and stations by a paid supervisory force. The Dutch project nevertheless remains appropriately classified as primarily a situational crime prevention experiment because the key mechanism for achieving crime reduction was the reduction of the perceived opportunity to offend.

But there are other ways in which one can attempt crime prevention, of a more fully social kind. To take a simple example from domestic life, some parents might lock cupboards or drawers to prevent their children from helping themselves to loose cash, chocolates and so forth (opportunity reduction); others will prefer, at as early an age as is possible, not to lock up anything in the house but so to socialize their children that they will not steal even if the opportunities are available. What scope is there, in a wider context, for this sort of social crime prevention?

The first point to make is that, under certain circumstances, considerable changes in social behaviour can be achieved by social processes, even in apparently unpromising circumstances. One example of this, from a slightly different context, is to be found here in Scotland in the recently published research evaluation of the Special Unit at Barlinnie Prison, where it has been shown that a particular kind of regime, within a particular set of social circumstances, has led to a marked reduction in aggressive behaviour among certain prison inmates with a long history of aggression

8   A. E. BOTTOMS

(Cooke, 1989). This result has been achieved by the Unit without, for the most part, placing any situational barriers on opportunities to offend; indeed some such opportunities, such as the availability of knives, have been increased by comparison with other regimes that the men might have found themselves in.

I have used this example to illustrate the kind of effect that can in principle be achieved by the mechanisms of social crime prevention. It has been necessary to make this point because, just as there were once those who tended to ridicule situational crime prevention, so there were (and still are, though to a diminishing extent) arch-situationalists who ridicule, or at least severely play down, the possibilities of social crime prevention. Any objective evaluation of completed crime prevention projects would have to concur with the author of a recent major review of the literature that:

there is little hard evidence to show that the social problems approach to community crime prevention is effective in reducing community crime rates or building community cohesion (Rosenbaum, 1988, p.354).

However, that does not mean, as Rosenbaum goes on to stress, that the approach actually is ineffective, only that, "there have been few strong evaluations of program effects in this rediscovered policy area". The Barlinnie example is useful because it does provide hard evidence that, under certain conditions, the mechanisms of a social crime prevention approach can be successful. The question therefore becomes one of whether mechanisms of a like kind can be translated across into a more general social context.†

It is to be hoped that they can, because there is plenty of evidence to suggest that in certain contexts a social crime prevention approach is badly needed. Let me give just two specific examples. The first is from a Home Office Crime Prevention Unit examination of crime and nuisance in a city centre shopping complex. It was noted that the complex was, "a meeting place for members of the prevailing youth subcultures" (p.23), and that young people were frequently involved in nuisance behaviour, and sometimes in crime, in the complex. Various situational crime prevention measures were suggested, but the researchers went on to note that, in a region with 13% unemployed,

leaving the problem as just one of nuisance, to be controlled by improved security measures, ignores the moral dimension in which planners, traders and marketing managers have contributed, albeit haphazardly, to the development of a town centre in which young people find it hard to *avoid* (sic.) being a nuisance. Resolution of the problem at this broader level has wider implications—not least for avoiding friction between police and young people, especially in this case black young people (Phillips and Cochrane, 1988, p.23).

The researchers then go on to point to an apparently promising Rotterdam experiment, designed to promote greater harmony between shopkeepers and young people in city centres, which involves a set of clear minimum rules for behaviour in

---

† This statement leaves open the issue of the theoretical basis of these mechanisms. This is a large question which cannot be adequately tackled here: however, it can perhaps be said that Braithwaite's (1989) "theory of reintegrative shaming" offers an integrated theoretical approach which is capable both of explaining the Barlinnie result and offering a number of leads to those concerned to develop social crime prevention approaches. As an overall criminological theory, however, Braithwaite's approach needs to be supplemented with at least the following: (i) greater attention to opportunity theory and situational crime prevention, and (ii) greater attention to middle-level social structures, some of which are capable of being creatively altered so as to promote crime prevention possibilities (see, for example, Bottoms and Wiles, 1988 on housing policy).

shopping complexes, the communication of these rules to youngsters, the provision of attractive alternative meeting places and leisure facilities (within and outside the shopping complex), and the employment of an autonomous detached street worker with credibility with youth.†

The second example comes from the recently published British Crime Survey. This has shown that British residents of Asian origin are more likely to be victims of robberies and thefts from the person, and of vandalism, even when it is taken into account that Asians live disproportionately in high-risk neighbourhoods. It seems to be particularly the case that Asian-origin residents are much more likely than other residents to be the subject of random attacks by passing groups of strangers in open spaces, often linked with overt racial hostility (Mayhew *et al.*, 1989, ch.5; see also Dawson *et al.* 1987).‡ Such attacks are clearly an unpleasant aspect of British social life; there is often little that can be done about them in purely situational terms, and the need for a social crime prevention response, perhaps centred upon racial awareness programmes in schools, youth clubs, and other community contexts, is highlighted (see also Ekblom and Simon, 1988 on crime and racial harassment in Asian-run small shops).

A 1984 report of an official committee in The Netherlands postulated that the rapid post-war growth in crime had come about partly because of greatly increased opportunities for theft following the economic expansion and the increasing demand for consumer goods of recent decades; and partly because of a decline

in the influence of many traditional social institutions within which the behaviour of individuals is effectively normalised, such as the family, clubs and associations, the church and the schools. Society has become more individualistic. In some cases this individualism leads to a tendency to satisfy personal needs at the expense of others or of the community. The increased use of alcohol and drugs also forms part of this pattern of greater individualism (Netherlands Ministry of Justice, 1985, p.10).

If this analysis is correct, then perhaps the growth of crime created both by greater opportunities and key changes in the social fabric needs to be tackled by opportunity-reducing initiatives and by imaginatively planned social crime prevention.

The most ambitious programme of social crime prevention yet attempted in Britain is probably the group of NACRO housing estate projects referred to above—though it should be pointed out that most of these projects also include elements of situational prevention. The estates chosen for NACRO projects normally suffer from multiple disadvantages, and have high crime rates. The NACRO strategy is one of active consultation with the key agencies providing services in the neighbourhood, while small-group meetings are held with random samples of residents, "to tease out possible solutions to the problems from their knowledge of the area" (Whiskin, 1987). This leads to the formulation and, it is hoped, the implementation of an Action Plan

---

† Some of these measures, particularly the provision of alternative meeting places, bear some resemblance to situational crime prevention measures, but they are not opportunity-reducing in a direct sense. Clarke (1983, p.244) similarly notes that, "certain measures of environmental management have some but not all of the characteristics of the situational approach, and some are opportunity-reducing only in an extended sense".

‡ The British Crime Survey also found that British residents of Afro-Caribbean origin were more at risk than whites for many types of crime: however, when relevant demographic and social factors were taken into account, they did not have a statistically significantly greater chance of victimisation than whites, even though the rates were still higher (Mayhew *et al.*, 1989, ch.5).

for the estate. Nigel Whiskin (1987, p.27) comments that the method of working, "is not strikingly original, and is based on the idea of involving all the different elements of a problem in the process of identifying key issues and finding common acceptable solutions".

Research evaluations of projects of this kind, often involving the simultaneous implementation of a range of different social (and some situational) measures, are notoriously complex and difficult to mount. Despite this, NACRO have arguably done themselves, and those with whom they have worked, a disservice by not devoting greater attention to project evaluation. But we do have a few evaluative clues to help us to address their work. In the original Widnes pilot project from which all other programmes stemmed, there appeared to be a genuine reduction in burglary, as measured by a victim survey (although this was not evenly achieved in different parts of the estate); a reduction in vandalism of houses and shops (though an increase in vandalism of trees and shrubs); and a marked improvement in the appearance and social atmosphere of the estate (Hedges *et al.*, 1980). The only subsequent formal evaluation of NACRO projects is that by Barry Poyner and his colleagues from the Tavistock Institute, and this is difficult to comment upon because aspects of it are strenuously contested by NACRO spokespersons. Two points do however seem reasonably clear from the Tavistock report. First, it appears that in a number of NACRO projects the level of implementation of the proposed action plan has been relatively poor: in such circumstances, one would not expect to find a successful crime-reduction outcome (see Hope and Murphy, 1983 on the problems of implementation in crime prevention projects). Secondly, Poyner and his colleagues do identify one project, the Bushbury Triangle project in Wolverhampton, where on the basis of recorded crime figures there seemed to be a genuine crime reduction which could be attributed "primarily to NACRO consultations and the implementation of an Action Plan" (Poyner *et al.*, 1986, p.61). Whiskin (1987, p.38) also provides, for the same estate, some rather sketchy victim survey data which point in the same direction. Although the research purist could wish for a more rigorous evaluation than any of this provides, it seems reasonable to conclude, with Poyner and his colleagues (1986, p.61), that, "providing action plans are well implemented, more projects will emerge which can justify the claim of crime reduction".† In other words, there does seem to be reasonable evidence here that the NACRO crime prevention approach can sometimes work. If this is the case, then fuller future evaluations might establish under what conditions the approach works, and under what conditions it fails. In the meantime, the limited data that are available do not encourage us to be disparaging either about NACRO's projects, or about the possibilities of social crime prevention in general.

As is well known, the most thoroughgoing approach to social crime prevention in Europe in recent years has been that adopted in France (see King, 1988). Much is claimed for the French programmes, including a general nationwide reduction in juvenile delinquency; and also larger crime reductions in areas where well-developed

---

† Poyner *et al.* (1986. p.66) go on to argue that the evidence from their study, "suggests that when crime prevention measures are targeted on specific crime problems they can reduce crime, whereas measures designed to operate in a more general way to improve the physical and social environment of an estate tend to have little effect on crime". However, I am bound to say that my own reading of the Tavistock report suggests that this conclusion seems to owe more to the authors' general views on crime prevention than to specific evidence arising from the research study.

programmes are in place than in areas where they are not (Waller, 1988, p.15). However, it remains the case, as far as I am aware, that adequately rigorous empirical evaluation of the French programmes is still to be accomplished (Waller, 1988, p.17). We should nevertheless continue to watch French developments with interest, for it may well be that they have things to teach us if, as I am advocating, we move into the 1990s with an imaginative mixed programme of situational and social crime prevention.

At this point I should like to draw especial attention to two current crime prevention projects being undertaken in England. Both of them, in different ways, mix elements of the situational and the social, and both of them seem to have promise in terms of the future of crime prevention, although that judgement must remain tentative at present as neither project has yet completed a final evaluation. What is of particular interest is that both projects are in high-crime-rate urban areas, and, as Dennis Rosenbaum (1988, p.378) noted in his important review of the crime prevention literature, "the biggest challenge facing crime prevention today is to implement effective programs in high-crime neighbourhoods". Indeed, as is now fairly well-known, one of the difficulties about neighbourhood watch schemes is that they have been established with least frequency in the areas with the highest rates of household crime (see Husain, 1988; Mayhew et al., 1989, ch.6).

The first of the two projects I want to discuss is the Kirkholt Burglary Prevention Project in Rochdale, carried out in a large local authority housing estate with an exceptionally high rate of domestic burglaries (Forrester et al., 1988). A key feature of this project was that the crime prevention measures which were developed relied very strongly on careful prior analysis of information about crime in the area, including some gleaned from interviews with burglars, and some from interviews with crime victims and their next-door neighbours. It was found that those households which had been burgled once were disproportionately likely to suffer burglaries in the future, and the main thrust of the crime prevention initiative in the area was therefore focused upon those recently victimised. A complex package of measures was used, including removal of cash pre-payment fuel meters; target-hardening of houses and more rapid repairs to houses after a burglary; the employment of a community support team to offer social support, a security survey, and property marking to recent victims of burglary; and the establishment of so-called "mini" or "cocoon" neighbourhood watch schemes. These "cocoon" neighbourhood watch schemes involved the victimised house and its immediate neighbours. Prior analysis had shown that many victimised households had, according to their neighbour households, some obvious reason for being burgled (such as low occupancy, or attractive video equipment); and many neighbours had said they were willing to help. It was believed by the project developers that the "cocoon" neighbourhood watch idea "mirrors what happens in well-established communities, where close groupings of dwellings share information and support each other" (Forrester et al., 1988, p.17); and that (as proved to be the case) these close groupings were capable of organic development into larger units. The "cocoon" neighbourhood watch schemes pre-sumably (this is not made entirely clear in the project report) incorporated both opportunity reduction through increased neighbourly vigilance, and the attempt to develop stronger social networks and social cohesion in the area.

This project mixed situational measures and social measures in an interesting package. In the first stage, situational measures were perhaps predominant, but in a second stage the project is moving on to incorporate additional social initiatives, focusing on the drugs, alcohol, unemployment and debt problems revealed in the offender interviews (Forrester *et al.*, 1988, p.29). The results of the first stage were spectacular, with a massive drop in recorded burglary not matched in the rest of the police sub-division; only limited spatial or offence displacement; and a specific reduction in multiple victimisations. I understand from the researchers that these good results have been maintained beyond the seven months reported in the initial publication of results. Although from a technical point of view a few methodological doubts could be raised about the results,† the size of the recorded burglary reduction is so large as to render such doubts essentially improbable. Because a whole set of measures were implemented simultaneously, it is not possible to ascertain clearly in research terms exactly how the crime reduction was achieved, but the achievement nevertheless remains an impressive one.

The second project I want to mention is in the Hilldrop project in the London borough of Islington. Following surveys of residents, which included questions about the social problems of the area and about residents' preferences as to policing priorities, researchers and policymakers devised a set of crime prevention measures which included (Lea *et al.*, 1988, p.61ff):

● target-hardening;

● lighting improvements;

● increased beat policing;

● women's self-defence classes;

● changes in the curriculum of local schools, including teaching on civic responsibility and on issues of racism and sexism, linked to the problems of assaults against ethnic minorities and against women in the area;

● action against "fences" for property crime;

● the development of a form of "neighbourhood watch".

As at Kirkholt, "neighbourhood watch" in Hilldrop has been assigned a different meaning from that adopted in most areas. In Hilldrop it is seen as a kind of neighbourhood forum, whose central role is, "in receiving and discussing public grievances in the area, and consulting with the police, particularly the beat officers" (Lea *et al.*, p.65). It can also involve residents joining together to tackle a range of local issues such as the support of crime victims; mediation over noisy parties; and the problem of dog mess on pavements.

I understand from the project developers that the implementation level of most of the proposed elements of this crime prevention package has been good, though implementation difficulties have been encountered in some areas; for example, the schools proposals and the action against fences (private communication from Trevor Jones, September 1989). The project awaits formal evaluation: initial indications are not unpromising, but enthusiasm should be restrained until proper results are forthcoming.

Once again, a particularly interesting feature of this project is that it has been

---

† In particular (i) the study relies only on police-recorded data for its analysis of crime rates; and (ii) there was an increase in criminal damage on the Kirkholt estate, and the authors do not adequately investigate the extent to which these recorded offences of damage could have been failed burglaries (Forrester *et al.*, 1988, pp.20–1).

mounted in a relatively high-crime area. Other important elements of the project include the specificity of its policy recommendations, following close prior analysis of crime and other social problems of the area; the project's determination to consult and to remain sensitive to the views of local people; and its inclusion, as a priority feature, of a close relationship and joint action with the local police.

Dennis Rosenbaum (1988, p.380) has remarked that:

> there is no need for communities to choose *a priori* between [the situational and the social] approaches to crime prevention; each has its purpose and they can be used jointly as complementary tactics.

Kirkholt and Hilldrop both, in different ways, well illustrate this point, and they both appear, at this interim stage, to be promising approaches.†

I should like to add one further point, which arises directly from these two projects. Both of them incorporate what might be described as unorthodox versions of neighbourhood watch. As such, they might be models to bear in mind for the future, because I suspect that, despite its current popularity, the orthodox version of neighbourhood watch may shortly need much more careful scrutiny than it has so far received. The most methodologically rigorous examination of the effects of orthodox neighbourhood watch that we have in this country so far is that carried out in the Metropolitan Police District by Trevor Bennett (1989) of the Cambridge Institute of Criminology. Bennett's research found, as have some comparably rigorous evaluation projects in the United States (see Rosenbaum, 1988, pp.361–4), no effect of neighbourhood watch on local crime rates; though Bennett did find a significant reduction in the fear of household victimisation in one of his two target areas. Although no-one, least of all Bennett himself, would wish to over-generalize from these results, nevertheless it could prove to be the case that neighbourhood watch, "has been oversold as a stand-alone strategy in the war against crime" (Rosenbaum, 1988, p.363).

Trevor Bennett (1989, p.176) reached the conclusion that the most convincing explanation of the failure of his London neighbourhood watch schemes to reduce crime lay in what he calls "programme failure". This, he thought, was not because the schemes were poor examples of neighbourhood watch as normally practised in London (they probably were not); but rather because of what Bennett calls the tendency to "minimalism" (p.177) in orthodox neighbourhood watch—that is to say, not too much actually happens in the standard neighbourhood watch scheme, and within the police service in London,

> the reward structure favours quantity (number of schemes implemented per division) rather than quality (how well they operate and how long they last for) (Bennett 1989, p.177).

Perhaps, then, the essentially simple concept of neighbourhood watch as that of neighbourhood notices, stickers in windows, and encouragement to be the, "eyes and ears of the police" is not enough. Bennett argues that either the situational or

---

† The English 1984 circular (Home Office *et al.* 1984, para.3d) argued that 'there is a need to address the social factors associated with criminal behaviour', but that this required 'long-term measures'. In the short term, the circular went on to argue, 'the best way forward is to reduce, through management, design, or changes in the environment, the opportunities that exist for crime to occur'. The danger with this approach is, of course, that attention will be so focused on the short-term situational measures that the social measures will never be attempted. It is interesting that the Scottish circular (Scottish Office 1984, para.2d) modified the stark English equation of short-term = situational, long-term = social. The message of the Kirkholt and Hilldrop projects is that this equation is unnecessary.

14   A. E. BOTTOMS

the social dimension of neighbourhood watch could be strengthened for possible
greater programme effect. Situationally, this could be done, for example, by the more
systematic creation of signs of occupancy, which we know from interviews with
burglars to be one of the main deterrents to burglary (Bennett and Wright, 1984).
As regards social crime prevention, it is known from North American research that

community crime prevention meetings are more likely to be constructive and long-lasting if the group
meets to pursue a number of objectives rather than just the one objective of crime prevention (Bennett
1989, p.185).

Nigel Whiskin, the Chief Executive of Crime Concern, highlighted some of these
issues when he wrote recently, in the editorial column of the neighbourhood watch
movement's own magazine, that, "not everyone seems to be agreed about where
neighbourhood watch should be going or what it should be aiming to do"; he went
on to make a number of specific suggestions, and concluded that "we need to put
the emphasis on *neighbourhood* rather than *watch*" (*Good Neighbour*, summer 1989,
p.3). The message of Trevor Bennett's research is that the debate started by Nigel
Whiskin is a necessary one, and that it needs to be open, honest and explicit. And
for me at least, the Kirkholt and Hilldrop approaches to neighbourhood watch are
models which will be worth the most careful scrutiny as this debate develops.

I have argued for a strategy of careful and creative synthesis of situational and
social approaches to crime prevention. But there is one further point to be made on
the substance of crime prevention strategies. It is clear from much recent research in
criminology that the distribution of *offences* as between different *offenders* is very
skewed: for example, in a study by the Home Office Statistical Department it was
found that nearly 1 in 3 of males born in 1953 had been convicted of a standard list
offence by the age of 28, but only a small proportion ($\frac{1}{2}$%, or 18% of those
convicted) had six or more court appearances before this age, *and they accounted for
70% of all the known offences committed by the group* (Home Office, 1985). Similar
(although less extreme) results have been found in other cohort studies in the United
States and in Britain, and the conclusions are supported by self-report research as
well as by research on official arrests and convictions (Farrington, 1987, pp.27–8;
Balvig, 1988). It is clear, therefore, that if this small number of persistent offenders
could be identified at an early age, then one form of crime prevention worth
attempting would be to work with them in a range of voluntary preventive programmes; the indications are that early identification, on the basis of troublesome
behaviour and other data available at age 10, is possible although difficult (Farrington, 1985). A further difficulty which would then have to be faced by such a strategy
is that the state of knowledge about which delinquency prevention programmes might
be successful for a group such as this is patchy (see Rutter and Giller, 1983,
pp.323–336). However, David Farrington (1989) has recently made some interesting
suggestions in this regard on the basis of up-to-date research—these suggestions
include behavioural parent training, Head Start educational programmes, increased
economic resources for deprived families, and techniques to help children to avoid
peer-group pressures. Many intermediate treatment (I.T.) workers in England (though
fewer in Scotland) have rather eschewed preventive programmes in recent years, but,
on the basis of the research by Farrington and others, a case can be argued that I.T.
workers should develop programmes of this sort, albeit in a more targetted fashion
than they have sometimes adopted in the past (see Bottoms *et al.*, 1990).

It is striking that, at the level of official policy and major local initiatives, most
U.K. crime prevention thinking in the 1980s has been situationally or socially focused

on adults or young adults. There is, as it seems to me, a very good research-based case for us to add a developmental dimension to strategic thinking on crime prevention in the 1990s, and it is a dimension that I hope the Government and other agencies will address in a sensitive way. What we need for the future, in my judgement, is a balanced strategy embracing the situational, the social and the developmental.

INTER-AGENCY CO-OPERATION

A view often expressed in official policy on crime prevention in the 1980s has been that the police cannot do it all themselves, but need the active co-operation of other statutory and voluntary agencies and of the public; and, further, that there is a particular need for the main statutory agencies to pool their efforts and to work creatively together on crime prevention projects in local communities. This so-called "inter-agency co-operation" is such a new theme that, as yet, it has been little researched. Such research as we have, however, suggests a number of difficulties which will have to be borne in mind for the future.

The most important research so far completed in Britain is that conducted by a team from Lancaster University and Middlesex Polytechnic as part of the Economic and Social Research Council's 'Crime and Criminal Justice' research initiative of the mid-1980s (the "ESRC project team"). This research group identified two dominant prior theoretical perspectives on inter-agency co-operation (Sampson *et al.*, 1988): these they described as the benevolent approach, whose fundamental orientation is one of, "a paternalistic corporatism, itself implying an unproblematic consensus on aims and objectives" (p.481); and, secondly, the conspiratorial approach, sometimes adopted by left-wing writers, in which, "the policies of the state are portrayed as being inevitably and irreducibly both instrumental and coercive" (p. 480). On the basis of their own research fieldwork with a number of local crime prevention projects (see Blagg *et al.*, 1988; Sampson *et al.*, 1988), the ESRC researchers concluded that neither of these perspectives could account for, or explain, the complexities of the real situation on the ground.

For present purposes, two points in the ESRC project team's research are of particular importance. First, they showed that there can be, and are, sometimes real conflicts or confusions as between different state agencies themselves (see also, for the field of intermediate treatment, Bottoms *et al.*, 1990, Chapters 3 and 5). Thus, for example, different agencies may have quite different perceptions of what the problem is in a given area, based on the main tasks and priorities of each particular agency:

one of our most consistent findings is the tendency for inter-agency conflicts and tensions to re-appear, in spite of co-operative efforts, reflecting the oppositions between state agencies at a deep structural level. We have also found consistent and persistent struggles between local authority departments over limited resources, power and prestige (Sampson *et al.* 1988, p.482).

Within this context of struggle, it should be noted that not all agencies are equally powerful, and that, in crime prevention projects in residential areas, the police and the housing department were the most dominant voices. A particularly strong comment was made by the ESRC project team about the role of the police in the projects they studied:

The police are often enthusiastic proponents of the multi-agency approach, but they tend to prefer to set the agendas and to dominate forum meetings, and then to ignore the multi-agency framework when it suits their own needs (Sampson *et al.* p.491).

16 A. E. BOTTOMS

In research carried out at Cambridge on intermediate treatment, a number of interesting comments were made by agency representatives about inter-agency liaison and co-operation. So, for example, one said, "it's a reality that (in inter-agency work) you lose a degree of autonomy"; another added, "if you are going to co-operate you have got to give and take"; while a third commented that at the end of the day, "the role of the police and the role of social services isn't the same", and that it was a mistake automatically to assume that because an inter-agency panel was in existence there would be cross-agency consensus (Bottoms *et al.*, 1990, ch.5).

We have been, I think, rather slow to recognize the importance of these issues, because of the strong pressures in the 1980s to achieve greater degrees of inter-agency co-operation in a number of fields related to crime and criminal justice. Understandably, because there was so little inter-agency co-operation before the 1980s, the major effort of policy has had to be to get across the message of the desirability and importance of increased collaboration. But as we begin to move beyond this initial phase of simply stimulating greater degrees of inter-agency co-operation, all of us have to confront more honestly and openly some of the real issues and potential tensions which the empirical evidence in this field raises. These include the following questions:

- do different agencies have different amounts of power in inter-agency crime prevention forums, and does it matter?

- how much autonomy is it necessary for each agency to lose for the sake of the collective good, and are they willing to lose it?

- to what extent is it right to recognise that different agencies (such as the police and social work departments) have different assigned functions, and that *these functions will necessarily limit the extent to which co-operation between agencies may properly (and ethically) extend?*

If we are honest, I think we have to say that we have hardly begun to tackle this agenda. It will be, in my view, an important agenda for crime prevention projects in the 1990s.

The second point to arise from the ESRC project team's research concerns the relationship between statutory agencies and local residents in crime prevention projects. The truth is that these different groups can have quite different priorities: for example, both the police and local residents may agree that motor cars present a problem for a given area, but the police may want to stress, within this, issues of thefts of and from cars; while residents may be more concerned about illegal parking, untidy parking, and the problem of abandoned cars, all of which may be seen as essentially trivial problems by the police (Sampson *et al.*, 1988, p.488). In this kind of context, the very real anxieties of minorities, or of groups of residents who are afraid to speak out, may easily get submerged: and this can mean, for example, that crimes against women and crimes involving racial harassment do not receive the attention, in local crime prevention projects, that they merit by reason of their real incidence and the anxieties that they engender (see Sampson *et al.*, 1988; Blagg *et al.*, 1988; Jones *et al.*, 1986). For reasons such as these, it does seem to me to be important to consult as closely as possible with residents at every stage of crime prevention projects in residential areas, as NACRO projects and the Hilldrop project have in different ways tried to do (not wholly successfully, but they have tried much harder than some).† I confess to some anxiety, therefore, about the message contained towards the end of the Home Office's Five Towns booklet:

While local surveys are important as a means of assessing residents' concerns about crime and the extent of unrecorded crime, the experience of the '5 Towns' initiative suggests that projects which are time constrained and pressed for resources would do better to act initially on police statistics which, if necessary, can be supplemented by other information as the project progresses (Home Office 1988a, p.13).

EVALUATION

In the United States, Arthur Lurigio and Dennis Rosenbaum (1986, p.23) have commented in relation to crime prevention projects:

Not everyone has the same level of interest in presenting the 'hard facts'. To obtain program funding from public or private sources, grant applicants often have a strong motivation to convince the funding agency that it will be investing in a proven, highly effective program for preventing crime in their community. Likewise, the granting agencies, although wanting to remain neutral in the absence of hard data, also want to believe that they were supporting a good 'product'. Moreover, the media are very interested in success stories ...

Similar issues arise in this country; one local crime prevention co-ordinator remarked to me, "co-ordinators really have to hype up effectiveness for the local politicians".

The only antidote to this kind of thing is properly rigorous research. This point was recognized by the recent Home Office Working Group on the Costs of Crime (Home Office 1988b, pp.36–8), which concluded that, in crime prevention, there was often 'an absence of detailed evaluation', and that:

by neglecting monitoring, few crime prevention schemes effectively incorporate the ongoing management which is so often necessary for achieving a successful outcome (p.37).

The Working Group went on to make the valuable additional point that low priority was often given to cost factors even when rigorous evaluations were attempted.

At this particular stage in the development of crime prevention, as local programmes multiply and everyone is becoming more conscious of the possible real benefits of crime prevention initiatives, there is a very real danger that the political and practical pressures to get on with the job could easily take over, and overrun what would be the more sensible course of proceeding creatively but cautiously, with adequately rigorous research attached to the most important local developments. A particular disappointment, it has to be said, is that no proper research evaluation was built in by the Home Office to the Five Towns Initiative,‡ despite the fact that this initiative was, as I have previously noted, basically a demonstration project for the 1984 Circular. It is especially pleasing to note, therefore, that the Home Office

---

† In the light of the ESRC project team's research, the limitations of the conclusions of Poyner *et al.* (1986) are starkly apparent. Poyner *et al.* argued that, "for the purposes of crime prevention, consultation is comparatively unimportant ... consulting the residents of an area will certainly yield insights into the local problems as residents perceive or experience them, but this is not a very effective way to find out what the crime problems of an area are like. What seems essential is a properly conceived analysis of crime problems" (p.67).

‡ However, some of the five areas have produced their own reports: see for example West Glamorgan County Council (1989).

Research and Planning Unit has been commissioned to evaluate the new and larger Safer Cities Programme. Unless we continue to be rigorous about evaluation, there is a serious risk that we shall embark expensively on too many false trails in the crime prevention field.

One other matter that must be addressed in considering evaluation concerns how we respond to published research reports when they become available. Johannes Knutsson (1988), a researcher with the Swedish National Council for Crime Prevention, has published an interesting short paper discussing the reactions in Sweden to his research on Operation Identification, a property marking scheme. The research reached negative conclusions on the effectiveness of this scheme: no crime reductive efforts were found; victims stood no greater chance of recovering their property if it was marked; and the detection rate for burglaries was not affected (see Knutsson, 1984). The police, we are told, found it difficult to accept these conclusions, and tried to explain them away; the Crime Prevention Council, on the other hand, decided simply to ignore the results of the study. As Knutsson points out, all this points to an interesting paradox. On the one hand, there is often a demand from politicians and others to demonstrate effectiveness before investing, or investing further, in crime prevention programmes. On the other hand, all researchers know that research, and especially methodologically rigorous research, does sometimes produce disappointing results which are unwelcome to politicians and to sponsoring organizations. Indeed, sometimes the very same people who at one time demand evidence of *prima facie* effectiveness before embarking on a scheme, will at a later date resist the negative conclusions of methodologically rigorous research. Nor is all this just a Swedish phenomenon: in this country, some of the same responses which Knutsson encountered have been evident in the reactions to Trevor Bennett's neighbourhood watch evaluation.

Yet there is a further twist to all this. As Knutsson himself points out, "no-effect" research results do not necessarily mean that the measures evaluated are wholly ineffective. In particular, there is a possibility that they may work in social conditions other than those investigated by the researcher, and indeed there is some research evidence of precisely that phenomenon with regard to property marking schemes.†️ Thus, we should not over-generalize from negative research results, though we should also not try to pretend that they do not exist; and we should maintain a similarly balanced appraisal with regard to positive research results. The required qualities in assessing and responding to research results are adequate attention to technical rigour; a good sense of judgement in knowing how to place the results in a wider research and social context; a steady nerve in handling the political clamour, from one side or the other or both, which may arise from any particular set of results; and a creativeness in shaping policy in accordance with research results as they emerge. Needless to say, this prescription is easy to offer, but very hard to carry out in practice.

---

† So, for example, in the United States and Canada "households that participated in the [property-marking] program ... generally experienced significantly lower burglary rates than non-participants", even though—given generally low participation rates—"there is little evidence that property-marking programs influence citywide burglary rates" (Rosenbaum 1988, p.345). A study by the Home Office Crime Prevention Unit in South Wales showed a more positive result, with a highly significant reduction in burglary incidents for participants, no reduction for non-participants, and an overall reduction in rates (Laycock, 1985). In this project, a very high participation rate (72%) was achieved, and the project area was ringed with uninhabited hills, limiting the scope for geographical displacement to other areas.

CRIME PREVENTION AND THE WIDER SOCIETY

Professor Norval Morris, the distinguished Australian-born criminologist, was at one time the director of the United Nations Asia and Far East Institute for the Prevention of Crime and the Treatment of Offenders. In that position, he has recalled, he was occasionally questioned by trainees from underdeveloped Asian countries with low crime rates who, anxious about signs of increasing crime in their societies, sought his advice on how these trends could be halted. Norval Morris's reply was straightforward. He used to sketch, he has told us,

with a wealth of detail, the horrors of increased delinquency and crime that would flow from any serious attempt to industrialise, urbanise, or educate their communities. He would conclude with a peroration against the establishment of an international airline (Morris and Hawkins, 1969, p.49).

Early in the 1980s, Barry Poyner, a British researcher in the field of environmental criminology, suggested that, in the interests of burglary prevention,

areas of wealthy or middle-class/middle-income housing should be separated as far as possible from poorer housing (Poyner 1983, p.36).

The first of these two pieces of advice was given ironically, and the second seriously. But they both draw attention to an important point, namely that, at the end of the day, some things are more important than crime prevention. Norval Morris's suggestions were universally rejected, as he expected them to be, because although in strictly criminological terms the advice was entirely sound,† the fact was that his Asian trainees were prepared to put up with a probable increase in crime as a by-product of what they perceived to be the necessary economic expansion and modernisation of their countries. As for Barry Poyner's proposal, many people would, I hope, join with me in rejecting this suggestion, even if (which is debatable) it were sound in crime prevention terms, since we should wish to try to foster a sense of community and common interest among people of different social classes and income levels, rather than to emphasize social separateness by deliberately creating the greatest possible degree of residential segregation.

Tensions of a not dissimilar kind can arise, though naturally in a more mundane way, in local crime prevention projects. In one area studied by the ESRC project team, for example, it was found that

as a result of [a high-technology crime prevention] initiative, old age pensioners were trapped inside a fortress of heavy doors and electronic card-key devices which they found difficult to understand and to operate, while neighbours were no longer able to keep a friendly eye on them (Sampson *et al.*, 1988, p.484).

I mentioned earlier that the 1984 crime commission in The Netherlands postulated increasing individualism, and the weakening influence of many traditional social institutions, as a major reason for the increased criminality of the post-war period (Netherlands Ministry of Justice, 1985). If this analysis is correct, it poses an important challenge for social crime prevention. But an alternative interpretation might be that perhaps the thrust towards individualism will be so strong that it will place severe limits upon the ultimate effectiveness of all crime prevention programmes

---

† Or at least, it would be so in the usual case. However, Japan is an interesting counter-case of a society which, in the post-World War II period, experienced a decline in crime rates despite rapid modernisation: see Braithwaite (1989, pp.61–5). The evidence suggests that there have been special reasons for this experience in Japan, and that the counter-example does not invalidate the general validity of Morris's claim.

20   A. E. BOTTOMS

that we now attempt, just as any crime prevention programmes we might seek to establish in a rapidly-modernising Asian country would probably be of limited effect.

I profoundly hope that this alternative interpretation of our own situation is an over-pessimistic one. For if individualism really is unstoppable, the end result, or nightmare, could ultimately be a society with massive security hardware protecting individual homes, streets, and shops, while all adult citizens would carry personal alarms, and perhaps guns, for individual protection while moving from place to place. But even if this heavy investment in defensive technology were to decrease crime rates, all the evidence suggests it would increase people's fear of crime (Rosenbaum 1988, pp. 330–339). It would also create a society which I, for one, would find a good deal less attractive than the kind of society in which we now live. There are thus good social as well as criminological reasons for advocating, as we move forward into the 1990s, a balanced programme of crime prevention measures embracing not only situational and developmental measures, but also an emphasis upon social integration and social relationships.

ACKNOWLEDGEMENTS

I am most grateful to Mark Liddle, a Ph.D. student at the Cambridge Institute of Criminology, for research assistance in the preparation of the James Smart Lecture. I also wish to thank a number of researchers and crime prevention project co-odinators, and officials at the Home Office and the Scottish Office, who kindly gave of their time to provide information either to Mark Liddle or to myself. Naturally, none of these persons should be held responsible for any of the views expressed.

References

Allatt, P. (1984*a*) Residential security: containment and displacement of burglary, *Howard Journal of Criminal Justice*, **23**, 99–116.
Allatt, P. (1984*b*) Fear of crime: the effect of improved residential security on a difficult to let estate, *Howard Journal of Criminal Justice*, **23**, 170–182.
Balvig, F. (1988) *Delinquent and Not-Delinquent Youth* (Kriminalistisk Instituts Stencilserie No.43), Copenhagen: Institute of Criminal Science, University of Copenhagen.
Barr, R. and Pease, K. (1990) Crime displacement, in: M. Tonry and N. Morris (Eds.) *Crime and Justice: A Review of Research*, vol.12, Chicago: University of Chicago Press.
Bennett, T. (1989) *Evaluating Neighbourhood Watch*, Aldershot: Gower.
Bennett, T. and Wright, R. (1984) *Burglars on Burglary*, Aldershot: Gower.
Blagg, H., Pearson, G., Sampson, A., Smith, D. and Stubbs, P. (1988) Inter-agency co-operation: rhetoric and reality, in: T. Hope and M. Shaw (Eds.) *Communities and Crime Reduction*, London: HMSO
Bottoms, A. E., Brown, P., McWiliams, B., McWilliams, W. and Nellis, M. (1990) *Intermediate Treatment: Key Findings and Implications from a National Survey*, London: HMSO.
Bottoms, A. E. and Wiles, P. (1988) Crime and housing policy: a framework for crime prevention analysis, in: T. Hope and M. Shaw (Eds.) *Communities and Crime Reduction*, London: HMSO.
Braithwaite, J. (1989) *Crime, Shame and Re-Integration*, Cambridge: Cambridge University Press.
Clarke, R. V. (1983) Situational crime prevention: its theoretical basis and practical scope, in: M. Tonry and N. Morris (Eds.) *Crime and Justice: An Annual Review of Research*, vol.4, Chicago: University of Chicago Press.
Clarke, R. V. and Hough, M. (1984) *Crime and Police Effectiveness*, Home Office Research Study No.79, London: HMSO
Clarke, R. V. and Mayhew, P. (Eds.) (1980) *Designing Out Crime*, London: HMSO
Coleman, A. (1985) *Utopia on Trial*, London: Hilary Shipman.
Coleman, A. (1989) Disposition and situation: two sides of the same crime, in: D. J. Evans and D. T. Herbert (Eds.) *The Geography of Crime*, London: Routledge.

Cooke, D. J. (1989) Containing violent prisoners: an analysis of the Barlinnie Special Unit, *British Journal of Criminology*, **29**, 129–143.

Crime Concern (1989) *Working in Partnership with Local Government, the Business Sector and the Police to Meet the Challenge of Crime: A Briefing Paper*, Swindon: Crime Concern.

Dawson, J., Middleton, S. and Sill, A. (1987) *Fear and Crime in the Inner City*, Leicester: Community Consultants.

Ekblom, P. and Simon, F. (1988) *Crime and Racial Harassment in Asian-Run Small Shops*, Crime Prevention Unit Paper No.15, London: Home Office.

Farrington, D. P. (1985) Predicting self-reported and official delinquency in: D. P. Farrington and R. Tarling (Eds.) *Prediction in Criminology*, Albany: State University of New York Press.

Farrington, D. P. (1987) Early precursors of frequent offending, in: J. Q. Wilson and G. C. Loury (Eds.), *From Children to Citizens: vol.III, Families, Schools and Delinquency Prevention*, New York: Springer.

Farrington, D. P. (1989) Implications of Criminal Career Research for the Prevention of Offending, paper delivered at the British Criminology Conference, Bristol, July 1989 (unpublished: copy lodged in the library of the Institute of Criminology, University of Cambridge).

Forrester, D., Chatterton, M. and Pease, K. (1988) *The Kirkholt Burglary Prevention Project, Rochdale*, Crime Prevention Unit Paper No.13, London: Home Office.

Heal, K. and Laycock, G. (Eds.) (1986) *Situational Crime Prevention: From Theory into Practice*, London: HMSO.

Heal, K. and Laycock, G. (1988) The development of crime prevention: issues and limitations, in: T. Hope and M. Shaw (Eds.), *Communities and Crime Reduction*, London: HMSO.

Hedges, A., Blaber, A. and Mostyn, B. (1980) *Community Planning Project: Cunningham Road Improvement Scheme, Final Report*, London: Social and Community Planning Research.

Home Office (1985) Criminal careers of those. born in 1953, 1958 and 1963, *Home Office Statistical Bulletin 7/1985*, London: Home Office.

Home Office (1988a) *The Five Towns Initiative: A Community Response to Crime Reduction*, London: Home Office.

Home Office (1988b) *Report of the Working Group on the Costs of Crime*, London: Home Office.

Home Office (1988c) *Safer Cities Programme*, London: Home Office.

Home Office, Department of Education and Science, Department of Environment, Department of Health and Social Security. and Welsh Office (1984) *Crime Prevention* (Home Office circular 8/1984), London: Home Office.

Hope, T. and Murphy, D. J. I. (1983) Problems of implementing crime prevention: the experience of a demonstration project, *Howard Journal of Penology and Crime Prevention*, **22**, 38–50.

Husain, S. (1988) *Neighbourhood Watch in England and Wales: A Locational Analysis*, Crime Prevention Unit Paper No.12, London: Home Office.

Jones, T., Maclean, B. and Young, J. (1986) *The Islington Crime Survey*, Aldershot: Gower.

King, M. (1988) *How to Make Social Crime Prevention Work: The French Experience*, London: NACRO.

Knutsson, J. (1984) *Operation Identification: A Way to Prevent Burglaries?*, Research Division Report No.14, Stockholm: National Council for Crime Prevention.

Knutsson, J. (1988) Crime preventive councils in Scandinavia: possibilities, problems, evaluations, in: J. Jäger (Ed.) *Gewalt in Unseren Städten: Als Beispiel für Aufgaben der Kommunalen Kriminalpolitik*, Munster: Polizei-Fuhrungsakademie.

Laycock, G. (1985) *Property Marking: A Deterrent to Domestic Burglary?*, Crime Prevention Unit Paper No.3, London: Home Office.

Laycock, G. and Heal, K. (1989) Crime prevention: the British experience, in: D. J. Evans and D. T. Herbert (Eds.) *The Geography of Crime*, London: Routledge.

Lea, J., Jones, T., Woodhouse, T. and Young, J. (1988) *Preventing Crime: The Hilldrop Environmental Improvement Survey, First Report*, Enfield: Centre for Criminology, Middlesex Polytechnic.

Lurigio, A. J. and Rosenbaum, D. P. (1986) Evaluation research in community crime prevention: a critical look at the field, in: D. P. Rosenbaum (Ed.) *Community Crime Prevention: Does It Work?*, Beverly Hills: Sage.

Mayhew, P., Elliott, D. and Dowds, L. (1989) *The 1988 British Crime Survey*, Home Office Research Study No.111, London: HMSO.

Morris, N. and Hawkins, G. (1969) *The Honest Politician's Guide to Crime Control*, Chicago: University of Chicago Press.

NACRO (1989) *Crime Prevention and Community Safety: A Practical Guide for Local Authorities*, London: NACRO.

Netherlands Ministry of Justice (1985) *Society and Crime: A Policy Plan for the Netherlands*, The Hague: Ministerie van Justitie.

Northumbria Police (1989) *Chief Constable's Annual Report for 1988*, Newcastle: Northumbria Police.

Painter. K. (1988) *Lighting and Crime Prevention: The Edmonton Project*, Enfield: Centre for Criminology, Middlesex Polytechnic.

Phillips. S. and Cochrane, R. (1988) *Crime and Nuisance in the Shopping Centre: A Case Study in Crime Prevention*, Crime Prevention Unit Paper No.16, London: Home Office.

Poyner. B. (1983) *Design against Crime*, London: Butterworths.

Poyner. B., Webb, B. and Woodall, R. (1986) *Crime Reduction on Housing Estates: An Evaluation of NACRO's Crime Prevention Programme*, London: Tavistock Institute of Human Relations.

Rosenbaum, D.P. (1988) Community crime prevention: a review and synthesis of the literature, *Justice Quarterly*, **5**, 323–395.

Rutter. M. and Giller, H. (1983) *Juvenile Delinquency: Trends and Prospects*, Harmondsworth: Penguin.

Sampson, A., Stubbs, P., Smith, D., Pearson, G. and Blagg, H. (1988) Crime, localities and the multi-agency approach, *British Journal of Criminology*, **28**, 478–493.

Scottish Office (1984) *Crime Prevention* (circular issued by the Scottish Home and Health Department (SHHD Police Circular No.4/1984) and the Scottish Development Department (SDD Circular No. 20/84)), Edinburgh: Scottish Office.

Shapland, J. and Wiles, P. (Eds.) (1989) *Business and Crime: A Consultation*. Swindon: Crime Concern.

Van Andel, H. (1989) Crime prevention that works: the care of public transport in The Netherlands, *British Journal of Criminology*, **29**, 47–56.

Waller. I. (1988) *Current Trends in European Crime Prevention: Implications for Canada*, Ottawa: Department of Justice Canada.

West Glamorgan County Council (1989) *West Glamorgan County Council Crime Prevention Initiative: The Progress of the Initiative 1986–1989*, Swansea: West Glamorgan County Council.

Whiskin, N. (1987) Crime prevention: an inter-agency approach at neighbourhood level, in: J. Junger-Tas, A. Rutting and J. Wilzing (Eds.) *Crime Control in Local Communities in Europe*. Lochem: J. B. van den Brink.

26

Policing and Society, 1991, Vol. 2, pp. 17–30
Reprints available directly from the publisher
Photocopying permitted by license only

GREY POLICING: A THEORETICAL FRAMEWORK

BOB HOOGENBOOM

Leiden University, Department of Public Administration, Postbox 9555,
2300 RB Leiden, The Netherlands.

(Received 6 July 1990; in final form 2 January 1991)

In the Netherlands regulatory bodies and private policing increasingly undertake different repressive police tasks. The growth of these forms of policing is related to crises in the welfare state. The welfare state encounters financial pressures hence the need for control in social-economic processes grows. Increasingly regulatory bodies investigate different forms of 'welfare crime'. At the same time the welfare state is faced with pressure of continuing privatization in many policy areas including policing. The Netherlands has witnessed the dispersal of the police function. On a theoretical level this is analyzed with notions developed by Foucault (disciplinary power) and Cohen (dispersal of social control and blurring). Although criminal policy in the Netherlands advocates a 'multi-agency' approach, attention is drawn to 'grey policing': forms of cooperation between different social control agencies, mostly on a 'rank and file' level, that take on the form of using each other's (police) powers, exchanging legally protected information and passing on the 'dirty work'. Dispersal of the police function on the one hand and (possible) accompanying 'grey policing' on the other hand could have important consequences for the accountability-debate in matters of policing.

KEY WORDS: Policing, regulatory bodies, private policing, social control, accountability, welfare state.

1 INTRODUCTION

When we think of policing the colour blue comes to mind. The blue uniform is the symbol of police forces throughout the western world. For the general public it signifies police visibility. Of course, policing involves more than visible surveillance. However, for arguments sake I take the 'blue' methaphor as a starting point. Visibility on the streets of cities is but one of the characteristics that ensures 'transparency' in matters of policing. In general transparency in a political system refers to notions like accountability, control and power over the police. Law, and more specifically criminal law and the criminal code, are among the forces that shape the form of policing. Theoretically, policing in western democracies can be influenced and controlled through various political channels at the state, regional and local levels, dependent on the specific structure of the police system in a given country. The exercise of the monopoly of force by the state ought in this sense, to be transparent. Through parliament, city-councils and varying complaint procedures democratic control can be exercised. Given the fact that 'police accountability' is a recurrent theme on the political agenda both in the United Kingdom and different continental countries, it is more appropriate to speak of the existence of a delicate equilibrium (Morgan and Smith 1989, Nogala 1989). From time to time, the actual degree of police accountability is called into question—not only with respect to policing within different countries, but also regarding matters of international police cooperation, such as the Schengen-treaty and Trevi-arrangement (Busch, Funk, and Werkentin 1990).

This article also touches upon the issue of accountability, but takes a somewhat different perspective. I aim to broaden the discussion on police transparancy/accountability by extending the focus beyond the police to so called regulatory units or inspectorates and the private security sector. I will argue that criminological research, and more specifically police research in the Netherlands, is too narrowly focused on the traditional police and the criminal justice system. Other forms of policing, and agencies of informal and semi-formal social control play an increasingly important role. However, I will not discuss these developments in extenso. Some excellent research has been done in this field (Shearing and Stenning 1987, Henry 1987). Instead of discussing these developments separately I shall focus on: the increased interconnections between the regular police and other social control agencies; the factors that positively influence this process, and the possible consequences of this blurring in view of the transparency-debate. In doing so, I shall introduce the concept of 'grey policing': informal forms of cooperation between different social control agencies for which traditional mechanisms of accountability appear obsolete. This 'grey policing' can take on different forms: the inordinate use of each other's (police) powers, the exchange of legally protected information and the sharing of technological gadgets.

To arrive at this conclusion some analytical steps are necessary. In the next section the political and social-economic crises of the welfare state will be discussed. Subsequently, emerging patterns of social control will be analyzed. This will be done by introducing theoretical notions developed by Michael Foucault and Stanley Cohen. In the Netherlands some of these notions have been used to analyze developments within regulatory bodies and the private security sector; a short overview of this work will be given in section four. In the fifth section, criminal policy with regard to these domains will be the central focus: the emerging 'Police Complex'. In the final section the concept of 'grey policing' is introduced as a possible (and plausible) scenario for developments of policing in the nineties.

2 CRISES OF THE WELFARE STATE

Usually the debate on crime and policing focuses on specific events: the Brixton-riots, the Miner's strike, poll-tax riots and IRA-bombings. These events receive much attention. Specific parts of a conflict are highlighted. For instance police violence is criticized or criminalization of politically motivated social protest takes place. Policing in this way is often depoliticised and decontextualized. The inherently political nature of policing and structural social-economic conditions of western domocracies do not figure prominently (Reiner 1985). For this reason I shall discuss some developments within the welfare state. In doing so emphasis will be placed on the relationship between the crises of the welfare state and developments within the regulatory bodies or inspectorates and the private security sector.

In the field of political sociology and public administration crises of the welfare state are analyzed from different perspectives. Government bureaucracies have come under scrutiny. One school of thought focuses on the weaknesses of traditional decision making, constraints on available resources, ever growing demands on governmental services by the public, the lack of a dominant ideology of the welfare state, and organizational and administrative problems in formulating and implementing policies (Peters 1989). Claus Offe (1984), in a neo-marxist perspective, draws attention to the existence of structural contradictions of the welfare state. In his view the welfare state is a political solution for societal divisions. The welfare state consists of three subsystems: the administrative-political system, the social system and the economic system. Each system processes different and at times incompatible demands. The following problems complicate the relationship between the three systems:

—the pressure of continuing privatization;

—the need of the state to guarantee accumulation in the economic system because the state depends on this for the financing of the social systems;

—the fiscal bottleneck: to what extent can the state interfere in the economic system through taxation?

Conservatives, liberals and neo-marxists are in agreement about the financial problems of the welfare state, although differences about causes and solutions exist of course. For decades, the institutions of the welfare state have developed and elaborate social programs have been initiated. The Netherlands witnessed the emergence of what has been called a 'Welfare Complex' (Rosenthal 1986). Alongside the repressive complex of the state with its traditional departments like Defence, the Home Office, Foreign Affairs and the Financial department, state intervention in social-economic processes has become apparent. Within the welfare complex, state intervention took on a whole new meaning. Through an extensive system of subsidies and social security schemes the state positively influenced education, housing, medical arrangements and (temporarily) unemployment. Growing state intervention is illustrated by new departments like Agriculture, Economics, Social Security and Cultural and Educational departments. From the early seventies onward this welfare complex encountered financial pressures. In the last 15 years efforts were made to cut budgets, improve the effiency of state bureaucracies and delegate tasks to the private sector.

   In the same period crime figures rose ten fold. In the political arena this rise in crime has been largely ascribed to the decline of many traditional social institutions within which the behaviour of individuals is effectively normalized, such as the family, clubs, associations, churches and schools (Society and Crime 1985). As in many European countries a neo-conservative discourse dominates discussions on crime: the relative decline of traditional values is said to induce people to commit crimes (Nogala 1989). Criticism by social scientists, and criminologists in particular, stresses the fact that these kind of analysis are somewhat superficial. The crime-issue is detached from structural developments both in society at large and from changes taking place in social control agencies. It is not only that the socio-economic context and the relationship with crime is their primary focus—that in itself is a mere reflection of the 'battle' in criminology between different schools of thought. The rhetoric and symbolism of the neo-conservative discourse is also contradicted by structural analyses of changes in the pattern of social control that actually indicate a reverse development: a dispersal of social control is taking place. This argument will be the subject of the following section.

3   THE DISPERSAL OF SOCIAL CONTROL

Criminological research in the Netherlands is almost entirely devoted to the criminal justice system of the state. Of course, studies exist of informal justice and more recently the field of regulatory bodies and private policing has been opened up. But the mainstream of criminological research focuses on the traditional criminal justice system. In this respect Dutch research fits the pattern observed in criminological research in general: "Inherent in the idea of a nation state is the notion that the state is the public authority and all other authorities operating within its terrority are subordinate to it" (Shearing and Stenning 1987). State formation processes from the 16th century onward have led to the monopolization of force by the state. Within this framework crime control and to some extent also formal social control in general have come to be viewed as the exclusive responsibility of the police and the criminal justice system. This framework has all the characteristics of a paradigm in Kuhn's sense of the word: the 'normal science' of crime is state-oriented (Shearing and Stenning 1987, Kuhn 1962).

Researchers like South (1988) who challenge this framework make use of the work done by Michel Foucault (1975) and Stanley Cohen (1985). Foucault's importance lies in his analyses of what he calls the 'Disciplinary Society'. He breaks the state-oriented framework because he places the juridico-political structure of a society only at the top of the social control pyramid. The criminal justice system, and other state agencies, only deal with specific forms of deviant behaviour. In focusing on the criminal justice system criminology reinforces the commonly held view in which the police, the courts and the prison system are seen as the 'crime fighters'. Foucault stresses the fact that the criminal justice system actually deals with a limited number of deviants and categories of deviancy. Outside the criminal justice system other forms of social control with different goals are operating. Foucault puts the position of police and other state-institutions into a broader social perspective, amidst other forms of social control. Underneath, or next to, the juridico-political structure operate so called disciplines: types of power, techniques for assuring the ordering of human multiplicities. Disciplines can be regarded as a sort of infra-law. They fulfill three main functions: Firstly, to achieve the exercise of power at the lowest possible costs, both economically and politically. Disciplines obtain the latter by discretion, low exteriorization and relative invisibility.

Second, they serve to bring the effects of social power to their maximum intensity and to extend them as far as possible. Third, they link this 'economic' growth of power with the output of the apparatuses (educational, military, industrial or medical) (Foucault 1975).

How is this done? Foucault mentions time tables, training, exercises, total and detailed observations, hierarchical surveillance, continuous registration, perpetual assesment and classification. Social control then is exercised by a wide variety of organizations and agencies.

Stanley Cohen also challenges the neo-conservative discourse: the crime control net is actually expanding and being strengthened. Control mechanisms are dispersed into the community, they penetrate even deeper into social fabric, touching more and more people. The control machine 'sucks in its prey'. New categories and sub-categories of deviance and control are constantly being created. Agencies concerned with these new forms of deviance are marking out their own territories of jurisdiction, competence and referral, and produce their own 'scientific' knowledge (Cohen 1985).

How is this done? Cohen mentions screening devices, diagnostic tests, treatment modalities and evaluation scales. For Cohen the emerging patterns of social control are: dispersal, penetration, blurring, absorption and widening.

The differences between Cohen and Foucault is that the latter sees the formation of disciplines—or infra-laws—operating underneath, or outside, the juridico-political structure. Cohen, on the other hand, sees net-widening in terms of the strengthening of state intervention. The decarceration movement of the sixties has not replaced the prison with 'community alternatives'. Instead of diverting deviants away from the criminal justice system it led to a disguised dispersal of social control by the state. The boundaries between controllers and those being controlled are blurred: pre-trial diversion projects; community, foster, and group homes; forestry camps; outward-bound projects; day, training, and community centres; community service centres; electronic monitoring and reparation projects; and reconciliation schemes.

Rule of law?

We are prisoners of our own thinking: Weber's definition of the state in terms of its monopoly of violence, the pervasive definition of crime in judicial terms and subsequent pleas for more police, more prisons, harsher punishments and more extensive powers, conjures up an image of the state not only as the sole but also as the effective answer to crime. Media mystification further builds and maintains this image. Relevant in this context is the fact that the exercise of state power is limited by criminal law. But if the criminal justice system is predominantly oriented towards only a relatively small fraction of deviant behaviour (street crimes and traditional crimes like murder, robbery etc.) and more and more behaviour is monitored, controlled and influenced by other agencies and corporations outside the state realm, how does this development relate to the rule of law?

Foucault questions the democratic character of some of the institutions in which he analyzes disciplinary power-relations. The rule of law does not apply in disciplinary settings. Disciplinary power signals a total rejection of universal norms like equality, justice for all, and fairness, in certain setting like the educational system, mental hospitals, the military, bureaucracies and in the business community. Disciplines are essentially nonegalitarian and asymmetrical and therefore undermine the limits that are traced around the law (Foucault 1975). All of us have had some experiences with disciplinary power: the drill exercises in the army, the house rules of companies, the rules and regulations of schools, the wheelings and dealings of a superior in a bureaucratic setting for whom you trade freedom of speech for career advantages, yet we hold onto the universal norms like the rule of law and other domocratic ideals when in every day life these are sometimes phantoms of the opera. In the available literature the examples of such (sexual) abuse of power in therapeutic settings as rape and child abuse are sufficient to open our eyes further. Perhaps the most incisive analyses of disciplinary power, although from a different theoretical perspective, have been made by Goffman (1962) in his study *Asylums*.

How do disciplines and the juridico-political system interact? According to Foucault disciplines serve as intermediaries: they support and reinforce their political counterpart. They are somehow linked together, interwoven with each other. Of course this goes without saying: if a person is disciplined through a number of different agencies the chance of getting into contact with the criminal justice system will probably be small. In this respect disciplines support the juridico-political system. But what of the opposite? This juridico-political system operates within the boundaries of the rule of law. What if the disciplines—with their essentially non-egalitarian character—get mixed up with the workings of the criminal justice system? This raises the question of blurring, mentioned by Cohen, i.e. the disappearance of boundaries between different types of social control agencies: it is no longer obvious who controls whom, and the public-private distinction withers away through neighbourhood-watch, community-policing schemes, the growth of private policing and the overall dispersal of social control.

Neither Foucault nor Cohen question these developements from a rule of law perspective: whether or not the growing interweaving of the criminal justice system and these dispersed other forms of policing and social control. could negatively affect the formal system. For example, if forms of disciplinary powers. methods of operation, the infra-structure, the sometimes extensive information gathering and administrative or quasi police powers of (informal) social control get mixed up with the operations of the criminal justice system, this could threaten the rule of law.

In the following two sections I shall argue that this is what actually happens in a specific part of the social control map of the Netherlands. The concepts of dispersal and blurring have been instrumental in my analysis of regulatory bodies and private policing in the Netherlands and consequently in the formulation of the concept of 'grey policing'.

4 REGULATORY BODIES AND PRIVATE POLICING: THE DISPERSAL OF THE POLICE FUNCTION

Within the Dutch welfare complex we find some 40 to 45 regulatory bodies, or inspectorates, as they are sometimes called. It is estimated that they employ some 20,000 officials who have different police powers but also have at their disposal extensive controlling powers. They have controlling tasks in such diverse fields as education, labour matters (safety, working hours), environment (permits to dump toxic wastes), social security (unemployment benefits) and economics (transportation rules, import and export regulations). Special social-economic laws, covering subjects from the closing hours of shops to the export of military products, stipulate the activities of the regulatory bodies. These agencies have a different approach to the enforcement of economic laws from the police enforcement of criminal laws. The latter is characterized in the Netherlands by what is called a normative approach: theoretically an offence will always be processed through the criminal justice system. However, the regulatory bodies employ a more pragmatic approach: with negotiation, information, guidance and persuasion an offender is 'talked into' changing his behaviour. Criminal law is only the last resort. In the Netherlands criticism of these regulatory bodies or inspectorates is growing. Fundamentally this criticism is directed at the fact that controllers find themself in an ambivalent position. On the one hand they have to enforce economic laws, on the other hand they have to carry out the policies of their respective departments. A tension is apparent because these policies are aimed at improving the position of certain industries and trades. Strict enforcement of economic laws could hinder this. In the summer of 1990 this tension has become very prominent in the case of the inspectorate of the Department of Agriculture. In parliament questions were asked about supposed neglect by the inspectorate in controlling fishermen, who overstepped fishing limits set by the European Community, and farmers, who, for years, have dumped manure on a scale that has become detrimental to the environment.

However, from the early seventies onward changes took place in the structure and modus operandi of these organizations (Hoogenboom 1985).

Firstly, there emerged new inspections in the social security system. On the local level, special social security investigators were increasingly integrated into different social security departments. Other agencies responsible for the collection and payment of unemployment benefits within the social security sector underwent similar changes.

Secondly, these changes were accompanied by a new recruitment policy: former police officials, especially detectives, found their way into the regulatory units. At the same time training and infra-structure (computerization, communications of the units, criminal observation units) were professionalized.

This development has been described in terms of a dispersal of the police function in the Netherlands: organizations within the welfare complex gradually take over characteristics and modus operandi of the repressive complex. The welfare and repressive complex become blurred. An explanation for this can be found in the crisis of the welfare state. Large sums of money have come to be distributed through the welfare complex. Yet, the economic crisis has led to a policy of financial cuts. Subsequent retrenchment policies magnified the perceived problems of misuse (frauds) of subsidies and especially social security benefits. Moreover, the relationship between industrial growth and the accompanying consequences for the environment increasingly dominate the political agenda. Hence, a need for more control developed, which the welfare agencies—under strong cutback pressures—were eager to take upon themselves. There are obvious limits to the pragmatic approach. However, some nuances must be noted. Although inspectorates gradually take over characteristics of the regular police a tension in the enforcement of economic laws still exists between repressive objectives and underlying economic interests. This conflict of interest seems to be more dominant in matters of environmental crimes and frauds with EG-subsidies than in the social security system. Perhaps an explanation for this can be found in the tension between the different subsystems of the welfare state, as mentioned by Offe. Although the welfare complex seems to have taken over characteristics of the repressive complex, investment in manpower, budgets and equipment are directed primarily at improving the detection of social security frauds. Is there not only a fiscal bottleneck but also an economic control bottleneck? In other words, although a more repressive approach can be found towards certain forms of welfare crime (frauds with subsidies etc.), an uneven distribution seems to have taken place: detection of unemployment benefits seems to have priority over intensifying the detection of different forms of white collar crime.

Private policing

It can be argued that the social-economic crisis also influences developments within the private security industry. Loss-prevention is the main objective of private policing. 'Policing for profit' and 'Justice for profit' are used to describe the objectives of private policing which definitely differ from the state objectives of crime control (Spitzer and Scull 1977). 'Justice for profit' draws attention to conflict resolution schemes which by-pass the criminal justice system. Private policing is an integral part of the structure of companies whose objective is to maximise profits and thus minimize losses. In other words private policing fullfills all three criteria of disciplinary power as defined by Foucault. Private policing introduces disciplinary forms of power into the structure of companies to improve the economic output. The

24   B. HOOGENBOOM

existence of private justice furthermore indicates the point mentioned by Foucault about the discretion and relative invisbility of disciplinary power.

Private policing antedates public policing. The United States especially has a long tradition of private policing. The industry started expanding worldwide in the late sixties. A causal relationship between this growth and the international recession of the early seventies probably exists.

In the Netherlands, the growth rate of private security in the seventies drew the attention of the Justice department. In 1979, adjustments were made in the law regulating the industry. After 1979 the private sector kept expanding. In that year 9,000 private guards were registered. In 1989 there were 14.000 guards.

A parallel can be drawn with the regulatory bodies. Increasingly, former police officials at management and executive levels are being employed by security companies. This in itself is nothing new. Recruitment of police officers has been a recurrent theme in the history of private policing. However, what is new is the higher turn-over rate and the fact that more and more former police detectives are employed by multinationals, insurance companies and banks to investigate internal-, insurance-, and cheque frauds (Hoogenboom 1988). Once again it can be argued that the police function is being dispersed throughout Dutch society: characteristics and modus operandi of the public police are integrated into the structure of private enterprises. A blurring between private and public sectors is the result.

5   THE POLICING COMPLEX

Commentators on Dutch policing forecast a development in which public policing will inevitably cooperate intensively with regulatory bodies and the private sector (Fijnaut 1985, Heyder 1989). The end result of such an integration process would be the existence of a 'Policing Complex'. Discussions on this topic evolve around subjects like information-sharing, the joint use of training facilities and combined investigations in specific cases. There are several reasons why a 'Policing Complex' is likely to develop.

First, the government, faced with an ever increasing crime-problem looks for ways of solving the capacity limits of the police and criminal justice system in general. As remarked earlier crime figures rose tenfold in the last twenty years. An influential criminal policy report *Society and Crime*, published in 1985, emphasized: "the co-responsibility of all sectors of society (that) must be activated in the prevention of petty crime". This led to encouragement by financial incentives, of occupational surveillance by public transportation personal, janitors, shopstaffs, sportscoaches, youthworkers etc.

The introduction of occupational surveillance was backed up by changes in criminal law, aimed at improving efficiency in criminal procedures, expanding prison capacity and organizational changes in the CID-organisation (larger scale of operation, computerization of criminal intelligence branches), primarily aimed at improving the war against organized crime (especially drug trafficking). Part of this policy program of occupational surveillance led to stimulation of the private sector.

Secondly, in the years following the publication of *Society and Crime*, and also during the implementation of the program, a heated discussion about privatization of police tasks took place. A lot of criticism was directed at the security industry. Much of the criticism was smothered by public officials who embraced the philosophy of

Society and Crime. Representatives of the private sector did not question their line of reasoning. The Junior-Partner position of the private sector was loudly advocated. The political function of this theory could play a role: it legitimizes the position of the industry and clouds issues like private investigations and private justices.

Thirdly, organized crime became an important topic. Annual reports from the Prosecuting-Attornies continually touched upon the subject of developing better information exchanges with the regulatory bodies, especially in matters of organized crime. The underlying reason was that these organizations, operating in specific areas of economic life, in the course of their duties gather useful information about criminal activities. Due to the fact that the line between organized crime and the respectable business community has come under scrutiny, and more and more attention is being given to corporate crimes (most particular in the field of environmental crimes), the regulatory bodies are sometimes looked at with envy by agencies in the regular criminal justice system.

Fourthly, another parallel exists with the private sector. The position of regulatory bodies, because of the publication of some highly critical research reports, became controversial. A governmental report *Re-assessment of Inspection Tasks* questioned the functioning of these inspections. Discussions on whether or not the regular police could take over certain tasks challenged the legitimacy of the regulatory bodies. The large departmental regulatory forces, combined forces, in reaction and created the 'Platform Regulatory Bodies'. In a policy-program cooperation amongst themselves and with the office of the Public Prosecutor was promoted. Again, it can be argued that political motives played a part in this.

6 GREY POLICING

Integration of the three different forms of policing is influenced by these different factors. Yet, this integration on both a management and rank and file level, is probably structurally limited by the large number of conflicting interests within the emerging Policing Complex. Different department policies, bureaupolitics and commercial interests intermingle. If we incorporate the 'Private Justice' argument—the tension between commercial interests and criminal law objectives—the complexity becomes clear. Different organizations have different objectives. Although forms of cooperation exist there are obvious limits to the proclaimed integration. In conclusion we can say that a number of political, symbolic and rhetorical mechanisms are at work.

This must not blind us to the fact that the rank and file of different organizations are probably only marginally interested in ongoing political, symbolic and ethical discussions. Their daily work is in a demanding environment, and their attention is focused on the problems of individual cases. Success is the paramount objective. In his study of 'street level bureaucrats', Lipsky (1980) analyzes the problems of policy implementation by lower bureaucrats interacting with the public: these officials have a need to structure their workload in a way that enables them to successfully counter demands from the management and the client-level. In practice, this means that street level bureaucrats autonomously decide what and how in a given situation is the best course of action. The choice he/she makes could well involve overstepping of authority or by-passing regulations and even laws.

26   B. HOOGENBOOM

The favour bank

In his novel *The Bonfire of the Vanities* Tom Wolfe (1988) writes about the informal dimension of policing: "You ever hear of the Favour Bank (..) everything in the criminal justice system in New York runs on favours. Everybody does favours for everybody else. Every chance they get, they make deposits in the Favour Bank (..) A deposit in the Favour Bank is not quid pro quo. It's saving up for a rainy day. In criminal law there's a lotta grey areas, and you gotta operate in 'em (..) if you've been making your regular deposits in the Favour Bank, then you're in a position to make contracts (..) What goes around comes around. That means if you don't take care of me today, I won't take care of you tomorrow".

Of course, this is fiction. However, as Edelman states, forms of art can function as an antidote to political mystification because works of art depend for their power upon properties that contrast revealingly with the characteristics of political language (Edelman 1988).

Lipsky developed the concept of 'street level bureaucracy' for the relationship between bureaucrats and their clients. I aim to broaden the theme to professional relationships between officials of different social control agencies. The reasons for this are the following:

Firstly, in research on the private security sector, especially with regard to cooperation with the regular police, emphasis is placed on the existence of so called 'old boy networks': informal communication networks through which (classified) information is passed on (Hollingsworth, Norton-Taylor 1988).

Second, police personnel is employed by private security companies on a free lance basis ('moonlighting') (Reiss 1988). Third, the 'Dirty Work-argument', introduced by Gary Marx (1987), is relevant in this context: officials of different social control agencies could make use of their respective (in)formal opportunities to do things their 'partners in crimefighting' are prohibited or unable to do. In this way the dirty work is passed on. Marx mentions the 'hiring' of private undercover agents by regular detectives.

Empirical evidence of the latter is absent. But research, both in the United States, Canada (Shearing, Stenning 1987) and the Netherlands (Hoogenboom 1988), has shown that 'old boy networks' and 'moonlighting' are to some extent present. Although, due to the nature of these subjects, the empirical basis of these findings is indeed a small one.

However, the three points mentioned have been instrumental in the formulation of the concept of grey policing. I must stress the fact that what follows is a hypothetical exercise.

Firstly, as we have seen, recruitment policies of regulatory bodies follow similar lines to those of security companies: increasingly former police officials find their way into different social control agencies in the welfare complex. Logically, it follows that the 'old boy' line of reasoning can be extended to these regulatory bodies. Are we indeed witnessing the emergence of a police culture that transcends existing boundaries between agencies?

Second, both the regulatory bodies or inspectorates and the private sector, have at their disposal extensive administrative and civil powers. Regulatory bodies, for example the Fiscal and Economic Investigation departments, have the right to examine accounting figures of private individuals and companies. Investigators in the social security system have the right to check on financial backgrounds of clients.

These administrative powers are limited to regulatory bodies. The regular police can only conduct these kinds of investigations with a court order. Similarly, the sector, on the basis of the laws of property and contract, possess wider powers to search employees and visitors of private property than the regular police. In this context the 'Dirty Work' argument could play a role: contacts on a personal basis could be used for investigations. On an informal basis one seeks criminal, financial, medical and other relevant personal information depending on the nature of a specific investigation. Information gathered in this way has different functions. Firstly, 'grey information' can be used as a case screening device. One can determine whether or not investments in time, organizational resources and personnel positively relate to the possible outcome of the investigation (conviction, restitution or for instance tax revenues).

Second, 'grey information' can be used as a guide in the investigation. For instance, if a (private) detective, from financial sources (tax-department, banks, insurance companies) receives information, it can be helpful in determining the direction in which the investigation should go.

Of course, a problem arises if 'grey information' has to be used in a criminal procedure. Regulatory bodies and the private security sector encounter this problem only if they resort to handing over a case to the Public Prosecutors Office. If they choose not to they can make use of it in a number of ways. For instance private companies can refuse to employ someone because of his/her criminal record and insurance companies can refuse to accept an insurance application because of medical information etc. This in itself illustrates the point that control over (semi-) official and private policing is problematic. But let us assume that 'grey information' has to be used in a criminal case. If this happens one seeks ways to make the information 'official'. A parallel with money-laundering can be made: information-laundering. This can be done in a number of ways.

Firstly, this kind of information can be used in an interrogation situation. The 'suspect' can be confronted with the far-reaching knowledge of the investigators in such a way that the psychological pressure on the 'suspect' increases enormously.

Second, different criminal and social-economic laws allows investigators to demand institutions to hand over information. However, the Public Prosecutor has to sanction this procedure. For instance, if an investigation into drug trafficking has produced 'grey information' that the 'suspect' has large deposits in bank X, the investigators confront the Public Prosecutor with the euphemism 'that they have strong indications about large sums of money' without specifying the exact source. Usually, the Public Prosecutor on the basis of this approves a formal request to bank X to hand over the suspect's account figures. In this way 'grey information' is used as a lubricant in criminal procedure.

Third, so called 'multi-agency' policy, advocated within the Policing Complex, has led to different ad hoc arrangements in which various social control agencies join forces. The political climate favors this development. An instrumental policy objective dominates the discourse: all goals seem to justify the combining of forces. Crime figures have risen and the government, in the policy plan *Society and Crime*, has actually promoted the 'multi-agency' approach. Evidently, advantageous aspects of this policy can be mentioned: the increased emphasis on prevention for instance. On the other hand this policy stimulates a further dispersal of social control, which according to Foucault and Cohen, is already structurally proceeding throughout society and its different control agencies.

Dispersal and blurring seem to be the appropriate concepts for developments in the field of crime control. They are used by authors like Foucault and Cohen. For the Netherlands I think it is justified to use them for the emergent Policing Complex: to a certain extent the boundaries between the welfare complex, repressive complex and the private security sector have become diffuse.

Until now this development has been analyzed within the traditional state framework, in which the state (police, criminal justice system) is exclusively responsible for crime control. Evidently, this framework is no longer sufficient: beside the criminal justice system an evergrowing number of social control agencies deal with an increasing amount of deviant behaviour. South (1984) proposes to use a continuum-approach. Instead of the classic state-oriented framework it is better to use a continuum of social control: 'a spectrum of 'formal' to 'informal' institutions of rule enforcement, investigation, abjudication and discipline'.

However, the rule of law with its balance between instrumental objectives and values like fairness and equity, only applies to the traditional criminal justice system. For this reason I think it is justified to incorporate in this continuum-approach the question of accountability, and of general democratic control by the political system over these agencies.

Political realitites

However, in the Netherlands a one-sided argument came to the force: regulatory bodies and the private security sector took over the modus operandi of the repressive complex of the state. Subsequently, criminal policy has redefined these developments in instrumental terms. A 'multi-agency' approach was the result. This policy neglects the various conflicting interests within the Policing Complex.

Furthermore, this policy neglects the following aspects: because of their uniforms, the general public ascribes police powers to private guards; the limited control by the Public Prosecutor's Office over the priorities adopted by Inspectorates and private security companies, and consequently its limited control on modus operandi of these agencies; the existence of extensive (controlling) powers and their possible effect on citizens; the use of illegal equipment (listening devices) by the private sector and the possible use of 'economic coercion' in private justice settings.

In these sectors the dispersal of the police function increasingly leads to quasi legal and informal forms of social control about which the Public Prosecutor's Office has only limited knowledge. The Inspectorates and the private policing sector autonomously decide when offences will be processed through the criminal justice system. Due-process safeguards, or rather the possible lack of them, are not perceived as a problem in crime control policy. If they are mentioned at all it is in passing. Predominantly, the dispersal of the police function is viewed in positive terms: a welcome development that supplements the overburdened criminal justice system.

Moreover, this policy neglects what I propose to call 'grey policing': possible forms of cooperation, mostly on a personal basis, between various officials of social control agencies outside the boundaries of (criminal) law (privacy-laws, criminal code) on which democratic control, and also control by the management of different agencies, is absent. Transparency in matters of policing could well be affected by this 'grey policing'.

The following observations are also theoretically relevant. Firstly, the criminal policy of the Dutch government advocates the multi-agency approach. On the level of political symbolism both regulatory bodies and the private security community probably pay lip service to this approach: cooperation is only sought if this is to the advantage of an agency in a specific case. A large number of conflicting interests intermingle. Together they hinder, or at least slow down, the integration of different forms of policing. In this way a top-down approach towards the Police-complex has only a limited value. Secondly, the rank and file of different agencies at the same time could gradually weave a grey pattern of informal cooperation between them. In this way a bottom-up approach towards the Police-complex would be more appropriate.

On a theoretical level it is necessary to develop a framework that does justice both to organizational conflicts of interests at the management-level, and to street-level cooperation on an ad hoc basis, differing in time and form from case to case, which actually neglects the existence of elite conflicts of interests. What is evident however is the fact that the bottom-up and top-down approach contradict each other.

The implication of this is that the expansion of 'grey policing', given these contradictions, is actually a classic management problem: in what way is it possible to control the 'street-cops'? This is problematic, as we know from organizational sociology research, both in public administration at large and in the police organization in particular. The fact that different factors actually stimulate cooperation on the rank and file level can only increase the scope of grey policing. Individuals or parts of the executive branch in this way detach themselves, from case to case, not only from bureaucratic control but in doing so also from democratic control in general: blue policing becomes grey policing.

Returning once again to the continuum-approach this concept of 'grey policing' problematizes the debate on dispersal even more by emphasizing the possible negative consequences of blurring. At the same time it must be stressed that 'grey policing' is only applicable to a specific form of cooperation, especially in certain parts of the (criminal, civic and private) investigation process. Of course. numerous forms of legitimate cooperation exist. In a complex society such as ours this is self evident. Yet, 'grey policing' could very well be the unwanted by-product of the emergent Policing Complex. Because of its implications for the rule of law, especially with regard to the accountability debate, it could well be the challenge of the 90's. (to paraphrase Shearing and Stenning 1982).

References

This article is a revised version of a paper, presented at the World Congress of Sociology, Madrid, July 9–13, 1990. The theoretical notion of 'grey policing' is part of a framework developed for an ongoing research project in Rotterdam in which forms of cooperation between different social control agencies are researched. I would like to thank my colleague Paul 't Hart for his criticism and textual improvements.

Bush, H., A. Fund und F. Werkentin (1990) Nicht dem Staate, sondern den Bürgern dienen—Ein Gutachten zur demokratische Neubestimmung polizeilicher Aufgaben, Strukturen und Befugnisse. Berlijn.
Cohen, S. (1985) Visions of Social Control. Cambridge: Polity Press.
Edelman, M. (1988) Constructing the Political Spectacle. Chicago: The University of Chicago Press.
Fijnaut, C. (1985) De Toekomst van de Politie in Nederland. Tijdschrift voor de Politie, 606–611.
Foucault, M. (1975) Discipline and Punish. Harmondsworth: Penguin Books.
Goffman, E. (1961) Asylums.
Henry, S. (1987) Private Justice and the Policing of Labour: the dialectics of industrial discipline. In C. D. Shearing and P. C. Stenning (eds) Private Policing. Newbury Park: Sage.
Heyder, A. (1989) Het Management van de Politiefunctie, Arnhem: Gouda Quint.
Hollingsworth, M. and Norton-Taylor, R. (1988) Blacklist. The Inside Story of Political Vetting. London: The Hogarth Press.

30 B. HOOGENBOOM

Hoogenboom, A. B. (1985) Bijzondere Opsporingsdiensten en Politie. Den Haag: Staatsuitgeverij.
Hoogenboom, A. B. (1988) Particuliere Recherche: een verkenning van enige ontwikkelingen. Den Haag: Staatsuitgeverij.
Kuhn, T. S. (1962) The Structure of Scientific Revolutions. Chicago: The University of Chicago Press.
Lipsky, M. (1980) Street-level Bureaucracy: Dillemas of the Individual in Public Services. New York.
Marx, G. T. (1987) The Interweaving of Public and Private Police in Undercoverwork. In C. D. Shearing and P. C. Stenning, Private Policing. Newbury Park: Sage.
Morgan, R. and Smith, D. J. Coming to Terms with Policing. London: Routledge.
Nogala, D. (1989) Polizei, avancierte Technik und soziale Kontrolle. Pfaffenweiler: Centaurus-Verlagggesellschaft.
Offe, C. (1984) Contradictions of the Welfare State. London.
Peters, G. (1989) The Politics of Bureaucracy. New York: Longman.
Reiner, R. (1985) The Politics of the Police. Brighton: Wheatsheaf.
Reiss, A. J. Jr. (1988) Private Employment of Public Police. Washington.
Rosenthal, U. (1986) The Welfare State: sticks no carrots. N. Furniss (ed.) Futures for the welfare state. Bloomington: Indiana University Press, 357–386.
Shearing, C. D. and P. C. Stenning (1982) Private Security and Private Justice: The Challenge of the 80's. Montreal.
Shearing, C. D. and Stenning, P. C. (1987) Private Policing. Newbury Park: Sage.
Society and Crime. A Policy Plan for the Netherlands. (1985) The Hague: Staatsuitgeverij.
South, N. (1988) Policing for Profit. The Private Security Sector. London: Sage.
South, N. (1984) Private Security, the Division of Policing, Labor and the Commercial Compromise of the State. Research in Law, Deviance and Social Control, vol 6, 172.
Spitzer, S. and A. Scull (1977). Privatization and Capitalist Developments: The Case of Private Police. Social Problems, 25 (1), 18–29.
Wolfe, T. (1988) The Bonfire of the Vanities. London: Picador.

[27]

THE
MODERN LAW REVIEW

| Volume 55 | November 1992 | No. 6 |

Policing a Postmodern Society

Robert Reiner*

Introduction: Paradise Lost?

Four decades after his first appearance, PC George Dixon, eponymous hero of the long-running TV series *Dixon of Dock Green*, remains for many the embodiment of the ideal British bobby. Dixon, more than any other symbol, conjures up a cosier era when thanks to the wonders of glorious nostalgiavision, life — like TV — was better in black and white.

The Dixon character was unique as a cultural phenomenon, historically and comparatively.[1] In no other country, at no other time, has the ordinary beat-pounding patrol officer been seen as a national hero. If the police were represented as heroic figures at all, it was the glamorous crime-busting detective.[2] The enormous influence and popularity of the Dixon character speaks volumes about the peculiarity of the English veneration of their police in what is often described as the 'Golden Age' of policing.

Public attitudes towards the police in Britain have changed dramatically since the Dixon era. The erosion of the Dixon image is a long process, with roots going back to the late 1950s, the last years of the 'Golden Age' itself, but it has become increasingly precipitous in the last decade of the century. This article will describe and attempt to explain this process of demystification. It will be suggested that underlying the immediate symptoms and causes is a more fundamental transformation of social structure and culture, the advent of what is often described as a 'post-modern' society. The conclusion will assess the ways in which the police have tried to tackle this problem and their chances of success.

The question of why the image and substance of policing in Britain has changed is of fundamental importance to understanding current social change in general. The function of policing is essentially to regulate and protect the social order, using legitimate force if necessary.[3] The dominant theoretical analyses of the state, deriving from Weber, see the hallmark of the modern state as the monopolisation

---

*Professor of Criminology, London School of Economics and Political Science.
This is a revised version of an inaugural lecture given at the School on 7 May 1992.

1 For fuller discussions see Clarke, 'Holding the Blue Lamp: Television and the Police in Britain' (1983) 19 *Crime and Social Justice* 44, and Sparks, *Television and the Drama of Crime* (Milton Keynes: Open University Press, 1992) pp 25–30.
2 Reiner, *The Politics of the Police* (Hemel Hempstead: Wheatsheaf, 2nd ed, 1992) Ch 5.
3 Bittner, 'Florence Nightingale in Pursuit of Willie Sutton: A Theory of the Police' in Jacob (ed), *The Potential for Reform of Criminal Justice* (Beverly Hills: Sage, 1974).

The Modern Law Review   [Vol. 55

of legitimate force in its territory. The police are the domestic specialists in the exercise of legitimate force. Thus policing is at the heart of the functioning of the state, and central to an understanding of legal and political organisation. The character and style of policing, in particular the extent to which resort has to be made to legitimate force, will be affected by most changes in the social order. The police are like social litmus-paper, reflecting sensitively the unfolding exigencies of a society. Thus understanding policing requires a consideration of the broadest features of social structure and change. Although the almost complest neglect of the police by social science twenty years ago has now been remedied by an explosion of research and comment, almost all of this is narrowly policy-oriented, governed by the immediate practical concerns of the police and police authorities.[4] This is valuable and welcome, but there is also a need for more fundamental social analysis of the determinants, nature and consequences of policing, apart from anything else to make sense of the disparate body of research studies.

This requires a return to the eighteenth-century notion of 'police science,' when it was regarded by Adam Smith, Bentham, Colquhoun, and other major social and political thinkers, as a fundamental aspect of political economy. Indeed, Adam Smith referred to it as 'the second general division of jurisprudence ... which properly signified the policy of civil government.'[5] The term 'police' then had a much broader connotation than its contemporary one of large people in blue uniforms, but the eighteenth-century conception of police science as the art of 'government-ality'[6] sensitises us to the mutual interdependence of policing and political economy as a whole. This is obscured by the narrow focus on specific technical aspects of policing which all too often pervades current research and policy. An analysis of the troubled state of policing today, and the sources of the malaise, will have to range much further than the police themselves.

I Singing the Blues: The Police in a Millennial Malaise

The modern British police were established in the 19th century in the face of protracted and widespread opposition.[7] But as new police forces spread out from the Metropolitan heartland established by Sir Robert Peel in 1829 to encompass the whole of England and Wales by the mid-nineteenth century, gradually and unevenly they began to cultivate increasing public consent and support. Painstakingly the police leadership, beginning with Rowan and Mayne, the first two Commissioners of the Metropolitan Police, strove to develop an image of the British bobby as the impartial embodiment of the rule of law and the ethic of public service. This rapidly became the prevailing conception of the police amongst the middle and upper classes, who had little direct personal experience of their stalwart servants in blue. The working class, who were far more likely to encounter what contemporaries dubbed 'the plague of the blue locusts,'[8] held more negative attitudes towards the new regulators of their social and political activities.

---

4 Reiner, 'Police Research in the United Kingdom: A Critical Review' in Morris and Tonry (eds), *Modern Policing* (Chicago: Chicago University Press, 1992).
5 Smith, *Lectures on Jurisprudence* (Oxford: Oxford University Press, 1978. Originally published 1763).
6 In Foucault's terminology: cf M. Foucault, 'On Governmentality' (1979) 6 *Ideology and Consciousness* 5.
7 For syntheses of recent research on the origins and development of the British police see Emsley, *The English Police* (Hemel Hempstead: Wheatsheaf, 1991) and Reiner, *op cit* n 2, Chs 1 and 2.
8 Storch, 'The Plague of Blue Locusts: Police Reform and Popular Resistance in Northern England, 1840–57' (1975) 20 *International Review of Social History* 61.

As the working class came gradually to be incorporated into the political, social and economic fabric over the next century, so acceptance of the police spread down throughout the social order. The economically and socially marginal — the 'rough' residuum of the reserve army of labour and indeed young men in general — continued to bear the brunt of the moral street-sweeping which constitutes the core of practical police-work. But the bulk of the settled and respectable working class followed in the footsteps of those higher up the social scale, and began to join in their veneration of the bobby as the very embodiment of the citizenly ideal. This support was brittle, and always fragile at times of industrial conflict. However, in the long social peace of the mid-twentieth century, symbolised successively by the Battle of Britain and the Festival of Britain, the bobbies had their finest hour in terms of popular affection.

Much contemporary evidence, apart from the Dixon myth, underlines the status as totems of national pride which the police enjoyed in the 1950s.[9] The most solid evidence is provided by the major survey conducted for the 1962 Royal Commission on the Police Report. This found 'an overwhelming vote of confidence in the police . . . No less than 83% of those interviewed professed great respect for the police.'

In the three decades since then, there has been a growing questioning of the institution, culminating in recent years in a veritable haemorrhage of public confidence. Optimists could, if pressed, still tell the story another way. The 1988 British Crime Survey (BCS) for instance found that 85 per cent of the public rated the police as very or fairly good in the job they did.[10] Most institutions (including universities and the legal profession) would be delighted with such approval ratings. But there is evidence of continuing erosion of confidence throughout the 1980s. This has now become precipitous in the wake of the great escape of miscarriage of justice skeletons from the Home Office cupboard since the 'Guildford Four' opened the door in 1989.

The regular *British Social Attitudes* surveys conducted by Jowell and his colleagues,[11] as well as the series of national *British Crime Surveys* by the Home Office,[12] show a clear decrease in the standing of the police. One-off surveys conducted since the series of miscarriage of justice scandals came to light, and during the current boom in the crime rate, suggest yet further decline. The *Operational Policing Review* conducted in 1990 for the three police staff associations found that only 18 per cent of a national sample considered that their local police did a 'very good' job.[13]

All these surveys show that opinion of the police is most negative amongst particular groups, those who are routinely at the receiving end of police powers: the young, males, the economically marginal, especially if they are also black and live in the inner-cities. Local surveys in city areas have for many years indicated that amongst these groups, who have been graphically described as 'police property,'[14] rejection

9 Royal Commission on the Police, *Final Report*, Cmnd 1782 (London: HMSO, 1962) pp 102—103. For other contemporary evidence of the high status of the British police in the 1950s, see Gorer, *Exploring English Character* (London: Cresset, 1955) and Almond and Verba, *The Civic Culture* (Princeton: Princeton University Press, 1963).
10 Skogan, *The Police and Public in England and Wales: A British Crime Survey Report* (London: HMSO, 1990).
11 Jowell, Witherspoon and Brook (eds), *British Social Attitudes: The 5th Report* (Aldershot: Gower, 1988) pp 117—118.
12 Skogan, *op cit* n 10, p 1.
13 Joint Consultative Committee of the Police Staff Associations, *Operational Policing Review* (Surbiton, Surrey: The Police Federation, 1990).
14 The term was coined by Cray, *The Enemy in the Streets* (New York: Anchor, 1972). It was developed analytically by Lee, 'Some Structural Aspects of Police Deviance in Relations with Minority Groups' in Shearing (ed), *Organisational Police Deviance* (Toronto: Butterworth, 1981).

of the practices of the police (though not the principles of law and order) is the norm.[15]

Most significantly of all for the police, they seem to have become increasingly estranged from the Conservative Government, whose pet public service they were not many years ago. The police fear a 'hidden agenda' in which they are to be made the scapegoats for the failure of the party of law and order to deliver on its election promises. The screws of financial and managerial accountability to the centre have been tightening remorselessly for several years and, much worse from the police point of view is fearfully anticipated.[16]

II The Deconstruction of Dixon

The declining status of the police is related to a number of changes in organisation and policy which have had the unintended effect of undermining legitimacy of the police. These will be considered, prior to analysis of the underlying causes.[17]

(i) Recruitment, Training and Discipline

The first element in the undermining of police legitimacy was the erosion of the image of an efficient, disciplined bureaucracy. Partly this was a question of standards of entry and training which had not kept pace with general educational improvements.

There have been many attempts in the last thirty years to raise police educational and training standards. Since the 1960s, various schemes have been introduced to attract graduates to the service and encourage higher education for serving police officers. However, significant results have only been achieved during the 1980s, when as a result of pay increases (and unemployment outside the service) the intake of graduates has accelerated sharply to about 12 per cent of recruits per annum. There has also been increasing interest from serving officers in specialist criminal justice degrees.[18] Significant changes have occurred in recruit training as well, largely following from the 1981 Scarman Report.[19] Despite the merit of these developments, they have not prevented an erosion of public confidence in police professional standards.

The main way that the image of the police force as a disciplined, rule-bound bureaucracy came to be dented was by the series of corruption scandals which rocked Scotland Yard in the early 1970s. Although there have been no major cases alleging

---

15 Smith, Small and Gray, *Police and People in London* (London: Policy Studies Institute, 1983); Kinsey, *The Merseyside Crime Survey* (Liverpool: Merseyside County Council, 1984); Jones, MacLean and Young, *The Islington Crime Survey* (London: Gower, 1986); Crawford, Jones, Woodhouse and Young, *The Second Islington Crime Survey* (Middlesex Polytechnic: Centre for Criminology, 1990); McConville and Shepherd, *Watching Police, Watching Communities* (London: Routledge, 1992).

16 Police concern was accentuated by the fact that the 'Inquiry into Police Responsibilities and Rewards,' recently announced by the Home Secretary Kenneth Clarke, consists almost entirely of people from industrial and commercial rather than legal backgrounds, under the chairmanship of Sir Patrick Sheehy of British and American Tobacco. ('Clarke sends for BATman,' *Police*, July 1992, pp 8–9; Loveday, 'A Murky Business,' *Police Review*, 17 July 1992, pp 1318–1319; Butler, 'Paying the Service Charge,' *Police Review*, 24 July 1992, pp 1360–1361.)

17 The organisational and policy changes are discussed in more detail in R. Reiner, *op cit* n 2, Ch 2.

18 Brogden and Graham, 'Police Education: The Hidden Curriculum' in Fieldhouse (ed), *The Political Education of Servants of the State* (Manchester: Manchester University Press, 1988); Tierney, 'Graduating in Criminal Justice' (1989) 5 *Policing* 208.

19 Scarman, *The Brixton Disorders*, Cmnd 8427 (London: HMSO, 1981); Fielding, *Joining Forces* (London: Routledge, 1988); Southgate (ed), *New Dimensions in Police Training* (London: HMSO, 1988).

personal corruption since Sir Robert Mark's clean-up of the Yard and the 'Country-man' inquiry in the 1970s, it is undoubtedly true that those scandals damaged severely the image of the police as disciplined law enforcers. While in the 1962 Royal Commission survey 46.9 per cent of the public did not believe bribe-taking occurred, by 1981 the Policy Studies Institute study of Londoners found that only 14 per cent believed that the police 'hardly ever' took bribes.[20] During the 1980s, personal corruption has become less of an issue, and attention has switched to abuses of police powers undermining the rule of law.

(ii) The Rule of Law

The issue of police violations of legal procedures in the course of dealing with offences has become acutely politicised since the 1970s. On the one hand, civil liberties groups have publicised much evidence of police malpractice, while on the other, the police have lobbied for greater powers to aid the 'war against crime.'

The Police and Criminal Evidence Act 1984 (PACE)[21] purported to provide a balanced codification of police powers and safeguards over their exercise, synthesising the concerns of the 'law and order' and the civil liberties lobbies. It is highly debatable how far it succeeds.[22] What is certain is that the issue of police abuse of powers has increased rather than abated, especially in the late 1980s and early 1990s. Between 1989 and 1991, public confidence in the police was further shaken by an unpre-cedented series of scandals revealing serious malpractice. The cases of the 'Guildford Four', the 'Birmingham Six' and Judith Ward are only the most prominent of a large number of miscarriage of justice scandals which have surfaced in the 1990s.

Although these cases profoundly shook public opinion, police representatives often argued that they had occurred before the recent reforms and could not happen under the procedures now in force. This argument was itself weakened by a number of *causes célèbres* which have involved more recent abuses,[23] as well as by the implications of academic research on PACE.

The anxiety produced by these revelations of abuse was enough to make the Home Secretary announce in March 1991 (after the release of the 'Birmingham Six') the establishment of a Royal Commission on Criminal Justice, chaired by Lord Runciman, the first Royal Commission in twelve years.

(iii) The Strategy of Minimal Force

The preparedness of the police to cope with public order problems began to be expanded and refined during the 1970s, as political and industrial conflict increased.

---

20 Smith *et al*, *op cit* n 15, p 249.
21 PACE was itself the product of a complex political balancing act, unevenly incorporating the major recommendations of the 1981 Report of the Royal Commission on Criminal Procedure. Cf Symposium on the Police and Criminal Evidence Act, *Public Law*, Autumn 1985, pp 388–454, and Leigh, 'Some Observations on the Parliamentary History of the Police and Criminal Evidence Act 1984' in Harlow (ed), *Public Law and Politics* (London: Sweet and Maxwell, 1986).
22 McConville, Sanders and Leng, *The Case for the Prosecution* (London: Routledge, 1991); Reiner, 'Codes, Courts and Constables: Police Powers Since 1984' (1992) 12 *Public Money and Management* 11; Reiner and Leigh, 'Police Power' in Chambers and McCrudden (eds), *Individual Rights in the UK since 1945* (Oxford: Oxford University Press/The Law Society, 1992).
23 Such as the series of cases involving the West Midlands Serious Crimes Squad (disbanded by the then Chief Constable Geoffrey Dear in 1989) and the Court of Appeal decision to uphold the appeals of the 'Tottenham Three,' who had been convicted of the murder of PC Keith Blakelock during the 1986 Broadwater Farm riots.

This militarisation of policing proceeded apace in the 1980s in the wake of yet more serious disorder, beginning with the 1981 urban riots in Brixton and elsewhere.[24]

Without much public debate *de facto* 'third forces' have developed, specifically trained and readily mobilisable to cope with riots. They are coordinated in a crisis by the National Reporting Centre, established in 1972 and located at Scotland Yard. When in operation it is controlled by the current President of the Association of Chief Police Officers (ACPO). Its most controversial and prominent use was during the 1984–85 miners' strike, when a massive, centrally coordinated policy operation was directed by the Centre, amid much criticism of 'police-state' tactics.[25] During the trial of miners on riot charges, it was revealed that in the early 1980s ACPO had produced a secret document, the Tactical Options Manual,[26] setting out the blueprint for a finely graded response to public disorder.

Neither the tougher methods available since the 1981 riots, nor the wider reforms inspired by Lord Scarman's Report, were able to avert the even more serious urban riots of 1985, on the Broadwater Farm estate in Tottenham and elsewhere. Serious public disorder occurred again in an industrial context at Wapping in 1986–87, during picketing outside the News International plant. Many complaints of undue violence were made against the police and the Police Complaints Authority upheld some of these after an investigation.[27] Other controversial uses of public order tactics have occurred in the late 1980s during the policing of hippy convoys converging on Stonehenge.[28] During 1990, anti-poll demonstrations were the source of severe public order clashes, especially following a rally in Trafalgar Square on 31 March.

In recent years, however, the greatest public order concerns have not been industrial or political conflicts. A 'moral panic' has developed about disorder occurring in a variety of leisure contexts. In 1988, ACPO raised fears about growing disorder in rural areas caused by so-called 'lager louts.'[29] In 1989–90, there was great police concern about the spread of 'acid-house' parties. During the summers of 1991 and 1992, serious violence and disorder has broken out on a number of housing estates in different parts of the country, ranging from Bristol to Tyneside, after police attempts to curb 'joy-riding.'[30] The police were subject to criticism, both for under-reacting to the joy-riding and from other quarters, for harassing teenagers suspected of joy-riding. Although the police response to riots remains lower in profile than most foreign forces, there has undoubtedly been a stiffening of strategy and more resort to technology, equipment and weaponry.

Apart from the growing use of riot control hardware, there has been a rapid proliferation of use of firearms by the police. Although still unarmed (apart from the traditional truncheon) on routine patrol, the number of occasions in which firearms are issued to the police has escalated inexorably. Many forces now deploy cars

---

24 For conflicting assessments of the militarisation of public order policing, see Jefferson, *The Case Against Paramilitary Policing* (Milton Keynes: Open University Press, 1990) and Waddington, *The Strong Arm of the Law* (Oxford: Oxford University Press, 1991).

25 McCabe, Wallington, Alderson, Gostin and Mason, *The Police, Public Order and Civil Liberties* (London: Routledge, 1988).

26 Northam, *Shooting in the Dark* (London: Faber, 1988).

27 Police Complaints Authority, *Annual Report 1989* (London: HMSO, 1990).

28 Vincent-Jones, 'The Hippy Convoy and Criminal Trespass' (1986) 13 *Journal of Law and Society* 343.

29 Subsequent Home Research has challenged the police view of growing disorder in rural areas, as distinct from towns inside what are formally county force boundaries, of M. Tuck, *Drinking and Disorder: A Study of Non Metropolitan Violence*, Home Office Research and Planning Unit Study 108 (London: HMSO, 1989).

30 cf the reports in *Police Review*, 24 July 1992, pp 1356–1357, and 31 July 1992, pp 1404–1405.

Policing a Postmodern Society

carrying guns in their lockers, which can be used on orders from headquarters. The number of occasions when guns are fired by the police remains small, and the rules are tight. Nonetheless, the traditional unarmed image of the British bobby has faded.

(iv) Non-Partisanship

The spectacle of James Anderton (Manchester's former Chief Constable) or representatives of the Police Federation preaching at the drop of a helmet about the sinking state of our national moral fibre first became familiar in the 1970s. By 1980 the police, at all levels from Chief Constable down to the rank and file, almost seemed to set the terms of debate on law and order and social policy.

In 1975, the Police Federation launched an unprecedented campaign for 'law and order,' which was revived in 1978 specifically to influence the 1979 general election. This proved to be an investment which reaped handsome dividends. The new Conservative government immediately implemented in full the pay increase recommended in 1978 by the Edmund-Davies committee. There ensued a prolonged honeymoon period in which the police were the Conservatives' most favoured public service. This love affair cooled as public expenditure cuts began to bite on the police and a 'hidden agenda' of incipient privatisation, coupled with strict central financial control, began to emerge in the late 1980s.[31]

For its part, Labour has tried hard to repair bridges which had been broken in the early 1980s, following the election of radical local authorities in the metropolitan areas, who adopted policies which were often perceived as 'anti-police.' The highpoint of tension between Labour and the police came during the 1984–85 miners' strike.[32]

There is now a tendency to return to cross-party consensus on law and order (accentuated in this and other areas by the replacement of Margaret Thatcher by John Major as Prime Minister in late 1990). The prototype of the outspoken Chief Constable, Sir James Anderton, retired in 1991. He had become ever more controversial in the late 1980s for his supposedly divinely inspired utterances on AIDS and other topics. By then, most other Chief Constables had come to believe overt police interventions in political and social debates were unwise.[33] Nonetheless, the years of partisanship had tarnished, possibly irretrievably, the sacred aura hitherto enjoyed by the British police of being, like the Queen, above party politics.

(v) The Service Role

The dominant current of police thinking stresses that, contrary to the popular image of the police as primarily crime-fighters, much if not most of uniformed police work (measured by time or number of incidents dealt with) consists of calls for help, in response to which the police act as a social service more than as law enforcers. The community policing philosophy, which emphasises this, has become influential amongst police chiefs in the UK, the USA and elsewhere.[34] There is evidence,

---

31 Rawlings, 'Creeping Privatisation? The Police, the Conservative Government and Policing in the Late 1980s' in Reiner and Cross (eds), *Beyond Law and Order: Criminal Justice Policy and Politics Into the 1990s* (London: Macmillan, 1991).

32 Reiner, *op cit* n 2, Preface and Ch 7.

33 Reiner, *Chief Constables* (Oxford: Oxford University Press, 1991) pp 210–219.

34 *ibid* Ch 6, and Skolnick and Bayley, *The New Blue Line* (New York: Free Press, 1986) and *Community Policing: Issues and Practices Around the World* (Washington DC: National Institute of Justice, 1988).

however, that most rank-and-file policemen believe the service aspects of the work should have low or no priority.[35] Since the Scarman Report in 1981 endorsed a kind of community policing philosophy, this has become the orthodox analysis of the police role for all Chief Constables. The evidence of recent decline in public support has led to a redoubling of the effort to define policing in service terms, in the Plus Programme of the Metropolitan Police and the ACPO Statement of Common Purpose and Values.[36] The success of these worthy attempts at relegitimation has yet to be seen, but initial research evaluations have not been optimistic.[37]

(vi) Preventive Policing

Peel's original conception of policing emphasised preventive patrol by uniformed constables as fundamental. The notion of the bobby on the beat as the essential bedrock of the force, to which all other specialisms are ancillary, remains a philosophy to which most Chief Constables pay homage. But in practice, specialist departments have proliferated and foot patrol has been downgraded.[38]

The meaning of prevention shifted away from the scarecrow function of uniform patrol to the development of specialist crime prevention departments, whose function is to provide advice to citizens on methods of minimising the risk of victimisation and alerting them to the dangers of some kinds of offences. At first, crime prevention departments were Cinderellas of the service, low status, low budget and low key. However, as crime prevention became increasingly central to the Government's law and order policy in the 1980s, so they blossomed into belles of the ball. A proliferation of specialist and plain clothes units, reversing the original Peelite philosophy, has been one consequence of an apparent crisis of police effectiveness in controlling crime.

(vii) Police Effectiveness

Police effectiveness is a notoriously slippery concept to define or measure. But the official statistics routinely produced by police forces and published by the Home Office seem to record an inexorable rise in serious criminal offences and decline in the clear-up rate since the mid-1950s, and especially since the late 1970s. Whereas in the mid-1950s there were less than half a million indictable offences recorded as known to the police in most years, by 1977 this was over 2 million and, by 1991, over 4 million. Before the war, the percentage of crimes recorded as cleared-up was always over 50 per cent. By the late 1950s, it had dropped to about 45 per cent and it is currently around 38 per cent.[39]

The inadequacy of these figures is well known.[40] Many crimes are not reported

---

35 For a recent national survey, see the *Operational Policing Review, op cit* n 13, s 6.
36 See the statements by the HM Chief Inspector of Constabulary, Sir John Woodcock, ACPO president Brian Johnson, 1991 and Michael Hirst, Chief Constable of Leicestershire (and one of the main architects of the 'quality of service' initiative) in *Policing*, Autumn 1991.
37 McConville and Shepherd, *op cit* n 15. But for a vigorous defence see Hirst, 'We're Getting It Right,' *Police*, July 1992, pp 40–42.
38 Jones, *Organisational Aspects of Police Behaviour* (Farnborough: Gower, 1989), and McConville and Shepherd, *op cit* n 15.
39 *Report of Her Majesty's Chief Inspector of Constabulary 1991* (London: HMSO).
40 Bottomley and Pease, *Crime and Punishment: Interpreting the Data* (Milton Keynes: Open University Press, 1986).

to the police, so increases in the rate may indicate a greater propensity to report rather than suffer victimisation.[41] The clear-up rate is affected by many other determinants apart from detective effectiveness, including massaging the figures. Nonetheless, it is hard to argue that the recorded trends do not correspond to basic changes in the same direction, and they are certainly associated with a growing public fear of crime and a popular sense that police effectiveness is declining. In addition to the direct effect on public confidence of apparently declining police efficiency, concern about crime has led to the controversial new tactics and law and order campaigns which have already been discussed.

(viii) Accountability

All the above concerns have converged on the central issue of accountability: how can the police be brought to book for poor performance? This was the nub of controversy for most of the 1980s. The independence of the British police force from control by any elected governmental institutions has usually been seen as a virtue, although there has also been a long-standing radical critique arguing that it was anomalous in a democracy.[42]

As policing has become more controversial in Britain in the last two decades, so the perception of the mechanisms of accountability has changed. The old mystical substitute of police identification with the public came under strain as the police were seen increasingly as unrepresentative in terms of race, gender and culture, and alienated from the groups they typically dealt with as offenders and victims.[43]

At the bottom of every specific conflict, critics pinpointed the problem of the police being out of control by any outside bodies and hence unresponsive to the popular will. They have sought to reform the structure of police governance so as to make police policy-making fully accountable to the electoral process. Sophisticated critiques of the existing system by constitutional lawyers appeared[44] and the view that the police were not adequately accountable came to be the orthodoxy of mainstream liberal as well as radical analysis of the police. While the police themselves have strongly resisted the full radical package, they have conceded increasingly the legitimacy of some aspects of the critique, especially about the complaints system and the absence of a local police authority for London.[45] For their part, the Conservatives have wanted to maintain the constitutional *status quo*. They have, however, become increasingly concerned to render the police more accountable for their use of powers and, even more crucially, the effective use of resources.

At the same time, it is becoming increasingly evident that local accountability to police authorities has atrophied. It is being replaced by a degree of central control amounting to a *de facto* national force.[46] Thus, accountability has been transformed, rather than simply reduced. What is clear is that the perceived lack of adequate local accountability has been a major factor undermining police legitimacy in recent years.

---

41 Hough and Mayhew, *The British Crime Survey* (London: HMSO, 1983); Mayhew, Elliott and Dowds, *The 1988 British Crime Survey* (London: HMSO, 1989).
42 Jefferson and Grimshaw, *Controlling the Constable* (London: Muller, 1984); Lustgarten, *The Governance of the Police* (London: Sweet and Maxwell, 1986) are the seminal discussions.
43 Hanmer, Radford and Stanko (eds), *Women, Policing and Male Violence* (London: Routledge, 1989); Cashmore and McLaughlin (eds), *Out of Order?: Policing Black People* (London: Routledge, 1991).
44 Notably L. Lustgarten, *op cit* n 42.
45 Reiner, *Chief Constables, op cit* n 33, Ch 11.
46 *ibid.*

The Modern Law Review   [Vol. 55

III The Calculus of Consent: Social Divisions and Desubordination

These eight aspects of police organisation and policy have all been specific, concrete issues of controversy and concern in recent years, symptoms of the erosion of the public standing of the police. Underlying them, however, are a combination of deeper social changes which form the social context of the declining legitimacy of the police.

Police activity has always borne most heavily on the economically marginal elements in society, the unemployed (especially if vagrant), and young men, whose lives are lived largely in the street and other public places, 'police property.'[47] Whereas the historical incorporation of the working class modified their resentment of policing, police conflict with the residuum at the base of the social hierarchy remained. Studies of policing in all industrial societies show this to be a constant. The police themselves recognise this and their argot contains a variety of derogatory epithets for their regular clientèle drawn from this stratum. In California they are 'assholes,' in Toronto 'pukes,' in London 'slag' or 'scum' and on Tyneside 'prigs.'[48] Drawn mostly from the respectable working class, the police are responsive to their moral values and adopt a disdainful scorn for those whose lifestyles deviate from or challenge them. But however conflict-ridden, relations between the police and 'slag' have not usually been politicised. Membership in the marginal strata is temporary (youths mature, the unemployed find jobs) and their internal social relations are atomised, so a sense of group identity is hard to develop.

One important factor which politicised policing in the 1960s and 1970s was the development of social groups with a clear consciousness of antagonism towards (and from) the police. This owes something to the development of more self-conscious youth cultures, the return of long-term unemployment and the increasing militancy of industrial conflict.

The most crucial change, however, has been the catastrophic deterioration of relations with the black community. There is a long history of police prejudice against blacks and complaints of racial harassment. By the mid-1970s, clear evidence had mounted of blacks (especially black youths) being disproportionately involved in arrests for certain offences, largely but not only because of police discrimination.[49] A vicious cycle of interaction developed between police stereotyping and black vulnerability to the situations that attract police attention, resulting from racial discrimination in society generally.

The burden of recent research on police-public relations suggests that while these still remain relatively harmonious with the majority of the population (including most of the working class), they are tense and conflict-ridden with the young, the unemployed, the economically marginal and blacks.[50] What has happened to politicise policing since the 1970s is a growth in the size of these vulnerable groups, primarily due to economic failure and a heightening of their self-consciousness as targets of policing.

This is due to structural changes in the political economy of Western capitalism.

47 E. Cray, *op cit*, J. Lee, *op cit*.
48 Skolnick, *Justice Without Trial* (New York: Wiley, 1966); Ericson, *Reproducing Order: A Study of Police Patrol Work* (Toronto: University of Toronto Press, 1982); Smith *et al*, *op cit* n 15; Young, *An Inside Job: Policing and Police Culture in Britain* (Oxford: Oxford University Press, 1990).
49 Lea and Young, *What Is To Be Done About Law and Order?* (Harmondsworth: Penguin Books, 1984) Ch 4; T. Jefferson, 'Race, Crime and Policing: Empirical, Theoretical and Methodological Issues' (1988) 16 *International Journal of the Sociology of Law* 521; Reiner, 'Race and Criminal Justice' (1989) 16 *New Community* 5.
50 Smith *et al*, *op cit* n 15; Jones *et al*, *op cit* n 15; Skogan, *op cit* n 10.

Long-term structural unemployment (increasingly never-employment) has re-emerged, leading to the *de-incorporation* of increasing sections of the young working class, especially amongst discriminated against minorities, 'who are being defined out of the edifice of citizenship.'[51] A new underclass has formed which is not simply a result of unemployment, but of its seeming structural inevitability. 'The majority class does not need the unemployed to maintain and even increase its standard of living . . . The main point about this category — for lack of a better word we shall call it the "underclass" — is that its destiny is perceived as hopeless.'[52] There is much debate about the now popular concept of an underclass, and its conservative culturalist version has unacceptable connotations of 'blaming the victim.'[53] But the structurally generated formation of a completely marginalised segment of society is a major source of the huge growth recently of crime, disorder and tensions around policing.

Unemployment is certainly not linked to crime or disorder in any straightforward automatic way, as the Conservatives are ever ready to tell us. But there is now much evidence that in the present period at any rate it is a factor in the emergence of a young underclass which has the motive, the opportunity and the lack of those social controls which are brought by social integration, and thus becomes a key part of the explanation of crime and disorder.[54]

The conflicts between the socially marginal and the police are perennial, although they are now more extensive and structural than during the postwar boom. However, the key to how this is translated into political debate is a long-term cultural change in the articulate opinion-forming middle class.

The police have lost the confidence of certain small but influential sections of the 'chattering classes,' what may be described roughly as *The Guardian* or *The Independent* reading circles. This process of a developing gulf with some educated middle-class opinion has a variety of roots, stretching back to the invention of the car. But the most significant are the growth of middle-class political protest since the early 1960s (CND, the anti-Vietnam War demonstrations, the 1960s' student movement and counter-culture) and the politicisation of forms of marginal deviance which involve some middle-class people, notably drug-taking and homosexuality. This conflict with highly articulate and educated sections of the population has been of enormous significance in converting policing into an overt political issue.[55]

Underlying the change in educated middle-class opinion is a broader cultural trend: the decline of traditional patterns of deference and unquestioning acceptance of authority, a process which has been aptly termed 'desubordination.'[56] This is reflected both in the attitudes of those at the receiving end of police powers and the general public audience of policing. Arrests are much less likely to be perceived as the legendary 'fair cop,' either by arrestees or by others. The police as symbols of social authority evidently suffer from a culture of desubordination.

The sources of declining public confidence in the police thus lie deeper than any

---

51 Dahrendorf, *Law and Order* (London: Sweet and Maxwell, 1985) p 98.
52 *ibid* pp 101–107.
53 Murray, *The Emerging British Underclass* (London: Institute of Economic Affairs, 1989); Field, *Losing Out: The Emergence of Britain's Underclass* (Oxford: Blackwell, 1989).
54 Farrington, Gallagher, Morley, St Ledger and West, 'Unemployment, School-Leaving and Crime' (1986) 26 *British Journal of Criminology* 335. Box, *Recession, Crime and Punishment* (London: Macmillan, 1987); Field, *Trends in Crime and their Interpretation*, Home Office Research Study 119 (London: HMSO, 1990).
55 Waddington, 'Why the "Opinion-Makers" No Longer Support the Police,' *Police*, December 1982.
56 Miliband, 'A State of Desubordination' (1978) 29 *British Journal of Sociology* 399.

The Modern Law Review   [Vol. 55

changes in police tactics or policies. We can postulate an equation predicting public consent to policing in which public acceptance is largely a function of the extent of social and cultural consensus. Increasing social divisions and declining deference equal a decline in the public standing of the police. This is because police tactics will move up the menu of coerciveness to deal with the symptoms of division and to overcome the decline of consent. At the same time, controversial tactics, as well as outright abuse, are more likely to be perceived as malpractice by recipients, opinion-formers and policy makers, as well as the general public, due to declining deference.

One possibility this raises is that the obvious response to increasing police scandals and falling public sympathy may be misguided. The conventional assumption across the political spectrum is that standards of police behaviour have declined since the 'Golden Age' of the mid-century. But is this really so?

It is inevitably difficult to assess the extent of police abuse at any particular time, let alone to measure changes over time. Police malpractice, like all deviance, is covert and subterranean. All we know is the amount which comes to light by the uncertain processes of revelation or detection. Criminologists have long stressed this issue when interpreting recorded crime trends, but they have been prepared to accept at face value the apparent increase in deviance amongst the police.

It is clear, however, that there was an enormous amount of hidden police deviance lurking behind the Dixon façade in the middle of this century. This is shown clearly by the evidence of memoirs and oral histories, both from the side of the police and the policed.[57] That most of this police deviance did not come to light was testimony to the more deferential if not authoritarian culture of the policed, as well as the legal establishment.

Whilst there was probably considerable under-reporting of police deviance in the 'good old days,' there is reason to believe that today there may actually be less gross malpractice. One reason is that there has been a set of changes which are likely to have diluted, although far from eliminated, the 'canteen cop culture' which numerous studies have pinpointed as the engine of abuse.[58] As mentioned above, the educational background and training standards of officers have been transformed out of all recognition, although much scope for improvement remains. In addition, whilst they remain grossly under-represented from an equal opportunities standpoint, the proportion of women and ethnic minority officers has risen substantially. So too have the number of part-time volunteers (the 'Specials') and civilian employees. The result is that the backstage areas of police stations now regularly contain people who are far removed from the identikit white macho working-class model of traditional police culture. In addition, a set of legal and policy reforms has tried, with partial success, to make police work more 'transparent' in order to secure more effective stewardship by courts and managers of the exercise of police powers.[59] These include the extensive recording requirements (by tape as well as paper records)

---

57 Mark, *In the Office of Constable* (London: Collins, 1978); Cohen, 'Policing the Working Class City' in Fine *et al* (eds), *Capitalism and the Rule of Law* (London: Hutchinson, 1979); White, *The Worst Street in London* (London: Routledge, 1990); Brogden, *On the Mersey Beat* (Oxford: Oxford University Press, 1991).

58 Holdaway, *Inside the British Police* (Oxford: Blackwell, 1983); Reiner, *op cit* n 2, Ch 3; Young, *op cit* n 48.

59 Morgan, 'Police Accountability: Developing the Local Infrastructure' (1987) 27 *British Journal of Criminology* 87. These measures may, however, have the ultimate function of preserving police autonomy as Morgan has also argued, cf Morgan, 'Policing by Consent: Legitimating the Doctrine' in Morgan and Smith (eds), *Coming to Terms with Policing* (London: Routledge, 1989).

of the Police and Criminal Evidence Act 1984, the introduction of lay station visiting schemes and the rise in access to legal and social work advisers facilitated by PACE. There have also been relevant advances in forensic science, such as DNA profiling and ESDA testing.

Many of the miscarriages of justice and allegations of malpractice which have been substantiated in recent years have come to light because of these changes. The role of scientific developments in clearing Stefan Kiszko, the Tottenham Three and the Irish cases is well known. The recent conviction of several Metropolitan Police Constables for a brutal assault was the product of evidence from a woman Special Constable, illustrating the importance of the dilution of cop culture.[60] The crucial change, however, is a general cultural one. There is a greater willingness on the part of those in power, in the media and the legal system, to pursue cases and seek the relevant evidence, and to believe it when it is found. The new Lord Chief Justice, Lord Taylor, revealed as much when he recently admitted that judges had been too ready to believe the police without question in the past, but should and would not be prepared to do so in the future.[61] Several reviews of the case law interpreting PACE have underlined the greater propensity of judges to apply the requirements of its Codes of Practice against the police, rather than the permissive approach which prevailed with respect to breaches of the old Judges' Rules.[62]

These changes all suggest that the apparent wave of police deviance may really be the product of a change in social reaction, not of a real increase in police wrongdoing. This chimes in with the general view of many experienced police officers who believe there is now less flagrant and regularised malpractice than in the not very distant past.[63] They feel somewhat frustrated at the paradox that public trust in them is at its lowest ebb precisely when professional standards are at an all-time high. This may or may not be a more valid view than the conventional one of a rotting of the police institutional framework. What is certain is that the relationship between the extent of police wrongdoing and the revealed amount is as problematic as that between all offending and the official crime rate. There are many mediating processes of perception, labelling, reporting and recording.

The decline in the public standing of the police is thus far from straightforward and due to complex and social changes rather than simply an increase in police malfeasance. The key roles played by increasing social divisions, and declining cultural deference, have already been emphasised. It is in theorising these processes that the concept of postmodern society is helpful.

IV Policing a Postmodern Society

In the last decade, the related clutch of terms 'postmodern,' 'postmodernism,' 'postmodernity' and 'postmodernisation' have become increasingly fashionable as labels for what is widely seen as a qualitative break in the development of contemporary society. The earliest usage of 'postmodern,' in precisely the sense in which it tends

---

60 See the report in *Police Review*, 10 April 1992, p 662.

61 *The Guardian*, 29 April 1992, p 1.

62 Feldman, 'Regulating Treatment of Suspects in Police Stations: Judicial Interpretations of Detention Provision in the Police and Criminal Evidence Act 1984,' *Criminal Law Review*, July 1990, p 452.

63 It must be emphasised that whilst gross malpractice may have declined, subtle forms no doubt remain rife, as indeed is shown by much of the research evaluating PACE: see for example M. McConville, A. Sanders and R. Leng, *op cit* n 22.

to be used today,[64] was by the late C. Wright Mills in a public lecture delivered at the LSE in 1969.[65] Mills' uncanny prophetic ability to anticipate the shape of things to come gives him a fair claim to be regarded as the H.G. Wells or Jules Verne of social science. Mills declared 'We are at the ending of what is called The Modern Age. Just as Antiquity was followed by several centuries of Oriental ascendancy, which Westerners provincially call the Dark Ages, so now The Modern Age is being succeeded by a postmodern period.'[66]

Mills' characterisation of this 'postmodern period' captures the gist of what contemporary analysts mean by the term: 'Our basic definitions of society and of self are being overtaken by new realities.' This is not, argues Mills, merely because of the pace of change and the struggle to grasp the meaning of it. Fundamentally, Mills claims, the explanatory and ethical frameworks which we inherited from the Enlightenment and which have dominated the 'modern' age, primarily liberalism and socialism, 'have virtually collapsed as adequate explanations of the world and of ourselves.' Referring to common threads in the work of Bentham, Mill, Freud and Marx, the giant shapers of modern understanding, Mills concludes: 'the ideas of freedom and of reason have become moot . . . increased rationality may not be assumed to make for increased freedom.'[67]

The rate at which new volumes bearing the word 'postmodern' in their titles appear on library shelves is alarming, and it is impossible here to deal systematically with all the varying interpretations, diagnoses, periodisations, explanations and political reactions in the debate.[68] The basic idea is, of course, that what is now occurring is a qualitative transformation from one kind of social order to another, as Mills' prescient remarks indicate. The use of the term 'postmodern' itself implies that, while it is claimed that there is a break from the 'modern' (itself variously interpreted), the precise contours of the new social formation are hard to pinpoint other than in the negative: they are fundamentally different from the 'modern.'

The key aspect of what is different is usually said to be epitomised by a concept developed by Lyotard.[69] Whereas the hallmark of 'modern' culture was its underpinning by 'grand' or 'meta-narratives,' such overarching stories about the direction

---

64 The term 'postmodern' itself has been in use for a long time. Arnold Toynbee used it before the Second World War in his *A Study of History*, but to refer to the whole period since the eighteenth century Enlightenment and Industrial Revolutions, ie precisely the heyday of 'modernism' in most current accounts. The *reductio ad absurdum* of attempts to find antecedents for postmodernism was the claim by Kroker and Cooke that the 'postmodern scene . . . begins in the fourth century . . . everything since the Augustinian refusal has been nothing but a fantastic and grisly implosion of experience as Western culture itself runs under the signs of passive and suicidal nihilism.' (Kroker and Cooke, *The Postmodern Scene*, London: Macmillan, 1988) p 127. No doubt we shall soon be told that postmodernism began with the Big Bang itself.

65 Published as 'On Reason and Freedom' in Mills, *The Sociological Imagination* (Glencoe: Free Press, 1959) pp 165—176.

66 *ibid.*

67 *ibid.*

68 For some recent general surveys and discussion of the issue, see Bauman, *Legislators and Interpreters: Modernity, Postmodernity and Intellectuals* (Cambridge: Polity Press, 1987); Bauman, *Modernity and the Holocaust* (Cambridge: Polity Press, 1989); Bauman, *Intimations of Postmodernity* (London: Routledge, 1992); Harvey, *The Condition of Postmodernity: An Inquiry into the Origins of Cultural Change* (Oxford: Blackwell, 1989); Turner (ed), *Theories of Modernity and Postmodernity* (London: Sage, 1990); Giddens, *The Consequence of Modernity* (Cambridge: Polity Press, 1990); Rose, *The Post-Modern and the Post-Industrial* (Cambridge: Cambridge University Press, 1991); Rosenau, *Postmodernism and the Social Sciences* (New Jersey: Princeton University Press, 1992); Crook, Pakulski and Waters, *Postmodernisation: Change in Advanced Society* (London: Sage, 1992). An excellent critique is provided by Callinicos, *Against Postmodernism* (Oxford: Blackwell, 1989).

69 Lyotard, *The Postmodern Condition: A Report on Knowledge* (Manchester: Manchester University Press, 1984).

and meaning of history have lost credibility. In one sense, of course, this claim is evidently self-defeating. For the notion of a breakdown of grand narratives is itself a meta-narrative. But clearly what is meant is the exhaustion of such grand-narratives as the ideas of Progress or Enlightenment, the unfolding of Reason or Revolution, which purported to give a positive and unitary meaning to the historical process as a whole.

Claims about the development of postmodernity falls into three distinct yet related thematic clusters. The origin of the recent fashionable use of the term was primarily in aesthetics and art criticism, where commentators like Baudrillard and Lyotard discerned the emergence of a fundamentally new set of styles which they labelled 'postmodernism.'[70] Another line of thought has primarily been philosophical, suggesting an epistemological break in conceptions of knowledge and ethics. This is often referred to generally as 'post-structuralism' or 'post-objectivism.'[71] Finally, analysts from a variety of theoretical and political persuasions have argued that there has occurred a basic transformation in the political economy, culture and social order of contemporary societies. These may be labelled as theories of 'post-industrialism' or 'post-capitalism.'[72] All these theories point to profound changes in knowledge, popular culture and social order, and the relationship between these.

Knowledge

In a vivid image, Bernstein has characterised the history of modern theories of knowledge as a variety of attempts to cope with 'Cartesian anxiety.' The twin harbingers of the modern — the Renaissance and the Reformation — undermined the absolute framework of understanding provided by Catholicism in the Middle Ages.[73] Descartes provides the prototypical example of a modern philosopher seeking a rational first principle, an Archimedean leverage point for knowledge after the removal of the absolute guarantees of religious revelation. From Descartes' *cogito*[74] to the twentieth-century positivists' falsification principle and logical coherence, modern philosophy has sought some secular substitute for clerical authority. Lurking behind the pursuit of a basis for objectivism was the fear that the only alternative was relativism and cognitive chaos.

MacIntyre tells a similar story about modern moral philosophy in his influential *After Virtue*.[75] The Enlightenment shattered the common language and conceptual framework which allowed meaningful discourse about morality. Although the simulacra of moral discourse remain, words are used with no shared conception of what they refer to. The concept of virtue lacks an agreed underpinning, just as knowledge does. In the postmodern era we have become conscious of what was always implicit in the project of modernity.

To this predicament there are two main responses. It can be celebrated as liberation from authoritarian epistemological or moral shackles. All that counts is what works

70 *ibid*; Poster (ed), *Jean Baudrillard: Selected Writings* (Cambridge: Polity Press, 1989).
71 Bernstein, *Beyond Objectivism and Relativism* (Oxford: Blackwell, 1983).
72 Bell, *The Coming of Post-Industrial Society* (New York: Basic Books, 1973).
73 This does not mean that all people in medieval times shared a monolithic world view any more than that in modern times there was a single hegemonic dominant ideology, cf Abercrombie, Hill and Turner, *The Dominant Ideology Thesis* (London: Unwin, 1980). But the Church did provide the basic parameters within which disputes and divergences occurred.
74 Hintikka, '*Cogito, Ergo Sum*: Inference or Performance?' in Doney (ed), *Descartes: A Collection of Critical Essays* (New York: Anchor Books, 1967).
75 MacIntyre, *After Virtue: A Study in Moral Theory* (London: Duckworth, 1981).

for particular protagonists in specific contexts, as implied by the pragmatism of philosphers like Rorty.[76] Alternatively, it is only possible to adopt a stoic stance in these new Dark Ages, as recommended by MacIntyre, and shelter in congenial small communities awaiting some new charismatic restorer of the grand tradition of the virtues.[77]

In either optimistic or pessimistic variants, postmodernity is the realisation of the relativist potential implicit in modernity from the beginning. It is the realisation that 'Cartesian anxiety' will not be dispelled by the discovery of some new Archimedean point but has to be lived with. As Bauman, one of the foremost theorists of postmodernity puts it, the role of intellectuals changes from 'legislators,' mapping a brave new world, to 'interpreters' of pluralism.[78]

These changes in intellectual culture do not just trickle down into the culture of people in general. However, the abandonment of absolutes is paralleled in popular culture. As Bauman puts it, in postmodern culture the 'pleasure principle' displaces Puritan asceticism and discipline.[79] Consumerism becomes the driving force of social action and the brittle basis of social order.

However, instead of a single dominant conception of the good life, postmodernity is characterised by cultural pluralism and ambivalence. A mosaic of different lifestyles is on offer, none able to trump the others in legitimacy. The exclusion of an underclass from participation in the opulent spectacle needs and can have no ideological justification. Religion is no longer the opium of the people, so they will have to make do with opium itself (or its cheaper substitutes).

Social Structure and Political Economy

The theorists of postmodern society depict it as following a similar path of disorganisation, structural pluralism and decentring. In Giddens' words: 'The postmodern order is split into a multitude of contexts of action and forms of authority ... The nation state declines in importance and the cohesive totality is replaced by a multiplicity of sites of social reproduction.'[80]

Many analysts have offered similar accounts of the dispersion and fragmentation of the concentrated and centralised structure of economic organisation which reached a climax in the corporatist state regulation of the post-Second World War period up to the 1970s. Western societies are now experiencing a transition from 'organised' to 'disorganised' capitalism, in the terminology of Offe.[81]

The influential analysis of 'New Times' by writers associated with *Marxism Today* echoes similar themes.[82] In their account, contemporary capitalism is witnessing the erosion of 'Fordism.' 'Post-Fordism' is consumption not production-led. It involves the disaggregation of the market into specialised sectors, with design as a major selling point, based on the connotation of varying lifestyles rather than simply use-value. This is made possible by the development of information technology to

---

76 Rorty, *Philosophy and the Mirror of Nature* (Oxford: Blackwell, 1979); *Contingency, Irony and Solidarity* (Cambridge: Cambridge University Press, 1989).
77 MacIntyre, *op cit* n 75.
78 Bauman, *op cit* n 68.
79 *ibid.*
80 Giddens, 'Uprooted Signposts at Century's End,' *The Higher*, 17 January 1992, pp 21–22.
81 Offe, *Disorganised Capitalism* (Cambridge: Polity, 1985). See also Lash and Urry, *The End of Organised Capitalism* (Cambridge: Polity, 1987).
82 Hall and Jacques (eds), *New Times: The Changing Face of Politics in the 1990s* (London: Lawrence and Wishart, 1989).

coordinate far-flung and specialist markets and labour processes.[83]

Instead of a mass labour force of mainly semi- or un-skilled workers, a smaller multi-skilled core workforce is required.[84] The peripheral workforce of unskilled workers is low-paid, temporary, often part-time, and increasingly consists of women and ethnic minorities.[85] An underclass of the permanently excluded develops while the core labour force increases its income and freedom, though not security: the so-called 'two-thirds' society.[86] Instead of the primarily bifurcated class structure of competitive or monopoly capitalism, a much more complex system of stratification with cross-cutting lines, such as gender, ethnic identity and region, develops.[87] New forms of oppositional politics emerge, but the position of Conservative parties becomes more secure as the two-thirds of beneficiaries from 'New Times' consistently outvote the one-third who are excluded.[88] The nation state becomes a less significant locus of power, usurped by a growing internationalisation of capital and division of labour on the one hand, whilst the vitality of local identities also increases as the sites of production and reproduction become more scattered and fragmented.[89]

The themes of pluralism, contingency, the undermining of absolutes, ambivalence and disintegration pervade accounts of postmodern society, culture, knowledge and morality. There is much room for argument about the interpretation and significance of all this. What, if any, is the relationship between the material, social and cultural developments? Is there really a 'break' in capitalism, or just an unfolding of its logic to a new stage, as many Marxists argue.[90] Is the project of the Enlightenment unfinished in its emancipatory potential, although threatened by current developments, as Habermas would argue?[91] Or does the present malaise just make explicit the relativist dark side of Enlightenment liberalism, as MacIntyre implies?[92]

Whatever the outcome of such debates, what is clear is that the factors which were outlined earlier as underlying the police fall from grace — deepening social divisions and a less deferential culture — are not temporary aberrations changeable by an election, an upturn in the economy, calls for a return to Victorian values or changes in Government or police policy. They are deeply rooted structural trends, not a passing *fin de siècle* malaise.

V The Prospects of Police Reform

What are the implications for the prospects of success of current police initiatives to restore their legitimacy? During the late 1970s and 1980s, as the creeping crisis

83 Murray, 'Fordism and Post-Fordism' and 'Benetton Britain' in Hall and Jacques, *op cit* n 82; Allen, 'Fordism and Modern Industry' in Allen, Braham and Lewis (eds), *Political and Economic Forms of Modernity* (Cambridge: Polity, 1992).
84 Braham, 'The Divisions of Labour and Occupational Change' in Allen, Braham and Lewis, *op cit* n 83.
85 *ibid*; McDowell, 'Social Divisions, Income Inequality and Gender Relations in the 1980s' in Cloke (ed), *Policy and Change in Thatcher's Britain* (Oxford: Perganion, 1992).
86 Dahrendorf, *op cit* n 51, p 103; Therborn, 'The Two-Thirds, One-Third Society' in Hall and Jacques, *op cit* n 82.
87 Bradley, 'Changing Social Divisions: Class, Gender and Race' in Bocock and Thompson (eds), *Social and Cultural Forms of Modernity* (Cambridge: Polity, 1992).
88 Galbraith, *The Culture of Contentment* (London: Sinclair-Stevenson, 1992).
89 Held, 'The Decline of the Nation State' in Hall and Jacques, *op cit* n 82.
90 Jameson, *Postmodernism: Or the Cultural Logic of Late Capitalism?* (London: Verso, 1992); Callinicos, *op cit* n 68.
91 Habermas, 'Modernity — An Incomplete Project?' in Foster (ed), *Postmodern Culture* (London: Pluto Press, 1985).
92 MacIntyre, *op cit* n 75.

of confidence in the police began to unfold, there emerged a succession of competing agendas for reform. In the late 1970s and early 1980s, debate became increasingly polarised between a conservative 'law and order' approach advanced by the police themselves and the Thatcher Government, and a radical rejectionist position, the organisational heart of which was in the Left-wing Labour Metropolitan local authorities elected in 1981.[93] Whilst the Conservatives advocated greater powers for the police, Labour saw the problem as the unfettered autonomy the police enjoyed and sought to reinforce their accountability to elected local authorities. The Scarman Report in 1981 proposed a sophisticated synthesis of these two positions, but with strict law enforcement subordinate in the last analysis to the diplomatic requirements of keeping the peace. This was a policy of back to the future. The ideals of the British police tradition epitomised by Dixon remained intact in principle but had been undermined in practice. Scarman advocated a blend of community consultation and police professionalism, predicated upon an adequately maintained iron fist, to deal with disorder should the velvet glove tactics fail.[94]

Scarmanism rapidly became the orthodox wisdom of government and police policy makers, to which at least lip-service had to be paid. In the hands of such influential police leaders as Sir Kenneth Newman and Sir Peter Imbert, it gave rise to a host of interrelated reforms throughout the 1980s. These were implemented in conjunction with innovations in management style which owed much to the new emphasis on professional management techniques and especially the concern for value for money, which increasingly pervaded the whole public sector. The style of the contemporary police chief correspondingly changed from bobby to bureaucrat.[95]

Opposition to these approaches was rapidly won over, or bludgeoned over. Middle of the road opinion could not resist the *bien pensant* tones of the new philosophy of community policing. The radical end of the spectrum was subject to cruder tactics. The Local Government Act 1985 dealt with the radical critique of policing by abolishing its material base — the Metropolitan local authorities — and replacing them for police purposes with the more manipulable Joint Boards.[96]

The problem with this accumulating avalanche of reforms was that while much changed in the leadership styles and presentational front of policing, the desired end products were not achieved. As discussed above, the end of the 1980s saw all-time record crime increases, renewed public disorder, spectacular scandals involving miscarriages of justice and plummeting public confidence in the police.

The leadership of the service has responded by seeking to model the mission of policing on the service style which their own research suggests is what the majority of the public wants. As described earlier, it has also sought to introduce a variety of managerial changes to monitor and improve the quality of service delivered.[97] The key is seen as changing police culture to incorporate quality of service values. In short, the police elite has turned to the language and style of consumerism — market research, prominently displayed mission statements, codes of ethical service and the like. This chimes in with the general approach to the public sector promulgated by John Major, and is policing designed for the age of the Citizen's Charter.[98]

Like its ideological first cousin, community policing, this consumerist ethos has

---

93 Reiner, *op cit* n 2.
94 Scarman, *op cit*.
95 Reiner, *op cit* n 33.
96 Loveday, 'The New Police Authorities in the Metropolitan Counties' (1991) 1 *Policing and Society* 193.
97 Woodcock, *op cit* n 36; Johnson, *op cit* n 36; Hirst, *op cit* n 36.
98 Barron and Scott, 'The Citizen's Charter Programme' (1992) 55 MLR 526.

the great virtue that it is almost impossible to be against it in principle. The issue is whether it fully confronts the realities of policing in the postmodern age. In so far as an emphasis of theorists of postmodern culture is on the centrality of style, design and image rather than use-value, it is clear that the consumerist tack is itself a prime expression of postmodernism.

However, neither this nor any other conceivable strategy will restore the police to the status they enjoyed in Britain in the middle years of this century. This was based on unique social and cultural conditions which are unlikely to re-occur and have certainly never been replicated elsewhere. In all other countries, the police have wielded power rather than authority (in the traditional Weberian distinction). The power of the British police was transmuted into authority primarily because they came to stand for a (largely mythical) national culture of order, harmony and restraint. Their power was legitimated by tradition. In other countries, any legitimation the police have achieved has been rational-legal or charismatic (again using Weber's famous ideal-typical categories).[99] These are more brittle and tenuous sources of legitimacy for the police than the authority of tradition. A first condition for the police to re-attain legitimacy is for them and the public to recognise that the traditional British bobby myth is anachronistic — indeed, it never corresponded to reality.

Beyond this, however, the deeper social changes of postmodernity are transforming the role of the police institution within the whole array of policing processes. The rise of *the* police — a single professional organisation for handling the policing function of regulation and surveillance, with the state's monopoly of legitimate force as its ultimate resource — was itself a paradigm of the modern. It was predicated upon the project of organising society around a central, cohesive notion of order. In Storch's striking phrase, the police were 'domestic missionaries.'[100] The role of the police, especially in Britain, was always more important for its dramaturgical function, symbolising social order, than for any instrumental effects in successfully controlling crime.[101] The changes in social structure and culture which have been labelled postmodernisation render this conception of policing increasingly anachronistic. There can be no effective symbol of a unitary order in a pluralistic and fragmented culture.

Nor can the instrumental functions of the police be straightforward in the 'two-thirds' society. The United States, as the Los Angeles riots of 1992 dramatically showed, indicates the dark end-point of processes which can be seen in less stark form throughout the Western world. The police are confronted with a social order bifurcated between the 'dreadful enclosures' of the underclass (often constructed on racial lines) and the castles of conspicuous consumerism in which the majority live, work and play.[102] The latter are increasingly taking the form of what the Canadian criminologists Shearing and Stenning have called 'mass private pro-

---

99   For a recent general discussion of the Weberian tradition in the analysis of power and legitimacy, see Beetham, *The Legitimation of Power* (London: Macmillan, 1991).
100 Storch, 'The Policeman as Domestic Missionary' (1976) IX *Journal of Social History* 481.
101 Manning, *Police Work* (Cambridge, Mass: MIT Press, 1977) is the most cogent presentation of a dramaturgical analysis of policing.
102 As Davis put it in his account of Los Angeles as prism of the postmodern future (written before the 1992 riots), 'the historical world view and quixotic quest of the postwar LAPD' (Los Angeles Police Department) was 'good citizens, off the streets, enslaved in their high security private consumption spheres; bad citizens, on the streets (and therefore not engaged in legitimate business), caught in the terrible jehovan scrutiny of the LAPD's space programme.' Davis, *City of Quartz* (London: Vintage, 1992) p 253.

perty,'[103] huge privately owned facilities like shopping centres, leisure parks, office or educational campuses, large private residential estates or apartment blocks. The role of the police in regulating the order of these areas is residual at most. A police officer is seldom, if ever, seen in Disneyland or indeed Brent Cross (except as a customer). Instead, control is maintained by architecture, the technology of surveillance and informal social mechanisms, with even the specialist input of private security personnel being vestigial, and primarily concerned with maintaining perimeter security.[104] The role of the police is the rump one of maintaining the order of public spaces, which increasingly are the preserve of the excluded social residuum.[105]

In addition, there remain higher level policing functions which the state must exercise: the control of serious professional and international crime, and the maintenance of state security. But these are increasingly remote from the world of the beat police.

In short, policing now reflects the processes of pluralism, disaggregation and fragmentation which have been seen as the hallmark of the postmodern. Hitherto, the British police have been unique in combining within a single omnibus organisation the disparate functions of patrol, public order, serious criminal investigation, political policing and regulating corporate crime. In most other countries, a variety of specialist organisations cope with these separately. It would seem, indeed, that they call for very different skills and tactics of mobilisation. It is most unlikely that the British police will survive the pressures towards an organisational division of policing labour in the last decade of the millennium. There will probably be a fundamental reorgani-sation, bifurcated between a variety of high-level units for national and international crime, public order and security functions, with local police forces on the other hand increasingly focused on small-scale crime, order and service tasks.[106] The latter will find it increasingly difficult to find a suitable niche in the face of competition from private and environmental security mechanisms. The local police role will increasingly be the Fort Apache syndrome: patrolling the borders between respectable and rough reservations. These processes have been referred to by several commen-tators as the 'greying' of policing: its diffusion between a variety of institutional processes, with the human element increasingly not clad in blue uniforms.[107] Sadly, Dixon is dead. Unlike his first demise in *The Blue Lamp*, we shall wait in vain for a second coming.

---

103 Shearing and Stenning, 'Private Security: Implications for Social Control' (1983) 30 *Social Problems* 493.
104 As Davis puts it, 'In cities like Los Angeles, on the bad edge of postmodernity, one observes an unprecedented tendency to merge urban design, architecture and the police apparatus into a single, comprehensive security effort ... Los Angeles in its usual prefigurative mode, offers an especially disquieting catalogue of the emergent liaisons between architecture and the American police state.' Davis, *op cit* n 102.
105 Important accounts of the increasing role of private security in contemporary social control are Shearing and Stenning (eds), *Private Policing* (Beverly Hills: Sage, 1987); South, *Policing for Profit* (London: Sage, 1988); Johnston, *The Rebirth of Private Policing* (London: Routledge, 1992).
106 Anderson, *Policing the World* (Oxford: Oxford University Press, 1989); Dorn, South and Murji, 'Mirroring the Market? Police Reorganisation and Effectiveness Against Drug Trafficking' in Reiner and Cross, *op cit* n 31.
107 Hoogenboom, 'Grey Policing: A Theoretical Framework' (1992) 2 *Policing and Society* 17; Johnston, *op cit* n 105.

Postscript: Postmodern Policing

There are three strategies which must be adopted if the police are to achieve what legitimacy is available in the postmodern period. All are already in place as policy aspirations of the more progressive police leaders. The first is the recognition of the chimerical character of the Dixon ideal and its replacement by more pragmatic conceptions of acceptability. The police are providers of a mundane public service, not sacred totems of national pride.

Second, the personnel of the police must reflect the more diverse and plural demographics of postmodern societies. Specifically, the proportions of women and ethnic minorities must parallel at all levels in the police their numbers in the population policed.[108] Third, local policing must be adjusted to the plural priorities and cultures of a much more diverse social world. Disaggregation downwards of policy making is already the main aspect of leading reforms such as the sector policing experiments in the Metropolitan Police.[109] One vital ingredient which must be taken on board, however, is the integration of elected local authorities into the policy-setting process. For London, this means the creation of such a local authority. Opinion polls and market research techniques, on which the police increasingly rely, cannot substitute for the electoral process as a means of registering public opinion.

The above analysis contains much intellectual pessimism. Is there room for optimism of the will?[110] Postmodern culture may have eclipsed the Enlightenment's modern conceptions of social justice, as well as the more ancient prophetic religious ideas of justice which modernism had displaced earlier. But certain harsh realities will not be pushed aside. As Los Angeles, the modern world's dream factory, showed us in May 1992, the backlash of the oppressed can turn complacent reveries into nightmare. To paraphrase Rosa Luxemburg,[111] in the final analysis the only alternatives are social justice or barbarism. Unfortunately at present, the odds seem strongly to favour barbarism.

---

108 For accounts of the formidable obstacles to achieving this, see Heidensohn, *Women in Control? The Role of Women in Law Enforcement* (Oxford: Oxford University Press, 1992); Holdaway, *Recruiting a Multi-ethnic Police Force* (London: HMSO, 1991).

109 Although this may not be how it is working out in practice. Weeks, 'Sector Policing,' *Police*, July 1992, p 38.

110 In Gramsci's famous formulation, cf Anderson, *Considerations on Western Marxism* (London: New Left Books, 1976) p 89.

111 Luxemburg, *Political Writings* (New York: Monthly Review Press, 1971) p 24.

[28]

THE
MODERN LAW REVIEW

| Volume 56 | November 1993 | No. 6 |

Privatisation and Protection: Spatial and Sectoral Ideologies in British Policing and Crime Prevention

*Les Johnston**

Introduction

In Britain, ideological differences about policing and crime prevention occupy two dimensions: one sectoral, the other spatial. First, there is debate about the relative roles of the public and private sectors in policing and crime prevention. Second, there is dispute about the appropriate spatial level (central state or local state) from which police and crime prevention services should be provided and controlled. This article considers two aspects of these debates, both of which illustrate the complexity of the issues arising. Part One of the article examines police responses to the emergence of private, quasi-private and 'hybrid' police forces in some towns and cities, paying particular attention to the resurgence of municipal policing bodies. Part Two considers some of the changes which have occurred in crime prevention policy, changes which raise serious concerns about the nature and extent of public accountability, the rights and obligations of citizens and the relationship between central and local politics.

A The Resurgence of Private and 'Hybrid' Forms of Policing

(i) Who Polices? Sectoral Changes in Policing

At present British policing is undergoing a crisis, the symptoms of which are many and varied. Recent exposure of police malpractice, following several cases of wrongful conviction, has exacerbated the problem of declining public confidence in the police. There is also widespread public criticism of the police due to their apparent inability to cope with escalating levels of recorded crime. At the same time, government continues to look for new ways of maximising output and

*Deputy Director of the Centre for Police & Criminal Justice Studies, University of Exeter.
This is a revised version of a paper previously presented at the 44th Annual Conference of the American Society of Criminology, New Orleans, November (1992) and at a meeting of the British Criminology Society Southern Branch, London, February (1993). Research for this article was undertaken whilst the author was in receipt of a Hallsworth Fellowship at the University of Manchester. The author also thanks Chief Inspector Bryce-Bennet and Inspector Walker of the Metropolitan Police, Mrs J. Killian and Inspector Scullion of the Royal Borough of Kensington & Chelsea, and Chief Inspector Dennis and Mr Stevens of Wandsworth Parks Constabulary. Any opinions expressed here are those of the author alone.

eliminating waste from police organisations.[1] There is, however, a more fundamental issue at the root of the crisis: the question of 'who polices'?

Had one asked the question 'who polices?' twenty years ago, one would have been met with blank incomprehension by British police and public alike. At that time it was assumed — however mistakenly — that public police forces enjoyed exclusive rights over those social functions which we call 'policing.' Historical analysis tells us, however, that policing has always consisted of a complex division of labour: a varying balance between public elements, private elements and those 'hybrid' elements whose status is neither unambiguously private nor unambiguously public.[2] At present in Britain, that sectoral division of labour is being renegotiated. In the words of the Audit Commission:

> A debate about the boundaries of the core public role of police forces should be valuable, not least in defining the long term functions of the service at a time when its structure, and the scope for contracting out areas of law and order services, are increasingly under discussion.[3]

In fact, there has been surprisingly little genuine public debate — and even less rational political decision — on this issue. Instead, market forces and consumer demand are being allowed to redefine the division of labour within policing. This process is occurring in three ways.

First, there is privatisation of functions, hitherto undertaken by public police forces. In recent months there have been several examples of this sort. Private security companies have been contracted by residents to patrol streets and housing estates in Hightown, near Liverpool[4] and at Wigan in Lancashire,[5] the latest in a long line of similar examples.[6] Arguably, a more significant event occurred some months ago when the Port of London Authority Constabulary, a body established by Act of Parliament in 1802, became the first statutory police force to be privatised.

A second development has been the re-emergence of what one might call 'citizen self-policing,' activities ranging from citizen street patrols to the summary justice imposed by 'vigilance committees.' Though such activity is difficult to document, it would seem to be on the increase, various cases having come to light in recent years.[7] Concern about the problem of vigilantism was again sparked off recently, following incidents in Manchester, North Wales and Norfolk.[8]

Finally, there has been increasing activity in the 'hybrid'[9] or 'grey'[10] areas of policing, those forms undertaken by bodies occupying an ambiguous position with

1 This process began with the demand for 'effectiveness and efficiency,' Home Office, *Circular 114/83 Manpower, Effectiveness and Efficiency in the Police Service* (London: Home Office, 1983) and led on to the policy of 'civilianization' of police posts, Home Office, *Circular 105/88 Civilian Staff in the Police Service* (London: Home Office, 1988). Its latest manifestation is the 'Sheehy Report' on police pay, conditions of service and rank structure: *Inquiry Into Police Responsibilities and Rewards* (London: HMSO, 2 vols, 1993) Cm 2280.1.
2 Johnston, *The Rebirth of Private Policing* (London: Routledge, 1992).
3 Audit Commission, *Taking Care of the Coppers: Income Generation by Provincial Police Forces* (Audit Commission for Local Authorities and the National Health Service in England and Wales, Police Paper No 7, November 1990: 13–14).
4 *Police Review* (1992) 7 February, p 244.
5 Beatt, 'Market Forces,' *Police Review* (1992) 4 September, pp 1628–1629.
6 Boothroyd, 'Nibbling Away at the Bobby's Patch' *Police Review* (1989) 13 January, pp 64–65.
7 Factor and Stenson, 'At the End of the Line,' *Youth in Society* (1987) January, pp 18–19; Boothroyd, 'Angels With Dirty Faces,' *Police Review* (1989) 6 January, pp 64–65; Craig, 'Vigilantes Fill Police Shoes and Stop Thefts,' *Sunday Times* (1989) 5 March; Johnston, *op cit* n 2.
8 Rawling, 'Vigilantes v Villains,' *Police Review* (1992) 11 September, pp 1680–1681.
9 Johnston, *op cit* n 2.
10 Hoogenboom, 'Grey Policing: A Theoretical Framework' (1992) 2 *Policing and Society*, pp 17–30.

respect to the public-private sectoral divide. In Britain, such organisations are many and varied.[11] Some are organised police forces of substantial size whose personnel have full constabulary powers such as the Atomic Energy Authority Constabulary,[12] the Ministry of Defence Police[13] and the British Transport Police. Others, such as the Post Office Investigations Department, though public bodies, are increasingly involved in selling services to private customers. Particular controversy has arisen recently with the growth of 'municipal' police forces — bodies engaged in the policing of parks and open spaces and in the protection of council property, an issue considered below.

(ii) Power to the Centre: Spatial Changes in Policing

As regards the spatial balance of policing, this too is subject to change. British policing has been undergoing a process of centralisation for much of the past century. The pace of that centralisation has, however, been accelerated in recent years by three forces.

The first of these was legislative change. In this respect, two pieces of legislation have had a significant impact on policing in England and Wales. First, the Police Act of 1964 (following the Royal Commission of 1962) established a 'tripartite' system of police governance. The character of tripartism need not concern us here, other than to say that one effect was to confirm an erosion of municipal influence over policing policy which had been evident for several decades. The 1964 Act was also accompanied by a series of amalgamations of police forces. This process was hastened by a second piece of legislation, the Local Government Act of 1972, which led to the reorganisation of local authorities in 1974. The effect of these amalgamations was striking. In the 1960s there had been more than 150 'Home Office' police forces in England and Wales. By the mid-1970s there were only 43.

A second catalyst for centralisation was the political and industrial unrest which spanned the period from the early 1970s to the mid-1980s. The culmination of this period of conflict occurred with the Miners Strike of 1984–85. It was during this period that mutual aid arrangements between the various forces achieved such co-ordination that critics charged Britain with having a national police force. It was also during this period that the 'tripartite' arrangements were exposed as a sham, local police authorities discovering that they had little, if any, influence over their forces.

Finally, there has been the influence of Europe. Debate about the prospects for a European Police Force has gone on for more than 20 years. Since 1976 there has been formal co-operation at government levels through the Trevi Conferences which were instigated to counter the terrorist threat. In 1985 the Trevi Conferences broadened their brief to include issues of international crime and, in so doing, put the policing issue back at the centre of the political agenda. The goal of European police integration was further enhanced by the signing of the Schengen Agreement in June 1990 by Germany, Belgium, Luxembourg, the Netherlands and France. By the terms of that agreement, police checks at the frontiers of signatories were abolished, hot pursuit across borders was permitted and the co-ordination and

---

11 Miller and Luke, *Law Enforcement by Public Officials and Special Police Forces* (London: Home Office, 4 vols, 1977).
12 Johnston, 'Nuclear Policing in Britain,' *Brookfield Paper No 8, Exeter: Centre for Police & Criminal Justice Studies* (1992); Johnston, 'Policing Plutonium,' *Policing and Society* (forthcoming).
13 Johnston, 'An Unseen Force: the Ministry of Defence Police in the UK' (1992) 3 *Policing and Society*, pp 23–40.

sharing of computerised information was encouraged. Though talk of a 'Europol' developing after 1 January 1993 is somewhat precipitate, it is undoubtedly true that British policing has begun to adapt to the prospect of growing cross-border crime in Europe. One indication of this has been the establishment of the National Criminal Intelligence Service (NCIS). Indications are that an increasing number of functions relating to organised crime and terrorism will be nationalised, so making supra-national co-ordination more feasible.

(iii) The Re-emergence of Municipal Policing

Although the centralising tendencies of the British state have reduced municipal influence over the larger police forces of today, it is important to realise that the legislative basis for some form of municipal police provision remains intact. Two pieces of legislation, the Public Health (Amendment) Act of 1907 and the Ministry of Housing and Local Government Provisional Order Confirmation (Greater London Parks & Open Spaces) Act of 1967, empower local authorities to swear in employees as constables for the purpose of securing local bye-laws. Some municipal authorities have also used specific local acts to establish constabularies for policing parks and open spaces,[14] and it is right to say that a significant amount of local legislation still exists. Consider, for example, the 'Paving Act' of 1824, most of which is still in force.[15] This legislation permits 'Paving Commissioners' to appoint 'Watchmen and Patroles' for policing Regents Park in London at night. Such persons, once appointed, will be sworn in as constables, will enjoy full police powers in their jurisdiction and will be provided with proper 'Arms, Ammunition, Weapons and Clothing.'

In recent times, the development of municipal provision has been particularly marked in London. Three forces (in Brent, Wandsworth and Holland Park) have already been established and at the time of writing seven other boroughs are considering following their example.[16]

At Brent, staff from the Borough Security Department have been sworn in as constables since 1979, though the organisation only recently adopted the official title of 'Brent Parks Constabulary.' The Constabulary operates with seventeen police constables and two supervisors, none of whom receive any training, a fact which has caused some concern in the Metropolitan Police.[17]

In Wandsworth, the flagship of Thatcherite local government reform in the 1980s, a Parks Constabulary was established when personnel from the 'Mobile Parks Security Group' were attested as constables in 1985. The force has an establishment of thirty-five officers, six of whom are dog handlers trained to Home Office standards, though it also swears in Special Constables. Uniformed officers carry out both mobile and foot patrols in marked police vehicles, covering parks, cemeteries, play areas and other urban spaces. Officers receive training in fingerprints, taped interviewing and crime reporting from the Metropolitan Police.

---

14 Amongst those authorities are Birkenhead, Birmingham, Brighton, City of London, Epping Forest, Gloucester, Liverpool and Wirral CIPFA, *Financial Information Service, Vol 24: Law and Order* (London: Chartered Institute of Public Finance, 1989).

15 *Georgii IV Regis Cap 100* ('An Act for more effectually paving, lighting, watching, cleansing and regulating the Regent's Park together with the New Street from the Regent's Park to Pall Mall, and from the New Streets and Improvements in the Neighbourhood of Parliament Street and Privy Gardens; and for maintaining a convenient Sewage for the same,' 1824).

16 Information gained from interview with Chief Inspector Colin Dennis and Mr Jeff Stevens of Wandsworth Parks Constabulary, 29 September 1992.

17 Internal Memorandum, Metropolitan Police, December 1990.

The Constabulary also sells training to other organisations and provides an advisory service to other local councils interested in setting up constabularies of their own. In 1991, £135,000 was generated from selling services.[18]

Of the three forces mentioned, the most recently established is that at Holland Park where patrols began in October 1991. The decision to establish a police force was taken following public concern about anti-social behaviour, crime and vandalism in public parks. There was also evidence of increased bye-law violations: illegal parking, cycling, skateboarding, loose dogs and the occurrence of 'unseemly behaviour' after dark.[19] The force has an establishment of twelve, all three senior staff being former regular police officers. Four weeks training is provided through a special course run by the Metropolitan Police. Like Wandsworth officers, those from Holland Park are required to take arrested persons to the nearest Metropolitan Police station, though those from Holland Park, unlike their Wandsworth counterparts, do not take fingerprints.

The expansion of these municipal forces in London and elsewhere can be seen as an attempt by local authorities to respond to local concerns about crime and social disorder in public places. Essentially, the aim is to provide local solutions under local control. So what is the official police response to this development?

(iv) The Official Police Response

The Metropolitan Police response to the prospect of various London boroughs establishing their own constabularies — albeit for the specific task of maintaining public compliance with bye-laws on municipal open spaces — has been mixed. On the one hand, day to day relations with existing forces are fairly good and there is a general awareness that they perform duties which would otherwise fall on the hard-pressed Metropolitan Police Service.[20] On the other hand, there is evident concern in New Scotland Yard about the legal, constitutional and operational implications of changes in the policing division of labour.[21] In that respect, Metropolitan Police concern about the expansion of municipal forces has to be related to wider police concern about the expansion of private security, the growth of vigilantism and the plethora of hybrid bodies which are becoming involved in the policing of public space.[22]

Predictably, the official police response — like that of the Home Office — has been inconsistent. In 1989, one (non-London) local authority sought Home Office advice about the powers of parks constables under the Police and Criminal Evidence Act 1984. At this time the view expressed was that parks constables enjoyed all of the powers of Home Office constables within the jurisdictional confines of the park.[23] That view has now changed due to concern about two

---

18 *op cit* n 16.
19 Royal Borough of Kensington & Chelsea, *Report by Director General Service. Keepering Holland Park* (1991, unpublished); Royal Borough of Kensington & Chelsea, *Holland Park Police* (1992, pamphlet).
20 Information gained from interview with Chief Inspector Bryce-Bennett and Inspector Walker, Battersea Police Station, 29 September 1992.
21 Between 1990 and 1992, TO 15 Branch of the Metropolitan Police was receiving information from and disseminating advice to relevant police divisions. Much of this documentation expressed concern about the expansion of municipal provision.
22 Association of Chief Police Officers, *A Review of the Private Security Sector* (North Wales Police, 1988).
23 Home Office communication to Hertsmere Borough Council, September 1989.

issues: the Metropolitan Police's own involvement in training parks constables; and consideration of the full implications of the 1989 advice.

Training is a particularly controversial issue. The Metropolitan Police train both Wandsworth and Holland Park Police on the grounds that to refuse to do so would be counter-productive. First, Metropolitan Custody Officers receive prisoners from both forces on a regular basis and some training in custody procedures is imperative. Second, it is felt that the police would themselves be the principal victims of any negative publicity arising from untrained parks constables exceeding their powers. Here the reasoning is simple. To the average Londoner all police officers are Metropolitan police officers.[24] Despite this, there remains considerable uncertainty within the organisation about the benefits of continued involvement. On the one hand, it is felt that, without training, parks constables might exceed their powers and, by so doing, compromise the Service. On the other hand, there is a fear that should a trained parks constable exceed his or her powers (or simply make a mistake) the Metropolitan Police might be held accountable: even worse, that it might be open to civil litigation. As yet, this issue remains unresolved.[25]

There is equal uncertainty in respect of the legal powers of parks constables. The Home Office advice given in 1989 implied that since they enjoyed full police powers within their jurisdictions — rather than mere citizen powers — there was nothing to prevent them from carrying truncheons on duty and driving vehicles equipped with flashing blue lights. The Metropolitan Police regarded this prospect with trepidation and sought Counsel's advice on the matter of legal powers through the Solicitor's Branch. This opinion appeared in a lengthy report issued in February 1990, later advice being issued in May 1990 and in October 1991.[26]

The central proposition of Counsel's advice was that a distinction should be drawn between police officers and 'bodies of constables which are not police forces.'[27] In effect, this enabled a distinction to be drawn between parks constables (along with other bodies of constables such as the British Transport Police) and what one might call 'real' police (those officers in the 51 United Kingdom forces coming under the jurisdiction of the 1964 Police Act). In particular, it was said that the parks constable's authority does not extend to the enforcement of general law. This interpretation is based upon a key phrase contained in the 1967 Act.[28] That Act states that a local authority may procure officers appointed by them for the purpose of securing the observance of enactments and bye-laws, 'to be sworn in as constables for that purpose.'[29] In Counsel's view, the phrase 'for that purpose' suggests that constables have no authority to enforce the Theft Act, the Criminal Damage Act or other pieces of 'general' legislation — save for that enjoyed by any other citizen.

Counsel further advised that although section 1 of the Police & Criminal Evidence Act 1984 gives powers of 'stop and search' to all 'constables,' such powers cannot apply to parks constables. Similarly, it was said that constables who

---

24 View expressed in interview, *op cit* n 20.

25 *op cit* n 21.

26 The three instalments of Counsel's Advice appeared under the title *re The Constitutional Position of Bodies Such as the 'Wandsworth Parks Constabulary'* (London: New Scotland Yard, 1990–91, unpublished). All subsequent references in the text are to the February 1990 instalment.

27 *ibid* p 6.

28 Ministry of Housing and Local Government Provisional Order Confirmation (Greater London Parks & Open Spaces) Act 1967.

29 *ibid* s 18.

are appointed solely to enforce park regulations do not have the authority to carry truncheons, and that only constables who drive emergency vehicles are permitted to fit them with blue lights.

Although Counsel's advice has been adopted by the Metropolitan Police and the Home Office, far from resolving the issue it has merely generated uncertainty amongst municipal forces. Thus, whilst the Wandsworth Parks Constabulary continues to assert that, subject to their own jurisdiction, its constables possess powers under the Police & Criminal Evidence Act equivalent to those held by Metropolitan officers, the Holland Park Police have acceded to Counsel's view that such powers are 'circumscribed.'

The problem is that the basis upon which Counsel's advice is founded is itself open to different interpretations. Counsel's view on the circumscription of powers is founded upon the following statement in *Halsbury's Laws of England*:

> The jurisdiction of such a constable is limited to the purposes for which he is appointed, and his authority as a constable does not appear to extend to the enforcement of the general law.[30]

One alternative interpretation,[31] however, suggests that the term 'general law' refers here to the 'wide legal powers held by the police' — as distinct from common law powers held by all constables. In respect of the latter powers, a key consideration is the responsibility of any constable to 'maintain the Queen's peace.' In other words, some conception of 'securing the peace' — or, to put it in the conceptual framework of the sociology of policing, to go about the function of 'order maintenance'[32] — is inherent in any notion of 'the constable.' In short, an alternative view would maintain that to possess constabulary status is, of itself, to have the authority to deal with breaches of the peace — including the powers necessary to restrict a citizen's liberty.[33]

(v) Towards a New Division of Labour in Policing

Municipal policing provides a useful illustration of what has been referred to as the changing sectoral and spatial balance in British policing. At the spatial level it is an attempt to re-insert an element of local authority control into the policing of public space. At the sectoral level it raises the question of who polices?

Municipal policing is certainly not 'private policing,' though it is significant that commentators from the British police invariably refer to it as such: evidence of their conviction that they alone hold a public mandate. Yet, it is not 'public' in the same sense as Home Office forces are 'public.' The author has suggested elsewhere that municipal forces — whose development has to be seen as part of a wider expansion of municipal security in Britain — are, in fact, best conceived of as hybrid policing organisations.[34] Such hybrid bodies have been ignored by sociologists of policing in the past, though they often possess powers far in excess

---

30 Halsbury, *Laws of England*, Vol 36 (London: Butterworths, 1987).
31 Scullion, 'Powers of the Parks Constable,' *Royal Borough of Kensington & Chelsea*, unpublished discussion paper (nd).
32 Reiner, *The Politics of the Police* (Hemel Hempstead: Wheatsheaf, 1992); Wilson, *Varieties of Police Behaviour* (Cambridge, Mass: Harvard University Press, 1968).
33 There is a complex question here about whether constables sworn in for a given purpose can have their function restricted to that purpose; or whether constabulary status, by its very nature, endows them with general duties and responsibilities. This issue arises, for instance, in respect of constables of the Atomic Energy Authority Constabulary undertaking duties on public space (see Johnston, *op cit* n 12).
34 Johnston, *op cit* n 2.

of those held by traditional police forces.[35] Even in the relatively innocuous world of municipal policing, this much is evident:

> It shall be lawful for any officer of the Council to exclude or remove from any open space any person committing any breach of the ... bye-laws, and all gypsies, hawkers ... beggars ... rogues and vagabonds.[16]

Ultimately, the issue of municipal policing, like that of private policing itself, is about the question of which policing bodies should have a monopoly over public space. Some years ago a senior police officer, Susan Davies, suggested that Britain might develop a 'two-tier' policing system.[37] The first tier would consist of sworn officers with full powers. The second tier would consist of uniformed, but unsworn, 'street wardens' whose job would be to deal with everyday nuisances: 'the litter bug, youngsters with skate-boards, or careless pet-owners allowing dogs to foul pavements.'[38] This model has already been developed in other countries. In San Francisco, 'patrol specials' deputised with 'peace officer' powers have operated for many years. In Victoria in Australia, local shires employ 'bye-law officers' who possess authority over litter, environmental protection, marine regulations, fire hazards, parking offences and a variety of other local laws.[39]

There were two main aims behind the proposal by Davies. First, it was seen as a way of releasing sworn officers from mundane tasks, thereby permitting them to concentrate on duties requiring the exercise of constabulary powers. More significantly, it was seen as a preferable alternative to the expansion of private security and municipal sponsored security schemes, both of which Davies felt would 'erode the position of the police.'[40] Here, then, is the crux of the issue. In Britain, the police still look on overt attempts by private or hybrid bodies to challenge their monopoly of 'everyday' public space with suspicion.

That is not to say, of course, that public-private partnerships might not be accepted by the police in other ways. One recent event of some signififance was the invitation given by the Association of Chief Police Officers to David Fletcher, Chief Executive of the British Security Industry Association, to address the 1992 Association Conference. Fletcher's speech aimed to identify both areas of potential co-operation between police and private security (hostage taking, terrorist risks, etc) as well as areas which might, in future, be contracted out fully to the industry (such as traffic duties). The issue of the private sector's role in policing and protection is discussed more fully in the concluding section of this article.

B The Sectoral and Spatial Dynamics of Crime Prevention Policy

In crime prevention policy many of the same sectoral and spatial shifts are occurring as appear in policing policy. First, one can observe the growing involvement of private bodies in policy-making and implementation, though here there is significantly less controversy about the principle of such involvement than there is in the policing arena. Second, one can observe very real tensions between

---

35 Hoogenboom, *op cit* n 10; Miller and Luke, *op cit* n 11.
36 Royal Borough of Kensington & Chelsea, *Parks, Gardens and Open Spaces By-Laws* (nd).
37 Davies, 'Streets Ahead,' *Police Review* (1989) 10 November, p 2277.
38 *ibid* p 2277.
39 *Acts and Regulations*, Shire of Mornington, State of Victoria, Australia (nd).
40 Davies, *op cit* n 37.

the rhetoric of crime prevention policy (expressed in terms of local autonomy) and the manner in which that policy is controlled from the centre. Finally, one can see the emergence of a complicated discourse about the rights, roles and responsibilities of 'citizens' *vis-à-vis* 'the community.' Before considering these developments, however, let us consider the wider context of crime prevention policy.

(i) The Context of Community Crime Prevention

Policies advocated in Britain for community crime prevention[41] reflect strategies found in other western countries. In the Netherlands, for example, the rationale of community crime prevention has been articulated forcefully. Here, after the setting up of the Roethof Committee in 1983, a comprehensive plan for the social prevention of petty crime was launched. Significantly, this entailed the development of a 'mixed' model of social control, where formal and informal, public and private, and local and national agencies were encouraged to combine in a network of supervision. This strategy involved a number of elements. First, it was stipulated that planning, architecture and design should aim to make the surveillance of young people in particular easier, and the commission of offences more difficult. Second, it was recognised that supervision by public officials was inadequate, the number of wardens, bus conductors and others having shrunk during the 1970s. Specifically, it was felt that 'surveillance of potential law-breakers by persons whose occupational duties cover a whole field, such as drivers, janitors, shop assistants, sports coaches, youth workers, etc, should be extended as far as possible.'[42] Third, it was recognised that the application of criminal law was not the best solution to petty crime. Instead, 'the strengthening of non-police surveillance of possible law-breakers' was to be developed in private, public and semi-public areas of life, by 'involving the citizen more and more in the maintenance of law and order,' as well as by 'strengthening the supervisory function of the intermediary structures' of family, work and recreation.[43]

Some of the ideas expressed in the Dutch model have parallels in Britain. One of the key features of the British experience, for example, has been the attempt to encourage the provision of services by informal and voluntary means, rather than through the state. As one prominent right-wing commentator put it: 'the more society can be policed by the family . . . and the less by the state, the more likely it is that such a society will be orderly and liberal.'[44] It would be a mistake, however, to regard voluntary and informal provision as a product of right-wing ideology alone. After all, much of the demand for informal mechanisms of justice (mediation, reparation, conciliation and arbitration) came from liberal lawyers and criminologists in the 1970s.[45] Moreover, both the welfare state in general, and the criminal justice system in particular, have long been characterised by a 'mixed economy' of public, commercial and voluntary elements.

---

41 Home Office, *Circular 84/1 Crime Prevention* (London: Home Office, 1984).
42 Van Dijk and Junger-Tas, 'Trends in Crime Prevention in the Netherlands' in Hope and Shaw (eds), *Communities and Crime Reduction* (London: Home Office Research and Planning Unit, 1988) pp 260–276.
43 *ibid* pp 264–265.
44 Johnson, 'Family Reunion,' *The Observer* (1982) 10 October, p 27.
45 Matthews, 'Privatisation in Perspective' in Matthews (ed), *Privatising Criminal Justice* (London: Sage, 1989) pp 1–23.

The relationship between these different elements is often complex. For example, the status of voluntary agencies is sometimes difficult to define. In Britain, the National Association for the Care and Resettlement of Offenders (NACRO) is regarded as a voluntary body. Yet, it has always had close ties with the state.[46] Examples of this sort suggest that any attempt to draw a rigid distinction between public, private and voluntary elements is fraught with difficulty. In effect, criminal justice is provided through a structural complex whose balance alters according to social and political conditions. A key feature of this complex is the 'blurring of the boundaries' between the public, private and informal sectors.

(ii) Private Sector Involvement in Crime Prevention

In Britain, as in the USA, private companies have begun to play an active role in crime prevention. This involvement can take a variety of forms. In 1989, for example, Royal Insurance donated £100,000 of property-marking kits for use in neighbourhood watch schemes. Another recent initiative, 'Crime Concern,' was established in 1988 through financial support from the Home Office and from Woolworths plc. The establishment of 'Crime Concern' followed a pledge made in the 1987 Conservative election manifesto to 'build on the support of the public by establishing a national organisation to promote the best practices in local crime prevention initiatives.' The organisation is run by an Advisory Board with representatives from the police, local government, business, trade unions, the voluntary sector, the judiciary, the Church and political parties. By the end of the first year, it had helped to establish crime reduction programmes in fifteen towns, was developing a national strategy to support neighbourhood watch and had raised £750,000 for local crime prevention projects.[47]

In certain respects, not least the fact that police resources are finite, the case for increased private sector involvement in crime prevention is a persuasive one. Recent Home Office policy has reflected this view, strong emphasis being placed upon the merits of 'partnership' between public and private agencies.[48] But to what extent is such partnership feasible? In a recent article, Roy Carter, Corporate Communications Director of Group Sonitrol Security Systems Ltd, and a consultant to the Home Office course for police community liaison officers, sought to demonstrate that there is 'no fundamental conflict between the private sector's commercial obligations and its support for community safety issues.'[49] Carter went on to suggest that support for community safety issues both offers commercial opportunities and contributes to business loss prevention: in short, that it can provide short-term and long-term commercial advantages ('added value') to companies.

Private sector involvement may, then, be feasible. But there are drawbacks. In a statement made shortly after the establishment of 'Crime Concern,' its Chairman, Steven Norris, touched on a critical issue. One of the main aims of the

---

46 Mawby, 'The Voluntary Sector's Role in a Mixed Economy of Criminal Justice' in Matthews, *op cit* n 33.
47 King, 'The Political Construction of Crime Prevention: A Contrast Between French and British Experience' in Stenson and Cowell (eds), *The Politics of Crime Control* (London: Sage, 1991) pp 87–108.
48 Home Office, *Partnership in Crime Prevention* (London: Home Office, 1990).
49 Carter, 'Community Safety and the Private Sector,' *City of London Crime Prevention News* 29 (1992) pp 18–21.

organisation, he said, was 'as far as possible to be financially independent, because with independence comes the ability to be constructively critical from time to time.'[50] Interestingly, Norris was referring here to 'independence' from Home Office influence. But it is the case that an organisation's priorities may equally be compromised by its dependence on private funding.

This issue has come to the fore with the development of commercially funded media campaigns to encourage citizen involvement in crime prevention activity. One issue raised by programmes such as 'Crimestoppers' and 'Crimewatch UK' concerns their potential for influencing crime prevention agendas. 'Crimewatch UK,' for example, focuses on stories with a potential for dramatic reconstruction (murder, armed robbery, rape, etc). This means that mundane crime is excluded, along with categories such as corporate and political crime.[51] However, the huge audience for such programmes raises the matter of their social impact. To what extent does an elite consisting of police, media and business representatives have the potential to shape public perceptions of crime? And, if so, to what extent do those representations conform with public experience — particularly at the local level?

(iii) Localism and Centralism

In Britain there is now general commitment across the political spectrum to the principle of crime prevention through multi-agency or inter-agency means. Most recently, this multi-agency principle has been re-cast as the 'Partnership Approach' to crime prevention. Despite this general support for multi-agency principles, however, two qualifications have to be made. First, the character of multi-agency work can be expressed in different ways. There is, in short, a political and ideological debate about how the process should work. Second, attachment to the principle is as much a matter of faith as of reason. This point was put forcefully in the report by James Morgan's Working Group to the Home Office Conference on Crime Prevention (hereafter the 'Morgan Report'): 'The case for the partnership approach stands virtually unchallenged but hardly tested.'[52]

Government commitment to multi-agency crime prevention began in the early 1980s. By 1984 the Home Office Crime Prevention Unit had been established and in the same year an interdepartmental circular was issued expressing commitment to the 'co-ordinated' approach. In 1986 the Crime Prevention Unit launched the 'Five Towns' initiative, effectively a demonstration project for the principles laid down in the circular. In 1988 a further scheme, the 'Safer Cities Programme,' was established to build upon lessons drawn from that earlier project. One of the problems identified by observers of these policies has been the relationship between central and local government with respect to funding and control. For example, Bright has noted that the circular of 1984, despite its successful promotion of the multi-agency approach, had serious flaws. In his view, 'its guidance on leadership was weak (reflecting its unwillingness to confer a central role on local authorities) and it offered no extra resources.'[53] As a result, many of the multi-agency bodies established either did not know what to do or, if they did,

---

50 Norris, 'Cracking Crime Together,' *Crime Prevention News* (1988) July—September, pp 14—15.
51 Schlesinger, Tumber and Murdock, 'The Media Politics of Crime and Justice' (1991) 42 *Brit J Sociology* 397—420.
52 Home Office Standing Committee on Crime Prevention, *Safer Communities: The Local Delivery of Crime Prevention Through the Partnership Approach* (London: Home Office, 1991) para 3.14.
53 Bright, 'Crime Prevention: The British Experience' in Stenson and Cowell (eds), *op cit* n 36, p 70.

lacked the resources to do it. Interestingly, the same author notes that the later circular, *Partnership in Crime Prevention*,[54] reproduces some of the original problems, 'leaving ill-defined the respective roles of the police, local government, statutory bodies, voluntary and private sectors, and failing to give a leadership role to local government.'[55]

Bright's comments are by no means isolated ones. King notes that the rhetoric of 'Crime Concern' and 'Safer Cities' emphasises the significance of locally organised initiatives. Yet control of these bodies and their related initiatives is in the hands of central government:

> In neither of these organisations is there any accountability to the local electorate or any local control over which local projects should receive major funding.[56]

This problem of allocating responsibility to the local level without granting local power is also recognised in the Morgan Report:

> A particular concern for the Group has been that the absence of elected members from crime prevention structures may have had the effect of marginalising crime prevention from mainstream local political issues. Any meaningful local structure for crime prevention must relate to the local democratic structure. Local authorities should decide for themselves how best this can be achieved.[57]

A relatively consistent picture appears, then, to emerge from commentary on the British experience of multi-agency approaches. First, there is widespread recognition that multi-agency strategies cannot work without local elected bodies being given a clear set of responsibilities. For this reason both the Morgan Report and the Labour Party[58] have, separately, proposed that local authorities be granted a clear statutory responsibility for community safety and crime prevention programmes. Second, there is recognition that without adequate funding at local levels — as distinct from costly publicity schemes orchestrated from the centre — there can be no effective implementation of the partnership approach. Again, this factor is recognised in the recommendations in the Morgan Report for the employment of co-ordinators, support staff and training for multi-agency schemes.

Beyond that, of course, there are other, somewhat broader questions about both the practicality and the ethics of multi-agency work. Bottom's review of recent research on inter-agency work in Britain identifies three issues for future consideration. First, what are the implications of power differentials between the different 'partners'? Second, are agencies willing to give up some of their autonomy for the collective good? Third, to what extent should we accept that the different functions of agencies (such as police and social workers) should properly (and ethically) limit their co-operation?[59] This last issue is a particularly important one. In Britain there is widespread support for the multi-agency approach. Such concern as has been expressed by critics has related, by and large, to the contradiction between the ideology of local autonomy and the reality of central control. There are, however, some critics who express deeper concerns about existing forms of the partnership approach. Left realist criminologists, for instance, though supportive of multi-agency work, would wish to see it reconstituted in a number of crucial respects. First, a rigorous distinction would be

---

54 Home Office, *op cit* n 48.
55 Bright, *op cit* n 53, p 73.
56 King, *op cit* n 47, p 105.
57 Home Office Standing Committee on Crime Prevention, *op cit* n 40, para 4.33.
58 Labour Party, *Tackling the Causes of Crime: Labour's Crime Prevention Policy for the 1990s* (London: Labour Party, 1991).
59 Bottoms, 'Crime Prevention Facing the 1990s,' *Policing and Society* 1 (1991) pp 3–22.

drawn between police and social work roles: 'Social work is social work and policing is policing.'[60] Second, policing, far from being permitted to colonise multi-agency work and invade new areas of social life through 'community' initiatives, would become 'minimal' in its scope. Effectively, its intervention would be limited to situations where the criminal law is broken and where there is public demand for police involvement.[61] Third, multi-agency work, far from seeking to eradicate conflict between agencies, would provide a forum for debate. In effect, politics would be re-inserted into the process, the local authority having an overall co-ordinating role for ensuring corporate decisions would be reached.

Whatever the strengths and weaknesses of the realist position, the issues being posed here are surely the right ones. The expansion of multi-agency work raises political and ethical problems which central government has either ignored or chosen to deal with as 'administrative' difficulties. Though a sanitised and apolitical multi-agency framework might, arguably, make implementation of policy a little easier — particularly if that policy is shaped from the centre — the ethical and political costs of such implementation would surely be excessive. Significantly, concern about the potentially oppressive consequences of multi-agency work has been expressed by commentators from both ends of the political spectrum. Gordon's Marxist critique[62] envisages a future where multi-agency co-ordination engenders a 'local police state' in which political interests completely absorb civil society. Interestingly, Alderson, the leading proponent of the multi-agency model of community policing, recognises the same danger when he remarks that the most effective form of multi-agency co-ordination arose in Nazi Germany.[63]

(iv) The Dynamics of 'Active Citizenship'

Finally, there is the issue of citizenship. 'Citizenship' has become a central concept in Conservative political discourse during the last few years. Specifically, it has provided the basis for political policies geared towards securing the rights of individual consumers and tax-payers through the idea of the 'Citizen's Charter.' In fact, the significance of citizenship as the focus of Conservative politics cannot be underestimated, for it encapsulates much of the dynamics of sectoral and spatial change discussed here. This point can be demonstrated most clearly in respect of policy on crime prevention.

For much of the last decade, Conservative crime prevention policy has been promulgated upon the mobilisation of the 'active citizen.' In concrete terms, the most direct consequence of this position has been government commitment to Neighbourhood Watch. The first British scheme was set up in 1982. By August 1989, the Home Office claimed that no less than 74,000 watch schemes were active. A year later, the total had risen to 81,000, new schemes appearing at the rate of 600 per week.

Proof of the effectiveness of watch schemes, like proof of the success of multi-agency work, is difficult to come by. This did not, of course, prevent Government Ministers in 1988 from making extravagant claims about the direct impact of watch

---

60 Young, 'Left Realism and the Priorities of Crime Control' in Stenson and Cowell (eds), *op cit* n 36, p 158.
61 Kinsey, Lea and Young, *Losing the Fight Against Crime* (Oxford: Blackwell, 1986).
62 Gordon, 'Community Policing: Towards the Local Police State?' *Critical Social Policy* 10 (1984) pp 39−58.
63 Alderson, 'Policing in the Eighties,' *Marxism Today* (1982) April, pp 8−13.

schemes on (at that time) declining rates of recorded crime: a case of evangelical zeal being inversely related to the quality of empirical evidence. Though Conservative opinion remained unaffected by subsequent empirical studies which demonstrated 'no measured impact [by neighbourhood watch] . . . on the crime rate,'[64] one would have anticipated that the escalating crime figures of 1990 would have encouraged a degree of prudence. In this context, the response from John Patten, then Home Office Minister, was interesting. In 1989 he had announced that the drop in recorded property crime was due to the coverage by neighbourhood watch of no less than 3.5 million households.[65] In 1990 he declared that the sharpest increase in recorded crime since 1857 was a result of the benefits of neighbourhood watch being restricted to 'only 4 million households.'[66]

The example is an important one because it demonstrates the extent of governmental commitment to a particular form of citizenship. The point about the Government's focus on neighbourhood watch, like its desire to boost the recruitment of volunteer special constables, is the desire to mobilise not just 'any old citizens' but 'responsible' ones. As the Government knows, the policy of encouraging active citizenship is fraught with danger since, once launched, it might be difficult to control. It is for this reason that the Home Office is horrified by any suggestion that neighbourhood watch might 'take to the streets' in the form of citizen patrol groups. Whilst 'responsible citizenship,' as encapsulated in neighbourhood watch, is an individualistic (privatised) form of self-protection, 'autonomous citizenship' (whereby groups engage in self-protective activity without the formal approval of the state) has been rejected consistently and forcefully by the Government.[67] Yet, as was indicated earlier, there is evidence that the latter form is re-emerging in its own right.

The Government's dilemma over active citizenship — having extolled its virtues, how to control it — is part of a more fundamental debate. The concept of active citizenship is, in fact, part of a wider discourse about the public-private divide (sectoral dynamics) and the appropriate locus of accountability and control (spatial dynamics). This much is confirmed in Douglas Hurd's celebrated declaration of principles. Active citizenship, Hurd insists, does not mean an abrogation of the state's responsibilities. The 'massive public services' (including public criminal justice) will continue to function. But 'alongside, and in the gaps between these services, are a myriad of needs which are *not* best met by creating or extending a bureaucratic scheme.'[68] Here, then, is a subtle mode of political intervention which, far from confronting public services head on, operates at the interstices of sectoral and spatial divisions (the 'gaps in between'). Ostensibly, the Government's concept of citizenship is about social rights and responsibilities. Fundamentally, it is a political agenda whose aim is to reconstruct sectoral and spatial boundaries in new forms.

---

64 Bennett, *Evaluating Neighbourhood Watch* (Aldershot: Gower, 1990).
65 Quoted in Jones, 'Surge in Crime Watch Schemes,' *The Independent* (1989) 9 August.
66 Quoted in Cowdry, 'Recorded Offence Climb by 15% to 4 Million,' *The Times* (1990) 29 June.
67 This rejection has been prolonged. Witness John Patten's denial of the Guardian Angels at the Young Conservatives Conference in February 1989 and his objection to neighbourhood watch 'taking to the streets' (interview with Jonathan Dimbleby, 'On the Record,' BBC1, March 1989). See also Travis and Donegan, 'Howard Picks Up Volunteer Village Constable Idea,' *The Guardian* (1993) 20 July, regarding the proposed recruitment of 'responsible citizens' who might 'take the sting' out of rural vigilantism.
68 Hurd, 'Freedom Will Flourish When Citizens Accept Responsibility,' *The Independent* (1989) 13 September.

Conclusion: Policing and Protection in Postmodern Society

What, then, are the social and legal implications of sectoral and spatial restructuring? First, let us consider the issue of hybrid policing with particular reference to municipal police organisations. Consideration of this issue is best approached by further examination of Counsel's Advice on municipal policing in London.

It will be recalled that that Advice sought to make a distinction between police officers and 'bodies of ·constables which are not police forces'[69] and 'which probably ought not to use such a name.'[70] The rationale for this argument needs to be examined carefully since it is meant to justify the restriction of the term 'police' to a specific and limited number of organisations. Moreover, it is intended to show that the powers of some constables (thereafter designated 'police') are inherently different from and superior to the powers of other constables (deemed to be 'non-police').

Counsel's Advice is constructed as follows. It is noted that the police originate from common law constables, statutory police forces only beginning to appear in the nineteenth century. In London, the Metropolitan Police Act 1829 and the City of London Police Act 1839 established police forces by statute. Subsequently, throughout Britain, a number of other bodies were established by statute, most for specific purposes in respect of the policing of designated areas such as docks, harbours, canals and railways. In Counsel's view, '[s]ome of these bodies may call themselves "police" because they are referred to as such in their statute of origin, but I consider that the others should not use the name.'[71]

This comment has interesting implications. Apparently, some organisations, such as the British Transport Police, may call themselves 'police' because the term is used in their statute of origin. (Here, Counsel insists that the full title of the Police Act 1964 — 'An Act to re-enact with modifications certain enactments relating to police forces in England and Wales, to amend the Police (Scotland) Act 1956, and to make further provision with respect to the police' — is significant precisely because it is directed at police forces, rather than other bodies of constables.) Likewise, the Ministry of Defence Police which, we are told, was 'set up by the Ministry of Defence Police Act 1987'[72] can also be regarded as a genuine police force.

There are, however, two problems with this position. First, the Ministry of Defence Police existed long before the 1987 legislation, having been established by the merging of the Admiralty, Army and Air Force Constabularies in 1971. Until the 1987 Act extended its already very considerable powers, the force owed its statutory basis to the 1923 Special Constables Act.[73] Yet, the Advice would have us believe that prior to 1987 this organisation was, somehow, not a 'police force.' Second, according to the principles outlined in the Advice, a body such as the Atomic Energy Authority Constabulary, whose powers are very similar to those of the Ministry of Defence Police, would also be precluded from describing its officers as 'police.'

---

69 *op cit* n 26, p 6.
70 *ibid* p 1.
71 *ibid* p 7.
72 *ibid* p 15.
73 Johnston, *op cit* n 13.

It is interesting to contrast Counsel's position on the question of what defines a police force with a number of others. Contrary to Counsel's Advice, most who have written about 'bodies of statutory constables' prefer to describe them as 'special police forces.' That view is particularly evident, for example, in Miller and Luke's lengthy study of law enforcement by such special police forces (namely, those statutory forces not attached to the Home Office). Miller and Luke also insist that nothing in law prevents a person from describing himself or herself as a 'constable' or a 'police officer.' Moreover, they argue that neither of these terms is necessarily restricted in law to those in possession of statutory powers.[74] Much the same point is made elsewhere:

> A special police force is made up of [constables sworn in under an Act of Parliament] . . . There is, however, no restriction on the use of the terms 'constable' and 'police' and they are sometimes applied to members of private, commercial security organisations.[75]

The interpretation given in Halsbury's *Laws of England* is also a matter of particular interest, given Counsel's reliance upon that same source to justify the argument that the powers of municipal constables are strictly limited. Here, Halsbury defines a police force in terms of the common law powers enjoyed by all constables: 'in essence a police force is neither more nor less than a number of individual constables whose status derives from the common law, organised together in the interests of efficiency.'[76]

There is one further element of Counsel's Advice which deserves consideration, namely the observation that the powers of statutory constables 'are always limited by the statute or statutes under which they were instituted.'[77] In Counsel's opinion, some constables might possess full police powers subject to a jurisdictional limit (for example, Royal Parks Constables, British Transport Police), whilst others possess only limited police powers within a given jurisdiction (for example, Wandsworth Parks Constabulary).

Two issues arise in respect of this position. First, the content of that Advice remains contested. In Wandsworth, following legal advice, the Constabulary's public relations leaflet continues to insist that constables possess full police powers within the perimeters of council property: 'Constables are responsible for all Law enforcement, including bye-laws and park regulations within the Boroughs parks [and] possess all the powers of arrest and search given to the Metropolitan Police whilst on patrol in the parks, commons and open spaces.'[78] As yet, this issue of constabulary powers remains unresolved.

A second issue is, however, equally important. Constabulary powers and the statutory limitations that surround them are not fixed for all time. It may be true to argue, as Counsel does, that parks police do not have the 'right of hot pursuit' beyond their specific territorial jurisdiction. Yet, the same could be said of the 43 'Home Office' police forces prior to the 1964 Act, for it was only then that police constables in England and Wales were granted unlimited jurisdictional powers. Prior to that Act, a constable's powers could only be exercised in force areas which were immediately contiguous to his or her own force boundary. This point is an important one because — as will be illustrated in a moment — at least two

---

74 Miller and Luke, *op cit* n 11.
75 CIPFA, *op cit* n 14.
76 Halsbury, *Laws of England*, Vol 30 (London: Butterworths, 1987) p 43.
77 *op cit* n 26, p 38.
78 Wandsworth Parks Constabulary, 'What Can They Do For You?' (nd).

hybrid police bodies in Britain have had significant expansion in their powers and operational jurisdictions in recent years.

Let us move on, then, to consider not just municipal policing but the hybrid policing of which it is a part. At present, there are about 125,000 police officers in the 43 constabularies in England and Wales. In fact, this figure represents a huge underestimation of the numbers engaged in formal policing activity. A 1977 review of law enforcement by agents other than police officers attached to Home Office forces calculated that there were about 10,000 persons with full constabulary powers employed by almost 40 special police forces in England and Wales. A further 16,000 prison officers held the office of constable. In addition to that, 33,000 persons employed by local and central government had law enforcement duties without possession of constabulary powers. In effect, during the mid-1970s more than 57,000 people — excluding private security personnel — were engaged in some form of policing.[79] Given what is known about subsequent developments in the UK and Europe,[80] it seems likely that the numbers engaged in such hybrid activity are significantly greater now than twenty years ago.

This activity comprises a mass of agencies whose formal status and operational activity cuts across the public-private divide in complex ways. Some are organised and uniformed police forces. Others consist merely of agents possessing specific legal powers. Some employ persons with full constabulary powers. Others do not. Classification is, therefore, difficult because of the wide variations between organisations.[81] Some are public agencies engaged in functions relating to state security (for example, immigration staff); others are public bodies which sell services on a commercial basis either to private companies or to the state (for example, the Post Office Investigation Department). In most cases, the powers of such bodies are more circumscribed than those of 'Home Office' police forces. In some situations, however, the legal powers of personnel far exceed those of ordinary police constables.

Consider two special police forces, the Atomic Energy Authority Constabulary[82] and the Ministry of Defence Police.[83] Originally, the powers of each of these organisations were contained in section 3 of the Special Constables Act 1923. Subsequently, both forces had their powers and jurisdictions extended by specific (and similar) Acts of Parliament: the Atomic Energy Authority (Special Constables) Act 1976 and the Ministry of Defence Police Act 1987. What is interesting in the context of current — sometimes hysterical — concern about the prospect of a 'national police force' emerging in the UK is that the 1976 and 1987 Acts established two such police forces without any apparent public awareness. The organisations concerned are armed, civil (that is to say non-military) police forces, whose personnel enjoy full constabulary powers, undertake training at Home Office establishments, engage in joint operations with (and in the case of the Ministry of Defence Police offer mutual aid to) 'Home Office' police forces, and carry out armed operational duties on public roads and in other public places.

Though these organisations are clearly public and civil police forces, their operational activity is overlaid by various private and military aspects. For

---

79 Miller and Luke, *op cit* n 11.
80 Johnston, *op cit* n 2; Hoogenboom, *op cit* n 10.
81 Compare the classifications in Johnston, *op cit* n 2, and Lidston, Hogg and Sutcliffe, *Prosecutions by Private Individuals and Non-Police Agencies*, Royal Commission on Criminal Procedure, Research Study No 10 (London: HMSO, 1980).
82 Johnston, *op cit* n 12.
83 Johnston, *op cit* n 13.

example, the Atomic Energy Authority Constabulary provides armed escort on public roads both for civil and military plutonium. Ministry of Defence sites are protected by a complex mixture of intersecting bodies: the Ministry of Defence Police, civilian guards, military guards, private security guards, and the local police constabulary whose chief constable has, in principle if not in practice, ultimate authority for determining operational policy in respect of on-site incidents involving crime and terrorism.[84]

To focus on whether such hybrid organisations are to be called 'police forces' or not is, surely, to miss the point. The critical question concerns the nature of the powers held by such organisations and the extent to which they are publicly accountable. Bodies such as the Atomic Energy Authority Constabulary and the Ministry of Defence Police are accountable to their 'users,' British Nuclear Fuels plc and the Ministry of Defence, through police committees. Despite the fact that a significant amount of their operational activity takes place on public space, however, their accountability to the general public is much more problematical, attempts by MPs to raise questions in Parliament invariably being unsuccessful.[85]

Some hybrid organisations are, then, relatively immune from the scrutiny of the general public. By contrast, others, such as municipal police organisations, emerge precisely because councils see them as a means of responding to policing needs and of exerting public influence over policing priorities at the local level. Yet, even this is uncertain. The Borough of Barnet, having recruited a constabulary, found that it was unable to determine policy to the extent that it wished and went back to a system of park wardens.[86] This is not, perhaps, unduly surprising. Much of the history of nineteenth-century English policing is characterised by conflicts between local watch committees seeking to determine policy, and chief officers seeking to exercise their constabulary discretion and independence.[87]

Given that historical tension between political and constabulary powers, it would be surprising if some local authorities did not opt for solutions other than the establishment of police forces with constabulary status. There are already indications that this route is being pursued. For more than a decade, each of the Merseyside metropolitan boroughs has operated its own security force. Each force has responsibility for the protection of council property and organises motorised patrols of educational, housing and other facilities.[88] The logical extension of this type of service would, of course, be to provide uniformed patrols of public streets and, in recent weeks, Sedgefield District Council in County Durham has established just such a 'Community Force.' Headed by an ex-Chief Inspector from the regular police, the force will undertake foot and motorised patrols of local streets, acting to all intents and purposes as a locally accountable police force, albeit one without police powers.[89] There is, of course, a further alternative. Dundee District Council has recently employed a private security company ('Securitay') to patrol the troubled Ardler and Kirkton areas of the city. Here, the response of the police has been interesting. Far from the repeating customary

---

84 *ibid* pp 34–36; Ministry of Defence, *Report of the Ministry of Defence Police Review Committee* (London: HMSO, 1986) Cmnd 9853.
85 Johnston, *op cit* n 12.
86 Internal Memorandum, Metropolitan Police, April 1991.
87 Jefferson and Grimshaw, *Controlling the Constable* (London: Muller/The Cobden Trust, 1984).
88 Johnston, *op cit* n 2; Wright, 'The Liverpool City Security Force,' *International Security Review* (1981) October, pp 106–112.
89 *Panorama*, 'To Catch a Thief' (1993) BBC1, 2 August.

police criticism of the expanded role of private security, the local commander has expressed his support: 'We see this initiative as being complementary to, rather than undermining, the role of the police.'[90]

Involvement of the private sector in policing and crime prevention obviously raises questions about standards of recruitment and training, mechanisms of public accountability, the dangers of private agents exceeding their powers and the implications of introducing commercial motives into the system of public justice. The issues raised here are far too complex to consider fully. Suffice it to say, there is already abundant evidence that standards of recruitment and training in the industry are poor[91]; that the existing system of self-regulation within the private security sector is hopelessly inadequate as a mechanism of accountability[92]; and that private security personnel, given the opportunity to do so, will attempt to replace formal and public standards of justice with private and informal ones to, sometimes, disturbing effect.[93]

The introduction of market principles and the involvement of private security companies in policing and crime prevention draws attention to two of the matters raised earlier in this article: first, the problem of the relationship between centre and locality in the determination of policy; and second, the question of how the services provided through such policy are to be made publicly accountable. Let us consider each of these in turn.

Recently, the apparent ease with which prisoners escaped from the custody of Group 4, the firm contracted to carry out the prisoner escort duties once undertaken by the police, has aroused public unease about the involvement of private companies in the public justice system. Much of this concern has, rightly, focused on the competence of the company in question. There is, however, a more fundamental issue at stake here regarding the involvement of international private security companies in the determination of criminal justice policy.

Despite government commitment to the free market, it is striking that competition for the contract to undertake prisoner escort duties was restricted to two international security companies, Group 4 and Securicor.[94] This attempt to invoke the principles of free market economics whilst, simultaneously, imposing oligopolistic conditions on the competitive process could have been predicted. In Britain, since the late 1980s a new policy-making elite, consisting of representatives from a few major private security companies, the building industry, the legal profession and the City has begun to influence both justice policy in general and penal policy in particular.[95] Increasingly, this process has global ramifications, there being growing evidence that a new 'military-industrial complex,'[96] composed of defence industries and international private security companies, is having an impact on justice policy in the USA and Europe.[97] In many respects, this process is to be anticipated since the concentration of the private security sector into larger and larger supra-national units had developed long before there was any talk of supra-national police forces in Europe. When

---

90 'Police are Ready to Work Alongside Council Guards,' *The Courier and Advertiser* (1993) 22 July.
91 Association of Chief Police Officers, *op cit* n 22.
92 Johnston, 'Regulating Private Security' (1992) 20 *Int J Soc Law*, pp 1–16.
93 South, *Policing for Profit* (London: Sage, 1988).
94 Warner, *Privatisation of Court Escort Duties* (unpublished MA Thesis, University of Exeter, 1992).
95 Johnston, *op cit* n 2.
96 Mills, *The Power Elite* (Oxford: Oxford University Press, 1956).
97 Lilley, 'An International Perspective on the Privatisation of Corrections' (1992) 31 *Howard J*, pp 174–192.

The Modern Law Review   [Vol. 56

these two developments are put alongside each other, however, the prospects for local influence over policing and crime prevention policy are seriously undermined.

The issues raised here relate directly to what Reiner has called the problem of 'policing a postmodern society.'[98] In such a society, the social structure is subject to fragmentation and the systems for maintaining order become increasingly pluralistic. In that situation, policing is subject to what Reiner calls an organisational 'bifurcation' or, to what one might call in the context of the present article, a 'spatial polarisation': on the one hand, a small number of centralised (and, arguably, co-ordinated) agencies at national and supra-national levels; on the other hand, a large number of decentralised (and, arguably, fragmented) agencies at the local level. Clearly, given the preceding discussion, it is apparent that that bifurcation will consist of a complex of public, private and hybrid agencies intersecting at different spatial levels.

It is interesting to examine the recent White Paper on the police in the context of these developments.[99] The White Paper makes three key proposals. First, there is recognition that future rationalisation of the structure of policing may be necessary if there is to be a co-ordinated regional, national and supra-national response to crime. Though concrete amalgamations are not yet proposed, the machinery for bringing them about will be put into place: 'The Government considers that . . . it may be desirable in the long term to reduce the number of police forces . . . The procedures for amalgamating police forces will be simplified so that changes where justified can be implemented.'[100] Second, there is renewed encouragement for police forces to engage in the contracting out of services. Though, as yet, existing contracts have been for things like catering, cleaning and vehicle services, we are assured that 'the Government will continue to apply compulsory competitive tendering in other areas where this is appropriate.'[101] Third, there is commitment to financial decentralisation and operational devolution, something which is already under way in many police forces. Here, the White Paper expresses support for 'devolution of resources and responsibility': 'The main responsibility for local policing must go [to] the local commanders who are in touch with their local communities.'[102]

The message of the White Paper is clear. There will be increased centralisation of structures and greater co-ordination of policy in respect of the 'big' policing issues, such as organised crime, terrorism and public order. By contrast, there will be increased decentralisation of structures, together with a corresponding devolution of policy making, in respect of 'everyday' policing and crime prevention. Further complexity will be added to this polarised structure, of course, by the involvement of private and hybrid bodies, alongside public ones, at each level. It is this pluralistic model of policing and crime prevention which is encapsulated in Reiner's concept of 'bifurcation.'

'Big' policing policies will, then, be determined at national and supra-national levels. So, does this mean that local policing and crime prevention matters will be determined locally? Or, to put it in the terms of our second question, to what extent and in what ways will local services be made publicly accountable? The answer to

98 Reiner, 'Policing a Postmodern Society' (1992) 55 MLR 6, pp 761–781.
99 *Police Reform: A Police Service for the 21st Century: The Government's Proposals for the Police Service in England and Wales* (London: Home Office, 1993).
100 *ibid* p 42 and p 3.
101 *ibid* p 16.
102 *ibid* p 3.

this question is, in fact, a complicated one. Though there is irrefutable evidence that policy making is being devolved to the local level, two points must be borne in mind. First, as the second section of this article has demonstrated, the central state has continued to maintain a strong role in the determination of local crime prevention policy, despite its rhetorical commitment to the principle of 'partnership.' There is little sign that this position will change. Despite the White Paper's commitment to the establishment of police authorities with 'broader local representation,' five of the 16 members of the new authorities will be appointed directly by the Home Secretary.[103] Second, even if the central state was to relinquish some of that control, the accompanying devolution would not be a straightforward one.

There are already clear indications of what that devolution would involve. In 1990 the Association of Chief Police Officers produced the *Strategic Policy Document* whose purpose was to ensure that in meeting community expectations, local police commanders would provide a 'quality service.'[104] This document has been very influential though, arguably, its main significance arises from its attempt to define the recipient of police services as a 'customer.'

This flirtation with the language of the market place is more than mere accident. To invoke the notion of the 'customer' is to expose policing to the language of 'customer choice,' a choice which is already inherent in postmodern policing. In so far as devolution offers local accountability, then, it is likely to involve customers choosing between alternative providers of policing and crime prevention services. Some of these providers will be public agencies, some will be private organisations and others will come from the hybrid sector. The growth of private security patrols and municipal police forces indicates that this process is already well under way. There are also indications that public police forces are beginning to respond to those developments. Elsewhere,[105] the author has outlined a hypothetical model whereby a police force ('Profitshire Constabulary') engaged in local competition with private security companies for a share of the policing market. In April 1993, two police forces (West Yorkshire and South Wales) announced that they were considering setting up companies to compete with the security industry in the provision of alarms, security patrols, escort services and security of housing estates.[106] As with any form of customer choice, however, the fear remains that 'quality service' and public accountability will follow those consumers best able to pay for them.

Finally, there is the question of citizenship. The implication of the previous paragraph is that people's relationship to policing is undergoing fundamental change. Those who, hitherto, regarded themselves as recipients of a public service are now prepared — either willingly or resignedly — to exercise consumer choice. A recent MORI poll found that 55 per cent of respondents supported residents setting up or paying for local security patrols. When asked, 27 per cent said that they would be prepared to take part in such patrols, the same proportion being willing to pay extra council tax in order for them to be run on municipal lines. In addition to that, 23 per cent of respondents said that they would be willing to pay for patrols run by private security companies.[107] Evidence of this sort appears to

---

103 *ibid* p 21.
104 Association of Chief Police Officers, *Strategic Policy Document: Setting the Standards for Policing: Meeting Community Expectation* (London: New Scotland Yard, 1990).
105 Johnston, *op cit* n 2.
106 Wainwright, 'Police Planning Secure Income,' *The Guardian* (1993) 27 April.
107 '55 Per Cent Favour Private Patrols,' *Police Review* (1993) 6 August.

The Modern Law Review   [Vol. 56

confirm two things. First, that people are willing to pay for security and protection. Second, that they are willing to become directly involved, or at least support the involvement of others, in the provision of that protection.

Public support for such active citizenship was most evident in the outcry surrounding the five-year gaol sentence imposed on two Norfolk men after they had kidnapped and threatened a youth suspected of involvement in burglaries.[108] There have been many recorded cases of vigilantism in the United Kingdom in recent years and there is growing evidence that such activity enjoys significant public support.[109] Its prevalence, together with the support that accompanies it, is indicative of two matters. First, that the public are increasingly aware of the police's inability to offer them effective protection against 'everyday' crime and disorder.[110] Second, that they are increasingly willing to regard active citizenship as the necessary means of ensuring such protection. As one commentator on vigilantism in America put it: 'If there is a widespread feeling that the state is no longer holding up its end of the bargain, then people will start "taking the law into their own hands" — which is where it was in the first place.'[111]

The Norfolk case raises one final issue. It has been alleged — though the police have denied it — that the information on which the two vigilantes acted was provided to them by a community constable, frustrated by his inability to accumulate sufficient evidence for prosecution against a 'known' offender.[112] Whether this allegation is true or not, the issue it raises is a critical one. For under conditions of postmodern policing, the question of how public police interact with other providers of protection is of fundamental importance. This is an issue which has already produced controversy in the USA where co-operation between public and private police is well advanced.[113] As that process develops here, a key issue will concern how the police relate to, and adjudicate between, modes of private protection which they deem legitimate and modes which they do not.

---

108 In June 1993, the Court of Appeal reduced that sentence to six months imprisonment on the grounds that the original sentence was 'manifestly grossly disproportionate'; Weale, 'Prison Term for "Vigilantes" Cut to Six Months,' *The Guardian* (1993) 29 June.
109 Johnston, 'Vigilantism and Informal Justice in the United Kingdom,' paper presented to British Criminology Conference, University of Cardiff, July 1993.
110 Sussex Constabulary, *Operational Policing Review: Demands and Resources* (London: Joint Consultative Committee, 1990).
111 Tucker, *Vigilante: The Backlash Against Crime in America* (New York: Stein & Day, 1985) p 27.
112 *Panorama, op cit* n 89.
113 Marx, 'The Interweaving of Public and Private Police in Undercover Work' in Shearing and Stenning (eds), *Private Policing* (California: Sage, 1987) pp 179–193.

A new agenda for
the old Bill? TIM NEWBURN AND ROD MORGAN

Tim Newburn is Head of Crime, Justice and Youth Studies at the Policy Studies Institute. Rod Morgan is Professor of Criminal Justice and Dean of the Faculty of Law at the University of Bristol. The authors are members of the Independent Committee on Police Roles and Responsibilities

The Police Foundation and Policy Studies Institute research into police functions has initiated debate on the desirability of a second tier police service.

We find ourselves at an important time in the development of policing in the UK. Crime levels remain high, public concern about crime and security grows apace, and new providers in the shape of Group 4, Securicor and a variety of self-help community patrol groups are hovering at the margins. Change seems inevitable. On what basis, however, will such change take place? A discussion document published in August by the Independent Committee of Inquiry into the Role and Responsibilities of the Police (Independent Committee, 1994) suggested that, despite the huge amount of time that has ostensibly been devoted to looking at the modern police service, the fundamental questions have not properly been addressed.

Although calls for a Royal Commission on the Police have been staunchly resisted throughout the 1980s and 1990s, the police have nevertheless been subject to intense official scrutiny. Just over one year ago three quite separate reviews of policing — the Royal Commission on Criminal Justice (Royal Commission on Criminal Justice, 1993), the Sheehy Inquiry (Sheehy, 1993), and the Home Office review which led to the White Paper on Police Reform (Home Office, 1993) — all reported within a week of each other. Much of Sheehy is now history, as indeed are elements of the original Police and Magistrates' Courts Bill which grew out of the White Paper. Police reform remains high on the agenda, however, and not just because of the new Police Act.

Towards the end of 1993 the Home Secretary, Michael Howard, announced the setting up of the Home Office Review of Police Core and Ancillary Tasks. Due to report in January 1995, its terms of reference are:

'To examine the services provided by the police, to make
recommendations about the most cost-effective way of delivering core police services and to assess the scope for relinquish-
ing ancillary tasks.'

The fear has been expressed that it is at heart merely a cost-cutting exercise
and, further, a means of extending the influence of the private security sector (see for example the editorial in *Police Review*, July 15,1994).

It might be thought that all the official scrutiny would make any further
investigation unnecessary. However, all these major inquiries have assumed
that the role and responsibilities of the police are well-known and subject to
overall consensus. Such a consensus does not in fact exist.

Furthermore, in describing the role of the police these various inquiries
contradict each other. Sheehy, for instance, names the four main aims of
policing as: to prevent crime; to pursue and bring to justice those who break
the law; to keep the Queen's peace; and to protect, help and reassure the
community. By contrast, the White Paper, and following it, the Police and
Magistrates Courts Act and the Review of Core and Ancillary Tasks, take
the view that 'fighting crime should be the priority for police officers . . . a
priority that local communities should share'. Keeping the Queen's peace is
not mentioned.

The Independent Committee

At present there is considerable muddle and concern about the role of the
police, in public opinion as well as in official documents. The models of
policing outlined in both the White Paper and the current Home Office
review depart from much previous thinking on this matter.

The Independent Committee, which is a joint initiative of the Police
Foundation and the Policy Studies Institute, arose therefore out of a
concern that changes in policing policy might be instituted without adequate reflection on the police role considered in the broadest terms.
Further, such initiatives might prejudice the British policing tradition
which, though the subject of some current concern, nonetheless remains
widely respected.

The key questions for the Committee include:

❑ What police services do the public want and need?
❑ What are the core tasks of the police? How and by whom should
those core tasks be defined? What systems are most appropriate
for accomplishing these tasks?
❑ What should be the role of other agencies — voluntary, private
and statutory — in delivering what might be termed policing services?
❑ Are the boundaries and the division of labour between these agencies and the police properly drawn and regulated?
❑ What works — how, for example, can crime best be prevented
and what role should the police play in its prevention?

A central dilemma

Before thinking about the future of policing, the Committee examined the pressures for change and, in doing so, identified a number of dilemmas that have to be confronted. One of them, and some options for responding to it, are considered in this article.

The Committee recognises that the causes of crime are complex and deep-rooted. It is totally unrealistic therefore to imagine that its prevention might be tackled by the police alone. A whole range of social and economic policies are relevant. And yet there is an ever-growing demand on the part of the public for more policing. One consequence of this has been the largely unregulated growth of private security and self-help organisations providing 'policing' services (for examples see Johnston, 1992).

Another major source of pressure comes from severe constraints on public expenditure, coupled with vigorous government efforts to introduce greater efficiency and market disciplines into all public services. There is, therefore, a complex problem to be addressed.

How is this ever-increasing demand by the public for more policing, and for better protection of person and property, to be satisfied given that public spending will need to be limited; that what the public demands may not have a significant impact on levels of crime; and that further extension of police powers and the reach of the law could have unwanted consequences?

The Independent Committee has taken the view that radical thinking is necessary. More particularly, it has accepted that the nature of the relationship between public police services and other policing services needs to be better defined. This cannot be achieved, however, by attempting to prioritise, hive off or even abandon what might currently be defined as ancillary tasks. The most that such a exercise can do is redistribute some resources and priorities, and do so in a way that is unlikely to have a significant impact on the public.

The Independent Committee, by contrast, has taken the view that the first step must be to set out some principles upon which the activities of officers not employed by constabularies can be limited. It is only by being explicit about what it is that must remain with public forces, that radical options for new partnerships between public and private agencies can be explored. The Committee therefore suggests a principle defining the essential powers of state police officers. It suggests that only sworn police officers, or other Crown servants responsible for policing within designated locations (such as prisons, places of entry to the country and so on), should have the power:

❑ to arrest, detain and search citizens, and to search and seize property under statutory powers;

❑ to bear arms and exercise force for the purpose of policing; and

❑ to have the right of full access to criminal records and criminal intelligence for the purposes of operational policing.

What then might the implications of the application of such a principle be? The discussion document included two illustrative examples of how such a principle (or a modified version) could be operated.

Two examples

In the first example, the Committee envisages the establishment of local patrolling forces, accredited by and under the direction of the public police. A wide variety of tasks could probably be almost as well achieved by non-sworn as sworn personnel were they to wear a uniform carrying insignia which the public might come to recognise and respect. It is known that most citizens are deferential to figures in uniform whether or not they have legal powers.

In fact most issues for which the public want a uniformed police presence do not require the use of legal powers. The respect in which the law is generally held allows it to be enforced most of the time without resort to force. Indeed, arguably, many incidents occurring during community patrols might be positively dealt with were legal powers not available and therefore not used. There is a powerful case for a more appropriate use of legal powers.

It is possible that such patrol work could be conducted under licence by approved personnel who might be employed by the constabulary, the municipality, local community groups or private security companies. But such personnel would carry out the task according to a binding, legally enforceable contract, compliance with which would be monitored by sworn officers.

An example such as this raises a host of practical questions. Would sworn officers be able to direct these patrols? What access to local intelligence would they have? Would they have their own stations and who would provide and own them? Would they have the power to develop files on the basis of which summonses might be served? How can equitable service delivery be assured? How would they be made accountable beyond the provisions of the enabling contract? Who would be the contract holder? What sort of complaints mechanisms would have to be introduced? Would there be a need for the private security sector to further regulate itself, for the staff in the private security sector to be vetted, or for a statutory regulatory body for the whole of the private security sector to be introduced? And so on.

The second example — which would require some modification of the principle outlined above — envisages the creation of 'designated' patrol officers. These officers would be part of the local constabulary and would be authorised to exercise certain limited 'street' powers such as arrest for minor public order offences, drunkenness, or theft, but not more complex offences. Their powers would be strictly limited and would not include the investigation of offences.

As with the first example, the intention would be to prevent crime, to maintain order and keep the peace and to provide public reassurance through visible patrol. Again, a number of practical questions arise. What exactly would the relationship between 'designated patrol officers' and other police officers be? How would lines of command operate and how would accountability be assured?

Although putting forward radical suggestions, the Independent Committee believes that the best aspects of the British policing tradition should jealously be preserved. Therefore, any options considered will have to demonstrate the benefits they provide in crime control, public reassurance and cost terms over those provided by the current public policing model. With greater financial and commercial freedom it might be argued that a 'reformed public model' might compete with the above examples. At the very least, it provides a benchmark for consideration of other options.

The primary aim of the Independent Committee at this stage is to stimulate a better informed public debate about the future of our public police and the potential role of the private and voluntary sectors in policing matters. The two examples outlined above are what might be considered to be points at either end of an alternative police patrol continuum. They are not recipes for change, merely stimuli for debate and, possibly, experimentation. What is crucial is that the high public regard that generally still attaches to public policing in the UK is not jeopardised by ill-thought through changes.

The response to the discussion document

What has been the response to the discussion document and, more particularly, to the examples outlined above? In some circles the response has been very positive. *The Times* for example described it as 'a welcome contribution to an emerging debate' in its editorial of August 4. Some commentators, however, have been very critical — the chairman of the Police Federation described the Inquiry as 'son of Posen' (Coyles, 1994). His objections were that the Committee had ignored the fact that the police are a cheap service when compared to other public services such as education and health and that, in its desire to find a cost-effective way to increase the number of uniformed people on patrol, it had put forward the option of 'second-rate', 'low-calibre' patrolling officers which would threaten the policing tradition that the Committee claimed to desire to protect.

Similar criticisms, but dressed up in Julie Burchill'esque language were offered by Suzanne Moore in *The Guardian* of August 5, 'Will the real PC Plod please stand up?'. She too, however, sought refuge in a 'money's no object' argument. Parodying the Committee's views as proposing 'glorified bouncers on our streets', she said 'we are asking for something much more complex and indeed expensive'. The essence of both these views is that the Independent Committee is proposing some form of policing on the cheap. These are not criticisms that should go without response.

Such views ignore what is happening by default in policing. Expenditure on the police rose by almost 70 per cent between 1979 and 1993. Police powers have also been increased — indeed, major criminal justice legislation is introduced in almost every parliamentary session. Yet the long-term growth in recorded crime and the public demand for additional police services grows apace. The police cannot meet the demand, and the suggestion that we should simply allow the bill to continue to grow is unlikely to be received favourably by any government, whatever its political hue.

It is also important to recognise what has happened in the private security industry. It has grown and is growing much faster than are the police. Private firms are, for example, already supplying patrol services on estates on a number of British cities (Fogg and Brace, 1994). Moreover, on August 24, 1994, Wandsworth Council in London announced that it was seeking the permission of the Home Secretary to establish its own police force with fairly extensive powers. As the Independent Committee pointed out:

> 'If present trends continue there is a danger that we may end up with the worst of all possible worlds: an increasingly centralised police force with ever-growing powers alongside the anarchic emergence of unregulated self-help and private police/security services in the hands of those pursuing sectional interests.' (para 7.9)

The second point that must be made is that the Independent Committee was clear that ancillary patrols must be appropriately trained for the tasks that are allocated to them; that they must be properly managed, and that this might be done by the local constabulary; that they should be uniformed, and should be made legally and democratically accountable. Furthermore, the idea that every employee has to be trained to deal with every eventuality would surely never be advanced in any other profession. Is one treated by a consultant surgeon for every minor ailment? Are fully qualified teachers the only people who can work in classrooms? Of course not. Suggesting that people with different training, qualifications and skills can and should undertake different tasks is surely simply sound pragmatism.

Further criticism in this area came from Sir John Smith in an article in *The Independent on Sunday* (Hyder and Victor, 1994). His criticisms were twofold. First, that the idea of designated patrol officers might lead to a situation akin to that observed in Los Angeles where the police has become 'obsessed with instant responses and crime statistics and were alienated from the community'. Second, that the Committee was really promoting the use of unregulated private services in place of police officers.

It is worth reiterating, briefly, what the Independent Committee actually said in relation to these issues. First, police-community relations. In its discussion document the Committee stressed repeatedly that it recognised the centrality and importance of the British tradition of 'policing by consent'. In the introduction to the document it stated:

> 'The police enjoy a high level of public regard and trust in the country. They remain largely unarmed, retain the principle of the minimum use of force, continue to patrol on foot, have strong local ties and encourage community consultation. The Police and Criminal Evidence Act 1984 (PACE) is regarded as a model of operational accountability in much of the rest of the world. The British policing tradition is something of which the country can be proud.' (para 1.7)

These are surely the words of a Committee that recognises that local knowledge and co-operation are central to police effectiveness. Furthermore, if the Committee was consistently critical of any tendency in current official thinking about policing, it was the tendency to place 'crime-fighting' — the detection and processing of offenders — ahead of maintaining public tranquillity and preventing crime. That the Committee should then be accused of proposing changes that would lead to the police occupying just such a crime-fighting role seems particularly ironic.

What then of the suggestion that the Committee proposed that patrol functions be taken over by the unregulated private market. Nothing could be further from reality. The Committee recognised that public demands for uniformed patrols that provide some reassurance are outstripping the capacity of the police to provide such a service. It therefore offered two examples, amongst what are no doubt numerous possibilities, of how other forms of provision might be organised.

One of these had no element of private provision in it at all, but envisaged the establishment of designated patrol officers within constabularies. The other envisaged the establishment of local patrolling forces, with limited powers, that might be employed by the constabulary, local municipalities or, yes, even private security companies. However, the Committee went on immediately to say that: 'such personnel would carry out the task according to a binding, legally enforceable contract, compliance with which would be monitored by sworn officers' (para 7.16), and it also raised the whole issue of regulating the entire private security sector.

The other interesting aspect of the response to the Independent Committee's document is that it focused almost exclusively on the idea of ancillary patrols. This is perhaps not surprising, but it does divert attention away from a number of other ideas which were also part of the Committee's thinking. The first was that the patterning of crime was now such that, in addition to forces with highly localised knowledge, it would be important to consider the pros and cons of enhanced regional and even national structures for policing. Given the ferocity of the debate that has arisen whenever the idea of a national force has been canvassed, it was slightly unexpected that the Independent Committee's statement that 'what is clear is that, increasingly, distinctions will have to be made between police functions at local, regional, national and international levels' (para 7.24) should pass without comment.

Finally, there is the Committee's suggestion that serious attention needs to be given to which agency should take the lead in crime prevention. The view taken by the Committee, and based on the large amount of research that has shown that failure to properly implement plans is perhaps the biggest barrier to successful crime prevention activity, is that the present confused position needs to be clarified. In particular, the Committee took the view that the main responsibility for crime prevention and community safety should lie with local authorities and that the police role, though extremely important, should remain secondary.

Furthermore, the Committee suggested that some form of statutory responsibility for crime prevention might have to be placed on local authorities, together with some method for holding constabularies accountable for the crime prevention services they provide to local communities if such initiatives are to be successfully promoted in the future. Although such ideas were picked up in the local press, and generally reported very favourably, the main commentators kept their gaze firmly fixed on the idea of ancillary patrols.

The central objective of the Committee is to provide a wider and deeper analysis of policy options, as a complement to the various official inquiries, and to ensure that this wider perspective is reflected in public debate and the process of change. The Independent Committee grew out of a feeling that there was insufficient public debate about the future of the police service, and a concern that radical changes might be imposed without consultation or indeed proper experimentation. The Committee still has much work to do, but if the debate that has started can be kept going then it will have achieved at least one of its primary objectives.

References

Coyles D (1994) 'Keep the best', *Police Review* August 12.

Fogg E and Brace M (1994) 'Private policing cuts crime on Islington estates', *The Independent*. London, August 16.

Home Office (1993) *Police Reform: A Police Service for the Twenty-First Century*, Cm 2281. London: HMSO.

Hyder K and Victor P (1994) 'Hiving off police jobs dangerous, chief warns', *The Independent on Sunday*, August 14.

Independent Committee of Inquiry into the Role and Responsibilities of the Police (1994) *Discussion Document*. London: Police Foundation/Policy Studies Institute.

Johnston L (1992) *The Rebirth of Private Policing*. London: Routledge.

Royal Commission on Criminal Justice (1993) *Final Report*, Cm 2263. London: HMSO.

Sheehy (1993) *Inquiry into Police Responsibilities and Rewards*. Cm 2280.1. London: HMS0.

THE REINER REPORT

LOOKING THROUGH THE GLASS
(OF A CRYSTAL-BALL)
DARKLY

Supercop or Robocop: what future for the police in a post modern post Sheehy brave new world asks Robert Reiner

There can be little doubt that the last few years have been exceptionally lean ones for the police. This is especially evident by contrast with the exceptionally fat ones of the Thatcher era. Following at least three decades of turbulence, the last couple of years have seen the launch of a package of 'reforms' on a scale without precedent certainly since 1964, or perhaps even since 1829 - the birth of the modern police. The Police and Magistrates Courts Act, the fallout from the Sheehy Report on Rewards and Responsibilities, the Criminal Justice and Public Order Act and the Posen Report on Core and Ancillary Tasks cover the gamut of policing issues. What should the police do? How should they be resourced and empowered? How should they be rewarded? To whom should they be accountable? On paper the changes have been revolutionary. All these separate components of the package are now becoming operational, so some crystal-ball gazing on what they may amount to in practice is timely.

Three profoundly different perspectives on the consequences of any major policy changes can be distinguished. These can be seen for example in the varying interpretations of the significance of the original creation of Peel's 'New Police' in 1829, and they are echoed today.

Opponents of the 'reforms' (and I count myself amongst their number) have been equally emphatic about the complete transformation they embody. We have been shrill, often apocalyptic, about how they will destroy the finest police system in the world

To contemporaries embroiled in the decades of heated controversy which preceded the 1829 Metropolitan Police Act the bobbies were either the saviours or the destroyers of British civilisation as they had known it hitherto. To some they represented either a necessary and legitimate guarantor of public order in a society reeling from the pressures of rapid industrialisation and urbanisation, to others they were the oppressive agents of an expansive state which was increasingly encroaching on traditional liberties. But, for good or evil, to contemporary commentators they embodied a massive change. This is the first perspective, taking reforms at their rhetorical face value.

THE NEW BLUE LOCUSTS

The second perspective is that offered by empirically minded historical and sociological researchers. At the level of the humdrum routines of everyday life far less changed than was implied by the formal organisational reforms. The daily life of Londoners was much the same in 1830 as in 1828 for all the advent of the new 'blue locusts'. As many have shown, the changes were in many ways largely cosmetic. Most of the early 'new' police officers were literally old constables in new uniforms. From this perspective change is usually old wine in new bottles: *plus ça change, plus c'est la même chose.*

But this seen-it-all scepticism implied by detailed empirical research, which emphasises the many continuities of detailed practice underlying the rhetoric of revolutionary transformation, is itself limited. Seeing only the trees it is blind to the wood. For, over the sweep of the 19th century as a whole, there were profound changes in daily life associated with the 'new police'. Britain moved from a society in which policing was a highly localised and spasmodic amateur patchwork to a policed society over which a professionalised bureaucratic organisation, still locally organised but subject to increasingly uniform standards, exercised regular surveillance. By the time a century had passed after their creation, the 'new police' were widely seen as a pillar of the social order, and a key symbol of the British way of life. The current transformations of the police can be seen from the same differing perspectives. During the exceptionally fierce debate which has attended the current reform package, inside and outside Parliament, they have been represented by friends and foes alike as amounting to a completely new departure in British policing.

UNDOUBTEDLY FINE

To the advocates of the reforms they will herald a timely and much-needed overhaul bringing a police system fashioned in the 19th century, and undoubtedly fine in its day, firmly into the brave new modern world of the 20th century (just in time for the advent of the 21st.). The new 'New Police' will be lean, clean, businesslike, giving true value for money. The post-Sheehy structure of pay and conditions will introduce the disciplines of the market to ensure properly motivated personnel. The revamped tripartite structure will provide a clear framework of objectives, carefully monitored centrally by the Audit Commission's league tables, with a keener, more efficient local input from the re-tuned businesslike police authorities. The police will be better able to concentrate on their core tasks if relieved of the ancillary burdens which have clogged past performance. Following PACE and the Criminal Justice and Public Order Act the police have all

the necessary legal powers for fighting crime, subject to a battery of safeguards to ensure this is not achieved unjustly at the expense of suspects.

Opponents of the 'reforms' (and I count myself amongst their number) have been equally emphatic about the complete transformation they embody. We have been shrill, often apocalyptic, about how they will destroy the finest police system in the world, replacing it with a nightmare organisation which will succeed in being at once both bumblingly incompetent and unfailingly oppressive.

Sheehy-style short-term contracts and performance related pay will erode the ethos of dedicated public service. The new accountability systems will replace democracy with accountancy, and produce a mock-businesslike hocus-pocus of policing by numbers. Behind the rhetoric of devolution of power locally it will be seen that the real levers of control will be concentrated at the centre. The police role will be stripped down to catching crooks, leaving all the people who currently call upon the police for help in a variety of other emergencies with nobody to turn to, thus alienating the public from the service. New criminal justice and public order legislation will give the police massive powers with only fig-leaf safeguards. The bottom-line will be a British-style police state, with inefficiency and incompetence as the only protections against centralised tyranny. This doomsday scenario envisages the police of the future as combining the least attractive characteristics of the Gestapo and the Keystone Kops.

EXCITEMENT AND A CUP OF TEA

Now that the bulk of the changes are *faits accomplis* I feel I can turn from polemic to sociological mode in considering their likely impact. The safest prediction in any social science is that there are always unintended consequences. The reforms are most likely to confound the rhetoric of both proponents and oppo-

nents. The best bet for the short to medium term is that policing tomorrow will closely resemble policing today. We will have neither the Supercops nor the Robocops anticipated by the contrasting rhetorics of political debate. Police officers will remain motivated by a complex and varying mixture of a search for interest, excitement, and a cup of tea. Loyalty and *esprit de corps*, commitment to public service, concern for the plight of victims will all play their parts, as will wanting to get through as trouble-free a shift as possible avoiding the rain and cold, and, yes, job security and a fair financial reward. But serving officers will not transmogrify overnight into the rational economic calculating machines dreamed of by the advocates of businesslike policing.

ORIGINAL DESIGN

The Home Office will be more busily involved in specifying and monitoring a national policing plan. They will be appointing some members of the new police authorities (although the government was frustrated in its original design of ending the locally elected members majority, and having centrally appointed chairpersons, by a revolt of Tory peers in the House of Lords). But these new Home Office appointees are unlikely to see their role as government puppets, as critics claimed. Conservative-minded or not, they will probably see their role as defending local interests, and side with the chief officer and other local authority members in disputes with the Home Office over such matters as funding levels.

Although opponents of the legislation by implication painted a rosy view of the status quo, major problems with the old police authorities have long been evident to everyone - not least the critics themselves. The new ones may prove more effective - if only because they are a less unwieldy size - albeit not necessarily as conduits of Home Office influence. Continuity and cock-up are always more likely outcomes than successful conspiracy. Targets and objectives are likely to be set at somewhere near current levels so that the impact on practice will not be major. Few sheddable ancillary tasks are likely to be discovered. People will still turn to the police as their first port of call in most emergencies, whether clearly related to crime detection or not. Although they are equipped with new legal powers on paper, the normal police style is still likely to regard the liberal use of discretion as the better part of valour – not to speak of community relations and the use of scarce resources. Under- rather than over- enforcement of the law is likely to continue to predominate, as shown for example in Tank Waddington's recent excellent empirical study of the impact of the 1986 Public Order Act, *Order and Liberty*. In short, the daily routines of policing and police culture will probably be robust enough to survive the new organisational brooms.

RHETORIC OF DEBATE

So far I have echoed the first two perspectives outlined earlier in relation to the 19th century creation of the police. The nightmares and utopias which dominated the rhetoric of debate were both confounded by the survival of mundane everyday routines. But now, as then, something big has happened, even if the world won't stand on its head overnight, and the end result is likely to be something different from the anticipations of both the advocates and the enemies of the reforms.

Some harbingers of more profound change are evident, and have been for a long time before the current package. Indeed they largely created the political space for it. Two important and related straws in the wind have become apparent recently. As common observation and media discussion indicate, and an important forthcoming paper by Trevor Jones and Tim Newburn in *Policing and Society* ('*How Big Is the Private Security Sector?*' Vol.5 No.2) demonstrates, the private security industry has grown massively of

late. So too has a variety of other means of substituting for sworn police personnel: civilianisation, voluntary citizen involvement (running the gamut from the Special Constabulary to Neighbourhood Watchers walking purposefully), and the technology of the security industry. The source of this growth of alternative policing forms is undoubtedly the increasing mismatch between hugely burgeoning demands for security and the expenditure on Home Office police forces. This has prompted the Policy Studies Institute/Police Foundation '*Independent Committee on Police Roles and Responsibilities*' to draw the logical conclusion. Only an explicit adoption of multi- tiered policing can cope with inevitably increasing demand for policing which cannot conceivably be met by boosting sufficiently the supply of sworn officers on the traditional model. So the first clear trend is the growth of competition in the supply of policing services.

> *Public policing is in effect increasingly restricted to a core rump. Those who are unsatisfied with this, and have the financial and other means to obtain private substitutes (of varying value for money and quality), are doing so*

The second is that there is now emerging clear evidence that the post-Sheehy cuts in police pay and conditions are resulting in an absolute decline in the number and quality of applicants joining the service (as reported by David Rose on the front page of The Observer on 16 April: 'Police recruiting squeezed as 25 per cent pay cut bites'). This absolute drop in police recruitment follows many years in which police numbers were declining relative to any measures of workload: crime, disorder, emergency calls and road traffic.

The two trends together indicate a clear *de facto* policy of privatisation. Public policing is in effect increasingly restricted to a core rump. Those who are unsatisfied with this, and have the financial and other means to obtain private substitutes (of varying value for money and quality), are doing so, and will have to more and more in the future.

The big question is how much is this a little local difficulty attributable to the present government, and how much is it a deeply rooted structural trend caused by more profound changes in contemporary culture and society. The present government has clearly added its own twist to what is going on. They are ideologically committed to the privatisation of everything with a pulse. Moreover there is resentment at the explosion of their own naive belief in 1979 that crime and disorder could be tackled merely by throwing money and powers at the police. In the Cabinet, As Kenneth Baker explicitly revealed in his memoirs in the early 1990s, "There was impatience that although we had spent more in real terms since 1979... there had still been a substantial rise in crime. 'Where is the value for money?' asked my colleagues."

PROFOUND CHANGES

It would be foolhardy to suppose that any prospective replacement of the present government of privatisers by one with a stronger commitment to public service would fundamentally alter the picture of the police. In all contemporary advanced industrial societies there are profound changes in social control and policing systems, corresponding to underlying transformations in society and culture. As the Canadian criminologists Clifford Shearing and Philip Stenning have put it, we are entering a 'new feudalism.' The more affluent two-thirds of society are increasingly living their work and recreational lives in forms of 'mass private property', such as private housing estates, shopping malls incorporating many leisure activities, amusement parks on a grand scale like Disneyland, and huge office complexes or industrial estates. The security of these castles of consumerism is provided by environmental design -- especially the 'moats' of roads, fences and walls cutting them off from the potentially threatening but excluded 'underclass'-- the technology of surveillance and prevention, notably the all pervasive CCTV systems, and private security personnel of various kinds. In these vast swathes of contemporary society the public police are increasingly rendered redundant.

A seminal study of the birth of the modern police (by Alan Silver) spoke of 'The Demand for Order in Civil Society'. In essence he argued modern industrial society required more predictability, harmony and order of a monolithic kind than did the less centrally organised societies of the past. The vast armies of workers huddled closely in cities to supply the voracious labour requirements of huge mass-production factories had to be disciplined inside and outside the gates. Even more than any practical peacekeeping role they may have had, the modern police were important for their symbolic function. Patrolling visibly, regularly and pervasively throughout society, they were walking totems of the uniform morality necessary for integrating complex modern societies.

QUALITY OF LIFE

What has changed above all is the erosion of this 'demand' for uniform order. Yes, crime and disorder have been increasing for decades, at great cost to victims and the quality of life. But with the overall decline of industrial work, the international dispersion and casualisation of what is left of it, and the advent of more permissive and fragmented cultures, there is no longer a single monolithic moral order for a single uniform type of police to enforce and symbolise. Have the police got a future in this brave new world? Or are we doomed to a loosely-coupled network of policing agencies and processors – pick 'n' mix policing for the more differentiated and diverse multicultures of a post modern age?

Name Index